Chris Leadbetter, Roger Blackford and Tony Piper

Cambridge International

AS and A Level

Computing

Coursebook

Completely Cambridge – Cambridge resources for Cambridge qualifications

Cambridge University Press works closely with University of Cambridge International Examinations (CIE) as parts of the University of Cambridge. We enable thousands of students to pass their CIE Exams by providing comprehensive, high-quality, endorsed resources.

To find out more about CIE
visit www.cie.org.uk

To find out more about Cambridge University Press
visit www.cambridge.org/cie

CAMBRIDGE
UNIVERSITY PRESS

CAMBRIDGE UNIVERSITY PRESS
Cambridge, New York, Melbourne, Madrid, Cape Town,
Singapore, São Paulo, Delhi, Mexico City

Cambridge University Press
The Edinburgh Building, Cambridge CB2 8RU, UK

www.cambridge.org
Information on this title: www.cambridge.org/9780521186629

© Cambridge University Press 2012

First published 2012

Printed in the United Kingdom at the University Press, Cambridge

A catalogue record for this publication is available from the British Library

ISBN 978-0-521-18662-9

Cover image: Gusto images/Science Photo Library

Contents

Introduction

This full-colour, highly-illustrated textbook has been written by experienced authors specifically for the University of Cambridge International Examinations AS and A Level Computing syllabus (9691). The four modules of the book follow the four sections of the syllabus, and there are syllabus codes <insert fig 1 here> throughout to provide an easy reference to the syllabus. This enables students and teachers alike to make sure they are on track to cover the complete course.

The narrative provides clear explanations that are supported by diagrams, screenshots and photographs, bringing the topics to life. At the end of each chapter, there are self-assessment questions with answers at the back of the book. These relate to the material covered in the chapter, and offer an opportunity to revise concepts just learned, or to test understanding. Whilst these are not examination questions, each comes with a mark allocation to get the students into the practice of always thinking carefully about each point they make. The questions often include useful 'Hints' from the authors, particularly with respect to mark allocations. The answers also include 'Comments' from the authors in places where there are common pitfalls or typical errors.

Throughout each chapter there are 'Activity' and 'Discussion' boxes (see images below). These are questions or points for individual or class discussion. These allow students to explore the topics in more detail and really test their understanding.

Activity

Discussion

At the end of each Module, there are examination questions from real past papers. These will cover content from all the chapters in the Module in a random order. Each has the real mark allocations indicated and gives the students targeted exam practice for the given topics of that unit. The answers to these questions are provided at the back of the book, complete with 'Comments' from the authors in places where, in their experience, students have struggled in the examinations. There is also a chapter at the end of the book devoted to exam preparation that offers student general advice for coping with the examinations.

However, learning is about more than passing an examination; it is about increasing knowledge. Therefore, there are numerous places where the book goes beyond the scope of the syllabus. This 'Extension' material (indicated by the boxes shown below) is there for those that want to carry out independent study or further research into the given topic. Please note that this material is not in the syllabus and therefore will not be in the examination.

Extension

Finally, there is the glossary of key terms. Here, you should find an easily accessible means to remind yourselves of the important terms you have learned as you progress through the course. We hope you enjoy the textbook and the course.
The author team.

Acknowledgements

We would like to thank the following for permission to reproduce images:

Cover: Gustoimages/Science Photo Library

1.2.7 Reproduced with the permission of Winzip Computing; 1.4.3 Shutterstock / Joel Dietle; 1.4.5 Shutterstock/ Kostia; 1.4.6 Shutterstock / Stephen Coburn; 1.4.7 Shutterstock / Vixit; 1.4.8 Shutterstock / Iakov Filimonov; 1.4.9 Shutterstock / OtnaYdur; 1.4.10 Shutterstock / shutswis; 1.4.11a Shutterstock / Daboos; 1.4.11b Shutterstock/ 3d brained; 1.4.12 Doug Steley A / Alamy; 1.4.13a Ted Foxx / Alamy; 1.4.13b Shutterstock Dja65; 1.4.13c Shutterstock / Robert Milek; 1.4.14 Courtesy of mucad.com; 1.5.1 Shutterstock / Deymos; 1.7.1 Chris Fertnig / Alamy; 1.7.2 Shutterstock / Yuri Arcurs; 1.7.3 Shutterstock / Chuck Rausin; 1.7.4 Shutterstock / SFC; 1.7.8 aberCPC / Alamy; 1.8.1 Courtesy of Tom Dalton, Assistive Technologies; 1.8.2 focus mankind / Alamy; 1.8.4 Shutterstock / Jiri Hera; 1.8.5 Len Holsborg / Alamy; 1.9.1 Reproduced with the permission of Articulate; 3.7.1 Reproduced with the permission of LEGO® MINDSTORMS®; 3.7.2a JHP Public Safety / Alamy; 3.7.2b Shutterstock / lenetstan; 3.7.2c Art Directors & TRIP / Alamy; 3.7.3 Shutterstock / John Kasawa; 3.7.4 Francisco Cruz / Superstock; 3.8.1a Wendy White / Alamy; 3.8.1b Sergey Galushko / Alamy; 3.8.1c: Hugh Threlfall / Alamy.

Examination questions are reproduced by permission of University of Cambridge International Examinations.

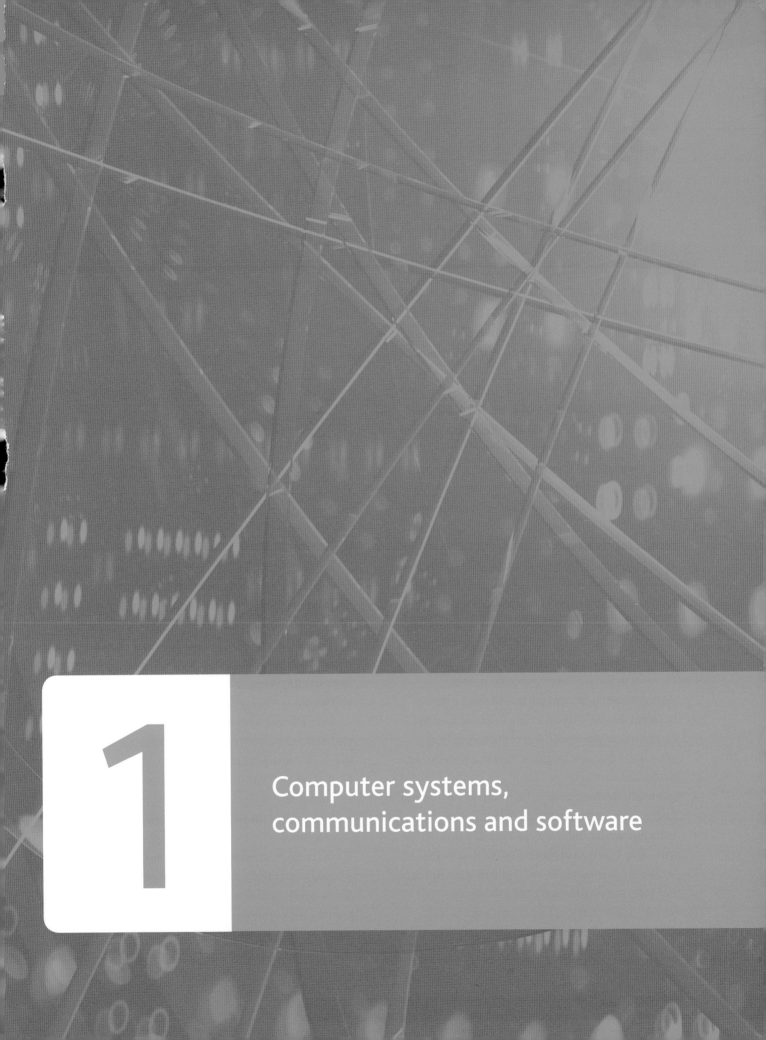

1

Computer systems,
communications and software

1.1 Components of a computer system and modes of use

A "computer system" is made up of hardware and software. In this chapter we explain the terms relating to a computer system that will be used throughout the rest of the coursebook.

1.1 a, b — Definitions and purposes of hardware devices

The **hardware** is the physical electronic and electrical components that make up the computer system. For example, these include the motherboard, a keyboard and a monitor. In this section, we explain terms relating to hardware devices that we use throughout the rest of the text.

Peripheral devices are hardware devices that are outside the central processing unit (CPU). They are normally connected to the computer by internal wiring (buses), cables or wireless technology. A printer is obviously a peripheral as it is separate from the computer. A **hard disk** drive is also a peripheral because it is not part of the CPU. This is less obvious because it is in the same box as the computer.

Most peripheral devices are one of three types:

- An **input device** transmits data from the user to the computer processor. A computer is only of value if it is possible to give it data and processing instructions.
- An **output device** conveys the results of processing from the computer processor to the user.
- A **storage device** can store data outside the processor. When a computer system is switched off, data in the processor are lost. Data that are needed for future use must be saved to a storage device

Figure 1.1.1 shows a typical set of hardware in a computer system. The arrows show the direction of flow of data and information. The storage device is both an input device and an output device.

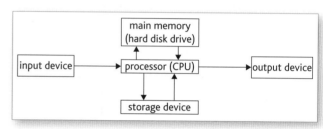

Figure 1.1.1 The typical hardware of a computer system.

In Chapter 1.4, we look at various types of hardware in more detail.

1.1 a, c — Definitions and purposes of software types

Software is the set of instructions that make the computer hardware usable. These sets of instructions are known as "programs". So, a computer program is a piece of software. It is important to distinguish between **operating system software** and **generic applications software**.

Operating system software is the set of instructions that make the hardware of the computer available for use. It includes programs:

- that allow the user to communicate with the computer
- that control the movement of data around the computer
- that turn instructions that people can understand into instructions that a computer can recognise.

Applications software is a set of instructions designed to make the computer do something for the user. For example, the user might want to write a letter, create a report or create a slide show presentation.

Software that can be used for many tasks is called *generic applications* software or *general purpose applications* software. Microsoft Office is a suite of generic applications, including Microsoft Word (a word processing application), Microsoft Excel (a spreadsheet application) and Microsoft PowerPoint (a presentation application).

Other applications software carries out a specific sequence of tasks. For example, a payroll application can process payroll data, print payslips and generate BACS payments. It cannot process electricity billing data.

In Chapter 1.2, we discuss types of system software in more detail. You will notice that applications software is covered throughout much of the rest of the syllabus, which should give you an idea of its importance. Chapter 1.7 looks specifically at applications software.

Summary

- Hardware is the physical components that make up the computer system.
- Software is the set of instructions (programs) that make the computer hardware usable.
- An input device is a physical component that transmits data to the computer.
- A storage device is a physical component that stores data for use by the computer.
- An output device is a physical component displays data transmitted from the computer.
- Operating system software comprises the programs that make the computer hardware available for use, often unseen by the user.
- Generic/general purpose applications software comprises programs that can be used for many tasks, such as a word processor, spreadsheet software and database software.

Test yourself

1. Explain the difference between hardware and software.　[2]

Hint

The question mentions two items ("hardware" and "software") and two marks are available. Therefore, you should make two points. Make sure that the second point is not just the opposite of the first. The word "explain" indicates that the two points need to say *how* the items differ.

2. Give **two** reasons why a computer system would need to have some type of external storage device.　[2]

Hint

Notice that the question asks for reasons *why* the system needs external storage. Do not say what is stored or what sort of device might be used. There are two indicators in the question that you should make two points: the word in bold and the marks awarded.

3. Describe the difference between system software and application software.　[2]

Hint

This question is similar in style to Question 1. Remember that you need to state two distinct points that are related to each other.

1.2 System software

1.2 a The purpose of an operating system

An operating system (OS) is the main item of **system software** used by a computer system. The OS is a set of programs designed to run in the background on a computer system and provide an environment in which application software can be executed.

Most operating systems comprise a large set of programs, only some of which are stored in the computer's memory all the time. Many of the routines available in the OS are stored on the hard drive so that they can be accessed when required. This saves space in the computer's main memory .

When you are using applications software, you are not communicating directly with the computer hardware. Your applications software communicates with OS program modules that communicate with the computer hardware on its behalf. Without an operating system, a computer is useless no matter how many programs you have.

There are many different types of operating system. Each type makes the computer behave differently and is appropriate to a given computer system and its applications. We look at some of the different types of OS in this chapter and again in other parts of the syllabus. All operating systems have some common purposes:

- The OS must manage the physical resources of the computer. Some resources are limited and must be managed to maximise the use of the computer system:
    - A simple system has only one processor.
    - Secondary storage is of a fixed size.
    - Some input/output devices (e.g. printers) are shared.
- The OS provides a means of communication (the user interface) between the human user, or the outside world, and the computer.

- The OS provides a platform on which the applications software can run.
- The OS hides the complexity of the hardware from the user.
- The OS controls access to the computer system so that you can put passwords on your files to stop other people seeing them. It controls the access rights of different users.

Whether or not a certain feature is classified as part of the operating system or as a utility program varies considerably across operating systems. We consider utility software in more detail at the end of this chapter.

1.2 b Types of operating system

Batch

When computing was still a new science, there were not enough machines to satisfy the demand for processor time. There was a "speed mismatch" between the user sitting at the keyboard, who was very slow, and the processing by the computer, which was very fast. One solution to this problem is to buy more machines. Another solution is to make the machines work more effectively by taking away the slowest part of the system – the human being. Nowadays we might well opt to buy more machines! When computers were very expensive, an aim for efficiency improvements gave rise to batch processing.

A **batch processing** operating system does not allow for interaction between the user and the processor during the execution of the program. Lots of programs (or lots of data to be run through the same program) are collected together (to form a batch). The batch operating system then controls their passage through the computer.

Nowadays, batch processing is used for applications where:

- there are large amounts of data to be processed
- the data are very similar in nature and require similar processing
- the computer system has identifiable times when it is not being used and so has available processor time
- the application does not require interaction by a user.

Typical examples of applications which use batch processing include:

- the processing of payroll information
- the production of bank statements from customer files at periodic intervals; e.g. all accounts with surnames starting A–E could be processed on the fifth of each month, surnames F–J on the tenth of each month, and so on
- the production of utility (gas, electricity and telephone) bills from customer records.

Real-time

A **real-time operating system** can react quickly enough to affect the next input or process that needs to be carried out. There is a continuous cycle of input–processing–output.

Most real-time systems are based on the control of some process in the real world (where the processing takes place on a timescale of milliseconds). Some information processing applications require the processing to be done within seconds; it still fits the description of the continuous cycle and is known as a **pseudo real-time operating system**.

The following examples of real-time applications show why immediate response can be vital:

- A chemical plant has a reaction vessel in which the temperature is critical to the result of the process. The temperature is monitored by a computer that accepts input from a sensor. The computer uses the sensor data to make decisions about adjusting the heating elements in the vessel. A delay in the decision-making process might corrupt the reaction.
- A robot trolley is controlled by a processor that takes input from a sensor following a black line

on the floor. The processor makes decisions about steering to keep the trolley on the black line. The trolley would very soon lose its direction if it was not steering quickly enough.

- A catalogue shop processes orders. The code for a product is input and the system compares it with information in its files. When it finds the correct code, it can report to the user the quantity of that product in stock. It is necessary to record a purchase before the next shopper's request is processed otherwise the second person might be sold the same item.

Single-user

A **single-user operating system** controls a system which has only one user, and their programs, at any one time. A perfect example of a single-user system is the PC or laptop that you may have at home. Only one person uses the computer system at any one time. Note that it does not mean a system that only ever has one user! This means that security measures are important so that the system only allows access to files that belong to the appropriate user.

Multi-user

Again, as the name implies, this type of operating system allows the computer to service more than one user simultaneously. A **multi-user operating system** has a single (normally powerful) computer which is connected to a number of terminals. These terminals are not computers, although they may have a very limited amount of processing power. They rely on the main computer to carry out any processing.

The computer sends a message to each of the terminals in turn, asking if it wants any processing to be carried out. This process is called a **time-share** system or a **round robin** system. Each of the small amounts of processor time is called a "time slice". The length of a time slice varies according to the system but is typically about a hundredth of a second.

A configuration in which a central computer (a server) processes data from several terminals (see Figure 1.2.1 on page 6) is called a "thin-client network".

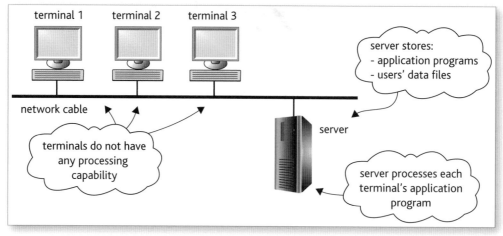

Figure 1.2.1 A multi-user computer system. Since terminals do no processing this is a thin client network.

There is a limit to the number of terminals that can be serviced. The system needs to be fast enough that a user at a terminal does not have to wait for too long before being given processing time. The system can be speeded up if the computer ignores terminals that are not active. Terminals can send a signal to the computer when they need processor time. Such a system is only satisfactory if the response time for all users is acceptable; no user should have to wait for a long time for a program to respond.

Multi-tasking

A **multi-tasking operating system** allows several applications to be available simultaneously. On a single-user system, you are probably used to having a number of processes loaded in main memory at the same time. One window may show a spreadsheet while another shows a word processing application; you may also be connected to the Internet through an email client; and you may be playing music while you work. It appears that more than one task is running simultaneously but they aren't, they just appear to be. The OS can switch between tasks so quickly that it seems to the user as if they are all being done at once. The method used to do this is very similar to the multi-user OS. The tasks are allocated time slices and the computer goes from one to the other servicing them.

Microsoft Windows is a multi-tasking operating system. You can view a list of the running processes in the Task Manager operating system utility (Figure 1.2.2). In Chapter 3.1, we further consider multi-tasking in Windows.

Network

A network comprises a number of computers linked together for the purposes of communication and the sharing of resources. Networks are important because they allow hardware and software to be shared. They require the computers to run a **network operating system**. Often, one of the machines is used to control the rest of the system; this machine is called the server.

A network OS must carry out tasks such as:

- control of access to the network
- management of the filing system
- management of all applications programs available from the server
- management of all shared peripherals.

A common misunderstanding is to confuse network systems with multi-user systems. A multi-user system has many users using one computer at the same time; a network system has many computers each using shared hardware and software.

In Chapter 3.8, we consider networking in detail.

1.2 c Application requirements for operating systems

In an examination, you will be asked to identify applications that require batch processing and applications that require real-time processing.

Applications that require batch processing include: payroll, the production of bills and the production of bank statements. Be very careful in choosing any other application – it must be clear that there are good reasons for using batch processing. For example, simply to say that an ATM machine uses batch processing is not enough. Requests for bank statements

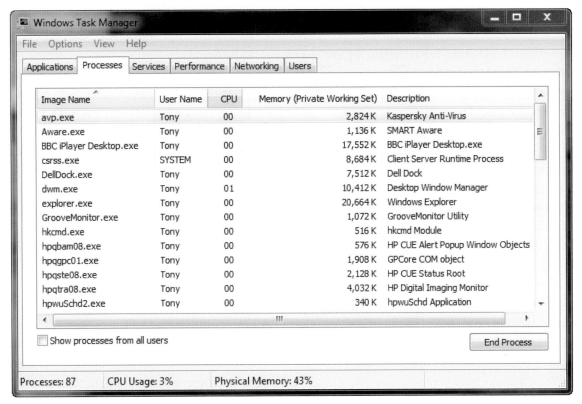

Figure 1.2.2 The Windows Task Manager utility.

are batched for later processing but the PIN for a customer must be checked in real time. You must be specific and justify your choice. For example, you could write "Because statements must be sent out by post, they can be processed while the computer is not doing other things. It makes sense to process a large number of statements at the same time as a batch."

Control applications, in which the results of a process are used to inform the next input, use real-time processing. A good example would be the control of a robotic machine on a production line. Information systems also require real-time processing. It is necessary to update the file of information before the next enquiry is dealt with. The classic example is the airline (or theatre) booking system. If a customer decides to buy a ticket for a flight, the number of tickets available must be updated before the next person makes an enquiry, otherwise another person may be sold the same seat.

In general terms, an examination question will ask you to decide which of these two types of processing is most appropriate for a given application. It is not sensible to try to memorise a list of applications for each type. You must learn to identify the characteristics of each of the types of processing for a given application.

1.2 d Types of user interface

The user interacts with a computer system through its **user interface**. The user gives input (e.g. the click of a mouse) and receives responses from the computer. A user interface (also called a human–computer interface (HCI)) consists of both hardware and software.

When a user types instructions into a computer and the computer responds by displaying details on a screen, then that is an interface. The keyboard and the screen are the hardware components; the software components of the interface allow the computer to understand the typed instructions. In the early days of computing, people could use a teleprinter instead of a monitor. The teleprinter was similar to a typewriter. As the user typed commands on it, the computer would print the commands and its response on paper. The hardware and software components of the interface need to be appropriate to the use. For example, a keyboard and screen are needed for an interface that enables the user to make enquiries about theatre tickets; a printer would enable the user to print a booked ticket.

There are many different types of interface. Their features vary depending on the application, the conditions in which it is to be used and the knowledge and skills of the user. From the many types of HCI, you are expected to be able to describe the five software interfaces discussed below and give a typical application for each of them. In Chapter 1.9, we discuss the hardware that is necessary to put the software interface into operation.

Form-based interface

If the majority of the input to a system is standardised, a typical interface is an on-screen form to be filled in. This type of interface is used by an operator inputting information while talking to a customer over the telephone.

The interface:

- prompts the operator to ask each of the questions in turn
- makes the operator input the information in the correct order and ensures that nothing is missed out
- ensures that the information is input in the correct format
- makes the checking of the information easier.

A **form-based interface** (see Figure 1.2.3) has a specific area for each piece of data. For example, there may be:

- a drop-down list for restricted input (such as the person's title or a date)
- boxes for textual information (such as the name or email address)
- check boxes for yes–no information (such as a box to indicate acceptance of conditions).

The form uses standard widget controls – text boxes, radio buttons, check boxes and drop-down lists.

When the user enters data, the cursor often moves automatically to the next box to be filled in. Sometimes a

Figure 1.2.3 Form-based interface.

box is highlighted to make it clear to the operator where the data are to be inserted. Some of the data are more important than others and the cursor does not move on until data have been supplied. The interface checks that the input is sensible for that box before moving on.

When a person orders something from a supplier on the Internet, a form-based interface is used. The customer fills in a number of standard personal and payment details.

Menu-based interface

A **menu-based interface** is used in situations where the user does not know what options are available. Examples of this are information systems for tourists and the on-screen menus for digital television. A list of choices is made available. When the user selects an option, a further set of choices is displayed, and so on until the result is obtained.

Imagine an information system at a train station in a popular holiday location. The first screen may ask for the general area of interest (accommodation, trips, shopping or entertainment). If the user selects "accommodation", the next screen may offer a choice

of types of accommodation (hotels, guest houses, etc.). The third screen may offer different price bands. Finally, the user may see a list of all the available properties that match the choices of type and price band. Such an information system often uses a touch screen because other peripherals are less appropriate. For example, a mouse connected to an information system in a train station might be vandalised or damaged by the weather.

Graphical user interface

A **graphical user interface** (GUI) uses windows, icons, menus, and a pointer (giving rise to the acronym WIMP). The user of a GUI expects to be able to view different applications or files on the screen at the same time. This is done by putting each into its own bordered area known as a *window*. The user can select a command by clicking on a small picture (an *icon*) that represents it. The user selects further options from *menus*. Icons and menu options are selected by using some sort of *pointing device* such as a mouse.

In Figure 1.2.4, the main menu is displayed horizontally as text options (File, Edit, etc.). Selecting *Shape* from the menu opens a drop-down menu of

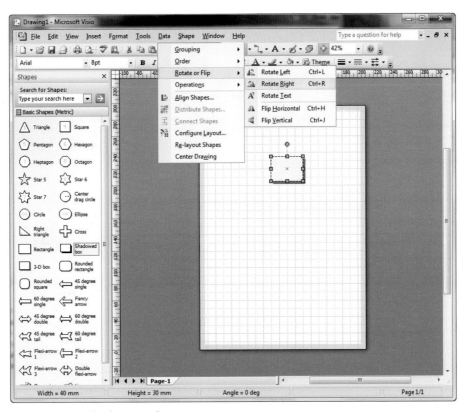

Figure 1.2.4   Graphical user interface.

selections. Selecting *Rotate* or *Flip* gives access to a final menu from which the user can select the final command – *Rotate Right*. The user can save a file in one step by clicking the "Save" icon (it represents a floppy disk); in Figure 1.2.4 you can see this button directly under the "Edit" button.

The whole principle of a GUI is to make using the system as simple as possible by hiding all the complicated bits! For example, when the user clicks an icon to bring a piece of software onto the screen, it involves only one action. In the background, the computer is executing a complicated process involving a lot of instructions. When the icon is chosen, the computer is simply told to run those instructions so the software will appear. The icon has hidden the complexity from the user.

Natural language interface

A **natural language interface** is sometimes referred to as a "conversational interface". The computer displays or speaks questions that give the user the impression that the computer is talking to them. However, the system restricts itself to questions that will provoke very simple responses which the computer can understand. If the user does not give one of the expected responses, a message is produced which makes it clear that the user must try again.

It is often assumed that a natural language interface is very close to a spoken language. This may be true but it is likely to be typed into the machine rather than actually being spoken. For example, some Internet search engines or large information systems can process natural language queries. This is the next step up from a simple keyword search, where the software picks out the keywords and then searches for matching documents or files.

Computerised telephone systems may use voice input to select menu choices. A true spoken interface might be used by a disabled person to communicate with a computer.

Command line interface

In a **command line interface**, or "command-based interface", the user types a series of commands at the keyboard and the computer displays appropriate output (see Figure 1.2.5). The computer does not

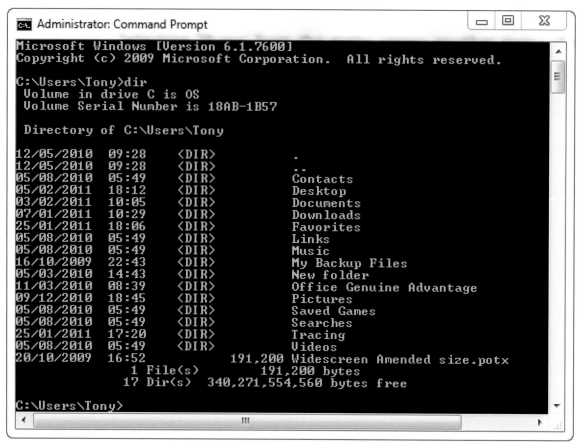

Figure 1.2.5 Command line interface.

prompt the user to enter any particular information. If the user enters a command incorrectly, the computer will give an error message.

To use a command line interface, the user needs:

- to know what commands are available
- to understand the commands
- to understand how material is stored in the computer system.

A command line interface, has two very important characteristics:

- The computer system is very much more open than in the other types of interface. Other interfaces restrict the options that the user has available to them. A command line interface allows anyone with a knowledge of the commands access to the entire operating system. Hence, they have access to the workings of the entire computer.
- Command line interfaces can only be used by people who are computer literate. Users need to understand the commands and their uses. They also need to understand something about how the computer operates and how information is stored.

1.2 e Utility software

Programs that carry out tasks necessary to the operation of the computer are known as **utility software**.

Disk formatter

When a disk is first produced the surface is blank. It cannot be used to store data until it has been formatted by **disk formatter** software. The formatting process divides the disk into smaller areas, each of which can be searched more easily (see Figure 1.2.6).

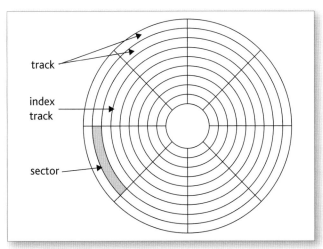

Figure 1.2.6 A formatted hard disk.

The disk surface is divided into a number of tracks and each track is divided into smaller blocks called sectors.

The amount of information that can be stored is enormous. One of the tracks is used as an index, to hold data about where the other data are stored. The formatting process removes all data from the disk so you should save the contents of a disk elsewhere before re-formatting it.

Hardware drivers

Any piece of hardware needs to be controlled and set up for communication with the processor. The **hardware drivers** are programs that control the communication between the device and the operating system.

File handling

Data stored on a computer system are organised as files. A set of utility programs is needed to handle the storage and use of these files. There are programs to store and retrieve the files and programs that allow files to be altered or deleted. Sometimes the contents of two files need to be combined (*merged*) or the contents of a file may need to be put into a particular order (*sorted*).

A file handling utility normally does all these tasks. If an examination question asks for two examples of utility software, you should not describe two file handling routines.

Automatic backup or archive

Files on a computer system need to be protected from being damaged. A backup or archiving utility is a simple routine that copies the contents of files to another location. If the original file is damaged, the copy can be used to replace the damaged file.

If an examination question asks for an example of a utility, simply saying "backup" is not a satisfactory response. You can make a backup manually as a simple file copy process. A good example of a utility program would be one that automatically backs up the changes to files since the previous backup copy was made (incremental backups).

Email client software encourages the user to regularly archive files to reduce storage space.

Anti-virus software

A computer virus is a small program that can reproduce itself. If it "infects" a computer system, a virus can cause a range of damage including deleting files. An **anti-virus software** utility program continually compares a dictionary of known viruses against the files accessed by the computer. It alerts the user if any of the files matches a virus "signature". It is crucial that the virus dictionary is kept up-to-date on a daily basis as new viruses are constantly appearing.

File compression software

Files containing sound and video information are usually large in size. **File compression software** reduces the size of a file by cutting out much of the duplication of data in the file.

If a file is to be sent electronically (e.g. as an email attachment), you can use a utility (such as WinZip, shown in Figure 1.2.7) to compress it. Files may also be compressed to save space on a secondary storage device.

Figure 1.2.7 WinZip file compression software.

Summary

- An operating system:

  - controls the hardware

  - provides a platform for application software to run on

  - provides an HCI

  - manages the resources of the computer system.

- A batch operating system controls the passage of jobs through the computer without user interaction.

- A real-time operating system reacts quickly enough to affect the next input or process that needs to be carried out. It operates a continuous cycle of input–processing–output.

- A single-user operating system enables only one user at a time to access the system.

- A multi-user operating system enables more than one user to access the system at the same time.

———→

Summary continued …

- A multi-tasking operating system gives the user the impression that they can carry out more than one task at the same time.
- A network operating system links a number of computers together and enables them to share peripherals.
- Applications that require batch processing include:
  - payroll
  - bank statements
  - utility bills
- Applications that require a real-time response include:
  - industrial control systems
  - robots
  - ticket-booking systems.
- A form-based user interface provides boxes into which the user can type data. It provides the user with help (on-screen prompts and validation) in completing the data.
- A menu-based user interface provides the user with a set of options that restrict the available information. An information system for tourists and on-screen menus for digital television are easy for users to operate.
- A graphical user interface (GUI) provides windows, icons, menus and a pointer to enable the user to interact with the computer in complex ways.
- A natural language user interface enables the user to use a natural language (such as English) to interact with the computer. It may be spoken or typed input.
- A command line user interface requires the user to type commands to give specific instructions to the computer. It enables a technician to get close to the workings of the computer.
- Disk formatting software prepares a disk for use by the operating system.
- File handling software enables the user to move, copy and delete files.
- Hardware drivers enable successful communication between devices and the operating system.
- File compression software allows data to be stored in a smaller amount of storage space.
- Virus-checking software monitors input and stored data to ensure that it does not contain malicious software.

Test yourself

There are some areas of the specification where the topic is so narrow that only one question can possibly be asked. It may look different from one exam paper to the next but really it is testing the same knowledge. Question 1 is from one of those sections.

1. State **three** purposes of an operating system as part of a computer system. [3]

Hint

There are many possible responses to this question. It asks for *three* purposes and awards *three* marks, one for each purpose. The word "state" indicates that you simply need to list the purposes.

2. a. Distinguish between a *multi-tasking* and a *multi-access* operating system. [2]

> **Hint**
>
> When a question asks you to "distinguish" two things, you must choose facts that compare the things.

b. State what is meant by a *network system* and give an advantage of this type of system over a set of stand-alone computers. [2]

> **Hint**
>
> When a question asks you to "give an advantage", it usually tells you what to compare. In this instance, you must compare a network system with stand-alone computers.

3. A company payroll system uses a personnel file.
   a. Explain the difference between batch processing and real-time processing. [2]
   b. Explain how both batch processing and real-time processing can be used sensibly in the context of the payroll being calculated using the personnel file. [4]

> **Hint**
>
> Notice that you are not asked for separate uses of batch processing and real-time processing. You must consider how batch processing and real-time processing apply to the given application.

4. A computer operator takes phone calls from the public who ring up asking whether a particular item in a catalogue is available. The operator needs to type in a series of responses to questions put to the caller, so that the computer can check the file and determine whether that item is available. Suggest what type of interface is appropriate and its possible contents in terms of options presented to the user. [4]

> **Hint**
>
> Notice that *four* marks are available. You are asked to suggest an interface design and its contents. Assume that *one* mark will be allocated to the interface type and give three or four contents of the interface you suggest. The contents must be based on the scenario described in the question.

5. The technician responsible for maintaining the system in Question 4 uses a command line interface.
   a. Explain what is meant by a *command line interface*. [2]

> **Hint**
>
> Two marks are available, so you should make *two* points.

b. Give **two** advantages and **one** disadvantage to the technician of using a command line interface rather than a menu-based interface. [3]

6. a. Explain the need to have driver software installed for a printer. [2]
   b. Give **three** different utility programs which would be part of a single-user operating system and state what each program would be used for. [6]

1.3 Data: its representation, structure and management

1.3 a **Representation of character sets**

Many different types of data have to be stored in computers, including numbers and character data. We look at the representation of numbers later in this chapter but first we consider how characters are stored in a computer.

Values are stored inside a computer as a series of 0s and 1s. A single 0 or 1 is called a binary digit or *bit*. Any group of 0s and 1s can be used to represent a specific character, for example, a letter. The number of bits used to store one character is called a **byte**. The complete set of characters that the computer uses is known as its **character set**.

Each of the characters in a character set must have its own binary value, which is the code by which the computer recognises it. For example, "A" could be represented as 000, "B" as 001, "C" as 010 and so on. However, there are only eight possible codes using three bits, so we could store the letters A to H but not the rest of the alphabet. We also need to represent the lower case letters, punctuation marks, digits and so on. The computer can store as many characters as necessary simply by using sufficient bits in the code.

The size of the character set depends on what the computer is meant to be able to do. Some systems don't need to be able to recognise a lot of characters so they use only a few bits for each character. A good example of this is an ATM (a cash machine) which needs very few characters to operate the interface.

Activity

Study the input requirements of a cash machine. Try to determine how many bits are necessary to code the required number of characters which are used to operate the interface.

A good way of thinking about the character set for a normal computer is to have a look at the characters that are available on its keyboard. For this character set eight bits are used to store a single character. Using a byte (eight bits) for a character, we have 256 codes (i.e. 256 different eight-bit binary values). This is enough to represent each of the characters on a standard keyboard.

Imagine that one computer stores "A" as 01000001 and another computer stores "A" as 01000010. Any document created on one of the computers will not make sense on the other, because they will interpret the codes differently. Computers can only communicate if they can understand each other's codes. In the 1960s, a meeting in the USA agreed a standard set of codes known as the American Standard Code for Information Interchange (**ASCII**). Most computer systems today use the ASCII coding system, so you can be fairly sure that when you type in "A" on any computer, it is stored in the computer's memory as 01000001 and will be read as "A" by any other computer.

The ASCII coding system uses seven bits to represent each character and the eighth bit as a means of checking the rest (we discuss this in Chapter 1.5). This means that 128 different characters can be represented in the standard ASCII character set. (As this is the most common character set, people generally consider a byte to be eight bits).

Unicode is a more recent, 16-bit code that uses two bytes. Using 16 bits makes it possible to represent over 65,000 characters. This means that all the characters used by the world's languages can be represented in Unicode. It is widely used to handle documents, particularly if a single document needs to be written in, for example, English, Arabic and Chinese. Unicode also allows the localisation of software, where standard software can be adapted for use by different cultures by modifying the layout and features of the interface.

Lots of different character sets are available to a computer for different tasks. Consider how many bits are needed for:

- the ANSI set, which includes graphical symbols, lines and shapes
- the standard Chinese character set, which has thousands of different characters.

Each applications program determines how to interpret a binary pattern by the context in which the value is used. In Module 2, we consider the fundamentals of programming. You'll see that the declaration of the data type for a program variable determines how its value is interpreted.

1.3 b Representation of data types

A computer needs to store and use different types of data in the operation of the system. All of these different types of data look the same in the primary memory as they are all stored in a binary representation.

Numeric data

The computer must be able to recognise different types of numbers: whole numbers (**integers**), negative numbers and fractions (**real numbers**). In this chapter, we consider only positive integers. The other types are discussed in Chapter 3.4.

Integers are stored by the computer as binary numbers (see the next section) using a whole number of bytes. It is usual to use one byte, two bytes (called a "short integer") or four bytes (called a "long integer"). A larger number of bytes makes it possible to store larger numbers. For example, a byte can only be used for positive integers in the range 0 to 255 but a short integer can store positive integers in the range 0 to either 32767 or 65535, depending on the programming language.

Boolean data

Sometimes there are only two possible answers to a question: yes or no, true or false. The computer uses binary data which consists of bits of information that can have the value of either 0 or 1, so it seems reasonable that the answer to such questions can be stored as a single bit with 1 standing for yes and 0 standing for no, or 1 standing for true and 0 standing for false. Data which can only have two states is known as **Boolean** data.

A simple example of its use would be in the control program for an automatic washing machine. One of the important pieces of information for the program would be to record whether or not the door was shut. A Boolean variable could be set to 0 if it was open and to 1 if it was shut. A simple check of that value would tell the program whether it was safe to fill the machine with water.

Character data

A **character** can be anything which is represented in the character set of the computer by a character code usually stored as a single byte. "A" is a character, as are "4" and "&". Each letter in a person's name may be a character, but the name consists of a lot of them. When the characters are put together, they form a string. The word "character" always refers to a single letter, digit or symbol.

String data

A **string** is a sequence of characters stored together, so "F" might be a character which represents "Female" but the sequence "Female" is known as a string. (You may come across alternative names that are used in various programming languages. A string is sometimes called "text", for instance; don't worry about this as either term is acceptable.)

Other data types

Some types of data are used so often by computer systems that they are considered to be special forms of data. Two examples of such data types are Date/Time and Currency.

These special forms of data can be set up by the computer system so that they are recognised when the user enters them. The computer is told the rules that govern such data types and then checks the data that is input against those rules. You are probably familiar with such data types through their use in database software.

Such data types are fundamentally different from the others mentioned here because the others are characterised by the operating system while these types are set up by applications software.

Activity

A shop's computer stores the following details about items that are sold:

- the name of the item
- the date of manufacture
- the number that are in stock
- the price of the item
- a letter (S, M or L) representing the size (small, medium or large).

State what data type should be used for each item stored and justify your answer.

Extension

Try to find out how your computer system stores dates. What is the connection between the two data types of Date/Time and Integer?

What is the maximum number of items that can be in stock if the quantity is stored as a short integer or as a long integer?

How would you store the quantity of items (such as flour and rice) that are sold loose?

Discussion

Consider the data that is held about students at your school. For each item of data decide what data type would be used. Consider some data that may be stored for which there is no sensible data type.

1.3 c Representation of positive integers

Counting is one of the first skills that a young child masters and none of us consider counting from 1 to 100 to be difficult. However, to count, we have to learn, by heart, the meanings of the symbols 0, 1, 2, . . ., 9 and also to understand that two identical symbols mean totally different things according to their "place" in the number. For instance, the 2 in 23 actually means 2 * 10. But why multiply by 10? Why not multiply by six? The answer is simply that we were taught to do that because we have 10 fingers, so we can count on our fingers until we get to the last one, which we remember in the next column and then start again.

We don't need to count in tens. The ancient Babylonians counted in a system that is similar to counting in 60s. This is very difficult to learn because of all the symbols needed but we still use systems based on 60s today: 60 seconds = 1 minute, 60 minutes = 1 hour; 6 * 60 degrees = 1 revolution. Instead of increasing the number of symbols in a system, which makes the system more difficult, it seems reasonable that decreasing the number of symbols makes the system easier to use.

A computer is an electronic machine. Electricity can be either on or off. If electricity is not flowing through a wire, the lack of electricity can stand for 0. If electricity is flowing, then it stands for 1. The difficulty is what to do for the number 2. We can't just pump through twice as much electricity, what we need is a carry system, similar to what happens when we run out of fingers. What we need is another wire (see Figure 1.3.1).

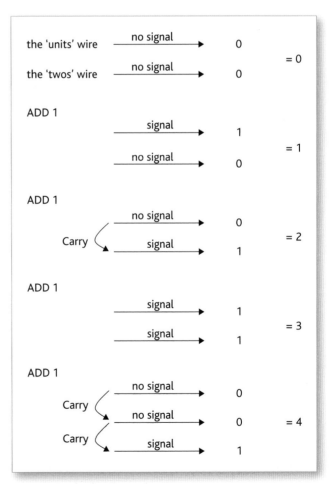

Figure 1.3.1 Doing arithmetic on wires.

The computer can continue like this for ever, just adding more wires when it gets bigger numbers. This system, which has only two digits, is known as the **binary** system. A single binary digit (0 or 1) is called a bit. And again, a group of eight bits is a byte.

The first thing we must be able to do with the binary system is to change numbers from our system of 10 digits (the **denary** system) into binary, and back again. There are a number of methods for doing this, but the simplest is to use a column diagram. In the binary system, the column headings go up in twos instead of tens.

←	32	16	8	4	2	Units

Convert a denary number into a binary number

To convert a denary number into a binary number, create a column diagram where the leftmost column heading is greater than the denary number and follow these steps:

1. Start on the left of the diagram.
2. If the column heading is less than the denary number:
   a. Put a 1 in the column.
   b. Subtract the column heading from the denary number.
   c. Move to the next column to the right.
   d. Go to step 2.
3. If the column heading is greater than the number:
   a. Put a 0 in the column.
   b. Move to the next column to the right.
   c. Go to step 2.

You are normally only expected to be able to do this with numbers up to 255, because that is the biggest number that can be stored in one byte. You may be asked to use more bits for larger numbers.

As an example, we change the denary number 117 into a binary number. First, we set up the column diagram up to column heading 128 (which is larger than 117).

128	64	32	16	8	4	2	1

Then we follow the algorithm. 128 is greater than 117 so put a 0 in the 128s column and move to the 64s column.

128	64	32	16	8	4	2	1
0							

64 is less than 117 so put a 1 in the 64s column, subtract 64 from 117 (giving 53) and move to the 32s column.

128	64	32	16	8	4	2	1
0	1						

32 is less than 53, so put a 1 in the 32s column, subtract 32 from 53 (giving 21) and move to the 16s column.

128	64	32	16	8	4	2	1
0	1	1					

If you continue this until you reach 1 or 0 in the denary number, the result is:

128	64	32	16	8	4	2	1
0	1	1	1	0	1	0	1

So 117 (in denary) = 01110101 (in binary).

Convert a binary number into a denary number

To turn a binary number into denary, simply put the column headings above the binary number and add up all the heading of each column with a 1 in it.

As an example, we change the binary number 10110110 into a denary number.

128	64	32	16	8	4	2	1
1	0	1	1	0	1	1	0

So 10110110 = 128 + 32 + 16 + 4 + 2 = 182 (in denary).

This principle can be used for any number system, even the Babylonians' 60s if you can learn the symbols!

The range of positive integers it is possible to represent is determined by the number of bits used. If they are represented by a byte, the smallest number is 00000000 (i.e. 0 in denary) and the largest number is 11111111 (i.e. +255 in denary).

We return to the subject of number representation again in Chapter 3.4.

1.3 d The structure of arrays

Data stored in a computer is stored at any location in memory that the computer decides to use, which means that similar pieces of data can be scattered all over memory. This, in itself, doesn't matter to the user, except that to find each piece of data it has to be referred to by a name (known as a "variable name"). For example, if we want to store the 20 names of students in a group then each location would have to be given a different variable name. The first, "Iram", might be stored in location `Name1`, the second, "Sahin", might be stored in `Name2`, the third, "Rashid", could be stored in `Name3`. Creating the 20 different variable names is possible but these names are separate (as far as the computer is concerned) and do not relate to each other in any way.

It would be far more sensible to force the computer to store them all together using the same variable name. However, this doesn't let me identify individual names. If I call the first one, `Name(1)`, the second one `Name(2)` and so on (see Figure 1.3.2), it is obvious that they are all people's names and that they are distinguishable by their position in the list. A list like this is called an **array**.

	Name
1	Iram
2	Sahin
3	Rashid
4	Tey
5	Smith
6	Allan
7	Patel
8	Che
19	York
20	Assan

Figure 1.3.2   An array.

Each element in the array is identified using its **subscript** or **index number**. The largest and smallest index numbers are called the *upper bound* and *lower bound* of the array.

Initialising an array

Because the computer is forced to store all the data in an array together, it is important to tell the computer so that it can reserve that amount of space in its memory; otherwise, there may not be enough space when the program uses the data, for example, when it starts assigning string values to the elements of the array. Warning the computer that an array is going to be used is called **initialising** the array.

Initialisation consists of telling the computer program:
- the identifier name of the array
- the sort of data that is going to be stored in the array, i.e. its data type
- how many items of data are going to be stored, so that it knows how much space to reserve.

Different programming languages have different statements for initialising the array but they all do the same thing. In Visual Basic, the statement is:

```
Dim Name(20) As String
```

This `Dim` statement declares:
- the identifier name: `Name`
- the upper bound: 20
- the data type: String.

The upper bound of 20 specifies that there can be a maximum of 21 data items, since Visual Basic starts with a subscript of zero. We do not have to fill the array; the upper bound of 20 indicates the maximum size.

The array that has been described so far is really only a list of single data items. It is possible to have an array which can be visualised as a two-dimensional table with rows and columns and a data value in each cell. The use of such two-dimensional arrays is developed further in Chapter 2.3.

Extension

All the data held in an array must be of the same data type in traditional programming languages. For many more recent languages, such as PHP, this restriction does not hold! We could extend our example to store each person's date of birth as well. This is possible as long as the dates are stored as strings. An alternative solution is to use a record with a user-defined data type. You may find it interesting to explore this in Chapter 2.3.

Reading data into an array

To assign data values to the elements of the array, we do this with assignment statements such as:

```
Name(6) = "Allan"
```

This places the string "Allan" at index position 6 in the array.

Similarly, the following statement places the string "Rashid" at index position 3 in the array.

```
Name(3) = "Rashid"
```

Searching in an array

Searching for a particular name in the array involves a simple serial search, looking at each name in turn. For example, the following code searches the `Name` array for "Liu".

```
Index ← 1
IsFound ← FALSE
WHILE Index < 21 AND IsFound = FALSE
   IF Name[Index] = "Liu"
      THEN
            IsFound ← TRUE
            OUTPUT "Found"
      ELSE
            Add 1 to Index
   ENDIF
ENDWHILE
IF IsFound = FALSE
   THEN
        OUTPUT "Name not in array"
ENDIF
```

Throughout the book we shall use square brackets for array subscripts in our pseudocode.

The assignment operator ← means that the value on the right hand side is assigned to the variable on the left hand side.

Discussion

Try to understand what is happening in the search algorithm. Notice that it is written in pseudocode. Could you produce the same algorithm as a flowchart?

Activity

Try to produce an equivalent algorithm using a REPEAT–UNTIL loop structure. Explain what the difference is between the two algorithms.

What would be the equivalent algorithm using a FOR–ENDFOR loop structure?

Extension

Arrays are normally numbered from zero so that the first value is in location `Name[0]`. What is the effect of this on your algorithms?

1.3 e The features of queues and stacks

Queues

Data arrives at a computer in a particular order. It may not be numeric or alphabetic but there is an order dependent on the time that the data arrive. Imagine that Zaid, Iram and Sahin send jobs for printing in that order. When these jobs arrive at the printer, they are put in a **queue** awaiting their turn to be printed. It is only fair that, when the printer is free, Zaid's job is sent first because his has been waiting longest.

These jobs could be stored in an array. The jobs are put in at one end and taken out of the other. All the computer needs is a *start pointer* (SP) showing it which job is next to be done and an *end pointer* (EP) showing the array index where to store the next job to arrive.

In Figure 1.3.3a, Zaid's job arrives and is put in position 1. The EP is moved to point at cell 2. When Iram's job arrives (Figure 1.3.3b), it is put into cell 2 and the EP moves to cell 3. Zaid's job is processed (the SP moves to cell 2) and Sahin's job arrives (the EP moves to cell 4), as shown in Figure 1.3.3c.

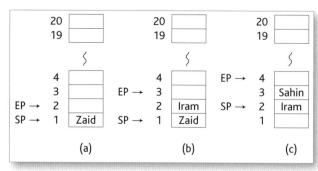

Figure 1.3.3 A job queue: the start and end pointers move as entries arrive and are processed. a) Zaid's job arrives, b) Iram's job arrives and c) Sahin's Job arrives.

Note: The array is limited in size and the contents of the array seem to gradually move up. Sooner or later, the queue will reach the end of the array.

In a queue, the first value to enter is also the first to be processed. A queue is described as a *First In First Out* (FIFO) data structure.

A queue does not have to be held in an array. It could be stored in a type of data structure which can change size. This sort of structure is called a linked list (see Chapter 3.4). The example of jobs being sent to a printer is not really a proper queue. It is called a "spool" but we don't need to know about the difference until Chapter 3.1.

In Chapter 3.4, we consider how queues are implemented.

Stacks

Imagine a queue where the data are taken off at the same end that they are put on. This is a grossly unfair queue because the first item to arrive is the last item to be processed. In other words, the "first in" would be the "last out". This structure is known as a **stack** and is more commonly described as a *Last In First Out* (LIFO) data structure.

A stack only needs one pointer because adding and removing items happen at the same end.

- Adding an item to the stack is called a *push* to the stack.
- Removing an item from the stack is called a *pop* from the stack.

This is illustrated in Figure 1.3.4. Zaid's job arrives and is put into position 1. The pointer moves to cell 2. When Iram's job arrives, it is put into cell 2 and the pointer moves to cell 3 (Figure 1.3.4a). The job below the cell that the pointer is indicating (Iram's job) is

popped from the stack and the pointer moves to cell 2 (Figure 1.3.4b). Sahin's job arrives and is put into cell 2, then the pointer moves to cell 3 (Figure 1.3.4c).

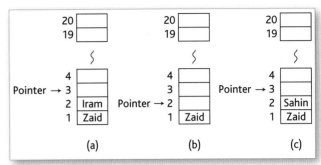

Figure 1.3.4 A job stack: the pointer always points to the top.
a) Iram's job arrives after Zaid's, b) Iram's job is popped from the stack and c) Sahin's job arrives.

We shall meet practical applications later in the course where we want a data set to behave in this way. In Chapter 3.4, we consider how stacks are implemented.

1.3 f **Fixed-length records**

Stored data are normally connected in some way. For example, data stored about the students in a class is connected because it all refers to the same set of people. Each student has his or her own data stored, for example, their name, address, telephone number and exam grades. The data for a number of students could be presented as a table (see Figure 1.3.5).

Name	Address	Telephone	Exam grades	...
Imsha Dar	13a New Town	7775874347	A,C,C,D	...
Nooshun Bilal	7b Old Town	7573456123	E,D,E,C,A	...
Alison Smith	15 Old Town	7573455723	B,E,D,D,B	...
...	...	...	...	...

Figure 1.3.5 Data records for a number of students.

All the information stored has an identity because it is all about the set of students. This large quantity of data are called a **file**. This particular file may be named `Student`. The information referring to a particular student is called a **record**. In Figure 1.3.5, each row represents the data stored for one student record. Each record contains exactly the same fields: name, address, etc. Each type of information is called a **field**. A number of fields make up a record and all records from the same file must contain the same fields. A single data value is called a **data item**.

It is important that each record in the file refers to a different student. A field (or combination of fields) must be used to ensure that the records are unique. This **key field** is used to identify the record. In our example, the records could have added a field called student number, which would be different for each student.

The name "Imsha Dar" is nine characters long (including the space character) and "Alison Smith" is 12 characters long. It makes it easier for the computer to store things if the same amount of space is allocated to the name field for all records. It might waste some space, but searching for a particular record can be done more quickly. When each of the records is assigned a fixed amount of space, the records are said to be **fixed-length records**.

Extension

A lot of storage space can be wasted if "short" data are stored. Alternatively, long data may have to be abbreviated to make it fit. The alternative is to use

→

Extension continued ...

variable-length records, in which the field size can change in every record. Investigate how computers can identify the start and end of each variable-length record.

Figure 1.3.5 illustrates two problems caused by fixed-length records:

- The name of a student may be too long for the length of the Name field.
- A student may take more subjects than the space allowed in the Grades field.

Both of these problems can be solved by variable-length records.

Activity

Identify the data that would be stored by a supermarket about each item that it sells. Explain what is meant by the terms file, record, field and item, giving relevant examples.

1.3 g Methods of accessing data

Computers can store large volumes of data. The issue is to be able to retrieve them! In order to be able to retrieve data, they must be stored in some sort of order. Consider the phone book. It contains a large volume of data which can be used, fairly easily, to look up a particular telephone number because the data are stored in alphabetic order of the subscriber's (person whose phone number is in the book) name. Imagine how difficult it would be to find a subscriber if they had just been placed in the book at random. The value of the book is not just that it contains all the data that may be needed but that it has a *structure*. It is the structure which makes the data accessible. Similarly, the structure of the data in a computer file is just as important as the data that it contains. There are a number of ways of arranging the data that aid (help) access in different circumstances.

Serial access

Data are stored in the file in the order in which it arrives. This is the simplest form of storage, but the data are effectively unstructured, so finding an item again may be very difficult. This sort of data storage is only used when it is unlikely that the data will be needed again or when the order of the data should be determined by when it is input. A good example of a **serial file** is the book that you are reading now. The words were all typed in, in order, and that is how they should be read. Reading this book would be impossible if all the words were in alphabetic order. Another example of the use of a serial file is discussed in the section "Backup and archiving data" (page 26).

Sequential access

A file of data can usually only be read from beginning to end. Data records are stored in sequence – using a key field – and this is known as a **sequential file**.

Consider again the example of a set of students whose data are stored in a computer. The data could be stored in alphabetic order of their name. It could be stored in the order that they performed in a Computing exam or by date of birth with the oldest first. However it is done, the data has been arranged so that it is easier to find a particular record. If the data are in alphabetic order of name and the computer is asked for Zaid's record, it must start looking from the beginning of the file.

We need to be aware of the file processing features available in the programming language we shall use. It is highly unlikely that you would be able to read records starting at the end of the file.

Indexed sequential access

Imagine a large amount of data, such as the names and numbers in a phone book. To look up a particular name still takes a long time even though it is held in sequence. Perhaps it would be more sensible to have a table at the front of the file listing the first letters of peoples' names and giving a page reference to where those letters start. For example, to look up "Jawad", J is found in the table which gives the page number 232 and the search is started at page 232 (where all the Js are stored in alphabetical order). This method of access involves looking up the first piece of information in an index, which narrows the search. The data are then searched alphabetically in sequence. This type of file organisation is called **indexed sequential**.

Random access

A file that stores data in no particular order (a **random access** file) is very useful because it makes adding new data very simple. In any form of sequential file, an individual item of data is very dependent on other items of data. Jawad cannot be placed after Mahmood because that is the wrong "order".

However, it is necessary to have some form of order because otherwise the file cannot be read easily. It would be wonderful if the computer could work out where data are stored by looking at the data that is to be retrieved. In other words, the user asks for Jawad's record and the computer can go straight to it because the word Jawad tells it where it is being stored. How this can be done is explained in the next section.

Discussion

What are the advantages and disadvantages of each of the different methods of storage considered?

Extension

What is the difference between random access storage and direct access storage?

1.3 h Implementation of file access methods

This section is about how we implement the different methods of accessing data in files. There is not a lot of detail and some questions remain unanswered; don't worry, they are discussed in later chapters.

Serial access

Serial files have no order, no aids to searching and no complicated methods for adding new data. The new data are simply placed at the end of the existing file (i.e. "appended"). Searches for data require the whole file to be read, starting with the first record and ending either when the requested record is found or the end of the file is read without finding the data.

Sequential access

Sequential files are held in key field order, so adding a new record is more complex because it has to be placed in the correct position in the file. To do this, all the records that come after it have to be moved in order to make space for the new one.

A section of a school student file might look like this:

. . .

Hameed, Ali, 21, . . .

Khurram, Saeed, 317, . . .

Khwaja, Shaffi, 169, . . .

Naghman, Yasmin, 216, . . .

. . .

If a new student arrives whose name is Hinna, storage space must be found between Hameed and Khurram. To do this all the other records have to be moved down one place, starting with Naghman, then Khwaja, and then Khurram.

. . .

Hameed, Ali, 21, . . .

Khurram, Saeed, 317, . . .

Khwaja, Shaffi, 169, . . .

Naghman, Yasmin, 216, . . .

. . .

This leaves a space into which Hinna's record can be inserted and the order of the records in the file can be maintained.

Discussion

Why is it necessary to move Naghman first and not Khurram?

Having to manipulate a file in this way is very time-consuming. This type of file structure is only used for files that have a small number of records or that change infrequently. Larger files could use this technique, but would be split up using indexing into a number of smaller sequential files.

For example, the account numbers for a bank's customers are used as the key to access the customer accounts. Imagine there are approximately 1 million accounts held in a sequential file. Every account number is a seven-digit code. Indexes could be set up which identify the first two digits in an account number (see Figure 1.3.6). Dependent on the result of this

first index search, there is a new index for the next two digits, which then points to all the account numbers, held in order, that have those first four digits. There is one index at the first level but each entry in it has its own index at the second level, so there are 100 indexes at the second level. Each of these indexes has 100 options to point to, so there will be 10,000 final index blocks. But each block of records has a maximum of 1000 records in it, so adding a new record in the right place is manageable, which it would not have been if the million records had had no underlying structure.

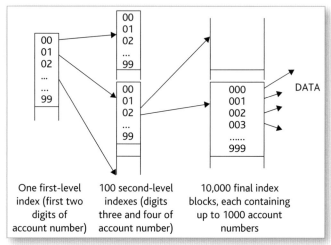

Figure 1.3.6   An index structure.

Activity

It is decided that the student file in your school should be stored using indexed sequential organisation. Design an index structure for it.

Repeat this activity for the items sold in a supermarket.

Random access

To access a random file, the data itself is used to give the address of where it is stored. This is done by carrying out some arithmetic (known as pseudo arithmetic because it doesn't make much sense) on the data that is being searched for.

For example, imagine that you are searching for Jawad's data. The rules that we shall use are that the alphabetic position of the first and last letters in the name should be multiplied together to give the address of the student's data. J is in alphabetic position 10 and D is 4, so Jawad's data are held at address $10 \times 4 = 40$ in memory.

This algorithm is particularly simplistic and does not give good results, as we shall soon see, but it illustrates the principle. Any algorithm can be used as long as it uses the same calculation for all records. This type of algorithm is known as a "hashing algorithm" or "hashing function".

The problem with this example can be seen if we try to find Jaheed's data. Jaheed's data are also calculated to be at address $10 \times 4 = 40$. The data for Jaheed cannot be there because Jawad's data are already there. This is called a *clash* or *collision*. When a clash occurs, the simple solution is to work down sequentially until there is a free space. So the computer would inspect addresses 41, 42, and so on until a blank space is found.

The algorithm suggested here will result in a lot of clashes which will slow access to the data. A simple change in the algorithm eliminates all clashes. If the algorithm writes the alphabetic position of all the letters in the name as a two-digit number and joins them together, there is only a clash if two people have the same name. For example:

Jawad = 10 01 23 01 04 giving the address
1001230104
Jaheed = 10 01 08 05 05 04 giving the address
100108050504

The problem of clashes has been solved, but at the expense of using up vast amounts of memory (in fact more memory than the computer has at its disposal). This is known as redundancy. Having so much redundancy in the algorithm is obviously not acceptable. A sensible hashing algorithm needs to be a compromise that minimises redundancy without producing too many clashes or collisions.

Discussion

Establish a hashing algorithm that could allow random access to a student file using the student name as the key field.

Selecting data types and structures

Data types

When a computer program stores data, the program code makes clear the type of the data.

Different data that needs to be stored requires different data types to be used. In some cases, the choice of data type is obvious. For example, if the data to be stored is the quantity of items left in the supermarket, it must be a whole number and therefore needs to be stored as an integer. If the item of data to be stored is the name of the item stocked by the supermarket, then it is obviously text or string data.

Things become more difficult when there is a choice that can be made. A date is one of these cases. It could be stored as a string because it is not written as all digits, but the programming language may have a specific data type, e.g. Date/Time, available. This can allow the data to be processed in particular ways. For example, an item arrives at the supermarket on a certain date and it is known that these items stay fresh for 10 days after arrival. If the date was stored as a string it would be difficult to work out the date by which the item should be sold, however if it is stored as a date then the computer is set up to be able to add 10 days to it and so calculate the sell by date.

If the data item is the Universal Product Code (a **barcode**), it is tempting to suggest that it should be stored as an integer, as the barcode is made up of digits. However, integers should make sense when arithmetic is done to them and two barcodes added together do not make any sense. They should therefore be stored as strings.

Data structures

We have so far studied two data structures: a stack and a queue. You should be able to justify the use of a particular type of structure for storing data in given circumstances. Examination questions based on this will be restricted to arrays, stacks and queues and will be unambiguous.

For example, a question might say "Jobs are sent to a printer from a number of sources on a network. State a suitable data structure for storing the jobs that are waiting to be printed, giving a reason for your answer."

The answer would be "A queue, because the next one to be printed should be the one that has been waiting longest."

1.3 j ## Backup and archiving data

Backing up

Data stored in files is often very valuable. It has taken a long time to input to the system and may be irreplaceable. If a bank loses the file of customer accounts because the hard disk crashes, then the bank is out of business, so it makes sense to take precautions against a major disaster. The simplest solution is to make a copy of the data in the file, so that if the disk is destroyed, the data can be recovered. This copy is known as a **backup**.

In most applications, the data are so valuable that it makes sense to produce more than one backup copy of a file. Some of these copies are stored away from the computer system in case of a hazard, such as a fire, which could destroy everything in the building.

The first issue with backing up files is how often to do it. There are no right answers but there are wrong ones; it all depends on the application. A file that is frequently altered needs to be backed up more often than one that is very rarely changed (what is the point of making another copy if it hasn't changed since the previous copy was made?). A school student file may be backed up once a week, whereas a bank customer file may be backed up hourly.

The second issue is that the backup copy is rarely the same as the original file because the original file keeps changing. If a backup is made at 9:00am and an alteration is made to the file at 9:05am, the backup does not include the change that has been made. It is very nearly the same, but not quite. Because of this a separate file of all the changes that have been made since the last backup is also kept. This file is called the **transaction log** and it can be used to update the copy if the original is destroyed. This transaction log is very rarely used. Once a new backup is made the old transaction log can be destroyed. Speed of access to the data in the transaction log is not important because it is rarely used, so a transaction log tends to use serial storage of the data. If an examination question asks for an example of using a serial file, a transaction log is a good one to use.

Archiving

Sometimes data are no longer used. A good example would be in a school when some students leave at the end of the year. Their data are still on the computer file of students, taking up valuable space. It is not sensible to just delete it because there are all sorts of reasons why the data may still be needed. For instance, a past student may ask for a reference. If all the data has been erased it may make it impossible to write a sensible reference. Data that is no longer needed on the file but may be needed in the future should be moved onto a long-term storage medium and stored in case it is needed. This is known as producing an **archive** of the data. (Schools normally archive data for seven years before destroying it.)

Notice that an archive is *not* used for retrieving the file if something goes wrong. It is *only* used for storing little used or redundant data in case they are ever needed again, so that space on the hard drive can be freed up.

Discussion

A small shop specialises in locally produced jewellery for the tourist industry. A computer system is used to keep a file of all the items that the shop has in stock. When new stock comes into the shop or stock is sold, the file is updated.
a. Devise a suitable backup routine for the manager of the shop to follow.
b. Describe how data could be archived on this system and why it is necessary.

Summary

- All data in a computer are stored in groups of bits. The complete set of characters that the computer uses is known as its character set. Character sets with standard codes (e.g. eight-bit ASCII and 16-bit Unicode) enable computers to exchange data.

- Integers (whole numbers) are stored in one byte, two bytes or four bytes.

- Boolean data has only two possible values and can be represented by one bit (0 meaning false and 1 meaning true).

- Date/time data and currency data have specific representations according to the applications software that uses them.

- Character data represents a single character in the character set of the computer and is stored in one or two bytes.

- Positive integers are stored in binary form:
  - The easiest way to convert from denary is to use a column diagram and put a 1 or 0 for each heading value in the number:

128	64	32	16	8	4	2	1

  - The easiest way to convert to denary is to add up the columns containing a 1.

- An array is similar to a table, with parallel columns and rows of data.

- When an array is initialised, the computer is told its identifier name, size and type of data.

- Data is often read into an array in a loop:

```
FOR Index ← 1 TO 10
   Name[Index] ← INPUT
ENDFOR
```

- A serial search on an array is also done in a loop:

```
WHILE Index < 11 AND DataFound = FALSE
   IF Name[Index] = SearchValue
      THEN DataFound ← TRUE
      ELSE Index ← Index + 1
   ENDIF
ENDWHILE
```

- A stack operates in a LIFO fashion: the last item to be added to the stack is the first to leave it.

- A queue operates in a FIFO fashion: the first item to be added to the queue is the first to leave it.

- When data is stored in fixed-length records, the same number of bytes is allocated to each data item (field) with no reference to how much data is stored. For example, if 10 characters are allowed for a forename and 15 for a surname, a record for "Peter Smith" will have a lot of empty space.

- Serial access to data means starting at the beginning of an unordered file (data stored in the order it is entered) and reading it to the end. Backup or archive files may be held serially.

- Sequential access to data means starting at the beginning of an ordered file (data stored in an key field order, such as alphabetically) and reading it to the end. Data files that are processed in batches (such as a payroll file) may be held sequentially.

→

Summary continued …

- Indexed sequential access to data means that the search can be reduced by reading an index to find an address closer to the required data. Once at the block, the data is read sequentially. Large files of data that are usually accessed in a particular order (e.g. phone numbers by subscriber surname) may be held in an indexed sequential manner.
- Random access to data means that data is stored in random order but that a series of indexes keeps the address of the data so that a search can go straight to it. Data such as a customer file that requires fast access to a particular customer record is held in a random access fashion.
- Serial organisation of files is implemented very simply: new records are added at the end of the file and the file must be read in order to find any record.
- Sequential organisation of files is implemented by inserting a new record in the correct order, so spaces must be opened up in the data to allow for insertion. The sequential order of the records is done using a key field.
- Random organisation of files may be implemented using a hashing algorithm. The hashing algorithm calculates a number which files the address of the record. This same number is used to retrieve the record.
- Data types and data structures should be appropriate to the problem. For example, a phone number is a string of characters rather than an integer because it usually starts with a "0" and no arithmetic is performed on it.
- Data is backed up to ensure that it is not lost in the event of a computer failure.
- Fast-changing data may be backed up daily (or more frequently) with a file of transactions since the last backup.
- Data is archived once it is no longer required by the organisation's operations. It is kept in an archive in case it is needed in the future.

Test yourself

1. Express the number 113 (denary) in binary in a byte.   [2]

> **Hint**
>
> You need to show a method of working out. The question states the size of the binary number (a byte), so you must use the correct number of bits. You can use a calculator to check the results.

2. Describe how characters are stored in a computer.   [3]

> **Hint**
>
> Remember to make *three* points.

3. A library keeps both a book file and a member file. The library does a stock take twice a year and orders new books only once a year. Members can join or cancel their membership at any time.
   a. Describe how the library can implement a system for backing up the files. [4]
   b. Explain the part that would be played by archiving in the management of the files. [4]

> ### Hint
>
> Remember that backing up and archiving are not the same thing. Consider the purpose of each process and when it would be used. Give specific suggestions based on the scenario. There are two files: a book file and a member file. Try to say two things about each file in part (a) and part (b).

4. a. Explain what is meant by an integer data type. [2]
   b. State what is meant by Boolean data. [1]

> ### Hint
>
> The key words are "explain" and "state". Part (b) does not require any detail.

5. An array is to be used to store data. State **three** parameters that need to be given about the array before it can be used, explaining why each is necessary. [6]
6. A stack is implemented using an array. Items may added to and removed from the stack.
   a. State a problem that may arise when:
      i. adding a new value to the stack
      ii. reading a value from the stack. [2]
   b. Explain how the stack pointer is used to recognise when such problems occur. [2]
7. A library stores details of the books that are available. Two fields stored are title and author.
   a. Suggest three other fields that it would be sensible for the library to store in this file, giving a reason why each of your chosen fields would be needed. [6]
   b. State which field would be used as the key field of the record and explain why a key field is necessary. [2]
8. a. Explain the difference between a serial file and a sequential file. [2]
   b. Describe what is meant by a hashing algorithm and explain why such an algorithm can lead to clashes or collisions. [3]

> ### Hint
>
> Only three marks are available. Do not go into too much detail. Check that you are answering the question asked.

1.4 Hardware

1.4 a ## The components of a processor

The first thing to be said in this section is what it does not include. The fetch–execute processing cycle and complex diagrams showing how the various parts of the processor connect up and communicate with each other are not introduced until Chapter 3.3. The requirements of this section are very simple. They are restricted to a basic understanding of what the parts of the processor are meant to do.

Control unit

All computers execute **program instructions**. These instructions are in a particular order in the program. By following them and carrying them out, the computer accomplishes whatever task it was meant to do. The job of the **control unit** is to manage the instructions and make sure that all the other parts of the processor do what they should be doing.

The control unit has a number of roles:

- It decides which instruction to carry out next and fetches it.
- It decodes instructions to work out what needs to be done to execute them.
- It tells other parts of the processor what they should do to carry out the instruction. It does this by sending control signals to other parts of the processor.
- It synchronises the actions of the processor using signals from its internal clock.

Arithmetic and logic unit (ALU)

The **arithmetic and logic unit** (**ALU**) is where things are actually done in the processor. The ALU contains circuitry that allows it to add numbers together (do arithmetic). It also allows for decisions to be made, by enabling logical comparisons (e.g. if a total is negative then report error).

The ALU acts as the gateway between the processor and other parts of the computer system. All input to the processor and output from the processor goes into the ALU and waits there while the control unit decides what to do with it.

Main memory

The third component of the central processing unit is the storage. **Main memory**, also referred to as **primary memory** or the **immediate access store** (**IAS**), stores everything that the processor is going to use. This includes all the program instructions and the data needed to carry out those instructions.

The programs which are part of the operating system also need to be stored in memory (see Figure 1.4.1).

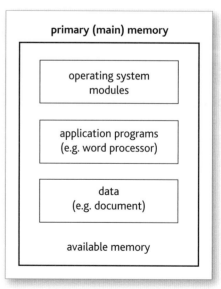

Figure 1.4.1   Main memory.

Types of primary memory

The first question that needs to be asked is "What is primary memory?"

In the previous section, we introduced a the concept of the processor needing to store data of all types in memory. However, there are plenty of other places that a computer can store data or programs e.g. on a disk drive or a CD-ROM. These are secondary storage and are discussed in the next section (page 32).

We stated that all the data and program instructions that the processor uses have to be in the processor's memory. This "memory" is usually described as RAM in a computer's specification. For example, a specification might say that the computer has "4 GB of RAM". This describes the capacity of the primary memory of the processor.

The alternative term of "immediate access store" conveys the meaning that data held in the main memory is immediately available to the processor. This means that it is available at speeds of the order of microseconds, which is an important consideration in the rest of this chapter.

There are many different types of primary memory, including PROM, EPROM, EAROM, SRAM, DRAM. They are all types of either RAM or ROM and you have no need to learn the details of any of them. We discuss the basic types of memory (ROM and RAM) in the rest of this section.

Read-only memory (ROM)

Read-only memory (ROM) is memory whose contents cannot be altered. Even when the computer is switched off, the contents of the ROM are not affected. There is very little that needs to be stored in ROM so it tends to be of a very small capacity.

In the past, the whole operating system was stored in ROM. As soon as the computer was turned on, programs would be there very quickly, ready for use. However, storing the operating system in ROM made it impossible to upgrade the operating system. For this reason, the operating system is normally stored on the hard drive of a computer along with all the other programs that may be used.

When the computer is switched on, it needs an operating system to be able to do anything useful. A small program stored in ROM has the job of loading the operating system from the hard drive so that the computer can work. This program is called the "bootstrap loader" and the process of retrieving the operating system is known as "booting up" the computer system.

Some processors are used in applications (such as a washing machine or a burglar alarm system) where all the processing follows a standard pattern. The program instructions are standard each time it is used and it is important that the user cannot alter the instructions. Consequently, it is sensible to store them on ROM. In this case, the ROM is sizable compared to the rest of the primary memory and the processor is said to be embedded.

Random access memory (RAM)

Random access memory (RAM) stores programs that are being used by the computer (including parts of the operating system) and the data that is being used with those programs. When the computer is switched off, all data in RAM is lost. RAM is said to be *volatile* memory because its contents are lost when the power is switched off, whereas ROM is *non-volatile*.

Activity

Explain why RAM and ROM are different. Describe what is stored in each justifying your answers.

A typical examination question will ask for an example of what is stored in ROM and RAM. The safest answers are that the bootstrap loader is stored in ROM and user software and data are stored in RAM. If you say that the operating system is stored in ROM, you may have a problem. You should talk about **embedded systems** in that case, because the operating system is *not* stored in ROM in most microcomputer systems.

The processor's BIOS (if you don't know what that is, don't worry because there is no reason why you should at the moment) includes user-defined parameters and hence is not stored entirely in ROM. It tends to be stored in a special type of RAM which is refreshed using battery power when the system is switched off. This is outside the scope of this course and you should not use the BIOS as an example of storage in ROM.

Secondary storage media

Primary memory is memory within the central processing unit (CPU). It is here that the computer stores data that are in current use because the control unit does not have direct access to data that is stored anywhere outside the main memory.

However, the storage available in the processor is limited in size and is volatile. Some form of permanent storage is therefore needed and this is called **secondary storage**. Secondary storage can be categorised according to:

- the means by which the data are stored: optically, magnetically or on a solid state device
- the technique used for storage of the data: sequential or direct access
- the capacity of the medium
- portability of the medium
- access times to read data from or write data to the device.

As technology develops, other types of secondary storage will become available. You need to keep up-to-date with the types of storage that are in common usage. The syllabus does not mention any types by name.

Magnetic tape

Magnetic tape is still widely used, particularly for long-term storage of archive material and for backup copies of large files (see "Backup and archiving data" on page 26 in Chapter 1.3). The big disadvantage of tape is that access to the data stored is sequential. If an application needs data from the far end of the tape, then it will take a long time to read because it will have to read through the rest of the tape from the start.

This sequential access makes magnetic tape unsuitable for most data-handling applications. Consider what would happen if a supermarket stored its price lookup file on magnetic tape. The assistant would scan the barcode and then you could have a chat to the assistant for five minutes while you waited for the price to be found on the magnetic tape.

However, magnetic tape can hold large volumes of data and it is easily transported. This makes it suitable for offline storage of data. It is these qualities which make it valuable for producing and storing backup and archive copies of files stored on a computer system.

Magnetic hard disk

Figure 1.2.6 (on page 11) shows the tracks and data blocks on the surface of a magnetic disk "platter", which may be single- or double-sided. It is made of a rigid material and the read/write heads skim very close to the surface. A **hard disk** consists of more than one disk platter contained inside a sealed unit.

The storage density can be very great, so the amount of data that can be stored on a single surface is very great. This means that it is important to have strategies to be able to find data on the surface of the disk. The basic unit of storage is called a *block* or *sector*. The process of dividing the surface of a disk up into these manageable areas is called "formatting" (see "Utility software" on page 11 in Chapter 1.2).

A hard disk drive is likely to be the main secondary storage for a computer system. Although portable hard disk drives are available, they are more likely to be mounted inside the chassis of the computer.

Optical disc

A CD or DVD drive is an optical storage device. Such devices use the reflection of a laser from the pitted surface of the disc to read information. Large quantities of data can be stored on the surface and the medium is portable from one machine to another. Most personal computer systems are fitted with a CD or DVD drive, which makes the data stored truly portable between machines.

There are different types of optical storage medium:

- The data on a **CD-ROM** or **DVD-ROM** cannot be altered. For this reason, manufacturers have tended to use CD-ROMs to distribute software and large data files, such as encyclopaedias. Data-rich systems are now more likely to be produced on DVD than CD because DVDs provide greater storage capacity.
- In **CD-RW** and **DVD-RW**, the "RW" indicates "read and write". The contents of such discs can be both erased and re-written. This makes them particularly useful for transporting files and for backing up or archiving files. It is sensible to use an RW medium for backup copies of files because they need to be recorded on a regular basis. For example, a school backs up the student file every evening and keeps the last three backups. Using an RW disc means that

it can be copied over when the old copy of a backup is no longer required.

- In **CD-R** and **DVD-R**, the "R" indicates "read only". These discs only allow data to be written once. Once it has been written it cannot be altered, although the disc may be written to a number of times until all the capacity is used. The school that backs up its student file onto an RW disc every day may take an archive of data files less frequently, perhaps once a year. The important thing about this archive file is that it is stored safely over a long period of time in case it is ever needed again. This makes the use of an R disc appropriate, as it cannot be accidentally erased.

Solid state technology

Devices such as USB sticks (also known as USB pens or cards) use solid state technology. The data are stored on a circuit which reacts in the same way as primary memory and hence provides very fast access to the data. The devices are activated simply by plugging them into the computer's USB port. They are fully portable and very small.

Modern laptop computers are increasingly fitted with solid state memory for their secondary storage in place of a hard disk unit.

DVD-RAM disc

A **DVD-RAM** disc is very like a DVD-RW disc but the data are stored in a different way. The different form of storage means that:

- the surface can be written to far more often than the surface of a DVD-RW disc
- access to the data and the reading time is faster
- reading and writing can take place simultaneously.

If a DVD-RAM is used as the storage medium in a television-recording machine, it is possible to record one television programme at the same time as watching a different one from the disc. They can also be used as a subsidiary system to support the memory of a computer. They have a greater capacity than other forms of DVD but they are more expensive and cannot be used in an ordinary DVD player.

Blu-ray disc

Blu-ray is an optical storage technology which became commercially available around 2008. Blu-ray has the advantages of much larger storage capacities than other optical storage devices while at the same time being able to provide high-speed data transfers. These two advantages combine to make possible the extra data required for recording and playing back of high-definition video. Film distributors are increasingly making films available in Blu-ray format due the to vastly increased picture quality. The disadvantage is the cost which is much higher than standard DVDs – both for the discs and the player–recorder unit.

Extension

The difference between Blu-ray and DVD is in the type of laser used. Different lasers use different parts of the available wavelength of light. The shorter the wavelength, the more data can be squeezed onto the surface. Try to explain why this type of disc is called "Blu-ray".

Comparison of backing storage media

It is not possible to state the storage capacity of each type of media. First, the media do not have fixed sizes – for example, the amount of storage on a magnetic tape depends on the length and packing density of the tape. Second, the volumes change frequently as technology changes. By the time of publication, any numbers we would give would be likely to have increased. Because of this, it would be misleading to state the capacity of any of the media. Instead, we divide the media into categories, as shown in Table 1.4.1.

Table 1.4.1   Volume of data held.

Very large capacity	Large capacity	Limited capacity
• Fixed hard disks • Portable hard disks • Magnetic tapes • DVD-RAM discs • Blu-ray discs	• DVD-R, DVD-RW and DVD-ROM discs • Memory sticks or pen drives • Flash memory cards	• CD-R, CD-RW and CD-ROM discs

Access times to data are not fixed. Table 1.4.2 (page 34) gives an indication of comparative speeds. Think carefully about why data access to solid state technology devices are much faster than data access to a hard disk.

Table 1.4.2 Access times to data.

Very fast access	Fast access	Slow access
• DVD-RAM discs • Flash memory cards • Memory sticks or pen drives	• Fixed hard disks • External hard disks • All CD, DVD and Blu-ray discs	• Magnetic tapes

Comparative portability (Table 1.4.3) is based on the size and weight of the device and, in the case of some devices, how easy it is to remove from the computer.

Table 1.4.3 Portability.

Very portable	Less portable (because of size)	Not portable
• All CD, DVD and Blu-ray discs • Flash memory cards • Memory sticks or pen drives	• Magnetic tapes (although some cartridges are small) • External hard disks	• Fixed hard disks

We measure robustness by considering how easy is it to damage the media or device and how easy is it to lose the contents. The more robust a device, the better (see Table 1.4.4).

Table 1.4.4 Robustness.

Very robust	Robust	Not robust (if moved or dropped)
• Flash memory cards • Memory sticks or pen drives • Magnetic tapes	• CD-ROM, DVD-ROM, CD-R and DVD-R discs (but can be damaged) • CD-RW, DVD-RW, Blu-ray and DVD-RAM discs (but may lose data if wrongly used)	• Fixed hard disks • External hard disks

The cost of the different media is very variable but Table 1.4.5 shows an attempt at categorisation.

Table 1.4.5 Cost.

Cheap	Medium cost	Expensive
• All CD, DVD and Blu-ray discs • Memory sticks or pen drives	• DVD-RAM discs • Flash memory cards • Magnetic tapes	• Fixed hard disks • External hard disks

Common uses of backing storage media

Obviously, no list of uses can be complete. However, there are some common uses for each storage type which take into account its advantages and disadvantages:

- Magnetic tape is used for backup and archive files because it can store a large amount of data.

The slow data access does not matter because it is rare that the files will be used.

- A solid state device can be used for storing personal confidential files because it can be written onto and taken away from the computer. All PCs and laptops now have USB ports and solid state devices provide a good way of transferring data from one machine to another.

- A hard disk drive is used for storing software and user data files because it can store very large amounts of data and access to the data is fast. The disadvantage of being attached to one machine is not important if the same users always use the same machine.

- A CD-ROM or DVD-ROM disc is used to store software for installing onto a system, large reference files (such as encyclopaedias) and all forms of multimedia material. The main reason that they are good for this purpose is that the contents of the disc cannot be altered.

1.4 d ## Transferring data between primary and secondary storage

Data in a computer system can be stored in primary memory or in secondary storage.

It is necessary to transfer data from primary memory to secondary storage before the computer is switched off, otherwise the data in primary memory are lost. It is necessary to transfer data from secondary storage to primary memory when the processor wants to use them. Whichever direction the data are transferred, the method of transfer must be planned.

As shown in Figure 1.4.2, primary memory is part of the central processing unit (CPU). There is a continual exchange of data between primary memory and the secondary storage.

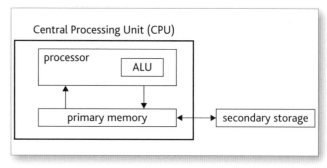

Figure 1.4.2 Central processing unit.

Primary memory operates at great speed (measured in microseconds) because it is part of the processor; secondary storage is probably a disk which is comparatively slow at reading or writing data (measured in milliseconds). This means that the processor should be able to get on with something else because the secondary storage is so slow. This problem is overcome by the use of a buffer.

A **buffer** is a small amount of fast memory used as a temporary store. The processor can send data to the buffer or receive data from the buffer very quickly and then get on with something else while the storage device takes its time in reading (or sending) the data. Saving data from primary memory to secondary storage has two stages: fill the buffer from the processor and then empty the buffer to storage.

This system is fine if the buffer can hold all the data that needs to be sent to the storage device. However, if there is more data than will fit in the buffer, the storage device has to be able to tell the processor (actually the control unit) that it has used up all the data in the buffer and is ready for more data. The storage device sends an **interrupt** to signal the processor that it needs attention. When the processor receives an interrupt, it stores it and carries on with what it is doing. When it finishes, it checks all the waiting interrupts and services the most important one. In this case, the processor would fill the buffer with more data.

The use of interrupts is widespread in any computer system. Any device (e.g. a printer or a keyboard) can use an interrupt to signal that it needs the attention of the processor.

Every interrupt has program code which is run to deal with or 'service' that interrupt. This code is called the **Interrupt Service Routine (ISR)**.

Activity

Describe how a large data file can be transmitted from the hard drive of a computer to primary memory.

Extension

Investigate the concept of "double buffering". Explain why it is useful when transmitting large data files.

 Common peripheral devices

A peripheral is any hardware device that is part of the computer system but is not part of the CPU.

Peripheral devices can be categorised under four headings:

- communication devices (covered in detail in Chapter 1.5)
- storage devices (described in "Secondary storage media" on pages 32–34)
- input devices
- output devices.

Input devices

There are too many input devices for you to be familiar with all of them. However, there are a number of common devices that you should know about. Some devices, e.g. mouse and keyboard, are so common that you are expected to have experience of using them. You should also learn about a variety of contemporary devices so that you can use them when answering questions that ask for a hardware configuration for a specific application.

Keyboard

A standard keyboard uses keys that generate the different character codes that the computer recognises in its character set. Most keyboards contain the letters of the alphabet. Calculator keypads are very different, as are the keypads for use at cash machines. They potentially reduce keying errors. Indeed, cash machine keypads have the added sophistication that the different keys stand for different characters or values at different times in the application. Mobile telephone keypads are sometimes numerically based, although some handsets now allow a full keyboard to be used. The characters needed for specialist machines are determined by the use to which the machines are to be put. Keyboards are the most common form of input device to a system because they are universally available and understood.

A QWERTY keyboard (Figure 1.4.3 on page 36) is so named because those are the first six characters on the top line of letters. The design is not very good because the arrangement of characters comes from the original typewriter layout – it was arranged to be difficult to use in order to slow typists down so that they did not jam the mechanism of the mechanical machines. It is difficult to improve the layout now because of all the experienced operators that can use the present keyboard so well. Retraining them to use a different arrangement of keys would not be feasible.

Figure 1.4.3   A standard QWERTY keyboard.

The keyboard is also difficult to use comfortably because the keys are arranged in rigid rows. Various attempts have been made to address this problem by arranging the keys in curves that fit the palm of the hand rather than in straight lines. These are called natural or ergonomic keyboards.

Concept keyboard

A standard keyboard is prone to damage from dirt or liquids. A "touch-sensitive" keyboard, or concept keyboard, has the keys as part of a continuous surface which has pressure-sensitive areas (Figure 1.4.4). Concept keyboards are ideal for use outside because rain does not damage them as it would a normal keyboard.

Figure 1.4.4   A concept keyboard used in a restaurant.

Concept keyboards can be programmed so that the individual keys represent different things within different application software. For example, a fast-food

establishment may use a concept keyboard for the input of orders. This is possible because the number of items on the menu is small (it must be less than the number of keys on the keyboard) so that one key stands for "burger" and another represents "regular fries". If the menu changes, the individual key mappings are reprogrammed. This not only makes data input far easier but it also allows for changes to be made very easily. The keyboard is less prone to damage in what may well be a greasy environment.

MIDI keyboard

A musical instrument digital interface (MIDI) keyboard is normally arranged like a piano keyboard. A special piece of hardware connects the musical keyboard to a computer system.

Mouse

A mouse is designed to be used with a pointer on the screen (Figure 1.4.5). It is particularly useful because it mimics the natural human action of pointing. A mouse is really two input devices in one. The physical movement of the mouse is an analogue input. The click of a switch (a mouse button) is a digital input.

Figure 1.4.5   A standard mouse.

Variations have been developed which use the same basic principles but are designed for particular applications. For example, many laptop computers include a tracker ball, which the user rolls rather than moving an object around a flat surface. Other laptops use a pressure (touch) pad which registers the movement of the user's finger over the surface. These are necessary because someone using a laptop may not have a flat surface available.

Investigate different mouse-type devices. The basic one described here registers the movement of a ball and selection using a button.
- What other forms of movement recognition are there, apart from registering a ball underneath the mouse?
- Many mice have more than one button; what are they used for? Explain what the wheel on the top of many mice is used for.
- Consider different forms of data communication between the mouse and the computer (it is not always connected by a wire).

Barcode reader

A barcode reader is a scanner that reads laser light reflected from dark and light lines of varying thicknesses (Figure 1.4.6). The lines are read in pairs and the widths of two lines together represent a particular character. The pairs of lines make up a code that can be converted into a number. When a barcode is scanned, the level of reflected light is captured as an electrical signal and converted to a digital (numerical) reading. This number can be used as the key field for a file of items.

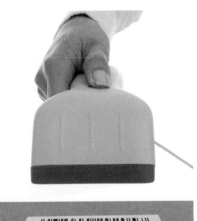

Figure 1.4.6　A barcode with the code number printed beneath it.

Barcodes can easily be misread, so one of the digits is used to check that the rest of the code has been read properly. This **check digit** is explained in detail in Chapter 1.8. At the moment, it is enough to know that this check is carried out every time a barcode is read.

Extension

Investigate the difference between the Universal Product Code (UPC) and the European Article Number (EAN). These are the most common barcode systems. This exercise should give you more idea of how barcodes represent values.

When an item is passed over a laser scanner in a shop, the terminal beeps to tell the shop worker that the code has been read properly. How does it know to beep?

Barcodes are particularly useful because they do not rely on human interaction to input the data. Barcodes can be printed on original packaging as the data does not change. We go into more detail about barcodes in Chapter 1.8.

Optical Character Reader

An optical character reader (OCR) is a device that can read and distinguish the different characters in a given character set. It works by comparing the shape of a scanned character with a library of stored shapes. OCR tends to be an unreliable form of input and works more effectively when it is restricted to a standard character set produced by printing rather than handwriting. OCR is used for reading post codes on printed documents. It is also the input part of a system for reading documents to blind people; the contents of the documents are output using a voice synthesiser.

The technique is in widespread use for billing systems. A utility bill is in two parts where the bottom section of the bill is returned by the customer with their payment. All the data about the bill (account number, amount, etc.) is encoded on the bill in characters which are then read by the computer system, hence capturing the data about the received payment. A document which is used in this way is called a **turnaround document**

It is possible to read OCR as "**optical character recognition**" (i.e. the technique, not the device). In Chapter 1.8, we consider OCR as an automatic data capture method.

Optical Mark Reader

An optical mark reader (OMR) is a device that can recognise the presence of a mark on a sheet of paper. The position of the mark is scanned and converted to a digital reading by the scanning software. For example, a school register may consist of a list of names of students in a class with two columns of small rectangles, one for present and one for absent. The same action (shading in a rectangle) stands for both being present and being absent. The difference is the position that the mark occupies on the paper. The sensitive areas of the sheet are printed in special ink that the optical scanner does not see (OMR documents tend to be printed in light blue or pink). Another widespread application of OMR is answer sheets for multiple-choice examinations (see Figure 1.4.7).

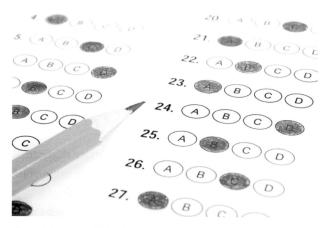

Figure 1.4.7   A multiple-choice exam paper for use with an OMR.

The big advantage of both OCR and OMR is that data can be input to a computer system without having to be transcribed, thereby reducing the number of errors at the **data capture** stage.

It is possible to read OMR as "**optical mark recognition**" (i.e. the technique, not the device). In Chapter 1.8, we consider OMR as an automatic data capture method.

Scanner

A **scanner** (Figure 1.4.8) is a device that converts a document into a series of pixels. Picture elements (pixels) are small squares that, when put together, form a picture. The larger the number of pixels, or the smaller each individual pixel, the better the definition of the final picture. There are different types of scanner, but they all use the same principle to capture the image. A typical use for a scanner would be to input a

photograph of a house that is for sale so that it can be included in an estate agent's publication or website.

Figure 1.4.8   A flatbed scanner.

Graphics tablet

A **graphics tablet** (Figure 1.4.9) is a flat glass surface on which the user can draw with a special pen. The tablet senses where the pen is pointing and converts the movements of the pen to a digital reading that is then interpreted by the software as a line, for example.

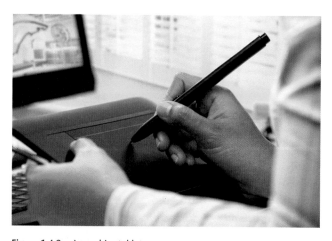

Figure 1.4.9   A graphics tablet.

Microphone

A microphone (Figure 1.4.10) can be used to input sound into a computer. The sounds can be used to provide an audio commentary for a slideshow or they can be converted to text.

An advantage of speaking into the computer is that input is more intuitive than typing at a standard keyboard. Software on the computer can translate the

Figure 1.4.10   A microphone.

sounds of spoken words into digital form for use in a word processor. Microphones are also used by disabled people for whom the use of some more commonly used input devices is simply not possible.

A disadvantage is that the software used to translate the spoken word into text can be unreliable. The first stage in using any voice-recognition software is to teach the software to understand the voice of the specific user.

Discussion

A microphone can capture input for a processor that controls a burglar alarm system in a car. The processor might be programmed to identify the sound of broken glass. This would be picked up by the microphone if someone broke into the car through a window. What would happen if a bottle was smashed outside the car? How could the microphone and processor recognise that this is not damage to the car?

Output devices

There are too many output devices to be able to document them all. However, you must be familiar with a range of output devices and know enough about them to apply them to specific applications. You are not expected to explain precisely how they work.

Screen

Monitor screens (Figure 1.4.11) are categorised according to the number of pixels displayed by the screen, known as the **screen resolution**. The more pixels, the better quality the picture.

(a)

(b)

Figure 1.4.11   Common computer monitors: a) a TFT and b) an older CRT screen. For a long time on CRT screen a resolution of 800 pixels × 600 pixels was common. Although higher resolutions, usually with screens with a larger physical size, were possible. Modern TFT and LCD screens have resolutions up to 1680 pixels × 1050 pixels. Programmers and media developers who find this still insufficient will often use two screens.

This text has been typed using a monitor with a very low-resolution, monochrome screen. If you consider the task, there is no reason for a more sophisticated device. However, a computer system running modern games software needs high-definition colour in order to produce a satisfactory picture. The more pixels that there are on the screen, the higher the resolution.

Touch screen

A **touch screen** (Figure 1.4.12 on page 40) acts as both an input device and an output device. Information is output by the system onto the screen and the user is invited to answer questions or make choices by pointing at a particular area of the screen. The device can sense where the user is pointing and can report the position to the processor. The processor can then deduce the user's response according to the screen position. Touch screens are particularly useful in areas where keyboards are not appropriate, for example where the device may suffer from vandalism. They are also useful for users who would find difficulty using other input devices, for example very young children.

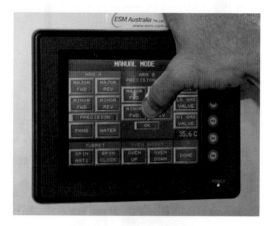

Figure 1.4.12   A touch screen.

Printer

A printer (Figure 1.4.13) is a device that provides the user with permanent, printed output from the system. The output is also known as **hard copy**. There are many different types of printer and you should be aware of a number of them, their uses, advantages and disadvantages. However, again there is no need to understand how they work.

Dot-matrix printers are slow by modern standards and the output is of poor quality. The output is produced by using a print-head made up of a matrix of pins. The print-head travels across the paper a line at a time. A carbon strip lies between the print-head and the paper. Characters are produced by striking the pins against the carbon strip on to the paper, hence a dot matrix printer is called an "impact printer". Unlike other types of printer, dot-matrix printers can produce multiple copies by using carbon paper or self-carbonating paper. For example, when a shopper makes a purchase with a credit or debit card, two copies of the receipt are produced – one for the shop and the other for the customer.

Inkjet printers produce output by spraying coloured inks onto the paper. The print-head consists of a number of ink cartridges – black, cyan, magenta and yellow – which each spray ink onto the page to produce a vast range of colour combinations. The print-head travels across the page a line at a time, in a similar way to a dot-matrix

Figure 1.4.13   Common types of printer: a) dot-matrix, b) inkjet and c) laser.

printer. The ink reservoir is heated and this vaporises droplets of ink, which then forces a small ink blob onto the paper. The ink is usually cool by the time the final line of output is produced. An inkjet printer is ideal for home use where colour is required, for example to produce photos. The price of the unit is reasonable but the cost of replacement ink cartridges must be considered.

Laser printers produce very high-quality output at high speed and at relatively low cost. A laser printer is a page printer. A print drum is negatively charged.

The printer generates a bitmap image of the page and a laser beam is shone onto the rotating drum. The laser creates an electrostatic charge which attracts negatively charged toner from the laser toner cartridge. The toner is fused onto the paper page with a heated roller. Typical applications include:

- an office environment in which the laser printer is used for general office administration, e.g. a mailshot to customers
- a school network where several network users have access to a shared printer.

Plotters

Plotters come in various configurations but the most common is a flatbed plotter (Figure 1.4.14). The paper is placed on the flat surface and set of pens move above the paper under the control of the software. Plotters are commonly used for applications that draw lines and geometric designs rather than characters. Plotters tend to be used for drawing blueprints, for example in an architect's office to produce detailed drawings of a building.

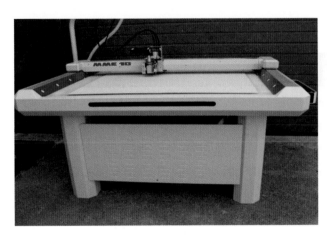

Figure 1.4.14   A flatbed plotter.

Speakers

Speakers (or a set of headphones) are used to output sound from a computer system. A specific use could be a machine which uses OCR to read documents for a blind person and then uses speakers to relay the contents by using a voice synthesiser.

Sensors and actuators

Sensors and **actuators** are devices that are used for automatic input and control in real-time systems. These devices and their uses are described in Chapter 3.7.

1.4 f Select appropriate peripheral hardware for an application

There are many other peripheral devices used for both input and output. A knowledge of some of them will be useful. However, we have discussed a sufficient range of devices for you to be confident answering questions in the exam. The questions normally take the form of presenting a given scenario and then asking for a description of the hardware required. The important thing to remember is that marks are not awarded for every device mentioned but for sensible suggestions for peripherals in a specific scenario. In other words, the mark is not given for "a keyboard" or "a mouse" but for suggesting sensible methods of input to a system. This section deals with the requirements of applications, rather than with the peripheral devices themselves.

When you choose peripheral devices, you must take into account a number of factors:

- Who are the people that are going to use the application? Specifically, consideration must be given to their age (whether they can read is an obvious issue), their ability with computer systems, their understanding of the software (whether they need to be given instruction on how to use it) and any physical disabilities which may make some hardware impossible to use.
- Under what circumstances will the system be used? If the input and output devices are to be used in the open air then the environment will dictate restrictions which would not be necessary if the system was being used inside a building.
- What software is being used? The software dictates the type of input required and the type of output that is produced. Consequently, it also has an influence on the peripherals that are suitable for that input and output.
- Is the system automated in any way? If so, the peripherals may include sensors and actuators. This point is included here but becomes relevant in Chapter 3.7.

When answering questions drawn from this section, compare the requirements of the application with the characteristics of the available hardware devices and be prepared to justify your choice.

It is also important to think in terms of four issues: input devices, output devices, storage devices and communication devices. We consider communication devices in Chapter 1.5.

Activity

A small shop has a single counter at which sales are made. The owner decides to replace the manual system of recording sales with a computerised system. Suggest a hardware configuration which would be sensible, justifying your choices.

(1.4 g) Speed mismatch between peripheral and processor

The power of the computer is the ability to store and process data at high speed. The different tasks that computers carry out are done by different pieces of hardware and there are unavoidable clashes between them. For example, a processor can calculate the results from data very quickly and it can very quickly send the results to a storage device or a printer. However, the peripheral devices to which the data are being sent are comparatively very slow in operation. Processor tasks are measured in the amount of time it takes electronic signals to be sent (microseconds) whereas peripheral devices are partly mechanical and operate on a timescale of milliseconds. For example, a hard drive needs to physically move the read/write head to the correct track and wait for the disk to rotate until the required block is under the head. To us, these actions are carried out incredibly quickly, but to the processor they are extremely slow.

This difference in the operating speeds of different parts of the computer system is referred to as the "speed mismatch of the system". One solution is the use of buffers (see "Transferring data between primary and secondary storage" on page 34).

Activity

Identify the slowest part of most computer systems. Try to describe what can be done to remove the problem of speed mismatch between this part of the system and the processor.

Summary

- The control unit contains the arithmetic and logic unit (ALU) and fetches and decodes program instructions and data.
- The main memory (RAM) transfers data to and from the processor and secondary storage.
- Random access memory (RAM), which is volatile, stores programs and data when in use.
- Read-only memory (ROM), which is non-volatile, has a smaller capacity than RAM and is used to store the bootstrap loader software.
- Secondary storage devices include:
  - magnetic tape which has the major disadvantage that it is a sequential access media only
  - hard disk, which allows direct access to data and encodes data magnetically on a disk surface organised into tracks and sectors
  - optical discs, which come in many variants, e.g. CD, DVD and Blu-ray, and encode data with pits and are read and written to the disc with a laser
  - solid state memory, which is becoming increasing widely used.
- A buffer is an area of temporary memory used to compensate for the speed mismatch between the processor and various input/output devices.
- An interrupt is a signal sent to the processor from a peripheral to seek the attention of the processor, e.g. a printer telling the processor it is out of paper. The interrupt is serviced by running its Interrupt Service Routine (ISR) code.

→

Summary continued ...

- Common input devices include the standard keyboard, the concept keyboard and the mouse.
- Input devices designed for automating data entry include optical mark readers (for OMR), optical character readers (for OCR) and barcode readers.
- More specialised input devices include:
  - a graphic tablet, where the user draws freehand on a glass tablet
  - microphone, which captures analogue sound data and converts this, using an analogue-to-digital converter, to digital data
  - sensors, which read data from the real-world environment such as pressure, temperature and movement
- Common output devices include:
  - a monitor, printer, plotter and speakers
  - actuators are used with a computer system which receives data from sensors. The actuator receives a signal from the processor to change the state of a mechanical device such as switching on/off a heater or motor
  - combined input and output device is a touch screen

Test yourself

1. State **three** functions of the arithmetic logic unit. [3]

   > **Hint**
   >
   > The key word is "state". Only simple statements are required.

2. a. State **two** differences between RAM and ROM. [2]
   b. Explain what types of data would be stored in each of RAM and ROM, giving reasons for your answers. [4]

3. A student has a home computer system. State what storage devices would be used on a home computer system and justify the need for each one. [8]

   > **Hint**
   >
   > The question does not specify the number of devices. Each device has to be named and justified. There are 8 marks for the question, so mention four devices.

4. Describe how buffers and interrupts can assist in the transfer of data between primary memory and a secondary storage device. [4]

   > **Hint**
   >
   > Clearly identify the process you are describing.

5. A department store decides to place a computer system by the main entrance so that customers can locate specific items in the store. The departments remain in the same places, but the articles available in each department change on a regular basis. State a sensible hardware design for such a computer system, giving reasons for your choices of hardware. [6]

   > **Hint**
   >
   > You must give a reason for each piece of hardware. Do not make a comprehensive list.

6. Explain what is meant by speed mismatch in computer systems. [3]

1.5 Data transmission and networking

1.5 a **The characteristics of LANs and WANs**

All the systems that have been mentioned so far have been stand-alone computers. This means that the systems we have discussed so far are not connected to other machines.

Consider a classroom with 20 stand-alone computers. Every time a lesson ends, you need to store your files on secondary storage. It would be possible to store the files on a USB stick and take them away with you, but the likelihood is that the files are stored on the hard disk. The next time you want to use those files, you need to sit at the same computer. It would be much more sensible to have a system that allowed access to the same files through any of the 20 computers. To allow for this, the computers need to be connected to each other so that you can store your files on a shared disk drive. When computers are connected together to share files, they form a network.

A network of 20 computers in a school classroom is obviously on a small scale, not because 20 is a small number, but because communication is easier when short distances are involved. If a business with a head office in London and factories in Lahore and Mumbai want to connect their computers between the three sites there is an obvious problem of distance to be overcome.

Generally, a network over short distances is called a **local area network (LAN)** while those over great distances are **wide area networks (WAN)**. Whether a network is a WAN or a LAN, it allows the computers to:

- communicate with one another
- share information centrally
- share copies of software
- give access to data and program files to multiple users.

In a LAN there is the added benefit of being able to share hardware. For example, the classroom with 20 computers may only have one or two printers. Also, those printers may be of different types and used for different tasks. This means that the type of printer used is dependent on the job that the user wants it to do rather than on the type of printer that happens to be connected to the computer from which the printout is sent.

To summarise:
- Computers can be linked together to form networks.
- If the distances are short – typically in the same building – the network is a LAN.
- If the distances are longer – regional national or global – the network is a WAN.
- Networks allow computers to communicate and share hardware and software.

There are two major issues with linking computers in a network. The first is that it is more difficult to control access to a network and to files that are stored on the network. This means that files are less secure than they would be on a stand-alone machine. The second disadvantage applies to machines on a LAN. These machines share hardware, such as printers and hard disk storage. This is an advantage if all is working well, but if the shared disk drive fails then work has to be stopped across the LAN.

In Chapter 3.8, we discuss the issues around the implementation of a network.

Discussion

What are the advantages and disadvantages of linking a set of computers in a LAN?

1.5 b Network hardware and software

- In a network, each computer needs a special piece of hardware attached to the processor, called a **network card** or **network interface card** (**NIC**).
- The computers need to be connected in some way. A LAN uses cables or wireless signals to carry data from one machine to another.

Wired networks

Typically, the cable used in a LAN is coaxial, similar to the cable used to connect an aerial to a television set. The signal gradually deteriorates as it is sent down the cable, which means that the maximum possible length of the cable is about 300 metres. This maximum depends on a number of factors, not least the quality of the cable used, but all cable is ultimately going to be limited in length.

Wireless networks

For wireless communication, there needs to be a central router (Figure 1.5.1) that broadcasts a signal to which the computers on the network can connect.

Wireless communication means that computers on the network do not need to be fixed in position. If a legitimate computer can gain access to the **wireless network**, it is also possible for an unauthorised computer to pick up the wireless signal and log on to the network. A wireless network tends to have more security systems than a cable network because the

Figure 1.5.1   A router.

more powerful the wireless signals that are used, the greater the area where the signals can be picked up and the greater the chance that someone will be able to receive the signal that shouldn't. It is not possible to restrict wireless signals to being inside a building so the security of the data becomes an issue.

With a number of computers attached to the network, a device is needed for the central storage of files. This task is carried out by a computer whose job is to control the network. It is known as a **server** or a network server. There are many roles the server must carry out:

- A file server is responsible for the storage of program files, the network operating system and users' data files.
- A domain controller server is responsible for the authentication of user log-ons.
- A print server is responsible for the management of shared devices.

On many LANs – typically in a small business environment – these server functions are all carried out by a single network server.

The communications around such a system are obviously quite difficult to control. It is necessary to have a set of instructions that the network must follow. A network operating system provides those instructions.

Wide area networks

A wide area network differs because the distances involved tend to be far greater than for a LAN. It is not possible to connect all the computers by a cable or by a wireless signal. In the UK, network cabling is already in place in the form of the public service telephone network (PSTN). Two computers that are a long distance apart can simply ring each other up!

Unfortunately, the type of signals produced by a computer are different from the type of signals that can be sent down a telephone line. In order to send a computer signal down a telephone line, it must be converted from a digital signal (used by the computer) to an analogue signal (used by the telephone network). This is done by hardware called a **modem**. There must be a modem at the other end of the line in order to convert the analogue signal back to a digital signal.

This not the whole story by any means and more detail about communications are covered in the remainder of this chapter, but the full story has to wait until we return to the topic of networking in Chapter 3.8.

Types of data transmission

Serial transmission of data

Data needs to be transmitted between devices in a computer system. The easy way is by using a single wire that links the two devices. Data are transmitted down the wire in the form of bits, so a byte that represents a single character is transmitted as eight bits in sequence, one signal for each bit. Figure 1.5.2 shows the data byte 01101101 in the process of being transmitted from Device 1 to Device 2. As there is only one wire, only one bit can be transmitted at any time. This is known as **serial transmission** of data.

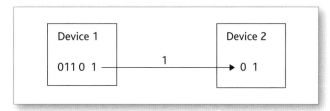

Figure 1.5.2 Serial transmission of data.

Serial transmission has the advantage of being simple and reliable because the next bit is not transmitted until the current one has been received. However, because only one bit can be transmitted at a time, the transmission is slow. All peripheral devices that connect through a Universal Serial Bus (USB) use serial data transmission.

Parallel transmission of data

If the devices are connected by more than one wire, then more bits can be sent simultaneously. A sensible number of wires would be eight, because then a whole byte can be sent at the same time (Figure 1.5.3).

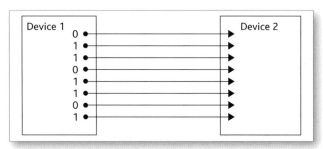

Figure 1.5.3 Parallel transmission of data.

This type of data transfer is called **parallel data transmission**.

Parallel transmission of data is obviously faster than serial transmission because all the bits are travelling at the same time. However, because of the fine tolerances in the transmission, it is less reliable as the bits can become muddled up. If one bit is delayed because of the resistance on its wire, for example, it may arrive in time to be counted as a bit in the next byte! This problem, where the bits become out of sequence, is called "skew". Parallel transmission is only suitable for short distances.

Modes of transmission

If data can travel in only one direction then it is known as a **simplex** transmission (Figure 1.5.4a). A good example of simplex transmission of data is teletext information which is passed to a television receiver. There is no way to send data in the other direction.

When data can pass in both directions at the same time it is known as **duplex** transmission of data (Figure 1.5.4b). An example of duplex transmission would be a telephone conversation as both users can speak and be heard at the same time. Duplex transmission is sometimes called "full duplex" in order to distinguish it from "half-duplex" transmission.

When data can pass in both directions but in only one direction at a time, the transmission is called **half duplex** (Figure 1.5.4c). An example of half-duplex transmission is a CB radio system in which each handset can be set to either receive mode or send mode.

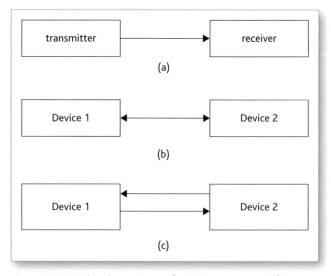

Figure 1.5.4 Modes of transmisson: a) simplex transmission, b) duplex transmission and c) half-duplex transmission.

1.5 d Bit rates and time sensitivity of data

Data needs to be sent to devices in a computer system from other devices. For example, a picture stored in the memory of the computer may need to be sent down a telephone line to another computer. Remember that the more pixels that there are and the more colours that can be represented, the better the picture quality. However, there is a limit to the amount of data that can be transmitted in a given time down the phone line, so a decision needs to be made. One choice is to have as much detail as possible and accept that it takes a long time to transmit. The other is to limit the resolution of the picture and the number of colours used to depict it, meaning that there is less data to send (i.e. a smaller file size) so that the message is sent more quickly.

The number of bits that can be sent in one second is known as the "bit rate". The units used to measure the bit rate are baud: 1 baud = 1 bit per second. (It may be more complicated than this, as 1 baud = 1 bit per second assumes that one signal change represents a single bit.)

Note that text can seemingly be sent much more quickly than other forms of data. The rate at which data are sent is the same but there is less data to be sent for each item of text. This means that many pages of text can be sent in the same amount of time that it takes to transmit a single image, so it seems that text is transmitted more quickly.

When data other than text is being transmitted, e.g. on the Internet, it is important to limit the amount of data that needs to be sent to stop the time taken to download the data being unreasonably long. The amount of data can be limited by reducing the file size of pictures so that they take up only a small part of the screen or restricting them to a few colours. Speeding up the transmission of the data is achieved by reducing the amount of data that is sent. This is known as **file compression**.

We are talking about the *rate* of data transmission, not the *speed* of data transmission. Imagine a pipe which is used to fill a pool with water. If we want to fill the pool more quickly, we can either force the water through more quickly (increasing the speed of the water flowing through the pipe) or use a larger diameter pipe (increasing the rate of water flowing through the pipe). In terms of computer transmissions, the speed of data transmission remains roughly the same however it is done. If we want to increase the amount of data in a given time period, we need to increase the rate at which the data are sent. A measure of the amount of data that can be sent in a given time period is the **bandwidth** of the medium being used. The higher the bandwidth, the more data can be sent in a given time. In an examination question about this, be careful not to say "the speed at which data are sent" but instead talk about "the rate at which data can be sent".

The size of the transmitted file is not an issue as long as we have time to wait for it to be downloaded or uploaded. In simple terms, if a file consists of 100,000 bits of data and the baud rate is 1000 bits per second, then the file will take 100 seconds (nearly two minutes) to be transmitted. If the file of data is a text file which the recipient will read after they have finished another task, then the two minutes taken to transmit the file does not matter; it does not make the file less useful.

If the file is a video clip, transmission time does not matter if the file is going to be watched after the recipient has done some other work. It begins to matter if the file is a video that the recipient wants to watch as it is being transmitted. This technique is called **streaming**. For streaming, it is important that the file can be transmitted quickly enough to let the person watch the video as it is being transmitted. In other words, the data must arrive quickly enough to compose and display the media. If the bit rate is not high enough then the video will appear to judder, or even to freeze, while the computer waits for the next download of data.

This difference between the files that makes the baud rate so important is not the size of the file, but how it is used. If a file is going to be watched in real time as it is received then the data are said to be "time sensitive". Time-sensitive files need a high baud rate, not necessarily just large files. Much recent research has been done on streaming as computers are increasingly used for the download and viewing of media files.

1.5 e Errors in data transmission

When data, of whatever type, are transmitted from one device to another, they are transmitted as a series of binary digits. Any data that are transmitted are going to be made up of a very large number of bits.

Consequently, there are bound to be occasions on which the data are not transmitted correctly or on which they become corrupted during transmission.

There are only two possible types of error that can occur; either a 1 is received as a 0 or a 0 is received as a 1. Mistakes rarely occur, but when they do occur they can be very serious, as the data are no longer correct. This makes it important that there should be methods for checking the data when they are transmitted.

Echoing back

The simplest way of checking the transfer of the data is to send the data back again. If the data sent back are the same as the data sent in the first place then the original data must have reached the destination unaltered. If not, the data must be sent again. This is known as echoing back. Echoing back is very effective, but suffers from having to send data twice. The transmission mode needs to be either duplex or half-duplex to allow data transfer in both directions.

Checksum

Data are normally sent as blocks of bytes rather than as individual bytes. Whatever the data represent, they are in binary form and hence could be treated as numbers that can be added together. Another checking procedure is to add all the bytes that are being sent in the block of data. Any bits lost at the most-significant end as a carry are ignored, so the answer is an eight-bit number. This "check byte" or **checksum** is calculated before the data are sent and then calculated again when they are received. If there are no errors in the transmission, the two answers match. If, however, the two bytes are different there must be at least one checksum that has been corrupted and the whole block of data has to be re-sent.

Parity check

A **parity check** involves checking that the number of 1 bits in a byte totals to an even number (called "even parity") or an odd number (called "odd parity").

If two devices that are communicating decide to use odd parity, there must always be an odd number of 1s. If a byte is received with an even number of 1s, an error must have occurred. For example, the byte 01011000 is

sent. It has three 1 bits so it passes the odd parity check. When it is transmitted, the byte received is 11011000. This has four 1 bits, which is an even number, so there must have been an error in transmission. The receiving device would ask for it to be sent again. Although this example uses odd parity, even parity can equally well be used. The two devices have to agree which type of parity to use.

Parity is used not only during data transfer between devices but also when data are transferred between different components of the CPU.

If two mistakes are made in the same byte, they cancel each other out and the faulty data are accepted. This problem can be overcome and a clever way of identifying mistakes can be implemented by using **parity blocks**.

A byte can represent a character code in eight bits, giving potentially 256 different characters. However, an ASCII character reserves one of the bits for a parity bit. This leaves seven bits for the character code, reducing the number of different characters to 128.

Parity blocks

A further check can be made on the data bytes which are transmitted. An additional byte, called the parity byte, is calculated and transmitted for each group of bytes. The data bytes and parity byte together are called a parity block.

A parity block is like a rectangle made up of rows and columns. The last bit in each row, i.e. in each data byte, is the parity bit, which checks if there is an error in the byte. One possible problem with a parity bit check is that two errors in the same byte are not picked up by the parity bit check. They are however detected by the check which the parity byte performs.

Think of the parity byte not as data but as a whole row of parity bits, each of which is there to check the column of bits above it in the grid.

Consider the following transmission in which four data bytes are followed by the parity byte using odd parity. The correctly transmitted parity block (four data bytes followed by the parity byte) is shown in Figure 1.5.5.

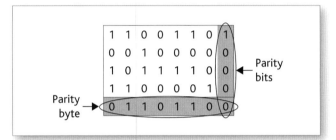

Figure 1.5.5 Correctly transmitted parity block.

Assume that there was an error in the transmission and the bytes shown in Figure 1.5.6 were received by the device. The parity bit for data byte three is calculated as 1. A 0 bit was received, so the conclusion is that there must be an error with it. The parity byte shows that there is an error with the calculation in column three. The conclusion is that the incorrect bit in byte three must be the one in column 3, so change this from 0 to 1.

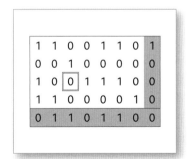

Figure 1.5.6 Received parity block with one bit in error.

Consider Figure 1.5.7, which shows two bits received in error in the same data byte. Byte three passes the parity bit check. The point here is that the parity bit is in error! The parity byte, however, shows that there

is an error – the bits in positions 4 and 8 of the parity byte do not match the calculation for columns 4 and 8.

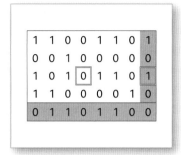

Figure 1.5.7 Received parity block with two bits in error.

It is claimed that checking the parity bits and using a parity block check will identify 99% of all transmission errors.

(1.5 f) Packet switching and circuit switching

When a message is sent from one computer to another, particularly over a wide area network, the message may have to pass through other devices. This may be forced on the system because there is no direct route between the sending and receiving computers.

In the network shown in Figure 1.5.8, it would be easy to send a message from A to D or from A to B because A is directly connected to both of them. However, sending a message from A to C is more involved as there is no direct route.

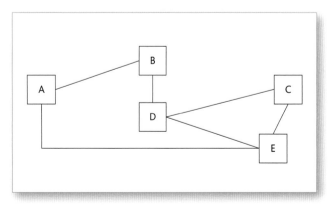

Figure 1.5.8 A network. Each sending and receiving point is called a node.

The message can be sent from A to C using **packet switching** or **circuit switching**.

In packet switching, the message is split into a number of equal-sized packets (or datagrams). Each packet has a label – its destination address – saying where it is meant to be going and a packet sequence number. These packets are sent along communication lines towards the destination. Each time a packet reaches a node (a point of intersection) on the network, the node decides which direction to send it on. For example, one packet in the message from A reaches node D. The obvious route to take is the one directly to C. If it is in use for another message, D decides to send the packet to E. When the next packet arrives at D, the line to C is free, so the packet is sent direct to C. The packets are likely to arrive at C out of sequence. When all the packets have arrived, the message has to be re-assembled in the correct order.

Packet switching allows optimum use of the connections around the network. It maximises the number of routes in use at any one time. Packet switching is also valuable because it becomes almost impossible to intercept a whole message and therefore messages are more secure. However, some packets may take a long time on the network and the receipt of the complete message is only as fast as the slowest packet. When the packets have all arrived they need to be re-ordered in order to re-create the original message.

In circuit switching, the network reserves a route from A to C. The message can then be sent directly from A to C and does not need to be re-ordered when it arrives. Circuit switching ties up a large part of the network for the duration of the transmission but it does mean that the whole message is kept together.

(1.5 g, h) Protocols

When data are being transferred in a computer system there must be rules set up as to how the transfer is going to be done. The set of rules that needs to be established to allow the transfer of data to be carried out is known as a **protocol**. There are a number of protocols that you may have heard of, e.g. http or TCP/IP, but don't worry about specific examples. You do not need to know specific examples of protocols but you should be able to discuss some of the issues that go to make up a protocol.

Typical rules would define:

- the wire connecting the two parts of the system: errors would occur if one device had a serial connection and the other was expecting a parallel connection
- the bit rate used: if one device sent data at a particular bit rate and the other device was set to receive at a different rate, the message would not be received correctly
- the parity used: if one device used even parity and the other device used odd parity then no correctly sent byte of information would ever be accepted.

When two devices need to communicate, the initial contact between them is a signal called the **handshake signal**. This involves an exchange of data between the two devices to establish that they are both ready for the communication to start and that they agree on the rules that are going to be used for the communication.

(1.5 i) Physical and logical parts of a protocol

The interface between two devices is the connection between them through which data can be sent. The *physical* part includes the wires or other connection. The *logical* part includes the rules agreed about the form of error checking used. There are many other rules to the logical parts of the protocol, for instance:

- how messages are routed from one place to another
- how the flow of data is going to be controlled
- how the data transfer can be synchronised so that data are not mixed up.

Most modern protocols use the concept of *layering* the different aspects of the communication. For instance, first set up the rules about how the devices are to be connected physically, and – as a separate issue – decide on the rules to spot errors that have been made in the data transfer. This is known as "layering the interface" because the most basic layer has to be done first and then more layers may be put on top. The physical parts of the protocol are the basic layers and then the logical parts are built on those.

The main advantage of layering the interface is that changes may be made to one layer without having to make a change to any of the other layers. It also allows manufacturers to develop communication systems and software which use standard protocols.

Discussion

In the early days of personal computing, it was important to buy all the hardware from the same manufacturer. Devices from different manufacturers were not necessarily able to operate together. There were difficulties in establishing an interface between different parts of the system. Layered interfaces make such communication possible.

Discuss whether standardisation of protocols is a good or a bad thing in computing.

Summary

- Computers in a local area network (LAN) are geographically close to each other, e.g. in the same building.
- Computers in a wide area network (WAN) are remote from each other, e.g. regional, nationwide or global.
- Each computer in a network needs a network interface card (NIC) and a network operating system.
- Computers on a LAN are usually connected by cables (but can be wireless through a router).
- Computers on a WAN are connected by phone lines (through modems), dedicated lines or satellite communications.
- Serial transmission of data means transferring information, one bit at a time, down a single wire.
- Parallel transmission of data means transferring information down several wires at the same time, for example, one byte can be transferred along eight wires.
- In simplex mode, data can only be transmitted in one direction (e.g. teletext broadcast).
- In half-duplex mode, data can be transmitted in only one direction at a time (e.g. CB radio).
- In full duplex mode, data can be transmitted in both directions at the same time (e.g. telephone).
- The bit rate is the number of bits that can be sent in one second.
- The higher the bandwidth, the more data can be sent at one time (thus the bit rate is higher).
- Time-sensitive data (such as streamed video) must be sent at a high bit rate or the output will seem jerky to the viewer.
- Downloaded text documents will be read after the whole file has been transmitted so they do not need a high bit rate.
- In data transmission, one or more bits may be incorrectly received.
- A parity check ensures that number of 1s transmitted in a byte is odd (or even, as agreed between the computers). If the number of 1s in the received data is even, the receiver asks for it to be sent again.
- A parity block uses a byte to check the parity of the previously sent bytes.
- Echoing involves the receiver transmitting the received data back to the sender. If the echoed data are not the same as what was sent, the data are sent again.
- A check sum is calculated by adding all the bytes of data sent. The check sum is also sent and the receiver compares the received check sum with the check sum it calculates. If they are different, the receiver asks for the data to be sent again.
- In a packet switching system, packets of data are sent independently around the network. At the destination, they need to be put in order before the message is reassembled.
- In a circuit switching system, data are sent along the same route around the network. At the destination, data arrive in order. The circuit is only released for further use when the communication is completed.

- A protocol is a set of rules that define how data is transferred between devices and computers.
- Protocols define for example:
  - whether the connecting wire is serial or parallel
  - the bit rate used
  - the type of parity used.
- Physical protocols define the wires or other connections between the computers.
- Logical protocols define the types of error-checking and synchronisation of data.
- A communications interface (a protocol) involves a number of different issues that can be grouped. Each issue is called a layer and it is usually visualised with the physical protocol on the bottom and other parts of the protocol (such as error checking) layered on top.

Test yourself

1. Explain the difference between a wide area network (WAN) and a local area network (LAN). [2]

Hint

You need to give *two* distinct points of comparison. Saying that one covers a large area and the other a local area is insufficient.

2. a. State **three** pieces of hardware that are needed to create a LAN from a set of stand-alone computers. [3]
   b. Explain why the communication over a WAN differs from that across a LAN and state how the hardware necessary for communication would differ from that used in part (a). [3]
3. Explain the difference between:
   a. simplex transmission of data
   b. half-duplex transmission of data
   c. duplex transmission of data
   giving an example of the use of each. [6]

Hint

Don't try to be imaginative – give the standard examples.

4. Explain why the bit rate is more important when sending a colour picture from one device to another, than it is when sending a page of text. [3]

Hint

Make sure you say what the bit rate is.

5. Give an example of a computer file which would need a high bit rate (baud) when being transmitted to other machines on a network, justifying your answer. [3]

6. The following bytes of data are sent to a second device using even parity:

```
01001101
10001000
10101011
00011011
```

An automatic checking technique is used to check that the data has been transmitted without error.

a. State which byte has been received incorrectly, explaining how you arrived at your answer. [3]

b. Explain why it is possible that a byte of data could still be incorrect despite passing the test that you used in part (a). [1]

c. If the parity byte `11110101` had been transmitted with the data block, explain how the error could be self checked and corrected. [3]

Hint

Write the parity byte under the block to ensure that you can easily count the bits.

d. Describe **two** other methods of checking data that has been transmitted. [6]

7. Explain the difference between packet switching and circuit switching. [2]

Hint

You need to give two *distinct* points of comparison. Don't state the same comparison in two ways.

8. A computer is to use a printer to provide hard copy output of jobs. In order for the data to be transmitted and received properly, a protocol must be set up between the computer and the printer. State two parts of the protocol which would be essential in this example. Give reasons why they are necessary. [4]

9. a. Explain the term "layered interface" when describing intercommunication between devices. [2]

b. State a reason for arranging the interface between devices in a layered fashion. [1]

10. A school's computing department has decided to invest in new hardware for its two computer rooms. The teacher in charge has to decide between a network of computers or a collection of stand-alone machines. The teacher has asked your advice about which hardware to implement.

a. State **four** advantages of implementing a network solution. [4]

b. State a disadvantage of using a network in this context and suggest a solution to the problem. [2]

1.6 Systems development life cycle

When an organisation needs a computerised solution to a problem, it employs a specialist to manage the design, creation and implementation of the solution. This computing specialist is called a **systems analyst**.

The systems analyst probably knows nothing about the problem or even the company at the start. Before they can be expected to solve the problem they must make sure that they investigate the circumstances that have given rise to the problem in the first place. For all but the most trivial of problems, this is a complex process that requires the analyst to define the problem and then design a solution. After this, the analyst will probably hand the design to other specialists who implement the requirements from the design of the solution and then the analyst plans the installation of the solution into the organisation and arranges for its maintenance.

With all these processes to carry out it is important that the analyst has a working framework. This framework is called the **systems development life cycle**. One way to understand the systems life cycle is using a diagram. A common depiction is a waterfall model (Figure 1.6.1) that shows the stages in order.

When considering the systems development life cycle, it is important to think of the different stages as a continually developing process rather than each stage being an end in itself. Throughout this section keep referring back to Figure 1.6.1.

When one of the stages is completed, the previous ones may need to be re-considered. For example, if the problem definition agreed with the client proves to be impossible to implement, then the analyst needs to go back to the problem definition and re-negotiate it so that a solution is possible. If the required input proves not to be feasible then it may be necessary to alter the expected output. If, during the training of the staff, one of the input operators is found to be colour blind then the input screens may need to be re-designed in order not to have any clashes between red and green. This reliance of each stage on previous ones means that the process is said to be iterative, because we may need to keep going back to alter things.

If the process is not iterative then it becomes linear. In a linear process, the problem is defined and analysed and then a solution is designed and so on. This may be possible for a very simple problem but in most cases the problems, and hence the solutions, are too complicated for a linear process.

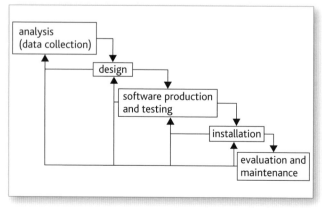

Figure 1.6.1   The waterfall model.

Discussion

It may be useful to discuss with your teacher the problem that you aim to solve in Module 4. You will follow the process in this section when you start your project. If something does not work properly and you have to go back to a previous stage in the project, you are doing exactly what is expected in the systems life cycle. A project that shows this iteration is superior to one that simply shows a linear process.

Problem definition

From the outset of a project to design of a new computer system, it is important to ensure that everyone involved agrees about the aims of the proposed system.

An individual, a company or an organisation has a problem that cannot be solved by current practices. Similar problems may seem to have been solved by computerisation elsewhere. The individual, company or organisation decides that it would benefit from computerisation. The owner of the problem probably understands the problem quite well but may not understand the consequences of using computers to try to solve the problem. For this reason, it is necessary for the organisation to employ a specialist who does understand computers and computerised solutions to problems; this is the systems analyst. The systems analyst is not likely to be an expert in the client's business area.

The system analyst's job is to solve the problem by planning and overseeing the introduction of computer technologies. The owner of the problem will be happy if the analyst can introduce a computerised solution. A problem can arise when the analyst, who doesn't know very much about the business, solves the problem that the analyst thinks needs solving rather than the problem that the business has! It seems obvious that analysts should make sure that they know what is required. If you are asked to answer questions 1 to 5 but you do 6 to 10, there is an obvious breakdown in communication. This is what can happen if you only listen to the instruction, "Do five questions".

To ensure agreement on a definition of the problem, there are discussions between all the interested parties and a list of objectives is drawn up. This list of objectives, if they are all addressed, will result in a solution to the problem, so the people involved must agree to the list of the objectives. The success or otherwise of the project depends on the completion of these objectives.

The initial definition of the problem is the all important first stage because, if it is not done correctly, the wrong problem may be solved. This will lead to a very dissatisfied client and the client may well withhold payment for the work.

The function and purpose of a feasibility study

When the organisation and the systems analyst have agreed the definition of the problem, a decision must be made about the value of continuing to develop the computerised solution. The organisation may be convinced that there is a problem to be solved and that its solution will be worth the effort and the expense. However, the systems analyst is paid to look at the problem, and its solution, from another point of view. The analyst is an expert in computer systems and what is possible with computer systems. This analyst must consider the problem from the point of view of the computerised part of the solution and make a report to the organisation saying whether the solution is possible and sensible. This report is called the **feasibility study** because it will report on whether or not the solution is feasible.

The feasibility study considers the problem from a number of perspectives:

- Is the solution technically possible?
  A car manufacturer may decide that using robots on the production line will improve the quality of work. However, if it is not possible to manufacture a robot arm of the correct dimensions to fit into the small areas under a car bonnet, it doesn't matter how big an improvement there would be in the quality of the finished product, it would simply not be feasible.
- Is the solution economic to produce?
  Perhaps robots exist that can be programmed to assemble the engines and the benefits will be worthwhile. However, if the cost of the robots and the new programs to control them is so great that it puts the car manufacturer out of business, the introduction of the robots is not feasible.
- Is the solution economic to run?
  The benefits of a robot production line may be tremendous and the robots may be cheap to buy, but if they need many electric motors and are too slow in carrying out the assembly work, it may be cheaper to employ people to do the job.
- What are the social effects?
  If the car plant is the only major employer in the region and the introduction of robots will put much of the workforce out of work, then the company may decide that the human cost is too great.

- Is the workforce skilled enough?
  It will be necessary to employ highly skilled technicians to look after the robots. If there are no workers with the necessary skills then computerisation is not feasible.
- What effect will there be on the customer?
  If the customer is likely to be impressed with the introduction of the new system then it may be worth the expense. However, if the customer sees no obvious benefits with the new system, what is the point?
- Will the introduction of the new system be economically beneficial in the long term?
  Put bluntly, will the introduction of robots increase the profits made by the firm?

Several of these points can be summarised as a "cost–benefit analysis".

1.6 c Determining the information requirements of a system

Following the feasibility study, if the decision is to go ahead with the proposed system, the next stage is for the systems analyst to collect as much information about what is required and to investigate current work practices. It is highly unlikely that there is not some system currently in place which the proposed new system is to replace. It could be a manual system or a computer system which requires replacing.

Other textbooks include this process as part of the general analysis stage. Analysis is simply "finding out" about the proposed system and establishing what is required.

When a computer system is being designed, it is necessary for the designer of the system to find out as much as possible about the requirements of the system. We have already mentioned the importance of defining the problem, but further difficulties can arise. Imagine an organisation that commissions an analyst to design a new payroll system. The analyst and the managers of the organisation agreed that the system needs to be able to communicate with banks, deduct tax at source and other important features. The analyst designs the solution and the software is then written. It is the best payroll program ever produced and is installed ready to process the first monthly payroll. Unfortunately, many of the workers are employed on a weekly basis. A meeting and discussion with one of the weekly paid staff would have highlighted this for the analyst and meant that this costly mistake was avoided. When a system's requirements are being drawn up there must be no room for errors caused by a lack of information.

Following the feasibility study, the analyst needs to collect as much information as possible. Obvious methods of collecting information are to ask staff, customers, etc. about the problem and the present system for solving it. It may not be feasible to ask everyone in the organisation for their views, but a representative sample of workers, management and customers should be given the chance to provide information. After all, the part-time worker on the production line probably knows more about the business than the analyst.

We now consider five accepted methods of collecting information.

Interviews

Interviews are particularly important because they allow the interviewee to talk at length and the interviewer to depart from a prepared script when conducting the interview. An example would be that the analyst may ask about the data that needs to be stored. It is only when the interviewee has answered the question that the analyst knows:

- that it is important to protect the files of data and so can ask about security procedures
- the types of data and so can discuss who in the organisation needs access to which particular data to do their job
- how widely spread data access needs to be and so can discuss the methods for communicating the data.

An interview makes it possible for the analyst to alter the questions dependent on the replies that are being given. This is a most important point about an interview. However, interviews are very time-consuming and, consequently, restrict the number of people whose views can be sought.

Questionnaires

Questionnaires make it possible to find out the views of a large number of people very quickly. Because the questions are pre-determined, the person supplying the answers may find it difficult to put their point of view across. Questionnaires also have the disadvantage that they usually have a low return rate (e.g. send out 120 questionnaires and you may get only 20 returns).

Group meetings

A group meeting allows a number of people to discuss points and make their views known. It can reduce the amount of time spent in interviews getting the same answers over and over again. The problem with a meeting is that one or two people can dominate, not allowing all the members of the group to express their opinions and viewpoints.

Existing documentation

If there is a system in operation that the proposed system is intended to replace, there will be written documentation describing its operation. The analyst must find out if what is written down is consistent with what staff actually do to operate the system.

Often the views of the people connected with the problem are clouded by years of familiarity, so it is important for the analyst to also gain first-hand knowledge of any existing systems. One way to do this is to collect printed documentation and study it in order to find out what data are required by the system and in what form information is output.

Observation

Another way for the analyst to gain first-hand knowledge is to observe the current system in action. Rather than just asking staff about their involvement with the current system, observation by the systems analyst will prove invaluable. The analyst may come across operational problems which none of the staff have described.

The analyst must take into account that workers being observed are unlikely to behave in their normal manner. This is the same effect as a television camera has on otherwise fairly sensible individuals!

Discussion

A small clothes shop, owned by Shikhar Sharma, has a paper-based point of sale operation. Six sales staff work in the shop at different times of the week. The shop manager deals with ordering new stock and discounting stock that is not selling very well. Shikhar decides to introduce a computerised point of sale system. What forms of information collection are sensible and what information can the analyst expect to find out?

1.6 d Analysing the requirements of a system

The planning of any system design must start by deciding on the requirements of the system. A system may need to store data for future reference or processing. However, simply being aware of that requirement is not enough.

- The types of data need to be determined as this decides the form in which the data are stored and the amount of storage space required.
- The volumes of data have to be calculated to determine which storage devices are appropriate. The volume of storage can also affect the structures that are used to store the data.
- The relative importance of different ways of accessing the data must be assessed. Will it be necessary to access individual items of data or will all the data be accessed at the same time?
- The frequency of changes to the data must also be determined.

It is important that these decisions can be supported by reference to the information that has been collected. The assumption must be that the analyst knew nothing of the organisation or of the problem to be solved until beginning to collect information and, therefore, they have nothing else on which to base decisions. The analyst should use information collected to justify each decision made so that the client can refer to the reasons why decisions were made.

It is at this stage that the analyst often finds out that not enough information was collected about a particular area to be able to make a sensible decision. At that point, the analyst needs to go back for clarification.

When decisions are made about the direction that a particular system is going to take, it is normal to produce a list of tasks that need to be carried out to progress with the system. These tasks should be in a specific order. For example, it would not make sense to consider inputting data into the system before designing the data structures for the data. This list is called a priority list and it forms the basis of the system design. Each of the tasks in the list should be considered separately to decide its important points. For example, the stock file held in a specific business may need to allow for:

- 1000 items (thus putting a lower limit on the size of appropriate storage)

- direct searching for individual stock items (thus ruling out some types of storage media and some data structures)
- an interface with other systems (they may share database or data files).

Design specification

Many facts must be considered and decisions made, but a set of constraints has already been placed on the design. This is known as the **design specification** and it should be agreed between the analyst and the organisation before the design is implemented.

Often, the inputs and outputs to a system and the storage and processing that goes on in the system is so complex that, in order to understand it, the system needs to be divided up into a number of connected sections or modules. Each one must be simple enough to be handled as an entity (i.e. a sub-system).

Requirements specification

The result of the analysis stage is a list of objectives (the **requirements specification**) that must be met before it is possible to state that the client's original problem has been solved. The individual requirements should be justified by reference to evidence in the investigative work. The final list must be agreed by the client. If the analyst satisfies all the requirements in the specification, the client must consider the problem solved and must pay the analyst, who has done what he or she was contracted to do. By agreeing to the list of requirements, the client has agreed to the boundaries for the proposed project.

Hardware and software requirements

The analyst should also be able to produce a reasoned list of the hardware and software that are needed for the new system. This gives an indication of the costs involved and the scale of any additional costs.

The analyst should consider the following questions:
- Should the proposed new system run on the existing hardware platform?
- Will additional computers be required?
- Will a new file server be needed for data storage?
- Is the proposed system a web-based application?

- Will new software have to be developed?
- Does existing software need to be modified?

(1.6 e) Data structures

The analyst must consider the data entered into the system and the information output from it. At this stage, the analyst also identify the hardware and software requirements of the system in more detail.

Designing data input

All computer systems require input. How the data are input to the system depends on a number of factors:
- the design of the user interface
- is the data graphical, textual or physical in nature?
- is the data already in existence or does it need to be collected?
- is the data to be entered via a keyboard by an operator or is there a way of automating the data input?

This section relates back to "Types of user interface" in Chapter 1.2 (pages 7–11), which covered the different forms of software interface. The main task in input design is to design the interface with the outside world so that data can be captured by the system.

Designing output

The results that are produced by the system must be presented in a way that is appropriate for the application. A system that produces bank statements for customers at an ATM machine would not use audio output. Audio output is sensible if the statements are to be delivered as part of a telephone banking application. Similarly, a burglar alarm system would not serve the purpose if it outputs a message onto a computer screen in the house. There is probably no-one in the house to read it, which is why the alarm was needed in the first place! However, a message on a computer screen would be a sensible output if it is sent to a central office which is manned continually in order to protect properties.

Decisions about the type of output depend upon the hardware available, the form that the output needs to be in and the experience of the operator (indeed, on whether an operator is present).

Equally as important as giving enough information is the danger of providing too much information.

In order for users to be able to understand the information presented, various techniques can be used:

- The same type of information can always be put in the same position on a monitor screen. The operator quickly becomes accustomed to the relative importance of different areas of the screen.
- Information can be colour coded. For example, important information may appear in red while less important information is in black. Notice that this implies some form of decision making on the part of the designer to determine what is important in the first place. It is also necessary to be very careful about choice of colours. People who are colour blind commonly find difficulty distinguishing between red and green, so choosing these colours to represent information that is dangerously near a limit or at a safe level, could have serious implications. Similarly, colour combinations have to be chosen carefully. Blue text on a black background is almost impossible to see, as is yellow text in some lighting conditions.
- Video reversal can be used to highlight a particular piece of information effectively. If the normal writing on the screen is black on a white background, the piece that needs to stand out can be shown as white on a black background.
- Very important pieces of information may be displayed in a dialogue box that obscures the rest of the screen until it is dealt with.
- A printer may be reserved for special messages so that a hard copy of the information is preserved. Again, the fact that the information appears on that printer means that it has a particular importance.
- Information can be made to flash or can be printed in a different size – anything that makes the operator's eye go to that part of the screen.

Designing data structures

The data used in a computer solution needs to be stored. What is important is getting the data back again when it is needed. Chapter 1.3 described the data structures of array, queue and stack (others are covered later in the text). When a solution is designed, it is necessary to decide how access to the data will be handled and to choose appropriate data structures.

Examination questions on this part of the syllabus tend to ask for the sort of choices that need to be made rather than any complex analysis of fitting a data structure to a given situation, although simple examples (such as modelling a queue at a shop's checkout) may be asked.

Many of the design decisions can be illustrated by the use of diagrams. The requirement to be able to produce specific types of diagram is no longer a part of the syllabus, but you should be aware of some of the types of diagram and should be able to follow and explain the logic behind an example diagram for an application. They are also useful tools for producing the documentation for the project work in Module 4.

A **Jackson diagram** starts with the original problem as the highest level. The next, and subsequent, levels show how the problems in the previous levels are split up to form smaller, more manageable problems (see Figure 1.6.2). This continues until each of the blocks at the lowest level is a self-contained and easily solvable problem. These individual problems can then be solved and combined according to the links that have been used. If the links between the different blocks are used correctly, the result is a solution to the original problem.

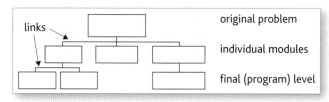

Figure 1.6.2   A Jackson diagram.

A Jackson diagram is a methodology for showing the individual modules that make up a solution and the relationships between them. The links between the modules can be conditional. For example, if a module calculates a mark out of 100, one print routine could be called if the mark is below a certain value and a different one if it is above that mark.

An example where a Jackson diagram could describe the design to be used is as follows.

An electronic register is taken of the 25 students in a class. Each student can be either present or absent. The teacher needs to print out the number of students present and the number absent. We can use a Jackson diagram to document the problem as shown in Figure 1.6.3.

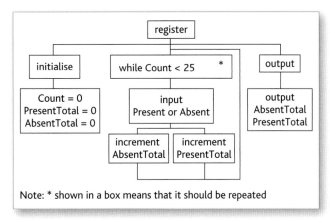

Figure 1.6.3   A Jackson diagram for student registration.

Designing the system processes

In order to transform input and stored data into output data, the computer system must carry out some processing. Many of the processing design decisions can be illustrated by the use of diagrams.

Dataflow diagram (DFD)

A **dataflow diagram (DFD)** uses symbols to describes the data flows present in a system. DFDs comprise symbols that represent:

- an entity – something from which data originates or which receives data, e.g. a customer or a printer
- a flow line – a line that shows the direction of the flow of information and is labelled with the information description, e.g. CustomerCode, ProductCode and Quantity
- a process – the processing that takes place, e.g. receive customer order or print invoice
- a data store – the file or database table in which data is stored, e.g. the customer file.

The symbols are all illustrated in Figure 1.6.4.

Discussion

Consider a mail order business. Customers phone in orders to an operator or post orders on paper. Orders are validated and stored in an order file and an acknowledgement is sent to the customer. The accounts department produces an invoice and the warehouse department sends the invoice with the goods. Try to explain the diagram by numbering the arrows in the order in which the process is carried out.

Discussion continued …

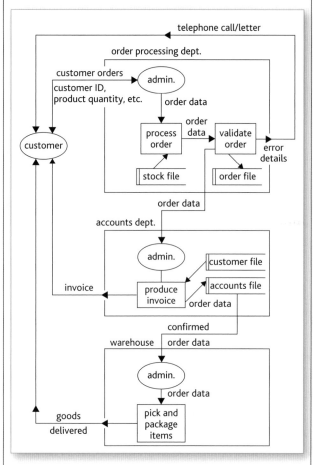

Figure 1.6.4   A dataflow diagram for an ordering process.

The diagram does not show the acknowledgement of the order. What will this look like on the diagram?

When a customer receives their goods and invoices, either they return the goods (and the invoice is cancelled by the accounts department) or they send a cheque for the payment. Show these two processes on a diagram similar to the one shown.

Draw a diagram that shows the flow of data if an item is out of stock. The customer must be informed.

System flowchart

A **system flowchart** is similar to a DFD but it does not necessarily show the people or departments involved. Instead, it shows the processes and their data sources. The validation routine which is part of its "validate order" process may look like Figure 1.6.5 on page 61.

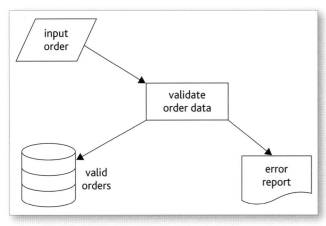

Figure 1.6.5 A system flowchart for a validation routine.

Activity

Draw system flowcharts for the other stages of the mail order process.

1.6 f ## Evaluating the system against initial specifications

A system must meet certain criteria if it is to be considered successful. This does not only apply to a computer system–it applies to any system. For example, a car must satisfy various criteria before it can be called a car:

- It must move under its own power.
- It must be possible to steer it.
- It must have three or four wheels.
- It must have seats.

There would be many other facts which would have to be true before most of us would recognise this system as a car. However, some assumptions have been made in just the four criteria mentioned here. A toy, radio-controlled car fits all these criteria, but it was not the sort of system that we had in mind when designing the criteria. Perhaps the second bullet point should have specified that it has to be controlled from within the car itself or there should be a new criterion that gives a minimum size for the vehicle.

When systems are being designed, the list of criteria that the finished system must match is of paramount importance. It must also be agreed between the designer of the system and the commissioner of the design, so that there are no misunderstandings. We can imagine a situation where the Ford motor company commission a new car design, only to find that it is 30 centimetres long when delivered.

Note that these criteria are all decided before the system is created. They are used to decide how well the system works. In other words, does it do what it is meant to? This question can only be answered if it is known what the system was meant to do in the first place.

As stated at the beginning of this chapter, the problem must be defined properly if we are going to be able to adequately assess whether or not it has been solved. This assessment is very important to the client, who needs to ensure that the final system carries out all the tasks that the organisation needs. It is also very important to the analyst, who is only paid for the work if the original requirements have been met.

1.6 g ## Documentation

The documentation of a system consists of text and graphics that explain how the system was produced, how it should be used and how it can be maintained. Documentation is created at the different stages in the systems life cycle and for different people to use. We discuss some of the different types of documentation in this section and others later in the course. Indeed, much of the project work that is done in Module 4 consists of producing the documentation for your chosen problem.

Requirements specification

This is a list of the requirements of the customer for whom the system is being designed. It consists of the criteria that are used to evaluate the finished system (see "Analysing the requirements of a system" on pages 57–58). It is usual for the systems analyst and the customer to "sign off" the list of requirements so that there is no confusion when the work is finished.

Design specification

Taking the requirements specification and working out the stages necessary to produce the required end product is known as the design specification. This includes the different stages and also the criteria for each stage of the solution.

For example, one part of a solution may be the production of a file of data. The design specification includes the following information:

- the ways in which this file of data relates to the other parts of the system
- the specifications of the file (what is the key field?)
- how many records the file will contain
- the most appropriate storage medium.

Program specification

Program specifications include detailed algorithms showing the method of solution for all parts of the problem. These algorithms may well be in the form of program flowcharts or pseudocode. The language to be used, the data structures necessary and details of any library routines to be used are also in the program specification.

The program specifications are given to the programmers in order for them to write the program code.

Technical or maintenance documentation

The technical documentation includes:

- the program specifications
- the program code
- details of hardware configurations.

Generally, the technical documentation includes any documentation that assists the technician in maintaining or updating a system. Indeed, technical documentation is also known as "maintenance documentation". This type of documentation is not intended to be accessible to the user of the system, who does not need any of these details to be able to use the system correctly.

User documentation

User documentation is the documentation for the person who will use the system. It contains the details needed to make the system operate as it should. The user documentation normally includes the following information:

- examples of output screens
- examples of valid input
- methods for the input of data
- error messages and what to do when they appear
- instructions for installing the system on specific hardware
- tutorials

- FAQs
- reference addresses, email addresses and websites for further sources of assistance.

Some user documentation is part of the software and can be called up onto the screen when it is needed. This type of documentation is called **on-screen help**. Indeed, some problem solutions *require* on-screen help because it is not possible to provide a hard copy user guide for the user. An obvious example of this is a website, where any necessary instructions for the use of the site need to be provided on the screen.

Help for software is now often provided as web pages which are available centrally from the software house's website. This has advantages for the software house as the documentation can be updated when required and any software fixes can be made available from the website as a download.

A software house may organise information as a **knowledge base** which can be accessed using a keyword search.

(1.6 h) Testing and implementation planning

Testing

Any system needs to be extensively tested to ensure that it works. This is a fairly obvious statement but, in reality, comprehensive testing is impossible in all but the simplest of systems. It is simply not possible to test the results of every conceivable input or follow the path of every logical construction in the system. This difficulty means that testing must be carefully planned and should relate directly to the criteria referred to earlier in this section.

We cover specific types of testing in Chapter 2.6, where we consider carrying out tests that provide evidence as to whether the requirements have been met or not. This type of testing can take many forms but is broadly referred to as *functional testing*. The software is being tested to see if it carries out the different functions for which it was designed.

Implementation of the system

When a system has been completed, it has to be implemented so that it is performing the tasks for which it was designed. Initially, this involves:

- ensuring that the correct hardware is available
- arranging for staff to be trained in the use of the new system

- inputting data to the data files, either manually or by downloading them from the original system.

There are four possible strategies for implementation:

- **Parallel running:** Until the system can be considered fault free, the old and new systems are run side by side, both doing the same processing. This allows results to be compared to ensure that there are no problems with the new system. Such a system is "safe" and also allows staff training to be carried out, but it is obviously very expensive because of the need to do everything twice. Parallel running is used in situations where the data are so valuable that there must be no possibility of failure.

- **Pilot running:** Key parts of the new system are run alongside the old system until it is considered that they have been fully tested. This is a compromise with the idea of parallel running but it does not give a clear idea of the effects on the system of the large amounts of data that are going to be encountered in the full application.

- **Direct changeover:** The old system is removed and the "live" new system replaces it completely and immediately.

- **Phased implementation:** Parts of a system are replaced while the remaining parts are covered by the old system. This allows for some testing of the new system and for staff training to take place, but also allows for a backup position if the new version does not work as anticipated.

The four methods of implementation can be best distinguished from each other by considering the following example. A publishing firm that produces textbooks decides to invest in a new computerised system for running the accounts part of the business. The present accounts system is out-of-date and is not suitable for use with new hardware. The analyst appointed to oversee the introduction of the new software has to consider different methods of implementation:

- If they choose parallel running, all accounts and invoices have to be dealt with twice, in the old system and in the new system. If something goes wrong with the new system, data from the old software can be used. However, everything must be done twice, which will slow down the accounts department and cost money in additional staff. It is a safe system and the new software can be rigorously tested as every transaction can be compared with the result from the old system.

- If they choose pilot running, they may decide to move the accounts for A-level Maths textbooks onto the new system. All the other types of book will be dealt with using the old system until they are sure that the new system works perfectly. This reduces the risk involved in the changeover. If something goes wrong, only a small part of the accounts are affected and they can probably be recovered fairly easily. This system also gives an opportunity for all the workers to receive training on the new system before a complete changeover is implemented. However, it remains awkward because two systems are running side by side. It will be difficult to deal with a centre that has ordered some Maths books and some English books because they will be dealt with by different systems.

- If they choose direct changeover, the old system is removed and the new one is implemented, possibly over a weekend when the accounts staff are not working. It is the cheapest and simplest form of changeover but is a potentially dangerous strategy. There is no fallback position if something goes wrong. The staff must be fully trained before the changeover and all the files must be input to the new system before it goes live.

- If they choose phased introduction, the accounts department would continue to use the old system for all but one part of the accounts. Perhaps the discounting subsystem would change to the new system whereas all other parts would still use the old system. This means that the two different systems must be compatible because both will be used on the same accounts. If the new system does not work, the effects are not critical.

The four methods of implementation must not be thought of as the only issue to consider when asked a question about implementation. Remember, there are other issues that are equally important e.g. the way the data files are going to be created and how the staff will be trained.

System maintenance and the software lifespan

Systems are designed for a well-defined purpose and should realise that purpose; if they do, they are considered successful.

During use it may become necessary to alter the system for some reason – this is known as **maintenance**. There are three different types of maintenance to be considered:

- **Corrective maintenance** is necessary when a fault or bug is found in the operation of the new system. These are software bugs which were not picked up at the formal testing stage. A technician or the original programmers will be needed to correct the error.

- **Adaptive maintenance** is necessary when conditions change from those that existed when the original system was created. This may be because of a change in the law (tax rates may change, for example) or the hardware may be changed, so that changes need to be made to the software for it to remain functional.

- **Perfective maintenance** is required to "tweak" the system so that it performs better. For example, searching for a particular stock item may be quite slow. The technician decides that supplier details should be stored in another file rather than with the details of the stock, the size of the stock file is reduced and it is far quicker to search. This has not changed how the system operates as far as the user is concerned but the performance improves.

Computing and computer applications is a subject that changes regularly through advances in technology, new ideas, different legal frameworks and different business practices. A system should never be considered to be finished. Rather than being a linear process with a beginning, a middle and an end, it should be thought of as a circular process, continually returning to previous stages to fine tune them and take advantage of changing circumstances.

In addition to the need for continual maintenance, all systems have a natural lifespan and eventually need to be replaced. The limited lifespan of a system is known as **obsolescence**. Even the most up-to-date and most expensive system eventually becomes out-of-date. This may be because a piece of hardware needs to be replaced and it is not possible to find anything that is compatible with the software; because the competitor for a business updates all its systems and customers find their service more impressive; or because customers expect more to be done for them.

Summary

- The accurate definition of a problem is important to ensure that the correct problem is solved.

- A feasibility study considers whether a solution to the problem is possible and economic.

- The information requirements of a system must be defined to ensure that all data is collected and the correct outputs are produced.

- The information requirements are established by conducting fact-finding exercises:

  - Interviews involve the analyst talking to and asking questions of a representative set of users. Interviews can be adjusted to the answers given by the respondent. However, they are time-consuming and cannot be carried out with many people.

  - Questionnaires involve many people in an organisation answering a standard set of questions on paper. The questions are fixed in advance so some information may be missed and not everyone may return the questionnaire.

  - Group meetings involve a number of people discussing the system with the analyst. It is a good way to collect information quickly but group dynamics may mean that a few people dominate the discussion.

  - Existing documentation can be examined to see how the current system works.

  ⟶

Summary continued …

- – Observation involves the analyst watching the current system in use. It can be a good way to find differences between the documentation and what people do. However, people do not necessarily behave normally when they are observed.
- • The requirements of a system must be analysed:
  - – The requirements specification must state all the things that the new system must do.
  - – User requirements must be defined with criteria for each requirement.
  - – Hardware and software requirements must be identified, including any specialist input or output.
- • Data structures, inputs, outputs and processing must be defined:
  - – A Jackson diagram breaks down the problem into sub-problems that are easier to solve.
  - – A dataflow diagram (DFD) shows how data flows around the system.
  - – A system flowchart shows the processes of the system, their inputs and outputs and storage of data.
- • A new system must be evaluated against initial specifications to ensure that it solves the defined problem.
- • Documentation must be created and revised throughout the system life cycle. Each phase produces a document (e.g. requirements specification, design specification and program specifications).
- • User documentation helps a user to use the system.
- • Technical documentation gives programmers and computer operators information about running and maintaining the system.
- • Testing is carried out on individual modules and sub-systems as well as on the complete system.
- • The installation of a new system must be planned. Methods of installation include:
  - – parallel running
  - – pilot running
  - – direct changeover
  - – phased implementation.
- • A system is maintained after going live:
  - – Corrective maintenance fixes software bugs which were not picked up at the formal testing stage.
  - – Adaptive maintenance changes the system to cater for changes in the law, or hardware or new business procedures.
  - – Perfective maintenance makes the system perform better.

Test yourself

1. a. State **three** different stages in the systems life cycle. [3]
   b. Describe the purpose of each of the stages you have chosen from the systems life cycle. [6]

1.7 Choosing appropriate applications software

1.7 a Custom-written and off-the-shelf software packages

In Chapter 1.6, we discussed how software is designed and produced to meet the requirements of a proposed computer system. Such software is applications software, designed to make the computer system do something useful. There are many types of applications software but all can be divided into two types:

- **Special-purpose applications software** is designed to carry out a specific task and may only used by one organisation or to solve a specific problem that needs solving.
- General-purpose applications software is designed to be general purpose and can be used for many tasks in a broad area of problem solution.

Note, this simply describes the end result. The terms in the syllabus – "custom-written" and "off-the-shelf" – are more about the way in which the software is developed and produced.

Off-the-shelf software

If a person or an organisation has a problem that needs to be solved, it may be possible that a piece of software has already been produced that does all the tasks that are required. There are many pieces of software that have already been written and are immediately available to buy. This type of software is called **off-the-shelf software** because you can literally go into a computer shop (Figure 1.7.1) or a "software house" and purchase a copy of the software.

There are a number of advantages in buying an off-the-shelf package:

- The software is available immediately. The user does not have to wait, sometimes a considerable time, for it to be designed and coded.

Figure 1.7.1 Software for sale.

- The software is used by many people or organisations, therefore they share the development costs. This implies that the software will be considerably cheaper.
- Copies of the software may have been in use for some time and so any bugs in the software should have been found and rectified, consequently it can be expected to work without errors.
- If it is part of a suite of software, it is compatible with other applications. For example, data can be imported from or exported to another piece of software. If an organisation uses a desktop publisher and a spreadsheet from the same suite, graphs drawn in the spreadsheet can be imported into the publisher in order to illustrate a report.
- Because the software is in general use there are likely to be well-established training courses for the staff to be sent on to learn about the software.
- There is help available from staff or user-group forums on the Internet who already know how to use the software.

Most general-purpose software has many features and only some of them are appropriate to the problem that needs to be solved. In most cases, an off-the-shelf package needs to have parts taken out of it and other parts adapted so that it solves the problem properly. For example, a company needs to have a payroll package tailored to mirror the exact way in which it administers the payroll:

- The software must allow for both monthly paid and weekly paid employees but the company may only have monthly paid employees.
- All the output documents must show the company logo.
- Different countries have different procedures for taxation.

All of this will require tailoring of the software to meet the exact needs of each company that decides to purchase the payroll software. This process of altering the software to fit what the user wants it to do is called "tailoring" and the finished product is *tailored software*.

Custom-written software

Software that is specially written to solve a specific problem is known as **custom-written software**. There may be no freely available piece of software that satisfies the needs of the company. Custom software designed by an analyst (Figure 1.7.2) should mean that the organisation gets software that does all the tasks that it requires doing and, equally importantly, does not contain extra routines that will never be used.

Software written for a particular client is called **bespoke software**.

Figure 1.7.2   An analyst meeting a client.

1.7 b Business, commercial and industrial applications

Stock control

As the name implies, stock control systems are used to keep track of the stock sold by an organisation. There are typically three areas that need to be handled by a stock control program:

- data about individual items that the organisation holds in its stock – these details differ depending on the nature of the business. A shop needs to store the colour of towels but a plant hire firm does not need to store the colour of bulldozers. The engine size of the bulldozers would be stored, which obviously does not apply to towels!
- data related to the product – e.g. details of suppliers or the location of goods in the shop or warehouse, which are not directly about a specific product
- data about the use of the goods – e.g. when they were acquired; when they were sold, hired or written off; how many are in stock.

Stock control systems record stock levels, describe the condition of the stock and keep track of where the stock is. Stock control systems record the number or amount of the goods that are in stock. If the quantity in stock falls below a pre-determined number, the system automatically initiates a re-ordering process. It uses the details of the supplier and may involve a human manager, to allow for variations caused by season, fashion, etc.

Order processing

The stock control system must be integrated closely with the order processing system. Customers may telephone an order or send a paper form in the post. A copy of each order is sent to the accounts department so that an invoice can be raised. When the goods are delivered, the ordering system is informed so that the live order can be shown to have been fulfilled. The accounts department is told that the order has arrived and that clearance has been given for payment to take place.

Activity

Design an algorithm to show the process of automatic stock control.

Each record in the stock file needs a Boolean value to show that an order has been sent to the supplier. Explain why this is important.

Payroll

Payroll is a perfect example of a batch process (see "Types of operating system" in Chapter 1.2):

- The employee records need to be processed in one run because the workers need to be paid at the same time.
- Each record undergoes the same type of processing: working out the number of hours worked, multiplying by the hourly rate, doing the tax calculations and producing the final outputs.
- The processing requires no human intervention.

Traditionally, the master file of workers and the transaction file that holds the workers' details for that week. The two are arranged in the same order and are processed together. The results are stored on a new master file. This gives rise to the ancestral filing system form of backups described in Chapter 1.3. In this system, the old files are kept so that if the new version gets corrupted it can be reproduced using the old master and transaction files.

While easy to understand if the files are stored on tape, the file is now more likely to be held on a disk with an index to allow fast access to individual records. This would imply that the records are overwritten and that no new version of the master file is created.

Electronic point-of-sale (EPOS)

An **electronic point-of-sale (EPOS) system** is used at the point-of-sale (the checkout) in a shop. It needs to carry out three actions:

- identify the goods being bought
- carry out whatever processing is required and produce satisfactory output
- receive the customer's payment.

The identification of the goods can be done in a number of ways, but the standard method is to read a barcode. This code is then validated (see "Validation and verification techniques" in Chapter 1.8) and sent to the processor. The processor uses the barcode as the key field when searching the product file. When the item record is found, the contents of the record are used to produce a printout for the customer (a till receipt). The price is added to the total value of the goods that have been bought. Finally, payment can be made electronically by sending details of the customer account to the bank or credit card company, which then pays the store. Note that this system is closely linked to the shop's stock control system.

Marketing

When a product or service is developed it is important to make potential customers aware of it. The term given to this process is "marketing". In computer terms, it would include the use of systems to produce advertising literature, the promotion of the product on the World Wide Web and the use of techniques such as direct mailing.

Direct mailing systems use purchased files of people's details. It identifies people who may reasonably be expected to have some interest in the product and then mail merges their details with details of the product for an email or paper mailshot.

Computer aided design (CAD)

Computer aided design (CAD) is the use of a computer system to design an item. It may be used for applications as diverse as a house, a carburettor to fit a particular engine, or a new traffic flow system around a town. CAD software (Figure 1.7.3) can be used to:

- make calculations (will the roof be well enough supported by walls made from that particular product?)

- make decisions about the way the product is manufactured (will the robot tool be able to manoeuvre into position to screw the two halves together?)
- make predictions (what will happen if this street is made one way?)
- cost a solution (the prices of individual components can be used with the known costs of production to calculate the cost of each unit).

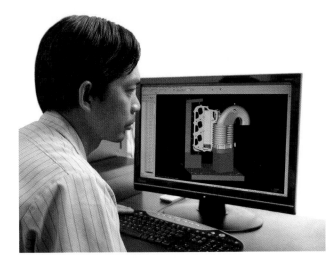

Figure 1.7.3   A CAD application.

Computer aided manufacture (CAM)

Computer aided manufacture (CAM) is the use of a computer for the manufacturing process. If the two principles of CAD and CAM are combined then it should be possible to produce a seamless process whereby the computer software produces a design, which is sent electronically to another system where the design is produced by a computer-controlled robot.

Process control

As the name implies, process control systems use a computer to automatically control some process (Figure 1.7.4). The computer receives information about the process from sensors which allow it to make decisions. The results of these decisions are actions that are carried out. The next set of input from the sensors not only tells the system about the current state of the process, but also allows the computer to compare with the last set of inputs to decide whether the actions that

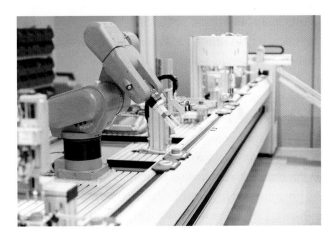

Figure 1.7.4   A computer-controlled robot.

it previously took had any impact. There is a continual cycle of input-processing-output which forms a **feedback loop**.

A process control application may automatically control some part of a manufacturing process which would otherwise have to be done by human beings. An example is given in the activity on page 67 in "Custom-written and off-the-shelf software packages". A person would have to monitor the thickness of the glass if the computer system was not available to do it. The computer system will be costly to produce and install, so why is it done?

- The computer system takes measurements at precise intervals.
- Measurements are taken accurately.
- The computer system performs the same repetitive task without complaint or boredom.
- The computer system can immediately take action to correct any problem that might arise from the measurement.

Activity

Other examples you could consider include:
- a flight control system in an airplane
- a process-controlled greenhouse (for temperature control)
- a process-controlled bakery oven.

For each application, consider what sensors are used. Does the application fit with our description of the input–processing–output feedback loop?

Generic applications software

It is necessary to provide a few definitions so that we have a clear starting point.

- *Applications software* does a task that would be carried out even if there were no computer. For instance, business letters are sent without technology, so a word processor is an applications program.
- An *applications package* is an applications program and its documentation. The project that you create in Module 4 will contain software to solve a problem (applications software) and a user guide (this makes it an *applications package*). The definition is sometimes widened to mean a set of applications programs that communicate with each other.
- *Generic applications software* (or **generic software**) is software that can be used as the "starting point" to solve a number of different tasks. For instance, a word processor is generic because it can be used to solve lots of different problems. Tax calculation

software is not generic because it has a specific use and cannot be adapted for other uses.

In the examination, you should be able to suggest sensible generic software for a given application. You should be able to identify important characteristics from a description and decide which of the generic software applications is best suited to the application requirements.

Word processor

A word processor is used for applications where the user needs to communicate with others using text. Writing letters, mail merging and preparing text for use in other software packages are all typical uses of a word processing software.

Spreadsheet

A spreadsheet is a type of software that allows data to be stored and displayed as a grid with rows and columns (Figure 1.7.5). If this were all that a spreadsheet could do then there would be other, more satisfactory types of

	A	B	C	D	E	F	G	H
1								
2								
3	INCOME			EXPENSES				
4	from Accounts software summary	£3,272.55			**EXPENSES 2009 - 2010**			
5								Postage
6		06/04/2009		Website updates	Blueshift Internet LTD	17.25		10.87
7		01/05/2009		Stationery	Viking Direct	75.73		1.22
8		09/06/2009		Accounts software upgrade	Quickbooks	153.47		1.28
9		10/06/2009		Software	Digital River	17.48		8.82
10		08/07/2009		Software training course	AQA	195.00		0.61
11		20/07/2009		Cable	Maplin	12.98		4.68
12		14/01/2010		Accessories	Argos	54.99		74.40
13		18/01/2010		Stationery	Viking Direct	105.68		4.95
14		18/01/2010		Software	SwiftDisc	20.54		5.56
15		01/02/2010		Software	NCH Software	25.00		24.00
16		02/02/2010		Reference texts	Amazon	16.03		15.80
17		02/02/2010		Reference texts	Amazon	10.75		1.46
18		04/02/2010		Reference texts	Amazon	16.03		21.23
19		07/02/2010		Software	MoleskinSoft	15.33		
20		18/02/2010		Stationery	Lanes	0.99		
21		18/02/2010		Stationery	Staples	21.65	Total:	174.88
22		02/03/2010		Stationery	CPC	25.12		
23		03/03/2010		Web site hosting	Blueshift Internet LTD	141.00		
24		09/03/2010		Stationery	Viking Direct	10.99		
25				Printing	Express print	30.00		
26				Heating contribution (5%)		100.00		
27				Phone bill contribution		100.00		
28				Web site domain registration renewal	Blueshift Internet LTD	22.99		
29				SKY broadband connection (£10 pm X 50%)	Sky	60.00		
30				O2 mobile (£50 pm and 30% usage)	Vodafone	180.00		
31				House electricity (10%)	EDF	100.00		
32				Postage		221.01		
33				Laptop computer (100% business usage)	PC World	485.94		
34								
35				**Total Expenses**		**2235.95**		

Figure 1.7.5   A spreadsheet.

software available. A spreadsheet is particularly useful because it can store different types of data, including numerical data, and can perform calculations on the areas (cells) where the data are stored.

A spreadsheet should be considered for any example where data are stored and calculations need to be carried out on them. Examples are profit and loss accounts, budgeting, payroll (although more specialised payroll software would be used in a large-scale application), indeed any example that requires the manipulation of figures to give accurate results, forecasts or predictions.

A spreadsheet is particularly suited to a "what-if" type application. Consider a sheet showing the income and expenditure for a planned music concert. We could try increasing the cost of a ticket by $10, keep all other variable costs the same and see the effect this change has on the profit made. We are posing the question "what if we increase the ticket price by $10?".

You may have used a spreadsheet to store and present data from an experiment in the science lab at school. You will have used a spreadsheet because the sensors that you used can send data straight to the computer where it can be loaded into the spreadsheet. The data can then be manipulated and presented in such a way that the user can interpret the data easily.

Desktop publisher (DTP)

Desktop publishing (DTP) software is characterised by the ability to produce a page of printed output that has been designed using advanced layout techniques. The page may well contain text, graphics, tables and many other types of output each of which may be better produced using a word processor, a drawing package or a spreadsheet. The value of DTP software is that it contains powerful tools for arranging these individual items on the page. The output can be used directly as the starting point for a printing process.

DTP software is used for the production of leaflets, posters, proof copies of books, magazines and product catalogues. Many word processors now have features which previously would only have been found in a DTP package, for instance the ability to produce text in columns or to surround graphics with text, and the distinction between a DTP package and a word processor has become increasingly unclear.

The output device (a printer) needs to be top quality otherwise the other parts of the system are let down.

Presentation software

The growth of the use of **presentation software** has followed the development of portable computers. If a salesperson is to do a presentation to a group of people, he or she can take a computer to the meeting with a prepared presentation. The software allows for the preparation of a show which typically follows a storyboard of individual screens. The presentation can morph from one screen to another, include **animation** and use text and graphics in individual screens. If required, a soundtrack can be added to complement the slides being shown.

A presentation can be set to produce a rolling display, with each slide shown for a set time. A single monitor would be fine for an automated rolling display in a department store but a projection screen would be needed for a larger audience. This could be accomplished using a data projector linked to the computer.

The use of presentation software is now so prevalent that there is a backlash against its use, with audiences being turned off by "yet another PowerPoint". The reason for this is that presenters have not been sensible or discerning in its use.

Drawing packages

Drawing, or graphics, software allows for the creation and manipulation of images. Often such output is exported to a DTP package for inclusion in some publication, to presentation software for inclusion in a display or to provide content on a web page.

There are two basic types of graphics package, determined by the way the graphic is formed and stored.

In **bitmap graphics**, the picture is made up of a series of square pixels of different colours. The colours available determine the type of bitmap:

- black and white (monochrome)
- grey-scale
- 16-colour
- 256-colour
- true colour – where millions of colours are possible.

In general, the higher the definition and the more colours which are used, the greater the final file size of the image.

A problem can arise when we attempt to increase the size of a bitmap image because each of the pixels increases in size, losing definition. If the size increase is too great, the individual pixels can become visible (Figure 1.7.6). This is known as the "staircase effect". In **vector graphics**, a drawing is composed from a toolbox of available shapes – rectangle, straight line and thousands of others – called "drawing objects" (Figure 1.7.7). The properties of each object are stored as a set of mathematical equations, coordinates, etc. Hence when an object is re-sized, none of its definition is lost as the re-sizing is achieved by re-calculating all the properties.

Different software packages create graphics in different ways. Microsoft Paint creates bitmap graphics while Microsoft Visio creates vector graphics.

Discussion

The officers of a swimming club use a computer system to run the club. Explain how the different generic applications could be used in the club.

Figure 1.7.6   An enlarged bitmap graphic showing the "staircase effect".

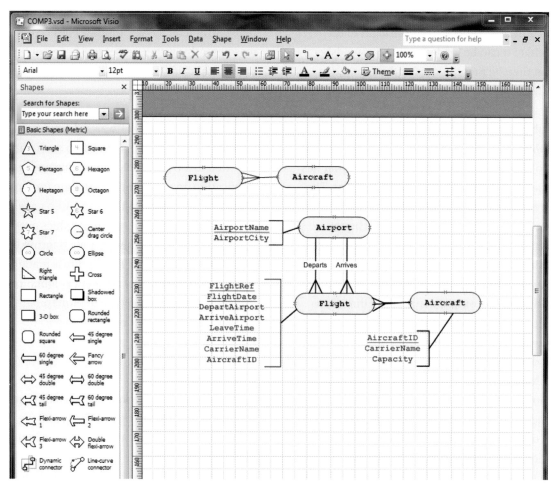

Figure 1.7.7   A vector graphics program.

Areas in which generic applications software is not appropriate

Generic software is the starting point for an application that performs a required task. For example, a user may wish to maintain a list of 100 customers. The user is satisfied that a spreadsheet (a generic software package) is capable of doing this. The developer must be satisfied that all the requirements of the final software solution can be produced using the features and functions of the generic software.

However, generic software is not capable of producing an acceptable solution for many tasks. This is due to:

- the specialised nature of the task
- the lack of features that can be engineered to produce the required solution.

The user must then research a **special-purpose application** program which does meet their needs. Special-purpose software is designed for one task. For example, the following types of application (and thousands more!) are available off the shelf:

- route-planning software
- garden design software
- games.

These are all applications that the user has to purchase. The solution cannot be developed from generic software packages.

The impact of generic applications software

The purposes of the different types of generic software have been covered earlier in this chapter. The impact of the different types of software has been profound.

Word processor

Expectations have changed markedly since the days of the typewriter, which can be thought of as the direct predecessor of the **word processor**. Letters or other documents are now perceived to be unacceptable if they contain an error. If an error is spotted, then it is corrected and the document is reprinted.

The advent of electronic machines was heralded as the start of the "paperless office", whereas the fact is that the amount of paper consumed in office applications has increased! The use of computers running word processing programs was greeted with fear by most typewriter operators for two reasons. The first was because of the fear of unemployment. The logic went along the lines of: "Each operator will be able to work much faster and hence produce more output; therefore some of the operators can be made redundant". While this happened in some organisations, the truth was far from this and there are now more computer operators than there ever were typists. The second fear was that, in order to use one of the new machines, typists would have to undergo considerable training. While this was true to some extent and there were some typists who found great difficulty in changing their old practices, most had no problems. Some people learned new skills that made them better qualified, giving more job satisfaction.

Spreadsheet

In its simplest form, a **spreadsheet** is simply a data storage system. However, spreadsheets begin to take on added significance when formulae are applied to numeric data in the sheet to make calculations, particularly calculations that make predictions about what would happen if some value were to be changed.

Spreadsheets can also be expected to have presentation tools such as graphing features to produce the results in easily understandable form. The addition of an inbuilt programming language, so that algorithms can be programmed, makes a spreadsheet a very powerful software tool. It goes beyond simply juggling with figures necessary for doing a payroll or keeping the accounts and makes it possible to model mathematical problems.

Desktop publisher (DTP)

Printing used to be a specialised task in which a typesetter physically created a page from metal type (letter blocks) and used a mechanical machine to print out multiple copies. A DTP package combines software and output devices so that published quality material can be produced from a desktop computer system. Commercial printing is now electronically set up, meaning that the publication and the process can be controlled from a PC.

In the 1970s, fewer than 200 magazine periodicals were available in Australia because of the difficulty of setting up a new publication and the cost which could only be recuperated if there were sufficient sales of the magazine. The cost of producing a magazine has fallen so much that a small circulation title can now make a profit and the production is very simple, often a one-person job. This has led to there being many thousands of specialist titles available.

Presentation software

When presentation software was first available, those who used it produced presentations that were out of the ordinary and consequently it was seen as something to aspire to (Figure 1.7.8). There was a novelty factor in being able to hold the attention of an audience. However, as the use of such presentations became more common, more and more complex techniques were needed to maintain the novelty factor. Presentations became overloaded with tricks that could distract from the key message of the content. Presentation software can be used to make a message more accessible to the audience, but no amount of clever gimmickry can hide a poor message.

Figure 1.7.8   A presenter using PowerPoint.

Drawing or graphics software

Strictly speaking, drawing software enables the creation of vector graphics, as opposed to painting software that creates bitmaps. However, the syllabus uses the term "drawing package" to refer to the concept of the user being able to create images (vector or bitmap graphics) that can be imported into other software packages. No longer does a school worksheet need to be a simple text document – diagrams, pictures and photographs can all be included.

Summary

- Custom-written software is specially written to solve a specific problem.
    - It may take a long time to become available to users.
    - It is expensive.
    - Bugs in the software may not be found for a long time.
    - Any training must be specially developed.
    - No help is available on the Internet.
- Off-the-shelf software is available for purchase from a shop or website:
    - It is available immediately.
    - It is used by many people or organisations that share the development costs, making it cheap.
    - Bugs in the software are found and rectified more quickly.
    - It may be compatible with other applications from the same software house.
    - There may be training courses available for it.
    - There may be help available from staff or user-group forums on the Internet who already know how to use the software.
- Common business, commercial and industrial applications:
    - Stock control systems keep track of the stock sold and bought by an organisation.
    - Payroll systems use employee details to produce payslips and bank transfer transactions.

Summary continued …

- Process control systems monitor physical processes in a factory or plant and report the results or adjust inputs.
- Point-of-sale systems calculate the value of purchases in shops and record customer payments.

- Generic applications software:

  - Word processors are used to process text documents, such as letters, mail-merged documents and reports. They ensure that documents look better and have fewer errors.

  - Spreadsheets are used to store data and apply calculations to it. They make it easier to try out different scenarios (such as price changes) and to present numerical data in graphs.

  - Desktop publishers (DTP) are used to lay out documents for print output. They make it easier and cheaper for small and voluntary organisations to produce a magazine.

  - Presentation software is used to create animated and interactive on-screen presentations. They can engage the audience's attention and help to put across a message.

  - Drawing packages are used to create bitmap and vector images. The images can be included into other types of document, such as word-processed reports or presentations.

- Generic applications software is not appropriate for specialised problems (such as games and garden design).

Test yourself

1. Describe how CAD/CAM software can be used to produce prototype designs in a manufacturing process. [4]
2. A firm produces widgets for sale to the baking industry. A baking company may come to the firm with a proposal for a widget to fit a particular container. The firm needs to produce the widget, ship the finished product in batches and invoice the baking company. Sometimes the sales team will be sent to try to persuade the baking company of the advantages of the firm's widgets. Explain how the firm can use applications software in the running of its business. [6]

> **Hint**
>
> There are six marks available. Do not go into detail about any piece of software. Find one thing to say about each of six pieces of software.

3. Discuss why the manager of a solicitors' practice might decide to change the currently used word processing package for a more up-to-date one. [4]

> **Hint**
>
> There are four marks available and the key word is "discuss". You are expected to go into detail.

4. State **two** reasons why custom-written software might be more appropriate to the solicitors' practice than readily available software. [2]

1.8

Handling of data in information systems

Manual and automatic methods of capturing data

All computer systems need to have data input, otherwise they have nothing to process. Methods used for collecting the data can be divided into two types: automatic and manual data collection.

Automatic data collection

Automatic data collection can be considered to be any data collection that does the two stages of data collection and data input to the system without going through the intermediate phase of data preparation to make it suitable for computer use.

Sensors

The most obvious type of automatic data collection is in a control system where the computer collects its data from sensors that give information about the physical environment. The data collection is continuous but the reading of the data is at fixed time periods. The processor does not want to know the temperature in the room all the time, but perhaps every 5 minutes. This gives a previous decision, for example about whether or not to turn the heating on, long enough to have had some effect. The use of only some of the available data is known as **sampling**.

Many sensors that measure physical values are analogue sensors while the data required by the processor needs to be digital. Analogue data are physical data that create a signal which consists of a continuously changing voltage. For example, a thermistor increases the voltage output as the temperature which it is measuring increases. This signal must be changed into a stream of 0s and 1s that the computer can recognise. This is done by hardware called an **analogue-to-digital converter**.

When data are collected offline, often by sensors in remote locations, and then stored until ready for input to the system at a time that is convenient to the system, it is known as **data logging**. A typical data logger is in the form of a disk drive on which the data are stored until a set has been collected. The data can then be entered into the system in one operation. Obviously, this would not be suitable data input for a system which was controlling the central heating in a house. It would, however, be suitable for a remote weather station on a mountain top where readings are taken every 10 minutes and radioed back to the weather centre once every 24 hours. The system would need just such a device to store the data until it was required.

There are many different types of sensor depending on the data that they are intended to measure. Whatever the value to be measured, if it is a physical value there is almost certainly a type of sensor to measure it. Be careful not to confuse the use of sensors in a computer system with the idea of a mechanical control system. Consider a thermistor (temperature sensor) collecting data about the temperature of a room and passing it to a computer which can then make decisions about the need for heating or cooling according to an algorithm. This is very different from a switching device such as a bi-metal strip which bends as it cools and when it has moved enough it trips a switch to turn on a heater. This is a mechanical switch with no decision-making element in it.

Barcodes

A less obvious form of automatic data collection is the barcodes used in retailing. A barcode is printed as a series of dark coloured bars on a light background. The data can be input to the barcode reader without any further preparation. You need to be aware of the need to check the input by use of a check digit in the code (see "Validation and verification techniques" on page 80). A question about barcodes will almost certainly be contained within another question about automatic data collection or stock control systems.

Voice recognition

Another method of automatically entering data is by **voice recognition**, which is particularly important for disabled users. It is done by using a microphone to communicate with the computer (Figure 1.8.1). The sound waves produced by the microphone are sampled and digitised. The digital values are then compared with a library of digital values stored on the computer and interpreted by the computer.

The computer must be trained to recognise a particular voice. Background sound can distort the data capture. The smaller the vocabulary of the system and the better the masking of background noise, the more effective it is. Voice recognition is particularly useful for simple menu commands in telephone-enquiry systems.

Figure 1.8.1   A user speaking into a microphone.

Optical mark recognition (OMR)

In Chapter 1.4, you learned that an optical mark reader (OMR) is an input device. A school registration system can record marks on a sheet of paper which can then be read directly into the computer by an optical mark reader, with no human intervention.

Data are read by translating the position of the marks on the paper into a digital reading (Figure 1.8.2). The position of the mark on the sheet is read as a pair of coordinates so that two marks side by side on the paper mean different things because of where they are rather than because of their appearance. A school register is only one of many applications of OMR. The basis of an examination question could be about how information is contained and read or about the suitability of OMR for a particular application.

Figure 1.8.2   A data capture form for a money lottery.

Optical character recognition (OCR)

In Chapter 1.4, you learned that an optical character reader (OCR) is an input device. Computer systems are available that read individual characters and input them without the data having to be transcribed (Figure 1.8.3). This qualifies as automatic data collection (it is known as "optical character recognition"). OCR has become very much more accurate as algorithms to recognise the characters have improved. Rather like sound recognition methods, the computer samples the letter that is scanned and compares it to a library of stored images, selecting the best fit. Major improvements in reliability have come about because of improvements to the algorithms by increasing the sampling and expanding the library (e.g. by increasing the number of fonts) and by improving predictive algorithms so that combinations of characters can be accepted or rejected.

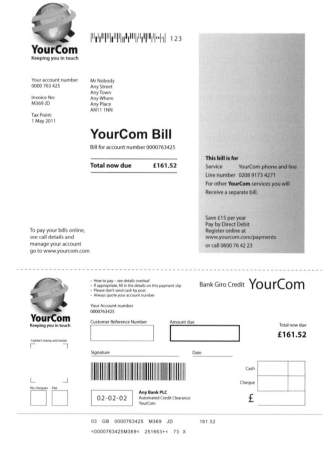

Figure 1.8.3   A utility bill showing characters which will be read by OCR.

Touch screen

This has already been described in Chapter 1.4 in the section "Common peripheral devices". The data handling capability of a touch screen is to act as both an input and output device. The technology has become increasingly widespread in devices such as the iPad, iPhone and other smartphones with the provision of an on-screen keyboard for texting, etc.

Chip and PIN technology

Personal information is extremely sensitive and valuable. It needs to be protected as far as possible. Credit and debit cards initially stored data on a magnetic stripe. Car park tickets and hotel room keys still use magnetic stripes because the information is not confidential. Credit and debit cards now tend to store personal information on a computer chip embedded into the plastic card and requiring an identification code (PIN) to gain authorisation (Figure 1.8.4). The system is known as **chip and PIN**.

Figure 1.8.4   A plastic card with embedded chip.

Image capture

Taking and storing pictures is also described as "image capture". Mobile phones are now used as cameras (even video cameras) and all sorts of devices can capture an image. Some credit cards even include a picture chip.

It can take a large amount of memory to store images with an acceptable resolution, so electronic images are compressed to save space on the storage device. There are many ways to take, capture, compress and store images. Two of the most popular file formats are JPEG format for still images and MPEG for moving pictures, i.e. video clips.

Manual data entry

Many data collection methods rely on a person completing a paper-based form. The questions on the form must be unambiguous. The form must contain clear areas where the answers can be written. Exam questions will concentrate on the need to use forms and check the input data (see "Validation and verification techniques" on page 80). Chapter 2.1 covers various aspects of interface design.

Data collected on a form are not in a form acceptable to the computer. An operator must read the data and type them into the computer via a keyboard. The data may have to be prepared before being typed in. For example, a response may require a date. Different people may write a date in many different ways. The person inputting the data may have to interpret the date into a standard format. The form should be designed to force the provider of the data to prepare the data themselves, perhaps by using boxes headed DD/MM/YY.

Most data needs to go through three stages before being stored in a computer:

- collection (ask someone to fill in a form)
- preparation (ensure that the data collected is in the correct format)
- input (enter the data into the computer system).

In some systems, measures are taken to remove the need for one or more of these stages.

Activity

Try to identify the stages that data goes through when gathered by:

- a paper form used by customers to place an order by post
- a paper form used by operators to record customer orders received by telephone
- an on-screen form used by customers to order goods over the Internet.

When the method of input does not rely on a keyboard, one of these stages is removed. Touch screens (Figure 1.8.5) tend to be used when there are a finite number of possible choices. The user's choices are restricted to what is available on the screen. Use of this technology is often determined by the environment: a keyboard cannot be used where it would be at danger from the weather; a mouse is not sensible where a system is susceptible to vandalism.

Figure 1.8.5   A touch screen for buying rail tickets.

(1.8 b) Image capture

Scanner

A scanner shines a laser at a source document and reads the intensity of the reflected light. The surface of the document is divided into small rectangles (pixels). The light intensity is recorded as an electrical signal which is converted to a digital value for each pixel.

Scanners can be of different sizes. On an A4 flatbed scanner, the image is placed on a sheet of glass and is scanned line by line. A handheld scanner is rolled across the image, collecting a band each time. The bands are matched up by software to produce a complete image. Once an image is stored electronically, a user can manipulate it using image editing software or convert it to text characters using OCR software.

Video capture card

A video picture is made up of a series of images that change approximately 26 times per second. A **video capture card** is an analogue-to-digital converter which reads the analogue signals from the video camera or video tape and digitises them ready for storage in a computer. Many video cameras are now digital cameras and consequently do not need a video capture card, but video capture cards are still used to provide other functions such as colour correction capabilities. The algorithm which processes the signal and prepares it for storage and use is called the "codec". There are many different codecs that use different algorithms to do the same job. This means that video which was prepared using one codec can only be re-created by using the same codec.

A video capture card fits into one of the expansion slots of a computer system and allows the processor to store the values of the screen pixels for a specific picture. In other words, it allows the action to be frozen. A typical example of the use of a video capture card is the selection and storage of a single frame taken from a video file. If a computer is able to receive and display television pictures, the video capture card could store a single picture frame.

Digital camera

A digital camera works in a similar way to an optical camera but it does not store the image on film. Instead, the image is stored electronically, enabling the user to download it into a computer and then manipulate and print the image.

Image editing

Each of these image capture systems results in an electronic image being stored in the computer system. Image editing software can then be used to alter or edit the image in any way that is required. While this allows the user to use their imagination and to tidy up pictures or crop them, it also allows unscrupulous people to produce pictures with very little foundation in reality. It used to be said that: "The camera never lies" – this is no longer true!

Discussion

Realistic images can be manufactured to show what is simply untrue. What are the implications of this?

(1.8 c) Validation and verification techniques

When data are input to a computer system, they are only valuable if they are correct. No amount of care in programming can make up for erroneous data and the results produced can be expected to be unreliable. There are three types of error that can occur with the data on entry.

The first is that the data, while reasonable, is wrong. John's date of birth is 8 November 1993 but is written onto a data capture form incorrectly as 18 November 1993. It can be typed into the computer with the utmost care (in the form DD/MM/YY) 18/11/93; it can be checked by the computer to make sure that is a sensible

date; and it is accepted as the date of birth despite the fact that it is wrong. There is no reason for the computer to imagine that it may be wrong. There is nothing that the computer system can do to identify this type of error.

There is very little that can be done about faulty data except to let the owner of the data check it on a regular basis. The personal information kept on the school administration system about you and your family may well be printed off at regular intervals. You can then check it to ensure that the stored information is still correct. There are many operational reasons why data may become inaccurate; for example, a student may move house and forget to inform the school. The school computer system is now storing inaccurate data for the student's address.

The second type of error is a **transcription error**. For example, suppose this time the date of birth on the paper form is correct but the operator typing in the data selects the wrong key and types in 18/11/83. An error-checking technique, called a **verification check**, requires the data to be entered twice. The actual error is not obvious but the user knows that the two data values entered do not match. This is the usual process when you change your password for your user account on a network of computers.

The third type of error is when a data value is typed in which simply is not sensible. The computer software knows that there are only 12 months in a year so it knows that 08/13/93 must be wrong. A check on the sense or "validity" of data is called a **validation check**.

Data verification

Verification means checking the input data with the original data to make sure that there have been no transcription errors (transcription means copying the data). The standard way to do this is to input the data twice to the computer system. The computer then checks the two data values (which should be the same) and, if they are different, the computer knows that one of the inputs is wrong. It won't know which one is wrong but it can ask the operator to check that particular input.

Data validation

The first thing is to dispel a common misinterpretation of validation. Checking of data, specifically the use of parity bits, was mentioned in Chapter 1.5. This is not what is understood by validation. Parity bits and echoing back are techniques that are used to check that data has been *transmitted* correctly within a computer system (e.g. from the disk drive to the processor) or between sending and receiving devices. Validation checks are used to check the input and capture of data.

Validation is a check on data input to the system by comparing the data input with a set of rules that the computer software has been programmed to implement. If the data input does not match up with the rules then there must be an error. In Chapter 2.4, we look at programming algorithms for implementing data validation.

There are many different types of validation check that may be appropriate and these include:

- Range check: A mathematics exam is marked out of 100. A simple validation rule that the computer can apply to input data is that the mark must be between 0 and 100 inclusive. Consequently, a mark of 101 would be flagged as being outside the acceptable range.
- Character check: A person's name consists of letters of the alphabet and sometimes a hyphen or apostrophe. This rule can be applied to input of a person's name so that "dav2d" is immediately rejected as an unacceptable name.
- Format check: An application is set up to accept an identity card number. Each person has a unique identity card number, but they all have the same "format", for example, two letters followed by six digits followed by a single letter. The computer could then identify "DH098765G" as valid and "ABC12345Z" as invalid.
- Length check: A product code has exactly five digits. If more or fewer than five characters are keyed in then the data value is invalid. Hence the product code 56744 is valid but 6744 is invalid. Notice that this is not the same as a range check.
- Existence check: A barcode is read at a supermarket check out till. The code is sent to the main computer which searches for that code on the stock file If the code is found in the stock file then it is known to exist and is accepted.
- From a list check: Only a limited number of values are allowed. The gender of a person must be entered

as M or F. Usually implemented with a drop-down list containing the permitted values.

- Presence check: A value must be present. When filling in an online form, the system does not allow the user to progress to the next data item unless some input to the present value is provided. The Microsoft Access database software calls this check a "Required" validation check. Be careful about distinguishing between existence and presence checks: they are often confused by candidates in exam questions.
- Uniqueness check: Each new product entered must be allocated a unique ProductID number. The data value must be unique in the file.

Some systems can also use a check digit to ensure that input is valid. When the barcode is read on an item at the supermarket, it consists of numbers. One number is special: it is called the check digit. If the other numbers have some arithmetic done to them using a simple algorithm, the answer should be this special digit. The scanner reads the code and applies the algorithm to the digits. If it does not result in the check digit, the barcode must have been read wrongly. It is at this point that the beep sound indicates correct or incorrect reading of the barcode.

Check digits are used as an automatic data input validation check for many numeric data values, such as membership numbers, universal product codes (barcodes), employee numbers and the ISBNs that identify books (Figure 1.8.6). Check digits are used on any numbers where it is imperative that they are valid.

Figure 1.8.6 An ISBN on the back cover of a book.

An examination question will not ask for the details of the algorithm that is used for the calculation, however, the Extension shows how a check digit is calculated.

(1.8 d) Output formats

When data has been processed by a computer system, it is necessary to report the results of the processing. There are a number of different ways that the results can be reported to the user. We revisit the topic of output in Chapter 2.4 when we consider writing programs.

Reports

A report is usually a printout, known as hard copy. An on-screen report (also known as **soft copy**) is transient (temporary). The output disappears when the computer system refreshes the screen or the screen is turned off, unlike hard copy output which can be filed for future reference.

If a weather station prints the outside temperature at 12 noon each day, it is unlikely that any valuable information could be learned. However, if the temperature was measured at the same time each day for a given period of time, the system could create a report showing all the temperatures at noon. Valuable information could be learned about the temperature in different seasons. If they are produced as a hard copy report, they can be studied at leisure and can be referred to in the future should there be a need to revisit the data.

In order to make data easier to read it is normally structured in some way, typically in tabular form, perhaps all the temperatures divided into 12 columns according to month. This has the advantage of producing the actual figures according to the values specified by the user. However, skill is often needed to interpret the significance of such figures. Presenting figures out of context may not be useful.

Graphs and charts

Graphs show trends very clearly. Different types of graph can illustrate different characteristics of a data set:
- A pie chart can give a very simple comparison between data. A pie chart could be drawn showing the number of people who rent their home compared to the number who own their home. It is not possible to read off accurate measurements but the areas of the graph can be compared. It is easy to see which is most common and approximate the difference.
- A bar chart can provide a scale on the vertical axis to indicate the numbers represented by each bar.
- A line graph can be used to show trends. For example, it can show the numbers who owned and rented their homes over ten years.

Care needs to be taken in reading data values off a graph. This is particularly true if the scale does not start at zero or is shown differently for different values represented on the graph. Also, the specific values are not easily read from a graph, indeed, in a continuous distribution such as a line graph, it may not be possible to "read off" values from the graph at any degree of accuracy. The chart gives the "big picture" but for actual data values the user must have available the original data sets.

Other forms of output

- Sound: Many applications do not lend themselves to a standard on-screen or printed report. Sound can be used for output from some systems. Examples could be voice synthesis for reporting to blind people or an alarm system designed to protect property against burglars.
- Video: Video is a visually satisfying form of output that takes large amounts of memory to produce because it requires large quantities of pictures to produce the feel of continuous motion. Video is useful for demonstration of techniques; there is little value in pages of instruction if a simple video can illustrate something better. One of the most recent computing developments has been the availability of video from websites such as YouTube.
- Images: Graphical images (graphs, pictures, photographs…) can be used to illustrate output to make it more instructive and able to hold the viewer's attention.
- Animation: Moving images can provide a good stimulus for an audience. Presentation software contains a wealth of animation effects and care should be taken to use them sparingly and effectively.

1.8 e Suiting output format to the target audience

Consider an intensive care ward at a hospital. There are six beds, each with a patient who is being monitored by a computer. The outputs provided by the computer systems are available to a variety of users. There is a nurse at a desk at one end of the ward. The nurse has other duties, but is expected to make rounds of the patients to check on their progress at regular intervals. Doctors visit the ward twice a day to check on the patients and may make adjustments to their medication.

If the computer system senses a patient to have suffered a relapse, a sensible output would be an audible alarm to alert the nurse that something is wrong. This may be accompanied by a flashing light, or some other device, to quickly attract the nurse's attention.

When a nurse makes a visual check of a patient's condition, it is not necessary to have exact figures for heart rate or blood sugar. A quick glance at a screen showing a scrolling graph of the patient's vital signs is perfectly adequate. If a graph looks in any way abnormal, it may be necessary to get a printout of the actual values

to determine what action needs to be taken. A doctor may well want to see a printout of all the values for the last 24 hours, particularly if there is something happening to the patient which is difficult to understand. Historical data may indicate the cause of present symptoms.

The doctor may change the medication or the parameters within which the patient can be considered to be stable. This will involve the nurse resetting values on the scales of the graphical output, or even resetting the parameters for triggering the audible alarm. This involves the nurse in using an interactive presentation with the system.

Once a week the nurse leads a first aid class at the local college. There are too many students for a one-to-one presentation so the college computer system has been loaded with demonstration software showing an animation of the technique used for artificial respiration.

When considering output always consider the importance of timeliness and relevance. Data tends to have a limited "shelf life" which can be different for the same data in different situations. The data on heart rate from three hours ago is not going to be of importance to the nurse looking after the patient, but it may be of great value to the doctor in providing a clue as to the reason for a sudden change in their condition. Some data are not relevant to particular situations, however up-to-date it is. The colour of the patient's eyes has no bearing on their physical state and consequently should not be considered relevant.

Activity

Consider teaching situations in which your teacher uses computerised output. Decide on a sensible form of output for each case. Justify your choices according to the advantages and disadvantages of the different forms of output.

Extension

Consider other forms of output that are becoming available. You might start by considering 3D printers and 3D screen output. Try to decide on suitable uses for them.

1.8 f Knowledge-based (expert) systems

A knowledge-based system is a system that brings together all the knowledge of a human expert about a particular topic and makes it available to a user who is not an expert in that area. The computer system uses the **facts** in its knowledge base and applies **rules** to it.

Human knowledge encompasses so much data that it is not reasonable to try to distil it all into one computer database. Knowledge-based systems are restricted to a narrow area of knowledge, such as geological patterns in the oil exploration industry, medical diagnosis or personnel information in a company. They tend to be used in well-delineated areas of expertise where there are no grey areas of whether data should be included. In a knowledge-based system, or **expert system**, all the information that has been collected is stored in a database called a **knowledge base**.

The access to this knowledge can be very haphazard unless the system follows certain rules. That is why all expert systems include a **rule base** that determines how the data within the system relate to each other. A set of algorithms determines how the rules in the rule base should be applied to the knowledge in the knowledge base. These algorithms are implemented using an **inference engine**, which gives a method for using the rule base to search and query the knowledge base.

Finally there must be a user interface which allows the user to interrogate the knowledge base. The question which is posed by the user to the expert system is called the *goal*. The user interface passes requests on to the inference engine which, in turn, interrogates the knowledge base.

The user interface prompts the user with a series of questions, each of which has a limited number of possible answers. One answer may lead to another question. Gradually, the amount of data in the knowledge base that matches the data given by the user reduces. When it is sufficiently narrowed, the small amount of relevant data must provide the answer to the query.

The user interface also allows the user to ask for explanations of the reasoning behind the advice that has been given. The results are given as conclusions with the probabilities of those conclusions being correct. This ability to display the reasoning – i.e. which facts and rules were used in arriving at a decision – is called "backtracking".

An expert system may use data collected automatically by sensors and may even use data from other computer systems.

Software which allows an expert system (i.e. the knowledge base and rules) to be created is called an **expert system shell**. This software is usually written using a declarative, high-level programming language, such as Prolog.

1.8 g Knowledge-based diagnostic tools

Many applications of an expert system are diagnostic in nature. For example, an expert system about plumbing could consider reasons for no hot water being available in a house. The system would then report possible reasons with an explanation for each one.

A medical diagnostic expert system contains an enormous amount of knowledge about medical conditions. To read all of it would be a Herculean task. A knowledge-based system can enable a doctor or nurse to ask questions – i.e. the goal – about the patient's condition. If the user interface asks whether the patient has a high temperature there are two possible answers which immediately divide the knowledge base into two parts and hence restricts the number of possible results. A series of similar questions will allow the inference engine to report its conclusions.

The patient may be being monitored by various devices. A temperature sensor can read the patient's temperature automatically without a user asking about it through the HCI. Data logging may be used and the data can be downloaded from the monitoring system straight to the knowledge-based system.

The result may well be more than one possible diagnosis. In this case, probabilities are assigned to each diagnosis to give an indication of which are more likely than others. Notice that in such an important application the final decision is left up to the human being (the doctor). The information from the system is simply used to inform the doctor.

Summary

- Automatic methods of capturing and inputting data into a system include:
  - barcodes to read product details from labels with black and white stripes
  - optical mark recognition (OMR) to translate marks made by hand on a piece of paper into digital readings
  - magnetic stripe cards to provide data encoded directly in the magnetic stripe
  - optical character recognition (OCR) to distinguish characters printed in a known font on a document
  - sensors that record information from the environment by means of an analogue-to-digital converter and data logging
  - chip and PIN cards that provide data encoded on the chip and authorised by the PIN.
- Data can be entered manually into a system by a person using a keyboard to enter data into forms or a touch screen.
- Images can be captured by using:
  - a scanner that converts a sheet of paper into an image
  - a video capture card that digitises data from an analogue video device
  - a digital camera or camcorder.
- Verification means checking the input data against the original data to make sure that there have been no transcription errors, e.g. by entering the data twice and comparing it.
- Validation means checking that input data is reasonable and matches rules applied to it (such as checking that months of the year are numbers from 1–12).
- The following validation tests can be carried out on data:
  - range check: values must be within a specific range, e.g. 0–100.
  - character check: values must only include certain characters, such as letters of the alphabet.
  - format check: values must conform to a specific pattern, for example, two letters followed by six digits followed by a single letter.
  - length check: values must be a specific length.
  - existence check: values must exist in another list.
  - presence check: a value must be present.
  - uniqueness check: values cannot be repeated in the file (e.g. a product ID in a product file).
- Output formats include:
  - graphs that clearly show trends and comparisons between data
  - reports, usually on hard copy, that can be taken away from the computer and studied
  - interactive presentations containing sound, video, images and animations.
- The output format needs to be appropriate to the target audience and the environment. For example, someone whose eyes are engaged in another task may have an audible signal when an unexpected event happens.
- Knowledge-based (expert) systems bring together knowledge about a particular topic and make it available to non-expert users.
  - The expert knowledge is collected into a knowledge base as facts and rules.
  - The user poses a problem through a user interface.

$\longrightarrow$

- An inference engine processes the query/goal set by the user.
- When only a few solutions are left, the engine provides probabilities and explanations of its reasoning.

• Knowledge-based (expert) systems are used for diagnosis, for example, in medicine or engineering. The computer can consider many possibilities and lead the user into tests that narrow down the options.

Test yourself

1. a. State **two** methods of data entry used by banks for the processing of cheques. [2]
   b. Explain why banks find the use of your two methods suitable for this application. [4]

2. A small stall is to be opened, as part of a market, where the customer can have their likeness printed on to the front of a sweatshirt. Describe **two** possible methods of capturing the image to be printed. [4]

Hint

There is one very obvious answer. Give it and then think about another method.

3. A mail order firm receives orders from customers on a paper order form. These are keyed into the computer system by operators. The data keyed includes the five-digit article number, the name of the customer and the date that the order is received.
   a. Explain how the data input would be verified. [3]
   b. Describe **three** different validation checks that could be performed on the data. [6]

4. A reaction vessel in a chemical plant is monitored, along with many others, by a computer system using a number of sensors. Describe **three** types of output that would be used by such a system, stating why such a use would be necessary. [6]

5. a. Describe what is meant by a knowledge-based system. [4]
   b. Explain how a knowledge-based system could be used in a garage for servicing cars. [3]

1.9 Designing the user interface

Issues relating to user interface design have already been covered in Chapters 1.2 and 1.6. It features again in Chapter 2.1. This chapter should be read in conjunction with those sections.

1.9 a The importance of good interface design

However complex the software, however expensive and powerful the hardware, a computer system is unusable if there is no intuitive, simple-to-use interface with the human being who is in control of the system or for whom the system is producing results. The human–computer interface (HCI) must:

- be unambiguous so that decisions made are clearly understood by both the user and the software
- allow the user to input all the data that the user thinks is important and that is necessary to allow the system to produce results
- produce the output to the user in a format which is easily understandable.

There are a number of factors that need to be considered when designing an interface:

- who it is for?
- what information needs to be conveyed?
- the circumstances under which the interface must operate
- the effectiveness of the communication
- the satisfaction with using it – i.e. is it intuitive to use?

The intended user of the interface must be considered. An interface designed for very young children to learn number work is going to be very different from an interface designed for the manager of a chemical factory to keep a check on the reactions around the plant. A complex user interface (Figure 1.9.1 on page 88) is not necessarily inappropriate.

The information that the interface is intended to convey to the user is a factor in the design. The interface that the manager would use to study a particular reaction is very different from the interface the same person would use if they wanted to see the flow of a chemical around the whole factory. The reaction would be shown in tables of figures or graphs. The flow around the factory would probably be in the form of a diagrammatic representation of the factory, i.e. "visual".

The circumstances under which the interface is to operate are also important. At the end of Chapter 1.8 we considered the case of a nurse looking after a group of patients. In those circumstances, an audible warning is far more sensible than a visual one, which may be ignored if the nurse is working away from the computer for a short period of time.

Finally, the designer of the interface needs to take account of the purpose for which the interface was designed. If the user is using the computer to play a game, then of paramount importance is that the interface adds to the enjoyment of the user.

All these factors are important when the interface is being designed, although some are more important than others in particular applications.

Activity

Explain why software designed to teach students about volcanoes needs good interface design. What are the factors that need to be taken into consideration?

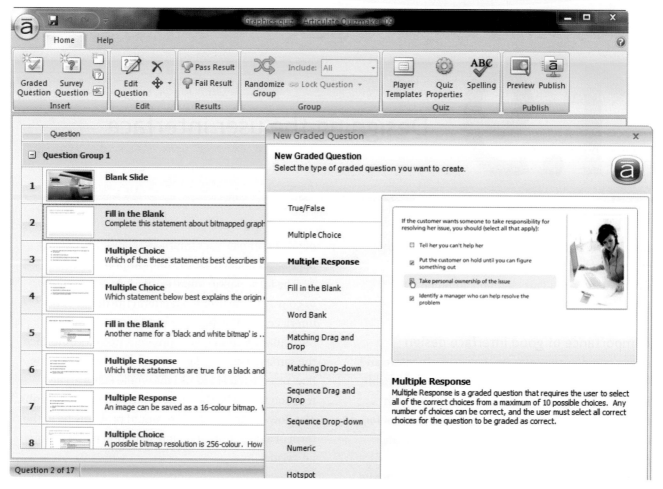

Figure 1.9.1   A modern user interface.

Behind the interface is the software that produces what is used for communication. An equally important part of the interface is the hardware that will be used for the communication. When choosing peripheral devices, a number of factors need to be taken into account:

- Who are the users that are going to use the application?
  - the age of the user
  - their reading ability
  - their ability to use a keyboard and a mouse
  - their ability with computer systems
  - their understanding of the software
  - whether they need instruction in how to use it
  - any physical disabilities which may make some hardware impossible to use
- Is the system automated in any way? If so the peripherals may include sensors and actuators.

- Under what circumstances will the system be used? If the input and output devices are to be used in the open air, then the environment will dictate some restrictions which would not be necessary if the system was being used in a computer room.
- What applications or system software is being used? The software dictates the type of input required and the type of output produced. Consequently, it also has an influence on the peripherals that are suitable for the input and output.

When answering questions drawn from this section, compare the requirements of the system with the characteristics of the available hardware devices. Be prepared to state why a particular choice has been made.

1.9 b HCI design issues

Before attempting the design of any interface the developer must be clear exactly what each screen is attempting to do. Any computer program is likely to include the following aspects:

- input of data to the computer application
- output of information to the screen
- a warning message to indicate a potential problem
- an indication that the computer is currently processing (e.g. downloading a large file) and requires no input from the user.

The developer must be aware of the volume of information which is to be presented and whether or not the user is expected to retain this information. For example, will the user be comfortable with a data entry form that scrolls vertically? Should the data entry be split across two screens?

The three fundamental features which must be considered for any interface are colour, layout and content.

Colour

Colour is an important consideration when designing any HCI. The contrasting use of colours can highlight the more important information or can be used to distinguish one type of information from another. The different levels of contrast between colours are necessary if the individual items of information are to stand out. Black on white provides the highest possible contrast, while dark blue on black would be very difficult to read.

Colour choice can also be very important to the organisation for whom the software is being produced. It is important in many instances to ensure that corporate colour schemes are used.

Colour can be used as an indicator of the data being highlighted. For example, red is often used as a warning colour and green to signify that there is no problem. Care, however, must be taken with the choices; colour-blind users may not be able to tell the difference between green and red and other colour combinations.

Layout

The layout of data on the screen is important. The eye naturally scans in the direction required for reading (e.g. from left to right and from top to bottom in English). This means that more important information should be positioned on the screen where the user will read. The volume of information on the screen

at any one time is also important. There is a limit to the amount that the eye can follow, and the brain can process, in one sweep of the screen content.

If information should be read in order, then the correct screen order is the same as for reading in the language of the interface (e.g. left to right).

It is also important to maintain a similar layout across software which is part of a software suite. For example, common commands should be placed in the same screen locations in all the software that controls a chemical factory, so that users get used to the layout of the interface. The same word should be used for the same command on all screens.

Activity

Consider software that you use in school or college: a database, a spreadsheet, a word processor or a web page creation program. Look at how the interface is set out. Note all the similarities and differences in the interfaces for each piece of software. You should end up with a much bigger list of similarities than of differences. If the differences are too many then either the software comes from different manufacturers or has been badly designed. Users do not want to have to learn different things for all the different pieces of software that they use.

Content

The content of the information presented is important. A user soon learns to ignore unnecessary items of information that are put on the screen. Similarly, if a piece of information is highlighted but the operator does not perceive the urgency, then all such highlighted information is ignored.

1.9 c The characteristics of a user interface

This material has been covered in previous sections:

- Chapter 1.2 covers the different types of interface that we study on this course. This includes a distinction between different interface types according to the information that the application uses and the intended user of the system.
- Chapter 1.4 covers the hardware that is used to support the interface. It also considers the requirements of different applications and justifies the choices made.

- Chapter 1.6 covers the design of interfaces, discussing the importance of different decisions about input and output design.

Module 2 discusses the design and implementation of interfaces. The topics are included in this part of the syllabus to test candidates on the theory of interface design and the design of interfaces for practical situations.

Summary

- There are a number of factors that need to be considered when designing an interface:
  - who it is for?
  - what information needs to be conveyed?
  - the circumstances under which the interface must operate
  - the effectiveness of the communication
  - the satisfaction with using it – i.e. is it intuitive to use?
- A good interface design:
  - is unambiguous so that decisions made are clearly understood by both the user and the software
  - accepts the data that the user thinks are important and the data that are necessary to allow the system to produce results
  - produces output in a format that is easily understandable.
- The three fundamental features which must be considered for any interface are colour, layout and content.

Test yourself

1. A company has a workforce of around 2000 employees. Some employees work in the office using the computer system for administrative tasks, while others use the computer system on the production line manufacturing goods to satisfy orders received.

   a. Describe the factors that would have been considered in the design of the software interfaces to be used by the office workers and the production line workers. [6]

   ### Hint

   Relate your answer to the scenario and do not stray into other areas that are not relevant.

   b. Select appropriate peripheral hardware for the application areas, giving reasons for your choices. [12]

   c. A clerk has to key in the details of all new employees from a standard form which the new employees complete. Explain how a form-based software interface would be useful to the clerk who has to key in the data. [4]

   d. Explain the types of output that would be expected from the computer in the factory, if it is used to control the speed of the production line as well as being a tool for the workers. [4]

1.10 Logic gates

In Chapter 1.3, we considered how a computer can store and use data. The method is equivalent to having a lot of wires through which electric pulses can be sent. At any one time, no electronic pulse represents a 0 and an electronic pulse represents 1. These are the only types of data that can be represented.

All computer hardware is constructed from circuit boards each of which require various inputs and outputs. All data values are produced as electrical signals which are either on or off, and these are represented by the circuit designer as binary digits 0 and 1.

Imagine a wire with a switch. In Figure 1.10.1, the switch is open. The output is 0 because no electric pulse can pass along the wire. In Figure 1.10.2, the switch is closed. The output is 1 because an electric pulse can pass along the wire.

Figure 1.10.1 A wire with a switch: open.

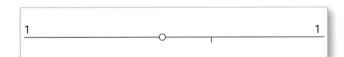

Figure 1.10.2 A wire with a switch: closed.

If a number of switches are arranged in a particular pattern they can have a predictable outcome for all possible combination of inputs. The fundamental building block of an electronic circuit is a logic gate which is known to behave in a certain way.

A note of warning is required before we start. If you look in other textbooks you may find a different set of symbols to the ones used here to represent the various gates. The advice is to use the ones that are featured here and to ignore the others. Any circuit diagrams that appear on an examination paper will feature these symbols and no others. If you are asked to draw a diagram then try to use the correct shapes.

1.10 a The effect of logic gates on binary signals

A set of switches is arranged in a particular pattern to produce a specific outcome. The symbol used to represent the switches is called a **logic gate** because it is a very logical process underneath it to decide whether it should be a 0 or 1 that is output. Each of the gates receives a set of inputs which have some rules applied to them and then a result is allowed through to the other side.

Other books consider six types of logic gate but you need to be familiar with five logic gates for this examination.

Imagine the single switch that we considered. If it is open, then no pulse is output so we can think of it as representing 0 and if it is in the closed position then it represents 1. Now think of two of these switches on the same line (Figure 1.10.3). Both switches are in the 0 position so the result is 0.

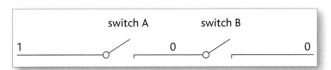

Figure 1.10.3 Two open switches.

What if switch A is in the 0 position but switch B is in the 1 position (Figure 1.10.4)? The result is still 0 because although switch B would have produced a 1 if it was given a 1 as input, the output from A is a 0 so switch B cannot produce a 1.

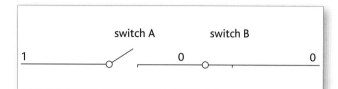

Figure 1.10.4   One open (A) and one closed switch (B).

AND gate

There are two other possible positions for the switches in Figure 1.10.4. Switch A could be in the 1 position and switch B in the 0 position; this results in a 0 overall because switch B does not allow a pulse through. The final position is for both switches to be in the 1 position. This is the only combination that produces a 1 output.

The blob over the switch in the Figure (1.10.4) is really the logic gate. The logic gate needs to be given a name in order to distinguish it from other sets of switches which behave differently. Because this combination of switches needs switch A *and* switch B to be in the 1 position to produce a 1 output we call it an **AND gate**.

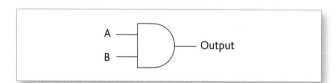

Figure 1.10.5   An AND gate.

The other thing that we need to do is to find some way of writing down all the possible inputs and outputs from a logic gate without having to write it all out in words. The accepted method is to list all the possible inputs (states of the switches) in a table and then to write down the column of outputs which match the combinations of inputs. The table is called a **truth table.** The truth table for the AND gate is shown in Table 1.10.1.

Table 1.10.1   The truth table for an AND gate.

A	B	Output
0	0	0
0	1	0
1	0	0
1	1	1

OR gate

Imagine the switches being rearranged so that they look like Figure 1.10.6. The diagram shows the only combination of positions that results in a 0. If either of the switches is set to the 1 position then a 1 is output.

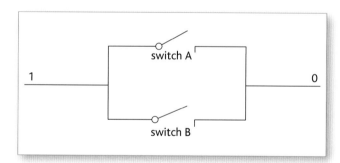

Figure 1.10.6   An OR circuit.

To put it another way, if switch A *or* switch B is set to a 1 then the output is a 1. For this reason the logic gate is called an **OR gate.** An OR gate with two inputs is shown in Figure 1.10.7 and its truth table is in Table 1.10.2.

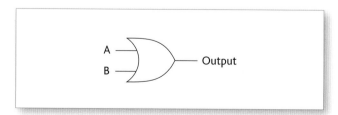

Figure 1.10.7   An OR gate.

Table 1.10.2 The truth table for an OR gate.

A	B	Output
0	0	0
0	1	1
1	0	1
1	1	1

Table 1.10.3 The truth table for a NOT gate.

A	Output
0	1
1	0

Activity

Draw the truth table for an OR gate with three inputs: A, B and C.

NOT gate

Consider Figure 1.10.1 on page 91. We saw that if it is in the open position then a 0 is the result and if it is switched to closed a 1 is the result. This is not very useful at all but if we change the position of the output line then we get a more interesting and useful result. If the switch is in the open position (Figure 1.10.8a), we get a 1 as the output. If the switch is in the closed position (Figure 1.10.8b), then the output is 0.

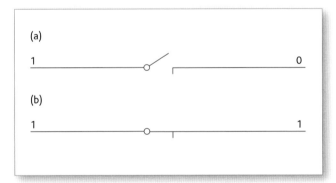

Figure 1.10.8 A NOT circuit: a) switch open, b) switch closed.

This type of arrangement makes the input (and it can only ever be a single input) swap from 0 to 1 or 1 to 0. It outputs the opposite of what was input. It is called a **NOT gate** (Figure 1.10.9) and its truth table is given in Table 1.10.3.

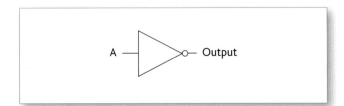

Figure 1.10.9 A NOT gate.

NAND gate

A **NAND gate** (Figure 1.10.10) is a single logic gate that is equivalent to an AND gate followed by a NOT gate (Figure 1.10.11).

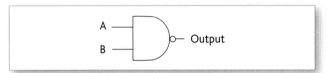

Figure 1.10.10 A NAND gate.

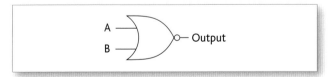

Figure 1.10.11 An AND gate followed by a NOT gate.

The truth table (Table 1.10.4) is most easily worked out if we compute the intermediate values at P in the circuit (Figure 1.10.11).

Table 1.10.4 The truth table for a NAND gate.

A	B	P	Output
0	0	0	1
0	1	0	1
1	0	0	1
1	1	1	0

NOR gate

A **NOR gate** (Figure 1.10.12) is a single logic gate that is equivalent to an OR gate followed by a NOT gate (Figure 1.10.13).

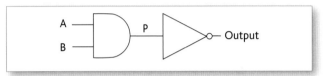

Figure 1.10.12 A NOR gate.

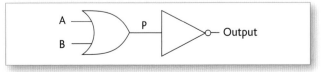

Figure 1.10.13 An OR gate followed by a NOT gate.

The truth table for a NOR gate (Table 1.10.5) is most easily worked out if we compute the intermediate values at P in the circuit (Figure 1.10.13 on page 93).

Table 1.10.5   The truth table for a NOR gate.

A	B	P	Output
0	0	0	1
0	1	1	0
1	0	1	0
1	1	1	0

(1.10 b) Calculate the outcome from a set of logic gates

In arriving at the truth tables for the NAND and NOR gates, we drew a combination of logic gates to form a logic circuit.

Logic circuits can get very complicated, with many 1s and 0s and it is easy to make a careless mistake. The technique to producing the final outputs is to compute the intermediate outputs as appropriate.

Consider the circuit with three inputs in Figure 1.10.14. We have added intermediate outputs D and E, which we show in the truth table (Table 1.10.6).

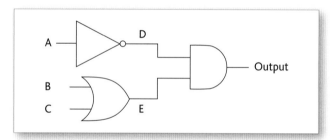

Figure 1.10.14   A circuit with three inputs.

Table 1.10.6   The truth table for a circuit with three inputs.

A	B	C	D	E	Output
0	0	0	1	0	
0	0	1	1	1	
0	1	0	1	1	
0	1	1	1	1	
1	0	0	0	0	
1	0	1	0	1	
1	1	0	0	1	
1	1	1	0	1	

Once D and E have been worked out, we just need to compute "D AND E" to get the final output (Table 1.10.7).

Table 1.10.7   The completed truth table for a circuit with three inputs.

A	B	C	D	E	Output
0	0	0	1	0	0
0	0	1	1	1	1
0	1	0	1	1	1
0	1	1	1	1	1
1	0	0	0	0	0
1	0	1	0	1	0
1	1	0	0	1	0
1	1	1	0	1	0

Columns D and E are not necessary to the answer, but using them means we are less likely to make a careless mistake.

Activity

Try working out the truth table for the circuit in Figure 1.10.15.

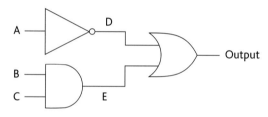

Figure 1.10.15   A second circuit with three inputs.

Compare your result with the one in Table 1.10.6. The three gates are the same as in Figure 1.10.14. All that has changed is the order in which they appear. Produce the truth table using D as the output from the NOT gate and E as the output from the AND gate.

Try working out the truth table for the circuit in Figure 1.10.16.

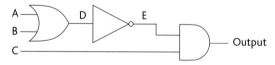

Figure 1.10.16   A complex circuit.

1.10 c Logic gates used as an accumulator and memory

Logic gates as an accumulator

This section is about a particular combination of logic gates called an accumulator, that can be used to add binary digits in a computer. Remember the digits that we work with: 0 or 1. You learned how to add binary numbers in Chapter 1.3, but here the addition is easy if we restrict our thinking to sum just two digits:

$$0 + 0 = 0$$
$$0 + 1 = 1$$
$$1 + 0 = 1$$

So far, so good but $1 + 1$ is the difficult one. We would like to say 2 but there is no digit 2, so we write down the 0 and carry the 1, just as we do when we add 9 and 1 with decimal numbers. So, $1 + 1$ in binary = 0 and carry 1.

Now consider the logic diagram in Figure 1.10.17. The first thing to notice about the diagram is that there are two outputs, labelled C and S.

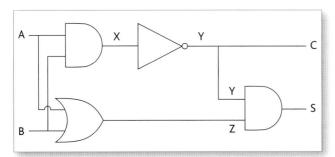

Figure 1.10.17   A 2-bit adder circuit.

The second thing to notice is that the A input is used more than once. Don't worry about this. We just label all the outputs from the individual gates and make extra columns in the table for the intermediate stages in the circuit.

Logic gates as memory

For many years, logic gates have been used to form memory.

A circuit can be used to form a sequential logic circuit that has feedback from an output that then acts as an input back to the circuit. The various outputs depend upon both historical inputs and current inputs. This means that for a certain arrangements of gates in a sequential logic circuit, the circuit can act as memory elements. This type of RAM which has to be continually refreshed to retain its contents is called **dynamic RAM**. The alternative is **static RAM**, which retains its contents as long as the power supply to the computer system is on. These memory elements can be used to act as a *register* (specialised small fast-access storage space) or Accumulator on the CPU. A RAM chip is made from thousands or even millions of these elements. Both static and dynamic RAM is volatile.

The expression "**memory refresh**" is used for the process of reading the contents of area of computer memory and immediately rewriting amended data to the same area of memory. The process can be best understood for an output monitor which is "memory mapped". That is an area of memory is dedicated to store the bytes which represent each of the pixels on the screen. For a graphical user interface the screen display will need to be continually updated as the result of (say) a mouse movement or dragging a window to a new position. This is achieved by refreshing the memory contents to ensure that the display to the user is updated. Hence this memory mapped area is achieved with a memory refresh.

Summary

- Logic gates combine or alter signals to produce an output:
    - An AND gate produces TRUE only if both inputs are TRUE.
    - An OR gate produces TRUE if either input is TRUE.
    - A NOT gate produces TRUE if the input is FALSE and vice versa.
    - A NAND gate produces FALSE only if both inputs are TRUE.
    - A NOR gate produces TRUE only if both inputs are FALSE.
- To calculate the outcome from a set of logic gates, make sure that you calculate the outcome of each of the intermediate stages.
- Logic gates can be used within the processor as a form of refreshable memory and as an accumulator.

Test yourself

1. a. Draw truth tables for:
    - i.   An AND gate with inputs A and B and output Z. [2]
    - ii. An OR gate with inputs A and B and output Z [2]
    b. Study the circuit shown in Figure 1.10.18.

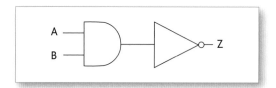

Figure 1.10.18   A circuit for Question 1b.

    - i.   Draw the truth table for this circuit. [2]
    - ii. What single gate could replace this circuit? [1]
    c. Why is it desirable that any circuit is constructed from as few gates as possible? [1]
2. Complete the truth table for the circuit shown in Figure 1.10.19. [4]

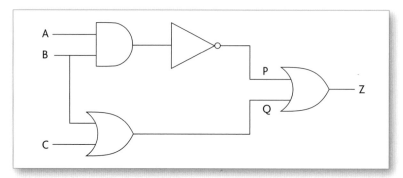

Figure 1.10.19   A circuit for Question 2.

A	B	C	P	Q	Z
0	0	0			
0	1	0			
1	0	0			
1	1	0			
0	0	1			
0	1	1			

3. A two-door car has a sensor on each door (S1 and S2) which detects whether or not the door is open. If either door is open, then the interior light (L) is switched on.

- 0 represents door closed; 1 represents door open
- 0 represents light off; 1 represents light on.

Draw the truth table which describes this logic circuit for the control of the interior light. [2]

Module 1 Exam questions

1. State what is meant by the
   i. hardware of a computer system, [1]
   ii. software of a computer system. [1]
   iii. an input device [1]
   iv. an output device [1]
   v. a storage device [1]

   Adapted from questions 1a and 1b Cambridge AS Level & A Level Computing 9691 Paper 1 June 2008

2. Describe the purpose of the following in a computer system:
   i. an input device,
   ii. an output device,
   iii. a storage device. [3]

   Question 1a Cambridge AS Level & A Level Computing 9691 Paper 1 June 2009

3. State what is meant by
   i. generic applications software,
   ii. operating system software. [2]

   Question 1a Cambridge AS Level & A Level Computing 9691 Paper 1 June 2005

4. State **four** purposes of the operating system of a stand-alone computer. [4]

   Question 6 Cambridge AS Level & A Level Computing 9691 Paper 1 June 2006

5. Describe **three** features which an operating system would be expected to provide in a single user
   computer system. [6]

   Question 1b Cambridge AS Level & A Level Computing 9691 Paper 1 June 2005

6. A large factory employs many thousands of workers. The workers' times of arrival and departure are noted. At the
   end of each week the pay for each worker is calculated by a computer system and the pay slips are produced.
   Explain why this is an example of batch processing and give reasons why batch processing is sensible. [4]

   Question 2a Cambridge AS Level & A Level Computing 9691 Paper 1 November 2006

7. Give an example of a computer application which would need to be processed in real time. Justify your choice. [2]

   Question 2c Cambridge AS Level & A Level Computing 9691 Paper 1 November 2006

8. a. i. Describe a GUI (Graphical User Interface). [2]
      ii. Describe a form-based computer interface. [2]
   b. i. State a computer application for which a GUI would be suitable. Justify your answer. [2]
      ii. State a computer application for which a form-based interface would be suitable. Justify your choice. [2]
   c. A computerised information system is set up in a busy town centre.
      The system gives details of transport, shops, sales of goods, places to eat and hotels. Describe the hardware
      and the software of the HCI (Human Computer Interface) giving reasons for your answers. [4]

   Question 1 Cambridge AS Level & A Level Computing 9691 Paper 1 November 2007

9. One purpose of most operating systems is to provide a set of utility programs designed to perform common tasks.
   i. Describe the purpose of a disk formatting utility. [2]
   ii. Describe the purpose of a virus checking utility. [2]

   Question 4a Cambridge AS Level & A Level Computing 9691 Paper 1 June 2007

10. A student decides to upgrade her computer system by buying a larger hard disk drive. She will use it to store large video files which she downloads from the internet.

For each of the following types of utility software, state their purpose and how the student would use them:

i.   disk formatter,

ii.   hardware driver,

iii. file compression,

iv.   virus checker. [8]

Question 2 Cambridge AS Level & A Level Computing 9691/11 Paper 1 November 2009

11. When texts are transferred large amounts of data are transmitted.

The characters are sent as ASCII characters.

Explain what is meant by an ASCII character. [2]

Question 7b(i) Cambridge AS Level & A Level Computing 9691 Paper 1 November 2006

12. A variety of goods are stored in a warehouse.

All goods enter and leave the warehouse at a specific point.

All goods are barcoded.

The number of each item in the warehouse is stored as a binary number.

Change 83 into a binary number stored in an 8 bit byte. [2]

Question 2a Cambridge AS Level & A Level Computing 9691 Paper 1 November 2007

13. The names of 20 students in a computing class are to be stored in an array called NAME(X) where X stands for a number between 0 and 19.

Describe an algorithm to find the position of a particular student in the array, using a serial search. [5]

Question 9a Cambridge AS Level & A Level Computing 9691 Paper 3 November 2008

14. A stock file in a company has records of all the different items held in stock. The records each hold a number of fields:

- the name of the item in stock
- description of the item
- cost
- whether or not in stock
- number in stock

Give **one** advantage and **one** disadvantage of storing files in the form of fixed length records. Relate each of your answers to the example of the stock file. [4]

Question 2b Cambridge AS Level & A Level Computing 9691 Paper 1 June 2009

15. A large factory employs many thousands of workers. The workers' times of arrival and departure are noted. At the end of each week the pay for each worker is calculated by a computer system and the pay slips are produced.

The employee file is stored as a sequential file.

i.   Explain what is meant by a sequential file. [2]

ii.   Give **two** reasons why a sequential file is a sensible choice of file type in this case. [2]

Question 2b Cambridge AS Level & A Level Computing 9691 Paper 1 November 2006

16. Data can be held in different ways in a computer system. This question is about different forms of access to data.

A company holds a file of workers' pay details. The company has a large number of workers. The file of pay details is used in the production of the weekly payroll for the workers.

a.   Explain why this file is accessed sequentially. [2]

b. Workers can enquire about details in their record. They can go to the office and their enquiry will be dealt with immediately.
    i.   Explain why sequential access to data is **not** suitable for this. [2]
    ii. State a more suitable type of access to the data, justifying your answer. [2]

c. Details of when workers arrive at and leave work are stored on a temporary file in the order in which they occur.
    State the type of file access most suitable for the data in this file, justifying your answer. [2]

d. i.   Identify a task from this application which will require batch processing, justifying your answer.
    ii. Identify a task from this application which will require rapid response processing, justifying your answer. [4]

Question 5 Cambridge AS Level & A Level Computing 9691/11 Paper 1 November 2009

17. Each part stored by the parts department [in a garage] has a 6 digit key.

- The first two digits refer to the model of the car for which it is designed.
- The third digit is used to indicate the year of manufacture.
- The last three digits are used to ensure the key for this part is unique.

    i.   Devise a hashing algorithm which would be suitable for storing 10,000 parts. [2]
    ii. State **two** key values which hash to the same address. [1]
    iii. Describe a method of handling collisions when using a hashing algorithm. [2]

Question 12b Cambridge AS Level & A Level Computing 9691 Paper 1 June 2007

18. A garage sells cars. The data in the car file is stored in fixed length records. The data held about each car includes:

- colour,
- size of engine,
- whether or not it has air conditioning,
- price.

State a suitable data type for each of the items of data listed. [4]

Question 8c Cambridge AS Level & A Level Computing 9691 Paper 1 June 2007

19. [An office worker] is responsible for making backup copies of [customer files and the records of expenditure for a company] and for archiving data.
    i.   Explain the difference between backing up data and archiving it. [4]
    ii. Describe a sensible procedure that this worker could adopt for backing up the data files. [4]

Question 1b Cambridge AS Level & A Level Computing 9691 Paper 1 November 2005

20. Explain the purpose of
    i.   the control unit,
    ii. the memory unit,
    iii. the arithmetic/logic unit (ALU) [6]
       in a computer.

Question 6 Cambridge AS Level & A Level Computing 9691 Paper 1 November 2005

21. State **two** differences between random access memory (RAM) and read only memory (ROM). [2]

Question 2a Cambridge AS Level & A Level Computing 9691 Paper 1 June 2005

22. Describe what is stored on
    i.   RAM,
    ii. ROM

explaining why that type of memory is appropriate. [4]

Question 2b Cambridge AS Level & A Level Computing 9691 Paper 1 June 2005

23. The workers in an office use stand-alone machines.

A decision is made to network the machines.

The workers in the office use three different types of storage medium.

For each of the three types, state a use to which the medium could be put and justify your answer.

i.   Hard Disk

ii. DVD-RW

iii. CD-ROM   [6]

Question 8 Cambridge AS Level & A Level Computing 9691 Paper 1 November 2008

24. Describe the stages of the process of transferring data from memory to backing store. Your answer should include references to buffers and interrupts.   [6]

Question 7 Cambridge AS Level & A Level Computing 9691 Paper 1 June 2005

25. A printer is a hard copy output device.

State **three** different types of printer.

For each of your choices give an example application where it would be used, justifying your choice.   [9]

Question 1b Cambridge AS Level & A Level Computing 9691 Paper 1 June 2009

26. Cashcard machines (ATMs) provide keyboards to allow users to input data.

Computers are often supplied with QWERTY keyboards to allow users to input data.

Discuss the differences between these different types of keyboard, explaining why the differences are necessary.   [6]

Question 4b Cambridge AS Level & A Level Computing 9691 Paper 1 June 2005

27. A student uses her home computer to:

- play games which she gets from a library;
- finish work that she brings home after starting it at school;
- produce a finished copy of the work to hand in to her teacher;
- communicate with her friends.

State the peripheral devices, apart from keyboard, mouse and monitor, which she would need.

Explain why each would be necessary.   [8]

Question 1 Cambridge AS Level & A Level Computing 9691 Paper 1 June 2007

28. Speed mismatch is a problem that arises with the use of computer systems.

a.   Describe what is meant by the speed mismatch between user, peripheral and processor.   [2]

b.   Identify an application which would use batch processing.   [1]

c.   Explain how batch processing can overcome problems caused by speed mismatch.   [2]

Question 2 Cambridge AS Level & A Level Computing 9691 Paper 1 June 2007

29. State **two** ways in which a local area network (LAN) differs from a wide area network (WAN).   [2]

Question 4a Cambridge AS Level & A Level Computing 9691 Paper 1 June 2006

30. The workers in an office use stand-alone machines.

A decision is made to network the machines.

State **two** extra pieces of hardware and **one** piece of software which would be necessary to create the network.   [3]

Question 6a Cambridge AS Level & A Level Computing 9691 Paper 1 November 2008

31. a. State what is meant by the following types of data transmission.
    i. Simplex.
    ii. Half duplex.
    iii. Serial.
    iv. Parallel. [4]

Question 5a Cambridge AS Level & A Level Computing 9691 Paper 1 November 2006

   b. State **two** of the modes of data transmission mentioned in part (a) which would be used to transfer data from primary memory to a hard drive. Give reasons for your answers. [4]

Question 5c Cambridge AS Level & A Level Computing 9691 Paper 1 November 2006

32. Explain why the bit rate is an important part of any protocol. [2]

Question 4c(ii) Cambridge AS Level & A Level Computing 9691 Paper 1 June 2006

33. Errors can occur when data is transmitted from one device to another. Explain how a checksum can be used to monitor a transmission for errors. [3]

Question 5a Cambridge AS Level & A Level Computing 9691 Paper 1 November 2005

34. Data which is transmitted between survey sites and head office is liable to errors. Data which is received is checked for errors.

   a. One method of checking for errors is to use parity checks.

      The following four bytes have been received:

      01101001 10111100 10101010 00100100

      i. One of the bytes contains an error. State which byte. [1]
      ii. Explain your choice of answer in (i). [2]
      iii. Explain why a byte may still be in error even if it passes the parity test. [1]

Question 11a Cambridge AS Level & A Level Computing 9691 Paper 1 November 2007

      iv. Describe how a parity block may be used to identify the location of the error if one occurs. [4]

   b. A second method of checking for errors is to use echoing back.

      Explain how echoing can be used to check data for transmission errors. [4]

Question 11b Cambridge AS Level & A Level Computing 9691 Paper 1 November 2007

35. Data is transmitted from one computer to another by using packet switching.
    i. Explain how packet switching works. [3]
    ii. Give **one** advantage and **one** disadvantage of using packet switching rather than circuit switching. [2]

Question 5b Cambridge AS Level & A Level Computing 9691 Paper 1 November 2005

36. Explain what is meant by the term protocol. [2]

Question 4c(i) Cambridge AS Level & A Level Computing 9691 Paper 1 June 2006

37. The workers in an office use stand-alone machines.

    A decision is made to network the machines.

    A protocol will be required.

    Explain what is meant by a protocol. [2]

Question 6b Cambridge AS Level & A Level Computing 9691 Paper 1 November 2008

38. A systems analyst is commissioned by a company to produce a computerised system in its offices.

    Explain why it is important to define the problem accurately. [2]

Question 3a Cambridge AS Level & A Level Computing 9691 Paper 1 June 2007

39. Give **four** points that need to be considered when a systems analyst produces a feasibility study. [4]

Question 4a Cambridge AS Level & A Level Computing 9691 Paper 1 November 2007

40. When a new piece of software is being planned it is necessary for the analyst to collect information about the present system.

State **three** ways of collecting information about the present system and give an advantage of each. [6]

Question 1a Cambridge AS Level & A Level Computing 9691 Paper 1 November 2006

41. A systems analyst is commissioned by a company to produce a computerised system in its offices. The analyst needs to collect information about the current system.

State **two** methods which the analyst can use to collect information and give an advantage of each. [4]

Question 3b Cambridge AS Level & A Level Computing 9691 Paper 1 June 2007

42. Describe what is involved in the analysis stage of the systems development life cycle. [6]

Question 4b Cambridge AS Level & A Level Computing 9691 Paper 1 November 2007

43. A company specialises in creating web sites for customers.

As part of the process of designing a site the company will use diagrams in order to make understanding easier.

Describe **two** types of diagram that may be used by the company. [4]

Question 8a Cambridge AS Level & A Level Computing 9691 Paper 1 June 2009

44. A systems analyst is commissioned by a company to produce a computerised system in its offices.

State the importance to

i.   the end user

ii. the systems analyst

of evaluating the system against the initial specification. [2]

Question 3c Cambridge AS Level & A Level Computing 9691 Paper 1 June 2007

45. A company specialises in creating web sites for customers.

It will be important to produce user documentation for new systems. By referring to the **two** different types of user of the new system, describe the documentation which will be produced. [4]

Question 8b Cambridge AS Level & A Level Computing 9691 Paper 1 June 2009

46. State **three** things which would need to be considered for the implementation (installation) of new software. [3]

Question 3c Cambridge AS Level & A Level Computing 9691 Paper 1 November 2008

47. It is important to maintain a system after it has been installed.

Give **two** reasons for system maintenance. [4]

Question 1b Cambridge AS Level & A Level Computing 9691 Paper 1 November 2006

48. State what is meant by

i.   custom-written software,

ii. generic applications software. [2]

Question 3a Cambridge AS Level & A Level Computing 9691 Paper 1 November 2008

49. A company specialises in creating web sites for customers.

The company stores details of customers and their accounts in a database.

i.   Distinguish between custom-written software and off-the-shelf software packages. [2]

ii. Explain why the company chose to use off-the-shelf software for their database. [2]

Question 12a Cambridge AS Level & A Level Computing 9691 Paper 1 June 2009

50. A variety of goods are stored in a warehouse.

All goods enter and leave the warehouse at a specific point.

All goods are barcoded.

The warehouse uses stock control software.

Explain how this software maintains stock levels in the warehouse. [5]

Question 2b Cambridge AS Level & A Level Computing 9691 Paper 1 November 2007

51. An office worker is responsible for communicating with other businesses and managing the computer systems in the office. The worker needs to
   i.   send letters to customers,
   ii. keep a record of expenditure,
   iii. keep records of customers.
   State types of software which would be used for each of these tasks. [3]

   Question 1a Cambridge AS Level & A Level Computing 9691 Paper 1 November 2005

52. A company specialises in surveying land for oil companies. Part of their work involves using radar and other scientific procedures to search underground for likely oil-bearing formations. The results of the surveys are stored numerically, ready for processing.
   a. Much of the processing of the data is carried out using a spreadsheet.
       Explain why the features of spreadsheet software would be useful for processing this data. [3]
   b. The results of surveys carried out must be presented to the oil company that has commissioned them. This is normally done at a special meeting with the managers of the company.
       Explain the features of presentation software which make it appropriate for use in this situation. [2]

   Question 10 Cambridge AS Level & A Level Computing 9691 Paper 1 November 2007

53. A computer controlled machine on a production line is designed to produce components for cars. When the firm decides to change the car model, the machine must be reprogrammed.
   State which of the types of software in [Question 48] is appropriate as the software for the computer controlled machine and justify your answer. [3]

   Question 3b Cambridge AS Level & A Level Computing 9691 Paper 1 November 2008

54. The servicing department of a garage sends letters to all customers who have bought cars from the garage. The letters are to remind customers that their car needs a service. The letters are sent, each year, on the date that the customer bought their car.
   Explain how the software is used to create a personalised letter for each customer. [5]

   Question 9b Cambridge AS Level & A Level Computing 9691 Paper 1 June 2007

55. A company makes and sells office furniture. Records of sales and customers are stored on a computer system.
   When the company completes a contract, the customer is asked to fill in a data capture form that asks about their satisfaction with aspects of the job.
   The intention is that the data on the forms should be input using optical mark reading (OMR) techniques.
   a. State the hardware necessary and describe the input method used, if the system is off-line. [4]
   b. Explain how the form and its contents are likely to be affected by the need to use OMR. [3]

   Question 9 Cambridge AS Level & A Level Computing 9691 Paper 1 June 2005

56. A large store has a number of departments, each selling different types of goods.
   Customers are allowed to open personal accounts so that they can buy things and pay with a single payment once a month.
   As a security measure, customers have to use a store card to buy something on their account.
   The card has the customer's picture on it.
   Describe how the customer's picture is produced digitally on the card. [5]

   Question 7a Cambridge AS Level & A Level Computing 9691 Paper 1 June 2008

57. a. Describe what is meant by verification of data. [2]
   b. Give an example of an application which would require the data input to be verified and explain why it would be necessary. [2]

   Question 5 Cambridge AS Level & A Level Computing 9691 Paper 1 June 2007

58. A company specialises in creating web sites for customers.

    The company stores details of customers and their accounts in a database.

    The data input to the database must be verified and validated. One piece of data which will be input to the database is the amount of money when a customer makes a payment.

    i. State what is meant by verification of data and describe how the customer payment will be verified when it is input to the database. [3]

    ii. State what is meant by validation of data and describe how the customer payment will be validated when it is input to the database. [3]

    Adapted from questions 12b and 12c Cambridge AS Level & A Level Computing 9691 Paper 1 June 2009

59. A computer system is implemented to control a production line in a factory. It is controlled from an operations room.

    Describe **three** ways in which information could be presented to the operator. [6]

    Question 9 Cambridge AS Level & A Level Computing 9691 Paper 1 November 2005

60. A company specialises in surveying land for oil companies. Part of their work involves using radar and other scientific procedures to search underground for likely oil-bearing formations. The results of the surveys are stored numerically, ready for processing.

    i. The results of the analysis of the data are often output on a plotter. Give **two** advantages of outputting this data to a plotter. [2]

    ii. Apart from the output to the plotter, the system produces many other output formats. State **two** forms of output which would be produced by this application and explain why each is appropriate. [4]

    Question 8b Cambridge AS Level & A Level Computing 9691 Paper 1 November 2007

61. A company specialises in surveying land for oil companies. Part of their work involves using radar and other scientific procedures to search underground for likely oil-bearing formations. The results of the surveys are stored numerically, ready for processing.

    Data collected during the search is input to a knowledge-based (expert) system.

    a. Describe **three** of the parts of a knowledge based system. [6]

    b. Explain how this knowledge based system was set up and how it is used. [5]

    Question 7 Cambridge AS Level & A Level Computing 9691 Paper 1 November 2007

62. Describe how a knowledge-based (expert) system can be used to aid geologists in carrying out geological surveys. [4]

    Question 7 Cambridge AS Level & A Level Computing 9691 Paper 1 June 2009

63. The water level in a reservoir is controlled by a computer system. During normal operation the water level (**W**) is between the high water (**H**) and low water (**L**) marks. At these times, the input valve (**I**) and output valve (**O**) are both open.

    - If the level reaches **H** then the input valve is shut off until the level falls below **H** again.
    - If the level falls below **L** then the output valve is shut off until the level rises above **L** again.
    - If the level falls below **L** for more than 1 hour, the system sends an alarm signal to the operator.

    The alarm signal, together with all the other values from the system, is sent to a central control room. All the water supplies in the city are controlled from this central room by a single operator.

    Explain the importance to the operator of good interface design, stating any features which should be considered. [5]

    Question 4b Cambridge AS Level & A Level Computing 9691 Paper 1 June 2008

64. An analyst needs to design the human computer interface (HCI) for a control room in a manufacturing plant. Describe the factors that the analyst should consider when designing the interface. [6]

Question 4b Cambridge AS Level & A Level Computing 9691 Paper 1 November 2006

65. Complete the tables to show the outcomes from these logic circuits:

a.

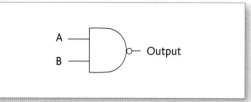

A	B	Output
0	0	
0	1	
1	0	
1	1	

[2]

b.

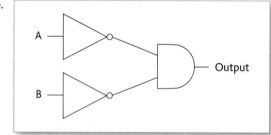

A	B	Output
0	0	
0	1	
1	0	
1	1	

[2]

c. Comment on your results. [2]

2

Practical programming techniques

2.1 Designing solutions to problems

2.1 a) The importance of good interface design

Any interface must ask for relevant input and report any results of processing clearly to the user. The input may be by various means: questions, forms, speech and so on. The output may be on a screen, as a written report or as sound.

Whatever the format of the interface, it must not be confusing or ambiguous. Users should instinctively know what is required of them or there must be clear instructions explaining what they need to do. There should also be on-screen help available whenever possible.

Order of input

The layout of the interface should be natural to use. For example, if input has to be copied from a printed form, the form on the screen should be similar and items should be in the same order as on the paper form. The order of data should be natural. For example, an address in the UK should be in the expected order: street, town, county and postcode. Wherever possible, the interface should guide the user towards correct data entry. This can be done using drop-down list boxes, radio buttons and check boxes.

Navigation

If input requires more than one screen, make sure that the screens allow **navigation**, as appropriate. The first screen should allow the user to move to the next screen. The last screen should allow the user to move to the previous screen. All other screens should allow the user to move to both next and previous and all screens should allow the user to quit (without saving). When all the required data have been entered, the user should be able to save them. When data are entered, it should be validated as appropriate and a clear error message produced if necessary.

Choice of fonts and colour

Often in a question about interface design, candidates give long discussions on font, colour and so on. Although they are relevant, take care not to over emphasise them. A good interface will use few colours and very few different fonts. Emphasis should be on size, the use of bold, italic and so on. Don't try using too many styles on the same interface. Text that is underlined and is in bold italics is extremely difficult to read and very tiring on the eyes. Look at newspapers and magazines to see the use of few fonts but many sizes and styles.

Key design points

However complex the software, however expensive and powerful the hardware, a system is unusable if the interface is not intuitively simple. The human being who is inputting data to the system must be clear about what is expected. The human–computer interface (HCI) must be unambiguous, allow the user to input all the important data and produce output in an easily understandable form.

Chapter 1.9 summarised the following issues concerning interface design:

- Who it is for?
- What information needs to be conveyed?
- Under what circumstances must the interface operate?
- How effective is the communication?
- How enjoyable is it to use?

Designing input and output

Refer back to Chapter 1.9 ("HCI design issues" on page 88) for a discussion of the design features that should be considered for form-based data input.

Data may be captured in many ways, including by means of a form. Form design requires a lot of thought. It is not simply a list of headings. The order of the headings is important. There is a need for clear instructions on how to complete the form. It is worth studying some sample forms and noting the order of the questions and the clarity of the instructions. Make a note of a few that you think are good and list your reasons. This will help you to design your own forms.

Users should find that the order of entering data on a form is natural. If the full name and address are required, then keep the forenames and surname close together. Do not have surname, address and then forenames. Make sure there is sufficient space for the data required and that the instructions for completing the form are clear. For example, if the date of birth is required, use one of the good layouts in Figure 2.1.1.

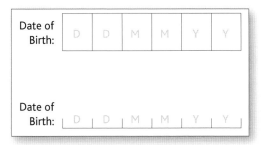

Figure 2.1.1 Date of birth field on a form.

Activity

Design a paper form to collect personal data from pupils in a primary school.

First, decide what data are needed. Clearly, forenames, surname and address are needed. You also need the date of birth of the pupil, details of parents/guardians and emergency contact details.

Now you must decide whether to use free format or indicate the maximum number of characters for each piece of information.

Finally, what about the size of the form? Should the form be printed on both sides? Should it be in landscape or portrait orientation?

One solution is given in Figures 2.1.2 and 2.1.3 (on page 110) but there are many good solutions. You will be marked for content, order of data entry and clarity of instructions. In this solution, A5 paper is used and the form is on both sides of the paper, which is in landscape orientation.

Poor design

When the data are entered into a computer system, the system may ask a series of questions or the user may complete a form on the screen. In either case, be careful that the screen does not become cluttered and that it is possible for the user to backtrack and correct errors.

If the system asks a series of questions, it is easy for the screen to become cluttered. It can also be difficult to correct early errors. Figure 2.1.4 (on page 111) is a poor design as the screen scrolls and it is not possible to correct errors made earlier. (The italicised data are entered by the user.)

Who is the typical user?

When designing a screen layout, you should consider very carefully the experience of the user. Most users for whom you design an interface will be novices or knowledgeable but intermittent users. We consider the needs of the novice user:

- The user is not confident of what the system requires. The computer system must make it clear what is to be done.
- Responses should be brief so that users can remember what is needed.
- Responses should be expected and consistent.
- Screens should have a consistent layout so that the user can find similar information in the same part of the screen throughout the software.
- Input should be obvious so that no, or very little, training is necessary.
- Any messages to the user should be clear, unambiguous and free of jargon. Use simple English in which the grammar is correct and sentences are short, concise and to the point. A suitable message to a novice user may be completely different from that for an expert.
- Do not give the user too many options from which to choose (although more experienced users can cope with a few more options than novice users). Consider using short menus with sub-menus so that the user is guided through the choices available.

HIGH TOWN PRIMARY SCHOOL

PUPIL'S DETAILS

Please complete using BLOCK LETTERS

SURNAME:

FORENAME(S):

ADDRESS:

STREET:

TOWN:

COUNTY:

POSTCODE:

DATE OF BIRTH: D D M M Y Y

SEX (Tick one): ☐ Boy   ☐ Girl

Figure 2.1.2   Paper form: pupil's details.

PARENT/GUARDIAN DETAILS

TITLE (DR, MISS, MR, MRS, MS, etc.):

SURNAME: INITIALS:

ADDRESS(If different from pupil's):

STREET:

TOWN:

COUNTY:

POSTCODE:

TELEPHONE: Please include area code.

EMERGENCY CONTACT:

NAME:

TELEPHONE 1:

TELEPHONE 2:

Figure 2.1.3   Paper form: parents' details.

```
A    Amend a record
B    Add a record
C    Delete a record
D    Quit

Choice: A

Enter key of record to be amended: SY14

Surname: SMYTH

Do you wish to change this surname? Y
What is the new surname? SMYTHE
Forenames: WILFRED BRIAN

Do you wish to change the forenames? N

Address:  17 Sun Street
          New Town
          Blackshire
          NT1 7SS

Do you wish to change line 1? N
Do you wish to change line 2? N
```

Figure 2.1.4   Poor design for on-screen data entry.

- Remember that novice users vary considerably – some understand more quickly than others. Let the user define the pace. If there is a message for the user, make sure that the user can decide when to move on.
- The user should know when a response is required. Do not create a situation where the user is left trying to work out what to do next. The interface should be intuitive to use.

Example of interface design

We consider a software learning game called *Roberta's Diamond*. This is an adventure game for 8–10-year-old pupils that involves moving through a house and garden to find a stolen diamond. In order to move, pupils must solve mathematical problems, some of which are easy and some of which need further investigation. Pupils must be able to save their position so that they can continue when they have solved the problem.

Figure 2.1.5 shows the initial screen. Most of the screen is taken up by the title but command buttons on the left state what can be done. There are only four options.

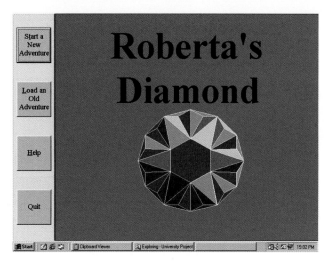

Figure 2.1.5   *Roberta's Diamond*: initial screen.

If pupils choose *Start a New Adventure*, the screen in Figure 2.1.6 appears. Notice that two of the buttons shown in Figure 2.1.5 have disappeared and a new button has appeared. To the right of the command buttons are two window panes. The upper pane describes the position in the game and the lower pane enables user input. This is the layout used throughout the software. In Figure 2.1.6, users are told where they are and then asked a simple question with only two possible answers.

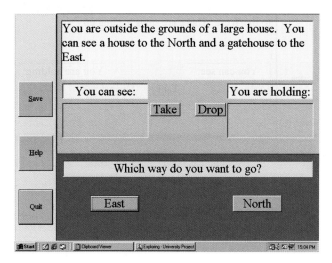

Figure 2.1.6   *Roberta's Diamond*: new adventure screen.

A similar screen is shown in Figure 2.1.7 (on page 112). The centre of the screen shows two list boxes from which the user can take objects.

The purposes of the *Take* and *Drop* buttons are obvious. If a user clicks one of these buttons without first choosing what to take or drop, an error message appears (Figure 2.1.8 on page 112). Notice that this

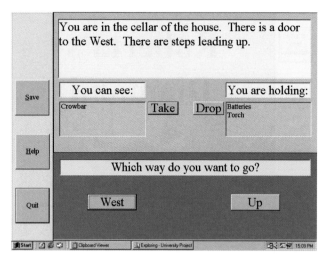

Figure 2.1.7 *Roberta's Diamond*: adventure screen 2.

window has a red background to attract the player's attention. It has a simple error message positioned at the bottom of the screen, which is where nearly all input occurs. There are two reasons for this. Firstly, it is where the user naturally looks to input data. Secondly, it prevents the user entering anything until they have selected something to drop. (All windows, except for the error message window, are disabled so the user has to click the O.K. button in order to continue.)

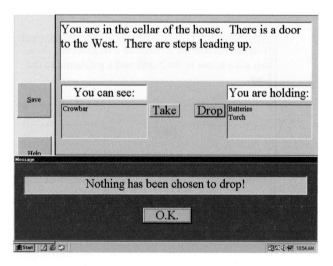

Figure 2.1.8 *Roberta's Diamond*: error message.

In order to move in the game, users must solve mathematical problems. Figure 2.1.9 shows that the problem fills the screen. The user's attention is thus concentrated on the problem. The upper part of the screen gives details of the problem while the lower part is for input. This is consistent with the other screens. Consistency is very important as it trains the user to look at the correct part of the screen for information and for entering data.

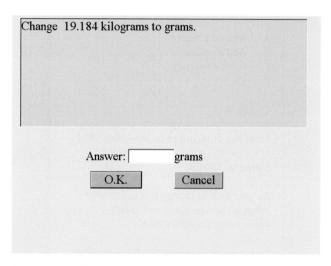

Figure 2.1.9 *Roberta's Diamond*: mathematical problem.

Users should not have to keep scanning the screen to find out what to do next. In order to maintain consistency, the designer must try to think of all the possible scenarios that may occur when running the software.

Figure 2.1.10 shows the message that appears when a problem has not been solved. As before, the background is red and the message is displayed at the bottom of the screen.

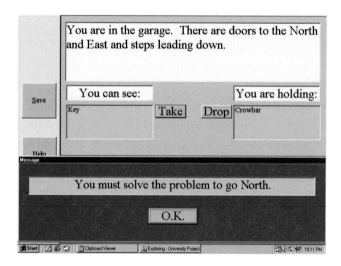

Figure 2.1.10 *Roberta's Diamond*: error message.

Sometimes a problem needs a diagram. Diagrams are consistently placed in the centre of the screen, between the description and the input pane (Figure 2.1.11). Notice how easy it is to move a disk in Figure 2.1.11b. On all screens on which input has to be typed in, the user may click the *O.K.* button or press the Enter key on the keyboard. This means that users can use the interaction method that is most natural or intuitive for them.

(a)
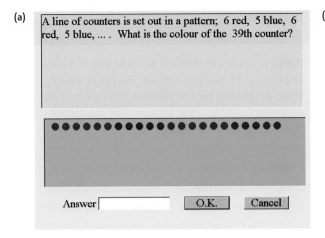

(b)
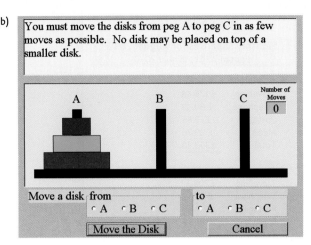

Figure 2.1.11 *Roberta's Diamond*: diagrams.

Report design

Now we consider the design of **reports**. It is important that reports are appropriate to the intended reader. Figure 2.1.12 shows a report of the expenses for four people in the form of a spreadsheet. This enables the user to compare expenses very easily.

B & L Publications

Monthly Expenses for August 2010
Printed 3rd September 2010

	Travelling	Telephone	Postage	Meals	Totals
A. Beans	176.48	83.49	3.45	89.76	**353.18**
C. Doncaster	298.31	97.52	4.95	187.95	**588.73**
E. Franks	158.23	76.48	2.50	76.45	**313.66**
G. Harris	167.41	85.93	3.74	0.00	**257.08**
Totals	**800.43**	**343.42**	**14.64**	**354.16**	**1512.65**

Figure 2.1.12 Expenses spreadsheet.

A spreadsheet is useful if the user wishes to make comparisons or needs a detailed analysis. However, it can be very confusing for some people and contains too much detail for the needs of some readers. A graph may be more appropriate in these circumstances (Figure 2.1.13).

However, in some circumstances a printed report such as that shown in Figure 2.1.14 (on page 114) is more appropriate.

When producing a paper-based report, you should consider the following aspects:

- a title and appropriate sub-titles
- an indication of the time period to which the report pertains
- clearly labelled columns, if used

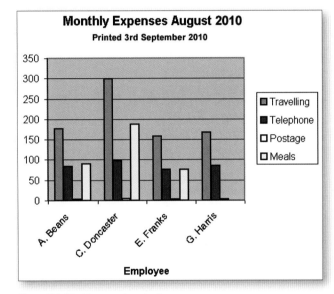

Figure 2.1.13 Expenses bar chart.

- abbreviations (if used) that are meaningful to the end user
- grouping information according to the needs of the end user
- making field sizes sufficiently large
- numbered pages
- aesthetic appeal.

Be careful numbering the pages as <page number> of <number of pages> (e.g. 63 of 67). This can cause problems if a page is deleted or inserted as the whole of the report has to be re-printed.

On-screen reports

When designing screen output, you need to make similar decisions to those made for printed output.

B & L Publications

Monthly Expenses for August 2010
Printed 3rd September 2010

A. Beans
Travelling	£176.48
Telephone	£ 83.49
Postage	£ 3.45
Meals	£ 89.76
Total	£353.18

C. Doncaster
Travelling	£298.31
Telephone	£ 97.52
Postage	£ 4.95
Meals	£187.95
Total	£588.73

E. Franks
Travelling	£158.23
Telephone	£ 76.48
Postage	£ 2.50
Meals	£ 76.45
Total	£313.66

G. Harris
Travelling	£167.41
Telephone	£ 85.93
Postage	£ 3.74
Meals	£ 0.00
Total	£257.08

Totals
Travelling	£800.43
Telephone	£343.42
Postage	£ 14.64
Meals	£354.16
Total	£1512.65

Figure 2.1.14   Printed expenses report.

However, remember that an on-screen report is transient. It is not permanent like a printout.

When producing screen output, you should consider the following aspects:

- The size of the screen restricts the amount of information that can be displayed. Do not try to put too much on the screen at once. Will horizontal and vertical scrolling to the edges and bottom of the report be acceptable?
- Use linked screens if there is a lot of information. The first screen should be linked to the next screen. The second and further screens should be linked to their next and previous screens and possibly back to the first screen.
- Large characters and different fonts can be useful for headings, as can the judicial use of colour.
- Do not overdo the use of different fonts and colours; the eye cannot cope with too many changes.

Activity

Design a report that displays the expenses of the four employees of B & L Publications. The report should group the data by type of expense (not by employee, as in Figure 2.1.14). Show the layout of this second report using the same data as Figure 2.1.14.

Figure 2.1.15 shows a typical initial layout design. Figure 2.1.16 shows the final report with data. The reports in Figures 2.1.15 and 2.1.16 are long and thin to fit on this book page. Normally, such reports would fill an A4 (or A5) page.

B & L Publications

Monthly Expenses for August 2010
Printed 3rd September 2010

Travelling
A. Beans	£
C. Doncaster	£
E. Franks	£
G. Harris	£
Total	£

Telephone

Postage

Meals

Totals

Figure 2.1.15   Initial layout design for expenses report.

B & L Publications

Monthly Expenses for August 2010
Printed 3rd September 2010

Travelling
A. Beans	£176.48
C. Doncaster	£298.31
E. Franks	£158.23
G. Harris	£167.41
Total	£800.43

Telephone
A. Beans	£ 83.49
C. Doncaster	£ 97.52
E. Franks	£ 76.48
G. Harris	£ 85.93
Total	£343.42

Postage
A. Beans	£ 3.45
C. Doncaster	£ 4.95
E. Franks	£ 2.50
G. Harris	£ 3.74
Total	£ 14.64

Meals
A. Beans	£ 89.76
C. Doncaster	£187.95
E. Franks	£ 76.45
G. Harris	£ 0.00
Total	£354.16

Totals
A. Beans	£353.18
C. Doncaster	£588.73
E. Franks	£313.66
G. Harris	£257.08
Total	£1512.65

Figure 2.1.16   Expenses report with data.

Activity

Design a set of screens to show the information on the expenses report for the four employees of B & L Publications.

Figures 2.1.17 to 2.1.19 show some possible screen designs for the on-screen expenses report in the Activity at the bottom of page 114. In this solution, a table of contents (Figures 2.1.18) is used to enable a user to jump to a particular screen. This is not the only possible solution.

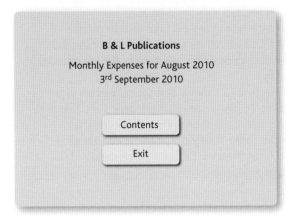

Figure 2.1.17   On-screen expenses report: title screen.

Figure 2.1.18   On-screen expenses report: contents screen.

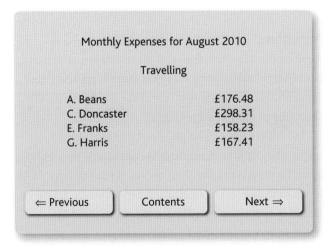

Figure 2.1.19   On-screen expenses report: detail screen.

2.1 c Advantages of top-down design of a solution

When a piece of software needs to be produced, the problem to be solved is likely to be complex. For example, it is unlikely to be as straightforward as a mathematical formula, such as the calculation of the perimeter of a rectangle. An **algorithm** like that is easy for a human being to think about. However, most useful problems involve such complex algorithms that it is not possible to consider them as a whole. For this reason, problems are normally divided up into a number of smaller problems. Each of the smaller problems is solved separately. The individual solutions are combined to give a solution to the whole problem.

Consider that you have been asked to produce a solution to the problem of computerising a set of traffic lights at a pedestrian crossing in the centre of a town. The problem is very complex, but it can be broken down into the following more manageable problems:

- How are data going to be collected from sensors and stored in the system?
- How is the decision going to be made about changing the lights?
- How are data going to be collected from the pedestrian crossing and then stored and processed?
- What outputs are necessary and how are they controlled?

This approach to problem solving is using a top-down design or a **modular approach**. We start with the original problem (the top) and split the problem into smaller and smaller parts until they become manageable. These individual parts of the solution are known as **modules**. When each of the individual problems has been solved, the solutions are combined to produce a complete solution to the whole problem.

There are other advantages in this top-down approach:

- More than one person can be engaged on solving parts of the same problem simultaneously.

   Different people are good at different things. Vicki solves the problem of collecting the information from the sensors. Leon is an expert on controlling devices using a computer, so he can design and code the processing module.
- The person producing a module is likely to make fewer mistakes.

Because the module algorithms are much shorter than for the whole problem, the programmers make fewer mistakes. It is also much easier to test the program code and eliminate errors. This means that the final software should be more reliable.

- Modules can be used in more than one project.

The company may have produced a similar solution for traffic lights in a different town. Different sensors were used, so Vicki still has to produce her module. Also, the number of roads is different so Leon still needs to come up with a solution for his module. However, the lights and other output devices are the same, so the same module can be used as last time.

Software developers store the modules that they have produced so that they can be used again if the opportunity arises. Collections of modules like this are known as software or program libraries.

2.1 d Top-down design of a solution

A diagram can be used to show a **top-down design** (Figure 2.1.20). It starts with the original problem at the highest level. The next, and subsequent, levels show how the problems in the previous levels are split up to form smaller, more manageable problems. This continues until each of the blocks in the lowest level is a self-contained, easily solvable problem. These individual problems can then be solved and combined according to the links that have been used. If the links between the blocks are used correctly, the result is a solution to the original problem. Imagine a diagram as a method for showing the individual modules that go to make up a solution to a problem and the relationships between them.

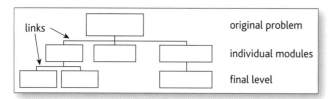

Figure 2.1.20   Top-down design diagram.

This diagram should be familar – it was introduced on page 59 called a Jackson diagram.

Some of the modules may involve iteration; this is not a problem. The links between the modules can be conditional. For example, if the result of a module

was a mark out of 100, then there could be two print routines. One would be used if the mark was below a certain level and the other if it was above the level.

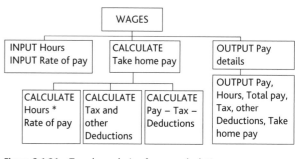
2.1 e Producing an algorithm using program flowcharts and pseudocode

In order to be able to solve a problem, someone has to know what to do. In maths, for example, you are given instructions telling you how to isolate the unknown value in simple equations. These are algorithms!

Algorithms

An algorithm is a set of instructions that either solves a problem or informs the user that there is no solution. Algorithms take many forms and are used extensively throughout Modules 2 and 3.

Here is a simple example. An electronic toy can move over the floor according to commands that it is given through a keypad. As it moves, it draws a line. It can obey the instructions shown in Table 2.1.1. The task is to write an algorithm for the toy to draw the diagram shown in Figure 1.2.22.

Table 2.1.1   Instructions understood by a toy.

Instruction	Meaning
Forward *n*	Move forward *n* cm
Backward *n*	Move backwards *n* cm
Left *n*	Turn left *n* degrees
Right *n*	Turn right *n* degrees
Repeat *n*	Repeat the instruction which follows *n* times

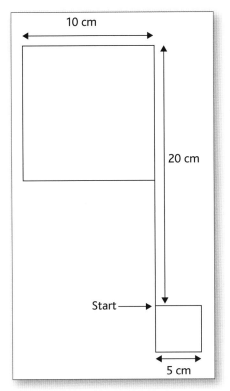

Figure 2.1.22   Drawing made by electronic toy.

The following algorithm would produce the diagram in Figure 2.1.22:

```
Repeat 4 Forward 5 Right 90
Left 90 Forward 20
Repeat 3 Left 90 Forward 10
```

Activity

It is usual to make sure that the toy is back where it started and facing its initial direction. Amend the algorithm to do this.

We can also write an algorithm to describe how to make a cup of tea. The following solution is not the only solution and may not be the exact way in which you do it:

```
Put water in the kettle

IF it is an electric kettle
    THEN
        Switch the kettle on
    ELSE
        Put it on lit gas
ENDIF

Set up the cup and saucer
Put a spoon on the saucer
Get a teapot
Put tea in the teapot

IF you take milk
    THEN
        Add milk to cup
ENDIF

IF you take sugar
    THEN
        Put sugar in cup
ENDIF

WHILE water has not boiled
    Wait
ENDWHILE

Add water to teapot
Wait 3 minutes
Pour tea into cup

IF there is sugar in the cup
    THEN
        Stir the tea
ENDIF

REPEAT
    Wait
UNTIL tea is cool enough to drink

Drink tea!
```

Notice the four `IF` statements; these are used when a decision needs to be made. Also note the `WHILE ...` `ENDWHILE` and `REPEAT ... UNTIL` statements. These pairs of statements act together to form a loop. The block of statements inside each loop are repeated a number of times. All these constructs are available when designing any algorithm and then coding the solutions.

There are many ways of representing algorithms. Which technique you choose to use is often a personal decision. You must be able to produce and use the two techniques of flowcharts and pseudocode.

Flowchart

A program **flowchart** is a diagram that can be very helpful to explain an algorithm. Program flowcharts use the symbols shown in Figure 2.1.23.

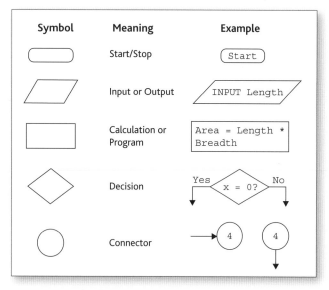

Figure 2.1.23 Flowchart symbols.

Study the flowchart in Figure 2.1.24. It asks the user to input a number, `n`. It asks for a sequence of `n` numbers and calculates the running total of the input numbers. It then outputs the average of the numbers. Consider the following questions:

- Why does it first check the value of `n`?
- What would happen if `n = 0` or `n = -5`?

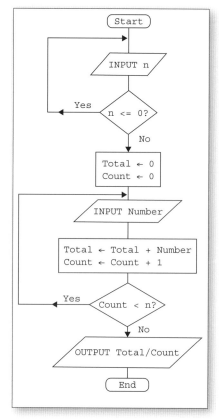

Figure 2.1.24 An algorithm as a flowchart.

Pseudocode

In the algorithms for moving the toy and making tea, we saw something between a high-level programming language and ordinary English. This is called **pseudocode**. As the name "pseudocode" implies, this is a halfway house between written English and the program code for the problem. The thinking is that, once the pseudocode is written, a programmer using any high-level language should be able to write the program code from the pseudocode algorithm design.

The following pseudocode is the algorithm from Figure 2.1.24:

```
n ← 0
WHILE n <= 0
    INPUT n
ENDWHILE

Total ← 0
Count ← 0

REPEAT
    INPUT Number
    Total ← Total + Number
    Count ← Count + 1
UNTIL Count = n

OUTPUT Total/Count
```

Note the use of the ← symbol for assignment of a value to a variable (you will see this symbol again throughout Modules 2 and 3). The statement containing the ← is an **assignment statement**.

Activity

Trace the pseudocode algorithm on page 118 for the following sequence of data input: 0, -5, 5, 2, 5, 4, 6, 3. (A trace shows how the values of the variables change and is done using a table with a column for each variable.) You should get a final output of 4.

Amend the algorithm to use a REPEAT loop (instead of the WHILE loop) and a WHILE loop (instead of the REPEAT loop). Trace through your solution.

Identifiers

What we have done – almost without thinking about it – is to make up names to represent the data items that the problem uses.

Different programming languages impose constraints on valid names. For example, identifiers in Visual Basic cannot be more than 64 characters and must not start with a digit.

Programmers also adopt a "style" to make the code or pseudocode easier to follow. In this textbook, we use *CamelCase* for all identifier names (e.g. `SquareRoot`). The exception is for identifiers that are a single

character (which is often used for a count-controlled loop). Single-character identifiers are in lower case.

Throughout the textbook, all pseudocode is shown using a Courier font.

Here is a second example of pseudocode:

```
INPUT a
INPUT b
INPUT c

d ← b * b - 4 * a * c

IF d < 0
  THEN
    OUTPUT "There are no real roots"
  ELSE
    SquareRoot = SQRT(d)
    Root1 ← (-b + SquareRoot) / (2 * a)
    Root2 ← (-b - SquareRoot) / (2 * a)
    OUTPUT Root1 and Root2
ENDIF
```

The algorithm assumes that the programming language has a **built-in function**, `SQRT()`.

Activity

Trace the execution of the algorithm on this page for the following data sets:
i.   1, -1, -6
ii   2, -3, 5

Note the use of **indentation** in these examples of pseudocode. The indentation shows the start and end of conditional statements to help with reading and understanding the algorithm. Indentation also shows the start and end of statements that are repeated.

Note also the use of **white space**. The examples have left a line of white space above and below the loop and conditional structures. White space and indentation are both designed to help with the "readability" of the code or pseudocode.

It is sometimes useful to number the steps of an algorithm. The need for this is more apparent in more complex algorithms.

Understanding algorithms

In the examination for Module 2, you might be given an algorithm and have to say what it does. You might also have to produce an algorithm to solve a given problem, which you will cover in Chapter 2.2. In order to be able to solve complex problems, you must be able to construct algorithms, using flowcharts or pseudocode, in order to clarify the solution.

Module 2 will also ask you to write program code using the language you are familiar with.

Summary

- A good user interface design is not confusing or ambiguous:
  - The layout of the interface should be natural to use.
  - Screens should allow appropriate navigation.
  - Few colours and very few fonts should be used.
- Data captured from forms:
  - The screen layout should have fields in a natural order.
  - The screen should not be cluttered.
  - Novice users should be able to see where to go next and what to enter.
  - There should not be too many options.
- Report layouts need to be appropriate to the user:
  - Graphs and charts are easier for people unfamiliar with the data.
  - Users familiar with the data may need the underlying numbers.
  - The screen or page should not be cluttered.
- Advantages of top-down design include:
  - More than one person can be engaged on solving parts of the same problem simultaneously.
  - The person producing a module is likely to make fewer mistakes.
  - Modules can be used in more than one project and are stored in software or program libraries.
- A structure diagram shows the overall problem at the top and each level below shows a further refinement, breaking it into smaller problems.
- An algorithm is a set of instructions to solve a problem.
- An algorithm can be illustrated as a program flowchart.
- An algorithm can be written in pseudocode, which is a form of structured English:

```
REPEAT 4
    FORWARD 5 RIGHT 90
FORWARD 20
REPEAT 3
    LEFT 90 FORWARD 10
```

Test yourself

1. A user will use a database to store data about customers. State **three** features that the designer of the software should consider in order to produce a good interface. [3]

2. A touch-screen interface is required for an octal (base 8) calculator that can perform the four arithmetic functions (addition, subtraction, multiplication and division). A user should enter the first number, choose the operation, enter the second number and indicate that the calculation is to be performed.

   Design a suitable interface. [7]

   ### Hint

   Notice that there are many points available. You should sketch a layout and describe it in words.

3. Give **four** advantages of using top-down design to solve a problem. [4]

4. Consider the top-down design in Figure 2.1.25 and explain what it shows. [7]

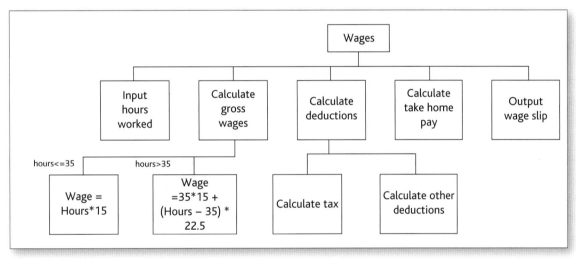

Figure 2.1.25

5. Draw a program flowchart to solve the following problem:

   The program inputs the value of an integer, n, and outputs the values of n and $n!$ ("factorial n") where:

   $n! = 1 \times 2 \times 3 \times 4 \times \ldots \times n$.

   For example, $5! = 1 \times 2 \times 3 \times 4 \times 5 = 120$. [8]

6. Write a description of the algorithm from Question 5 using pseudocode. [8]

2.2 The structure of procedural programs

(2.2 a) Procedural programming terms

This section of the syllabus refers to procedural high-level programming languages. These are languages that require the programmer to specify precisely how a computer is to solve a problem. They consist of a number of instructions that must be executed in the order specified.

There are a large number of such languages that have been designed to solve different types of problem:

- FORTRAN (FORmula TRANslation) was developed to solve mathematical/scientific problems
- PASCAL (named after the mathematician Pascal) was developed as a teaching language
- BASIC (Beginners All-purpose Symbolic Instruction Code) was developed so that as many people as possible could write computer programs.

All these languages have developed over the years and some languages are derivatives of others. For example, Modula-2 was developed from Pascal. All versions of Visual Basic are derived from the original BASIC.

This text does not teach you how to program in a particular language. Each centre may choose its own language for use in the examination and in the project. There are numerous textbooks on the market and (free) online tutorials available on the Internet which provide all that is necessary to learn programming. However, many examples of programs are given in this section and we use the Visual Basic .NET programming language. These examples are used to explain the theory of programming in a procedural language. They are not designed to provide you with an in-depth knowledge of Visual Basic .NET.

Program statements

A *statement* in a programming language is simply an instruction that can be executed. Each statement can be simple or complex. The simplest statement is the assignment statement, which takes the form:

```
<variable> = <arithmetic expression>
```

or

```
<variable> = <logical expression>
```

In this notation, anything in angle brackets has to be replaced by a valid expression in the programming language being used.

A typical arithmetic expression is:

```
Mass / Volume
```

A typical logical expression is:

```
Count < 10
```

Thus the following are valid assignment statements:

```
Density = Mass / Volume
NotFinished = Count < 10
```

Identifiers

All the above examples use identifiers. Since the value of the identifiers `Count`, `Density` and `NotFinished` may all change throughout the execution of the program, they are declared as *variables*. We would say "The variable `NotFinished` has been declared with this identifier name".

Subroutines

A **subroutine** is a self-contained block of code that has an identifier name. A subroutine can be either a procedure or a function.

A **procedure** is a block of code that can receive values from another program and can return none, one or many values back to that program. If the algorithm design has been produced using a top-down approach, then the different steps or stages in the design might each be coded as a procedure.

A **function** is given an identifier name and can also receive values from another program but returns only one value to the calling program. Much more detail about subroutines, procedures and functions are discussed in later sections.

When passing values between a main program and a subroutine, the values must be given variable names. When the main program calls a subroutine, the values being passed to the subroutine are called **arguments.** In the subroutine, the values are called **parameters.**

Loops

A **loop** is used when a block of program instructions is executed a finite number of times according to some condition. You saw examples of loops in Chapter 2.1. Because the instructions are repeated, these loops are called **iteration**, or **repetition**, constructs.

For example, you might want to write a program to read an integer, n, and output the squares of the first n integers. The following Visual Basic code carries out this algorithm:

```
Dim Num As Integer
Dim Square As Integer
Dim Count As Integer

Do
    Num = InputBox("Enter a positive integer ", _
                "number of iterations")
Loop Until Num > 0

lstResults.Items.Clear()

For Count = 1 To Num
    Square = Count * Count
    lstResults.Items.Add(CStr(Count) & "   " & CStr(Square))
Next Count
```

Notice that Visual Basic calls it a Do loop, not a Repeat loop, but it works in the same way. The Do loop makes the computer keep asking for the value of Num until the user enters a positive number. What would happen if the user entered 6.8 or 5.3? You will learn later how to avoid this problem.

Notice the new loop structure called a FOR loop. It causes the computer to repeat the following two instructions the required number of times:

```
Square = Count * Count
lstResults.Items.Add(CStr(Count) &""&CStr(Square))
```

Typical output from this code would be as shown in Figure 2.2.1.

More details of these constructs are given in the following sections.

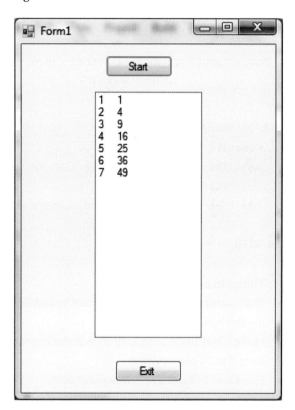

Figure 2.2.1   Output from code calculating the first n squares.

(2.2 b) Basic programming constructs

Read the following Visual Basic code and identify:

- a **sequence** of instructions
- an iteration construct
- a selection construct.

```
1   Dim Num As Double
2   Dim PosCount, NegCount As Integer

3   Num = InputBox("Enter a number (zero to end)", _
4                  "Next Number")

5   NegCount = 0
6   PosCount = 0

7   Do While Num <> 0
8      If Num < 0 Then
9         NegCount = NegCount + 1
10     Else
11        PosCount = PosCount + 1
12     End If
13     Num = InputBox("Enter a number (zero to end)", _
14                  "Next Number")
15  Loop

16  With lstResult.Items
17     .Clear()
18     .Add("The number of negative numbers is " & _
19         CStr(NegCount))
20     .Add("The number of positive numbers is " & _
21         CStr(PosCount))
22  End With
```

Things to note:

- The instructions 1 to 6 are executed *in sequence* as are the instructions 16 to 21.
- Lines 7 and 15 create a loop so that the instructions from 8 to 14 are *repeated*.
- Lines 8 to 12 form a *selection* construct.

This code illustrates the three fundamental constructs of all procedural high-level languages.

(2.2 c) Selection constructs

You have seen the **IF statement** used in pseudocode and in Visual Basic .NET (a procedural language). In this section, we put the two together to illustrate good programming practice. We also look at another **selection** construct, called the **Select Case** construct.

For example, we must write an algorithm and then the program code to input an examination mark and output the grade awarded. The maximum mark is 100 and Table 2.2.1 shows the grades that correspond to the marks gained.

Table 2.2.1   The grades corresponding to marks.

Mark	Grade
0–39	FAIL
40–59	PASS
60–79	CREDIT
80–100	DISTINCTION

There are many possible solutions to this problem. The following pseudocode is one option:

```
INPUT Mark

IF Mark < 40
    THEN
        Grade ← "FAIL"
ENDIF

IF Mark >= 40 AND Mark < 60
    THEN
        Grade ← "PASS"
ENDIF

IF Mark >= 60 AND Mark < 80
    THEN
        Grade ← "CREDIT"
ENDIF

IF Mark >= 80
    THEN
        Grade ← "DISTINCTION"
ENDIF

OUTPUT Grade
```

The equivalent Visual Basic code is:

```
Dim Mark As Integer
Dim Grade As String

Mark = InputBox("Enter the Mark out of 100. ", _
                "Examination Mark")

If Mark < 40 Then Grade = "FAIL"
If Mark >= 40 And Mark < 60 Then Grade = "PASS"
If Mark >= 60 And Mark < 80 Then Grade = "CREDIT"
If Mark >= 80 Then Grade = "DISTINCTION"

MsgBox("The Grade is " & Grade, , "GRADE")
```

What happens if the user enters 101 or –40 as the mark?

Clearly this program could be improved. Consider this amended pseudocode:

```
REPEAT
    INPUT Mark
UNTIL Mark >= 0 AND Mark <= 100

IF Mark < 40
    THEN
        Grade ← "FAIL"
ENDIF
...
```

The equivalent Visual Basic code is:

```
Dim Mark As Integer
Dim Grade As String

Do
    Mark = InputBox("Enter the Mark out of 100. ", _
                    "Examination Mark")
Loop Until Mark >= 0 And Mark <= 100

If Mark < 40 Then Grade = "FAIL"
If Mark >= 40 And Mark < 60 Then Grade = "PASS"
If Mark >= 60 And Mark < 80 Then Grade = "CREDIT"
If Mark >= 80 Then Grade = "DISTINCTION"

MsgBox("The Grade is " & Grade, , "GRADE")
```

The input from the user has now been validated to check that the mark entered is between 0 and 100 inclusive.

Consider the following pseudocode algorithm:

```
REPEAT
    INPUT Mark
UNTIL Mark >= 0 AND Mark <= 100

IF Mark < 40
    THEN
        Grade ← "FAIL"
    ELSE
        IF Mark >= 40 AND Mark < 60
            THEN
                Grade ← "PASS"
            ELSE
                IF Mark >= 60 AND Mark < 80
                    THEN
                        Grade ← "CREDIT"
                    ELSE
                        Grade ← "DISTINCTION"
                ENDIF
        ENDIF
ENDIF
```

This is called a **nested** IF structure. It has one IF statement nested (sitting inside) another.

The corresponding program code is shown on page 126.

```
Dim Mark As Integer
Dim Grade As String

Do
    Mark = InputBox("Enter the Mark out of 100. ", _
                    "Examination Mark")
Loop Until Mark >= 0 And Mark <= 100

If Mark < 40 Then
    Grade = "FAIL"
Else
    If Mark >= 40 And Mark < 60 Then
        Grade = "PASS"
    Else
        If Mark >= 60 And Mark < 80 Then
            Grade = "CREDIT"
        Else
            Grade = "DISTINCTION"
        End If
    End If
End If

MsgBox("The grade is " & grade, , "GRADE")
```

Which algorithm is the more efficient? In the first solution, every IF statement has to be checked. With the nested-IF solution, as soon as a TRUE answer is found, `Grade` is assigned and all other IF statements are ignored.

However, if we had more comparisons to make, this solution could become very difficult to understand. The following solution uses an alternative structure to IF-THEN-ELSE:

```
    REPEAT
        INPUT Mark
    UNTIL Mark >= 0 AND Mark <= 100

    SELECT CASE Mark
        CASE 0 TO 39
            Grade ← "FAIL"
        CASE 40 TO 59
            Grade ← "PASS"
        CASE 60 TO 79
            Grade ← "CREDIT"
```

(code continues ...)

```
        CASE >= 80
            Grade ← "DISTINCTION"
    END SELECT

    OUTPUT Grade
```

The corresponding program code is as follows:

```
Dim Mark As Integer
Dim Grade As String

Do
    Mark = InputBox("Enter the Mark out of 100. ", _
                    "Examination Mark")
Loop Until Mark >= 0 And Mark <= 100

Select Case Mark
    Case Is < 40
        Grade = "FAIL"
    Case 40 To 59
        Grade = "PASS"
    Case 60 To 79
        Grade = "CREDIT"
    Case Is >= 80
        Grade = "DISTINCTION"
End Select

MsgBox("The grade is " & Grade, , "GRADE")
```

This version – using the SELECT CASE structure – is efficient and easy to follow.

A discussion of further programming terms follow in Chapters 2.3 and 2.4. More details of good programming practice are given in Chapter 2.5 and testing strategies are in Chapter 2.6.

2.2 d) Iteration constructs

We have already used two loop structures in the examples of algorithm design. They are:

```
    REPEAT ... UNTIL <condition>
    WHILE <condition> ... ENDWHILE
```

The third loop structure which is available in all procedural programming languages is the

FOR ... NEXT construct. This construct takes the form:

```
FOR <variable> ← <start value> TO <end value>
   <block of program statements>
ENDFOR <variable>
```

The `<variable>` is called the **loop counter**. It can usually be omitted from the NEXT statement. The following pseudocode shows an example of the FOR construct:

```
FOR Count ← 1 TO 10
   OUTPUT StudentName
ENDFOR
```

The loop counter may be used to do some processing inside the loop:

```
FOR Count ← 1 TO 10
   OUTPUT Count, Count * Count
ENDFOR
```

In these examples, the initial value of `Count` is 1. When the pseudocode reaches the ENDFOR statement, it increments `Count` by 1 until it reaches 10, its final value. The program then exits the loop.

`For ... Next` is the Visual Basic .NET **syntax** for the beginning and end of the loop. Here is the corresponding program code:

```
Dim Count As Integer

For Count = 1 To 10
   lstResults.Items.Add(CStr(Count) & "   " _
                        & CStr(Count * Count))
Next Count
```

Figure 2.2.2 shows the output from this program.

The incremental steps need not be 1 – this is the default value. For example, you can output the squares of the even numbers between 2 and 10. The following program code achieves this with the `Step` keyword. Figure 2.2.3 shows the output from this program.

```
Dim Count As Integer

For Count = 2 To 10 Step 2
   lstResults.Items.Add(CStr(Count) & "   " _
                        & CStr(Count * Count))
Next Count
```

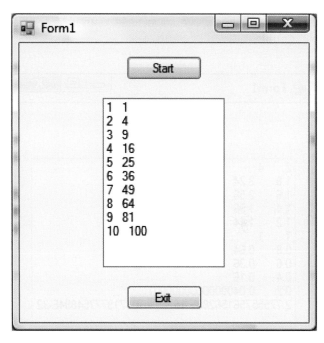

Figure 2.2.2   Output from code calculating the squares of numbers from 1 to 10.

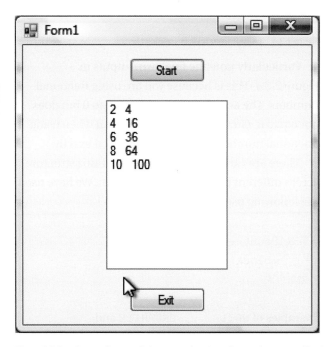

Figure 2.2.3   Output from code incrementing the values to be squared by 2.

It is also possible to change the loop counter up or down in fractional steps. Consider the following code and its output, shown in Figure 2.2.4:

```
Dim Count As Double

For Count = 2 To 0 Step -0.2
    lstResults.Items.Add(CStr(Count) & "  " _
                    & CStr(Count * Count))
Next Count
```

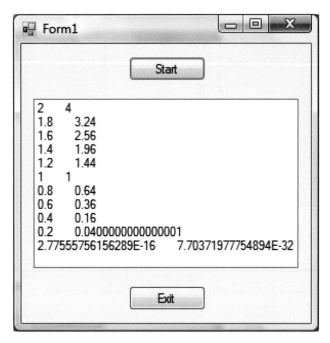

Figure 2.2.4 Output from code decreasing the values to be squared by 0.2.

Particularly note the final two outputs in Figure 2.2.4. This is because you are using fractional numbers. The actual value is very close to 0 but does not equal it. Great care needs to be taken when using fractional numbers as they are not stored exactly.

There are variations in the syntax for this structure across different programming languages. We have used the following pseudocode description:

```
FOR Count ← 1 TO 10
    <block of statements>
ENDFOR
```

Examples of WHILE ... ENDWHILE and REPEAT ... UNTIL loops have already been seen in earlier sections.

Nested selection and nested iteration statements

The following code was given in the "Selection constructs" section (page 124). It consists of three IF statements which are nested inside one another.

```
If Mark < 40 Then
    Grade = "FAIL"
Else
    If Mark >= 40 And Mark < 60 Then
        Grade = "PASS"
    Else
        If Mark >= 60 And Mark < 80 Then
            Grade = "CREDIT"
        Else
            Grade = "DISTINCTION"
        End If
    End If
End If
```

A **nested structure** (such as an IF statement) is containted inside another similar structure (e.q. IF statement) This is emphasised by indenting the code to show how the statements are nested. Loops can also be nested.

Consider a program that inputs a student's name followed by a set of examination marks. The process repeats for a number of students and terminates with input of the student name END. The list of marks for each student is terminated by a negative mark. The program outputs the average mark for the student.

The test data to be used is:

```
ROGER, 56, 48, 30, 89, -1
MARY, 78, 67, 97, -1
BRIAN, 67, 56, 78, 88, 45, -1
END
```

The pseudocode is as follows:

```
INPUT StudentName

WHILE StudentName <> "END"
    Sum ← 0
    Count ← 0

    INPUT Mark
    WHILE Mark >= 0
        Sum ← Sum + Mark
        Count ← Count + 1
        INPUT Mark
    ENDWHILE

    AverageMark ← Sum / Count
    OUTPUT "The average Mark for " StudentName,
                            " is  " Average
    INPUT StudentName
ENDWHILE
```

The Visual Basic .NET for this algorithm is:

```
Dim Mark, Sum, Count As Integer
Dim Average As Double
Dim StudentName As String

StudentName = InputBox("Enter StudentName of student _
                    (END to terminate.)", "StudentName")

Do While StudentName.ToUpper <> "END"
    Sum = 0
    Count = 0
    Mark = CInt(InputBox("Enter next Mark (-1 to end).", "Mark"))
    Do While Mark >= 0
        Sum = Sum + Mark
        Count = Count + 1
        Mark = CInt(InputBox("Enter next Mark (-1 to end).", _
                        "Mark"))
    Loop
    Average = Sum / Count
    MsgBox("The Average Mark for " & StudentName & " is " & _
            CStr(Average), , "Average Mark")
    StudentName = InputBox("Enter StudentName of student _
                    (END to terminate.)", "StudentName")
Loop
```

Notice that, in both the algorithm and the code, one loop is contained inside the other loop, i.e. we have an algorithm with "nested loops".

(2.2 f) Subroutines

Subroutines are used to split a problem into simpler tasks in order to solve a complex problem. A subroutine has an identifier name – which must follow the same rules as for variables – performs a task and is a program in its own right. Subroutines can be either procedures or functions (they are discussed again in Chapter 3.5).

Procedures

Consider the following problem. The user enters two numbers and the algorithm outputs their product. One possible solution is shown by Figure 2.2.5 on page 130. The interface is shown in Figure 2.2.6 on page 130. When the user clicks the button labelled *Calculate Product* (Figure 2.2.6a), the purpose is displayed (Figure 2.2.6b). The user clicks *OK* to continue and the output is shown (Figure 2.2.6c).

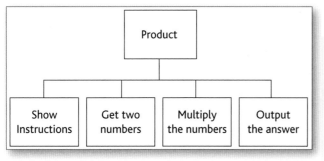

Product

Show Instructions | Get two numbers | Multiply the numbers | Output the answer

Figure 2.2.5 Design for an algorithm to output the product of two numbers.

(a)
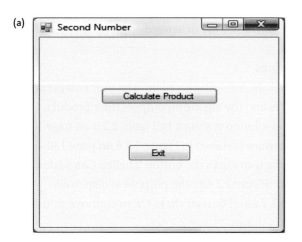

(b)
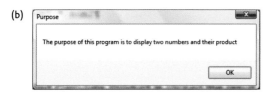

(c)
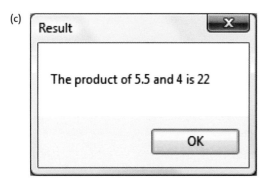

Figure 2.2.6 Interface for an algorithm to output the product of two numbers: a) start the process, b) display the purpose and c) output the result. Note the screen is not shown for the input of the two numbers.

One coded solution to this problem is:

```
Private Sub btnCalculate_Click _
                (ByVal sender As System.Object, _
                 ByVal e As System.EventArgs _
             Handles btnCalculate.Click

    Dim Num1, Num2 As Double
    Dim Product As Double

    MsgBox("The purpose of this program is to display _
            two numbers and their product", , "Purpose")

    Num1 = 5.5
    Num2 = 4.0

    Product = Num1 * Num2

    MsgBox("The product of " & Num1 & " and " & Num2 &
                                            " is " _
                        & Product, , "Result")
End Sub
```

An alternative solution is to design the code with two procedures. This solution is shown on page 131. The `ExplainPurposeOfProgram ( )` procedure displays the purpose dialog. The `OutputResult` procedure displays the result of the calculation. The interface is the same as for the first solution, as shown in Figure 2.2.6.

The line numbering in the code on page 131 is *not* part of the code. It allows us to refer to the lines in our comments. The meaning of this code is explained in detail in later sections. Here we concentrate on calling and using procedures.

Line 9 *calls* the procedure `ExplainPurposeOf Program`. This call passes control to line 19 and the instruction at lines 20–22 is executed. Line 23 passes control to the instruction immediately after the calling instruction, that is, to line 10.

```
1    Private Sub btnCalculate_Click _
2                  (ByVal sender As System.Object, _
3                  ByVal e As System.EventArgs) _
4           Handles btnCalculate.Click
5
6       Dim Num1, Num2 As Double
7       Dim Product As Double
8
9       ExplainPurposeOfProgram()
10
11      Num1 = 5.5
12      Num2 = 4.0
13
14      Product = Num1 * Num2
15
16      OutputResult(Num1, Num2, Product)
17   End Sub
18
19   Sub ExplainPurposeOfProgram()
20      MsgBox("The purpose of this program is to _
21             display two numbers and their product", _
22             , "Purpose")
23   End Sub
24
25   Sub OutputResult(ByVal FirstNumber, _
26                  ByVal SecondNumber, _
27                  ByVal Result)
28      MsgBox("The product of " & FirstNumber & _
29             " and " & SecondNumber & _
30             " is " & Result, , "Result")
31   End Sub
```

The instructions on lines 11, 12 and 14 are now executed. The instruction on line 16 calls the procedure OutputResult. This looks different from the call on line 9 as the name is followed by three **arguments**. The call passes control to line 25. The procedure name is followed by three **parameters** (the word ByVal will be explained in a moment and you can find more information about parameters in Chapter 3.5). The computer matches the arguments in line 16 to the parameters in line 25, as shown in Figure 2.2.7.

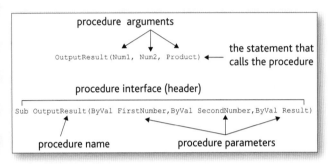

Figure 2.2.7 Matching arguments to parameters.

The values of Num1, Num2 and Product are passed to the variables FirstNumber, SecondNumber and Result, respectively. This is called passing **by value**. Hence the syntax ByVal in front of the parameters. Diagrammatically, this can be represented as shown in Figure 2.2.8.

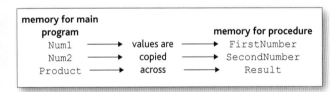

Figure 2.2.8 Copying argument values to parameters.

The memory for the main program can only be accessed by the main program (not by the procedure). Similarly, the memory for the procedure can only be accessed by the procedure (not by the main program).

So far we have passed values only one way. Now study the following code:

```
1   PrivateSub btnCalculate_Click _
2                   (ByVal sender As System.Object, _
3                   ByVal e As System.EventArgs) _
4           Handles btnCalculate.Click
5
6       Dim Num1, Num2 As Double
7       Dim Product As Double
8
9       ExplainPurposeOfProgram()
10
11      Num1 = 5.5
12      Num2 = 4.0
13
14      CalcProduct(Num1, Num2, Product)
15
16      OutputResult(Num1, Num2, Product)
17  End Sub
18
19  Sub ExplainPurposeOfProgram()
20      MsgBox("The purpose of this program is to _
21              display two numbers and their product",_
22              , "Purpose")
23  End Sub
24
25  Sub OutputResult(ByVal FirstNumber, _
26                  ByVal SecondNumber, _
27                  ByVal Result)
28      MsgBox("The product of "& FirstNumber & _
29              " and "& SecondNumber & _
30              " is "& Result, , "Result")
31  End Sub
32
33  Sub CalcProduct(ByVal FirstNumber, _
34                  ByVal SecondNumber, _
35                  ByRef Result)
36      Result = FirstNumber * SecondNumber
37  End Sub
```

This version gives exactly the same results as the previous code, but the calculation of the product is done in the procedure CalcProduct instead of in the main body of the program. In lines 11 and 12, the values of Num1 and Num2 are assigned as before. However, line 14 calls the procedure CalcProduct, which is defined in lines 33 to 37. Notice the definition of its parameters. The Result parameter is defined as ByRef. This means that the *address* of this parameter is sent to the procedure, not the value – it is passed **by reference**. Thus, the variable Product in the main program and the variable Result in the procedure use the same memory, as shown in Figure 2.2.9. Notice that Product and Result point to the same memory location.

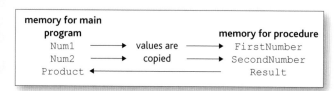

Figure 2.2.9   Referencing argument values.

Functions

If a subroutine needs to return only one value to the main program, a **user-defined function** can be used.

The code on page 133 is an alternative solution to the above problem. The CalcProduct procedure is replaced by the function CalcProduct. This function only requires two parameters, the two numbers. The result is returned via the function, as can be seen in line 14.

```
1   Private Sub btnCalculate_Click _
2               (ByVal sender As System.Object, _
3               ByVal e As System.EventArgs) _
4           Handles btnCalculate.Click
5
6       Dim Num1, Num2 As Double
7       Dim Product As Double
8
9       ExplainPurposeOfProgram()
10
11      Num1 = 5.5
12      Num2 = 4.0
13
14      Product = CalcProduct(Num1, Num2)
15
16      OutputResult(Num1, Num2, Product)
17  End Sub
18
19  Sub ExplainPurposeOfProgram()
20      MsgBox("The purpose of this program is to _
21              display two numbers and their
                                    product", _
22              , "Purpose")
23  End Sub
24
25  Sub OutputResult(ByVal FirstNumber, _
26                  ByVal SecondNumber, _
27                  ByVal Result)
28      MsgBox("The product of " & FirstNumber & _
29              " and " & SecondNumber & _
30              " is " & Result, , "Result")
31  End Sub
32
33  Function CalcProduct(ByVal FirstNumber, _
34                  ByVal SecondNumber)
35      Return FirstNumber * SecondNumber
36  End Function
```

The line that names and describes the function (line 33) is called the **function header** or the **function interface**. Notice how the result is returned by the function in line 35. The main program assigns the return value to the variable `Product` in line 14.

An alternative syntax is that line 35 would have been replaced with the following statement:

```
CalcProduct = FirstNumber * SecondNumber
```

That is, the value to be returned is assigned to the function identifier name. This is more in line with conventional function coding.

(2.2 g) Using subroutines to modularise a solution

In the previous section, we saw how to design the solution to a problem as a series of subroutines (i.e. sub-tasks). These subroutines are easier to understand than trying to write one program to do everything. This is called modularisation – using a modular approach to the design and coding.

To summarise:

- Any subroutine (procedure or function) can contain many statements just as any other program can.
- Each subroutine is designed to do a specific task.
- A complex task can be broken down into simple sub-tasks, each of which can be implemented by a subroutine.
- Functions and procedures must be given an identifier name.
- Functions may have any number of parameters, including none.
- Functions always return a value.

Figure 2.2.10 shows the algorithm for the problem posed in the "Subroutines" section (page 129) as a flowchart. Notice the new type of box. The double lines at the ends indicate that these are subroutines (i.e. procedures or functions). A separate flowchart can be drawn for each subroutine. This is left as an exercise for you.

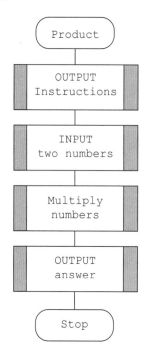

Figure 2.2.10 Flowchart for an algorithm to output the product of two numbers.

In pseudocode, we would write:

```
PROGRAM Product
    CALL ShowInstructions()
    CALL GetTwoNumbers(Num1, Num2)
    Product ← MultiplyNumbers(Num1, Num2)
    CALL OutputAnswer(Product)
ENDPROGRAM
```

Notice that no attempt has been made to describe the pseudocode for the three procedures (ShowInstructions, GetTwoNumbers and OutputAnswer) or the function MultiplyNumbers.

Any large problem needs to be broken down like this. A subroutine may also need to be broken down. This is fine. In fact, in very large problems this breaking down may go on for many stages.

2.2 h **Using recursion to solve a problem**

In Test yourself Question 5 in Chapter 2.1, we considered how to calculate the factorial of a given number. The algorithm showed an iterative solution (i.e a **loop**).

Consider again how to calculate 8! (factorial 8). It is defined as $8! = 8 \times 7 \times 6 \times 5 \times 4 \times 3 \times 2 \times 1$. Note that 0! and 1! are both defined as 1.

One possible solution to the problem is shown below as code. It uses a loop to calculate the value of a number entered by the user:

```
1   Do
2       Num = InputBox("Enter an integer number.", _
3                       "Input Data")
4   Loop Until Num >= 0
5
6   If Num = 0 Or Num = 1 Then
7       Fact = 1
8   Else
9       Fact = 1
10      Count = Num
11      Do
12          Fact = Fact * Count
13          Count = Count - 1
14      Loop Until Count = 0
15  End If
16
17  MsgBox("Factorial " & Num & " is " & Fact, , "Result")
```

- Lines 1 to 4 ensure that a positive number is entered.
- Lines 6 and 7 check for a 0 or 1 and set Fact to 1.
- If the number entered is not 0 or 1, then lines 9 to 14 are executed: Fact and Count are initialised and a loop calculates the factorial of Num.

Factorial 7 is defined as $7! = 7 \times 6 \times 5 \times 4 \times 3 \times 2 \times 1$. So, we conclude, $8! = 8 \times 7!$. This means that if we could calculate 7! we only need to multiply it by 8 to find 8! More generally, if n is a positive integer, $n! = n \times (n-1)!$.

In programming terms, we can write:

```
Factorial_N(n) = n * Factorial_N(n - 1)
```

Factorial_N is a function with a single parameter – the number. It should look something like this:

```
Function Factorial_N(ByVal Number
                        As Integver)
    Return Number * Factorial_N
                        (Number - 1)
End Function
```

A function that calls itself is known as a **recursive** function. However, this code does not do what we want. It will go on forever because there is nothing to tell the function when to stop. Details of how this works are discussed in the next section.

We know that 1! = 1. As soon as the function has a value of 1, it knows that it must return 1 as the result. The corrected version of the code is:

```
1   Function Factorial_N(ByVal Number
                            As Integer)
2
3       If Number = 1 Then
4           Return 1
5       Else
6           Return Number *
                    Factorial_N(Number - 1)
7       End If
8
9   End Function
```

Line 1 is the function definition. In line 6, the function calls itself so it is recursive.

The main program (excluding variable declarations) is:

```
1   Do
2       Num = InputBox("Enter an integer number.", _
3                       "Input Data")
4   Loop Until Num >= 0
5
6   If Num = 0 Or Num = 1 Then
7       Fact = 1
8   Else
9       Fact = Factorial_N(Num)
10  End If
11
12  MsgBox("Factorial " & Num & " is " & Fact, , "Result")
```

The function is called in line 9.

Activity

If the input is 5, what is the output of the following program?

```
Private Sub btnCalculate_Click
        (ByVal sender As System.Object,
        ByVal e As System.EventArgs)
            Handles btnCalculate.Click

    Dim Num As Integer
    Dim Answer As Integer

    Do
    Num = InputBox("Enter a positive
                    integer", "Input")
    Loop Until Num >= 0

    Answer = Power2(Num)

    MsgBox("The answer is " & Answer, ,
        "Result")

End Sub

Function Power2(ByVal Number As
                Integer)
    If Number = 0 Then
        Return 1
    Else
    Return 2 * Power2(Number - 1)
    End If
End Function
```

Study the code and state what it does.

Write down the output when the number entered is 10.

2.2 i Tracing the execution of a recursive subroutine

Study the following algorithm:

```
Private Sub btnCalculate_Click
        (ByVal sender As System.Object,_
        ByVal e As System.EventArgs)
        Handles btnCalculate.Click

    Dim Num As Integer
    Dim Answer As Integer

    Num = InputBox("Enter a positive
                    integer", "Input")

    Answer = Find(1, Num, Num)

    MsgBox("The answer is " & Answer, ,
            "Result")

End Sub

Function Find(ByVal First As Integer, _
            ByVal Last As Integer, _
            ByVal Number As Integer)

    Dim MiddleNo As Integer
    Dim Value As Integer

    MiddleNo = Int((First + Last) / 2)

    If (MiddleNo * MiddleNo <= Number)
                                And _
        (Number < (MiddleNo + 1) *
                    (MiddleNo + 1)) Then
        Value = MiddleNo
    Else
        If MiddleNo * MiddleNo > Number
                                    Then
            Value = Find(First,
                    MiddleNo - 1, Number)
        Else
            Value = Find(MiddleNo + 1,
                        Last, Number)
        End If
    End If

    Return Value

End Function
```

The programming language's built-in function `Int(n)` returns the largest integer not greater than n. For example, `Int(2.4)` returns 2 and `Int(5.9)` returns 5.

If the input for `Num` is 7, Figure 2.2.11 shows each step of the algorithm.

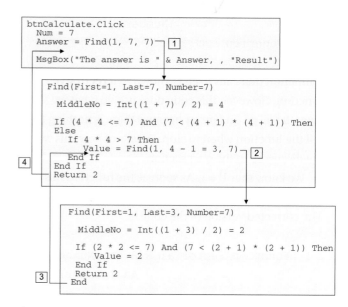

Figure 2.2.11 Executing a recursive program.

Each time the recursive function is called, new storage has to be allocated to `First`, `Last`, `Number`, `MiddleNo` and `Value`. This is because each time the function is called it has to have its own values for the variables.

Notice how the function returns to the instruction immediately after the one that called it. This process of returning to each exit point is called **unwinding** from each function call.

2.2 j Comparing iterative and recursive solutions to the same problem

Any recursive algorithm can be written as an iterative solution. Look again at "Using subroutines to modularise a solution" (on page 133). The solution to the factorial problem was written as an iterative algorithm and as a recursive algorithm.

There are clear advantages and disadvantages to each method:

- Recursion can be proved mathematically to produce a correct solution (or otherwise). Iteration can also be proved to be correct but sometimes it is more difficult.

- Iteration has the advantage that the storage required is fixed. In recursion, the storage required varies according to the number of times the recursive function is called.
- Recursion leads to simpler algorithms than iteration.
- Many problems are much easier to solve recursively, as was shown with computing *n*!.

Consider the Fibonacci sequence. The first two terms are 1 and subsequent terms are the sum of the previous two terms. This can be expressed as:

$$\text{Fibonacci}(n) = \begin{cases} 1 & \text{if } n = 1 \\ 1 & \text{if } n = 2 \\ \text{Fibonaacci}(n - 1) + \\ \text{Fibonacci}(n - 2) \\ & \text{if } n > 2 \end{cases}$$

The program to output the value of the *n*th term in the Fibonacci sequence is coded recursively as follows:

```
Private Sub btnCalculate_Click
        (ByVal sender As System.Object,_
        ByVal e As System.EventArgs)
    Handles btnCalculate.Click

  Dim Num As Integer

  Num = InputBox("Enter a positive
                 integer.", "Input")

  MsgBox("The " & Num & " th number is " _
         & Fibonacci(Num), , "Result")
End Sub

Function Fibonacci(ByVal Number As Integer)

  If Number = 1 Or Number = 2 Then
     Return 1
  Else
     Return Fibonacci(Number - 1) +
            Fibonacci(Number - 2)
  End If
End Function
```

Compare this solution with the iterative solution shown below.

```
Private Sub btnCalculate_Click
        (ByVal sender As System.Object,
        ByVal e As System.EventArgs)
    Handles btnCalculate.Click

  Dim Num As Integer
  Dim Num1, Num2, Num3 As Integer
  Dim Count As Integer = 2

  Num = InputBox("Enter a positive
                 integer.", "Input")
  If Num = 1 Or Num = 2 Then
     MsgBox("The " & Num & " th number
                 is 1", , "Result")
  Else
     Num1 = 1
     Num2 = 1
     While Count <> Num
        Num3 = Num1 + Num2
        Num1 = Num2
        Num2 = Num3
        Count = Count + 1
     End While
     MsgBox("The " & Num & " th number
            is " & num3, , _
            "Result")
  End If

End Sub
```

The recursive solution follows the definition very closely and is much shorter. The iterative solution involves implementing the algorithm using iteration.

- Procedural programming terminology:
  - A statement is an instruction that can be executed:

$$Density = Mass \ / \ Volume$$

  - A subroutine is a self-contained block of code that has an identifier name.
  - A procedure is a block of code that may receive values from another program and can return values.
  - A function is a block of code that may receive values from another program and returns only one value.
  - A parameter is a value supplied to a subroutine or function.
  - A loop is a block of instructions that are repeated.

    A loop is the programming construct for iteration.
- The three basic programming constructs used to control the flow of execution are:
  - sequence
  - iteration
  - selection
- Selection constructs are IF statements and CASE/SELECT statements.
- Iteration constructs are:
  - count-controlled (FOR ... NEXT) loops

```
FOR Count ← 1 TO 10
    OUTPUT StudentName
ENDFOR
```

  - condition-controlled (WHILE ... ENDWHILE and REPEAT ... UNTIL) loops.

```
Count ← 0
WHILE Count < 10
    OUTPUT StudentName
    Count ← Count + 1
ENDWHILE

Count ← 0
REPEAT
    OUTPUT StudentName
    Count ← Count + 1
UNTIL Count > 9
```

Summary continued …

- Nested statements are when a selection or iteration statement occurs inside another selection or iteration statement:

```
FOR i ← 1 TO 10
    FOR j ← 1 TO 10
        Name[i, j] ← i * j
    ENDFOR
ENDFOR
```

- Subroutines enable the modularisation of the solution to a problem.

- A recursive subroutine is one that calls itself. It needs a stopping condition.

- Recursive solutions can be implemented using iteration but recursion may be clearer.

Test yourself

1. Define the following terms:
   a. statement   [3]
   b. procedure   [3]
   c. parameter   [2]
   d. selection   [2]
   e. loop.   [2]
2. In the following program, identify:
   a. a sequence   [1]
   b. selection   [1]
   c. iteration.   [1]

```
lstResult.Items.Clear()
Number = InputBox("Enter a number (0 to end).", "Input")
While Number <> 0
If Number < 0 Then
        lstResult.Items.Add("The number is negative.")
Else
        lstResult.Items.Add("The number is positive.")
End If
    Number = InputBox("Enter a number (0 to end).", "Input")
EndWhile
```

3. Table 2.2.2 shows some abbreviations. Write an algorithm to input an abbreviation and then output its meaning. If the abbreviation is not in the table, a suitable message should be output. [5]

Table 2.2.2   Abbreviations and their meanings.

Abbreviation	Meaning
m	metre
kg	kilogram
s	second
A	ampere
K	kelvin

4. The following algorithm inputs two integer numbers and outputs all the integers from the first number to the last number.

```
INPUT FirstNumber
INPUT LastNumber
FOR Number ← FirstNumber TO SecondNumber
        OUTPUT Number
ENDFOR Number
```

Rewrite this algorithm using:
a. a WHILE-ENDWHILE loop [3]
b. a REPEAT-UNTIL loop. [3]

5. Write an algorithm to input a number.
   If the number is zero, stop.
   If the number is positive, output the number.
   If the number is negative, square the number, and output the square and square root of the answer. [5]

6. Consider the following program.

```
Dim Num1, Num2 As Double
Num1 = InputBox("Enter first number.", "First Number")
Num2 = InputBox("Enter second number", "Second Number")
    Mystery(Num1, Num2)
    MsgBox("The numbers are "& Num1 &" and "&_
Num2, , "Result")
Sub Mystery(ByRef FirstNumber As Double, _
ByRef SecondNumber As Double)
Dim Temp As Double
If FirstNumber > SecondNumber Then
        Temp = FirstNumber
        FirstNumber = SecondNumber
        SecondNumber = Temp
    End If
End Sub
```

a. State the output for the following inputs:
   i.   3 followed by 7 [1]
   ii. 8 followed by 4. [1]
b. State the purpose of the subroutine. [1]

7. The following function is supposed to return the sum of the first *n* integers. Explain what is wrong with it and correct the error.

```
FUNCTION Sum(BYVAL n: INTEGER)
    RETURN n + Sum(n - 1)
ENDFUNCTION
```
[3]

8. Study the following algorithm.

```
FUNCTION Mystery(m, n)
    r ← m - INT(m / n) * n
    IF r = 0
    THEN
        RETURN n
    ELSE
        RETURN Mystery(n, r)
    ENDIF
ENDFUNCTION
```

INT(Number) returns the integer part of the parameter, Number. For example, INT(4.2) returns 4 and INT(5.8) returns 5.

The function Mystery is called with

```
CALL Mystery(69,12)
```

Produce a diagram that traces each step of the algorithm and the function calls. [7]

2.3 Data types and data structures

(2.3 a) ## Defining data types

Some of this content has already been covered in Chapter 1.3. You might well want to re-read this before proceeding.

Different tasks carried out by various application programs require different types of data. All of these different types of data have to be stored as binary numbers. The computer can distinguish one type of data from another from the context in which it is used.

Integer

We must distinguish between different types of numbers that the computer stores and processes.

An integer is a whole number that may be positive or negative. It is stored by the computer as a binary pattern using a number of bytes. There will be variations across the different programming languages. Table 2.3.1 shows the integer data types available in Visual Basic.

Table 2.3.1   Integer data types.

Data type	Represents	Storage
Byte	positive integers 0–255 only	1 byte
Integer	–32 768 to +32 767	4 bytes
LongInt	Much larger range	8 bytes

Common sense tells us that the more bytes that are used, the larger is the range of possible integers.

Integers can be used for counting. For example, we already assumed the use of an integer variable `Count` when we introduced the `FOR-ENDFOR` loop structure.

Real numbers

A real number is one that has a fractional part. How these are stored internally is not covered until Chapter 3.4, when we discuss floating-point format. For the moment, we appreciate that many data values used in programs need to be real numbers:

- `AverageScore` – as the average may compute a decimal number
- `OrderTotal` – as a typical total would be 139.99.

In Visual Basic .NET, the common real data types are `Single`, `Long` (bigger range possible) and `Decimal`.

Variables would be declared for each data item with statements such as:

```
Dim AverageScore As Single
Dim OrderTotal As Single
```

Boolean data

Sometimes a data item may take only a "true" or "false" value. The computer uses binary data that consists of bytes of information, so it seems reasonable that this data value can be stored as a single byte. The computer stores True (Yes) as 1 and False (No) as 0. Data which can have only two states is known as Boolean data.

A simple example of its use would be in a program which is searching for a particular data value. A Boolean variable could be used to indicate that the value required has or has not been found.

```
Dim IsFound As Boolean
```

A value is assigned with:

```
IsFound = TRUE
```

This variable could be used in a conditional statement to determine whether or not a loop terminates:

```
WHILE IsFound = FALSE
    <Block of statements>
ENDWHILE
```

An actual data item can also be a Boolean data type:

```
Dim PermanentEmployee As Boolean
```

A value is assigned with:

```
PermanentEmployee = TRUE
```

Character data

A character can be any single character which is represented in the character set of the computer. Modern computer systems use either the ASCII coding system (each character a single byte of eight bits) or Unicode (two bytes of eight bits to represent a character).

Examples are such things as gender (we are expecting only the values 'M' and 'F') and category (e.g. 'F' for fiction and 'N' for non-fiction):

```
Dim EmployeeSex As Char
Dim BookCategory As Char
```

String data

A string is a sequence of characters. The programming language used may impose a limit on the length of a string – it's usually a maximum of 255 characters.

Examples could be surname (values such as "Patel"), product code (e.g. "D4532") and telephone number (e.g. "+44-823-786544"):

```
Dim EmployeeSurname As String
Dim ProductCode As String
Dim TelephoneNumber As String
```

2.3 b Using arrays

When the programmer declares a variable, the computer allocates a storage location for that data value. Where it is stored in memory is of no interest whatsoever to the user of the application program.

Consider an application where we know that the program needs to store and process at least 20 surnames. One strategy for the programmer is to use a different identifier name for each surname as follows:

```
Dim Surname1 As String
Dim Surname2 As String
Dim Surname3 As String
...
Dim Surname20 As String
```

And then later in the program code, assignment statements such as:

```
Surname1 = "Williams"
Surname6 = "Patel"
```

Note that this would work – the identifier names are all valid. The problem is that there is no relationship between the different variables – they are as different as using identifier names A, B and C.

Declaring an array

An array is a data structure that allows, for example, all 20 surnames to use the same identifier. Each surname is then referenced with an **index number** or **subscript**.

The programmer must make clear the size of the array with the **declaration statement**:

```
Dim Surname(20) As String
```

This declaration says that the highest subscript we shall use (the **upper bound** of the array) is 20.

Data values are then assigned with statements such as:

```
Surname(1) = "Williams"
Surname(6) = "Patel"
```

In summary, declaring the array tells the program:
- the identifier name for the array, e.g. Surname
- the sort of data that are going to be stored (i.e. the data type), e.g. String
- the size of the array or, more precisely, its upper bound, e.g. 20.

There are differences across different programming languages when declaring arrays. Visual Basic .NET assumes a **lower bound** of zero so our example could use subscripts 0 to 20 inclusive. Pascal requires both the lower bound and upper bound to be stated:

```
Surname[11:30]: String
```

Pascal also uses square brackets, *and we shall use square brackets in our pseudscode.*

Initialising an array

We wish to assign an initial value to all the array elements. This usually takes the form of some kind of "Null" value. For a string data type, it could be the "empty string":

```
FOR Index ← 0 To 20
    Surname[Index] ← ""
ENDFOR
```

Note the use of the `Index` variable – acting as a loop counter – to supply the index value for the array. This is a widely used programming technique.

`Surname` is a one-dimensional **array**. The values can be visualised as a one-dimensional table with a cell for each data item and the subscript or index number as a label (see Figure 2.3.1).

Index	Surname
0	Smith
1	Williams
2	Khan
3	Lee
4	Yung
5	Shah
6	Patel
.	
.	
.	
20	Carter

Figure 2.3.1   A one-dimensional array.

Two-dimensional arrays

It is possible to define a two-dimensional array. Indeed, most languages allow multi-dimensional arrays. The following code defines a two-dimensional array:

```
Dim HomeVisit(5,14) As Integer
```

This can be visualised as a table with six rows and 15 columns. The array is to represent the number of home visits made by five staff over a two-week period. We need two arrays:

- `StaffName` – a 1-D array to store the names of the five staff
- `HomeVisit` – a 2-D array to store the number of visits made by each staff member over the 14-day period.

We need to declare and initialise the arrays. The following code initialises the `StaffName` array to the empty string:

```
Dim StaffName(5) As String
Dim i As Integer

For i = 1 To 5
    StaffName(i) = ""
Next i
```

The following code initialises all of the entries of the `HomeVisit` array to zero (note the use of nested loops):

```
Dim HomeVisit(5, 14) As Integer
Dim Person As Integer
Dim DayNo As Integer

For Person = 1 To 5
    For DayNo = 1 To 14
        HomeVisit(Person, DayNo) = 0
    Next DayNo
Next Person
```

Note the programmer has decided not to use row 0 or column 0.

Let's return to our list of employee surnames. Now suppose you wish to input the values to the `Surname` array. Suppose we know that the maximum number of values is 20, but there may be fewer. First we need to declare an array to hold 20 strings (representing the surnames), then we must stop trying to read names when the maximum is reached or the last one has been read.

In the following code, we use the surname "END" to indicate the end of the list. Note that we can omit stating the upper bound when we declare an array in Visual Basic.

```
Dim Surname() As String
Dim NextName As String
Dim i As Integer

i = 1
NextName = InputBox("Enter the next
                     name (END to
                     finish).", _
                  "Input names")

While i <= 21 And NextName <> "END"
   Surname(i) = NextName
   NextName = InputBox("Enter the next
                        name (END to
                        finish)",_
                     "Input names")
   i = i + 1
End While
```

The next example uses a two-dimensional array to represent the multiplication tables from 0 to 10:

```
Dim MultiplicationTable(10, 10) As
Integer
Dim Row, Column As Integer

For Row = 0 To 10
   For Column = 0 To 10
      MultiplicationTable(Row, Column) =
                            Row * Column
   Next Column
Next Row
```

Notice again the nested FOR loops. A trace shows that Row takes the value 0 then Column takes each of the values 0 to 10. Next Row takes the value 1 and Column takes the values 0 to 10 again. This is repeated until Row = 10 and Column = 10 which is the last cell in the array MultiplicationTable. Each cell is assigned the value Row * Column, hence the multiplication table is produced.

Searching a one-dimensional array

It is a very common requirement in many programs to search an array for a particular value. A structured-English description of the algorithm could be:

```
Look at each element in the array

If the element is the required one
                    Output its position

If the end of the list is reached
                 without finding item
      Output "element is not in list"
```

This states what to do but is not detailed enough to attempt writing the code. Now study this pseudocode algorithm:

```
PROGRAM SearchListArray
   Index ← 0
   Found ← FALSE
   INPUT ThisName

   WHILE NOT ("End Of List" AND ThisName not found)

     IF MyList[Index] = ThisName
        THEN
           OUTPUT "Found - Position is ", Index
           Found ← TRUE
        ELSE
           Index ← Index + 1
     ENDIF

   ENDWHILE

   IF NOT Found
      THEN
         OUTPUT ThisName " is not in the list"
   ENDIF

ENDPROGRAM
```

The Visual Basic .NET code on page 146 assumes that n names have been entered into the array called MyList.

```
Dim MyList(20), ThisName As String
Dim n, Index As Integer
Dim Found As Boolean

Index = 0
Found = False

ThisName = InputBox("Enter the name to be found", _
                    "Enter Name")

Do While Index <= n And Not Found
   If MyList(Index) = ThisName Then
      MsgBox(ThisName & " is in  position " & Index, , _
            "Result of Search")
      Found = True
   Else
      Index = Index + 1
   End If
Loop

If Not Found Then
   MsgBox(ThisName & " is not in the list")
End If
```

The above algorithm and code assume that there is at least one name in the list. As an exercise, modify the algorithm and code to allow for an empty array.

2.3 c) Designing a record format

Data stored in computers is normally connected in some way. For example, data about 20 students has a connection because the data all refers to the same group of people. Each person has their own information stored and each person has the same type of information stored, for example their name, address, telephone number and exam grade.

Records and files

All the information stored has an identity because it is all about a set of students. This collection of data is called a **file**. Each student has data stored. The information referring to a particular student is called a **record**. Hence a file consists of a number of records.

Each record of information contains the same type of data, such as name. Each type of information is called a **field**. Hence we would say that a student record contains a name field, an address field, etc. A number

of fields make up a record and all records from the file must contain the same fields.

The data that goes into each field, for example "Jane Smith", "3 Canal Street" is different for most of the records. The data that goes in a field is called a **data item**.

Some fields may contain the same item of data in more than one record. For example, there may be two people in the set who happen to be called Jane Smith. Also if we record the class for the student there will be several students in the same class.

Fixed-length records

"Jane Smith" is ten characters long (including one for the space character) and "Christopher Patterson" is 21 characters. It makes it easier for the program to store records if the same amount of space is allocated to the name field in each record. It might waste some space, but searching for information can be done more quickly.

When each of the records is assigned a certain amount of space, the records are said to be of fixed length. Sometimes a lot of space is wasted and sometimes data may have to be abbreviated to make it fit into the space allowed. The alternative is to store some fields using a variable number of characters. These are then called **variable-length records**.

Key field

It is important to use a field to ensure that each record is unique. Choosing the student's name for this purpose could give problems – it is not unusual to have two people with the same name.

This is an important design decision. If there is not a natural field that is unique then the strategy is to allocate each record some form of reference number.

Designing a record

The first thing to do is to decide what data needs to be stored.

Consider the following scenario. A teacher is taking 50 students on a rock-climbing trip. The students may come from any one of five schools. The students are being charged $20 each and, because of the nature of the exercise, their parents may need to be contacted if there is an accident. The teacher decides to store the information as a file. The task is to design the record format for this file.

The fields needed are as follows:

- `SchoolNumber`
- `StudentName`
- `AmountPaid`
- `EmergencyNumber`
- `Class`

There are other fields that could be included but we will add just one more: `StudentNumber`.

For each of these fields it is necessary to decide what type of data they are. We also need to decide how many characters are needed for the data in that field – remember that these are fixed-length records.

Table 2.3.2 Data types for student records.

Identifier	Data Type	Storage	Example
SchoolNumber	Integer	2 bytes	10
StudentNumber	Integer	1 byte	2
StudentName	String	20 bytes	Jane Smith
AmountPaid	Integer	1 byte	12
EmergencyNumber	String	13 bytes	0778 436 5438
Class	String	3 bytes	3RJ

Notice that it would be perfectly reasonable to say that a String data type is more appropriate for the `SchoolNumber` and `StudentNumber` as we shall never carry out any arithmetic using these data values.

- `StudentName` is an arbitrary length. 15 bytes would be perfectly reasonable, as would 25 bytes, but five bytes would not. In other words, there is no single right answer but there are many wrong ones!
- `AmountPaid` is shown as an integer as the teacher will store the number of whole dollars paid so far. Thinking that it could contain a fractional part, e.g. 12.00, is equally valid.
- `EmergencyNumber` could be an integer but phone numbers often start with a 0 and integers are not allowed to. In order to retain the leading zero, we choose String as the data type.
- Three characters were allowed for `Class`. In an examination, give an example of what you mean by

the data. It can't hurt and it may confirm you a mark in the question.

How is all this implemented in a high-level programming language? Different languages use slightly different syntax. We use the following terms to describe a record data type using pseudocode:

```
TYPE <Identifier>
    <Field identifier> <Data type>
    <Field identifier> <Data type>
...
ENDTYPE
```

Record data in Visual Basic .NET

Visual Basic .NET uses the `Structure` syntax to declare a record data type:

```
Structure StudentRecord
    Dim SchoolNumber As Short
    Dim StudentNumber As Byte
    Dim StudentName As String
    Dim AmountPaid As Short
    Dim EmergencyNumber As String
    Dim Class As String
End Structure
```

The record structure has the identifier `StudentRecord` and contains six fields. Each field is given a name and a data type.

It is now possible to define a variable to be of this new data type. The following code defines an array of up to 21 students of data type `StudentRecord`:

```
Dim Student(20) As StudentRecord
```

The program which follows on page 148 reads data from a text file `Student.txt` into our `Student` array. Notice the "dot notation" used to refer to each field in `StudentRecord`.

```
Private Sub btnStart_Click
    (ByVal sender As System.Object, _
    ByVal e As System.EventArgs)
  Handles btnStart.Click

Dim Index, i As Integer
Dim FileStudent As IO.StreamReader
Dim Answer As String
Dim Student(20) As Student
Dim SchoolNum As Integer

FileStudent = IO.File.
            OpenText("Student.txt")
Index = 1

While FileStudent.Peek <> -1
    Student(Index).SchoolNumber =
            CInt(fileStudent.ReadLine)
    Student(Index).StudentNumber =
            CInt(fileStudent.ReadLine)
    Student(Index).StudentName =
            fileStudent.ReadLine
    Student(Index).AmountPaid =
            CInt(FileStudent.ReadLine)
    Student(Index).EmergencyNumber =
            FileStudent.ReadLine
    Student(Index).Form = FileStudent.
            ReadLine
    Index = Index + 1
End While

FileStudent.Close()
```

Don't worry if you cannot understand the **file handling** statements. The important content here is the use of the `StudentRecord` record type.

In addition to the "built-in" data types that are available in any programming language, we can now design our own "user-defined" (or, better, "programmer-defined") data types.

(2.3 d) Estimating the size of a file

In the previous section, we designed the record format shown in Table 2.3.3. We now need to calculate the **file size**.

Table 2.3.3 Data types for student records.

Identifier	Data Type	Storage
SchoolNumber	Integer	2 bytes
StudentNumber	Integer	1 byte
StudentName	String	20 bytes
AmountPaid	Integer	1 byte
EmergencyNumber	String	13 bytes
Class	String	3 bytes

Having decided on the size of each field, it is a simple matter of adding up the individual field sizes to get the size of a record, in this case 40 bytes. There are 50 students going on the trip. Each of them has a record, so the size of the data in the file is $50 \times 40 = 2000$ bytes.

All data files should make provision for expansion. A staff file when it is created may contain 50 employee records, but how many records do we anticipate it will contain in a year? Additionally, files will contain extra data like control characters. The usual guideline is to allow for an expansion of 10%. Therefore the size of the student file is 2000 bytes + (10% of 2000 bytes) = 2200 bytes.

The final stage is to ensure that the units are sensible for the size of files. There are 1024 bytes in 1 KB, so the size of this file is 2200/1024 = 1.95 KB.

Don't worry about dividing by 1024, because, after all, this is only an approximation anyway. If you were to give the final answer as 2 KB (approximately) then that is acceptable. Just make sure that you write down somewhere that you know that there are 1024 bytes in a kilobyte, otherwise you can't be given that mark.

(2.3 e) Storing, retrieving and searching for data in files

Opening a file

To store or retrieve data in a file requires that the file is "opened".

The data items are recalled in the same order in which they were stored. Most file types require that the data items can only be read in sequence starting with the first item. This is a very important point and means that to make a simple change to a file usually requires that a new file containing the change is created and the original file deleted.

Updating a file

Updating a file is a general term which means making a change to the contents of a file. For a file of customer records the change could be either to add a new customer, delete an existing customer or to amend a customer record. Each of these changes would results in an update of the file.

Closing a file

Once all the data has been written to a file, the file must be closed otherwise the file contents will not be saved.

Similarly a session which retrieves a file contents would open the file at the start of the session and finally close the file.

How data is retrieved from the file will be determined by how the data was originally written to the file and its subsequent organisation.

- Each item of data can be stored on a separate line which makes retrieving it straightforward. A spelling checker dictionary file would have one word on each line of the file.
- Separate each item of data by a comma; this is known as comma-separated variable (CSV) format. This format requires slightly more complex programming to retrieve the data and would be used when the data has a record format. For example one customer's data on each line of the file with the name, address, etc. each separated by a comma

Writing to a file

This simply means creating the file.

The sequence for the program would be:

```
OPEN the (new) file i.e. create it

REPEAT
   INPUT the data from the user
   WRITE this data to the file
UNTIL  no more data to input

CLOSE the file
```

When we are writing data to a file is it said to be an "output file" and this is made clear in the programming language OPEN statement. The file mode is "output".

Appending data to a file

This assumes that the file already exists and (say) contains 65 customer records. We now need to add a new customer record.

Open the file to add data (the file mode is called "append") and the new data is added *to the end of the same file.*

Retrieving data from a file

Retrieving data involves opening the file for reading (the file mode is "input") then reading each data item in sequence. The file must be closed when reading is complete.

Note: the records/data can only be read from a file in sequence. The only exception to this is for direct access files.

Assume we need to open the file and search for a particular customer. The simplest form of search is a sequential (linear) search. This involves looking at each item in turn until the item required is found or the end of the file is reached (when the program should report that the item was not found).

The algorithm for this file search is similar to searching an array as described earlier. The only difference is that the data are read from a file instead of from a one-dimensional array.

Further details of these file operations, including sample program code, are given in the next section.

2.3 f Using a procedural language to perform file operations

The methods used by procedural languages differ slightly so you must consult a textbook for the language you are using. However, the methods are very similar and here we use Visual Basic .NET.

Opening a file

To open a file you must first declare a variable of type StreamReader. You then assign the name of file to this variable and open the file for reading, writing or appending.

The following code opens a file for reading (as an "input" file):

```
Dim InputData As IO.StreamReader

InputData = IO.File.OpenText(<full
           pathname for the file>)
```

The following code opens a file for writing (as an "output" file):

```
Dim OutputData As IO.StreamWriter

OutputData = IO.File.CreateText(<full
           pathname of the file>)
```

Reading from a file

The following code reads an item of data from a file that has been opened as `InputData`:

```
<variable name> = InputData.ReadLine
```

This assigns a line of text from the file to the variable `<variable name>`.

Writing to a file

The following code writes an item of data to the file that has been opened as `OutputData`:

```
OutputData.WriteLine(<data to be
written>)
```

The data that is to be written to the file must be of data type String or one of the numeric data types.

Care! If you open for writing a file that already exists, it is erased and a new empty file is opened.

Amending data in a file

Two files are required. The first contains the data record to be amended; the second is a new file into which the updated data – and all the original data items – is written. The original file can then be renamed as the backup file and the new file is given the original file name. Both files must be closed before these actions can take place.

Here is an algorithm for amending a record in a file. The file to be changed is a serially organised file where the data items were written into the file in no particular order.

```
OPEN old file for reading - OLDFILE
OPEN empty file for writing to -
          NEWFILE

INPUT NameToChange
INPUT NewName
Found ← FALSE

WHILE NOT EOF(OLDFILE) AND NOT Found
    FILEREAD ThisName from OLDFILE
    IF ThisName <> NameToChange
       THEN
           WRITE ThisName to NEWFILE
       ELSE
           FILEWRITE NewName to NEWFILE
           Found ← TRUE
    ENDIF
ENDWHILE

WHILE NOT EOF(OLDFILE)
    FILEREAD ThisName from OLDFILE
    FILEWRITE ThisName to NEWFILE
ENDWHILE

CLOSE NEWFILE
CLOSE OLDFILE

IF NOT Found
    THEN
        OUTPUT message that NameToChange
               was not found
    ELSE
        DELETE any backup file
        RENAME OLDFILE to BACKUPFILE
        RENAME NEWFILE as OLDFILE
ENDIF
```

The corresponding program in Visual Basic. NET is shown on the next page. The program is referred to again and improved in Chapter 2.5, which discusses making code more understandable.

```
Dim NextName As String
Dim NameToChange, NewName As String
Dim Found As Boolean
Dim OldFile As IO.StreamReader
Dim NewFile As IO.StreamWriter

OldFile = IO.File.
OpenText("ListOfNames.txt")
NewFile = IO.File.
CreateText("NewListOfNames.txt")

NameToChange = InputBox("Enter the name
                   to be changed.", _
              "Name to Change")
NewName = InputBox("Enter the new
                   name.", "New Name")

Found = False

Do While OldFile.Peek <> -1 And Not
Found
   NextName = OldFile.ReadLine
   If NextName <> NameToChange Then
      NewFile.WriteLine(NextName)
   Else
      NewFile.WriteLine(NewName)
      Found = True
   End If
Loop

Do While OldFile.Peek <> -1
   NextName = OldFile.ReadLine
   NewFile.WriteLine(NewName)
Loop

OldFile.Close()
NewFile.Close()

If Not found Then
   MsgBox("The name was not in the
                   file", , "Error")
Else
   IO.File.Delete("listOfNames.bak")
   IO.File.Move("listOfNames.txt",
              "listOfNames.bak")
   IO.File.Move("newListOfNames.txt",
              "ListOfNames.txt")
End If
```

Inserting data into a serially organised file

This is simple if the programming language has a file mode of "append". The algorithm would be similar to:

```
INPUT NewDataItem
OPEN file in append mode
FILEWRITE NewDataItem
CLOSE file
```

The program code would be as follows, where `DataFile.txt` is the name of the file which is to have data appended to it:

```
Dim AppendFile As IO.StreamWriter
DimNewName As String

AppendFile = IO.File.AppendText("DataFile.txt")
NewFile.WriteLine(NewName)
AppendFile.Close()
```

Inserting data into a sequentially organised file

Two files are required to insert a new item into a file. The algorithm and program are similar to those for amending a record. The main difference is that records are in order of some key field. Before continuing, try to write an insertion algorithm and program to insert a new item into a file of names that are in alphabetic order.

A possible solution is shown on page 152.

Our algorithm is as follows:

```
OPEN file for reading - OLDFILE
OPEN file for writing - NEWFILE

INPUT NewName
Inserted ← FALSE

WHILE NOT EOF AND NOT Inserted
   FILEREAD NextName from OLDFILE
   IF NextName > NewName
     THEN
        FILEWRITE NewName to NEWFILE
        FILEWRITE NextName to NEWFILE
        Inserted ← TRUE
     ELSE
        FILEWRITE NextName to NEWFILE
    ENDIF
ENDWHILE

IF NOT Inserted
   THEN
      FILEWRITE NewName to NEWFILE
   ELSE
      WHILE NOT EOF
         FILEREAD NextName from OLDFILE
         FILEWRITE NextName to NEWFILE
      ENDWHILE
 ENDIF

DELETE any backup file
RENAME OLDFILE to a backup file
RENAME NEWFILE as OLDFILE
```

The corresponding program in Visual Basic .NET is given below:

```
Dim OldFile As IO.StreamReader
Dim NewFile As IO.StreamWriter
Dim Inserted As Boolean
Dim NextName, NewName As String

OldFile = IO.File.OpenText("List Of
                          Names.txt")
NewFile = IO.File.CreateText("New List
                       Of Names.txt")

NewName = InputBox("Enter name to be
               inserted.", "New Name")
Inserted = False
Do While OldFile.Peek <> -1 And Not
                            Inserted
   NextName = OldFile.ReadLine
   If NextName > NewName Then
      NewFile.WriteLine(NewName)
      NewFile.WriteLine(NextName)
      Inserted = True
   Else
      NewFile.WriteLine(NextName)
   End If
Loop

If Not Inserted Then
   NewFile.WriteLine(NewName)
Else
   Do While OldFile.Peek <> -1
      NextName = OldFile.ReadLine
      NewFile.WriteLine(NextName)
   Loop
End If

OldFile.Close()
NewFile.Close()

IO.File.Delete("List Of Names.bak")
IO.File.Move("List Of Names.txt", "List
                     Of Names.bak")
IO.File.Move("New List Of Names.txt",
              "List Of Names.txt")
```

Summary

- An integer is a whole number.

- A real number is one that has a fractional part.

- Boolean data can have only two states: True (Yes or 1) and False (No or 0).

- Character data is any single character from the character set of the computer.

- String data is a sequence of characters.

- An array is a data structure that allows multiple similar items to be referred to by the same identifier:

```
Dim Surname(20) As String
Dim HomeVisit(5,14) As Integer
```

- Arrays are written and read in loops:

```
FOR Index ← 0 To 20
    Surname[Index] ← ""
ENDFOR
```

- A record is a data structure that allows data items to be grouped and referred to with an identifier name.

```
Structure StudentRecord
    Dim StudentNumber As Byte
    Dim StudentName As String
    Dim Class As String
End Structure
```

- The size of a file is calculated from adding the size of the items in each record and multiplying by the number of records. If `StudentRecord` has 25 bytes and there are 2000 students, then the file is 25 × 2000 bytes, or about 50 KB.

- There are 1024 bytes in 1 KB.

- You should allow an additional 10% file space for overheads.

- A file must be opened before data is written to it.

- A file must be closed and re-opened before it can be read.

- A sequential or linear search involves opening a file and reading through it from the beginning until the required record is found:

$\longrightarrow$

```
OPEN file for reading - STUDENTFILE

INPUT SearchName
Found ← FALSE

WHILE NOT EOF(STUDENTFILE) AND NOT Found
    FILEREAD ThisName from STUDENTFILE
    IF  ThisName = SearchName
        THEN
            Found ← TRUE
    ENDIF
ENDWHILE

CLOSE STUDENTFILE

IF Found
    THEN
        OUTPUT SearchName was found
    ELSE
        OUTPUT SearchName was not found
ENDIF
```

Test yourself

1. A computer program will simulate a die thrown 1000 times. The program will calculate and output:
    *   the total number of 1s, 2s, 3s, 4s, 5s and 6s
    *   the average of all 1000 throws.
    Define the variables that will be needed, clearly stating their data types. [5]

    ### Hint

    Consider presenting the information in a table.

2. Write an algorithm for the problem presented in Question 1. You may assume the existence of a function RND ( ) which generates a random number in the range 0 to just under 1. [7]
3. A file is to be created to store data about university modules. Each module has:
    *   a unique four-digit code from 1000 to 4999
    *   a module name
    *   the number of credits it is worth (30 or 60)
    *   the number of the room in which it is taught (two uppercase letters followed by three digits).
    a. Design the variables for this data. Give the length of each field and its data type. [5]
    b. Define a record data type for this data. [3]
    c. Estimate the size of the file if there are about 500 different modules. [5]
    d. The records are stored as a sequentially organised file in module code order. Write an algorithm to find the module with code 3542. [5]

2.4 Common facilities of procedural languages

Using assignment statements

We have already used **assignment statement** in many of the programs in earlier sections. An assignment statement takes the form:

```
<variable> = <expression>
```

For example:

```
i = 15
Found = True
Surname(i) = "Tey"
Count = Count + 1
```

The right hand side of the statement is evaluated and its value is assigned to the variable on the left hand side of the statement.

Arithmetic operators

An **operator** is a symbol that *operates* on one or more values. The arithmetic operators are +, -, *, / and ^, which stand for addition, subtraction, multiplication, division and exponentiation. Examples of their use are illustrated with the following assignment statements:

```
Total = 4.6 + 7.8
Difference = 3.6 - 8.78
Product = 4.54 * 6.43
Dividend = 23.87 / 5.86
Cube = 5 ^ 3
Total = Num1 + Num2
Difference = FirstNumber - SecondNumber
Product = Number1 * Number2
Dividend = Numerator / Denominator
AreaOfSquare = Length ^ 2
```

MOD and **DIV** are special operators that are available in some high-level languages.

a MOD b returns the remainder when integer a is divided by integer b. For example, 7 MOD 3 is equal to 1 and 15 MOD 4 is equal to 3.

a DIV b means divide integer a by integer b. The DIV operator computes the "whole number of times" that b divides into a. For example, 7 DIV 3 is equal to 2 and 19 DIV 5 is equal to 3.

Thus, we can summarise:

```
Remainder = Num1 MOD Num2
WholeNumber = Num1 DIV Num2
```

You need to check whether or not these operators are available in your programming language. If not, there is probably an INT function in the language so the equivalent would be:

```
Remainder = (a/b - Int(a/b)) * b
WholeNumber = Int(a/b)
```

Relational operators

A couple of relational operators have been used in programs in previous sections. For example,

```
Name <> OldName
Name > NewName
```

These expressions compute a value of TRUE or FALSE. That is, if Name has the value "DAVIS" and OldName also has the value "DAVIS", then the value of the first expression is FALSE.

In the second expression, if `Name` has the value "JONES" and `NewName` has the value "CRADDOCK", then the value of the second expression is TRUE. Note that we can use these relational operators to make a comparison between two strings. Table 2.4.1 contains a summary of the relational operators.

Table 2.4.1   Relational operators.

Operator	Meaning
=	Equals
<	less than
<=	less than or equal to
>	greater than
>=	greater than or equal to
<>	not equal to

2.4 d Boolean operators

The Boolean operators AND and OR operate on two Boolean values (or conditions that evaluate to a Boolean value).

Assume we have two Boolean variables `Value1` and `Value2` (which can each be TRUE or FALSE). Tables 2.4.2 and 2.4.3 summarise the effects of the AND and OR operators.

Table 2.4.2   The AND operator.

Value1	Value2	Value1 AND Value2
TRUE	TRUE	TRUE
TRUE	FALSE	FALSE
FALSE	TRUE	FALSE
FALSE	FALSE	FALSE

Table 2.4.3   The OR operator.

Value1	Value2	Value1 OR Value2
TRUE	TRUE	TRUE
TRUE	FALSE	TRUE
FALSE	TRUE	TRUE
FALSE	FALSE	FALSE

The NOT operator requires only a single input (see Table 2.4.4).

Table 2.4.4   The NOT operator.

Value	NOT Value
TRUE	FALSE
FALSE	TRUE

We have already used both the AND and NOT operators in earlier programs. The following code only returns TRUE if the value of `Index` is less than or equal to the value of n and `Found` is FALSE (which makes `Not found` TRUE):

```
Index <= n And Not Found
```

Further examples using the Boolean operators may be found in many of the programs in this text.

2.4 e Precedence of standard operators

Operators have an order of precedence – the order in which they are evaluated. The arithmetic operators have the order of precedence shown in Table 2.4.5. This means that expressions are evaluated as in the following examples:

$$5 + 6 - 3 = 11 - 3 = 8$$
$$4 * 5 / 8 = 20 / 8 = 2.5$$
$$2 \wedge 3 \wedge 4 = 8 \wedge 4 = 4096$$

Table 2.4.5   Order of precedence for arithmetic operators.

Order	Operator	Notes
1	^	Left to right in an expression
2	* /	Left to right in an expression
3	+ -	Left to right in an expression

The order of precedence can be overridden by using left and right parentheses (brackets) in pairs. The innermost pair is always evaluated first. For example:

$$2 * 7 - 3 = 14 - 3 = 11$$
$$2 * (7 - 3) = 2 * 4 = 8$$

$$14 - 3 \wedge 2 = 14 - 9 = 5$$
$$(14 - 3) \wedge 2 = 11 \wedge 2 = 121$$

If there is more than one pair of parentheses, then they are evaluated from the innermost pair outwards and from left to right. Here is an example:

$$(5 - 2) * ((16 - 1) / (2 + 3)) = 3 * (15 / 5) = 3 * 3 = 9$$

Be careful with expressions such as $\frac{a}{bc}$.

Mathematically this means divide a by the product of b and c. However, in programming, `a/bc` contains two errors. In a program, `bc` is read as a variable name rather than an expression. The product of b and c is written as `b*c`. However, `a/b*c` means "divide a by b and multiply the result by c". In a program, it must be written as $a/(b*c)$. Assume $a = 20$, $b = 2$ and $c = 5$ and we want to evaluate $\dfrac{20}{2*5} = 2$. If the program says 20/2*5, it evaluates to 10 * 5 = 50. We have to write 20/(2*5) = 20 / 10 = 2.

Logical operators also have an order of precedence (Table 2.4.6).

Table 2.4.6 Order of precedence for logical operators.

Order	Operator	Notes
1	NOT	Left to right in an expression
2	AND	Left to right in an expression
3	OR	Left to right in an expression

As with the arithmetic operators, parentheses can be used to change the order of precedence. For example,

TRUE AND NOT FALSE OR TRUE

evaluates as

TRUE AND TRUE OR TRUE

= TRUE OR TRUE

= TRUE

but

TRUE AND NOT (FALSE OR TRUE)

= TRUE AND NOT TRUE

= TRUE AND FALSE

= FALSE

If in doubt, use parentheses. You may use as many sets of brackets as you like to make the intended order of evaluation clear.

2.4 f Evaluating expressions

You have already used many of the relational operators which are given in Table 2.4.7.

Table 2.4.7 Relational operators.

Mathematical notation	Programming notation	Meaning
<	<	Less than
≤	<=	Less than or equal to
=	=	Equal to
≠	<>	Not equal to
≥	>=	Greater than or equal to
>	>	Greater than

Activity

1. Evaluate the following arithmetic expressions where a = 3, b = 4 and c = 5. Show your working.
   a. a * b + c
   b. a * (b + c)
   c. a ^ b
   d. b * a ^ c
   e. (c – a) ^ b
   f. 8 * (a + c) / b
   g. (b + c) /a * b
   h. (a + b) * (b + c) / (c – a)
2. Evaluate the following logical expressions where a = 3 and b = 4. Show your working.
   a. 4 * a = 3 * b
   b. b <= a
   c. (a + b) < (b – a)
   d. 3 ^ a = b ^ 2
   e. (5 – a) * (b + 1) > (a * b – 6)
   f. NOT (a < b)
   g. ((a + b) > 3) AND ((2 * a – b) < 2)
   h. (a * b < 10) OR (a < 5) AND NOT (b > a)

2.4 g Operators and built-in functions for string manipulation

Built-in functions can be used in algorithms. Different programming languages have similar functions but they do not always use the same syntax. For example, older versions of Visual Basic use LEFT(), RIGHT() and MID() functions but Visual Basic .NET uses *methods* because it is an object-oriented programming (OOP) language. You study OOP in Chapter 3.5.

Manipulating strings

The formats of some functions are given in Table 2.4.8 (on page 158), together with their purposes. In the table, Str, Str1 and Str2 are all variables of data type String and n and m are positive integers. Each character of a string has a position relative to the start of the string. The first character is numbered 0 (some languages start numbering at 1). Thus, the position of the character "p" in the string "computer" is 3.

Note: You should use these pseudocode function names in any algorithms you are asked to produce. In the examination you will be expected to be familiar with the list shown in Table 2.4.8.

Examples of these functions in use are as follows:

- `LOCATE("Technology", "chno")` returns 2
- `LOCATE("Technology", "Chno")` returns –1 (notice that "C" does not equal "c")
- `LEFT("Technology", 6)` returns "Techno"
- `MID("Technology", 2, 4)` returns "chno"
- `RIGHT("Technology", 5)` returns "ology"
- `LENGTH("Technology")` returns 10

Table 2.4.8 String manipulation functions.

Function	Purpose
LOCATE(`Str1`, `Str2`)	Return the start position of `Str2` in `Str1` or –1 if `Str2` is not in `Str1`
LEFT(`Str`, `n`)	Return the first n characters of `Str` as a string
MID(`Str`, `m`, `n`)	Return, as a string, the next n characters of `Str`, starting at the mth character
RIGHT(`Str`, `n`)	Return the last n characters of `Str`
LENGTH(`Str`)	Return the number of characters in `Str`

Converting between a character and its ASCII number

ASCII was introduced in Chapter 1.3.

Every character has to be stored in the computer, as a pattern of binary digits. A standard set of character values is known as American Standard Code for Information Interchange (ASCII). Using this code, each character is represented by seven binary digits (the eighth digit of a byte is used for parity checking). In this system, "A" has the code 10000001 or 65 in denary, "B" is 1000010 or 66, "C" is 67 and so on. The digits "0" to "9" are represented by the denary numbers 48 to 57.

Note: Most modern computer languages use ANSI codes, which use eight bits and can therefore represent more characters.

The **function ASCII**(`<character>`) returns the ASCII value of `<character>`. For example:

- `ASCII('A')` = 65
- `ASCII('a')` = 97

The **function CHAR**(`<number>`) returns the character with ASCII value `<number>`. For example:

- `CHAR(67)` = `'C'`
- `CHAR(56)` = `'8'`

Again, think of these function names as you create pseudocode.

Note: In Visual Basic .NET the corresponding functions are `Asc(<character>)` and `Chr(<number>)`.

Concatenating strings

Two strings can be joined by using the + or & operators. This is known as **concatenation**.

Consider these examples:

- "Tech"&"nology" = "Technology"
- "David" + "Beckham" = "DavidBeckham". Why is there no space character included in the final string?

Note: Visual Basic .NET allows the use of either the & or the + operator.

Isolating a sub-string

We have already documented these functions in Table 2.4.8 and suggested pseudocode identifiers. In Table 2.4.9 we make the point that these functions are all available in Visual Basic .NET but with different names and implemented as methods (not functions).

Table 2.4.9 String manipulation functions in Visual Basic .NET.

Pseudocode function	Visual Basic .NET method
`LOCATE(Str1, Str2)`	`Str1.IndexOf(Str2)`
`LEFT(Str, n)`	`Str.Substring(0, n)`
`MID(Str, m, n)`	`Str.Substring(m, n)`
`RIGHT(Str, n)`	`Str.Substring(Str.Length-n, n)`

The reason that Visual Basic .NET uses methods and not functions is that it is an object-oriented language, as are most modern programming languages. You will get more details in Chapter 3.5.

(2.4 h) Relational operations on alphanumeric strings

Because each character has a number value, characters can be compared in the same way as numbers. This means that:

- "A" < "C" returns FALSE
- "X" > "x" returns TRUE

The comparison is essentially based on each character's position in the ASCII code table. Characters are compared one by one – just like searching a dictionary.

This means that:

- "a" > "ab" returns FALSE
- "3" <> "3.0" returns TRUE

Let's design an algorithm that inputs a name in the format <surname><space><first name>and outputs it in the format <first name><space><surname>:

```
INPUT MyName
LengthOfName = LENGTH(MyName)
PositionOfSpace = LOCATE(MyName,
                         '<Space>')
FirstName = LEFT(MyName,
                 PositionOfName)
Surname = RIGHT(MyName, LengthOfName -
                PositionOfName - 1)
OUTPUT Surname &'<Space>'& FirstName
```

In Visual Basic .NET, this algorithm can be implemented as:

```
1   Dim MyName As String
2   Dim FirstName, Surname As String
3   Dim LengthOfName As Integer
4   Dim PosnOfSpace As Integer
5
6   MyName = txtInputName.Text
7
8   LengthOfName = MyName.Length
9   PosnOfSpace = MyName.IndexOf(" ")
10  FirstName = Name.Substring
                      (0, PosnOfSpace)
11  Surname = MyName.
            Substring(PosnOfSpace + 1, _
12          LengthOfName - PosnOfSpace - 1)
13  txtReversedName.Text = Surname & "
                    " & FirstName
```

On line 6, the name is keyed into a text box control called txtInputName. On line 13, the final string is displayed in a text box control called txtReversedName.

Inputting and validating data

Chapter 1.8 looked at techniques for verifying and validating data. This section contains some algorithms that demonstrate what you can do in your practical programming. Remember, all data should be validated on input, if possible. This does not ensure the correctness of data, only that it is reasonable and satisfies some agreed rules.

Suppose you are entering the gender of a person. You could use the following algorithm to validate the value. It ensures that only "F" or "M" is accepted; no other value is allowed:

```
REPEAT
    INPUT Gender
UNTIL Gender = "F" OR Gender = "M"
```

The Visual Basic .NET version of this algorithm is:

```
Dim Gender As Char

Do
    Gender = InputBox("Enter the gender (F or M)", _
                "Get gender")
Loop Until Gender = "F" Or Gender = "M"
```

Suppose a program requires the entry of the number of computers ordered by a school. How can you validate the data? It seems reasonable to argue that the order must be for at least one computer and no more than 250. We can use the following algorithm to validate the data input:

```
REPEAT
    INPUT NumberOfComputers
UNTIL NumberOfComputers > 0 AND
            NumberOfComputers <= 250
```

What type of validation check is being used? Is this sufficient? What happens if someone enters 15.6 instead of 156?

The Visual Basic .NET version of this algorithm is:

```
Dim NumberOfComputers As Integer

Do
    NumberOfComputers = InputBox( _
    "Enter the number of computers
    required", _
    "Number Required")
Loop Until NumberOfComputers > 0 And
            NumberOfComputers <= 250
```

2.4 j Outputting data

The normal output from a program is to a screen (other forms of output are discussed in Chapter 1.8). Output to a file was described in "Using a procedural language to perform file operations" in Chapter 2.3 (page 149).

Output to a printer depends on the programming language but usually contains formatting parameters. In fact, formatting information can also be used on screen output. Formatting information tells the printer (or screen) how to display the output.

One of the simplest methods that can be used is to simply print the output. For example, two numbers are input. The program computes and outputs their sum. One print statement could be:

```
PRINT Answer
```

The output might be:

```
6.1
```

This does not tell the user much. Now consider this:

```
PRINT Num1, Num2, Answer
```

It might produce:

```
2.6 3.5 6.1
```

This is still not very clear – so, now try this:

```
PRINT "The sum of ", Num1, " and ",
Num2, " is ", Answer
```

which produces:

```
The sum of 2.6 and 3.5 is 6.1
```

The following code is even clearer:

```
PRINT "The first number is ", Num1
PRINT "The second number is ", Num2
PRINT "and their sum is ", Answer
```

This produces:

```
The first number is 2.6
The second number is 3.5
and their sum is 6.1
```

These examples show some of the simplest ways of formatting the output.

All programming languages have built-in methods for formatting output. You should familiarise yourself with these methods and use them, particularly in your project work for Module 4. Very complex formatting can be used in all languages but they are dependent on the language.

You need to understand the need for formatting output in order to make it easy to read and understand. Consider these two outputs:

```
RogerBlackfordM04/09/3777.4165
DianaWardF15/05/4150.3150
BillWorthyM18/06/4681.3180
```

and

Name	Gender	DOB	Weight (kg)	Height (cm)
RogerBlackford	M	04/09/37	77.4	165
DianaWard	F	15/05/41	50.3	150
BillWorthy	M	18/06/46	81.3	180

Which is clearer?

These programming language features can be used to produce formatted output to both printer and screen. In fact, many languages allow you to use these methods to output to a text file – the idea being that we can then print the contents of the file later. For further information on output to file, see "Using a procedural language to perform file operations" in Chapter 2.3 (page 149).

Summary

- An assignment statement gives an identifier a value, e.g. `i=15`.

- Arithmetic operators are the symbols that cause arithmetic operations to be carried out on identifiers:

```
Total = 4.6 + 7.8
Difference = 3.6 - 8.78
Product = Number1 * Number2
Dividend = Numerator / Denominator
AreaOfSquare = Length ^ 2
```

- `a MOD b` returns the remainder when integer `a` is divided by integer `b`.
- `a DIV b` returns the number of times that integer `b` goes into integer `a`.
- Relational operators compare values and identifiers, returning a Boolean value, e.g. 3 > 2 returns TRUE.
- The Boolean operators AND, OR and NOT can be used to combine two Boolean values or expressions: `NOT Found AND i < 10`.
- Programming languages evaluate expressions according to a strict order of the operators (e.g. powers are evaluated before multiplication, which is evaluated before addition).
- Parentheses are used to ensure that the order of evaluation is as intended by the programmer.
- Strings can be manipulated using the standard comparison operators and built-in functions that are specific to the language, for example, LOCATE, LEFT, MID, RIGHT, LENGTH and conversion functions.
- The result of a relational operation on strings depends on the binary codes of the characters. Different character sets order characters differently.
- Data entered by the user can be validated using loops and relational operators:

```
REPEAT
    INPUT Gender
UNTIL Gender = 'F' OR Gender = 'M'
```

- Output data must be formatted to make it easy for the user to read.

Test yourself

1. Use the functions MOD and DIV to convert a sum of money in cents to dollars ($) and cents. You should use meaningful identifier names for any constants and variables you use. [5]
2. `Mark` is a variable that takes values between 0 and 100 inclusive. Write pseudocode which inputs a value for `Mark` until it is valid. [3]

3. Evaluate the following Boolean expressions when a = 8, showing your working.

   a. a < 5 AND a > 0 OR a = 10 [3]

   b. a < 5 AND (a > 0 OR a = 10) [3]

4. Evaluate the following expressions when p = 4, q = 6 and r = 10. Show your working.

   a. p + q * r [3]

   b. (p + q) * r [3]

   c. (q − p) ^ (p + q) / r [4]

5. The variable `MyString` stores "a sentence" and variable St2 stores the string "student".

   a. Describe the following string functions:

   `LOCATE(MyString, Str2)`

   `RIGHT(MyString, n)`

   `LENGTH(MyString).` [3]

   b. Write an algorithm, that uses the string functions `LOCATE(MyString, Str3)` and `RIGHT(MyString, n)` to count the number of words in `MyString`. [6]

2.5 Writing maintainable programs

2.5 a ## Programming terms

A **variable** is a data item associated with a location in memory. The value of the variable may change during the running of the program. The variable is given an identifier name. It enables a program to be written before the values are known, e.g. `NoOfChildren` is an identifier name and later it will hold the value 4.

A **constant** is a data item associated with a location in memory. Once a value is assigned, it cannot be changed while the program is running. Constants – just like variables – must have an identifier name and a declared data type. In the following example, `Pi` is the identifier name for a constant that is assigned a value:

```
Const Pi As Single
Pi = 3.141593
```

In Visual Basic .NET the declaration and assignment can be combined into a single program statement with:

```
Const VATRate = 0.175
```

Constants are useful as they can be referred to many times in the program code by their identifier name. In the UK, the rate of VAT changed in January 2011 from 17.5% to 20%. Assuming this number was used as a constant in programs, the program codes require only a change to a single line of code (i.e. where the constant was assigned the value) and not everywhere the constant value is used in the program.

An **identifier** is a name that is used to represent a variable, a constant, a function, a procedure, a user-defined data type (e.g. a record), an object or another element in a program. In forms-based programming and web programming, all the various controls used on the interface (text boxes, drop-down list, etc.) also have identifiers.

A **reserved word**, or keyword, is one that is defined in the programming language. It can only be used for the purpose specified by the language. Reserved words cannot, therefore, be used as identifier names. Typical reserved words are `For`, `Next`, `Loop`, `If`, `Case/Select`, `Integer` and `String`.

2.5 b ## Declaring variables and constants

Variables and constants need to be declared so that the compiler or interpreter can reserve the correct amount of memory for the values.

Allocating memory

In the case of an array, the compiler or interpreter has to save several memory locations as specified by the size or upper bound in the declaration statement. For example, consider the declaration:

```
Dim MyArray(10, 20) As Integer
```

`MyArray` is a two-dimensional array. Assume that the subscripts start at 1. The program must reserve enough memory space for 10 × 20, i.e. 200 integer values. Integers are usually stored with four bytes so the total memory space reserved for the array is 800 bytes. The compiler must also store the number of subscripts (two) and the upper bounds (10 and 20) for the subscripts – again, as integers, requiring four bytes for each.

The scope of variables

When a variable is declared, it may only be used in certain parts of the program. This is known as its **scope**.

Consider the following program, which produces the output in Figure 2.5.1:

```
Private Sub Button1_Click
        (ByVal sender As System.Object, _
        ByVal e As System.EventArgs) _
    Handles btnStart.Click

  Dim a, b As Integer
  a = 1
  b = 2
  lstResults.Items.Add("Now in main program")
  lstResults.Items.Add("a = " & a)
  lstResults.Items.Add("b = " & b)
  LocalVariables()

  lstResults.Items.Add("")
  lstResults.Items.Add("Now back in main program")
  lstResults.Items.Add("a = " & a)
  lstResults.Items.Add("b = " & b)
End Sub

Sub LocalVariables()
  Dim a, b As Integer

  a = 10
  b = 20

  lstResults.Items.Add("")
  lstResults.Items.Add("Now in Procedure")
  lstResults.Items.Add("a = " & a)
  lstResults.Items.Add("b = " & b)
End Sub
```

Notice how variables a and b have different values when they are in the procedure to those they have in the main program. We say that the scope of a = 1 and b = 2 is the main program; in the procedure the values are a = 10 and b = 20. This is because these variables are "in scope" inside the procedure. The main program cannot see a = 10 and b = 20. Similarly the procedure cannot see a = 1 and b = 2.

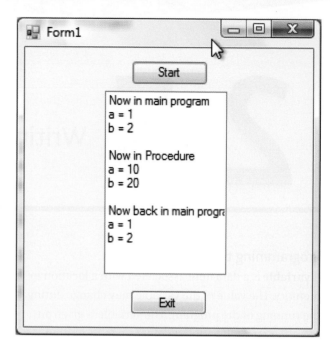

Figure 2.5.1 Local scope of variables.

In this example, "main program" refers to the event procedure Button1_Click. To be more precise, the scope of the original variable is only inside this event procedure. Had we been programming in console mode, then "main program" is taken to be the module Sub_Main.

Many programmers may work on a project, writing many procedures and modules. They do not need to worry that another programmer may use the same identifier name in their procedures. This is because the scope of each variable is different.

Other variables can be declared so that they are "in scope", i.e. recognised, throughout a program. These are called **global variables** and are declared at the start of a program. A variable which is declared inside a procedure or function is said to be a **local variable** with a scope which is local to that procedure or function. The scope of variables is a very powerful feature of high-level procedural programming.

Compare the output (Figure 2.5.2) of the program on page 165 with the code above.

Notice that in the program on page 165 the values of c and d are the same in the procedure as in the main program. Also notice that c and d are not declared in the procedure – this is because they are global variables.

```
Dim c, d As Integer

Private Sub Button1_Click
            (ByVal sender As System.Object, _
             ByVal e As System.EventArgs) _
         Handles btnStart.Click

  Dim a, b As Integer
  a = 1
  b = 2
  c = 3
  d = 4

  lstResults.Items.Add("Now in main program")

  lstResults.Items.Add("a = " & a)
  lstResults.Items.Add("b = " & b)
  lstResults.Items.Add("c = " & c)
  lstResults.Items.Add("d = " & d)

  LocalVariables()

  lstResults.Items.Add("")

  lstResults.Items.Add("Now back in main program")
  lstResults.Items.Add("a = " & a)
  lstResults.Items.Add("b = " & b)
  lstResults.Items.Add("c = " & c)
  lstResults.Items.Add("d = " & d)
End Sub

Sub LocalVariables()
  Dim a, b As Integer

  a = 10
  b = 20

  lstResults.Items.Add("")
  lstResults.Items.Add("Now in Procedure")
  lstResults.Items.Add("a = " & a)
  lstResults.Items.Add("b = " & b)
  lstResults.Items.Add("c = " & c)
  lstResults.Items.Add("d = " & d)
End Sub
```

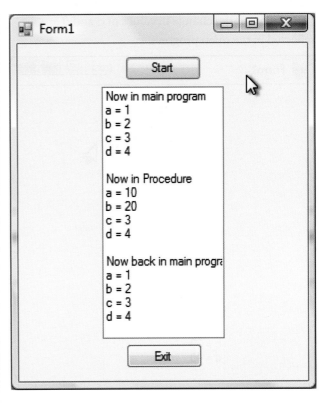

Figure 2.5.2 Global and local scope of variables.

What happens if c and d are given new values in the procedure? The new values only apply to c and d in the procedure. Outside the procedure, they remain the same as before entering the procedure. Here is a version of the procedure that assigns values to c and d (its results are in Figure 2.5.3 on page 166):

```
Sub LocalVariables()
  Dim a, b As Integer

  a = 10
  b = 20
  c = 30
  d = 40

  lstResults.Items.Add("")

  lstResults.Items.Add("Now in Procedure")
  lstResults.Items.Add("a = " & a)
  lstResults.Items.Add("b = " & b)
  lstResults.Items.Add("c = " & c)
  lstResults.Items.Add("d = " & d)
End Sub
```

Notice that the change in values of c and d are reflected in the main program.

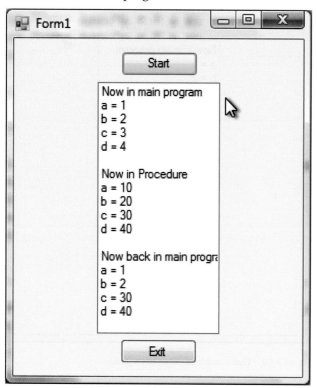

Figure 2.5.3 Assigning values to global variables in a procedure.

2.5 c Using meaningful identifier names

The programs used so far have used meaningful identifier names for all variables and constants. Consider the following code, which we studied in "Functions" in Chapter 2.2 (page 132).

```
Private Sub btnCalculate_Click _
             (ByVal sender As System.
                            Object, _
           ByVal e As System.
                         EventArgs) _
         Handles btnCalculate.Click
   Dim Num1, Num2 As Double
   Dim Product As Double

   ExplainPurposeOfProgram()
   Num1 = 5.5
   Num2 = 4.0
   Product = CalcProduct(Num1, Num2)
   OutputResult(Num1, Num2, Product)
End Sub

Sub ExplainPurposeOfProgram()
```

```
   MsgBox("The purpose of this program
                  is to display two _
          numbers and their product",
                        , "Purpose")
End Sub

Sub OutputResult(ByVal FirstNumber, _
             ByVal SecondNumber, _
             ByVal result)
   MsgBox("The product of " &
          FirstNumber & " and " & _
       SecondNumber & " is " &
                Result, , "Result")
End Sub

Function CalcProduct(ByVal FirstNumber,
             ByVal SecondNumber)
    Return FirstNumber * SecondNumber
End Function
```

Not only are the variables given meaningful names but so are the procedures and the button control. Each procedure name explains what the procedure does. Purists say that procedure and function names should always read like a verb, as they carry out some action. Note that `ExplainPurposeOfProgram`, `OutputResult` and `CalcProduct` all satisfy this condition.

Some programmers start variable identifiers with three letters that indicate their type. Thus integer variable identifiers would start with `int`, such as `intCount`, and variables of data type `Double` would start with `dbl`, such as `dblNum1`. It is important that every programmer sticks to the standard set down by the company for which they work.

Controls, such as buttons and text boxes in Visual Basic .NET, also need to have meaningful names such as `btnStart` or `txtAnswer`. If you do not change them, the default names (`Button1` or `Text1`) can make a program very difficult to follow and debug.

2.5 d Initialising variables

Most programs assign variables a value when they are declared. However, this practice varies from one language to another and some languages do not initialise any variables (or even, in some cases, ask for the data type to be specified!). Not initialising variables is considered bad practice. If an uninitialised variable is used, the program may simply use any random data in that memory location and the result of the program will be undefined.

The initialisation may take the form of an assignment statement or the user may be asked to enter a value. In the code shown below, Count is declared and assigned an initial value in the same statement. The initial value of Num is entered by the user. Count is declared and initialised before it is used.

The following code initialises the elements of a two-dimensional array to 0 before they are used.

```
Dim MyArray(10, 20) As Integer
Dim Row, Column As Integer

For Row = 1 To 10
    For Column = 1 To 20
        MyArray(Row, Column) = 0
    Next
Next
```

```
Private Sub btnCalculate_Click _
                (ByVal sender As System.Object, _
                ByVal e As System.EventArgs) _
        Handles btnCalculate.Click

    Dim Num As Integer
    Dim Num1, Num2, Num3 As Integer
    Dim Count As Integer = 2

    Num = InputBox("Enter a positive integer.", "Input")
    If Num = 1 Or Num = 2 Then
        MsgBox("The " & Num & " th number is 1", , "Result")
    Else
        Num1 = 1
        Num2 = 1
        While Count <> Num
            Num3 = Num1 + Num2
            Num1 = Num2
            Num2 = Num3
            Count = Count + 1
        End While
        MsgBox("The " & Num & " th Number is " & _
                Num3, , "Result")
    End If

End Sub
```

2.5 e Annotating code

To make clear what a program is doing, code should be annotated. The **annotation** is sometimes written before the code so that the programmer is clear about certain aspects of the design. Also, the annotation should be such that if the code were removed, it would be possible to re-create it.

Here is one of the programs we saw earlier but now with annotation:

```
Private Sub btnStart_Click(ByVal sender As System.Object, _
                    ByVal e As System.EventArgs) _
          Handles btnStart.Click

    'Declare variables to be used
    Dim OldFile As IO.StreamReader 'name for the original file
    Dim NewFile As IO.StreamWriter 'name for the new file
    Dim Inserted As Boolean      'Inserted is true when new name
                                 'has been inserted into file
    Dim Name, NewName As String    'current name and
                                   'name to be inserted
    Dim NextName As String         'next name in the list

    'Open files for reading from and writing to
    OldFile = IO.File.OpenText("List Of Names.txt")
    NewFile = IO.File.CreateText("New List Of Names.txt")

    'Ask the user for the name to be inserted
    NewName = InputBox("Enter name to be inserted.", _
                    "New Name")
    'Initialise Inserted to FALSE to show
    'name has not been inserted into file
    Inserted = False

    'While there are still records to be searched
    'and new name has not been inserted
    Do While OldFile.Peek <> -1 And Not Inserted
        'Read the next name in the file
        Name = OldFile.ReadLine

        If Name > NewName Then
            'insert new name and then old name into new file
            'and note that the name has been inserted
            NewFile.WriteLine(NewName)
            NewFile.WriteLine(Name)
            Inserted = True
        Else
            'write old name to file
            NewFile.WriteLine(Name)
        End If
```

```
Loop

If Not Inserted Then
    'insert the new name at the end of the list
    NewFile.WriteLine(NewName)
Else
    'write the rest of the original file to new file
    Do While OldFile.Peek <> -1
        Name = OldFile.ReadLine
        NewFile.WriteLine(Name)
    Loop
End If

'Close the files
OldFile.Close()
NewFile.Close()

'Delete the original backup file
IO.File.Delete("List Of Names.bak")

'rename the original file as the latest backup
IO.File.Move("List Of Names.txt", "List Of Names.bak")

'rename the new file so that it can be used again
IO.File.Move("New List Of Names.txt", "List Of Names.txt")

End Sub
```

2.5 f **Showing control structures within code**

All the examples in this text show control structures within code by using indentation. It is also good programming practice to insert blank lines – called "white space" – between control structures or, more generally, to separate out the various stages within the code.

The same style of indentation should be used with both pseudocode and program code.

Summary

- Programming terminology:

  – A variable is a data item associated with a memory location of which the value can change.

  – A constant is a data item associated with a memory location of which the value cannot change. If the value needs to change, it is changed once and the program is recompiled.

  – An identifier is a name that represents an element in a program (such as a variable, a constant, a function, a procedure, a user-defined data type or an object).

  – A reserved word, or keyword, is one that is defined by the programming language, such as INPUT or FOR.

- Variables must usually be declared so that the computer knows how much space to allocate and the type of data to which they refer.

- The identifier name for a variable or constant must be unique and not a reserved word. It should be meaningful.

$\longrightarrow$

- Variables should be initialised appropriately before using them:

```
Dim a, b As Integer
a = 1
b = 1
```

- Variables have a "scope" within the program code:
    - a variable which is recognised everywhere in the code is said to be a "global" variable
    - a variable may be "local" to a procedure or function.
- Someone else will find it easier to follow the logic of the solution if the code contains:
    - comments
    - indentation and formatting to show the control structures (i.e. IF statements and loops)
    - use of white space.

Test yourself

1. Define the following terms:
   a. variable [1]
   b. constant [1]
   c. reserved word [1]
2. Discuss the need for good programming techniques to facilitate the ongoing maintenance of programs. [8]

2.6 Testing and running a solution

Types of error in programs

Program errors may be of the following types:

- errors in syntax (incorrect use of the programming language)
- errors in logic (the program does not do what was intended)
- run-time errors (ones that are only discovered when the program runs).

Syntax errors

Syntax errors are errors in the grammar of the program language. That is, the rules of the language have been broken. Common errors are typing errors, such as `Selct` for `Select`. Other errors are more subtle, for example:

- an `If` statement without a matching `End If` statement
- a `For` statement without a matching `Next` statement
- an opening parenthesis without a closing parenthesis: `(a + b.`

Most syntax errors are spotted by the programmer before an attempt to run the code. Some program editors help with this. For example, the Visual Basic .NET editor underlines any variable in the code which has not been declared. Similarly, it highlights declared variables which have not been used in the code.

Syntax errors are finally picked up during the syntax analysis stage of the program's translation. In the case of an interpreter, the error is reported as soon as it is found. A compiler reports all errors found in the complete program in its error report. You should be aware that some editors can report syntax errors while the code is being entered. It is still the syntax analyser that spots the error. If an examination question asks when a syntax error is found, the answer is "during the syntax analysis stage of the program's translation".

Often the analyser reports program statements that are not correctly formed. For example, the following statement reports an error:

```
For Index 1 To 20
```

The correct Visual Basic syntax is:

```
For Index = 1 To 20
```

A similar example is a call to a function that requires two parameters in the function header; an error is reported if the programmer only provides one parameter. Similarly, the programmer may provide the parameter but it is of the wrong data type.

Logic errors

A **logic error** occurs when the programmer makes a mistake in their logic for some part of the program. Suppose a programmer wants the first 10 positive integers to be output and creates the following algorithm:

```
FOR Count = 0 TO 10
    OUTPUT Count
NEXT Count
```

This algorithm has no grammatical errors but it does not produce the correct result. It produces the integers 0 to 10 not 1 to 10. This type of error can only be found by thorough testing. The programmer can carefully check the code by reading it or can attempt to run the program. Another common error is to use the wrong arithmetic symbol, e.g. a+b instead of a−b, or to put parentheses in the wrong place, such as (a+b−c)*d instead of (a+b)−c*d. These errors should be identified during testing and are all a mistake in the logic of the programmer.

Run-time errors

Run-time errors occur during the execution (running) of the program. A typical error is to have an expression, such as (a+b)/(c−d), used in the program but c is equal to d, resulting in an attempted division by zero. The problem is that this error may be undetected for a considerable time because the equality of c and d rarely happens. However, it could be disastrous when it does. It is a good idea to test the denominator before division to ensure that this error doesn't crash the program. Instead, the programmer "traps" the error and displays an error message, as seen in the following code:

```
Dim A As Integer : Dim B As Integer
   Dim C As Integer : Dim D As Integer
   Dim Denominator As Single

   A = InputBox("A ...")
   B = InputBox("B ...")
   C = InputBox("C ...")
   D = InputBox("D ...")

   If C <> D Then
     Denominator = C - D
     MsgBox("Answer is ... " &
           Denominator)
   Else
     MsgBox("Denominator is Zero")
   End If
```

(2.6 b) Testing strategies

Software creation is a human activity and, as a result, is subject to errors. All software has to be tested. Only the simplest of programs work first time and most contain errors (or bugs) that have to be found. If a program has been designed and written in modules, it is much easier to debug because the programmer should be able to test each module independently of the others. There are several strategies the programmer can adopt for testing a program.

White box testing

White box testing is where testers examine each line of code for the correct logic and accuracy. This may be done manually by drawing up a table to record the values of the variables after each instruction is executed. Examples could include selection statements (If and Case Select), where every possible condition must be tested. Alternatively, debugging software can be used to run the program step by step and then display the values of the variables. You will find more about this in the final section of this chapter (page 174).

Black box testing

Black box testing is one of the earliest forms of test. Here the programmer uses test data, for which the results have already been calculated, and compares the results from the program with those that are expected. The programmer does not look at the individual code to see what is happening – the code is viewed as being inside a "black box". The testing only considers the inputs and the outputs they produce.

Alpha and beta testing

The terms "alpha" and "beta" testing are usually used to describe software which is "mass marketed".

Alpha testing is done inside the software developer's own company. A number of employees who have not been involved in the production of the software are given the task of testing it. The software may not be complete at this stage and may have errors that the programmers have not previously found.

Beta testing follows the alpha testing stage. The software is made available to a selected and limited number of testers:
- invited customers
- magazine reviewers
- authors of books about the use of the software
- other developers of software and hardware.

At this stage the software is virtually complete but there may still be bugs present. These testers are expected to provide constructive criticism.

Even Microsoft invites developers and users to be beta testers for new products. The only condition is that the user agrees to provide feedback on the new product.

Acceptance testing

When a large new system is finally delivered to the client's workplace, it goes through an **acceptance testing** phase. Some errors may not be discovered when the software was being developed. They may surface for the first time when the programs are run on the *client's* hardware and operating system platform. At this stage, the software is complete and the developer has to prove to the customer that it does everything specified in the design and the original requirements specification.

2.6 c Selecting suitable test data

It is impossible to test every possible data value that may be used by a program. Suppose a program requires the input of a date of birth. You can make sure the day, month and year are all reasonable by using a range test but you cannot test every value inside that range.

You must examine the problem and then choose data that can be used to test the program. Notice that you do not look at the program to choose the test data. This is because the program may appear to work without any bugs, but it does not prove that it correctly solves the problem.

Consider the problem of inputting a value that lies between 5.5 and 9 inclusive. Look at this pseudocode solution:

```
INPUT n
WHILE n <= 5.5 OR n >= 9
    INPUT n
ENDWHILE
```

Looking at the code, we might choose $n = 6$ as normal data and find that it is accepted. Now let us try a borderline value such as 5.5. This is rejected because $n <= 5.5$ is TRUE. This means that this algorithm works for $n = 5.5$. However, it is not correct for the *problem*, which required that the borderline values should be accepted. This means that the test data should be chosen by examining the problem, not the solution. You are trying to prove that the *solution* solves the *problem* correctly.

In this case, any value between 5.5 and 9 (excluding 5.5 and 9) are **normal data**, 5.5 and 9 are called **borderline data** (or **boundary data**), and **invalid data** could be 4, 10 or even 2000. You will probably use these terms for your Module 4 project to describe various test data to be used. (Note that you might have seen invalid data referred to as 'abnormal data' and boundary data as 'extreme data', such as in the *IGCSE Computer Studies Course*.)

2.6 d Using a trace table

Working through an algorithm using test data values is called a **dry run** or **trace**. The results are shown in a **trace table**.

Table 2.6.1 (on page 174) shows the results of a dry run of the following algorithm using the sequence of input data –2, 0, 3, 5, 12, 16:

```
1   n = 0
2   WHILE n <= 0
3       INPUT n
4   ENDWHILE

5   Total ← 0
6   Count ← 0

7   REPEAT
8       INPUT Number
9       Total ← Total + Number
10      Count ← Count + 1
11  UNTIL Count = n
12  OUTPUT Total/Count
```

Table 2.6.1 A trace table.

Instruction	n	Total	Count	Number	Boolean	Output
1	0					
3	−2					
3	0					
3	3	0	0			
2	2			5		
5		5				
6			1		FALSE	
7				12		
8		17				
9			2		FALSE	
10				16		
11		33				
7			3		TRUE	
8						11
9		7				
10			2			
11					FALSE	
7						
8			8			
9		15				
10			3			
11					TRUE	
12						5

Notice that you only need to record a variable's value in the table if it changes.

Activity

Draw up a new trace table for this algorithm and trace execution for the following sequence of inputs: −1, 2, 13, 29.

2.6 e) Debugging tools and facilities in procedural programming languages

During translation of a high-level language into **machine code** (or intermediate code), syntax errors are spotted and reported by the programmer.

Some text editors report a syntax error as the code is typed in. For example, if you write the instruction Mass = 56 and the variable Mass has not been declared, some editors report it immediately. In any case, it is reported during translation by the interpreter or compiler.

Many languages have an **integrated development environment (IDE)**. This enables the programmer to use some very sophisticated techniques. One such technique is to arrange for a program to stop at a given instruction and display the values of the variables at this point. These are called **break points**. The program can then be continued or stopped by the programmer.

```
Dim A As Integer : Dim B As Integer
Dim C As Integer : Dim D As Integer
Dim Denominator As Single

A = 1
Do While A <> 0
    A = InputBox("A ...")
    B = InputBox("B ...")
    C = InputBox("C ...")
    D = InputBox("D ...")

    If C <> D Then
        Denominator = C - D
        MsgBox("Answer is ... " & Denominator)
    Else
        MsgBox("Denominator is Zero")
    End If
Loop
```

The code now includes a loop. This shows that a break point has been set on the highlighted statement.

Figure 2.6.2 A break point in Visual Basic .NET.

A programmer may step through a program either by setting break points or by stopping after the execution of each instruction. When a programmer sets a break point, the program can then be run to this point. The programmer can then step through the following instructions one at a time, run the program to the next break point, or run to the end of the program.

A watch window (Visual Basic .NET calls this the "Immediate Window") can be used to display the values of variables and expressions. The window displays to the programmer the current value (and maybe the data type) of each variable. To obtain these values, the programmer simply types the name of the variable or the expression into the window and the information is displayed.

You should experiment with the **debugging tools** and facilities that come with your programming language environment.

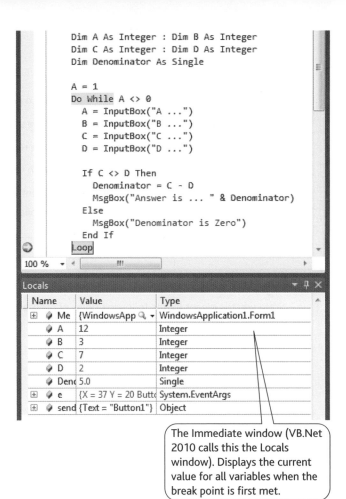

```
Dim A As Integer : Dim B As Integer
Dim C As Integer : Dim D As Integer
Dim Denominator As Single

A = 1
Do While A <> 0
    A = InputBox("A ...")
    B = InputBox("B ...")
    C = InputBox("C ...")
    D = InputBox("D ...")

    If C <> D Then
        Denominator = C - D
        MsgBox("Answer is ... " & Denominator)
    Else
        MsgBox("Denominator is Zero")
    End If
Loop
```

100 %

Locals			
Name	Value	Type	
⊞ ● Me	{WindowsApp 🔍 ▾	WindowsApplication1.Form1	
● A	12	Integer	
● B	3	Integer	
● C	7	Integer	
● D	2	Integer	
● Deno	5.0	Single	
⊞ ● e	{X = 37 Y = 20 Butto	System.EventArgs	
⊞ ● send	{Text = "Button1"}	Object	

The Immediate window (VB.Net 2010 calls this the Locals window). Displays the current value for all variables when the break point is first met.

Figure 2.6.3 The Immediate Window in Visual Basic .NET.

Summary

- Syntax errors involve incorrect use of the programming language (such as an IF without an END IF). They are detected by the compiler or interpreter.

- Logic errors mean that the program does not do what was intended (such as looping 9 times instead of 10). They are detected by testing.

- Run-time errors (such as division by zero) are only discovered when the program runs.

- Testing strategies include:

  - white box testing of individual modules, checking each line of code

  - black box testing of the output from modules, given specific input and noting the output produced

  - alpha testing of the system by technical staff 'in-house'

  - beta testing of the system by a limited number of users outside of the company

  - acceptance testing by the client.

Test yourself

1. a. State what is meant by the following types of programming error:
        i.   syntax error   [1]
        ii. arithmetic error.   [1]
    b. Explain what is meant by:
        i.   white box testing   [2]
        ii. alpha testing.   [2]

2. An algorithm is shown below.

```
1 X = 1
2 REPEAT
3     A = X * X
4     OUTPUT X, A
5     X = X + 1
6 UNTIL X = 3
7 END
```

Copy and complete the following table to dry run the algorithm.   [4]

Line	X	A	Output	Condition

3. When a computer runs a program, the program may fail to run successfully because there are errors in the code.
    Describe **two** types of error that may be present, giving an example of each.   [6]

4. When a programmer writes a program, it is necessary to ensure that the code is properly presented to allow technicians to maintain it.
    Describe **three** methods that the programmer can use to make the code understandable.   [6]

Module 2 Exam questions

1. Programs can be designed in modular form.
   Discuss the advantages and disadvantages of designing programs in modular form. [5]

   Question 5a Cambridge AS Level & A Level Computing 9691 Paper 1 June 2006

2. A program is to be written which will update the records in a sequential file and then produce a backup copy.
   Describe, using a diagram, the way that this problem can be split into modules to prepare it for coding. [5]

   Question 5b Cambridge AS Level & A Level Computing 9691 Paper 1 June 2006

3. An automatic fan is designed so that it turns on only when a person is in the room AND the temperature is above a set value (D).
   The fan receives information from two sensors:
   1. A motion sensor which returns a value (M) dependent upon a person being sensed in the room.
   2. A thermistor (electronic thermometer) which returns the temperature in the room (T).
   Produce an algorithm to control the fan. Your algorithm may be expressed in any form. [6]

   Question 3b Cambridge AS Level & A Level Computing 9691 Paper 1 November 2006

4. A washing machine is computer controlled. The full cycle consists of:
   - Check the door is shut
   - Heat water with heater (H) to 80 degrees if hot wash has been selected, 40 degrees if a cool wash has been selected
   - Run wash motor (M) for 20 minutes, checking water every 5 minutes to see if heater (H) should be turned on again
   - Sound buzzer to signify that wash cycle is complete.

   Note: M can be set to "on" or "off".
   Write an algorithm, in whatever form, to show the working of the washing machine. [7]

   Question 6 Cambridge AS Level & A Level Computing 9691 Paper 1 November 2007

5. Explain what is meant by a procedure. [2]

   Question 5c(i) Cambridge AS Level & A Level Computing 9691 Paper 1 June 2005

6. Describe how procedures and the programming construct "selection" can be used to code a simple menu system for a user. [3]

   Question 5c(ii) Cambridge AS Level & A Level Computing 9691 Paper 1 June 2005

7.
```
INPUT A,B
IF B = 0 THEN C = A
    ELSE C = A ÷ B
ENDIF
PRINT A,B
PRINT C
END
```

   Write down the outputs produced by the algorithm if
   i.   A = 8, B = 2 [2]
   ii. A = 6, B = 0 [2]

   Question 3a Cambridge AS Level & A Level Computing 9691 Paper 1 November 2006

8.
```
READ NUMBER
FOR COUNT = 1 TO NUMBER
    READ MARK
    IF MARK < 50 THEN OUTPUT COUNT,
"FAIL"
    ELSE IF MARK > 80 THEN OUTPUT
COUNT, "MERIT"
        ELSE OUTPUT COUNT, "PASS"
            END IF
        END IF
NEXT
END
```

The above algorithm is designed to read a number of examination marks and print out the result for each one.
It is intended that only marks from 0 to 100 inclusive should be awarded in this examination.
Describe how validation can be included in the original algorithm in order to ensure that only marks from
0 to 100 are included.   [5]

Question 4b Cambridge AS Level & A Level Computing 9691 Paper 1 November 2008

9.
```
D = 1
INPUT X,E
B = E
C = E
FOR I = 1 TO (X-1)
    INPUT  A
    IF   A>B
        THEN B = A
    ELSE
        IF A<C
            THEN C = A
        ENDIF
    ENDIF
    D = D + 1
    E = E + A
NEXT
F = E/D
OUTPUT B, C, F
END
```

   a. State the output values of B, C and F for the following input test data:
      4, 6, 3, 7, 0   [3]
   b. Give **three** other different sets of test data, explaining what condition each is meant to test. [3]

Question 6 Cambridge AS Level & A Level Computing 9691 Paper 1 June 2007

10. A garage sells cars.

    The data in the car file is stored in fixed length records.

    The data about each car includes:

    - Colour
    - Size of engine
    - Whether or not it has air conditioning
    - Price.

    State a suitable data type for each of the items of data listed. [4]

    Question 8c Cambridge AS Level & A Level Computing 9691 Paper 1 June 2007

11. A small business has one shop. It specialises in taking portrait photographs for customers.

    Details of customers are stored on paper.

    It is decided to buy a stand-alone computer and use it to store customer records in a file.

    The following fields are to be stored:

    - Customer name (to allow customer to be addressed properly when contacted).
    - Customer telephone number (so that customer can be contacted when their order has been completed)
    - Date of original commission (so that customers are not kept waiting too long).
    - Whether or not the order has been paid for.

    a. State a suitable data type for each of the four fields. [4]

    b. It is assumed that there will never be more than 1000 records.

        Estimate the total size of file needed for these records. [4]

    Adapted from questions 7a and 7b Cambridge AS Level & A Level Computing 9691 Paper 1 June 2006

12. Describe **two** methods of making the code of a piece of software more understandable to other programmers. [4]

    Question 4b Cambridge AS Level & A Level Computing 9691 Paper 1 November 2005

13. When a programmer writes a program, it is necessary to ensure that the code is properly presented to allow technicians to maintain it.

    Describe **three** methods that the programmer can use to make the code understandable. [6]

    Question 2a Cambridge AS Level & A Level Computing 9691 Paper 1 November 2008

14. When a computer runs a program, the program may fail to run successfully because there are errors in the code.

    Describe **two** types of error that may be present, giving an example of each. [6]

    Question 2c Cambridge AS Level & A Level Computing 9691 Paper 1 June 2008

15. i.   Describe the technique of white box testing. [2]

    ii. Describe **two** other methods of identifying program errors. [4]

    Question 2b Cambridge AS Level & A Level Computing 9691 Paper 1 November 2008

16. Use the code in Question 9 to produce a formal dry run with the test data given. [8]

    (This is not a question from a past paper).

17.

```
READ NUMBER
FOR COUNT = 1 TO NUMBER
    READ MARK
    IF MARK < 50 THEN OUTPUT COUNT, "FAIL"
    ELSE IF MARK > 80 THEN OUTPUT COUNT, "MERIT"
         ELSE OUTPUT COUNT, "PASS"
         END IF
    END IF
NEXT
END
```

The above algorithm is designed to read a number of examination marks and print out the result for each one.

Complete a table like the one below in order to dry run the algorithm with the data 4, 40, 90, 60, 50, 70

NUMBER	COUNTER	MARK	OUTPUT

[8]

Question 4a Cambridge AS Level & A Level Computing 9691 Paper 1 November 2008

18. When software is written the code will probably contain errors.

Describe **three** methods or tools available for identifying program errors. [6]

Question 4a Cambridge AS Level & A Level Computing 9691 Paper 1 November 2005

3

Systems software mechanisms, machine architecture, database theory, programming paradigms and integrated information systems

3.1 The functions of operating systems

Features of operating systems

The operating system (OS) must provide:

- management of all hardware resources:
  - processor
  - secondary storage filing system
  - input/output devices
- an interface between the user and the machine
- an interface between applications software and the machine
- security for the data on the system
- utility software to allow maintenance to be done.

Multi-tasking

The processor works much faster than the human user. To make full use of the processor, more than one program is stored in memory at the same time. The processor gives time to each of these programs in turn.

Suppose two programs are stored in memory. Input devices and output devices are very slow compared to the processor. If one program is waiting for input from the user, it makes sense for the other program to be able to use the processor. In fact, this can be extended to more than two programs, as shown in Figure 3.1.1.

The OS must manage the memory so that all three programs shown in Figure 3.1.1, and any data that they use, are kept separate. It must also schedule the jobs in the sequence that makes best use of the processor. We considered multi-user operating systems in Chapter 1.2.

Multiprogramming was one of the earlier techniques of computing and is still the basis of computing on modern computer systems, especially a PC. It makes possible the basic aim that we want the

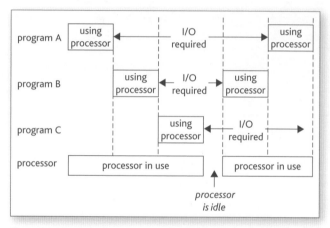

Figure 3.1.1   A processor sharing time between three programs.

computer to be able to do as much work as possible. Multiprogramming will be considered alongside the different strategies for memory management which follow and you need to be careful in the way you describe multiprogramming. "Several programs being executed at the same time" is wrong (see Figure 3.1.1). More than one program concurrently loaded in the main memory is our understanding of multiprogramming.

Loader software

A program may not occupy the same memory locations each time it is loaded and run. For example, consider three programs A, B and C loaded into memory on one occasion (Figure 3.1.2a). On another occasion they are loaded into different locations (Figure 3.1.2b).

The processor needs to know the whereabouts of every program instruction otherwise it cannot

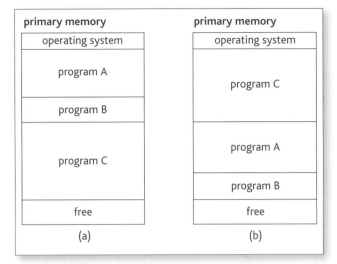

Figure 3.1.2   Programs loaded into memory on separate occasions.

execute the programs. This movement of the program instructions around in memory presents a major problem for the operating system. It is solved by a special program called the **loader**. The loader can remember exactly where everything is every time it is loaded. We consider loaders in more detail in Chapter 3.2.

A further problem occurs if two or more users wish to use the same program at the same time. For example, suppose user X and user Y both wish to use a compiler at the same time. Clearly it is wasteful of memory if two copies of the compiler have to be loaded into main memory. It would make much more sense if both programs are stored in main memory along with a single copy of the compiler, as shown in Figure 3.1.3.

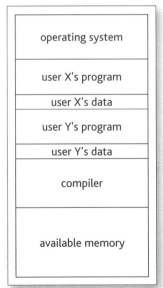

Figure 3.1.3   Two users sharing a single process.

Now, the two processes can use the compiler in turn. There are two different sets of data for the compiler, user X's program and user Y's program. These two sets of data and the outputs from the compiler for the two programs must be kept separate. Programs working in this way – where two data sets are worked on by the same program – are called *re-entrant*.

Memory management

The process of the operating system managing the use of the computer's primary memory (rather than the user doing it) is known as **memory management**. The issues are straightforward. The memory management module within the OS must:

- keep track of memory used
- keep track of memory which is available
- make memory available when a program finishes execution
- constantly check whether or not there is enough memory available to load a new program
- ensure that two loaded programs do not attempt to use the same memory space.

Scheduling

The OS must have a strategy for deciding which program is next given use of the processor. This process of deciding on the allocation of processor usage is known as low-level **scheduling**.

We need to be careful when using the term "scheduling". The allocation of processor time is strictly called **low-level scheduling**. The term scheduling can also be used to describe the order in which new programs are loaded into primary memory. This is **high-level scheduling**.

Memory management, scheduling and spooling are described in more detail in the following sections.

(3.1 b) Using interrupts

The fundamental process of the Von Neumann **computer architecture** executes a sequence of program instructions stored in main memory. The **fetch–execute cycle** is shown in Figure 3.1.4 (see page 184).

This is satisfactory so long as the processor successfully decodes (makes sense) of each program instruction and the program being run maintains the control of the processor. Unfortunately things do go

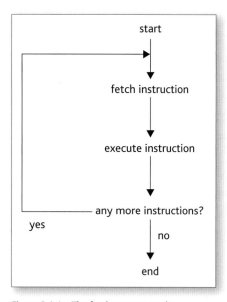

Figure 3.1.4 The fetch–execute cycle.

wrong and sometimes the normal order of operation needs to be changed. For example, if a program has used up all the time allocated for its use of the processor, it is necessary to stop that program running (in order to be fair to all the other loaded programs). This is the overall aim of any scheduling strategy. It must be "fair" to all the loaded programs, i.e. they all get some usage of the processor.

These changes in order are instigated by **interrupts**, which are messages sent to the processor. A device or program uses an interrupt to say "Can you stop what you are doing and give me some time, please?" There are a number of different types of interrupt:

- An I/O interrupt is generated by an I/O device to signal that a data transfer is complete or an error has occurred, e.g. that a printer is out of paper or is not connected.
- A timer interrupt is generated by an internal clock to indicate that the processor must attend to some time-critical activity (see "Scheduling, job queues and priorities" on page 185).
- A hardware interrupt is generated by, for example, a power failure which indicates that the OS must close down as safely as possible.
- A program interrupt is generated by an error in a program. For example, a violation of memory use (trying to use part of the memory reserved by the OS for some other program) generates a program interrupt. An attempt to execute an invalid instruction (e.g. trying to compute a "division by zero") also generates a program interrupt.

If the OS is to manage interrupts, the sequence in Figure 3.1.4 is modified as shown in Figure 3.1.5. After the execution of an instruction, the processor checks to see if an interrupt has occurred. If so, the OS services the interrupt if it is more important than the task already being carried out. This involves running a program called the **interrupt service routine (ISR)**. Every interrupt signal, e.g. "printer out of paper", has its own ISR that "services" the interrupt.

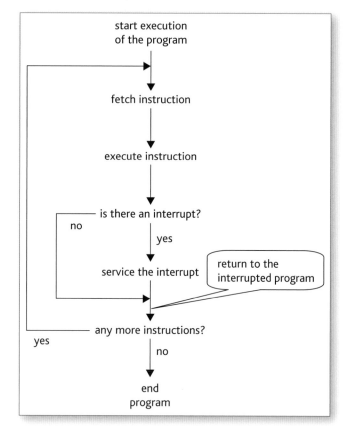

Figure 3.1.5 The fetch–execute cycle with an interrupt.

There is no problem in doing this (after all, the computer can follow sets of instructions very easily) but a problem arises from the fact that the original program has not completed. If interrupts are used too often, no program will actually complete its execution. The real problem here is "how can the OS arrange for the interrupted program to resume from exactly where it left off?" In order to do this, the contents of all the registers in the processor are saved so that the OS can later restore them to carry on with the execution of the interrupted program. Chapter 3.3 describes the registers and their purpose as well as explaining the fetch–execute cycle in detail.

Another problem the OS has to deal with is what happens if an interrupt occurs while another interrupt is being serviced. There are several ways of dealing with this but the simplest solution is to place the interrupts in a queue and only allow return to the originally interrupted program when the queue is empty. Alternative strategies are explained in the next section. Taking the simplest case, the order of processing is as shown in Figure 3.1.6.

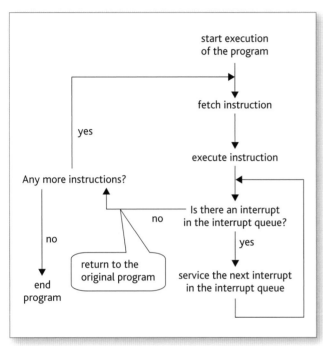

Figure 3.1.6 The fetch–execute cycle with multiple interrupts.

The interrupts are held in a queue, called a **priority queue**, very like the queue of customers waiting at the checkout in a supermarket. The position of individual interrupts in the queue is determined by their importance – the more important the process, the higher the priority. For example, the user pressing Ctrl–Alt–Del in the Windows OS has a high priority and pressing the computer's reset button has an even higher priority!

This concept of priorities is covered in detail in the next section and in Chapter 3.5.

Activity

Describe three different types of interrupt.

(3.1 c) Scheduling, job queues and priorities

One of the tasks of the OS is to allocate processor time in an appropriate way. This process is known as (low-level) scheduling because it creates a schedule of when things are done. The scheduling algorithm should ensure that the processor is working to its full potential.

The simplest strategy is to allocate each loaded program the same amount of time. When the "time slice" expires, the processor switches to the next program. However, we have already suggested that we might want to allocate priorities to jobs, i.e. to make one job more important than another.

Consider two programs loaded in a computer system owned by a large company: program A is printing wage slips for the employees and program B is analysing the sales of the company, which has a turnover of many millions of dollars. Program A makes little use of the processor because the calculations are very minor but it performs a lot of printing and is continually reading data from the disk drive. This is called an **I/O-bound job**. Program B makes a great deal of use of the processor. It collects one set of data from the drive and produces one printout at the end of processing. This is called a **processor-bound job**.

Which type of job should have a higher processor priority? If program B has priority over program A for use of the processor, it could be a long time before program A can print any wage slips because all program B's processing needs to be done before A gets a look in! Figure 3.1.7 (on page 186) shows what happens if program B has priority over A. Notice that the printer gets very little use.

It seems much fairer to let A do a bit of processing and then get on with using the printer (which takes a long time because of the comparatively slow speed of the printer) while B is allowed to use the processor. Figure 3.1.8 (on page 186) shows what happens if A is given priority over B. This shows that the I/O-bound program can run in a reasonable time and the printer is used more effectively.

In the discussion which follows, we use the term "job" to mean any program which is currently loaded into primary memory.

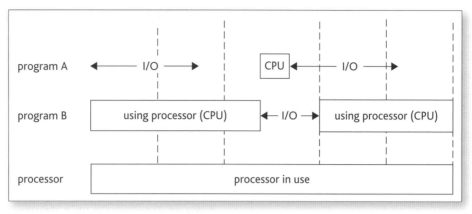

Figure 3.1.7   Scheduling two programs: B has priority so A spends time waiting.

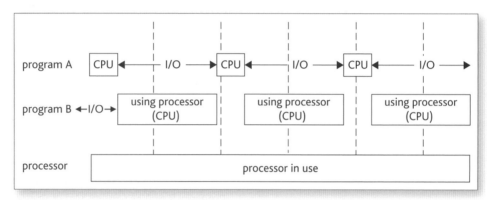

Figure 3.1.8   Scheduling two programs: A has priority so spends less time waiting.

Input/output-bound and processor-bound jobs

Different types of program need differing amounts of processor time. A program which is constantly re-calculating matrix computations in order to display 3-D graphics needs lots of processor time and is said to be "processor bound". A program that runs a database query and is constantly having to read data records from a hard disk is said to be "I/O bound".

These examples suggest that the OS should give:
- high priority to I/O-bound programs
- low priority to processor-bound programs.

Consider the following types of application. It should be clear that they should all have high priority:
- safety-critical applications
- online applications, e.g. users at terminals running interactive programs, customers using bank ATMs
- real-time applications (discussed in Chapter 1.2).

For example, a computer monitoring the temperature and pressure in a chemical process whilst analysing readings taken over a period of time must give high priority to the control program. If the temperature or pressure goes out of a pre-defined range, the control program must change immediately.

Batch-processing programs (discussed in Chapters 1.2 and 1.7) should have low priority.

Objectives of scheduling

The objectives of scheduling are to:
- maximise the use of the whole of the computer system
- be fair to all programs
- provide a reasonable response time:
  - to users in front of online applications programs at a terminal
  - to batch-processing programs (i.e. to meet the deadline for production of the final output)
- prevent the computer system failing if it is becoming overloaded
- ensure that the system is consistent by giving similar response times to similar activities.

The following factors need to be considered when assessing if the objective can be met:
- priority: low priority to processor-bound jobs

- type of job:
  - real-time processing must be done quickly so that the next input can be affected
  - batch processing only has to meet the deadline for final outputs
- resource requirements: the amount of processor time needed to complete the job, the memory required, the amount of I/O time needed
- waiting time: the time the job has been waiting to be loaded into main memory.

Job status

In order to understand how scheduling is carried out we must assess the current state of any program. All currently loaded jobs are in one of the following states:

- **ready** – the job is waiting for use of the processor
- **running** – the job is currently using the processor
- **blocked** – the job is unable to use the processor at present.

If we only have one printer and it is currently being used, a second job is blocked waiting for it to become available.

Figure 3.1.9 shows how jobs may be moved from one state to another. Note that a job can only enter the *running* state from the *ready* state. There may be several jobs at any one time which are in either the *blocked* state or the *ready* state. The OS maintains a queue of jobs in each state. On a single-processor computer, only one job can be in the *running* state at a time (look back to Figure 3.1.1). When first loaded to primary memory, all jobs are in the *ready* state and (normally) only leave the system from the *running* state.

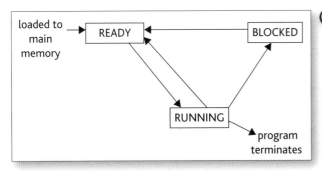

Figure 3.1.9   Moving a job between processor states.

When entering the system, a job is placed in the ready queue by the **high-level scheduler (HLS)**.

Moving jobs in and out of the ready state is done by the **low-level scheduler (LLS)**. The LLS decides the order in which jobs are placed in the running state, i.e. which job next uses the processor.

Scheduling strategies

How does the low-level scheduler decide which job uses the processor next if there is more than one job in the ready state?

The following "scheduling strategies" are common ways of deciding how jobs should be scheduled. They all have a "common sense" feel to them and are designed to address the basic aim to "get as much processing done by the computer system" as possible.

- Shortest job first: Jobs in the ready queue are sorted in ascending order of the total processing time the job is expected to need. New jobs are added to the queue in such a way as to preserve this order.
- Round robin: Each job is given a maximum length of processor time (a **time slice**) after which the job is put at the back of the ready queue and the job at the front of the queue is given use of the processor. If a job is completed before its time slice is used up, it leaves the system.
- Shortest remaining time: Jobs in the ready queue are sorted in ascending order of the remaining processing time the job is expected to need. This scheme favours short jobs. There is a danger of long jobs being prevented from running because they never manage to get to the front of the queue.

There are many other possible strategies the scheduler module could use.

3.1 d Memory management

In order for a job to be able to use the processor, the job must be loaded into the computer's main memory. If several jobs can be loaded – because the size of the memory permits it – the programs and their data must be protected from the actions of other jobs being processed.

Figure 3.1.10 (on page 188) shows jobs A, B, C and D loaded into the memory of a computer with a total of 130 MB available for application programs (remember that the OS itself uses some main memory). This is only one possible arrangement of the jobs.

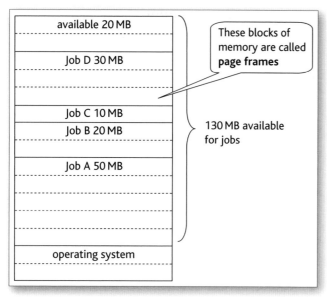

available 20 MB

Job D 30 MB

Job C 10 MB

Job B 20 MB

Job A 50 MB

operating system

These blocks of memory are called **page frames**

130 MB available for jobs

Figure 3.1.10 Jobs loaded into main memory.

Now suppose Job C terminates and Job E, requiring 25 MB of memory, is next to be loaded. Clearly Job E cannot be loaded into the space that Job C has relinquished. However, there is 20 + 10 = 30 MB of memory free in total. So the OS must find some way of using it. One solution is simply to move programs that are currently loaded and leave all the available memory in a continuous block. This would make heavy use of the processor as not only must all the instructions be moved, but all addresses used in the instructions would have to be relative addresses. Another way would be to leave A, B and D where they are and to split Job E into two parts, storing one part where Job C has been and the other part in the available space.

When jobs are loaded into memory, they may not always occupy the same locations. Instead of loading Jobs A, B, C and then D, assume that it is required to load Jobs A, B, D and E, in that order. Now Job D occupies different locations in memory to those shown in Figure 3.1.10. The programs would now use entirely different addresses.

Linkers and loaders

The OS has the task of loading the jobs (the high-level scheduler) and adjusting the addresses. The loader is a program that does both these tasks. The calculation of addresses can be done by recalculating each address

used in the instructions once the address of the first instruction is known.

An alternative is that relative addressing can be used. That is, addresses can be *compiled* as relative to the address used for the first instruction of the program. Software is required to link program blocks which are stored in non-continuous areas of memory – this is the **linker**. Linkers and loaders are integral to the management of the available memory space.

Paging

Notice in Figure 3.1.10 that the memory has been divided into equal-sized sections, called **pages**. (This is similar to the way in which the OS manages the filing system by dividing a program into allocation units.) Pages are of equal size and each job is allocated a number of pages. The allocated pages may be in order, as they are in Figure 3.1.10, or they may be scattered across the memory. The pages allocated to Job E in the above scenario will be scattered across the memory to gain enough space. Notice that the sizes of the pages are fixed and may not be totally convenient for the jobs being stored.

For example, the program instructions for Job E may need 21 MB of memory and the data may need 4 MB. If the work has to be split for storage, the logical way to do it would be 21 MB and 4 MB but this does not fit the predetermined page size of 10 MB. A characteristic of paging is that the divisions are pre-determined and the data and programs have to be loaded into the available memory to get the best fit possible.

The division of the available memory is into units called **page frames**. A program is divided into equal-sized blocks called pages.

Segmentation

Another way of splitting the job up is to see what the logical requirements of the job are. Job E may have 8 MB of program instructions, 4 MB of data and 13 MB of help files. The logical thing to do then is to divide the memory space required into three sections with sizes 4 MB, 8 MB and 13 MB. Now, these sizes required cannot be predicted in advance so it relies on the OS (or, to be precise, the linker and loader) to store each part of the program in memory. These "pieces" are called **segments** and this method of using memory is called **segmentation**.

Segmentation is far more complex to control than paging because of the different and unpredictable nature of the sizes of the segments.

Virtual memory

Paging and segmentation lead to another important technique called **virtual memory**. Jobs are loaded into memory when they are needed, using a paging technique. When a program is running, only those pages that contain required code need to be loaded.

For example, consider a word processor:

- Page 1 contains the program instructions to allow users to enter text and to alter text.
- Page 2 contains the code for formatting characters.
- Page 3 contains the code for formatting paragraphs.
- Page 4 contains the code for cutting, copying and pasting.

When the word processor program runs, only page 1 needs to be loaded initially. If the user wants to format some characters so that they are in bold, then page 2 must be available. Similarly, if the user wishes to copy and paste a piece of text, page 4 must be loaded. When other facilities are needed, the appropriate page can be loaded. If the user wishes to format more characters, the OS does not need to load page 2 again as it is already loaded.

The loading of program pages from the hard drive takes a relatively long time. If there is not enough space in memory to have all pages stored then the movement of pages into memory can take a disproportionate amount of time. This has led to the creation of small amounts of fast access storage between the drive and the memory. This storage is known as virtual memory because it is *virtually* as fast to access as the memory. The OS now has part of the program in memory and part on the hard drive. What it needs to do is to predict which pages are most likely to be accessed next and store them in virtual memory.

The use of **library (DLL) files** fits exactly with this strategy for managing the memory. A commercial program such as Microsoft Word has one main executable (EXE) file which is loaded initially. The code for other features, such as the spelling checker, could be contained in a separate DLL file which is only loaded into main memory when required.

3.1 e Spooling

In a multiprogramming, multi-access or network system, several jobs may wish to use the peripheral devices at the same time. It is essential that the input and output for different jobs do not become mixed up while they are waiting to be output. This can be achieved using **spooling**.

Two or more jobs may be sent to a printer at similar times (for example, in a classroom at the end of a lesson when everyone wants a printout). A printer can only cope with one job at a time so the jobs are sent to a spool queue on a fast access storage device, such as a disk. They are queued on the disk, ready for the printer to deal with them in order.

Be careful. The last paragraph is the usual explanation of spooling, but it gives the wrong impression. What actually happens is that the jobs for the printer are stored as files on the hard drive. The only thing that is stored in the spool queue is a reference to where the print file is located. When the reference to that job gets to the top of the queue, the file is retrieved from storage and sent to the printer (see Figure 3.1.11 on page 190).

Another problem is that a spool queue is not necessarily a "first-in–first-out" queue. Such a conventional queue would put new jobs (or references to them) at the end of the queue. In a spool queue, the more important jobs can be inserted further up the queue; in other words, they jump the queue. This is because some jobs can be more important than others.

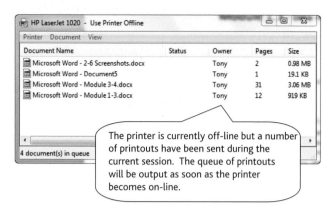

Figure 3.1.11   Print queue on the Windows operating system.

The printer is currently off-line but a number of printouts have been sent during the current session. The queue of printouts will be output as soon as the printer becomes on-line.

The data structure then becomes a **priority queue**. So, when talking about a spool queue of jobs remember that it isn't really a queue of the jobs, only a queue of *references* to them and it is something of a strange queue because it might allow "pushing in".

It should be noted that spooling not only keeps output from different jobs separate, it also saves the user having to wait for the processor until the output is actually printed by a printer (a relatively slow device). It lets the processor get on with further processing while the jobs are queued up. Spooling is used on personal computers as well as on large computer systems capable of multiprogramming.

Memory management in Windows 7

Figure 3.1.12 illustrates many of the points discussed. The Windows 7 Task Manager utility (top) shows the large number of programs and processes which are running before the user loads any applications software. The user then loads the Windows Media Player. The Task Manager utility (bottom) reports the large increase in processor usage.

The Task Manager utility also shows:
- the usage of the kernel part of the OS
- the current usage of memory
- that Windows uses paged memory allocation.

3.1 f   Components of a desktop PC

There are basically two types of OS used on PCs and they are distinguished by their user interface, command driven or graphical. Probably the best known of these are Unix (command driven) and various versions of Windows (GUI). They differ in the way the user uses them

and the tasks that can be carried out. In this discussion, we concentrate on Windows but other operating systems provide similar facilities, i.e. create folders or directories.

File management

File management allows the user to copy, delete and move files as well as letting the user create a hierarchical structure for storing files, i.e. create **folders** or **directories**.

Multi-tasking

Windows was preceded by a command-line OS known as MS-DOS. It used very limited main memory and could only run one program at a time.

Windows allows the user to use much more memory and it supports multi-tasking. This is when the user opens more than one program at a time and can move from one to another. It looks to the user as if the OS is handling both programs at once. In fact, the OS is swapping between the tasks so fast that the user is not aware of the swapping.

Activity

Try opening a word processor and the Clipboard in Windows at the same time. Adjust the sizes of the windows so that you can see both. Now mark a piece of text and copy it. You can see the text appear in the clipboard window although it is not the active window. This is because the OS can handle both tasks, apparently at the same time.

Another good example of multi-tasking is to run the Windows Clock application while using another program. You see that the clock is keeping time although you are using another software application.

Try playing a music file using Windows Media Player while writing a report in a word processor and keeping an eye open for any new emails that might arrive.

The OS guarantees the use of a block of memory to an application program and protects this memory from being accessed by other application programs or system files. If an application program needs to use a particular hardware peripheral, Windows loads the appropriate device driver.

The "boot up" process

The sequence of **boot up** actions that takes place when a PC is switched on is listed on page 192.

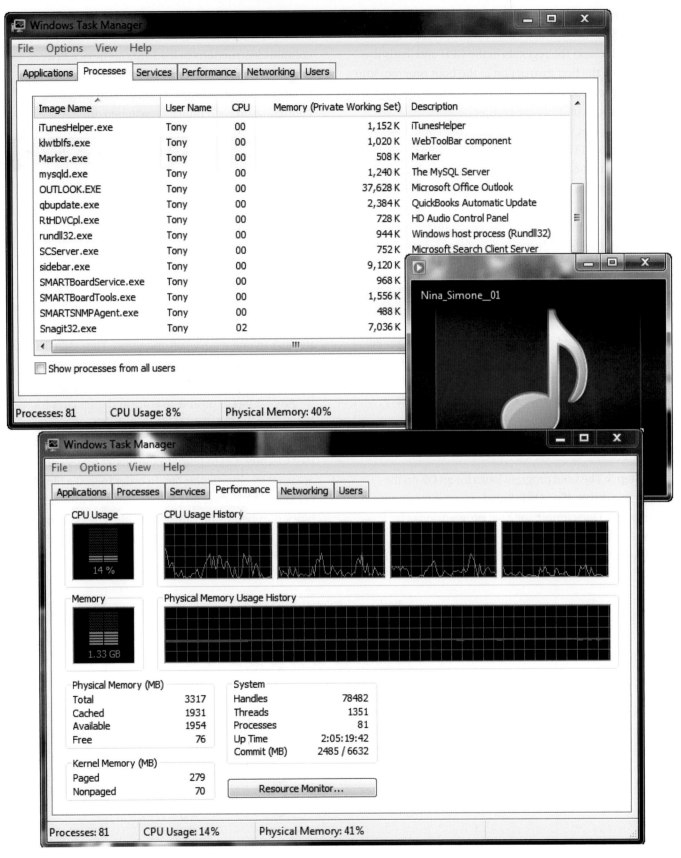

Figure 3.1.12   Processes running in Windows 7.

Step 1: Run the power-on-self-test (POST) routine. The POST routine resides in permanent memory (ROM). It clears the registers in the CPU and loads the address of the first instruction in the boot program into the program counter (PC) register (see Chapter 3.3 for details of special-purpose registers).

Step 2: Run the boot program, which first checks itself and the POST program. The boot program is stored in read-only memory (ROM) and contains the basic input/output system (BIOS) structure. The CPU then sends signals to check that all the hardware is working properly. This includes checking the buses, system clock, RAM, disk drives and keyboard.

Step 3: The boot program looks for an OS on the available drives. If no OS is found, an error message is produced. Once found, the boot program looks for files which contain the *kernel* – the core part of the OS. The prime task of the kernel is to act as the interrupt handler.

Step 4: The OS searches the root directory on the disk for a boot file (such as CONFIG.SYS) that contains instructions to load various device drivers. A file (such as AUTOEXEC.BAT) is then loaded to ensure that the computer starts with the same configuration each time it is switched on.

File allocation table (FAT)

The disk-formatting process divides each track on the disk into **sectors** or **blocks**. One block is the minimum amount of data which can be written to or read from the disk in one read/write operation. These blocks are called **file allocation units** and the size of a block in Windows 7 is 16 kilobytes.

Any OS has to be able to store and then later locate files on the disk. To do this, the OS uses a **file allocation table (FAT)**. This table uses a linked list (see Chapter 3.4) to point to the blocks on disk that are used by a particular file. In order to find a file, the OS looks in the directory for the filename and gets the block number for the start of the file. The OS can then follow the pointers in the FAT to find the other blocks used to store that file (Figure 3.1.13).

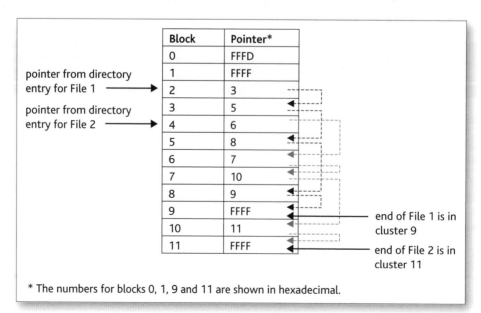

Block	Pointer*
0	FFFD
1	FFFF
2	3
3	5
4	6
5	8
6	7
7	10
8	9
9	FFFF
10	11
11	FFFF

pointer from directory entry for File 1 → 2

pointer from directory entry for File 2 → 4

end of File 1 is in cluster 9

end of File 2 is in cluster 11

* The numbers for blocks 0, 1, 9 and 11 are shown in hexadecimal.

Figure 3.1.13   A file allocation table (FAT).

In the FAT, unused blocks have a zero entry. Thus, when a file is deleted, the clusters that were used to save the file can be set to zero. In order to store a new file, the OS finds the first cluster with a zero entry. It enters the cluster number in the directory for the new file. Now the OS only has to search linearly for blocks with a zero entry to set up the linked list for the new file.

It may seem that using a linear search will take a long time. However, the FAT is normally loaded into RAM so that continual disk accesses can be avoided. This speeds up the searching of the FAT.

Summary

- The main aims and features of an operating system are to manage the resources of the computer system:
  - processor management – for multiprogramming, the low-level scheduler must decide which job will get the next use of the processor
  - decide on appropriate scheduling algorithms
  - file management – maintaining a list of files, directories and which file allocation units belong to which files
  - input/output management – control of all input and output devices attached to the computer
  - memory management – using strategies such as segmentation and paging and the high-level scheduler to decide which jobs will be loaded next.
- Peripherals and processes that want to use the processor send an interrupt:
  - a program interrupt signals an error in a program.
  - an I/O interrupt signals that a data transfer is complete or an error has occurred.
  - a timer interrupt signals that a time-critical activity needs attention.
  - a hardware error signals that some device has failed.
- After the processor finishes executing an instruction, it checks the priority queue of interrupts.
- High-priority interrupts are serviced before the processor continues with the next instruction.
- Every interrupt signal has its own interrupt service routine (ISR) that services the interrupt.
- The state of registers and memory is stored before an ISR runs in order that the interrupted process can resume from the same point.
- Scheduling tries to ensure that the processor is working to its full potential:
  - that the processor is not idle, waiting for I/O
  - that I/O-bound processes do not wait for the processor when they only need to use it a little
  - that processor-bound processes do not block other processes.
- The scheduler has a choice of strategy for deciding which job gets the use of the processor next:
  - shortest job first
  - round robin
  - shortest remaining time.
- Jobs must be loaded into the computer's main memory to use the processor.
- Each job must be protected from the actions of other jobs.
- Linker and loader software load and keep track of processes and their data.

⟶

Test yourself

1. Explain how an interrupt is handled by a processor which is working on another task. [4]
2. State **three** different types of interrupt that may occur and say in what order the three interrupts would be handled if they all arrived at the processor together, giving a reason for your answer. [5]
3. Explain the difference between:
   i.   an input/output-bound job
   ii. a processor-bound job.
   Explain how the computer should prioritise the two types of job if it is going to make maximum use of the processor. [4]
4. Describe **two** types of scheduling that are used by computer processing systems. [4]
5. Explain how interrupts are used in a round robin scheduling operating system. [3]
6. a. Explain the difference between paging and segmenting when referring to memory management by the operating system. [2]
   b. Describe how virtual memory can allow a word processor and a spreadsheet to run simultaneously in the memory of a computer even though both pieces of software are too large to fit into the computer's memory. [3]
7. Describe how a PC operating system uses a file allocation table when storing and retrieving files. [4]

3.2 The functions and purposes of translators

When computers were first used programs had to be written in **machine code**. This code comprised simple instructions, each of which was represented by a binary pattern in the processor. To write programs, a programmer had to code every instruction in binary. This not only took a long time but was prone to errors. The process of taking these programs and setting up a computer in such a way that it would follow the instructions was so complex that only mathematicians were capable of doing it. If this had not changed, then we would probably not be able to use computers in the way we do today.

The problems were caused by the fact that people had to present the instructions in a form the processor could understand, i.e. as machine operations. In order that computers could be used anywhere other than research institutions, human beings needed a method of communicating with the computer which was closer to *human* communication than to *machine* operations.

As the processor cannot understand anything but binary, this implies the need for a language which matches the computer's instruction set. If the program written by the programmer is not in machine code then it must be translated into machine code.

Turning assembly language into machine code
Machine code

Every processor has a set of basic machine operations which it can carry out. The complete set of machine operations is called the *instruction set* for that processor. Table 3.2.1 gives a flavour of what machine operations are like. Each operation is represented by a machine code (shown in binary). This is called the **operation code** or **opcode**.

Table 3.2.1 Machine operations.

Opcode	Operation
001	Add a number
010	Subtract a number
011	Input a value
100	Output a value
101	Store a value in a memory location
110	Get a value from a memory location

Some of the operations in Table 3.2.1 need a second or third piece of data in order to carry out the instruction. This "other" piece of data that makes up the program instruction is called the **operand**. It may be a number or a memory address.

A machine instruction consists of an opcode and an operand.

Table 3.2.1 is a restricted set of operations but it serves to illustrate the workings of a processor. Imagine that the processor stores every instruction as a byte. It would use:
- three bits for the opcode
- five bits for the operand.

This only allows 32 possible addresses but it serves as an illustration.

If the processor is given the program instruction 00100001, it splits the instruction into two parts: 001 and 00001. The opcode 001 means that something has to be added. The operand 00001 is the address in memory of the value that has to be added. The value stored in location 00001 in memory is added to the contents of the *accumulator* (see below and Chapter 3.3).

The program instruction 00100001 is therefore understandable by humans (as we have a list of the opcodes) and the processor. However, imagine a program with thousands of instructions that look like this. It really would be almost impossible for a human to follow. Human beings need a bit of help. They need a language other than binary if they are going to be able to understand a large program.

Assembly language

The first attempt at making programs more understandable was to use a mnemonic in place of the binary opcodes, as shown in Table 3.2.2.

Table 3.2.2 Assembly language mnemonics.

Opcode	Operation	Mnemonic
001	Add a number	ADD
010	Subtract a number	SUB
011	Input a value	IN
100	Output a value	OUT
101	Store a value in a memory location	STO
110	Get a value from a memory location	GET

Consider a program in binary and the equivalent program using mnemonics:

Machine code program	Assembly language program	Description
011 0011	IN 3	Load the value 3 to the processor
001 0101	ADD 5	Add 5 to this value
100 0000	OUT	Output the current value
101 1111	STO 15	Store the value at memory address 15

Note that some instructions, e.g. OUT, do not have an operand. The assembly language version assumes we can code numbers as decimal values.

Stop and think which program is easier for the programmer to code and understand.

Where exactly in the processor are these calculations taking place? The answer is in a special register called the **accumulator**.

Using labels for addresses

There are still problems because the references to locations in memory are written as binary or decimal numbers. The operand shows a particular memory address so we could give this location a name, or **label**. The program in the activity above simply adds two values together. Instead of referring to these values by their addresses (00100 and 00101), why not just call them NUM1 and NUM2?

The program then becomes:

```
IN
STO NUM1
IN
STO NUM2
GET NUM1
ADD NUM2
OUT
```

Using mnemonics to represent opcodes and labels to represent the memory locations makes the program code very much easier for the programmer to understand. The use of labels for memory addresses is called **symbolic addressing**.

The need for translator software

However, it is impossible for a computer to execute this assembly language code because it is not in machine code. It is now necessary for the computer to use a **translator** program to turn the original program into machine code. This translator program is called an **assembler** and programs written in this way are said to be written in **assembly language**.

The assembly process is relatively simple because assembly language has a one-to-one relationship with machine code. That is, every assembly language instruction translates into exactly one machine code instruction.

Basically, the assembler must translate the mnemonics into binary, which is done by having a simple lookup table with the mnemonics in one column and the binary machine code equivalents alongside. The labels are a bit more complicated. The assembler does the translation in the same way, but the table contents are not known before translation starts. The list of labels and their actual memory address values have to be created by the assembler. As the program is read, the assembler recognises the first label, NUM1, and allocates an actual memory location for NUM1 relative to the address used to store the first instruction. In this way, the assembler builds its own lookup table of labels used by the assembly language program.

3.2 c Interpretation and compilation

We have discussed how assembly language was used to make program writing easier. Assembly language allows the use of mnemonics and labels for memory addresses. Writing programs in assembly language, although easier than using machine code, is still tedious and takes a long time. Assembly languages are still "machine oriented", i.e. their instruction set is very much in terms of the what the computer architecture can do.

After assembly languages, high-level languages were developed. They are closer to the language that people use for communication. That is, the languages were designed to more closely resemble the *task* or problem the computer program was attempting to solve. However, programs written in these high-level languages also need to be translated into machine code. This is done by a compiler or an interpreter.

Compiler software

As high-level languages are more complex and further away from machine code, so the translators had to become more complicated. Each new programming language that was created led to the need for a translator for that particular language called a **compiler**. Hence to write high-level programs in language XYZ, the programmer must have compiler software for language XYZ.

A compiler takes a program written in a high-level language (called the **source program**, which is made up of **source code**) and translates it into an equivalent program in machine code (called the **object program** or object file, which is made up of **object code**). Once this is done, the machine code version can be loaded into the machine and executed without any further involvement of the compiler. The compilation process is shown in Figure 3.2.1.

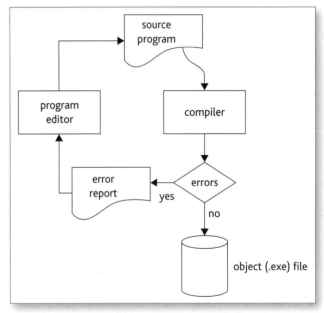

Figure 3.2.1   The compilation process.

The advantages of compilation are that:
- The final object (.exe) file can easily be distributed to many users.
- Once the .exe file is produced, users do not need the compiler software.
- Users have no sight of the original source code and so there is no risk that it could be changed.

The disadvantages of compilation are that:
- The final object file is only produced when *all* errors in the source code have been located and fixed.

- The development process can be long-winded with several runs of the compiler before finally all the errors are located and the object file produced.
- The compilation process uses a lot of computer resources.

During the compilation process, memory contains:

- the compiler software
- the programmer's source code
- the resulting object code
- sufficient memory for working storage while the translation is taking place.

Interpreter

Some programming languages are translated by an **interpreter**. In this process, the programmer can attempt to run the program as soon as (some of) the source code is created. The interpreter identifies each instruction in sequence and executes it until a statement is found which contains an error. At this point the program terminates and the programmer is shown the instruction in the program which generated the error.

Each instruction is executed before the next instruction is identified. This system was developed because early personal computers lacked the power and memory needed for compilation. It is also used in some programming for the web. Interpretation has the advantage of producing an error message as soon as an error is encountered. This means that the instruction causing the problem can be easily identified.

The advantages of interpretation are that:

- The programmer can attempt to run the program at any time, including before all the code has been written.
- Debugging is generally easier and faster using an interpreter.

The disadvantages of interpretation are that:

- Execution of a program is slow compared to that of a compiled program:
  - The original program has to be translated every time it is executed.
  - Instructions inside a loop are translated each time the loop is entered.
- The interpreter software has to be present in memory every time an attempt is made to run the program.

- No final .exe (object file) is produced:
  - So all users of the program must have the interpreter software available.
  - The code is not protected – other programmers could make unwanted changes to the code as the source code is always present.

The best of both worlds!

Earlier version of Visual Basic – up to version 6 – provided a programming environment which contained both an interpreter and a compiler. This enabled the programmer to use the interpreter during program development, making the finding of errors much easier. When the program was working, it could be translated by the compiler into machine code to speed up program execution. The machine code version (the .exe file) could then be distributed to users who would not have access to the original code.

Sadly the latest Visual Basic .NET versions carry out a "compilation" when the user attempts to run the program. If errors are found and reported then they must be corrected.

Activity

A piece of software is being developed for sale to the public. Explain when a compiler would be used and when an interpreter would be used.

The stages of translation

The problem with translation, once past the simple assembler standard, is that it is not simply a matter of looking things up in a table. The languages have command words in them that may need many simple machine code instructions to carry them out. This implies that the translator must have an "understanding" of what the various commands do.

The meaning of a command can change dependent on where in the code it is placed, what comes before it and what is included in the instruction itself. This means that there is an element of a need to "understand" what the code is doing. The word *understand* has been emphasised because the translator does not really understand the program in the sense that we do. However, there is certainly an understanding that goes beyond simple lookup tables.

In order to translate a high-level language program using a compiler, there are three stages to the compilation process:

- lexical analysis
- syntax analysis
- code generation.

At each of these stages, the compiler considers the code with a specific objective. The source program is broken down into its constituent parts in a process called **parsing**. The next three sections explain what the compiler does at each of the three stages.

3.2 d Lexical analysis

During **Lexical analysis**, the lexical analyser uses the source program as input. It turns the high-level language code into a stream of **tokens** for the next stage of compilation.

A token replaces a group of characters in the code. So, a keyword, such as PRINT, is replaced by a token, such as 0011110100011110, that represents this part of the high-level language statement. Single characters that have a meaning in their own right are replaced by their ASCII values (see Chapter 1.3).

Variable names need to have additional information stored about them and this is done by creating a *symbol table*. This table is used throughout compilation to build up information about the identifier names used in the source program. So when a variable name, for instance NoOfChildren, is met for the first time, it is placed in the table. During the lexical analysis stage, only the variable's name is noted. It is during the next stage that details such as the variable's type and scope are added to the symbol table.

The lexical analyser may output some error messages and diagnostics. For example, it can report errors such as a keyword which is not entered properly. If PINT has been entered the error may be found because there is no token that can replace it. Similarly, the lexical analyser has rules for valid variable names (e.g. fewer than 64 characters and not starting with a digit character) and it spots errors when it tries to enter them into the symbol table.

At various stages during compilation, it is necessary to look up details about, and add further details to, the names in the symbol table. This must be done efficiently; a linear search may not be sufficiently fast. In fact, it is usual to use random access to the name entries in the table. This is done by creating a hash table (see hashing Chapter 1.3). When two names are hashed to the same address, there must be a strategy for dealing with this (in common with any application where hashing is used).

The lexical analyser also removes redundant characters such as white space (spaces, tabs, etc.) and comments. The lexical analysis may take longer than the other stages of compilation. This is because it has to handle the original source code, which can have many formats. For example, the following two pieces of code are equivalent although their format is considerably different.

```
IF Num1 = Num2            IF Num1 = Num2
  THEN                        THEN Answer
    'square Num1           := Num1 * Num1
    Answer := Num1 *       ELSE Answer :=
    Num1                      Num2 * Num2
  ELSE                      ENDIF
    'square Num2           PRINT Answer
    Answer := Num2 *
    Num2
ENDIF
PRINT Answer
```

When the lexical analyser has completed its task, the code is in a standard format, which means that the next stage can always expect the format of its input to be consistent.

3.2 e Syntax analysis

This section should be read in conjunction with "Backus–Naur Form and syntax diagrams" in Chapter 3.5 (page 251).

The **syntax analysis** stage starts with the output produced from the lexical analysis stage. During syntax analysis, the code is parsed to see that it is grammatically correct. All languages have rules of grammar and computer languages are no exception. The grammar of programming languages can be defined by the use of **Backus–Naur Form (BNF)** notation or a **syntax diagram**. It is against these rules that the code has to be checked.

For example, taking a very elementary language, an assignment statement and an expression may be defined to be of the following forms:

```
<statement> = <variable><assignment_
              operator><expression>
<expression> = <variable><arithmetic_
              operator><variable>
```

In the syntax analysis stage, the parser must take the output from the lexical analyser and check that it is of this form.

If the original statement is:

```
Sum := Sum + NewNumber
```

The parser receives:

```
<variable><assignment_operator>
        <variable><arithmetic_operator>
                            <variable>
```

which can be simplified to:

```
<variable><assignment_operator>
                    <expression>
```

and then:

```
<statement>
```

which it concludes is a valid statement.

If the original statement is:

```
Sum := Sum + + NewNumber
```

It is parsed as:

```
<variable><assignment_operator> <variable>
        <arithmetic_operator><arithmetic_
                    operator><variable>
```

which does *not* represent a valid statement and an error message is returned.

At this stage, invalid identifier names can be found if they were not spotted earlier. PINT may have been read as a variable during lexical analysis. This means that the statement containing PINT is not a valid statement because it does not contain a keyword. In languages that require variables to be declared before being used, the lexical analyser may pick up this error because PINT is not declared as a variable and so is not found in the symbol table.

During syntax analysis, certain **semantic checks** are carried out. A semantic check simply means a check on the meaning of the statements; what they are meant to do. These include label checks, flow of control checks and declaration checks.

For example, some languages contain GOTO statements that allow control to be passed, unconditionally, to a statement that has a label. The GOTO statement specifies the label to which control must be passed by using the label in the program code. For example:

```
GOTO Start
```

The compiler must check that such a label exists.

Certain control constructs can only be placed in certain parts of a program. For example in C (and C++) the Continue statement can only be placed inside a loop. The compiler must ensure that statements like this are used in the correct places.

Many languages insist on the programmer declaring variables and their data types before they are used. It is at this stage that the compiler verifies that all variables and constants have been properly declared and that they are used correctly. Data types and other details, such as the parts of the code where it is valid, are added to the entries in the symbol table.

Most compilers report errors during syntax analysis as soon as they are found and attempt to show where the error has occurred. However, they may not be very accurate in their conclusions and the error message may not be clear.

To summarise, the word "syntax" means the set of rules that must be followed and it is syntax analysis which checks that the various rules of the language have been followed by every statement in the source code.

3.2 f Code generation and optimisation

After lexical and syntax analysis, all the errors due to incorrect use of the language have been removed and the source code has been transformed into a form that the compiler can understand. Code must now be produced which can be understood by the computer's processor. This stage is known as **code generation** because it produces the object code (i.e. the .exe file).

During lexical and syntax analysis, a table of variables and labels has been built up which includes details of the variable name, its type and the block in which it is valid. When a variable is encountered during code generation, the address of the variable is computed and stored in the symbol table.

The compiler can then produce the machine code that is required by the computer by directly translating from the tokens to the binary code, using lookup tables. A more detailed discussion of the process follows but the syllabus does not expect you to know this.

Extension

Two methods can be used to represent the high-level language in machine code. One uses a tree structure and the other a three-address code (TAC).

A TAC allows no more than three operands and instructions take the form:

```
Operand₁ := Operand₂ Operator Operand₃
```

For example, using three-address code, the assignment statement

```
A := (B + C) * (D – E) / F
```

can be evaluated in the following order, where R_i represents an intermediate result:

```
R₁ := B + C
R₂ := D – E
R₃ := R₁ * R₂
A := R₃ / F
```

This can also be represented by the tree shown in Figure 3.2.2.

→

Extension continued …

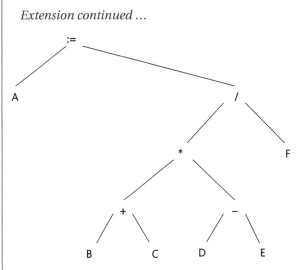

Figure 3.2.2   A parsed statement represented by a tree.

Other statements can be represented in a similar way and the final stage of compilation can then take place.

The compiler finally considers the type of code that is required. Code can be produced which has the following objectives:

- It executes as quickly as possible.
- The least amount of code possible is produced.

These two objectives will sometimes be in conflict and the final code is a compromise between the two.

Consider the following example code:

```
IN
STO Num1
IN
STO Num2
GET Num1
ADD Num2
OUT
```

(Note: It is reproduced here in assembly language form so that we can more easily understand what is happening.)

This code works perfectly well – it adds two numbers and produces the correct output. However, the two values `Num1` and `Num2` have been stored first when there seems to be no reason for doing so.

Consider the following sequence of instructions:

```
IN
STO X
IN
ADD X
OUT
```

This code produces the same result as the original program but requires two fewer instructions and less access to memory (always time consuming) and uses up less valuable memory space.

The two versions carry out the same task but one is far better in computing terms than the other. This process of trying to improve the code is called **code optimisation**.

Extension

In Figure 3.2.3, the code on the left has been changed to that on the right so that `r1 * b` is only evaluated once. These code fragments achieve the same result.

```
a = 5 + 3          a = 5 + 3
b = 5 * 3          b = 5 * 3
r1 = a + b         r1 = a + b
r2 = r1 * b        r2 = r1 * b
r3 = r2 / a        r3 = r2 / a
r4 = r1 * b        r4 = r2
r5 = r4 + 6        r5 = r4 + 6
c = r3 - r5        c = r3 - r5
   (a)                (b)
```

Figure 3.2.3   Optimising code – equivalent statements.

However, care must be taken when doing this. It does not work in Figure 3.2.4 because the value of `b` changes between the two evaluations of `r1 * b`. Hence the code on the right is not equivalent to that on the left.

Extension continued …

```
a = 5 + 3          a = 5 + 3
b = 5 * 3          b = 5 * 3
r1 = a + b         r1 = a + b
r2 = r1 * b        r2 = r1 * b
r3 = r2 / a        r3 = r2 / a
b = b + 2          b = b + 2
r4 = r1 * b        r4 = r2
r5 = r4 + 6        r5 = r4 + 6
c = r3 - r5        c = r3 - r5
   (a)                (b)
```

Figure 3.2.4   Optimising code – statements that are not equivalent.

In Figure 3.2.3b, there is a copy statement `r4 = r2`. This means that `r4` and `r2` represent the same value and hence one of them can be removed. This leads to the following code:

```
a = 5 + 3
b = 5 * 3
r1 = a + b
r2 = r1 * b
r3 = r2 / a
r5 = r2 + 6
c = r3 - r5
```

Another way of optimising code is to use algebraic transformations. This sounds very complicated but is really very simple. Table 3.2.3 shows some equivalent statements.

Table 3.2.3   Algebraic transformation.

Statement	Transformation
a = b * 1	a = b
a = b + 0	a = b

There are many other techniques for optimising code, but they are beyond the requirements of the syllabus.

3.2 g Linkers, loaders and library routines

Programs are usually built up from small, self-contained blocks of code called subprograms, procedures or modules. Each of these may be separately compiled so there is not only a high-level language version of the code but also the compiled object code. It seems sensible that, if a module for carrying out a particular task has been written and compiled and shown to work, it should be saved so that it can be used again within other programs under development. If this is possible, it is a very useful programming technique as it results in "reusable code".

These modules are stored in an area known as a program library and the modules made available are library routines. Library routines are very valuable to programmers because they have already been written and tested so the programmer is saved a lot of work; the code exists in compiled form so it does not need to be re-compiled when it is used.

However, a problem immediately arises because variable names and memory addresses are different from one use of the library routine to the next. These problems are solved by two utility programs. A loader loads all the modules into memory and sorts out difficulties such as changes of addresses for the variables. A linker links the modules together by making sure that references from one module to another are correct. If one module calls another, it is important that the correct module is called and that the correct data are sent to the called module.

No further knowledge of these techniques is expected.

Activity

Explain how linkers and loaders are used with a program library to help a programmer who is writing a complex program.

Extension

Investigate the use of linking loaders and link editors.

(3.2 h) Compilation errors

When lexical analysis is being carried out, the keywords in the program code are identified and turned into tokens of binary numbers ready for the next phase. The lexical analyser expects to find the keyword in a lookup table that contains the appropriate replacement token. If there is an error in a keyword, the analyser does not find a reference to it in the lookup table.

The analyser may decide that the incorrect keyword is a variable. In that case, it inserts the name into the symbol table and does not report an error. However, if the language requires that variable names should be declared, the name is not recognised and an error diagnostic is output.

At the syntax analysis stage, it is recognised that keywords are missing and errors are reported. The task of the syntax analyser is to ensure that statements in the code follow the rules that are laid down for particular keywords (see Chapter 2.5). Errors are reported if the remainder of the statement does not match the "pattern" laid down for the specific keyword.

The compiler does not stop at the first error that it finds, as an interpreter would. It collects a list of all the errors and outputs them at the end of the compilation process. If a listing file is asked for, then the original source code is printed along with the errors that have been produced.

Notice that logical errors, such as calling the wrong module or statement or an arithmetic error, are not found by compilation because they indicate an error in the algorithm to solve the problem, not an error in translating that algorithm into machine code.

Summary

- Machine code is the set of instructions or operations, in binary, that a computer's processor uses.
- Assembly language is a set of mnemonics that match machine code instructions.
- An assembler is software which translates an assembly language program into machine code.

⟶

- An assembler looks up an assembly language mnemonic in a table and reads off the matching machine code instruction.
- Interpretation involves software that reads one source code instruction, interprets it and executes it before moving onto the next instruction.
- Compilation involves software that reads a complete source code program, analyses it and produces object code. The object code is executed without reference to the source code, at a later time (or even on a different computer).
  - During lexical analysis, the source code is checked and turned into a stream of tokens. Errors in the use of the language (such as misspelled keywords or incorrectly formed identifiers) are reported.
  - During syntax analysis, the output from the lexical analyser is checked against the grammar of the programming language. Errors in the use of the language (such as missing keywords) are reported.
  - In the code generation phase, the output from the syntax analyser is turned into optimised object code.
  - Optimisation tries to improve the code so that it takes as little processing time and memory as possible.
- A library routine is a precompiled, self-contained piece of code that can be used in the development of other programs.
- A loader loads modules (including library routines) into memory and sorts out memory allocations.
- A linker links modules together by making sure that references from one module to another are correct.
- Errors recognised during compilation (by the syntax and lexical analyser) are reported to the programmer, who must fix them before recompiling.

Test yourself

1. Explain why translation is important to the development of software on computer systems. [3]
2. a. Describe assembly language and the advantages of using assembly language rather than machine code. [4]
   b. Explain why the relationship between machine code and assembly language can be described as one-to-one. [1]
3. The following table is a set of sample instructions from the processor's instruction set. All arithmetic takes place in the accumulator (Acc) register.

Operation	Opcode
Divide the contents of Acc by the given number	000
Add the number in the storage location to the contents of Acc	001
Subtract the given number from the contents of Acc	010
Input a number	011
Output the contents of Acc	100
Store the contents of Acc to a memory location	101
Get a value from a memory location to Acc	110

The machine code uses a byte for each instruction, with the first three bits being the opcode and the remaining bits the operand. Consider this program:

```
01100000
10101000
01100000
10101001
01100000
10101100
11001001
00101000
00001100
10000000
```

The input data are 4, 6, 2.

a. Write this program in assembly language. [4]

b. Describe what the program does. [4]

c. The program will produce a single result and the values are not needed again.

   i. State what is meant by optimisation of code. [2]

   ii. Produce an optimised version of the above code. [3]

4. a. Using the set of operations from Question 3, consider what additional machine operations are necessary to write code that prints out the first X multiples of 10. [4]

  b. Describe in structured English a solution for the problem. [6]

5. Explain why the size of the memory available is an issue for the compilation process. [4]

6. a. Explain the difference between the two translation techniques of interpretation and compilation. [2]

  b. Give **one** advantage of the use of each of the two translation techniques. [2]

7. State the **three** stages of compilation and briefly describe the purpose of each. [6]

8. Explain in detail the stage of compilation known as lexical analysis. [6]

3.3 Computer architectures and the fetch–execute cycle

(3.3 a) Von Neumann architecture

John von Neumann introduced the idea of the stored program. Previously data and programs were stored in separate memories. Von Neumann realised that data and programs are indistinguishable and can therefore use the same memory.

Von Neumann architecture uses a single processor. It follows a linear sequence of *fetch–decode–execute* operations for the sequence of instructions which make up the program. In order to do this, the processor has to use some special registers. A register is simply a location that can store data. Registers can be thought of in the same way as individual locations in memory in that they store data, although memory locations have no special purpose. The registers are outside the immediate access store and consequently allow faster access to the data they store.

The processor uses a group of **special-purpose registers** to execute a program:
- program counter (PC)
- current instruction register (CIR)
- memory address register (MAR)
- memory data register (MDR)
- index register (IR).

The following alternative names for the registers will not be used on your examination paper. However, it is worth noting them because you may see them used in other textbooks.
- The PC is sometimes called the sequence control register (SCR).
- The MDR is sometimes called the memory buffer register (MBR) because it acts like a buffer, temporarily storing a data value before passing it on (e.g. to the CIR).

In the "fetch" part of the cycle:
- The **program counter** (PC) stores the address of the next instruction to be fetched. As instructions are held sequentially in memory, it is normal for the value in the PC to be incremented every time an instruction is accessed so that it always stores the address of the next instruction to be fetched.
- When the next instruction is needed its address is copied from the PC and placed in the **memory address register** (MAR).
- This location, or address, is found and the contents are placed in the **memory data register** (MDR).
- The contents of the MDR are then copied to the **current instruction register** (CIR).
- The current instruction register holds the instruction that is about to be executed.

In the "decode" part of the cycle:
- The instruction in the CIR is split into its individual parts. We know of two parts of the instruction already from Chapter 3.2 – the operation code and the operand.
- If the operand is an address, the address is copied to the MAR and the data are fetched and placed in the MDR.
- The operation is decoded by referring to a lookup table which gives the control unit the instructions about what needs to be done.

The "execute" phase of the cycle varies depending on the nature of the instruction. Some instructions require arithmetic; other instructions require accessing a value (or storing a value) in main memory.

A typical processor is shown in Figure 3.3.1. The central processor contains the arithmetic and logic unit (also known as the ALU or the arithmetic unit) and the control unit. This is a very simplified model of a typical computer's processor architecture. A real processor is likely to have many **general-purpose registers**.

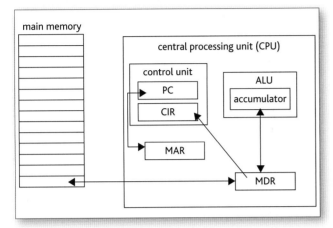

Figure 3.3.1 A typical processor.

The accumulator is a register inside the ALU. It is a single general-purpose register where all values are held when processed by arithmetic and logical operations. Arithmetic operations are those that add, subtract, multiply and divide numbers. Logical operations involve comparing binary patterns and making decisions, e.g. about whether two values are equal.

The control unit fetches instructions from memory, decodes them and synchronises the operations before sending signals to other parts of the computer using the control bus (see the section "Using buses to convey data" on page 208). The program counter and the current instruction register are in the control unit. The memory data register and memory address register are in the processor.

Figure 3.3.1 also shows the pathways along which data are transferred.

(3.3 b) The fetch–decode–execute cycle

A program is a set of instructions stored in a sequential block of main memory locations. The following sequence of steps describes the fetching and execution of a single program instruction. At the end the cycle, the sequence repeats until the program terminates.

The fetch stage:
1. Copy the address that is in the program counter (PC) into the memory address register (MAR).
2. Increment the PC (ready for the next fetch).
3. Load the instruction that is in the memory address given by the MAR into the memory data register (MDR).
4. Load the instruction that is now in the MDR into the current instruction register (CIR).

The decode stage:
5. Identify the type of addressing being used by the instruction (see "Low-level programming languages" in Chapter 3.5, page 249).
   a. If the address is a direct address, load a copy of the address into the MAR and retrieve the contents of the address.
   b. If the address is an indexed address, add the address to the contents of the index register (IR) and copy the result to the MAR. Retrieve the contents of this address.
6. Decode the instruction.

The execute stage:
7. If the instruction is a jump instruction then
   a. Load the address operand into the PC.
   b. Go to step 1.
8. Execute the instruction.
9. Go to step 1.

The memory data register is used whenever data are transferred from the central processing unit to main memory, or vice versa. Thus the next instruction is copied from main memory into the MDR and then copied from MDR into CIR.

Once an instruction has been fetched, the control unit can decode it and decide what has to be done. This is the execute part of the cycle. If it is an arithmetic instruction, this can be executed and the cycle restarted as the PC already contains the address of the next instruction. However, if the instruction involves jumping to an instruction that is not the next in sequence, the PC has to be loaded with this new address. This address is the operand of the current instruction, hence the address part is loaded into the PC and the next cycle started.

Our discussion of what happens in the fetch–decode–execute cycle is very wordy. It can be simplified by using register transfer notation. The notation [PC] denotes "the contents of the register PC". Note the use of the "assignment operator" (used extensively in Module 2 for our pseudocode algorithm descriptions).

1. MAR ← [PC]
2. PC ← [PC] + 1
3. MDR ← [[MAR]]
4. CIR ← [MDR]
5. Decode
6. Execute
7. Go to Step 1

Activity

List the special registers that are used in the von Neumann computer architecture. Describe the fetch–execute cycle, explaining the role that the special-purpose registers play in the cycle.

Extension

Here are two interesting questions:

1. Why might it be necessary to add 2 to the program counter rather than 1?
2. How does the processor deal with a conditional jump?

Activity

In Chapter 3.1, we saw that interrupts were used to temporarily stop one program from running so that another could be dealt with. We also said that when the interrupt service routine (ISR) was completed the original program could resume from where it had been interrupted. Can you explain how this is done, now that we have discussed the fetch–execute cycle? There is a hint in Chapter 3.1 where we said that even an interrupt has to wait for the cycle to finish before it is allowed to interrupt the program.

Extend the discussion to consider what can be done if there are a number of interrupts one after the other, so that there are a number of part-finished programs to be completed.

3.3 c Using buses to convey data

A **bus** is a pathway along which data can travel. If you think of a bus as being a set of wires in parallel which is reserved for a particular type of data transfer you won't go far wrong.

Three types of bus are present inside a typical microprocessor. The difference is in what data they are used to convey and their role:

- The **data bus** is used to carry the data that needs to be transferred from one hardware component to another. The memory data register (MDR) is at one end of the data bus (see Figure 3.3.1 on page 207). The processor has instructions in its instruction set to read values from main memory and store values in memory. Hence the data bus is bi-directional.
- The **address bus** carries the address of the main memory location or input/output device which is about to be used. The address bus sends address values in only one direction, i.e. from the processor to the memory address register (MAR).
- The **control bus** is used to send control signals from the control unit to the other components of the system. A separate wire is dedicated to a particular control signal, for example:
  - a completed data transfer (read or write) operation
  - reset button pressed
  - interrupt request
  - interrupt acknowledgement.

3.3 d Parallel processing systems
Co-processors

A **co-processor** is sometimes called a floating-point unit. Floating-point representation (Chapter 3.4) is a data representation which requires long strings of bits. A maths co-processor is a device which has a number of registers that have a sufficient number of bits to store the length of a floating-point number, thereby speeding up processing. It is particularly useful when handling on-screen graphics, which must be calculated fast enough to produce real-time changes to quickly refresh the screen display.

Pipelining

Using the standard fetch–decode–execute cycle, it is apparent that an instruction can be in one of the three phases. It could be being fetched (from memory), decoded (by the control unit) or executed (by the control unit). One approach would be to split the processor up into three parts, each of which handles one of the three stages. This would result in the situation shown in Figure 3.3.2, which shows how the process known as **pipelining** works.

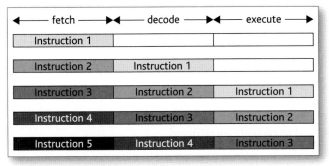

Figure 3.3.2   Pipelining.

The use of pipelining increases the speed of throughput of program instructions unless the next instruction in the pipe is not the next one that is needed. Suppose Instruction 2 is a jump to Instruction 10. Then Instructions 3, 4 and 5 need to be removed from the pipe and Instruction 10 needs to be loaded into the fetch part of the pipe. Thus, the pipe has to be cleared and the cycle restarted. The result is shown in Figure 3.3.3.

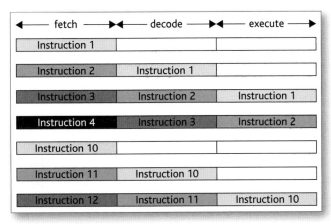

Figure 3.3.3   Pipelining: a jump.

Array processor

An **array processor** involves more than one arithmetic and logic unit but still only one processor. This is particularly useful when processing data held in a one-dimensional array when the same operation is to be applied to every element of the array. An example could be where all the values represent the cost of different stock items and it is required to compute selling prices calculated by adding the same percentage to each price value. An array processor is able to do the same calculation simultaneously to each of the input values.

Parallel processor

An extension of array processors is to use **parallel processors**. This system uses many independent processors working in parallel on the same program. One of the difficulties with this is that the programs running on these systems need to have been written specially for a parallel processor architecture. If the programs have been written for standard processor architectures, some instructions cannot be processed until others have been completed. Thus, checks have to be made to ensure that all prerequisites have been completed. However, these systems are in use, particularly in systems that receive many inputs from sensors and the data needs to be processed in parallel. A simple example that shows how the use of parallel processors can speed up a solution is the summing of a series of numbers. Consider finding the sum of n numbers. A single processor would involve $(n - 1)$ additions in sequence.

Using $n/2$ processors, we could simultaneously add $n/2$ pairs of numbers in the same time it would take a single processor to add one pair of numbers. This would leave only $n/2$ numbers to be added and this could be done using $n/4$ processors. Continuing in this way, the time to add the series would be considerably reduced.

Summary

- The basic von Neumann architecture has a single processor which uses a fetch–decode–execute cycle for the sequence of instructions which make up a program.
- The von Neumann architecture contains special registers that allow fast access to data and are used to execute a program:
  - program counter (PC)
  - current instruction register (CIR)
  - memory address register (MAR)
  - memory data register (MDR)
  - index register (IR).
- In the fetch stage:
  - The address in the PC is copied to the MAR and the PC is incremented.
  - The instruction in the MAR address is loaded into the MDR and then the CIR.
- In the decode stage:
  - If the CIR address is a direct address, it is loaded into the MAR and its contents are retrieved.
  - If the CIR address is indexed, the index register contents are added to the address (the operand of the instruction in CIR) and copied to the MAR. Its contents are retrieved.
  - The instruction is decoded.
- In the execute stage:
  - If the instruction is a jump instruction then its operand is loaded into the PC and a new fetch stage starts.
  - If the instruction is not a jump instruction, it is executed. A new fetch stage starts.
- A bus is a set of wires in parallel which is reserved for a particular type of data transfer:
  - The data bus carries data between hardware components.
  - The address bus carries the address of a main memory location or input/output device from the processor to the MAR.
  - The control bus carries signals from the control unit to other components.
- A parallel processing system speeds up processing by splitting a problem between several processors working in parallel.
  - Programs must be written particularly to take advantage of parallel processing.

Test yourself

1. The program counter (sequence control register) is a special register in the processor of a computer.
   a. Describe the function of the program counter.   [2]
   b. Describe **two** ways in which the program counter can change during the normal execution of a program, explaining, in each case, how this change is initiated.   [4]
   c. Describe the initial state of the program counter before the running of the program.   [2]
2. Explain what is meant by the term "von Neumann architecture".   [2]

> **Hint**
>
> The mark allocation shows that the answer needs to be more than one line.

3. Describe the fetch–decode part of the fetch–decode–execute cycle, explaining the purpose of any special registers involved. [7]

> **Hint**
>
> Consider using the "register transfer notation" and address only the information that is requested.

4. Describe **two** different buses used in the processor. [4]
5. Explain what is meant by the following types of processor and give a use for each.
   a. maths co-processor [3]
   b. parallel processors [3]
   c. array processor. [3]

3.4 Data representation, data structures and data manipulation

(3.4 a) ## Expressing numbers in binary coded decimal and hexadecimal

In Chapter 1.3, we learned about the use of binary to represent positive whole numbers. You should ensure that you understand binary representation before continuing with this section.

For example, make sure you understand how the table below shows the conversion of the denary number 117 into a binary number of eight bits (1 byte).

128	64	32	16	8	4	2	1
0	1	1	1	0	1	0	1

Binary coded decimal

Some numbers are not proper numbers because they don't behave like numbers. For example, a barcode looks like a number but if the barcode for a chocolate bar is added to the barcode for a sponge cake the result is meaningless. Values that are written as a string of digits but do not behave like numbers are often stored in **binary coded decimal (BCD)**. Each digit is changed into a four-bit binary number that is then placed after one another in sequence.

For example, to convert 398 into BCD, we convert the 3 to 0011, the 9 to 1001 and the 8 to 1000. Thus, in BCD, 398 is represented by 001110011000. Note that it is essential to retain the leading zeros.

Activity

Change these numbers into BCD representation:
i. 234
ii. 789
iii. 20348
Practise using BCD by finding some barcodes and changing them into BCD.

Hexadecimal number system

The base-16 number system (counting in 16s) is called **hexadecimal**. It uses the same principles as those we used in Chapter 1.3 to convert from decimal to binary numbers:

1. Start on the left of the diagram.
2. If the column heading is less than the denary number:
   a. Divide the denary number by the column heading and put the whole number in the column.
   b. The remainder becomes the denary number.
   c. Move to the next column to the right.
   d. Go to step 2.
3. If the column heading is greater than the number:
   a. Put a 0 in the column.
   b. Move to the next column to the right.
   c. Go to step 2.

Because hexadecimal is base 16, the column headings start at the right with 1 and then each column is the previous one multiplied by 16.

256	16	1

To convert 117 (in denary) to hexadecimal, we set up the column diagram and put 0 in the first column:

256	16	1
0		

117 can be divided by 16 seven times. We write the 7 in the 16s column and move to the 1s column with the remainder (5):

256	16	1
0	7	5

So, 117 denary is 75 H or 75 hex.

If we convert 75 H to BCD, we get 01110101 which is the binary value of 117. A quick way of translating a binary number into hexadecimal is to divide the eight bits into two groups of four and convert each group into a hexadecimal number.

Base 10 uses the digits 0, 1, 2, 3, . . . , 8, 9. Base 2 uses the digits 0 and 1. We can conclude that the largest digit we need in any number base is one less than the base. This means that for hexadecimal (base 16) we need digits for the values: 0, 1, 2, 3, . . . , 8, 9, 10, 11, 12, 13, 14 and 15. The values from 10 to 15 must be represented by a single symbol. By convention, they are represented by the letters A to F. In hexadecimal, we count 0, 1, 2, 3, . . . , 8, 9, A, B, C, D, E, F.

As an example, we translate the number BD H into denary and binary.

The hexadecimal number BD stands for 11 lots of 16 and 13 units

$$= 176 + 13$$
$$= 189 \text{ (denary)}$$

The hexadecimal number BD in BCD gives B = 1011 and D = 1101. This gives the binary number 10111101.

(3.4 b) ## Representing positive and negative integers

If a computer system uses one byte to store a number (as suggested in Chapter 1.4), three problems arise:

- The biggest number that can be represented is 255. This is solved by using more than one byte to represent a number. Most computer systems – in particular, high-level programming languages – use either two or four bytes to store integers. There is still a limit on the size of integer that can be represented, but it is now much larger.
- Fractions cannot be represented. This is discussed in the sections on real numbers and floating-point representation in this chapter.
- Negative numbers cannot be represented. This section considers two methods for representing negative integers.

The denary number 117 becomes 01110101 in binary. If we want to be able to store +117 and –117, the number needs a second piece of information to be stored, namely the sign. There are two ways of doing this.

Sign and magnitude

The first bit in the byte – i.e. the most significant bit (MSB) – will represent the sign. 0 represents positive and 1 represents negative. This means that:

$$+117 = 01110101 \text{ and } -117 = 11110101$$

We say the most significant bit is being used as a "sign bit".

Note that the range of possible integers represented by one byte is now –127 to +127 because we only have seven bits to store the size or "magnitude" of the integer.

The byte does not represent just the size of the integer but also its sign. This makes arithmetic unpredictable so there is still a major issue with using the "sign-and-magnitude" method.

Two's complement

The MSB still represents a number but is assumed to be negative. This means that the column headings, i.e. the "place values" of the number, become:

–128	64	32	16	8	4	2	1

The denary number +117 does not need to use the MSB, so it still becomes 01110101.

However, –117 must be thought of as –128 + 11:

–128	64	32	16	8	4	2	1
1	0	0	0	1	0	1	1

So the denary number –117 becomes 10001011.

Note that the range of possible integers represented by one byte is now –128 to +127. Two's complement has the major advantage over sign-and-magnitude representation that addition and subtraction of two numbers in two's complement form produces the correct result – as long as the result is within the permitted range of possible integers.

The following algorithm is another way of calculating the two's complement value of a negative number:

1. Work out the binary value of the positive number (make sure you write down all the leading zeros).
2. Change all the digits, 0 for 1 and 1 for 0.
3. Add 1.

This is usually remembered as: "Write down the positive number – flip the bits – add 1".

Let's apply this algorithm to our example of –117:

1. Work out the binary value of the positive number: 01110101.
2. Change all the digits: 10001010.
3. Add 1: 10001011.

This result matches the value we got using the method above.

Activity

Work out the sign-and-magnitude and two's complement representations of the following numbers, using a byte:

i. +63
ii. −63
iii. −11
iv. −58
v. −99

Explain why a problem is caused by attempting to represent −200. Suggest a solution to the problem.

3.4 c) Performing binary addition

The syllabus requires you to be able to add binary integers. The numbers and answers will be limited to ones which require only one or two bytes.

There are four simple rules:

$$0 + 0 = 0$$
$$0 + 1 = 1$$
$$1 + 0 = 1$$
$$1 + 1 = 0 \text{ and carry } 1$$

When you get a column that has two 1s and a 1 carried from the previous column, it is a bit more complicated.

That makes three 1s to add together which gives $1 + 1 + 1 = 1$ and carry 1.

You must always remember to show your working. This includes showing any carry bits. If an addition question is asked in an examination, there will always be marks for showing the working (see Figure 3.4.1).

Figure 3.4.1 shows that addition gives the correct result as long as the answer is within the range of possible integers. Using eight bits to represent a number in two's complement form, the range is −128 to +127 inclusive. Figure 3.4.1b gives an indeterminate answer – it is outside of the range possible.

3.4 d) Representing real numbers

You must fully understand how to represent integers in two's complement form before you learn how to represent fractional numbers.

The denary number 23.456 can be written as 0.23456×10^2. The decimal part of this representation, 0.23456, is called the **mantissa** and the number 2 is called the **exponent**. If we always stick to the same arrangement, we need only store the mantissa and the exponent to be able to define the number uniquely. (Notice that the decimal part of the representation is not the same as the decimal part of the number.)

Why do we sometimes want to express numbers like this? Very large and very small numbers contain a large number of zeros, so this representation is more concise.

We can apply the same rules to binary numbers. This is useful because binary representations are long

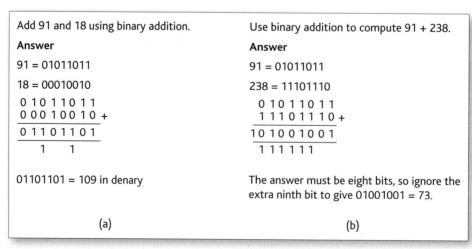

(a)

(b)

Figure 3.4.1 Binary addition.

anyway. For example, consider the binary number 10111. This could be represented by 0.10111×2^{101}, where 0.10111 is the mantissa and 101 is the exponent. This could be stored as 010111101 provided we are clear how many bits are used for the mantissa and the exponent.

When we deal with fractional values (numbers less than 1) in denary notation, the method for finding the mantissa and exponent is the same. We move the point until we have a number between 0 and 1. The only difference is that the point is being moved the other way so we have to make the exponent negative to compensate. So, 0.0000246 can be written as 0.246×10^{-4}. The mantissa is 0.246 and the exponent is −4.

Exactly the same methods and thinking can be used for binary. If we have 0.00010101 it can be written as 0.10101×2^{-11}, where 0.10101 is the mantissa and −11 is the exponent.

Remember from Chapter 1.3 that a real number is one which may (or may not) have a fractional part. Numbers that involve a fractional part, such as 2.467_{10} and 101.0101_2, are called real numbers.

Representing real numbers by storing the mantissa and the exponent is called **floating point representation** (because the binary or decimal point always floats into position).

3.4 e ## Normalising the floating point representation of a number

In the previous section, the point in the mantissa was always placed immediately before the first non-zero digit. Doing this allows us to use the maximum number of digits for the mantissa.

Suppose we use eight bits to store the mantissa and eight bits to store the exponent. The binary number 10.11011 becomes 0.1011011×2^{10} and can be held as:

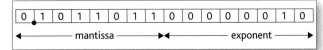

Notice that the first digit of the mantissa is 0 and the second digit is 1. The mantissa is said to be **normalised** if the first two digits of the mantissa are different:

- For a positive number, the first two digits of the mantissa are 01.

- For a negative number, the first two digits of the mantissa are 10.

The reason for normalising the mantissa is to preserve the maximum possible accuracy in the number. The exponent is always an integer and is represented in two's complement.

Consider the binary number 0.00000101011 which is 0.101011×2^{-101}. Thus the mantissa is 0.101011 and the exponent is −101. Again, using eight bits for the mantissa and eight bits for the exponent gives:

Care needs to be taken when normalising negative numbers. The easiest way to normalise a negative number is to:

1. Write down the normalised mantissa of the positive number.

2. Find the two's complement of the mantissa by changing all the digits (0 to 1 and 1 to 0) and then adding 1.

Consider the binary number −1011. The positive version is $1011 = 0.1011 \times 2^{100}$ and can be represented by:

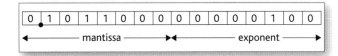

Now find the two's complement of the mantissa:

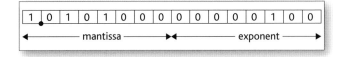

Notice that the first two digits in the mantissa are different. This must always be true if the number is to be considered to be in normalised form. Remember, for a normalised floating point negative number, the mantissa starts with digits 10.

For example, let's convert the decimal fraction −11/32 into a normalised floating point binary number.

$$11/32 = (1/4 + 1/16 + 1/32)$$
$$= 0.01 + 0.0001 + 0.00001$$
$$= 0.01011000$$
$$= 0.1011000 \times 2^{-1}.$$

Therefore, $−11/32 = −0.1011000 \times 2^{-1}$.

Representing the mantissa and exponent in two's complement, we have:

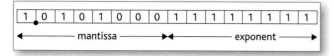

An alternative approach is to appreciate that the normalised representation has the mantissa as large as possible. So −11/32 can be written as:

$$-11/16 \times \tfrac{1}{2} = -11/16 \times 2^{-1}$$
$$= (-1 + 5/16) \times 2^{-1}$$
$$= (-1 + 1/4 + 1/16) \times 2^{-1}$$

which gives the mantissa and exponent shown above.

The fact that the first two digits are always different can be used to check for invalid answers when arriving at the final answer.

3.4 f **Trading accuracy for range in floating point representations**

However many bits are allocated for the storage of floating point numbers in a computer, there is always going to be a limit to the number of bits that can be used for storage of both the mantissa and the exponent. For any fixed number of available bits, if we use more bits for the mantissa, we have to use fewer bits for the exponent.

Let us start by using eight bits for the mantissa and eight bits for the exponent. The largest positive value we can have for the mantissa is 0.1111111 and the largest positive number we can have for the exponent is 01111111. This gives the representation: $0.1111111 \times 2^{1111111}$, which is almost 1×2^{127}.

The smallest positive mantissa is 0.1000000 and the smallest exponent is 10000000. This represents $0.1000000 \times 2^{10000000}$, which is very close to zero; in fact it is 2^{-129}.

The largest negative number (i.e. the negative number closest to zero) is $1.0111111 \times 2^{10000000} = -0.1000001 \times 2^{-10000000}$. Note that we cannot use 1.1111111 for the mantissa because it is not normalised. The first two digits must be different.

The smallest negative number (i.e. the negative number furthest from zero) is $1.0000000 \times 2^{01111111} = -2^{127}$.

Now suppose we use 12 of the bits for the mantissa and the other four for the exponent. This increases the number of bits that can be used to represent the number. That is, we have more bits in the mantissa and hence greater accuracy because we can keep more digits in the fractional part. However, the range of values in the exponent is much smaller; a four-bit exponent gives a range from −8 to +7 and this produces a very small range of numbers. The conclusion is that we have increased the accuracy at the expense of the range of numbers that can be represented.

Similarly, reducing the size of the mantissa reduces the accuracy, but we have a much greater range of values as the exponent can now take a wider range of values.

3.4 g **Linked-list, binary tree, stack and queue structures**

Linked lists

A **linked list** is a data structure that provides links between data items. For example, a list of surnames could be linked in alphabetic order.

Figure 3.4.2 shows an active linked list and a free list. The free list is a list of storage locations available for future insertions. The linked list is created by removing a cell from the front of the free list, inserting the new data item into the free cell and then inserting it in the correct position in the linked list.

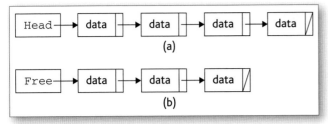

Figure 3.4.2   Linked lists: a) active and b) free space.

Data storage

A linked list can be represented as two one-dimensional arrays:

- a string array storing the data values, for example, `Surname(20)`
- an integer array storing the indexes that create the links, for example, `Link(20)`

The `Head` pointer stores the index position of the first item in the list. Figure 3.4.2 shows the order of the values starting with the value pointed to by `Head`.

Insertion

Consider the values held in an array (Figure 3.4.3). The integer pointer `Head` points to the array value which is first in the ordered list. The integer pointer `Free` points to the next available location (for when a new item joins the linked list).

Now suppose we wish to insert an element between the second and third cells in the linked list. The pointers have to be changed as shown in Figure 3.4.3.

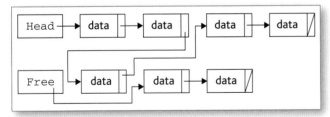

Figure 3.4.3   Linked lists: insertion.

An algorithm for inserting a value into the list is given below:.

```
PROCEDURE LinkedListInsert
    IF Free is NULL
        THEN
            OUTPUT error - no space for insert
        ELSE
            SET New to equal Free
```

```
        Change Free to point to next cell
        COPY data into cell pointed to by
                                        New
        IF Head is NULL
            THEN
                SET New pointer to NULL
                SET Head to New
            ELSE
                IF New data is less than
                        data in first cell
                    THEN
                        SET New pointer to
                                Head pointer
                        SET Head pointer to
                                        New
                    ELSE
                        CALL current cell
                                    Previous
                        SET Temp to Previous
                                    pointer
                        SET Previous pointer
                                    to New
                        SET New pointer to
                                        Temp
                    ENDIF
            ENDIF
        ENDIF
END PROCEDURE
```

The algorithm checks if the free list is empty. If it is, there is no way of adding new data. The algorithm also checks to see if the new data are to be inserted into an empty list (or the head of the list). In any other case, the algorithm must search the list to find the position for the new data.

Deletion

Suppose we wish to delete the third cell in the linked list shown in Figure 3.4.3. The changes to the pointers are shown in Figure 3.4.4 (see page 218).

The changes are that:

- the deleted item is bypassed in the active list
- the space becomes the new head of the free list.

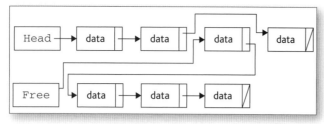

Figure 3.4.4 Linked lists: deletion.

```
PROCEDURE LinkedListDelete
    IF Head is NULL
        THEN
            OUTPUT error - nothing to delete
        ELSE
            'Search for cell before the
                    cell to be deleted
            IF the cell is not in the list
                THEN
                    OUTPUT error - cell not
                            found
                    STOP
                ELSE
                    Call current cell
                            Previous
                    SET Temp to Previous
                            pointer
                    SET Previous pointer to
                            deleted cell pointer
                    SET deleted cell
                            pointer to Free
                    SET Free pointer to Temp
                    STOP
            ENDIF
        ENDIF
    END PROCEDURE
```

Searching

Assume that the data in a linked list is in ascending order of some key value. The following algorithm shows how to move up the list of values until some required value is found. This algorithm would be needed for a sequential search and for insertion of a new item.

```
PROCEDURE LinkedListTraversal
    SET Current to Head
    REPEAT
        SET Next to Current pointer
        IF New data is less than Current
                                    data
            THEN
                SET Current equal to Next
        ENDIF
    UNTIL Found
ENDPROCEDURE
```

Trees

A tree is a data structure which – similar to a linked list – sets up link pointers between various data items. A tree with only two possible descendants from each value is called a **binary tree**.

Tree terminology
- Each data item in the tree is called a **node**.
- The first item added to the tree is called the root value.
- All items to the left of the root form the *left sub-tree*.
- All items to the right of the root form the *right sub-tree*.
- Any node may have its own sub-tree.
- An item which has no descendants is called a **leaf node**.

Data storage
A binary tree can be represented as three one-dimensional arrays:
- a string array storing the data values, for example, `Data(20)`
- an integer array storing the indexes for the left pointers, for example, `LeftLink(20)`
- an integer array storing the indexes for the right pointers, for example, `RightLink(20)`

The `Root` pointer stores the index position of the root item in the tree. The tree shown in Figure 3.4.5a contains data for subjects offered at a school. Figure 3.4.5b shows the contents of the data structures.

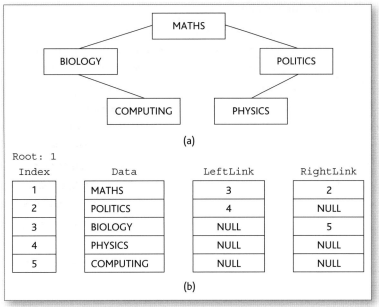

Figure 3.4.5 Tree representations: a) diagram and b) data structures.

Insertion

When inserting an item into a binary tree, it is usual to preserve some sort of order. To add a new value, we look at each node starting at the root. If the new value is less than the value at the node move left, otherwise move right. We repeat this for each node visited until there are no further nodes. The new node is inserted at this point by entering the data and setting up the link from the previous node.

If the tree data are stored as arrays, when the route through the array results in a Null value, the item is inserted into a free space in the array. The left and right pointers for the new item are both set to NULL.

The school subjects were inserted into the `Data` array in the following order to create the binary tree in Figure 3.4.5: MATHS, POLITICS, BIOLOGY, PHYSICS, COMPUTING.

The algorithm for an insertion to the tree is given in the next column.

```
PROCEDURE BinaryTreeInsert
    INPUT NewItem
    Allocate to next FreePosition in
            Data array
    IF tree is empty
        THEN
            Root = FreePosition
            SET FreePosition pointers
                to NULL
        ELSE
            'traverse the tree to find the
                insert position
            Current = Root
            REPEAT
                Previous = Current
                IF NewItem < Current item
                    THEN
                        'move left
                        Current = Current's
                                left pointer
                    ELSE
                        'move right
                        Current = Current's
                                right pointer
                ENDIF
            UNTIL Current = NULL
        ENDIF
        SET Previous pointer to FreePosition
END PROCEDURE
```

We trace this algorithm while inserting the new subject SOCIOLOGY:

```
INPUT SOCIOLOOGY
Data(6) ← "SOCIOLOGY"
LeftLink(6) ← NULL
RightLink(6) ← NULL

tree is NOT empty
    Current ← 1
    REPEAT
        Previous ← 1
        IF "SOCIOLOGY" is less than "MATHS"
            ELSE
                'go right
                Current ← 2
    UNTIL Current = NULL
        Previous ← 2
        IF "SOCIOLOGY" is less than "POLITICS"
            ELSE
                'go right
                Current ← NULL
        ENDIF
    UNTIL Current = NULL
ENDIF
RightLink(2) ← 6
```

The result is the tree shown in Figure 3.4.6.

Deletion

Deleting a node from a tree can be a very complex task. Suppose that we wish to delete the node BIOLOGY from Figure 3.4.6. What do we do with COMPUTING?

The difficulty is that each of the nodes is not only a data item but is also a part of the structure of the tree. If the data item is simply deleted, it is like sawing a branch off the tree – everything else on that branch also disappears. At least, we can't navigate to them. One node which does not give a problem is if the node to be deleted is a leaf node. Why?

The simplest strategy for all deletions is to leave the structure of the tree unchanged. The entry for BIOLOGY can be labelled as "deleted", so that the structure stays as it is but the value is not read when the tree is searched. Descendants of any deleted node can still be accessed as its left and right pointers are preserved. This strategy has the disadvantage that we waste storage space when we delete nodes.

To save space, we need to maintain only the values that are active, i.e. still members of the tree. To do this, we need to completely re-generate the tree structure.

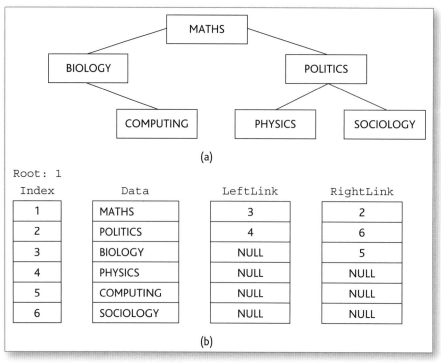

Figure 3.4.6 The subject tree after inserting SOCIOLOGY.

Benefits of a tree data structure

The major advantage of a tree structure is that –
provided the tree is a well-balanced tree – the access
time to an individual node is much quicker than by
using a simple serial search.

Consider a data set of 1024 items. A sequential
search requires on average 512 comparisons to find
a value. For a well-balanced binary tree with 1024
items, the average number of comparisons reduces
to only 11.

This is why trees are used for search engines and
other applications that require fast data retrieval,
e.g. searching for a user account and password for a
network that has several thousand user accounts.

Stacks

You studied the stack data structure in Chapter 1.3.
Any set of data values which is created as a stack
operates on the principle that the last item to join is the
first to leave.

Figure 3.4.7 shows a stack and its top-of-stack
pointer (TOS). In Chapter 1.3, we concluded that a
single pointer was needed to control the stack and
this pointer was to the next available location (which
means that the next item to leave is the one before this
position). In the discussion that follows, we adopt the
alternative strategy. The TOS pointer points to the item
which is currently at the top of the stack. Hence, a new
value joins at position TOS + 1.

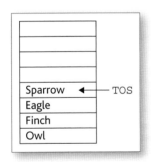

Figure 3.4.7   A stack.

Insertion and deletion are the only two operations
you can perform on a stack. The terms often used with
a stack are "push" for insertion and "pop" for deletion.

Insertion

If we are to insert an item into a stack, we must first
check that the stack is not full. If it is not, we must
increment the TOS pointer and insert the new data
item into the cell pointed to by TOS. This method
assumes that the cells in the array are numbered from 1
and that the pointer is zero when the stack is empty.

The algorithm for an insertion is:

```
PROCEDURE StackInsertItem
    IF Stack is full
        THEN
            OUTPUT "Stack full - insert
                    refused"
        ELSE
            TOS ← TOS + 1
            INPUT NewItem
            Stack[TOS] ← NewItem
    ENDIF
END PROCEDURE
```

Deletion

When an item is deleted from a stack, the item's value is
copied and the stack pointer is decremented. The data
itself is not deleted. This time we must check that the
stack is not empty before attempting to delete an item.
Note there is no choice about which item is retrieved –
the last item in is the item removed.

The algorithm for retrieving a stack item:

```
PROCEDURE StackDeleteItem
    IF Stack is empty
        THEN
            OUTPUT "Stack is empty"
        ELSE
            OUTPUT Stack[TOS]
            TOS ← TOS - 1
    ENDIF
END PROCEDURE
```

Queues

You studied the queue data structure in Chapter 1.3.
Any set of data values which is created as a queue
operates on the principle that the first item to join is
the first to leave. To implement a queue requires two
pointers Head and Tail. Figure 3.4.8 (on page 222)
shows a queue and its head and tail pointers.

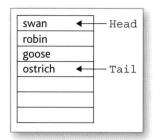

Figure 3.4.8 A queue.

Insertion and deletion are the only two operations you can perform on a queue.

Insertion

If we are to insert an item into a queue we must first check that the queue is not full. Having done this, we increment the `Tail` pointer and insert the new data item into the cell pointed to by the `Tail` pointer. This method assumes that the array cells are numbered from 1 downwards and that the two pointers point to the same cell when the queue has only one remaining.

The next item is added at position `Tail + 1`. The next item leaves from position `Head`.

The algorithm for an insertion is:

```
PROCEDURE InsertToQueue
    IF Queue is full
        THEN
            OUTPUT "Queue is already FULL"
        ELSE
            INPUT NewItem
            Tail ← Tail + 1
            Queue[Tail+1] ← NewItem
    ENDIF
END PROCEDURE
```

Deletion

Before trying to delete an item, we must check that the queue is not empty. Consider the representation in Figure 3.4.8.

The algorithm for deletion is given in the next column:

```
PROCEDURE DeleteFromQueue
    IF Queue is empty
        THEN
            OUTPUT "Queue is EMPTY"
        ELSE
            OUTPUT Queue[Head].
            Head ← Head + 1
    ENDIF
END PROCEDURE
```

You should appreciate that this implementation of a queue will eventually run out of storage space. As items leave, the space they occupied cannot be reused. The solution to this problem is to implement the queue as a circular queue. You would *not* be expected to produce the algorithm for a circular queue in an examination.

(3.4 h) Implementation of data structures

Static data structures do not change in size while the program is running. A typical static data structure is an array. Once you declare its size (or upper bound), it cannot be changed. Some programming languages do allow the size of arrays to be changed, in which case they are dynamic data structures. For the purposes of this syllabus, an array is considered a static data structure.

Dynamic data structures can increase and decrease in size while a program is running. A typical dynamic data structure is a linked list. Table 3.4.1 compares static and dynamic data structures.

Table 3.4.1 Comparison of static and dynamic data structures.

	Advantages	Disadvantages
Static structures	• Space allocated during compilation • Easier to program • Easy to check for overflow • Random access	• Space allocation is fixed • Wastes space when only partially used
Dynamic structures	• Only uses space required • Efficient use of memory • Emptied storage can be returned to the system	• Difficult to program • Searches can be slow • Serial access

Some high-level programming languages implement dynamic data structures with a "pointer". Two languages that support the use of pointers are Pascal (and its variants, e.g. Delphi) and C (and all its variants, e.g. C++). They are outside the scope of this syllabus.

3.4 i Binary searching and serial searching

There are many different algorithms for searching but only two are considered here. These methods are a serial search and a binary search.

Serial (or sequential or linear) search

A **serial search** assumes the data to be in consecutive locations, such as in an array. It does not require the data to be in any particular order. To find the position of a particular value involves looking at each value in turn – starting with the first – and comparing it with the value you are looking for. When the value is found, you need to note its position. You must also be able to report the special case that a value has not been found. This only becomes apparent when the search has reached the final data item without finding the required value.

A serial search can be very slow, particularly if there are a large number of data values. The least number of comparisons is one (if the requested item is the first item) and the maximum number is the size of the list (if the requested item is the last item). If there are n values in the list, the worst case is that we make n comparisons (if the required value is the last value or is not in the list). On average, the required value is in the middle of the list, requiring $n/2$ comparisons to locate it. Clearly, if n is large, this can be a very large number of comparisons and the serial search algorithm can take a long time.

The algorithm for a serial search is straightforward. Assume there are N values in the array MyList and we are to search for the data value ThisValue. A Boolean variable, Found, flags when the item is found.

```
PROCEDURE SearialSearch
    Found ← FALSE
    Index ← 1
    INPUT ThisValue

    REPEAT
        IF MyList[Index] = ThisValue
            THEN
                Found ← TRUE
                OUTPUT "Found at Position"
                    Index
        ELSE
            Index ← Index + 1
```

```
        ENDIF
    UNTIL Found = TRUE OR Index = N + 1

    IF Found = FALSE
        THEN
            OUTPUT "Requested item was NOT
                FOUND"
    ENDIF
END PROCEDURE
```

Binary search (or binary chop)

We discussed the **binary search** (also called **binary chop**) when we implemented a binary tree. We concluded that the major benefit of a tree data structure is to reduce the number of comparisons needed to locate a particular item.

Suppose the data items are sorted into ascending order as shown below:

1	Amsterdam
2	Bristol
3	Canberra
4	Dusseldorf
5	Edinburgh
6	Frankfurt
7	Glasgow
8	Hanover
9	Singapore

We wish to find the position of "Canberra". Compare "Canberra" with the value in the middle of the table, i.e. Edinburgh at position 5. As Canberra is before Edinburgh, we now look only at the new list, which only has four entries:

1	Amsterdam
2	Bristol
3	Canberra
4	Dussledorf

We compare "Canberra" with the new middle value. Convention says that if there is an even number of items, we take the middle value as the higher of the two – in this case item 3, i.e. Canberra. We have found the requested value and it has taken only two comparisons. This compares favourably with a linear search which, for a list of nine items, would have required four or five comparisons.

Clearly, the binary search is more efficient than the serial search algorithm and the benefits increase significantly for a large number of items. However, the data must first be sorted into order and this can take some time.

Table 3.4.2 compares the serial and binary search methods.

Extension

In order to compare the efficiency of the two methods, we need to use lists of different lengths. To do this we need to know the number of comparisons that need to be made for lists of different lengths. As a binary search halves the lists each time we do a comparison, the number of comparisons is given by m where $2m$ is the smallest value greater than or equal to n, the number of values in the list.

Suppose there are 16 values in a list. The successive lists compared contain 16, 8, 4 and 2 values. This involves a maximum of four comparisons and 2^4 is 16. Similarly, we only need 10 comparisons if the list contains 1000 values because 2^{10} is equal to 1024, which is close to and greater than 1000.

Figure 3.4.9 shows a comparison of the search times for the two methods. It includes the calculation of the midpoints in the lists used by the binary search and the time taken to make comparisons. It does not include sorting time before a binary search.

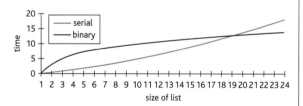

Figure 3.4.9 Comparison of search times.

Binary search algorithm

Be prepared! The idea of a binary search, that we keep looking at the middle value in smaller and smaller lists, is a simple one but the algorithm is less straightforward.

Assume that the data are held in an array, in ascending order. We must split the lists in two. If there is an even number of values, dividing by two gives a whole number and we split the list there. However, if the list consists of an odd number of values we need to find the integer part of it, as an array subscript must be an integer. All high-level programming languages have a function similar to `INT()` to perform this calculation.

We must also make sure that, when we split a list in two, we use the correct one for the next search. Suppose we have a list of eight values. Splitting this gives two lists– the four values in cells 1 to 4 and the four values in cells 5 to 8. When we started, we needed to consider the list in cells 1 to 8. That is the first cell was 1 and the last cell was 8. If we move into the first sub-list (cells 1 to 4), the first cell stays at 1 but the last cell becomes 4. Similarly, if we use the second sub-list (cells 5 to 8), the first cell becomes 5 and the last is still 8. This means that if we use the first list, the first cell in the new list is unchanged and the last is changed. However, if we use the second list, the first cell is changed and the last is not changed. This gives us a clue to how to do the search.

The following algorithm assumes we are searching for item `ThisItem` in the array `MyList` with upper bound `N`. For each sub-list considered, the algorithm calculates the position of `Bottom`, `Top` and `Middle`.

Table 3.4.2   Comparison of serial and binary search methods.

	Advantages	Disadvantages
Serial search	• Additional data are simply appended to the end of the list. • The search algorithm is straightforward. • A search works well if there is a small number of data items.	• A search is inefficient if there is a large number of data items. • Missing data items cannot be identified until every item has been compared.
Binary search	• Large numbers of data items can be searched very quickly. • Missing data items can be identified quickly.	• Data items must be sorted before the search is carried out. • Adding or deleting a data item is slow (as every change involves re-sorting the data).

```
PROCEDURE BinarySearch
    Found ← FALSE
    NotInList ← FALSE
    Top ← N
    Bottom ← 1
    REPEAT
        Middle ← Integer ((Top + Bottom)/2)
        If MyList[Middle] = ThisItem
            THEN
                Found ← TRUE
            ELSE
                IF Bottom > Top
                    THEN
                        NotInList ← TRUE
                    ELSE
                        IF MyList[Middle] < ThisItem
                            THEN
                                'Retain the top half of
                                            the list
                                Bottom ← Middle + 1
                            ELSE
                                'Retain the bottom half
                                        of the list
                                Top ← Middle - 1
                        ENDIF
                ENDIF
        ENDIF
    UNTIL Found = TRUE OR NotInList = TRUE

    IF NotInList = TRUE
        THEN
            OUTPUT "Requested item was NOT FOUND"
    ENDIF
END PROCEDURE
```

3.4 j Sorting algorithms

The binary search algorithm requires that the data items are sorted into order. Sorting involves placing values in an order, such as numeric or alphabetic order. For example, the values 3, 5, 6, 8, 12, 16 and 25 are in ascending numeric order and Will, Ross, Mark, Jami, Haz, Don, Ann are in descending alphabetic order.

There are many different sorting algorithms but the syllabus requires that you study only two of them: the **insertion sort** and the **quick sort**. This section describes the two sorts in general terms; the algorithms are given at the end of the section as extension work.

Insertion sort

We compare each number in turn with the numbers before it in the list. We then insert the number into its correct position.

Consider the following list of numbers: 20, 47, 12, 53, 32, 84, 85, 96, 45, 18. Figure 3.4.10 (on page 226) shows the sequence of actions to sort the list. The blue numbers are the ones before the one we are trying to insert in the correct position. The red numbers are the ones we are currently considering.

We start with the second number, 47, and compare it with the numbers preceding it. There is only one and it is less than 47, so no change in the order is made. We then compare the third number, 12, with its predecessors. 12 is less than 20 so 12 is inserted before 20. This continues until the last number is considered and inserted in its correct position.

Quick sort

At first, this method may appear to be very slow. This is only because of the length of time it takes to explain the method. In fact, for long lists, it is a very efficient algorithm.

Consider the same unsorted list: 20, 47, 12, 53, 32, 84, 85, 96, 45, 18. We use two pointers, one on the left and one on the right. In Figure 3.4.11 (on page 226), the number we are placing (20) is in red and the number being compared is in blue. We compare the two numbers. If they are in the wrong order, we swap them. We then move the blue pointer to the next item and compare the two values. If they are in the wrong order, we swap them.

We keep moving the blue pointer towards the red pointer until either the two pointers meet or the two numbers being pointed to are in the wrong order. If they are in the wrong order, we swap the numbers. When the

20	47	12	53	32	84	85	96	45	18	Original list, start with second number.
20	47	12	53	32	84	85	96	45	18	No change needed.
20	47	12	53	32	84	85	96	45	18	Now compare 12 with its predecessors.
12	20	47	53	32	84	85	96	45	18	Insert 12 before 20.
12	20	47	53	32	84	85	96	45	18	Move to next value.
12	20	47	53	32	84	85	96	45	18	53 is in the correct place.
12	20	47	53	32	84	85	96	45	18	Move to the next value.
12	20	32	47	53	84	85	96	45	18	Insert 32 between 20 and 47
12	20	32	47	53	84	85	96	45	18	Move to the next value.
12	20	32	47	53	84	85	96	45	18	84 is in the correct place.
12	20	32	47	53	84	85	96	45	18	Move to the next value.
12	20	32	47	53	84	85	96	45	18	85 is in the correct place.
12	20	32	47	53	84	85	96	45	18	Move to the next value.
12	20	32	47	53	84	85	96	45	18	96 is in the correct place.
12	20	32	47	53	84	85	96	45	18	Move to the next value.
12	20	32	45	47	53	84	85	96	18	Insert 45 between 32 and 47.
12	20	32	45	47	53	84	85	96	18	Move to the final value.
12	18	20	32	45	47	53	84	85	96	Insert 18 between 12 and 20.

Figure 3.4.10 Sorting a list of numbers: insertion sort.

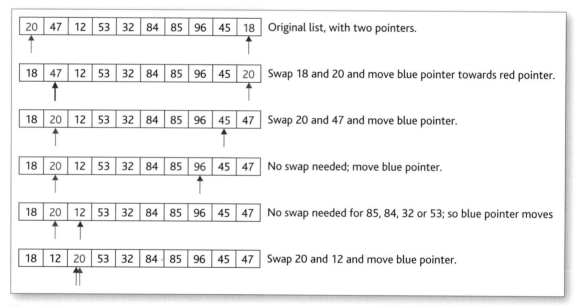

Figure 3.4.11 Sorting a list of numbers: quick sort.

pointers coincide, 20 is in its correct position. That is, all the numbers to the left of 20 are less than 20 and all the numbers to the right of 20 are greater than 20.

We now split the list into two; one to the left of 20 and one to the right of 20. We then "quick sort" each of these lists. Figure 3.4.12 shows the steps for the right hand list.

The number 53 is now in the correct position for this list. We split this list in two, as before, to give the two lists 47, 32, 45 and 96, 85, 84. We sort these two lists using the quick sort method. When all the sublists have a single number, they are put back together to form a sorted list.

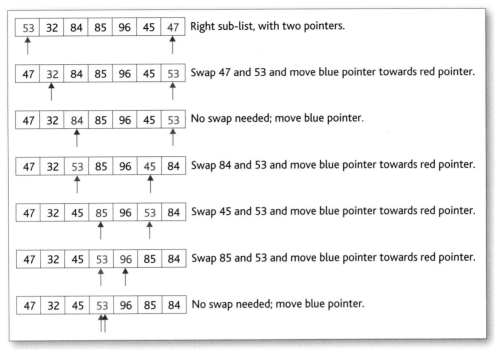

| 53 | 32 | 84 | 85 | 96 | 45 | 47 | Right sub-list, with two pointers.

| 47 | 32 | 84 | 85 | 96 | 45 | 53 | Swap 47 and 53 and move blue pointer towards red pointer.

| 47 | 32 | 84 | 85 | 96 | 45 | 53 | No swap needed; move blue pointer.

| 47 | 32 | 53 | 85 | 96 | 45 | 84 | Swap 84 and 53 and move blue pointer towards red pointer.

| 47 | 32 | 45 | 85 | 96 | 53 | 84 | Swap 45 and 53 and move blue pointer towards red pointer.

| 47 | 32 | 45 | 53 | 96 | 85 | 84 | Swap 85 and 53 and move blue pointer towards red pointer.

| 47 | 32 | 45 | 53 | 96 | 85 | 84 | No swap needed; move blue pointer.

Figure 3.4.12 Sorting a sub-list.

Extension

Insertion sort algorithm

There are N values in array MyList. The following algorithm uses an insertion sort to sort the values:

```
PROCEDURE InsertionSort
    'Look at each value in turn, starting
                     with the second value
    FOR Position ← 2 to N DO
       'store current number
       CurrentValue ← MyList[Position]
       'store it in position 0 in the array
       MyList[0] ← CurrentValue
       'look at numbers to the left of current
                                      number
       'move number right if it is greater
                        than CurrentValue
       If the number is not greater than
                           CurrentValue
    THEN
          insert CurrentValue
          Pointer ← Position - 1
       WHILE MyList[Pointer] >
                           CurrentValue DO
          MyList[Pointer + 1] ←
                       MyList[Pointer]
          'move left one place
          Pointer ← Pointer - 1
       ENDWHILE
       MyList[Pointer + 1] ← CurrentValue
    ENDFOR
END PROCEDURE
```

Quick sort algorithm

Clearly, the quick sort algorithm is more complex. When you have applied the quick sort to a list, you end up with two unsorted lists that still have to be sorted. These are sorted using a quick sort. Hence we have a recursive algorithm.

Suppose the data are held in a one-dimensional array, MyList, with a lower bound LB and an upper bound UB. For example, if the array is from

MyList [1] to MyList [10], LB is 1 and UB is 10.
 Similarly, if the list to be sorted are in cells
MyList [4] to MyList [7], LB is 4 and UB is 7.
 The algorithm for this is shown below.

```
PROCEDURE QuickSort(MyList, LB, UB)
   IF LB <> UB THEN
      'there is more than one
                     element in MyList
      LeftP ← LB    ' Left pointer
      RightP ← UB   ' Right pointer
      REPEAT
         WHILE LeftP <> RightP AND
         MyList[I] < MyList[J] DO
            'move right pointer left
            RightP ← RightP - 1
         ENDWHILE
         IF I<>RightP THEN swap
         MyList[I] and MyList[J]
         WHILE LeftP <> RightP AND
         MyList[I] < MyList[J] DO
            'move left pointer right
            LeftP ← LeftP + 1
         ENDWHILE
         IF LeftP <> RightP THEN swap
         MyList[I] and MyList[J]
      UNTIL LeftP = J
      'value now in correct
      position so sort left sub-list
      QuickSort(MyList, LB, LeftP - 1)
      'now sort right sub-list
      QuickSort(MyList, LeftP + 1, UB)
   ENDIF
END PROCEDURE
```

(3.4 k) Creating a binary tree

To create a binary tree from an unordered data list, we compare a data item with the current node:

- if the current node is greater than the new data item, we follow the left branch
- if the current node is less than the new data item, we follow the right branch.

The data item is inserted when we reach a null node, as was explained in the section on binary trees.

Consider the tree shown in Figure 3.4.13. The question that arises is "Why did we bother sorting it?" The answer involves a particular method of reading the values in the tree. Visiting the nodes in some particular order is called "tree traversal". There are a number of ways of traversing a tree.

Consider what happens if we output the values in the order "left node – then root node – then right node". We go as far to the left as we possibly can and output that node. Then we move to the root and finally we move right. We repeat the process, only returning when

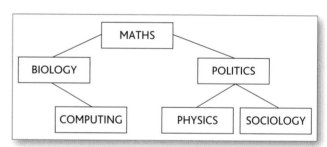

Figure 3.4.13 The subject tree.

we run out of branches to follow. On the way back we read any nodes that we haven't read yet.

That sounds complicated, as does the algorithm that we need to follow: Consider the sequence using the tree in Figure 3.4.13:

Start in the MATHS tree
It has a left node
    so move to the BIOLOGY tree.
    It has no left node
    so output its root value BIOLOGY

then move right

to the COMPUTING tree.

It has no left node

so output the root COMPUTING.

It has no right node

so backtrack to the BIOLOGY tree which is

completed.

Backtrack to the MATHS tree

Output the root MATHS

and move right to sub-tree POLITICS.

It has a left node

so move to the tree PHYSICS.

It has no left node

so output the root PHYSICS.

It has no right node

so backtrack to the POLITICS tree.

Output the root POLITICS.

It has a right node

so move to the tree SOCIOLOGY.

It has no left node

so output the root SOCIOLOGY.

It has no right node.

You should have concluded that visiting the node in this way has output the data values in order. Hence the name for the algorithm – an *in-order traversal*.

The algorithm arises from the concept that any tree can be visualised as built up from any number of sub-trees. Even a leaf node can be visualised as a tree with no left or right descendants. The algorithm is a good example of recursion.

```
PROCEDURE InOrderTraversal(Root)
    IF Root.LeftLink <> Null
        THEN
            InOrderTraversal (Root.LeftLink)
    ENDIF
    OUTPUT Root
    IF RootRightLink <> Null
        THEN
            InOrderTraversal (Root.RightLink)
    ENDIF
END PROCEDURE
```

Notice the "dot notation" used. `Root.LeftLink` describes the left pointer value of the current root node.

We return to a similar method in Chapter 3.5, where we look at a particular use for binary trees.

(3.4 l) Merging data files and lists

This merging algorithm assumes the two lists are in order. It creates a third merged list from the two original lists.

Consider the two sorted lists: 2, 4, 7, 10, 15 and 3, 5, 12, 14, 18, 26. In order to merge these two lists, we compare the first item in each list (2 and 3). The smaller is put into the new list, as shown in Figure 3.4.14.

Since we have used the number from the first list, we consider the next item in that list and compare it with the number from the second list (as we have not yet used it). 3 is less than 4, so 3 is placed in the new list. As 3 came from the second list we now consider the next number in the second list and compare it with 4. This is continued until one of the lists is exhausted. We then copy the rest of the other list into the new list. The full merge is shown in Figure 3.4.14.

The algorithm for merging two files is included here as extension work.

First List	Second List	New List
2 4 7 10 15	3 5 12 14 18 26	2
2 4 7 10 15	3 5 12 14 18 26	2 3
2 4 7 10 15	3 5 12 14 18 26	2 3 4
2 4 7 10 15	3 5 12 14 18 26	2 3 4 5
2 4 7 10 15	3 5 12 14 18 26	2 3 4 5 7
2 4 7 10 15	3 5 12 14 18 26	2 3 4 5 7 10
2 4 7 10 15	3 5 12 14 18 26	2 3 4 5 7 10 12
2 4 7 10 15	3 5 12 14 18 26	2 3 4 5 7 10 12 14
2 4 7 10 15	3 5 12 14 18 26	2 3 4 5 7 10 12 14 15
2 4 7 10 15	3 5 12 14 18 26	2 3 4 5 7 10 12 14 15 18
2 4 7 10 15	3 5 12 14 18 26	2 3 4 5 7 10 12 14 15 18 26

Figure 3.4.14 Merging lists.

Extension

The following algorithm merges two sets of data that are held in two one-dimensional arrays called `List1[1 to M]` and `List2[1 to N]` into a third one-dimensional array called `List3`.
`List1` and `List2` have been sorted into ascending order and if there are any duplicates they are only copied once into `List3`.

```
PROCEDURE Merge(List1, List2, List3)
    Posn1 ← 1
    Posn2 ← 1
    Posn3 ← 1
    WHILE I ≤ M AND Posn2 ≤ N DO
        IF List1[Posn1]< List2[Posn2]
            THEN
                List3[Posn3] ←
                List1[Posn1]
                Posn1 ← Posn1 + 1
                Posn3 ← Posn3 + 1
            ELSE
                IF List1[Posn1] >
                List2[Posn2]
                    THEN
                        List3[Posn3] ←
                        List2[Posn2]
                        Posn2 ← Posn2 + 1
                        Posn3 ← Posn3 + 1
                    ELSE
                        List3[Posn3] ←
                        List1[Posn1]
                        Posn1 ← Posn1 + 1
                        Posn2 ← Posn2 + 1
                        Posn3 ← Posn3 + 1
                ENDIF
        ENDIF
    ENDWHILE
    IF Posn1 > M
        THEN
            FOR R ← Posn2 TO N DO
                List3[Posn3] ← List2[R]
                Posn3 ← Posn3 + 1
            ENDFOR
        ELSE
            FOR R ← Posn1 TO M DO
                List3[Posn3] ← List1[R]
                Posn3 ← Posn3 + 1
            ENDFOR
    ENDIF
ENDPROCEDURE
```

Summary

- Numbers (such as codes) on which arithmetic are not carried out can be represented in binary coded decimal (BCD).

- BCD involves using four bits to represent each numeric character. For example, 398 is represented by 0011 (3), 1001 (9) and 1000 (8): 001110011000.

- The easiest way to convert from denary to hexadecimal is to use a column diagram. The column value is the number of times the heading value divides into the denary number. For example, 334 in denary becomes 14E in hexadecimal:

256	16	1
1	4	E

- The easiest way to convert to denary is to multiply each column value by its heading and add the results.

- To convert from hexadecimal to binary, convert each digit to a four-digit binary number: 9C becomes 10011100.

- To convert from binary to hexadecimal, break the binary number into groups of four digits and convert each to a hexadecimal character: 00111010 becomes 3A.

Summary continued …

- Sign and magnitude is one way of representing negative numbers. The first bit of the byte is used to indicated the sign (0 for positive and 1 for negative) and the other seven bits represent the size (magnitude). Numbers between −127 and +127 can be represented.

- Two's complement is another way of representing negative numbers. The easiest way to calculate the two's complement for a negative number is to write down the positive number in binary, flip the bits and add 1.

- Integer binary addition can be performed within the limits of the representation using two's complement.

- A real number can be represented by storing the mantissa and the exponent (floating point representation).

- In a normalised floating point representation, the first two digits of the mantissa are different.

- Increasing the number of bits for the mantissa and reducing the number for the exponent increases accuracy at the expense of the range of numbers that can be represented.

- Increasing the number of bits for the exponent and reducing the number for the mantissa increases the range of numbers that can be represented at the expense of accuracy.

- Static data structures (such as arrays) do not change in size while the program is running.

- Dynamic data structures (such as linked lists) can increase and decrease in size while a program is running.

- A serial search does not require the data to be in any particular order. Each value in turn is examined until the required value is found or the end of the data structure is reached.
  - A serial search algorithm can take a long time to execute as many comparisons are made.

- A binary search requires the data to be sorted into order. The list is then repeatedly divided until the item is found.
  - A binary search algorithm involves many fewer comparisons than a serial search and tends to take less time to run.

- The insertion sort algorithm is an iterative algorithm that moves one value at a time into place.

- The quick sort algorithm is a recursive algorithm that sorts successive sub-lists.

- A binary tree is traversed from left to right through the nodes to output the data values in order.

- Lists are merged by comparing successive values and inserting the smaller value from each comparison into the new list.

Test yourself

1. a. Express the number 113 (denary) as:
     i.   an unsigned binary integer
     ii. BCD   [4]
   b. Using the answer obtained in part (a) show how 113 (denary) can be expressed in hexadecimal.   [2]

2. Explain how the denary number −27 can be represented in binary using
   i.   sign and magnitude.
   ii. two's complement notation.
   Use a single byte for each answer.   [4]

3. Add together the two's complement representations of 34 and 83, using a single byte for each.
   Show your working.   [3]

4. Describe floating point representation for real numbers using two bytes. [4]

> **Hint**
>
> You could use an example or diagram to make it clear.

5. a. Explain how the mantissa can be normalised. [2]
    b. State the benefit of storing real numbers using normalised form. [1]
6. a. A floating point number is represented in a certain computer system with a single byte. Five bits are used for the mantissa and three bits for the exponent. Both are stored in two's complement form and the mantissa is normalised.

    i.   State the smallest positive value that can be stored.
    ii. State the largest magnitude negative value that can be stored

    Give each answer as an eight-bit binary value and show its denary equivalent. [4]
    b. Explain the relationship between accuracy and range when storing floating point representations of real numbers. [4]
7. State the difference between a dynamic and static data structure. Give an example of each. [3]
8. a. Show how a binary tree can be used to store the data items: Fred, Edna, John, Sean, Dave, Gail in alphabetic order. [4]
    b. Explain why problems may arise if John is deleted from the tree and how such problems may be overcome. [4]
9. Describe **two** search algorithms, giving an indication of when it would be advisable to use each. [6]
10. Describe the steps in sorting a list of numbers into order using an insertion sort. [4]
11. Given two sorted lists, describe an algorithm for merging them into a third sorted list. [6]

3.5 Programming paradigms

This section considers a number of different programming languages to illustrate the points being discussed. You are not asked to write program code in the examination for this module. However, you may well find it helpful to include code examples to support an answer. This is perfectly satisfactory; indeed it will often help you to clarify your answer. If you do write code, the accuracy of the syntax will not be marked. Only the logic that you manage to convey is under scrutiny. If your work contains code, then examiners will use it as evidence that you understand the question and can explain your answer.

Thus, treat the code contained in this section simply as illustrative of the different facilities available for different programming **paradigms**. Do not think that you have to be able to program all of these features in any specific language.

3.5 a Characteristics of programming paradigms

The syllabus says "Describe the characteristics of a variety of programming paradigms". "A variety of programming *whats*?" is the normal question. Don't worry about it, a *programming paradigm* is simply a way of programming. So why don't we say "a variety of ways of programming"? Simply because there is a specific technical term which we should use.

Low-level paradigms

Programming paradigms are simply methods of programming. Initially, computers were programmed using machine code. Machine code was called a **first-generation programming language**. It was difficult to write and led to many errors in program code that were difficult to find. Programs written in machine

code or assembly language are said to be a **low-level programming** paradigm.

As we saw in Chapter 3.2, assembly languages were developed to make programming easier. Assembly languages replace machine code operations with mnemonics and allow labels for memory addresses. Assembly language programming is also a low-level paradigm (remember, it simply means a method).

After having computers that you could only communicate with in binary, assembly languages were a great advance in programming. Assembly language was the second type of language to be developed after machine code and assembly languages are called **second-generation programming languages**. Figure 3.5.1 shows an assembly language program that adds together two numbers and stores the result. (Notice that it has been set out more formally than the examples in Chapter 3.2.)

Label	Opcode	Operand	Comment
	LDA	X	Load the accumulator with the value of X
	ADD	Y	Add the value of Y to the accumulator
	STO	Z	Store the result in Z
	STOP		Stop the program
X:	20		Storage for variable X
Y:	35		Storage for variable Y
Z:			Storage for variable Z

Figure 3.5.1   Assembly language program.

Although assembly language is an improvement over machine code, it is still prone to errors and code is still difficult to debug, correct and maintain.

Procedural paradigm

The next advance was the development of procedural languages. These are called **third-generation** programming languages and are also known as high-level languages. These languages are *problem oriented* as they use a language and syntax appropriate to the type of problem being solved. For example, FORTRAN (FORmula TRANslation) and ALGOL (ALGOrithmic Language) were developed mainly for scientific and engineering problems. BASIC (Beginners All purpose Symbolic Instruction Code) was developed as a teaching language. A later development is Visual Basic .Net which is designed to sit inside the Microsoft .Net framework and allow for the development of Windows-based applications.

Object-oriented paradigm

The difficulty with procedural languages is that it can be awkward to reuse code in other programs. Modifying solutions when there is a small change in the problem to be solved can prove very difficult, often resulting in the program needing to be rewritten. In order to address this issue, object-oriented languages (which include Smalltalk, Java and C++) were developed.

In these languages, the data and methods of manipulating the data are designed and coded as a single unit called an **object**. The only way that a user can access the data is via the object's **methods**. This means that, once an object is fully working, it cannot be corrupted by the programmer because they cannot change any of the design features of the object. A simple example could be that validation of an object's data values is included as part of the object's original definition. It also means that the internal workings of an object may be changed without affecting any code that uses the object.

Declarative paradigm

A further advance was made when declarative programming languages were developed. Procedural languages encode a sequence of steps that determines *how* to solve the problem. In declarative languages, the computer is told what the problem is, not how to solve it. Given a database or knowledge base of facts and a set of rules to apply to the facts, the computer program searches for a solution.

(3.5 b) Types of high-level language

Procedural languages

Procedural programming languages specify how to solve a problem as a sequence of steps. They use the constructs: sequence, selection and iteration. For example, to find the area of a rectangle the steps are:

1. INPUT the length.
2. INPUT the breadth.
3. Multiply the length by the breadth and store the result.
4. OUTPUT the result.

In C++, this can be coded as:

```
cout << "Enter the length: ";
cin >> Length;
cout << "Enter the breadth: ";
cin >> Breadth;
Area = Length * Breadth;
cout << "The area is " << Area << endl;
```

Each line of code is executed one after the other in sequence. Can you understand the code (even if you know no C++)? Relate it to the initial algorithm design (remember, no one is suggesting that you should learn C++) and simply try to understand the logic. This is a good example of the features available in high-level languages that are close to human language. High-level languages are *task oriented*. This program is not written in English but it is close enough for us to be able to understand what the code is doing.

A number of constructs are common to all procedural languages. The abilities to do **selection** (in Visual Basic this means `IF` statements and `SELECT CASE` statements) and **iteration** (any use of a loop structure) are the most obvious. Refer back to Chapter 2.2 if you are unsure of these ideas. The point to note with procedural languages is that the programmer has to specify exactly what the program has to do.

Procedural languages are used to solve a wide variety of problems. As stated earlier, there are procedural languages designed to solve scientific and engineering problems while others are more suitable for solving business problems or developing programs for a particular user interface. There are some languages particularly designed for solving control problems that need real-time solutions.

Procedural languages may include functions and procedures but they always specify the order in which instructions must be used to solve the problem. The use of functions and procedures helps programmers to reuse code, but there is always the danger of variables being altered inadvertently due to their scope being unclear.

Object-oriented programming languages

In the 1970s, it was realised that code was not easily reused and there was little security of data in a program. Also, the real world consists of objects, not individual values. My car, registration number W123 ARB, is an *object*. Kay's car, registration number S123 KAY, is another object. Both of these objects are cars and cars have similar **properties** such as registration number, engine capacity, colour, etc. That is, my car and Kay's car are *instance*s of a type of object, a **class**, called Car.

In order to model the real world, the **object-oriented programming (OOP)** paradigm was developed. In the early 1990s, OOP gained in popularity. True object-oriented languages, such as Smalltalk and Eiffel, became well established. Other languages – including Visual Basic – were slow to include object-oriented features. Although OOP languages are procedural in nature, the way that they hold the data and the methods that can be used on the data makes them different. OOP is considered to be a programming paradigm in its own right.

The class is the blueprint or definition of some type of object, e.g. a car. An object is an actual instance of the class, e.g. Car. Objects are referenced with a variable name, e.g. MyCar, and can use data structures we are already familiar with. For example, we can have an array of cars.

Declarative programming languages

Another programming paradigm is the declarative one and an example language is Prolog. **Declarative programming languages** tell the computer what is wanted but do not provide the details of how to do it.

These languages are particularly useful when solving problems in artificial intelligence, such as medical diagnosis or fault finding in applications. The idea behind declarative languages is shown in Figure 3.5.2.

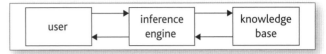

Figure 3.5.2   Declarative programming.

The user inputs a **query** to the inference engine, which then searches the knowledge base for the query results and returns them to the user. (Notice the similarity with expert systems which we studied in Chapter 1.8.)

In a procedural language, the data could be held in a two-dimensional array, Person:

	1	2
1	Female	Jan
2	Female	Ann
3	Female	San
4	Male	Cha
5	Male	Jaz
6	Male	Tom

The procedure to carry out the search using a procedural language must be coded by the programmer. In Visual Basic, it could be coded as follows:

```
For Index = 1 To 6
  If Person[Index, 1] = "Male" Then
    Console.Writeline (Person[Index, 2])
  End If
```

If we do this in a declarative language, we'll have a knowledge base that consists of the following facts:

```
female(jan).
female(ann).
female(san).
male(cha).
male(jaz).
male(tom).
```

In Prolog, data values start with a lowercase letter and all variables start with an uppercase letter. A user may want to output the names of all the males. The query `male(X)` returns the following data:

```
X = cha
X = jaz
X = tom
```

Notice that the user does not have to tell Prolog *how* to search for values of X that satisfy the query.

Suppose we now add the following data to the knowledge base:

```
parent(jan, mar).
parent(jan, raj).
parent(cha, mar).
parent(cha, raj).
parent(san, ati).
parent(jaz, ati).
```

The fact `parent(X, Y)` means X is a parent of Y. Suppose we wish to know the name of the mother of Ati. In Prolog, we set up the following query (notice that the comma denotes AND):

```
parent(X, ati), female(X).
```

Prolog finds that san and jaz satisfy the condition of being parents. It then goes to find which of them is female. That reduces the choices to one:

```
X = san
```

To get a list of all the fathers, we can write the following query:

```
parent(X, Y), male(X).
```

Prolog outputs:

```
X = cha Y = mar
X = cha Y = raj
X = jaz Y = ati
```

If we only want a list of fathers, we use an underscore and create the following query:

```
parent(X, _ ), male(X).
```

The result is:

```
X = cha
X = cha
X = jaz
```

The important point is that the programmer does not have to tell the computer *how* to compute the query results. There are no FOR . . . NEXT, WHILE . . . DO or REPEAT. . .UNTIL loops. Similarly, there are no IF. . .THEN statements. The programming environment simply consists of an inference engine and a knowledge base of facts and rules.

3.5 c Structured program development

A complex problem needs to be broken down into smaller and smaller sub-problems until all the sub-problems can easily be solved. This process is called *stepwise refinement*.

Consider the problem of calculating the wages for an hourly paid worker. The worker is paid £5.50 per hour for up to 40 hours and time-and-a-half for all hours over 40. Tax and health insurance contributions have to be deducted. The solution is represented in Figure 3.5.3.

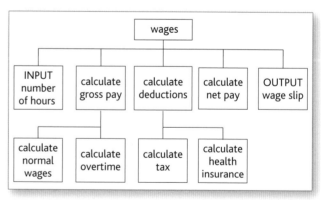

Figure 3.5.3 Calculating wages.

An alternative way of presenting the design is to use numbered statements. This can be easier to illustrate than the diagrammatic representation if there are many sub-problems to be solved.

```
1 Wages
   1.1 INPUT number of hours
   1.2 Calculate gross pay
       1.2.1  Calculate normal wages
       1.2.2  Calculate overtime
   1.3  Calculate deductions
       1.3.1  Calculate tax
       1.3.2  Calculate Health Insurance
   1.4 Calculate net pay
   1.5 OUTPUT wage slip
```

Either of these designs can be implemented as a number of functions and procedures. The program could be called Wages and consist of the following functions and procedures:

```
Wages
  InputHours()    ; returns an integer in the
                              range 0 to 60
  CalculateWage(Hours)    ; returns gross wage
  CalculateNormalWage(Hours)    ; returns the wage
                           for up to 40 hours
  CalculateOvertime(Hours)    ; returns the pay
                       for any hours over 40
  CalculateDeductions(GrossWage)    ;
                     returns total deductions
  CalculateTax(GrossWage)    ; returns tax due
  CalculateHI(GrossWage)    ; returns health
                             insurance due
  CalculateNetWage(GrossWage, Deductions)    ;
            returns net wage after deductions
  Procedure OutputResults(Hours, GrossWage, Tax, HI,
                      Deductions, NetWage);
                     prints the wage slip
```

A procedure is a block of program code statements designed to carry out a definable task. The procedure has an identifier name (see Chapter 2.2).

A function is a block of program code statements that returns a single value to the program that called it (see Chapter 2.2). As all programming languages have many "built-in" functions, we should call functions that are designed by the programmer "user-defined" functions.

In general if a single value is to be calculated, the simplest technique is to code a function. If there are no values to be returned, then a procedure should be used. If more than one value is to be returned, a procedure must be used.

For example, in the above design, the code could include the following function header:

```
Function InputHours() As Integer
```

The function header states that the function will return an integer and does not require any parameter values.

The following function header requires an integer value parameter and returns a number of data type Currency.

```
Function CalculateNormalWage(Hours As
Integer) As Currency
```

(3.5 d) Parameters and local and global variables

Stepwise refinement leads to a design from which the programmer can write modular code. Each module is a solution to an individual problem and each module has to interface with other modules. As long as the interfaces are clearly specified, each module could be given to a different programmer to code. The programmers need to know their problem and how its solution must communicate with the other modules that make up the overall design. The programmers need to pass values to other modules and be able to accept values from other modules.

Passing parameters

Let us first consider how data can be input to a module, be it a function or a procedure. This is done by means of parameters.

The function which follows on page 238, coded in Visual Basic, finds the perimeter of a rectangle given its length and breadth. This is not the only way of finding the perimeter and it is probably not the best way. However, it has been written like this in order to illustrate the definition of a simple function.

```
Public Function Perimeter(X As Integer, Y As Integer)_
As Integer
   X = 2 * X
   Y = 2 * Y
   Perimeter = X + Y
End Function
```

In this function, X and Y are integers, the values of which are passed to the function before it can find the perimeter of the rectangle. The variables X and Y are called *formal* parameters. To use this function, the program calls it and specifies the values for X and Y. This can be done by means of a statement of the following forms:

```
ThisPerimeter = Perimeter(4, 6)
ThisLength = 3
ThisWidth = 4
ThisPerimeter = Perimeter(ThisLength, ThisWidth)
```

Notice that the function follows the rules for any function:

- It has an identifier name, `Perimeter`.
- It requires two parameters of the stated data type, integer.
- Its definition says it will return a value (an integer).
- It returns a single integer value to the calling program variable, `ThisPerimeter`.

In the statements that call the function, the data values inside the brackets are called *actual parameters*. How the values are passed to the function or procedure depends on the programming language. We have two different ways of passing parameters.

In the first example of calling the `Perimeter` function, actual values (4 and 6) are passed to the function and stored in the variables X and Y. This is called passing parameters by value.

In the second example, the addresses of `ThisWidth` and `ThisLength` are passed to the function. This is called passing parameters by reference. A reference to the value is passed and the function then has to go and get the value.

Passing by reference

It is interesting to see the effect of passing values by reference (sometimes called passing by address). The following Visual Basic program calls the `Perimeter` function defined in the previous section:

```
Private Sub cmdShow_Click()
   Dim A As Integer
   Dim B As Integer
   Dim ThisPerimeter As Integer

   A = 3
   B = 4
   picResults.Print "Before call to Sub A = "; A; _
                    " and B = "; B
   ThisPerimeter = Perimeter(A, B)
   picResults.Print "Perimeter = "; ThisPerimeter
   picResults.Print "After call to Sub A = "; A; _
                    " and B = "; B;
End Sub
```

Note: `picResults` is the identifier name of a control that is used to display the output.

Figure 3.5.4 shows the output when this program is run. Notice that the values of A and B change after the function has been called. This is because the

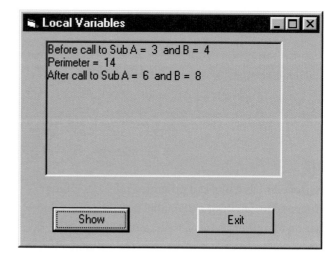

Figure 3.5.4   Output from perimeter program.

addresses of A and B were passed – not their values. When the algorithm doubled the values of X and Y in the Perimeter function, the effect was to change the values in the referenced variables.

Passing by value

Visual Basic can pass parameters by value as well as by reference. We have to use the ByVal keyword if we want to pass by value. Here is a modified form of the Perimeter function:

```
Public Function Perimeter(ByVal X As Integer, _
                 ByVal Y As Integer) As Integer
  X = 2 * X
  Y = 2 * Y
  Perimeter = X + Y
End Function
```

Figure 3.5.5 shows the output from running the modified program.

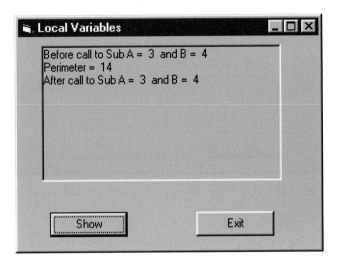

Figure 3.5.5   Output from modified perimeter program.

The scope of variables

Variables can have different values in different parts of the program. Study the Visual Basic code shown in the next column and its output shown in Figure 3.5.6 on page 240.

```
Private Sub cmdShow_Click()
  Dim A As Integer
  Dim B As Integer
  Dim C As Integer
  Dim ThisPerimeter As Integer

  A = 3
  B = 4
  C = 5

  picResults.Print "Before call to Sub A = "; A; _
                   " and B = "; B
  ThisPerimeter = Perimeter(A, B)
  picResults.Print "Perimeter = "; ThisPerimeter
  picResults.Print "After call to Sub A = "; A; _
                   " and B = "; B; " and C = "; C
End Sub

Public Function Perimeter(X As Integer, Y As Integer) _
               As Integer
  Dim C As Integer

  C = 10
  picResults.Print "In Sub C = "; C

  X = 2 * X
  Y = 2 * Y
  Perimeter = X + Y
End Function
```

Figure 3.5.6 (on page 240) shows that C has a different value in the function Perimeter from the value it has in the main program.

C is a local variable and the C used in Perimeter is a reference to a different address from the address referenced by C in the main program. Local variables only exist in the block in which they are declared. So the two variables called C that are declared in two different parts of an algorithm are two entirely separate variables.

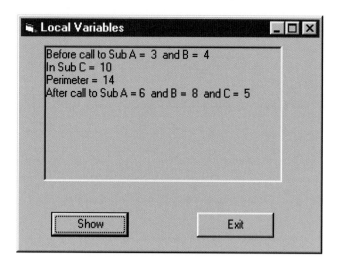

Figure 3.5.6 Output from perimeter program with local variable C.

This is very helpful as it means that programmers writing different routines do not have to worry about the names of variables used by other programmers.

However, it is sometimes useful to be able to use the same variable in many parts of a program. To do this, the variable has to be declared as *global*. In Visual Basic, this is done by means of a statement such as:

```
Public <variable name> As Integer
```

If we make C global in the example code, it becomes:

```
Public C As Integer

Private Sub cmdShow_Click()
  Dim A As Integer
  Dim B As Integer
  Dim ThisPerimeter As Integer

  A = 3
  B = 4
  C = 5

  picResults.Print "Before call to Sub A = "; A; _
              " and B = "; B; " and C = "; C
  ThisPerimeter = Perimeter(A, B)
  picResults.Print "Perimeter = "; ThisPerimeter
  picResults.Print "After call to Sub A = "; A; _
              " and B = "; B; " and C = "; C
End Sub
```

```
Public Function Perimeter(X As Integer, Y _
                          As Integer) _
                    As Integer
  C = 10
  picResults.Print "In Sub C = "; C

  X = 2 * X
  Y = 2 * Y
  Perimeter = X + Y
End Function
```

Figure 3.5.7 shows that the value of C, when changed in the function `Perimeter`, is also changed in the calling routine. In fact, it is changed throughout the program.

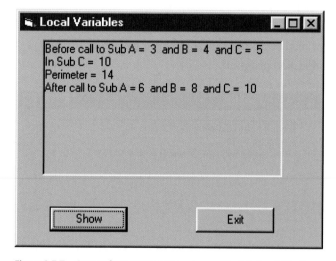

Figure 3.5.7 Output from perimeter program with global variable C.

To summarise:
- A *parameter* is a value that can be passed to a subroutine, whether a procedure or a function.
- If a parameter is passed *by value*, the actual value is passed and the original value is retained when the subroutine is finished.
- If a parameter is passed *by reference*, the address of the values is passed and any change to the value of the parameter in the subroutine changes the original value.

- The programmer must be careful about the intended scope of a variables:
  - A local variable only exists in the subroutine in which it is declared. A change to a local variable's value is seen only in the subroutine. The same local variable name can be used within many different subroutines.
  - A global variable exists throughout the entire program. A change to a global variable's value in one place is seen everywhere in the module. Variables are declared global as part of a module.

3.5 e) Calling procedures and passing parameters via a stack

When a procedure or function is called, the computer needs to know where to return to when the function or procedure call is completed. That is, the return address must be stored. Also, functions and procedures may call other functions and procedures, which means that not only must several return addresses be stored but they must be retrieved in the right order. This is achieved by using a stack (see Chapters 1.3 and 3.4).

Figure 3.5.8 shows what happens when three functions are called, one after another. The numbers represent the addresses of the instructions following the call to each function. The return addresses have to be stored.

The return addresses to be stored by this program execution are: 5, 204 and 305, in that order. They need to be retrieved in the order 305, then 204 and finally 5.

The last address stored is the first to be retrieved, i.e. it is a stack, as shown in Figure 3.5.9 (on page 242).

Notice that when the values are read (popped off the stack), they remain in the stack, it is just that they can never be used again and at some point the value is overwritten. They can be considered as deleted once they have been popped.

Using a stack to pass parameters

Now suppose that values need to be passed to or from a function or procedure. Again, a stack can be used. Consider a main program that calls two procedures:

```
ProcA(A1, A2)
ProcB(B1, B2, B3)
```

A1 and A2 are the formal parameters for ProcA. B1, B2 and B3 are the formal parameters for ProcB.

Figure 3.5.10 (on page 242) shows the procedures being called and the return addresses that must be placed on the stack.

Let us suppose that all the parameters are passed by value. When a procedure is called, the actual parameters are placed on the stack. The procedure pops the values off the stack and stores the values in the formal parameters. This is shown in Figure 3.5.11 (on page 243). Notice how the stack pointer is moved each time an address or actual parameter is pushed onto or popped from the stack.

Notice how the values X1 and X2 are deleted, not when they are read (popped) but when a new value is pushed.

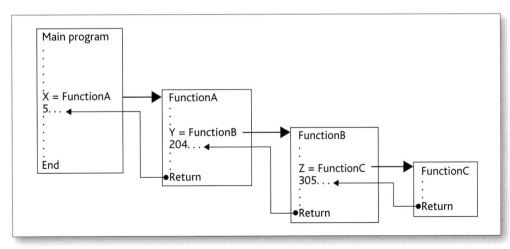

Figure 3.5.8   Calling multiple functions.

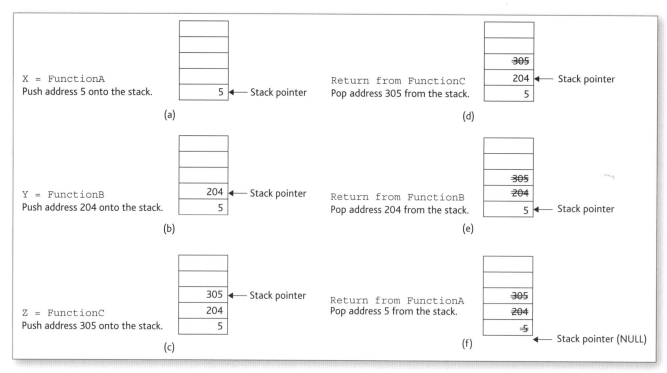

Figure 3.5.9 The changing stack as functions are called.

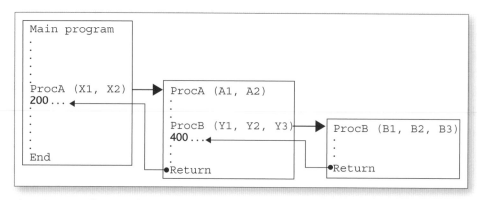

Figure 3.5.10 Calling procedures with parameters.

Next we must consider what happens if the values are passed by reference. This works in exactly the same way. The addresses of variables are passed so there is no need to return the values via parameters. The procedures or functions access the actual addresses where the variables are stored.

Finally, how do functions return a value? It simply pushes it onto the stack immediately before returning. The calling program can then pop the value from the stack. Note that the return address has to be popped off the stack before pushing the return value onto the stack.

The golden rule to think about when considering how stacks are used is where is the stack pointer? It points to the next item to be read.

One other thing about the stack: Do not worry if the diagram looks slightly different sometimes. Some textbooks implement the algorithm with the stack pointer pointing to the next available space. (This was the strategy we used when we introduced stacks in Chapter 1.3.)

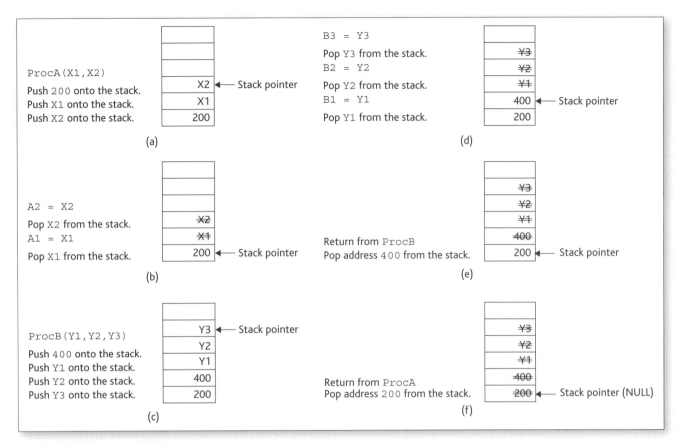

Figure 3.5.11 Passing parameters via a stack.

Object-oriented programming

All object-oriented languages have classes and use the concepts of encapsulation and inheritance. In this section, we consider these concepts in a general way, using diagrams rather than code for any particular language.

Encapsulation

Data **encapsulation** is the concept that data can only be accessed via the methods provided by the class. The class definition provides methods – coded as procedures or functions – for assigning and retrieving an object's data values, called its properties. Hence a class definition of an object is made up of:

- properties, e.g. a car object may include the EngineSize property
- methods to set a property value, e.g. SetEngineSize
- methods to recall a property value, e.g. GetEngineSize.

Objects can only access the data by using the methods provided. An object cannot manipulate the data directly. Consider a Rectangle class with Width and Length properties. An object of this class cannot directly calculate its Area. That is, we cannot write:

```
Area : = myRectangle.Width *
              myRectangle.Length;
```

where myRectangle is an object of type Rectangle.

To find the area of myRectangle, the class Rectangle must provide a suitable method. The only way to find the area is to use the write() method that outputs the area. If a user wishes to access the Width and Length properties of a rectangle, the class must provide methods to do this. Methods to return the Width and Length are given in the Java code on the next page.

```
Integer getWidth() {
    getWidth := Width;
} //end of getWidth method

integer getLength() {
    getLength := Length;
} //end of getLength method
```

myRectangle can use these methods to assign and retrieve the values for the width and length. However, it cannot change their values. To find the perimeter we write:

```
myWidth := myRectangle.getWidth();
myLength := myRectangle.getLength();
myPerimeter := 2 * (myWidth + myLength);
```

Here the "dot notation" denotes the use of the object's method, e.g. myRectangle.getWidth().

Thus, an object consists of the data and methods defined by the class. The concept of data being accessible only by means of the methods provided is very important as it ensures data integrity. Once a class has been designed, written and fully tested, neither its methods nor the data value of its properties can be tampered with. If the original design of a method is found to be inefficient, the design can be changed without the user's program being affected.

Inheritance and class diagrams

Another powerful concept in object-oriented programming is that of inheritance. Inheritance allows one class – called a *child class* – to inherit (i.e. use) all the properties and methods of its *parent class*.

Consider the Person **class diagram** shown in Figure 3.5.12. It has data about a person's name and address and three methods:

- outputData() outputs the name and address
- getName() returns the name
- getAddress() returns the address.

Now suppose we design a second class, Employee, that requires the same data and methods as Person

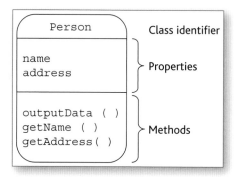

Figure 3.5.12   The class Person.

but also needs to store and output an employee's health insurance number. Clearly, we do not wish to re-design the Person class.

We implement the design with a new class called Employee that *inherits* all the properties and methods of the class Person and has properties and methods of its own. In Figure 3.5.13, the arrow signifies that Employee inherits the data and methods provided by the class Person. Person is the *super-class* (or *parent class*) of Employee and Employee is the *derived class* (or child class) of Person. An object of type Employee can use the methods provided by Employee and those provided by Person.

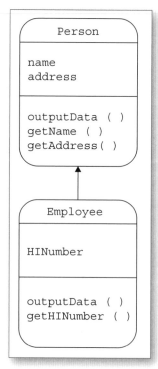

Figure 3.5.13   The class Employee inherits from Person.

Now suppose we have two types of employee; one type is hourly paid and the other type is paid a salary. Both of these employees require the data and methods of the classes `Person` and `Employee` but they each also need some additional properties. This is shown in Figure 3.5.14, which is called an *inheritance diagram*. Note the arrows always point up to the parent class.

Object diagrams

Think of classes as groups of real things. If there is a class called `Student`, it presupposes that there are some students that it represents. Each individual student has specific data stored for each of the properties. A specific student is an object of this class and a diagram which shows an individual student's properties is an *object diagram* (see Figure 3.5.15).

Definitions

An examination question may ask you to state the meanings of some basic terms. In this case, a simple definition is all that is required. There will only be one (or possibly two) marks for this type of question. The definitions given below would be a sufficient answer for questions that say "state the meaning of the term".

- A class describes the properties and methods of some real-world entity. The class definition is the "blueprint" from actual objects are later created.
- An object is an **instance** of a class, i.e. a real-world entity.
- Data encapsulation is the combining of the properties and methods for an object. Assigning and retrieving an object's property values are only done using methods to access the data.
- **Inheritance** is the ability of a class (the derived class) to use the properties and methods of another class (the parent class).

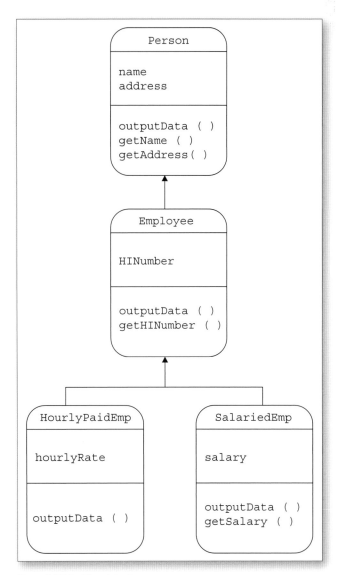

Figure 3.5.14 More inheritance.

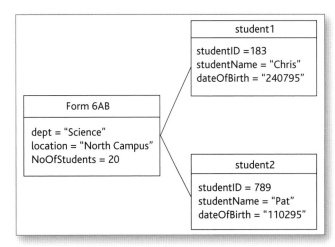

Figure 3.5.15 An object diagram.

Discussion

Referring to Figure 3.5.14, explain what is meant by the terms: object, class, inheritance, data encapsulation when referring to object-oriented languages.

3.5h Declarative programming

In "Types of high-level language" (on page 234), we saw that the programmer in a declarative language can simply state what data needs to be retrieved, once a set of facts and rules has been declared. We now look at how this is achieved using examples of Prolog scripts.

Prolog is called a declarative or **logic programming** language.

Consider the following knowledge base:

```
female(jan).
female(ann).
female(san).
male(cha).
male(jaz).
male(tom).
parent(jan, mar).
parent(jan, raj).
parent(cha, mar).
parent(cha, raj).
parent(san, ati).
parent(jaz, ati).
```

Remember that:
- variables start with an uppercase letter
- constants start with a lowercase letter.

Suppose we ask the query: `male(X)`. The query is known as a **goal**. The goal is to find all X that satisfy `male(X)`. If Prolog finds a match, we say that the search has succeeded and the goal is true. When the goal is true, Prolog outputs the corresponding values of the variable X.

Prolog starts searching the knowledge base and finds that `male(cha)` matches `male(X)` if X is given the value `cha`. We say that X is *instantiated* to `cha`. In other words, `cha` is an instance of something that matches the rules for clause `male`. Prolog outputs the goal and continues to search the knowledge base, until the whole knowledge base has been searched. The final output is:

```
X = cha
X = jaz
X = tom
No
```

The last line means that there are no more solutions. Now we add a rule that X is the father of Y *if* X is a parent of Y *and* X is male:

```
father(X, Y) :- parent(X, Y), male(X).
```

Notice that:
- The : - symbol denotes "if".
- The comma symbol denotes "and".

The knowledge base now looks like this:

```
female(jan).
female(ann).
female(san).
male(cha).
male(jaz).
male(tom).
parent(jan, mar).
parent(jan, raj).
parent(cha, mar).
parent(cha, raj).
parent(san, ati).
parent(jaz, ati).
father(X, Y) :- parent(X, Y), male(X).
```

Suppose our goal is to find the father of `raj`. That is, our goal is to find all X that satisfy `father(X, raj)`.

The components `female`, `male`, `parent` and `father` are called *predicates*. The values inside the parentheses are called arguments. Prolog looks for the predicate `father` and finds the rule:

```
father(X, Y) :- parent(X, Y), male(X).
```

In this rule, Y is instantiated to `raj` and Prolog starts to search the knowledge base for:

```
parent(X, raj)
```

This is the new goal and Prolog finds the match:

```
parent(jan, raj)
```

X is instantiated to `jan` and Prolog now uses the second part of the rule:

```
male(jan)
```

This new goal fails. Prolog does not give up but backtracks to the goal:

```
parent(X, raj)
```

Prolog finds another match:

```
parent(cha, raj)
```

With X instantiated to cha, the next step is to try to satisfy the goal:

```
male(cha)
```

This is successful so `parent(cha, raj)` and `male(cha)` are both true.

Thus `father(cha, raj)` is true. Prolog continues to see if there are any more matches. There are no more matches so Prolog finally outputs:

```
X = cha
No
```

We include here the definitions of terms used in this section. Remember, they can be used when a question says "State the meaning of the term".

- **Backtracking** means going back to a previous successful match in order to continue a search.
- *Instantiation* means giving a value to a variable in a statement.
- A goal is a statement that we are trying to prove either True or False. The goal effectively forms a query.

Activity

You are given the following facts and rules:

```
dog(fid)
dog(whi)
pig(spo)
cat(glo)
cat(pur)
chases(A, B) :- dog(A), cat(B)
```

where `dog(fid)` means Fid is a dog.

1. Explain the steps that are necessary to solve the goal `chases(X, Y)`.
2. Use the stages of your solution to explain what is meant by the following terms and give examples:
   i. backtracking
   ii. instantiation
   iii. a goal.

Extension

We were introduced to recursion in Chapter 2.2. Remember that we only need to be able to trace a recursive routine, not produce one, and there was an example of this in the coverage of binary trees in Chapter 3.4. Recursion can be used to create alternative versions of a rule.

Figure 3.5.16 shows that X is an ancestor of Y if X is a parent of Y. But it also shows that X is an ancestor of Y if X is a parent of Z and Z is a parent of Y. It also shows that X is an ancestor of Y if X is a parent of Z and Z is a parent of W and W is a parent of Y. This can continue forever. Thus the rule is recursive.

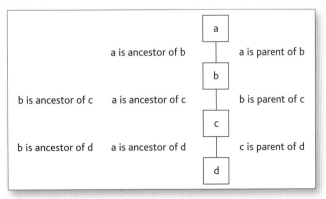

Figure 3.5.16   Recursive rules.

Extension continued …

In Prolog, we require two rules:

```
ancestor(X, Y) :- parent(X, Y).
ancestor(X, Y) :- parent(X, Z), ancestor(Z, Y).
```

The first rule states that X is an ancestor of Y if X is a parent of Y. Using the example in Figure 3.5.16, a is an ancestor of b, b is an ancestor of c and c is an ancestor of d.

The second rule is in two parts. Let us see how it works using Figure 3.5.16 as the knowledge base:

```
parent(a, b).
parent(b, c).
parent(c, d).
```

We set the goal `ancestor(a, c)`. Prolog finds the first rule and tries to match `parent(a, c)` with each predicate in the database. Prolog fails but does not give up. It backtracks and looks for another rule for `ancestor`. Prolog finds the second rule and tries to match `parent(a, Z)`. It finds `parent(a, b)`, so it instantiates Z to b.

This is now put into the second part of the rule to produce `ancestor(b, c)`. This means that Prolog has to look for a rule for `ancestor`. It finds the first rule and looks for `parent(b, c)`, which succeeds. This means that with X = a and Y = c, we have Z = b and the second rule succeeds. Therefore Prolog returns `Yes`.

Now try to trace what happens if the goals are:

```
ancestor(a, d)
ancestor(c, b).
```

You should find that the first goal succeeds and the second fails.

This form of programming is based on the mathematics of predicate calculus. Predicate calculus is a branch of mathematics that deals with logic. All we have done in this section is based on the rules of predicate calculus. Prolog stands for *programming in logic*.

In predicate calculus, the simplest structures are atomic sentences such as:

- Mar *loves* Har
- Phi *likes* Zak

The words in italics are part of the names of relationships.

We also have atomic conclusions such as:

- Mar *loves* Har if Har *loves* Mar
- Joh *likes* dogs if Jan *likes* dogs
- *Fra likes* Someone if Someone *likes* computing

In the last atomic conclusion, Someone is a variable. The meaning of the conclusion is that Fra likes anybody (or, in fact, anything) that likes computing.

Joint conditions use the logical operators OR and AND, examples of which are:

- Joh *likes* x if x is female AND x is vegetarian
- Mar *loves* Bil OR Mar *loves* Col if Mar *loves* Don

⟶

Extension continued …

The atomic formulae that serve as conditions and conclusions may be written in a simplified form. In this form the name of the relation is written in front of the atomic formula. The names of the relations are called "predicate symbols". Examples are:

```
loves(mar, har)
likes(phi, zak)
```

We use the symbol := to represent "if", thus:

```
loves(mar, Har) := loves(har, Mar)
likes(joh, dogs) := likes(jan, dogs)
```

AND is represented by a comma in the condition part of the atomic conclusion:

```
likes(joh, X) := female(X), vegetarian(X)
```

These examples show the connection between Prolog and predicate calculus. You do not need to understand how to manipulate the examples you have seen any further than has been shown in the earlier discussion.

3.5 i Low-level programming languages
Direct addressing

We have already used **direct addressing** in our assembly language discussion. The operand gives the actual memory address from which the data value is retrieved.

The following instruction means "retrieve the contents of location 10 and copy it to the accumulator":

```
LD 10
```

Figure 3.5.17 shows what happens when the statement is executed.

There are two problems with direct addressing:
- The number of bits used for the operand directly determines the number of memory addresses that can be used. A 16-bit operand give 63 536 different addresses. This is not significant if we can increase the number of bits used for an instruction.
- If we want to use the same instruction to refer to different memory locations – say, the contents of a continuous block of memory – we would write the same instruction many times. This can be avoided by using indexed addressing.

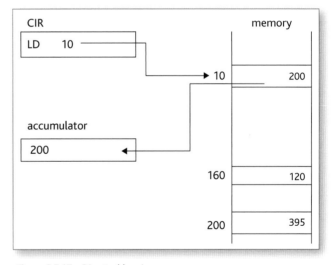

Figure 3.5.17 Direct addressing.

Indirect addressing

The following instruction means "retrieve the address in location 10 and copy the contents of that address to the accumulator":

```
LDI 10
```

Figure 3.5.18 (on page 250) shows what happens when the statement is executed.

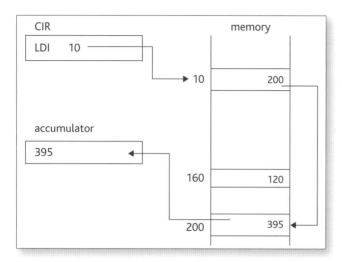

Figure 3.5.18 Indirect addressing.

Indirect addressing is very useful because it means that more addresses in memory can be used to store data.

Indexed addressing

The following instruction means "go to a memory location and add the contents of this address to the accumulator":

```
ADD <address>
```

Imagine that the contents of an array (a block of consecutive memory locations) of 100 items are to be added together. If the first item in the array is stored at location 10, then the sequence of instructions would be:

```
LD 10
ADD 11
ADD 12
...
ADD 109
```

Basically, it is the same instruction 100 times. It is far easier is to use a special register – called the **index register (IR)** – and calculate the address to be used as the one given in the operand plus the contents of the IR register.

Initially, IR is set to 0 so that the first actual address to use is calculated as 10 + 0. After each addition the IR is incremented and the same instruction is executed.

The second time, the address used is 10 + 1. When the IR is incremented and used again, the next address is 10 + 2 and so on all the way up to 10 + 99. Using **indexed addressing**, we only need one instruction inside a loop that is executed 100 times.

The assembly language instruction could be:

```
ADI <address>
```

This means "add to the accumulator the contents of the address calculated as <address> + the contents of IR". Figure 3.5.19 shows what happens when the instruction is executed.

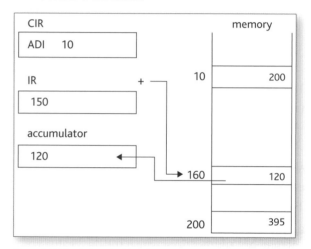

Figure 3.5.19 Indexed addressing.

Relative addressing

When a program segment is written or translated it is not always possible to predict where the program and its data are going to be loaded in the main memory. (Remember the issue of moveable code in our discussion about memory management in the operating system.) So there is no point in having an instruction of ADD 10 because the data may not be stored at location 10. We can't insist on that but we can insist that the program and data go into memory as a single block using continuous memory locations.

There is no problem then if we use **relative addressing**. This simply means that all the addresses are expressed relative to the address used for the first program instruction (the start of the program).

If the first instruction of the program is stored in location 10, the following instruction uses the data stored in 150 + 10, or location 160:

`ADR 150`

Every actual address is relative to the address used by the first instruction in the program (Figure 3.5.20).

Addressing mode

We have said more than once about the instruction that "some extra bits are reserved for other things". We now need to use two of these bits. If an instruction is `LD 10`, what does it mean? Does it mean that the contents of address 10 are to be sent to the accumulator or is it some other form of addressing that results in a totally different value being sent to the accumulator?

We have discussed four different types of addressing. In the mnemonics, we have tried to make clear the mode of addressing being used, i.e. `LD` uses direct addressing, `LDI` uses indirect addressing and `LDR` uses relative addressing.

An alternative strategy is that all three might use the same opcode and two additional bits to denote the mode of addressing. For example, the load opcode could be 010 and then we could use 00 for direct addressing, 01 for indirect addressing and 10 for relative addressing.

Activity

1. Direct addressing is not always suitable for low-level language instructions. Explain why this is.
2. Explain the other types of addressing that can be used in low-level language programming.

(3.5 j) Backus–Naur form and syntax diagrams

Since all programming languages have to be translated to machine code by means of software, they must be clearly defined.

The start of a FOR loop in Visual Basic is:

```
For Count = 1 To 10
```

Other languages use a different syntax. For example, C++ expects:

```
for (Count = 1, Count <= 10, Count++)
```

A Visual Basic compiler would not understand the C++ syntax and vice versa. We therefore need a set of rules, for each language, that specify precisely every part of the language. These rules can be expressed using **Backus–Naur form (BNF)** or **syntax diagrams**.

Backus–Naur form (BNF)

All languages use integers, so we shall start with the definition of an integer:

- a sequence of the digits 0, 1, 2, . . . , 9
- of arbitrary length – it can have any number of digits.

A particular compiler restricts the number of digits only because of the finite storage space set aside for an integer value. A computer language does not

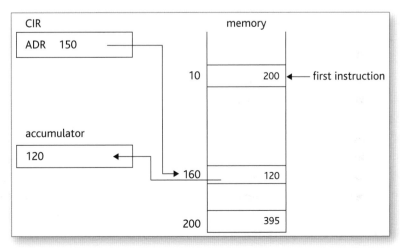

Figure 3.5.20   Relative addressing.

restrict the number of digits. The following are all valid integers:

$$0$$
$$2$$
$$415$$
$$3040513002976$$

Thus, an integer can be a single digit. We express this as:

```
<integer> ::= <digit>
```

The `::=` symbol means "is defined to be", so this is read as "an integer is defined to be a digit".
But we must now define a digit:

```
<digit> ::= 0|1|2|3|4|5|6|7|8|9
```

where the vertical line is read as "or".

Notice that all the digits have to be specified and that they are not inside angle brackets like `<integer>` and `<digit>`. This is because, unlike integer and digit, they do not have definitions elsewhere. The digits 0, 1, 2, . . . , 9 are called **terminal symbols**, i.e. they cannot be further simplified. We tend to start with the letters of the alphabet, the arithmetic operators or, as here, the digits. Anything else that we want as part of the programming language has to be defined. Anything that needs defining is put in <> brackets.

Our complete definition of a single digit integer is, therefore:

```
<integer> ::= <digit>
<digit> ::= 0|1|2|3|4|5|6|7|8|9
```

The language that we have used to express these rules is called Backus–Naur form (BNF).

But how are we going to specify that an integer may be of any length? Consider the integer 147. It is a single-digit integer (1) followed by the integer 47. But 47 is a single-digit integer (4) followed by a single-digit integer (7). Thus, all integers of more than one digit start with a single digit and are followed by an integer. Eventually the final integer is a single-digit integer.

Thus, an integer with any number of digits can be expressed as:

```
<integer> ::= <digit><integer>
```

Note that this is equivalent to:

```
<integer> ::= <integer><digit>
```

This is a *recursive* definition as `<integer>` is defined in terms of itself. Applying this definition several times produces the sequence:

```
<integer> ::= <digit><integer>

          = <digit><digit><integer>

          = <digit><digit><digit><integer>
```

To stop this we use the fact that, eventually, `<integer>` is a single digit and write:

```
<integer> ::= <digit> | <digit><integer>
```

That is, an integer is a digit or a digit followed by an integer. At any time `<integer>` can be replaced by `<digit>` and the recursion stops.

Strictly speaking we have defined an *unsigned* integer, as we have not allowed a leading plus sign or minus sign. This is dealt with later. We now have the full definition of an unsigned integer which, in BNF, is:

```
<unsigned_integer> ::= <digit> | <digit>
                        <unsigned_ integer>
<digit> ::= 0|1|2|3|4|5|6|7|8|9
```

Syntax diagram

The definition of an unsigned integer can be described using syntax diagrams (Figure 3.5.21). A syntax diagram is read from the left and then we just follow the arrows. All acceptable definitions are denoted by paths through the diagram from left to right. Any sequence that cannot be generated by following the arrows is therefore not allowed by the rules.

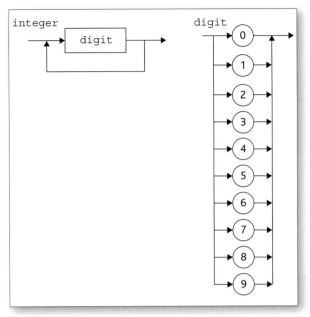

Figure 3.5.21 Syntax diagrams for an unsigned integer.

Now we define a signed integer, such as +2 and –3415. This is simply an unsigned integer preceded by a + or – sign. Thus we can use the earlier rules for an unsigned integer and create rules for a signed integer:

```
<signed_integer> ::= + <unsigned_integer>|
                     -<unsigned_integer>
```

or:

```
<signed_integer>::= <sign><unsigned_integer>
<sign>::= +|-
```

An "integer" is usually intended to mean a signed integer or unsigned integer. This then gives the following BNF rules for our definition of an integer:

```
<sign> ::= + | -
<digit> ::= 0|1|2|3|4|5|6|7|8|9
<signed_integer> ::= <sign><unsigned_integer>
<unsigned_integer> ::= <digit> | <digit>
                              <unsigned_ integer>
<integer> ::= <unsigned_integer>|<signed_integer>
```

Figure 3.5.22 shows the corresponding syntax diagrams.

It is better to use several rules than try to cater for all the possibilities in a single rule. In other words, start at the top with a general definition. Then break the definitions down into simpler and simpler definitions.

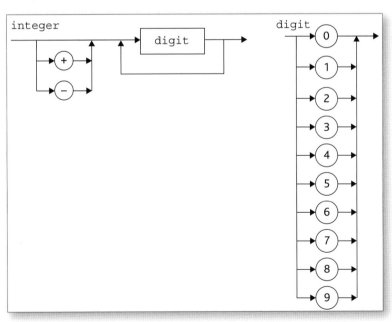

Figure 3.5.22 Syntax diagrams for an integer.

That is, we use a top-down design when creating these definitions.

Care must be taken when positioning the recursion in the definitions using BNF. Suppose we define a variable as a sequence of one or more characters starting with a letter. The characters can be any letter, digit or the underscore character. Examples of valid variables include:

```
A
x
sum
total_24
mass_of_product
MyAge
```

What happens if we use a similar definition to that for an unsigned integer?

```
<variable> ::= <letter> | <letter> <variable>
    | <letter> <character>
<character> ::= <letter> | <digit> | <underscore>
```

Note that the second alternative for `<variable>` is recursive and the order is important. The rule makes clear that A3 would be valid but 3A is an invalid variable name.

The revised rule definitions are:

```
<variable> ::= <letter>|<letter>|<variable>|<letter>|
                                      <character>
<character> ::= <letter>|<digit>|<underscore>
<letter> ::= <uppercase>|<lowercase>
<uppercase> ::= A|B|C|D|E|F|G|H|I|J|K|L|M|N|O|P|Q|R|
                                      S|T|U|V|W|X|Y|Z
<lowercase> ::= a|b|c|d|e|f|g|h|i|j|k|l|m|n|o|p|q|r|
                                      s|t|u|v|w|x|y|z
<digit> ::= 0|1|2|3|4|5|6|7|8|9
<underscore> ::= _
```

Activity

Draw the syntax diagram which matches the definition of `<variable>` given by the BNF rules.

Let us now use our definition of an integer to define a real number such as:

$$0.347$$
$$-2.862$$
$$+14.34$$
$$00235.006$$

We need only one additional rule:

```
<real_number> ::= <integer> . <unsigned_integer>
```

Discussion

Try to come up with a definition that covers all variations of signed, unsigned and fractional numbers.

Finally, suppose we do not want to allow leading zeros in an integer. That is, 00135 is not allowed but 0 is allowed.

This means that an integer can be:
- a zero digit
- a non-zero digit
- a non-zero digit followed by any digit.

This means that an integer is either zero or a digit string, where "digit string" must start with a non-zero digit. In BNF, this is:

```
<Zero> ::= 0
<NonZeroDigit> ::= 1|2|3|4|5|6|7|8|9
<Digit> ::= <Zero> | <NonZeroDigit>
<DigitString> ::= <NonZeroDigit> |
                <DigitString> <Digit>
<Integer> ::= <Zero> | <DigitSring>
```

Figure 3.5.23 shows the corresponding syntax diagram.

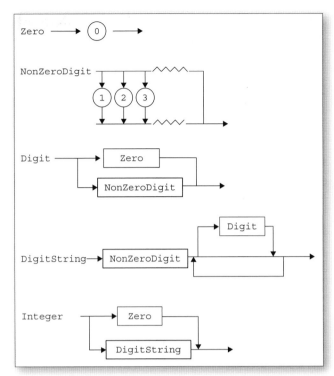

Figure 3.5.23 Syntax diagram for an integer without leading zeros.

(3.5 k) ## Reverse Polish notation

First, what is "reverse Polish notation"? If we want to add two numbers, A and B, we write the expression as:

```
A + B
```

This is called **infix notation** because the arithmetic operator (+) is placed between the two operands (A and B). The problem with infix notation is that if we have an expression such as 2 * A + B we need to have brackets in order to make clear whether to add the A and B first or whether to do the multiplication first. In other words, infix notation without brackets can be ambiguous about the order in which the parts of the calculation must be done.

A Polish mathematician came up with an alternative to infix notation that puts the operator at the front of the expression so that A + B becomes + A B.

This is not as strange as it at first looks. Instead of saying "Number A is added to number B", this Polish notation simply says "Add number A to number B". The important thing about Polish notation is that it is unambiguous; the operator always applies to the two operands that follow. Because there is no ambiguity, brackets are not needed. This makes understanding and evaluating Polish expressions a lot easier than expressions in infix notation. Polish expressions use **prefix notation** because the operator comes before the operands instead of between them.

Reverse Polish notation puts the operator after the two operands: A + B becomes A B + Polish. Reverse Polish is important in computing. Not only is it unambiguous, and so does not need brackets, but complex expressions can be evaluated with a technique involving a stack, which makes the algorithms to work out expressions very robust. Because the operator comes at the end, reverse Polish is called **postfix notation**.

The expression 2 * (A + B) means "add the numbers A and B and then multiply the answer by 2". How can we express this in reverse Polish notation? The first thing that needs to be done is the calculation inside the brackets, so that becomes A B +. After that, the answer is multiplied by 2, so the expression becomes 2 (A B +) *. But expressions in reverse Polish are unambiguous so we don't need the brackets (they are only there to make it more understandable). The infix expression 2 * (A + B) becomes 2 A B + * in reverse Polish.

To summarise, Reverse Polish is important in computing because:

- expressions written in postfix notation are unambiguous
- expressions do not need brackets
- expressions can be evaluated using a stack (see next section).

Activity

a. Work out the infix equivalents of these reverse Polish expressions:
  i.   ab−cd+*
  ii. ab*cd−+
  iii. xy+z+cd+−
b. Work out the reverse Polish equivalents of these infix expressions:
  i.   (a + b) − (c + d)
  ii. x * (y − z)
  iii. (a + b)/(c − d)

3.5 l) Converting between reverse Polish notation and the infix form of algebraic expressions

Using a binary tree

All expressions in infix notation consist of an operator and two operands, one on either side of the operator. This sounds very like "a node and its two branches", in other words a tree structure.

Consider the expression: 2 * (A + B). This expression can be represented by the binary tree in Figure 3.5.24.

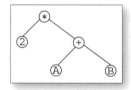

Figure 3.5.24   A binary tree for 2 * (A + B).

Consider the expression: (2A − B) / (C^3). This means "Divide the answer to 'subtract B from 2 times A' by the answer to C cubed". So which operator do we start with in this tree? Divide was the first one mentioned when we managed to write it out. Another way of deciding is to underline the options and you then get something that looks a bit like a tree but upside down:

    (2 * A − B) / (C ^ 3)

This gives the tree in Figure 3.5.25.

Why are trees relevant here? If the tree is traversed in a particular order, then the result is the reverse Polish form of the expression.

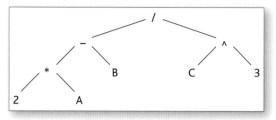

Figure 3.5.25   A binary tree for (2A − B)/(C^3).

If we traverse the tree in Figure 3.5.24 in the order left–root–right, then we output the nodes to give the infix notation (see Figure 3.5.26).

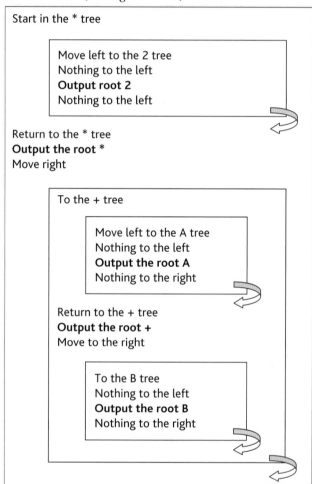

Figure 3.5.26   In-order traversal of the binary tree for 2 * (A + B).

We conclude that an in-order traversal produces the infix notation for the expression: 2 * (A + B).

Figure 3.5.26 shows how a move is made to deal with a sub-tree before the current tree is completed. This is an example of **recursion**. A new sub-tree traversal is started before the current one is completed. The arrows in Figure 3.5.26 illustrate the unwinding from each sub-tree to the return point inside the previous sub-tree or tree.

What happens if we traverse the tree in a different order? Consider the traversal order left–right–root, shown in Figure 3.5.27. Tracing this traversal shows that the order of output is 2 A B + *.

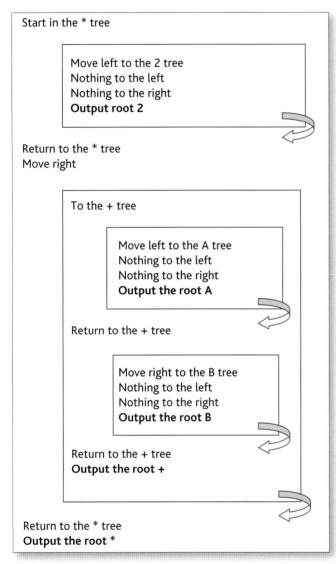

Figure 3.5.27   Post-order traversal of the binary tree for 2 *(A + B).

The order left–right–root is called a *post-order traversal*. For an expression tree, it outputs the reverse Polish representation of the expression.

To summarise:

- A binary tree can be used to represent an algebraic expression.
- A left–root–right traversal order is called an in-order traversal and produces the infix representation of the expression.
- A left–right–root traversal order is called a post-order traversal and produces the postfix (or reverse Polish) representation of the expression.

The numbering of the nodes in Figure 3.5.28 shows the order in which the nodes are output for a post-order traversal.

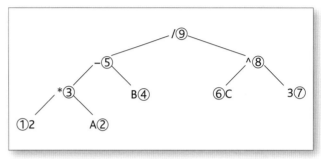

Figure 3.5.28   Post-order traversal of a binary tree for (2A − B)/(C^3) with numbered nodes.

Activity

Carefully trace the tree in Figure 3.5.28 to confirm that a post-order traversal gives the following output order: 2 A * B − C 3 ^ /, i.e. the reverse Polish for the expression.

Consider the expression:

X = (A − 2B) + 3(C / D − 3).

The first stage in converting it to reverse Polish is to write it out with all the operators present:

X = (A − 2 * B) + 3 * (C / D − 3)

Notice that this expression is actually a formula, so the X = must be included in the final tree. Assigning the expression to X is the last thing to be done, so the = must be at the root of the tree.

The only things outside brackets are the + and the *. We can't add the two parts together until the * has been done, so + must be the next thing in the tree. Then we unravel the two brackets, one on either side of the + sign. The tree is shown in Figure 3.5.29 (on page 258).

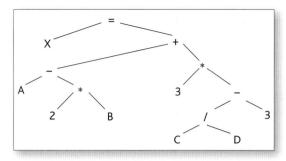

Figure 3.5.29 A binary tree for
$X = (A - 2B) + 3(C / D - 3)$.

This may look complicated, but only because of the volume. The general principles are exactly the same as we have already seen. To produce the reverse Polish expression, visit the nodes of the tree in the order left–right–root. The order of output is shown in Figure 3.5.30 with the nodes numbered.

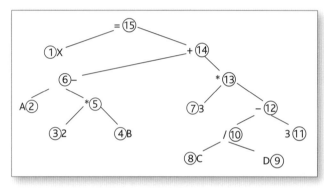

Figure 3.5.30 Post-order traversal of a binary tree for
$X = (A - 2B) + 3(C / D - 3)$ with numbered nodes.

Activity

1. Trace carefully the post-order traversal in Figure 3.5.30 to confirm that the expression

   X A 2 B * – 3 C D / 3 – * + = is

   the reverse Polish.
2. For each of the following expressions, draw the binary tree and use it to write the reverse Polish form:

   i. (a + b) * c
   ii. (2 * (a – b)) + (c – d)

Using a stack

To convert a reverse Polish expression to infix notation or to evaluate the expression, we can use a stack. The procedure is:

1. Each operand is placed (pushed) onto the stack in turn until it meets an operator.
2. Read the operator.
3. The two top values in the stack are read (popped).
4. The operator is carried out on them.
5. The result is placed on the stack.
6. Repeat until the final infix expression is the only item on the stack or the expression has been evaluated.

Figure 3.5.31 shows how the stack changes for the reverse Polish expression 2 a b + *. The procedure is:

1. 2, a and b are pushed onto the stack (Figure 3.5.31a).
2. The operator + is read.
3. a and b are popped from the stack and added.
4. The result is placed on the stack (Figure 3.5.31b).
5. The operator * is read.
6. (a+b) and 2 are popped from the stack and multiplied.
7. The result is placed on the stack (Figure 3.5.31c).

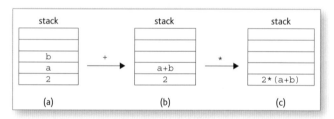

Figure 3.5.31 Changing stack for 2 a b + *.

Activity

Trace the operation of the stack in Figure 3.5.32.

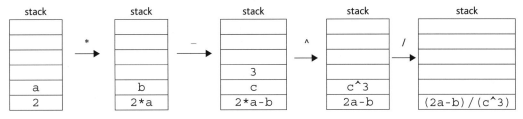

Figure 3.5.32 Changing stack for `(2A - B)/(C^3)`.

Summary

- The characteristics of programming paradigms:

  - Low-level programming languages are close to the way the computer works and are difficult to write, debug and correct.

  - Procedural languages are problem oriented and are easier to write, debug and correct.

  - Object-oriented languages make it easier to reuse code.

  - Declarative languages leave the computer to work out how to solve a problem from facts and rules.

- Types of high-level language include:

  - procedural languages that specify how to solve a problem as a sequence of steps
  - object-oriented languages that encapsulate properties and processing using objects
  - declarative languages that use an inference engine and a knowledge base of facts and rules.

- When a program is developed in a structured way, using stepwise refinement, the overall problem is broken down into smaller sub-problems until they are small enough to turn into code.

- The sub-problems can be coded as functions and procedures:

  - A parameter is a value passed to a procedure or a function.
  - If a parameter is passed by value, the actual value is passed and the original value is retained when the subroutine is finished.
  - If a parameter is passed by reference, the address of the values is passed and any change to the value of the parameter in the subroutine changes the original value.

- A local variable only exists in the subroutine in which it is declared.

- A global variable exists throughout the entire program.

- The return address for a called procedure or function can be pushed onto the stack, followed by the parameters to the subroutine. When control passes to the subroutine, it pops the parameters off the stack. At the end of the subroutine, the return address is popped off the stack.

- In object-oriented programming a class describes the properties and methods of a real-world entity:

  - An object is an instance of a class, i.e. a real-world entity.
  - Data encapsulation means that an object's data can only be accessed using its methods.
  - Inheritance is the ability of a derived class to use the properties and methods of its parent class.
  - Instantiation means creating an actual instance of an object.

Summary continued ...

- In a declarative language a goal is a statement that we are trying to prove either True or False. The goal effectively forms a query.
- Backtracking means going back to a previous successful match in order to continue a search.
- In low-level languages:
  - Direct addressing means that the operand is the actual address to be used.
  - Indirect addressing means the operand holds the address of the location that holds the value to be used.
  - Indexed addressing means the operand is added to the IR to calculate the address to be used.
  - Relative addressing means that the operand is added to the address of the first instruction to calculate the address.
- Backus–Naur form (BNF) is a way of defining rules for the syntax of a programming language.
- A syntax diagram is a visual way of defining rules for the syntax of a programming language.
- Reverse Polish is important because its expressions are unambiguous and can be evaluated using a stack.
- You can convert between reverse Polish notation and the infix form of algebraic expressions using a binary tree. Use an in-order traversal to get the infix notation and post-order traversal to get the reverse Polish notation.
- To convert a reverse Polish expression to infix notation or to evaluate the expression, we can use a stack.

Test yourself

1. Distinguish between procedural languages and declarative languages. [4]
2. Explain the passing of parameters by reference and by value. [4]
3. Explain the terms:
   i.   data encapsulation
   ii. inheritance
   iii. object
   when applied to programming in an object-oriented programming language. [6]
4. The class inheritance diagram in Figure 3.5.33 shows a design for staff employed at a school.

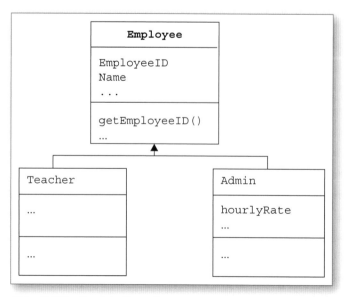

Figure 3.5.33   Class inheritance diagram.

a. Using Figure 3.5.33 and giving examples to illustrate your answers, explain the terms:

    i.   inheritance

    ii.   data encapsulation

    iii. class

    iv. object.   [8]

b. Cleaners should also be included on the diagram. Draw a diagram to show the class `Cleaner` and a property `AreaCleaned` with an appropriate method.   [3]

c. Some teachers are heads of department and others are individual members of department. These different types of teacher are each defined by a class. Explain where the three additional classes: `Cleaner`, `HeadOfDept` and `MemberOfDept` should be placed on the diagram.   [3]

5. Explain the difference between direct and indirect addressing and explain why indirect addressing allows access to more memory locations than direct addressing.   [6]

6. An amount of money can be written as the $ sign followed by either:

- a positive integer, or
- a positive integer, a point, and a two-digit number, or
- a point followed by two digits.

A positive integer has been defined as `<integer>`.

```
<digit>::= 0|1|2|3|4|5|6|7|8|9
```

Define, using Backus–Naur form, `<amount_of_money>`.   [3]

3.6 Databases

3.6 a ## Flat files and relational databases

Originally, all data held in computers was stored in files. A typical file used for a database-type application would consist of a large number of records, each of which would consist of a number of fields. Each field would have its own data type and hold a single item of data. For example, a stock file would contain records describing stock. Each record may consist of the fields in Table 3.6.1.

Table 3.6.1   Stock record.

Field Name	Data Type
Description	String
CostPrice	Currency
SellingPrice	Currency
NumberInStock	Integer
ReorderLevel	Integer
SupplierName	String
SupplierAddress	String

This approach led to very large files that were difficult to process. Suppose we want to know which items of stock need to be reordered. This is fairly straightforward. We search the file sequentially; if the number in stock is less than the re-order level, we output the details of the item and supplier.

The problem is that when we check the stock the next day, we create another order because the stock that has been ordered has not been delivered. To overcome this, we could introduce a new field called `OnOrder` of type `Boolean`. This can be set to True when an order has been placed and reset to False when an order has been delivered. Unfortunately it is not that straightforward. The original software is expecting seven fields, not eight fields. This means that the software designed to manipulate the original file must be modified to read the new file layout, i.e. the program code needs modifying.

Ad-hoc enquiries are virtually impossible. What happens if management ask for a list of the best selling products? The file has not been set up for this and to change it so that such a request can be satisfied involves modifying all existing software. Further, suppose we want to know which products are supplied by the company Food & Drink Ltd. In some cases, the company's name has been entered as "Food & Drink Ltd.", sometimes as "Food and Drink Ltd." and sometimes the full stop after "Ltd" has been omitted. This means that a match is very difficult because the data are inconsistent.

Each time a new product is added to the database, the name and address of the supplier must be entered. This leads to redundant data or data duplication as we already have the supplier address recorded as part of several other product records. Figure 3.6.1 shows how data can be proliferated when each department keeps its own files.

This approach to storing and processing data uses **flat files**. Flat files have the following limitations:

- Separation and isolation of data: Suppose we wish to know which customers have bought items from a particular supplier. We first need to find the items supplied by a particular supplier from one file and then use a second file to find which customers have bought those products. This difficulty can be compounded if data are needed from more than two files.
- Duplication of data: Figure 3.6.1 suggests that the supplier data will be duplicated for every stock

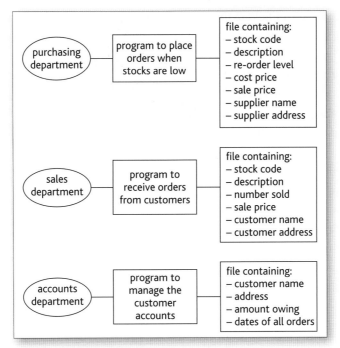

Figure 3.6.1 Redundant data.

record. Duplication is wasteful as it costs time and money. Data has to be entered more than once, therefore it takes up user time and storage space. Duplication is also likely to lead to a loss of data integrity and data inconsistency. What happens if a customer changes their address? The Sales Department may update their files but the Accounts Department may not do this at the same time. Worse still, suppose the Purchasing Department orders some parts and there is an increase in price. The Purchasing Department increases the cost and sale prices but the Accounts Department does not; there is now a discrepancy. When we have two copies of a data item which should be the same and they are not, this is called "inconsistent data".

- Data dependence: Data formats (typically a record description) are defined in the application programs. If there is a need to change any of these formats, whole programs may have to be changed. Different applications may hold the data in different forms, again causing a problem. Suppose an extra field is needed in a file, again all application programs using that file have to be re-coded.

- Queries/reports and the proliferation of application programs: Processing files by computer was a huge advance on the manual processing of queries on the

data. This led to end users wanting more and more information. Each time a new query was asked for by a user, a new program had to be written. Often, the data needed to answer the query were stored in more than one file, some of which were incompatible.

The need for database software

A solution to many of these problems with using flat files was the arrival of **relational database** software.

The data are stored in **tables** which have **relationships** between the various tables. Each table stores data about an **entity** – i.e. some "thing" about which data are stored, for example, a customer or a product. Each table has a primary key field, by which all the values in that table are identified. The table can be viewed just like a spreadsheet grid, so one row in the table is one record.

The practical design of relational databases is based in the theory developed in the late 1970s by Ted Codd. The theory called the entities relations and they are implemented as tables. Each record in the table is called a "tuple" (also known as a row). A data item is known as an attribute (or a column).

The records in the tables can be related to entities in other tables by having common fields within the entities. So, the problem of the supplier details being duplicated can be solved by the relevant field in the order table simply containing the key of the supplier entity. The likely data design here would be:

- The Supplier table has a primary key of SupplierID.
- The Product table also has the SupplierID field (to link back to the Supplier table).
- The SupplierID field in the Product table is called a **foreign key**.

The user can search the supplier table for details of the relevant supplier using the supplier key when it is necessary. In this way only the foreign key SupplierID needs to be stored in the Product table. The inclusion of other supplier data, such as the SupplierName and SupplierAddress, would be a duplication. We already have these details of the supplier stored in the Supplier table.

The differing needs of the departments are met by the software that is used to control the data. As all the data are stored somewhere in the system, a department only needs software that can search for it. In this way each department does not need its own set of data, simply its own view of the centralised **database** to which all users have access.

3.6 b, c Designing a relational database

Consider the delivery note from Easy Fasteners Ltd in Figure 3.6.2. The delivery note has more than one product on it. This is called a *repeating group*. In the relational database model, each record must be of a fixed length and each field must contain only one item of data. Also, since each record must be of a fixed length, this means that a variable number of fields is not allowed. In this example, we cannot say "let there be three fields for the products" as some customers may order more products than this and others fewer products. So, repeating groups are not allowed in a table design.

At this stage we should start to use the correct vocabulary for relational databases. We call the columns attributes and the rows are called records. The data are organised into tables. Table 3.6.2 is a first attempt at the database design for entity ORDER (Num, CustName, City, Country, ProdID, Description).

Normalisation is a set of formal rules that must be considered once we have a set of table designs. By following the normalisation rules we ensure that the final table designs do not result in duplicated data. If the initial designs were well thought through then the normalisation process will not result in any changes to the table designs.

Easy Fasteners Ltd
Old Park, The Square, Berrington, Midshire BN2 5RG

To: Bill Jones
London
England

No: 005
Date: 14/08/11

Product No.	Description
1	Table
2	Desk
3	Chair

Figure 3.6.2   A delivery note.

Table 3.6.2   The ORDER entity.

Num	CustName	City	Country	ProdID	Description
005	Bill Jones	London	England	1	Table
005	Bill Jones	London	England	2	Desk
005	Bill Jones	London	England	3	Chair
008	Amber Arif	Lahore	Pakistan	2	Desk
008	Amber Arif	Lahore	Pakistan	7	Cupboard
014	M. Ali	Kathmandu	Nepal	5	Cabinet
002	Omar Norton	Cairo	Egypt	7	Cupboard
002	Omar Norton	Cairo	Egypt	1	Table
002	Omar Norton	Cairo	Egypt	2	Desk

First normal form (1NF)

A table with no repeating groups is said to be in *first normal form*. Table 3.6.2 has repeating groups in the attributes ProdID and Description. We remove the repeating groups by:

- moving the ProdID and Description attributes to a new table
- linking the new table to the original table ORDER with a foreign key.

Tables 3.6.3 and 3.6.4 show the data in first normal form. The primary key of each table is shown in red.

Table 3.6.3   The ORDER table (1NF).

Num	CustName	City	Country
005	Bill Jones	London	England
008	Amber Arif	Lahore	Pakistan
014	M. Ali	Kathmandu	Nepal
002	Omar Norton	Cairo	Egypt
. . .			

Table 3.6.4   The ORDER-PRODUCTS table.

Num	ProdID	Description
005	1	Table
005	2	Desk
005	3	Chair
008	2	Desk
008	7	Cupboard
014	5	Cabinet
002	1	Table
002	2	Desk
002	7	Cupboard
. . .		

Second normal form (2NF)

A table is in *second normal form* if any partial **dependencies** have been removed. That is, every non-key attribute must be fully dependent on all of the primary key.

In our ORDER-PRODUCTS table, Description depends only on ProdID and not on Num. Hence the non-key attribute (Description) is not dependent on all of the primary key. We say that Description is dependent on ProdID or, turned around: ProdID *determines* Description or ProdID → Description.

We remove the partial dependency by:
- moving the Description attribute to a new table
- linking the new table to the ORDER-PRODUCTS table with a foreign key.

Tables 3.6.5 and 3.6.6 show the data in *second normal form*.

Table 3.6.5   The ORDER-PRODUCTS table (2NF).

Num	ProdID
005	1
005	2
005	3
008	2
008	7
014	5
002	1
002	2
002	7
. . .	

Table 3.6.6   The PRODUCT table.

ProdID	Description
1	Table
2	Desk
3	Chair
5	Cabinet
7	Cupboard
. . .	

At this stage, the ORDER-PRODUCTS table is fully normalised:
- 1NF – it does not have a repeated group of attributes
- 2NF – there are no non-key attributes

The PRODUCT table is also fully normalised:
- 1NF – it does not have a repeated group of attributes
- 2NF – it has a single-attribute primary key

Third normal form (3NF)

Third normal form (like second normal form) is concerned with the non-key attributes. To be in 3NF, there must be no dependencies between any of the non-key attributes. A table with no or one non-key attribute must be in 3NF, so PRODUCT and ORDER-PRODUCTS are in 3NF.

There is a problem with the original ORDER table. City determines the Country, so we have two non-key attributes which are dependent. This means that ORDER is not in 3NF. Tables 3.6.7 and 3.6.8 show the data in *third normal form*.

Table 3.6.7   The ORDER table (3NF).

Num	CustName	City
005	Bill Jones	London
008	Amber Arif	Lahore
014	M. Ali	Kathmandu
002	Omar Norton	Cairo
. . .		

Table 3.6.8   CITY-COUNTRIES (3NF).

City	Country
London	England
Lahore	Pakistan
Kathmandu	Nepal
Cairo	Egypt
. . .	

To summarise, we have been through the stages shown in Table 3.6.9. The primary key is underlined.

Table 3.6.9   Summary of design changes.

Stage	Tables
UNF	ORDER (Num, CustName, City, Country, (ProdID, Description))
1NF	ORDER(Num, CustName, City, Country) ORDER-PRODUCTS (Num, ProdID, Description)
2NF	ORDER (Num, CustName, City, Country) ORDER-PRODUCTS (Num, ProdID) PRODUCT (ProdID, Description)
3NF	ORDER (Num, CustName, City) CITY-COUNTRIES (City, Country) ORDER-PRODUCTS (Num, ProdID) PRODUCT (ProdID, Description)

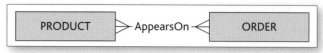

Figure 3.6.4 Many-to-many relationship.

Activity

1. A display is required showing all the customer names for orders that included the product with code 6. Which tables are needed to provide this view?
2. Consider if the PRODUCT table had included data about the supplier of each product. An initial design is: PRODUCT (ProdID, Description, SupplierID, SupplierName, SupplierAddress, SupplierTelNo).
   a. Carry out the discussion which concludes that this table is not in 3NF and arrives at the following re-designed tables:
   PRODUCT (ProdID, Description, SupplierID)
   PRODUCT-SUPPLIER (SupplierID, SupplierName, SupplierAddress, SupplierTelNo)
   b. i. Describe the relationship between the two tables created in part (a).
   ii. Explain how this relationship is formed.

Entity–relationship diagrams

An **entity–relationship diagram** (E–R diagram) can be used to illustrate the **relationships** between entities. In the earlier example, we started with the entities ORDER and PRODUCT. Each order can have one or more products on it and each product may appear on many orders.

To illustrate a situation diagrammatically, the first thing to do is to identify the entities that are being used and to draw them inside rectangles (Figure 3.6.3).

Figure 3.6.3 Entities.

Many-to-many relationship

The next step is to show the relationship between them (Figure 3.6.4). Actually there are two sides to this relationship:

- Many PRODUCTs appear on many ORDERs
- Many ORDERs contain many PRODUCTs

Many-to-many relationships are impossible to implement with relational database software. The

solution is always to introduce an intermediate table with two one-to-many relationships.

One-to-many relationship

We resolve the many-to-many relationship in Figure 3.6.4 by introducing an ORDER-PRODUCT entity and two one-to-many relationships (Figure 3.6.5):

One PRODUCT appears on many ORDER-PRODUCTs.
One ORDER contains many ORDER-PRODUCTs.

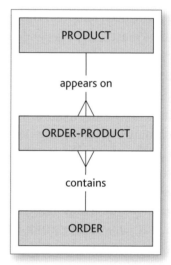

Figure 3.6.5 One-to-many relationships.

Think carefully and you should realise that we already have this design in our earlier discussion.

One-to-one relationship

One-to-one relationships are rare and probably only arise because the two tables were created at different times or originally for use with different databases.

General points

We would usually avoid showing many-to-many relationships (remember they cannot be implemented). It is usual to label relationships with a description (as shown in Figure 3.6.4).

The complete E–R diagram for our example is shown in Figure 3.6.6.

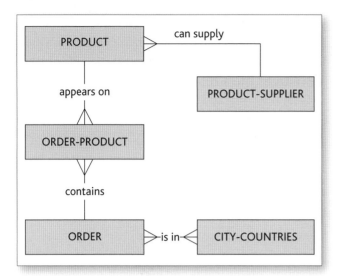

Figure 3.6.6　Entity–relationship diagram for our database.

3.6 d **Advantages of a relational database**

As we saw in the previous sections, there are a number of advantages of using a relational database (rather than flat files) to store data on a computer system.

Note that all the points listed under the "Relational database" heading in Table 3.6.10 offer a major advantage over the use of flat files for developing a database-type application. Several of the points in the "Relational database" column are considered plus points for using a database management system (DBMS).

3.6 e **Primary, secondary and foreign keys**
Primary key

The key used to uniquely identify a row in a table is called the **primary key**. A primary key may consist of a single attribute (e.g. the PRODUCT table) or more than one attribute. In the ORDER-PRODUCTS table, Num + ProdID together form the primary key, and this is called a **composite key**.

In a school database, the student table may have a "school admissions number" for each student and this would be the primary key. The problem with using the student name is that there may well be more than one student with the same name, hence the name could not be guaranteed to be unique.

Foreign key

Foreign keys and primary keys are the means by which tables are linked together and relationships are formed. A field is a foreign key in a table if it is the primary key in another table. The creation of foreign keys is done at the table design stage.

In our order processing example, ORDER has a primary key of Num and this links to a foreign key of Num in the ORDER-PRODUCTS table.

It would be good to decide on a formal way of describing each relationship and how each will be created. For example:

One record in the ORDER table refers to many ORDER-PRODUCTS records can be interpreted as

Table 3.6.10　Comparison of flat files and relational databases.

	Flat files	Relational database
Data storage	Data are stored in a number of files.	Data are contained in a single software application – the relational database or DBMS software.
	Data are highly likely to be duplicated and may become inconsistent – it can never be certain that all copies of a piece of data have been updated.	Duplication of data is minimised and so the chance of data inconsistency is reduced. As long as there is a link to the table storing the data, they can always be accessed via the link rather than repeating the data. Good database design avoids data duplication.
	Because of data duplication, the volume of data stored is large.	Because data duplication is minimised, the volume of data is reduced, leading to faster searching and sorting of data.
Program–data independence	When data structures need to be altered, the software must be re-written.	Data structures remain the same even when the tables are altered. Existing programs do not need to be altered when a table design is changed.
	Views of the data are governed by the different files used to control the data and produced by individual departments. All views of the data have to be programmed and this is very time-consuming.	Queries and reports can be set up with simple "point and click" features or using the data manipulation language. A novice user can write queries quickly.

Primary key Num (in the ORDER table) links to foreign key Num (in the ORDER-PRODUCTS table).

Activity

Refer back to Figure 3.6.6 on page 267 and write formal descriptions for the other three relationships as shown above.

Secondary key

A user often wants to search the database using an attribute which is not the primary key. For example, if the table contained details of students, we may want to search for all the students who live in a particular town. The town attribute is not the primary key. An attribute which is used to access the data in some way other than by using the primary key is known as a **secondary key**. The setting up of these secondary keys is called **indexing**.

The designer must decide which attributes to index (i.e. on which ones to set up a secondary key). The temptation is to index every attribute, but remember that indexes have to be kept up-to-date and this requires processing time. Every time the data in a table changes – e.g. a new record is added – the indexes must be updated.

Activity

A school uses a database which includes the following tables:

- STUDENT – stores data for each student
- SUBJECT – stores data for all taught subjects
- STUDENT-SUBJECTS – stores data showing which subjects are studied by each student

Use this database to define and give examples for the terms primary key, foreign key and secondary key.

(3.6 f) Specifying user access restrictions

Sometimes it must not be possible for a user to access the data in a database. For example, in a banking system, consider two customers who share the same bank account. There is an overdraft limit on the account and one customer may attempt to withdraw money (for example, at an ATM). While one customer is accessing the account using the ATM, the other customer must not be able to access the database.

Similarly, while a database system is checking stock levels for re-ordering purposes, the POS terminals cannot use the database as each sale would change the stock levels. Incidentally, there are ways in which the POS terminals could still operate. One is to use the database only to query prices. A transaction file of sales can be used later to update the database.

Database user accounts

The discussion of database user accounts that follows is nothing to do with a network user account, which provides access to a computer network.

It is often important that users have restricted views of the database. Consider a hospital that has a network of computers. There are terminals in reception, on the wards and in consulting rooms. All the terminals have access to the patient database, which contains details of the patients' names and addresses, illnesses and drugs to be administered. It is important that the receptionist can check a patient's name and address when the patient registers at reception. However, the receptionist should not have access to the drugs to be administered nor to the patient's medical history.

This access can be controlled by the database designer setting up different user accounts which are administered and controlled using passwords. It could be an account for an individual user or a "group account" such as that provided for all reception staff. That is, the receptionists' passwords only allow access to the information that receptionists need. A general rule is that users of the database should have sufficient sight of the data in order to do their job. When a receptionist logs onto the network, the database management system (DBMS) (see the next section) checks the password and ensures that the receptionist can only access the appropriate data.

The terminals on the wards are used by nurses, who need to see what drugs are to be administered. Therefore nurses should have access to the same data as the receptionists *and* to the information about the drugs to be given. However, they may not have access to the patients' medical histories. This can be achieved by setting up a group account for all nurses. In this case, the DBMS recognises the different userID and password and gives a higher level of access to nurses than it does to receptionists.

Finally, the consultants want to access *all* the patient data. This can be done by giving them another account and password.

All three categories of user of the database (receptionist, nurse and consultant) must only be allowed to see the data that is needed by them to do their job (and their job only).

Certain terminals only

So far we have only mentioned the use of passwords to impose levels of security. However, suppose two consultants are discussing a case as they walk through reception and they want to see a patient's record. Both consultants have the right to see all the data that is in the database but the terminal is in a public place and patients and receptionists can see the screen. This means that, even if the consultants enter the correct password, the system should not allow them to access all the data.

This can be achieved by the DBMS noting the address of the terminal and refusing to permit the logon. This is a hardware method of controlling access. All terminals have a unique address on their network card. This means that the DBMS can decide which logons – and consequently which data – can be allowed at each terminal.

> ### Discussion
>
> Find out about the levels of access allowed to the school database. You may want to consider what access is sensible for students, parents, teachers, admin staff and the headteacher.

3.6 g Database management systems

Many of the advantages of using relational database software over flat files would have been equally relevant here as plus points for using software called a **database management system (DBMS)**.

Software such as Microsoft Access is relational database software. This type of software is well suited to applications that store of the order of thousands of records. Some applications, e.g. an online retail database such as that used by Amazon, would generate thousands of order transactions in a day and software such as Microsoft Access would be inappropriate.

Applications which need high volume of transactions and other features must be implemented using DBMS software.

Commercial DBMS products include Oracle, SQL Server from Microsoft and MySQL from the free community.

Figure 3.6.7 (on page 270) shows a DBMS used to store and process data for a large hospital. The orange boxes represent application programs that are written in high-level programming languages to access and process the data held in the various database. The green boxes represent features that are available directly using features provided by the DBMS software.

What is a DBMS?

A DBMS is a piece of software that provides the following facilities:
- basic database design, including tables, relationship and user queries
- a data definition language (DDL) that the database designer uses to define the tables of the database
- a **data dictionary** that includes:
  - the descriptions of tables, relationships and all design information such as indexing
  - the rules about data integrity including validation rules for all attributes.
- a data manipulation language (DML) called SQL:
  - for inserting, amending and deleting data records
- backup of the database data
- control of multi-user access to the data.

The "centralisation" of data integrity is a key advantage of using a DBMS. It means that applications programs do not need hard coded validation checking. Validation is controlled by the DBMS.

Most large applications require that several users of the database have *concurrent access* to the data. This is done using features such as record locking. For example, if a user is currently editing a patient record, then access to this record is refused to other database users until the edit is completed. (Look back to the ATM example discussed on page 268.)

Data definition language (DDL)

The DBMS contains a **data definition language (DDL)** that the database designer uses to define the database. It allows the designer to specify the data types and

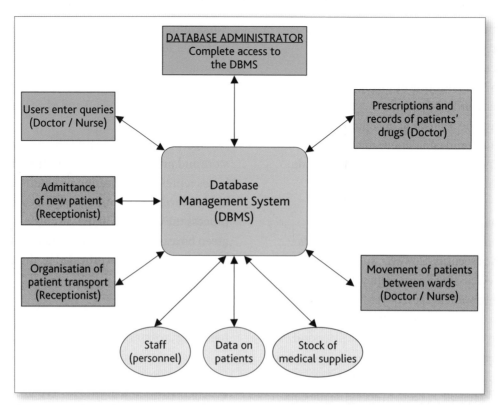

Figure 3.6.7   A hospital DBMS.

structures of the data. The DDL used by all popular database and DBMS software is **Structured Query Language (SQL)**.

A DBMS such as Microsoft Access allows the user to *avoid* direct use of a DDL by presenting the user with a design view in which the tables, relationship, queries, etc. are created with simple point-and-click features.

All current popular software uses SQL. Indeed, proficiency with SQL is one of the most sought after computing skills. This is the language that DBMS software or relational database software uses for:

- basic database design
- inserting a record
- deleting records
- amending records.

The following examples were done with the XAMPP software and uses the MySQL DBMS.

We consider a simple scenario where a hospital ward has a number of patients.

The following is a typical sequence of SQL scripts which would be run:

1. Create the database HOSPITAL.
2. Create the table PATIENT.
3. Create the table WARD.

```
CREATE DATABASE 'HOSPITAL';
CREATE TABLE 'HOSPITAL'.'PATIENT'
(
  PatientIDNumber INT NOT NULL ,
  PatientName VARCHAR(30) NOT NULL ,
  PatientAddress VARCHAR(50) NOT NULL ,
  NextOfKin VARCHAR(30) NOT NULL ,
  DateOfBirth DATE NOT NULL ,
  PRIMARY KEY PatientIDNumber ,
);
CREATE TABLE 'HOSPITAL'.'WARD'
(
  WardName VARCHAR(20) NOT NULL ,
  NoOfBeds INT NOT NULL ,
  NurseInCharge VARCHAR(30) NOT NULL,
  PRIMARY KEY WardName ,
) ;
```

4. Create the one-to-many relationship. This is illustrated by Figure 3.6.8.

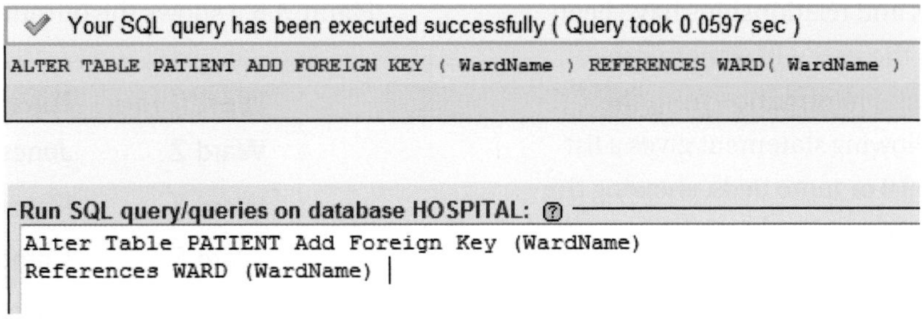

> ✓ Your SQL query has been executed successfully (Query took 0.0597 sec)
>
> ALTER TABLE PATIENT ADD FOREIGN KEY (WardName) REFERENCES WARD(WardName)
>
> ┌─ Run SQL query/queries on database HOSPITAL: ⑦ ──────────
> │ Alter Table PATIENT Add Foreign Key (WardName)
> │ References WARD (WardName) |

Figure 3.6.8   SQL query which adds a foreign key to the PATIENT table.

Data manipulation language (DML)

Part of SQL is a **data manipulation language (DML)**. The database designer can use it to write SQL scripts that:

- insert, amend and delete data records
- retrieve data from database tables based on search criteria specified by the user.

Again, this is likely to be done by the user with simple point-and-click features. What the DBMS does is create a SQL script that mirrors the actions of the user and then runs the script. In Microsoft Access, this is done using a facility called "Query By Example".

The following insert script creates 13 new WARD records:

```
INSERT INTO WARD (WardName, NoOfBeds,
                  NurseInCharge) VALUES
('Ward 1',10, 'Sellick') ;
INSERT INTO WARD (WardName, NoOfBeds,
                  NurseInCharge) VALUES
('Ward 2', 20, 'Jones') ;
INSERT INTO WARD (WardName, NoOfBeds,
                  NurseInCharge) VALUES
('Ward 3',15, 'Papandreou') ;
INSERT INTO WARD (WardName, NoOfBeds,
                  NurseInCharge) VALUES
('Ward 4',11, 'Mellas') ;
INSERT INTO WARD (WardName, NoOfBeds,
                  NurseInCharge) VALUES
('Ward 5',32, 'Comodi') ;
INSERT INTO WARD (WardName, NoOfBeds,
                  NurseInCharge) VALUES
('Ward 6',11, 'Mignini') ;
```

```
INSERT INTO WARD (WardName, NoOfBeds,
                  NurseInCharge) VALUES
('Ward 7',12, 'Philippe') ;
INSERT INTO WARD (WardName, NoOfBeds,
                  NurseInCharge) VALUES
('Ward 8',15, 'Bashir') ;
INSERT INTO WARD (WardName, NoOfBeds,
                  NurseInCharge) VALUES
('Ward 9',16, 'Kelly') ;
INSERT INTO WARD (WardName, NoOfBeds,
                  NurseInCharge) VALUES
('Ward 10',4, 'Morris') ;
INSERT INTO WARD (WardName, NoOfBeds,
                  NurseInCharge) VALUES
('Ward 11',4, 'Ocampo') ;
INSERT INTO WARD (WardName, NoOfBeds,
                  NurseInCharge) VALUES
('Ward 12',12, 'Sviridov') ;
INSERT INTO WARD (WardName, NoOfBeds,
                  NurseInCharge) VALUES
('Ward 13',12, 'Sekhina') ;
```

Writing SQL statements like this to insert a new record is extremely tedious. The database administrator (DBA) would make available to the users programs to do this (see Figure 3.6.8).

Once the data tables and relationships have been created and populated, the user will want to run queries that provide useful information from the database tables. The following statement gives a list of all wards which have 10 or more beds, showing the ward name and the nurse in charge:

```
SELECT WardName, NurseInCharge
FROM WARD
WHERE NoOfBeds >= 10;
```

Figure 3.6.9 shows the output of this query.

WardName	NurseInCharge
Ward 2	Jones
Ward 3	Papandreou
Ward 5	Comodi
Ward 8	Bashir
Ward 9	Kelly

Figure 3.6.9   Output of a query.

Summary

- A flat file consists of a large number of records each of which comprises a number of fields.
- Each field has its own data type and holds a single item of data.
- Flat-file systems tend to lead to:
  - separation and isolation of data
  - duplication of data
  - data dependence
  - data inconsistencies
  - difficulty in changing applications programs.
- Relational databases store data in tables.
- We ensure that database tables are in the third normal form (3NF):
  - 1NF – it does not have a repeated group of attributes
  - 2NF – there are no non-key fields attributes which are dependent on only part of the primary key.
  - 3NF – there are no dependencies between non-key attributes
- An entity–relationship (E–R) diagram shows the entities in the database and the relationships between them.
- A relational database gives the following advantages over flat files:
  - Data are contained in a single software application.
  - Duplication of data is minimised.
  - Data inconsistency is reduced.
  - The volume of data is reduced leading to faster searching and sorting of data.
  - Data structures remain the same even when tables are altered.
  - Existing programs do not need to be altered when a table design is changed or new tables created.
  - Queries and reports can be set up quickly.
- A primary key is used to uniquely identify a record or row in a table.
- A foreign key attribute links to a primary key in a second table.
- A secondary key is used to get fast access when searching on this attribute.

⟶

Summary continued …

- Different categories of user can see different views of the data – only what is needed for their job.
- Terminals in public areas may be refused access to sensitive data, even if the user has access.
- A DBMS is a piece of software that provides the following facilities:
  - a data definition language (DDL) that the database designer uses to define the tables of the database
  - a data dictionary that contains all design information
  - a data manipulation language (DML) for inserting, amending and deleting data records
  - backup of the database data
  - control of multi-user access to the data.
- The DML and DDL used by all modern database software is Structured Query Language (SQL).

Test yourself

1. A large organisation stores a significant amount of data. Describe the advantages of storing this data in a relational database rather than in a number of flat files. [4]
2. Explain what is meant by a table being in second normal form. [2]
3. Every student in a school belongs to a form. Every form has a form tutor and all the form tutors are teachers. Because some teachers are part-time, some forms have more than one form tutor although no teacher is a form tutor for more than one form. Students are identified by StudentID and each form has a unique name.
   a. Draw an entity–relationship diagram to show the relationships between the entities STUDENT, FORM and TUTOR. [6]
   b. Describe the relationship between FORM and STUDENT. [1]
   c. Describe how this relationship is formed. [2]
4. Consider the scenario from Question 3 with the addition of a DEPARTMENT entity. Each tutor can work in one or more departments and each department has many tutors. That part of the diagram is shown in Figure 3.6.10.

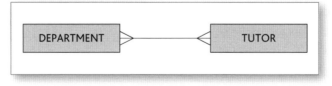

Figure 3.6.10   E–R diagram for DEPARTMENT and TUTOR.

This is a many-to-many relationship, which is not allowed, so a link table DEPARTMENT-TUTOR is produced and the relationship becomes two one-to-many relationships.
   a. Suggest labels that would describe each relationship. [2]
   b. Describe in words the data that is stored in the table DEPARTMENT-TUTOR. [1]
5. Define what is meant by a foreign key. [3]

3.7 Simulation and real-time processing

(3.7 a) Real-time applications

The term "real-time" has been already been used in Chapter 1.2, in the context of real-time operating systems. A real-time system is one that can react quickly enough to data input to affect the real world. This implies that the output from the system must be produced quickly enough to have an effect on the world outside the computer system before that world has enough time to alter.

Consider the case of an airline booking system. The "world" that we are talking about is the world of the database that contains all the booking transactions. The use of a real-time system here means that if a ticket is bought by a member of the public, the database must be updated before the next person has a chance to book a ticket. Notice that the idea of the computer system responding "incredibly fast" or "in billionths of a second" does not apply to this application. In some real-time applications, these descriptions may be reasonable but it depends on the "world" with which the application is concerned. When we discussed operating systems in Chapter 1.2, we called this pseudo real-time.

When asked to describe a real-time application, the first thing that needs to be described is the "world" of the application. Everything else then falls into place: you should describe the hardware necessary to allow the input and output needed to operate the system and the decisions that the software must take.

A nuclear reactor may start to react too violently. Sensors inform the control computer that this is happening. The computer takes the decision to insert graphite rods to slow the reaction down. This is a real-time application. The world of the application has been identified, the input devices are the sensors that inform the computer of the state of the reaction, the computer makes an immediate decision and the graphite rods are moved into place. Notice that the rods moving is not immediate – it takes place over a period of time – however the decision was taken immediately. Note also that the sensors simply report on the state of the world; there is no hint at decision making on the part of the sensors. Many students would phrase their answer in the form of "The sensors spot that the reaction is too violent and the processor . . .". This credits the sensors with interpreting the readings – this is not so.

You should also be able to identify when a real-time system is appropriate as opposed to a system where the decision making is in some way delayed.

Discussion

Consider the importance of real-time processing to data that is collected by sensors. Can other forms of input and processing be used?

(3.7 b) Sensors and actuators

A sensor is a device that measures some physical characteristic that can be read as a quantitative value (Chapter 1.4). A physical quantity is something that exists in the real world as opposed to the computer world. Examples include:

- length
- time
- temperature
- light intensity
- flow
- pressure

Digital and analogue data

Analogue data is generated from a physical property which may take a value on a continuous scale between certain values; analogue data includes temperature and pressure.

Sensors can be divided into two groups (see Figure 3.7.1): those that capture an analogue signal and those that are digital. Digital sensors produce an output that is digital. For example, a burglar alarm may have a pressure pad by the front door that produces a signal if it is trodden on. The signal is either that it has been trodden on or that it has not. It cannot be half trodden on. However, a temperature sensor that is measuring the temperature for a chemical reaction sends different signals according to the temperature that it detects. When the temperature increases, the voltage produced by the temperature sensor increases. It is this voltage which represents a temperature value. Note that any temperature value may be reported, hence the reading is analogue. The computer requires the signals from such analogue sensors to be passed through a hardware device called an analogue-to-digital converter because all computers which receive these readings as input are digital computers.

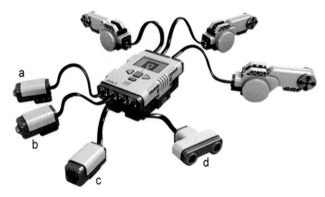

Figure 3.7.1   Sensors: a) touch; b) sound; c) light and d) ultrasonic.

Most sensors are surprisingly simple, relying on one of only two methods to capture a reading. They either use some type of spring mechanism to physically change the position of something in the sensor or they have a means of turning some reading into a variable voltage.

Spring sensors include a pressure pad held open by a spring which is overcome by the weight of the burglar. Similarly, a bumper around a robot vehicle can be kept away from the body of the vehicle by springs which are overcome if the robot or device moves too close

to something blocking its path. A temperature sensor, used to measure the room temperature for a central heating system, converts the ambient temperature to a voltage. A light-meter at a cricket match converts the current light intensity to a voltage so that the processor can produce a digital reading and the umpire decides if there is enough light for play to proceed.

Notice that the digital sensors are really switches. If the bumper around the robot is depressed, is it necessary for a processor to make a decision? Probably not; the switch would simply switch off the motor. The question arises whether this is a sensor in the true sense of a "sensor" in computing. The action of turning the motor off required no decision and hence no processing. However, the need to do so is reported to the processor because it now has to make a decision about what to do next and the input from the sensor is going to be an important part of that decision.

One last point about sensors. There are as many different sensors as there are physical quantities that need measuring (Figure 3.7.2 on page 276), but their actions need to be kept as simple as possible to allow the processor to make decisions quickly. The idea of a sensor being a TV camera because it can show the processor what is going on in a large area is unrealistic because it would provide too much information. What might be possible would be a TV picture which could be scanned by software for any kind of movement in order to indicate the presence of a burglar or a TV camera monitoring an area which never changes, perhaps a warehouse at night. If a burglar came into the picture, then the pixels would change. This could be used as a sensor to send a signal to the processor that the state of the warehouse has changed. Never lose sight of the idea that the processor is limited in the amount of data that can be interpreted, as is the software that is processing the inputs.

Actuators

When the processor makes its decisions, it must be able to instigate some action. In the type of scenario we are talking about, it is probably necessary to change something in the physical world. This may involve making the robot move in a different direction. It may be a matter of switching on some lights or telephoning the police station to report an intruder on the premises. Some of these are simple electric circuits that the computer can action itself. However, making the robot change direction is more complex. Such movement involves the use of an actuator. An actuator is the device that accepts a signal from the computer and turns it into a physical movement. An example of an actuator is an electric motor which can turn electrical signals from the processor into physical movement.

(a)

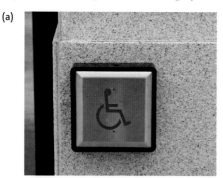

(b)

(c)

Figure 3.7.2 Sensors and actuators: a) an actuator in the form of a button to electronically open a door; b) The TV remote controller directs an infra-red beam to the front of the television which is received by a sensor on the front of the TV; c) a pressure pad on the road is a sensor that detects the number of cars that have driven over it.

Activity

Describe three types of sensor and explain how they might be used.

Extension

A modern motor car has many sensors for capturing data about the performance of the car.

Look at www.autoshop101.com/forms/h15.pdf for an account of sensors to be found in a motor car. The article also has a very readable introduction to the various types of modern sensors and actuators.

3.7 c) Using robots

The first thing to understand is what constitutes a robot. A robot is a movable, mechanical device that responds under the control of a computer program.

Consider a car production line. A typical production line organisation could operate as follows. Each car is built on a flat bed which is on wheels and runs along a track from one process to the next. It stops at the area where the wheels are fitted, then it moves along the track to have the engine fitted, then moves again to have the doors fitted and so on. This flat bed is not a robot, it is simply a machine following a pre-set course. Now imagine the same system but at the start of the production line the computer controlling the flat bed is told the parameters for that particular car: it is to be a three-door coupé with a 1700cc engine. It stops to have the wheels fitted but must then make a decision to go to the correct area for a 1700cc engine. From there it must go to the area that has the correct body shell for a three-door coupé. This machine is now making decisions and can be considered a robot. Note it satisfies exactly our initial definition of a robot.

Why are robots used?

- One of the first issues the manufacturing company would consider is cost. Never say that robots are used because they are cheaper. They are not. They are extremely expensive. What must be considered are two types of cost. The first is the capital cost of buying the equipment, the second is the cost of running the system. It is here that savings will probably be made in relation to the cost of employing a person.

- People can get tired and, when they do, the quality of their work may well suffer. The robot does not necessarily do a better job than the human (indeed, it is not as adaptable and therefore may produce worse results), but it is consistent. It never gets tired.

- There are some workplaces that are particularly hazardous for human beings, for example the inside of a nuclear reactor! However, maintenance must still be carried out. These are natural environments for a robot to work in because it would be inappropriate for a human to do so.

- A robot does not need the peripheral things that a human being needs as part of the business infrastructure. Humans need certain standards of light and air in a factory in which to work. For robots there is no need for a canteen or for rest rooms or for a transport infrastructure to get the workers to work and home again. There is no need for a car park or for an accounts department to work out the pay for all the workers.

There is a need, however, to employ technicians to service the machines and programmers to program the changing tasks which the robots must carry out. Notice the need for a human workforce has not disappeared but the workforce is made up of different types of worker, generally more skilled than was previously the case.

Discussion

Consider the uses of robots in an industry which is near your school. Your family members may work there. Think about any form of robot, from a robot cleaning device for the factory to computer-controlled machines and maybe even robotic arms on a production line. Try to work out why they are important and how the tasks were carried out before robots were used.

Extension

Investigate the uses of robots in the home. In the 1950s, people were predicting that by 2000 there would be no such thing as housework because every household would have a friendly robot to do all the work for them. Are we anywhere near this being a reality? Do we have any robots at the moment? Is an automatic washing machine a robot?

⟶

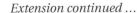

Extension continued …

Figure 3.7.3   A robotic vacuum cleaner.

(3.7 d) Reasons for using simulation

A computer processor has the ability to perform a large number of calculations in a short space of time. If a physical action can be portrayed as the result of a series of formulae and their results acting upon one another, then the computer can, by doing the calculations, pretend to be carrying out the physical action. This is what is meant by a **simulation**.

The rate of growth of a sunflower is known from observations taken over many years. The effects of different chemicals on the growth of sunflowers are known from simple experiments using one chemical at a time. The effects of different combinations of the chemicals are not known. If the computer is programmed with all the relevant formulae dictating how it should grow in certain circumstances, the computer can simulate the actions of the sunflower and show how a real sunflower can be expected to react. In this way the effects of different growing conditions can be shown in seconds rather than waiting six months for the sunflower to grow. One can imagine that in the course of a day, a programmer can come up with a suitable cocktail of additives to allow sunflowers to grow on the fringes of a desert and consequently create a cash crop for farmers where they had no cash crop before. This is an example of the use of a computer simulation to *speed up a process* in order to produce predicted results in a short time scale.

Simulation can be used to predict the results of actions, or model situations that would be otherwise too dangerous. What will happen when a certain critical condition is exceeded in a nuclear reactor? I don't want them to try it on the one down the road from where I live and I'm sure no one else does either. Program a computer to simulate the actions of a nuclear reactor and it is no longer necessary to do it for real.

Some things are impossible. It is not possible to fly through the rings of Saturn. Program a computer to pretend and a virtual reality world can be created. By using specialist peripheral devices , such as data gloves and helmets, we can make it seem possible (Figure 3.7.4).

Figure 3.7.4   Virtual reality equipment.

A car company is designing a new suspension system for a range of cars. One way of testing different designs is to build prototypes and road test them in different conditions to monitor how they work. This is very expensive, as well as time consuming. A computer can be programmed to take the characteristics of each possible system and report how well they will work, at a fraction of the cost. The same simulation can be made to vary the conditions under which it operates. A fairly simple change to the parameters of one of the formulae can simulate driving on a motorway or on a country lane.

Manufacturing designers can have ideas which need some initial investigation to see if they may be feasible. An engineer may design a new leaf spring for a suspension system. The hypothesis is that the spring will give more steering control when travelling on rough surfaces. The computer can be set up to simulate the conditions and give evidence to either support or contradict the hypothesis.

A financial package stores data concerning the economy. It can be used to provide information about past performance of the various criteria being measured or it can be set up to predict what will happen in the future. If the graph of a particular measure is linear then extrapolation of what will happen in a year's time is possible; in fact, you don't need a computer to provide the prediction. However, if the graph is non-linear the mathematics becomes more complex. More importantly, economic indicators do not exist in isolation. If the unemployment figures go up then there is less money in the economy, so people can buy less, so firms sell less, so more people are laid off. However, the National Bank may bring down interest rates which encourages people to borrow more and hence buy more, so firms need to employ more people in order to put more goods in shops. When the relationships become intertwined like this, the calculations of predictions become very complex and computers are needed.

Generally, as a student you are expected to understand that:

- there are usually a number of variables that control the outputs and the results that may be predicted
- the values of these variables do not just appear by magic but must be collected
- sensible limits should be set within which the variable values are expected to lie
- the results are going to be based on the use of these variables in specific formulae that relate the variables to one another
- the results produced are subject to a degree of error; the scale of the error results not just from the validity of the variable values and the relationships, but also the validity of the model that is used.

Weather forecasting involves a simulation and the use of predictions. Data are collected about present weather conditions from weather stations across the globe, from weather balloons and aircraft in order to make the model three-dimensional. More data are collected by satellite and they are all fed into a system together with relationships that the data are known to follow. A simple example would be that warm wind blowing off the sea becomes damp and there is more chance of rain. The values of the variables are arranged to be within sensible parameters, for example wind speed must be between 0 and 120 mph, temperature must be between 0 and 40°C degrees Celsius. The results are the best that can be expected for those data that are collected. However, there can always be unexpected problems, for example the sun may be particularly violent and such sun storms can have a pronounced effect on the weather. This was not a factor in the original simulation and consequently the reliability of the results is not as good as expected.

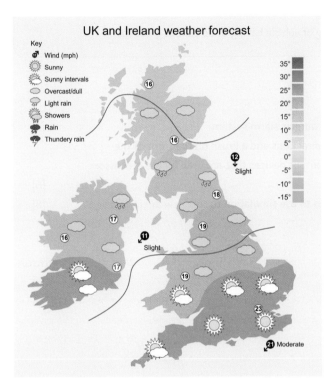

Figure 3.7.5 Output from a weather forecasting system.

(3.7 e) Simulation in testing design feasibility

Discussion

A property company is to build a new school. The school is not allowed to open unless it has a certificate from the fire authorities to say that escape procedures are acceptable. The company has a problem because in order to show the authorities that escape procedures are satisfactory, they have to build the school, make it operational and then set fire to it and see how many are able to escape! This would only test one possible fire.

What is needed is a simulation of the proposed building and the people in it and then a simulated fire could be started. The simulation could show how the evacuation procedures worked and where they did not.

Consider this simulation. What data would have to be input to the simulation process and what outputs would need to be produced to satisfy the fire authority?

Summary

- When you describe a real-time application, you must mention:

  - the "world" of the application

  - the hardware necessary to allow the input and output needed to operate the system

  - the decisions that the software must take.

- A sensor records information from its environment:

  - Light and temperature sensors convert the reading into a variable voltage reading. It must be converted by an analogue-to-digital converter.

  - A pressure pad gives a digital signal – pressed or not pressed.

- The processor makes a decision based on sensor input and then activates an actuator to take action.

- Robots are used in boring and hazardous environments.

- Robots perform to a consistent standard.

⟶

Summary continued …

- Robots do not get tired and do not need meal breaks.

- Simulation can be used to model a situation:

  - to produce results faster than carrying out the process (e.g. growing a generation of flowers)

  - to produce results that would be dangerous to obtain in real life (e.g. in a nuclear reactor)

  - to produce result more cost effectively than building a prototype.

- Simulation can test the feasibility of a design without the building or vehicle having to be built at great cost.

Test yourself

1. Describe the real-time application of a computer used to control a burglar alarm system. [4]

2. A robot is used to clean the floor in a factory. It travels in random directions and a brush on the front of the machine brushes up any litter. Describe the input devices and the output devices that are used by the processor in controlling the robot cleaner so that it can move about safely. [6]

3. Explain why a company that is producing a new aircraft would need to use simulation to test new aircraft designs. [8]

3.8 Networking

3.8 a ## Media for transmitting data

You need to be aware of the statement from the syllabus document regarding Paper 3: "This paper will be set according to the content of Section 3 of the syllabus *but will also assume knowledge learned in Section 1*" *(our italics)*. We discussed network operating systems in Chapter 1.2 and the low-level aspects of data transmission in Chapter 1.5.

When computers are able to communicate to form a network, they can share resources and allow communication between computers and users. An important consideration is the means used to provide the connection. There are two methods of connecting machines together:

- "hard wire" them
- wireless communication.

Whichever method of communication is chosen, each computer needs an interface card that connects the computer processor to the communication medium.

Hard wiring

The simplest method is to connect the computers using copper cable. It is in widespread use and is relatively cheap. However, as this is a physical method of connection, it must be remembered that the actual laying of the cables may cause disruption to the working environment and the physical infrastructure of the building.

Distance is also an issue; consider the difficulty of connecting all the computers for a business which has a warehouse on one side of a busy road with its retail shop on the other side of the road. It also means that the locations of the computers on the network are fixed by the position of the cable. An advantage of hard wiring over wireless communication is that it is potentially more secure because in order to tap into the signals transmitted on the network it is necessary to tap into the cable.

There are a number of different types of cabling (Figure 3.8.1):

- **Coaxial cable** consists of a copper wire with an insulation shield from another conductor and finally another insulator around the whole thing. It is used to send signals to a television from the aerial because of the way the outer conductor shields the central conductor from interference. For the same reason, coaxial cable is ideal for connecting computers on a network, although the distances which are possible are limited because of the natural resistance of the conductor.

- **Twisted pair** and *unshielded twisted pair (UTP) cable* consist of pairs of copper wires twisted together and then contained in an outer casing. The pairs of wires help to insulate each other from electrical interference. Sometimes many pairs of conductors are put within the same cable and it is often surrounded by an earthed screen which surrounds the core of conducting wires. If this screening is not used the signals become more susceptible to interference and the cable is called an unshielded twisted pair.

- **Fibre-optic cable** consists of a large number of very fine glass strands down which pulses of light can be sent (modulated light beams). Because the means of communication is light rather than electrical signals, the messages sent should remain interference free. They are also very difficult for outsiders to hack into and as they are not made of metal the cables do not corrode.

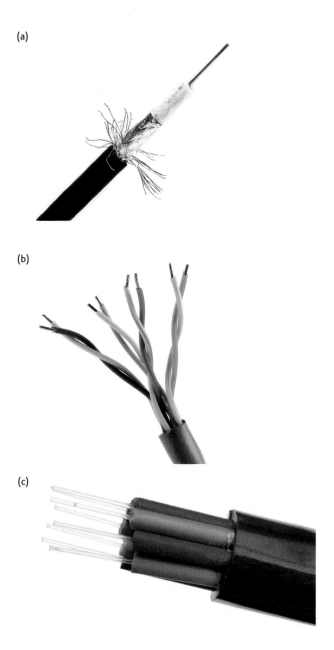

(a)

(b)

(c)

Figure 3.8.1 Network cables: a) coaxial, b) twisted pair and c) fibre-optic.

Wireless

Wireless communication is very convenient for the user, particularly if they are using any form of portable machine such as a laptop, netbook, PDA or mobile phone. Wireless communication allows the device to be used from any location which is in range of the transmitter/receiver.

The main disadvantages of wireless communication are concerned with issues of security. This can be overcome by having the necessary security measures on the system and many users do this, but home users often tend not to protect their systems as perhaps they should.

There is also a problem with interference to the signals. This is a radio signal and experience that we sometimes have with listening to radio stations illustrates the problem of interference. Wireless communication tends to be slower than an equivalent form of hard-wired communication. This is a very generalised comment but it is not possible to be any more specific because of the variations in speeds between the different media. There are a number of different types of wireless signal:

- **Infra-red communication** uses pulses of infra-red light to send coded signals. This is the communication used by remote controllers in the home. If you have a television with a remote controller, try pointing the controller away from the television and changing the channel. Infra-red signals travel in a straight line so any obstruction between the devices results in a communication failure. Infra-red could not be used to connect up a network in school where devices are sited in different rooms because the signals could not go through the walls. However, the earlier scenario of the business with the warehouse on one side of the road and the shop on the other could be solved by using infra-red transmission. Also, because they travel in a straight line, the signals are secure from third parties "listening in".
- **Microwave transmission** is also highly directional and is used to transmit large quantities of data between fixed positions.
- **Bluetooth** connections are wireless but only work over very short distances. They are also rather slow. A Bluetooth connection could be used to connect a peripheral device, such as a mobile phone, to a desktop computer or for transferring a music file between two mobile phones.
- **Wi-fi** is a true wireless connection using radio waves. The possible range is dependent on

environmental factors but is usually limited to cover a geographical area such as a school site. Users can move their devices around within the range of the transmitted signals. They can work as any other network communication but benefit from the freedom of not being tied to one particular location by a wired connection. The range of coverage can be extended by the use of wireless access points. This is often the setup in a large domestic house for the provision of broadband. The signal comes in to the house from the telephone point connected to a router. The router then broadcasts the signals to one or more wireless access points. The main disadvantage with Wi-fi is the difficulty of keeping the communications secure.

Discussion

Either discuss with your teacher or with the school technician:
- the types of network that are used in your school
- the media used for communication between machines in the school

What were the reasons for choosing those media?

3.8 b) Network components

Before starting to read this section you should familiarise yourself with the content of Chapter 1.5, which discusses the use of local and wide area networks.

The components that are used on a network rely heavily on the way that the network has been designed, i.e. its **topology**, and also depend on the scope of the communications expected on the network.

Bus topology network

A **bus topology** network (Figure 3.8.2) is a LAN (Chapter 1.5) that uses a hard-wired cable to pass messages along it to and from the various devices. If the message reaches the end of the cable, it is important that it does not "bounce back" otherwise it will come into conflict with other messages on the cable. A *terminator* is a simple device which is fitted to both ends of the cable run to stop such "echoing back" of signals onto the cable.

Common sense says that the more devices which are attached to the network, the slower the communication between them. This may degenerate to an unacceptable level in which case the solution is to split the devices into two separate network segments.

A server is a computer on a network that provides a resource to the other machines on the network. There are several different types of server on networks, distinguished from each other by the service that they provide on the network. Typical servers are the file server and the printer server. They offer services exactly as their names suggest and are there to provide a centralised resource. Many applications are now designed on the **client–server model**. Here the server provides a "service" – such as the sending and receiving of email – to a number of "client" computers on the network.

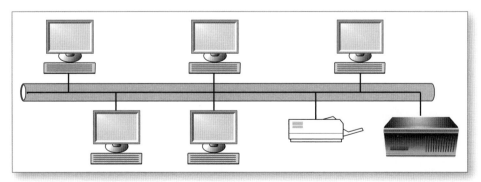

Figure 3.8.2   A bus network topology.

Star topology network

If the LAN is arranged with each of the computers having their own cable rather than sharing a cable with all the others (as in the bus network), the network is called a star network (Figure 3.8.3). With this type of network it is important to have something at the "centre" of the network that the individual wires can be connected into. There are two possible devices that can be used: a hub or a switch.

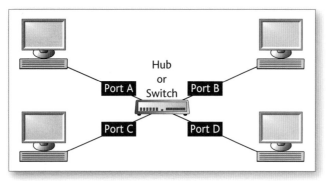

Figure 3.8.3   A star network.

A **hub** receives all the signals from the individual computers and then broadcasts them back to all the devices that are connected to it. There is no implication of any intelligence involved. The intended destination device receives the message but so do all others.

A **switch** receives the message, reads the destination label attached to it and only sends it to the device for which it is intended. This dramatically reduces the amount of traffic on the network. The switch sets up a temporary dedicated circuit between the sending and receiving devices. As soon as the transfer is complete, the circuit is released.

A star topology has a number of obvious advantages. The communication pathway between the central resource and the individual computers or networks may use a variety of different communication methods and transfer speeds. If one of the communication lines fails, none of the others is affected.

Connecting networks

Routers, bridges and gateways are used to connect two or more networks.

Bridge

A **bridge** is used to connect two LAN segments (Figure 3.8.4). If a school has a network for students and another for school administration, it may be necessary to link the networks together. Notice that there is no implication of signals being vetted as to their right to be transferred across to the other network. It is simply a link between the two segments.

Consider a LAN split into two segments to improve data transfer speeds. There is, however, a need for a device on one segment to communicate with devices on the other segment. The bridge maintains a table showing which **MAC addresses** are connected to each of its ports (Figure 3.8.5) A MAC is a unique address given to a device by the manufacturer.

Router

A **router** does a similar job to a bridge, in that it links two networks, but there is an implication of a degree

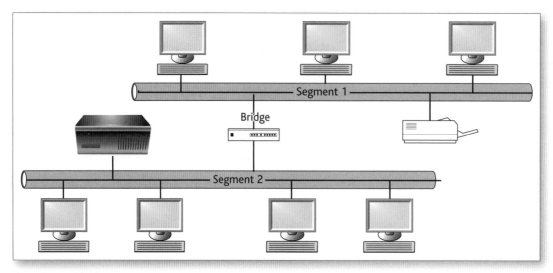

Figure 3.8.4   A bridge.

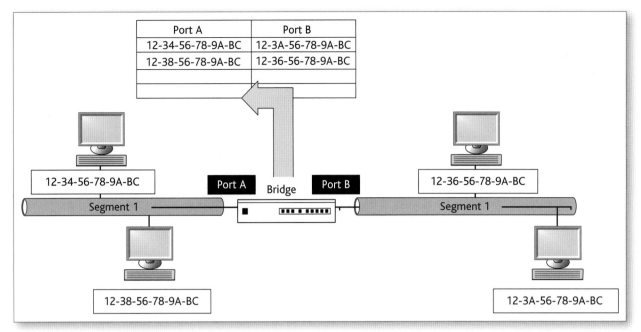

Port A	Port B
12-34-56-78-9A-BC	12-3A-56-78-9A-BC
12-38-56-78-9A-BC	12-36-56-78-9A-BC

12-34-56-78-9A-BC

Port A Bridge Port B

Segment 1

12-38-56-78-9A-BC

12-36-56-78-9A-BC

Segment 1

12-3A-56-78-9A-BC

Figure 3.8.5 A bridge and MAC table.

of decision making with a router. The router knows something about the two networks being connected. It is able to look at a message that is trying to pass from one network to another and read the header attached to the message. The header contains details about the message including the destination address.

The router maintains a table with all the hardware addresses of the devices to which it has a direct connection (Figure 3.8.6 on page 286). If the network communications protocol is TCP/IP then each hardware MAC address is mapped to an IP address for each device. Using the information in the router table, the router can direct any message to the correct device. It can also be used as a security device, ensuring that messages from one network cannot be sent across to the other one if inappropriate. In the example of the school system, it would not be appropriate for students to be able to request data from the administration system.

Figure 3.8.6 (on page 286) shows a LAN made up of a number of segments and three routers. Note the contents of the router table for Router 3.

Routers are generally used to provide the link between segments which use the same communications protocol.

Gateway

A **gateway** is a hardware device used to connect a LAN to a WAN (possibly the Internet). It provides a connection but also ensures that material passed from one to the other is appropriate and monitors the usage of the connection. It can be considered to be a single point of entry to a LAN from a larger network. The gateway deals with different communication protocols between the receiving LAN and the other networks to which it connects.

Modem

A modem is a hardware device that changes the digital signal produced by the computer into one that can be transmitted over the public telephone line, i.e. an analogue signal. A second modem is required at the receiving device in order to convert the analogue signal back into a digital signal, which can be then processed by the computer.

Discussion

Either discuss with your teacher or with the technician in your school the different components on the networks in your school and the role carried out by each device.

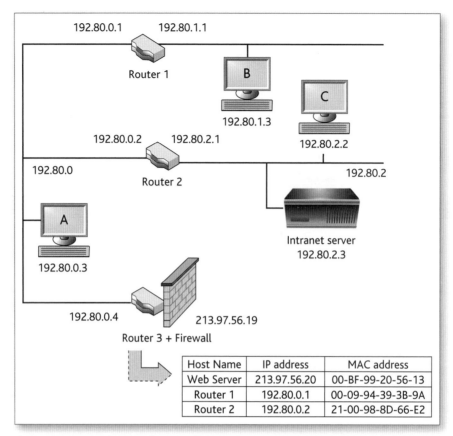

Figure 3.8.6   Routers being used on part of a network.

Common network environments

The Internet

The **Internet** is the largest example of a wide area network. Look back to Chapter 1.5; you should agree that the Internet satisfies our definition of a WAN and is the hardware infrastructure that makes global communication possible.

The Internet provides facilities to link computers worldwide, using telecommunications systems. It allows fast communication between computers and networks, the transfer of data between various computers and the distribution of information. Messages are passed from the source computer, through other computers, to the destination computer.

The Internet provides for the use of:

- content from the World Wide Web (www)
- electronic mail
- file transfer.

One thing to appreciate here before proceeding further is that the "Internet" and the "World Wide Web" definitely do not describe the same thing. The Web is all about content – the availability of web pages and other resources from web servers.

For a fee, an Internet Service Provider (ISP) connects subscribers to the backbone of the Internet. These providers then pass data between the subscribers' computers and other Internet users.

One issue with use of the Internet is the lack of control over users and the data that can be found on the www. The data can be misleading or simply incorrect as there is no body that is charged with policing the validity of the content. Data can be inappropriate for certain users and yet be freely available. For this reason ISPs provide some form of "parental controls". Viruses and other malware can be downloaded accidentally, causing many problems for a computer or network. Also the problem of hacking into personal communications and files that are transmitted can cause problems to any Internet user.

The open nature of the Internet means that some people who are active on it cannot be trusted because there is no control over them and any comments that they make cannot be trusted to be valid.

Intranets

An **intranet** is a network offering the same facilities as the Internet but solely from within a particular company or organisation. Information is made available from a web server and clients access material using web browser software.

Passwords and other measures, such as secure transmission lines, can be used to restrict not only the number of people who are allowed to access material placed on the intranet, but also the identities of those who are allowed access. Different levels of password can be used to ensure that only specific users can access specific facilities on the intranet.

The intranet web server has its own server address. For XYX College, it is likely to be:

http://intranet.xyzcollege.ac.uk

Note that www does not appear as part of the URL.

The lesser volume of material that is available from the intranet server ensures it is more likely to be relevant. Control over the material gives a greater likelihood that it is factually correct and relevant. Restrictions on membership of the intranet mean that comments from others are more likely to be relevant, sensible and correct.

Sometimes an organisation allows certain outside users to access all or parts of its intranet. This access to an intranet is called an **extranet**.

Structure of the Internet

Suitable software is required to make these systems work. *Browser software* allows a user to locate information using a **universal resource locator (URL)**. This is the address for any resource on the Internet. The URL includes the transfer protocol (see Chapter 1.5) to be used (for example, http), the domain name where the data are stored, and other information such as an individual filename.

For example, `http://www.bcs.org.uk/` is the URL for the British Computer Society's home page. The content that can be accessed from this page is part of the extranet run by the society. The contents of their intranet cannot be accessed by ordinary users of the Internet, only by members of the society.

Domain name

Domain names are held in a hierarchical structure. Each location on the World Wide Web has a unique domain name. The names in the various levels of the hierarchy are assigned by the bodies that have control over that area.

Consider the domain name `computing.wlv.ac.uk`. The high-level domain is `uk`. The `ac` part is assigned to a particular authority (in this case, UKERNA) and indicates this is the domain for an academic institution. The authority assigns the next part, i.e. `wlv`.

This makes `wlv.ac.uk` the domain name for the University of Wolverhampton. The university itself has added to the domain and `computing.wlv.ac.uk` is called a fully-qualified domain name (FQDN).

IP address

Each computer or device connected to the Internet has a physical address, called its **Internet Protocol (IP) address**. This 32-bit numeric address uniquely identifies the physical computer linked to the Internet. A domain name server is needed to convert the domain name into its corresponding IP address.

Domain name server (DNS)

The Internet is supported by domain name servers. The user requesting a web resource keys the URL into the address bar of the browser. The domain name is converted to its actual IP address by a device called a **domain name server (DNS)**.

> ### Discussion
>
> Does your school have an intranet? If so, what is it used for? If not, how could one be set up and what arguments could you use in a meeting with the headteacher to persuade him or her that a school intranet would be a good idea?

(3.8 d) Confidentiality of data on a network

Once an organisation opens up some of its network facilities, there is an issue of confidentiality of data. For example, an organisation may want potential customers to have access to their product database. However, they will not want them to have access to transactions from other customers.

A first step is to encrypt the confidential data and this is addressed in the next section. Along with encrypting the files that are transmitted, a simple procedure is to expect the use of passwords and user identities to identify users who are allowed access and verify any attempt to connect to the network.

Another solution is to install a **firewall**. This can be hardware or software (or a combination) that sits between the WAN and the LAN. The firewall interrogates all data packets that are intended for the LAN. There are two strategies for doing this:

- proxies
- stateful inspection.

With proxies, a **proxy server** (i.e. a server which is dedicated to this task) stops the packets of data at the firewall and inspects them before they are allowed onto the LAN. Once the packets have been checked and found to be satisfactory, they are passed through to the LAN. The message does not pass through the firewall but is passed to the proxy. This method tends to degrade network performance but offers better security than stateful inspection.

Stateful inspection tracks each packet and identifies it. To do this, the method uses tables to identify all packets that should not pass through the firewall. This is not as secure as the proxy method because some data do pass through the firewall. However, the method uses fewer network resources.

Techniques for addressing the issue of the privacy and security of data are the general techniques of **authorisation** and **authentication**. These are explained in the next section.

3.8 e Encryption, authorisation and authentication techniques

When data are sent from one computer to another over the Internet, they may pass through many different servers before reaching the destination computer. Consider the simple example of sending an email. It could be many days before the recipient retrieves the mail message from his or her mail server. Hence data is at risk from user interception or electronic tampering.

Encryption

Encryption involves applying a mathematical function, using a key value, to a message that can only be read by the sender and the intended receiver. There are many techniques for this. There are a number of specific terms used with encryption.

- **Plain text** describes the original unaltered text as created by the sender.
- Encryption algorithm is the calculation which is used to change the plain text into the encrypted text.
- **Cipher text** is the message text after the encryption has been performed.
- **Decryption** is the process of converting the message text back to the original plain text.

Be clear that the aim of encryption is not to prevent unauthorised access by some third party to the data but to make it impossible for them to "unscramble" the message, i.e. produce the plain text from it.

Clearly, whatever function is applied to the original message must be reversible as it would be silly to make a message unreadable to the recipient. The problem is to make it very difficult for anyone else to find the way to reverse the original encryption. It also means that there is a problem of many people needing to decrypt a message. All these people need the key to unlock the message.

Symmetric encryption

Symmetric encryption is the simplest technique for encryption. The same algorithm and key is used for both encryption and decryption. The receiver therefore must be in possession of both the algorithm and the key in order to decrypt the cipher text.

There are agreed standards for symmetric encryption and this includes the Data Encryption Standard (DES) which uses a 65-bit key and was first adopted in the United States in 1976.

Asymmetric encryption

Most modern systems of encryption use the idea of two keys working together – a **public key** and a **private key**. In general, the public key is universally known and the private key is known only to the holder.

To use **asymmetric encryption**, the user must purchase a digital certificate from a *Certification Authority*, such as Verisign. The certificate contains:

- the holder's name
- an ID number
- an expiry date (certificates are usually valid for one year)
- the public key
- a digital issue for the issuing authority.

A digital certificate would be the starting point for a user to send encrypted emails. Clients that you do business with may well insist that all email communication is encrypted.

Email client software – such as Microsoft's Outlook or any of its variants, e.g. Outlook Express – have detailed help about how to purchase a certificate and then set up the email software for sending and receiving encrypted email.

Who knows what when communicating via email?

Figure 3.8.7 assumes that Red and Blue each have a digital certificate which gives each their own public and private keys. The golden rule is that:

- Blue never knows Red's private key.
- Red never knows Blue's private key.

Figure 3.8.8 shows what happens when Blue sends an encrypted message to Red.

Authentication

Authentication is a general principle – not specific to computing. Consider these two examples:

Authentication procedures would be used when two parties communicate. The procedures in place are designed to ensure that the receiver is certain that the sender is who they claim to be and vice versa.

Also, when a user connects to a computer system using an account ID and a password, the computer system needs to check that this is an authentic user. The procedure assumes that the password has not been given to anyone and this would be stressed in

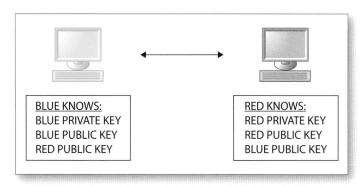

Figure 3.8.7 Who knows what?

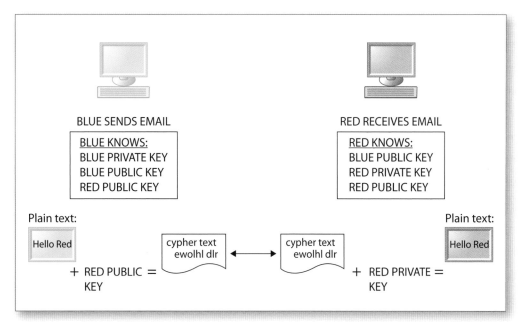

Figure 3.8.8 Sending and receiving an encrypted message.

the organisation's code of conduct. Hence a log-on using this account ID and password should confirm the identity of the user.

If the first example was email communication then the authentication that is needed is the proof that the message received by Red was indeed sent by Blue. This is achieved with another layer on the above process by computing a *digital signature* for the email and attaching it to the cipher text.

This level of detail – i.e. the use of digital signatures – is not expected for this syllabus, but does make for interesting discussion.

Extension

1. A primary advantage of public-key cryptography is the application of a digital signature, which helps combat repudiation, i.e. denial of involvement in a transaction. Since the owner keeps their private key secret, anything signed using that key can only have been signed by the sender. Can you modify Figure 3.8.8 on page 289 to show how a digital signature is calculated and then used in email communication?
2. Investigate the use of Secure Socket Layer (SSL) encryption.

Summary

- Data can be transmitted along cables or wirelessly.
- Types of cable include:
  - coaxial
  - twisted pair and unshielded twisted pair (UTP)
  - fibre-optic.
- Wireless technologies include:
  - infra-red communication
  - microwave transmission
  - Bluetooth
  - Wi-fi.
- Network components include:
  - switches that direct traffic to the appropriate node on a star network
  - routers that link networks and provide security
  - bridges that connect LAN segments
  - modems that convert a digital signal to an analogue signal for transmission down a phone line.
- Common network environments include:
  - the Internet, the largest WAN
  - intranets, private networks owned by an organisation.
- The Internet and intranets are accessed by the same software, a web browser.
- Every Internet location has a URL that is converted to an IP address by a domain name server.
- Confidentiality of data is addressed by using a firewall or a proxy server.
- Encryption scrambles a message so that someone who intercepts it will not be able to read it.
- Authentication ensures that a person is who they claim to be
  - implemented with passwords
  - implemented also with digital signatures.

Test yourself

1. A network can be created using a number of possible topologies (physical layouts of cabling and devices). One of these is a star network.

   Describe **two** advantages of using a star topology. [4]

2. Two business users who regularly communicate need to do so with encrypted emails.

   a. What is meant by encryption ? [2]

   b. What does each user need to set up in order to send and receive encrypted emails? [2]

   c. Describe the process – making reference to the keys which are involved at each stage – for User A to send an encrypted email which is received and read by User B. [4]

3. A national bank has a large number of offices spread throughout the country. It is important for information to be passed between the various bank offices.

   a. Explain why the bank uses an intranet to communicate between offices rather than the Internet. [4]

   b. Customers are able to use the Internet to do online banking.

   Discuss the problems of maintaining confidentiality of information on the Internet and the technologies used to address this issue. [5]

Module 3 Exam questions

1. Explain how interrupts are dealt with by a processor and how interrupted jobs may later be resumed. [6]

   Question 9 Cambridge AS Level & A Level Computing 9691 Paper 3 June 2009

2. One of the main features of an operating system is the ability to schedule job throughput.
   a. Explain the purpose of scheduling job throughput. [2]
   b. Describe **three** scheduling policies which lead to different scheduling algorithms. [6]

   Question 8 Cambridge AS Level & A Level Computing 9691 Paper 3 June 2008

3. Explain how memory is managed in a typical modern computer system.
   You should use the following as headings for your answer:
   i. Paging [3]
   ii. Segmentation [3]
   iii. Virtual memory [3]

   Question 6 Cambridge AS Level & A Level Computing 9691 Paper 3 November 2008

4. i. State what is meant by the term spooling. [2]
   ii. Describe the process of sending jobs for printing using a spooler. [3]

   Question 9b Cambridge AS Level & A Level Computing 9691 Paper 3 June 2006

5. Describe **two** of the main components of a typical desktop PC operating system. [4]

   Question 1b Cambridge AS Level & A Level Computing 9691 Paper 3 June 2007

6. Describe the difference between interpretation and the compilation of a high level language program. [4]

   Question 1b Cambridge AS Level & A Level Computing 9691 Paper 3 June 2006

7. Two of the stages which a high level language program undergoes during compilation are lexical analysis and syntax analysis.
   Discuss how errors are discovered during each of these two stages. [5]

   Question 6 Cambridge AS Level & A Level Computing 9691 Paper 3 November 2009

8. Explain the purpose of the code generation phase of compilation, including the principle of optimisation. [3]

   Question 4a Cambridge AS Level & A Level Computing 9691 Paper 3 November 2006

9. Explain the purpose of
   i. linkers
   ii. loaders
   in the running of a computer program. [4]

   Question 4b Cambridge AS Level & A Level Computing 9691 Paper 3 November 2006

10. Explain how errors in the
    i. reserved words
    ii. variables
    used in high level language instructions are recognised by the compiler during compilation. [4]

    Question 1c Cambridge AS Level & A Level Computing 9691 Paper 3 June 2006

11. Describe what is meant by von Neumann architecture. [2]

    Question 7a Cambridge AS Level & A Level Computing 9691 Paper 3 June 2007

12. Describe the fetch/decode/execute cycle when the next instruction to be executed is an unconditional jump instruction. [7]

    Question 5 Cambridge AS Level & A Level Computing 9691 Paper 3 June 2006

13. Describe the purpose of the following registers in a processor:

    i.   Current instruction register (CIR) [2]

    ii. Memory address register (MAR) [2]

    iii. Program counter (PC) [2]

    iv. Index register (IR). [2]

Question 1a Cambridge AS Level & A Level Computing 9691 Paper 3 November 2006

14. At a particular point in a program, the program counter (PC) contains the value 200.

    i.   State the expected value contained in the PC after the instruction held at location 200 has been processed.

       Explain your answer. [2]

    ii. The value contained in the PC is actually 180.

       Explain why the value has changed to 180. [2]

Question 5b Cambridge AS Level & A Level Computing 9691 Paper 3 June 2009

15. i. Using an example application, explain why some applications require parallel processing rather than serial processing. [3]

    ii. Describe what is needed to run a parallel process rather than a serial process. [3]

Question 8 Cambridge AS Level & A Level Computing 9691 Paper 3 November 2007

16. a. i. Express the number 93 as an 8-bit binary number. [2]

       ii. Express the number 93 as a number in hexadecimal. [2]

    b. Describe the connection between binary representation and hexadecimal. [2]

Question 4 Cambridge AS Level & A Level Computing 9691 Paper 3 June 2008

17. Show how the denary number −90 can be represented, using a single 8-bit byte, in:

    i.   Sign and magnitude;

    ii. Two's complement. [2]

Question 6a Cambridge AS Level & A Level Computing 9691 Paper 3 June 2009

18. A particular computer stores numbers as 8-bit, two's complement, binary numbers.

    01011101   and   11010010 are two numbers stored in the computer.

    Add the two binary values together and comment on your answer. [3]

Question 5b(ii) Cambridge AS Level & A Level Computing 9691 Paper 3 November 2006

19. A computer stores numbers in floating point form, using 8 bits for the mantissa and 8 bits for the exponent. Both the mantissa and the exponent are stored in two's complement form.

    a. Give the denary number which would have 01000000 00000000 as its binary, floating point representation in this computer. [2]

    b. Explain why it is not possible to represent zero as a normalised floating point number. [2]

Question 9b and c Cambridge AS Level & A Level Computing 9691 Paper 3 June 2007

20. The denary number 10¾ is to be represented as a floating point binary number using 12 bits. The first 8 bits are to be used for the mantissa and the remaining four bits are to be used for the exponent.

    i.   Explain what is meant by the mantissa of a floating point number. [2]

    ii. Explain what is meant by the exponent of a floating point number. [2]

    iii. Explain why 001010110101 is a floating point representation of 10¾. [3]

    iv. Normalise the floating point value given in **(iii)**. [2]

Question 6b Cambridge AS Level & A Level Computing 9691 Paper 3 June 2009

21. A computer stores numbers in floating point form, using 8 bits for the mantissa and 8 bits for the exponent. Both the mantissa and the exponent are stored in two's complement form.

Explain the effect on the

- range
- accuracy

of the numbers that can be stored if the number of bits in the exponent is reduced. [4]

Question 9a Cambridge AS Level & A Level Computing 9691 Paper 3 June 2007

22. a. With the aid of a diagram show how the names:

   SIHA   DIPO   GHIA   AMOR

   can be stored in a linked list in alphabetic order. [4]

   b. The linked list increases in size because of new entries being made. Explain, in whatever form you find appropriate, how the linked list can be searched for the name THEO. [4]

Question 3 Cambridge AS Level & A Level Computing 9691 Paper 1 June 2005

23. Jobs that require printing by a network printer are stored until the printer is ready. Their addresses are placed in a queue to await their turn for printing. Addresses of new jobs are placed at one end of the queue. These job addresses are taken from the other end when the printer is ready.

   a. State **two** reasons why it would be preferable to store the queue in a linked list rather than an array. [2]

   b. If the queue is held in a linked list, describe an algorithm for:

   i. inserting an address into the queue

   ii. reading an address from the queue. [5]

Question 3 Cambridge AS Level & A Level Computing 9691 Paper 3 June 2007

24. The names of 20 students in a computing set are to be stored in an array called NAME (X) where X stands for a number between 0 and 19.

   i. Explain why a serial search would **not** be suitable if the array was large enough to store the names of all 1000 students in the school. [2]

   ii. Suggest a better method of searching for a particular name, justifying your answer. [3]

Question 9b Cambridge AS Level & A Level Computing 9691 Paper 3 November 2008

25. List A is 2, 4, 7, 9

   List B is 15, 3, 8, 10, 1

   These two lists are to be merged into one list in numerical order, smallest first.

   List B must first be sorted into order.

   Describe how an insertion sort can be used to do this. [4]

Question 7a Cambridge AS Level & A Level Computing 9691 Paper 3 June 2008

26. A set of data items is stored in alphabetic order in a binary tree.

   Describe a procedure which will insert a new data item into the correct position in the binary tree. [4]

Question 2c Cambridge AS Level & A Level Computing 9691 Paper 3 June 2009

27. List A is 2, 4, 7, 9

   List B is 1, 3, 8, 10, 15

   These two lists are to be merged into one list in numerical order, smallest first.

   Describe how a merge sort can be used to do this. [4]

Question 7b Cambridge AS Level & A Level Computing 9691 Paper 3 June 2008

28. Describe each of the following programming paradigms:

   i. object-oriented [2]

   ii. declarative. [2]

Question 6a Cambridge AS Level & A Level Computing 9691 Paper 3 June 2006

29. Functions and procedures may be used to develop a program using stepwise refinement.

    i.   Explain what is meant by stepwise refinement. [2]

    ii.   Describe what is meant by a function. [2]

Question 2b Cambridge AS Level & A Level Computing 9691 Paper 3 June 2009

30. State what is meant by each of the following

    i.   a local variable

    ii.   a global variable

    iii. a parameter passed by value

    iv. a parameter passed by reference. [4]

Question 10b Cambridge AS Level & A Level Computing 9691 Paper 3 November 2006

31. Explain how a stack is used to handle procedure calling and parameter passing. [4]

Question 10c Cambridge AS Level & A Level Computing 9691 Paper 3 November 2006

32. Explain what is meant by the following terms when referring to object-oriented languages:

    i.   data encapsulation [2]

    ii.   inheritance. [2]

Question 11b Cambridge AS Level & A Level Computing 9691 Paper 3 November 2007

33. The following fish are all part of the same food chain:

    guppy, herring, roach, salmon, shrimp.

    The following facts apply:

        fresh (guppy)   eats (herring, shrimp)

        fresh (roach)   eats (salmon, herring)

        salt (shrimp)   eats (guppy, roach)

        salt (herring)   eats (salmon, roach)

        salt (salmon)

    where fresh (X) states that X is a fresh water fish

        salt (X) states that X is a salt water fish

        eats (X,Y) states that X eats Y

    By using examples from the facts given, explain what is meant by:

    i.   instantiation [2]

    ii.   a goal [2]

    iii. backtracking [4]

Question 10 Cambridge AS Level & A Level Computing 9691 Paper 3 June 2008

34. Explain the meaning of the following types of addressing:

    i.   indirect

    ii.   indexed.

    Give a reason why each may need to be used. [6]

Question 6b Cambridge AS Level & A Level Computing 9691 Paper 3 June 2006

35. A variable name is defined in a particular system as:

    one or two letters, followed by

    any number of digits (including zero) followed by either a

        $ sign if there are no digits, or an

        & sign if there are any digits.

    Draw a syntax diagram which describes a variable name. [6]

Question 10 Cambridge AS Level & A Level Computing 9691 Paper 3 June 2007

36. The following rules define <WORD> in a piece of text.

    <LETTER> :: = A|B|C|D|E|F|G|H|I|J|K|L|M|N|O|P|Q|R|S|T|U|V|W|X|Y|Z
    <WORD> :: = <LETTER>|<LETTER><WORD>

    i.   State why

         Hello

         is not a word.   [1]

    ii. <SENTENCE> is a set of words ending with a full stop (.) or a question mark (?)

         Define <SENTENCE>.

         There is no need to rewrite the rules for <LETTER> and <WORD>.   [5]

Question 10 Cambridge AS Level & A Level Computing 9691 Paper 3 November 2008

37. Three advantages of using a relational database rather than flat files are:

    i.   reduced data duplication

    ii. improved data security

    iii. improved data integrity.

    Explain what is meant by each of these and why they are features of a relational database rather than flat files. [6]

Question 8b Cambridge AS Level & A Level Computing 9691 Paper 3 November 2009

38. There are a number of TEAMs which represent a school.

    Each team has a TEACHER who runs it and a teacher may run more than one team.

    Each team has a number of PLAYERs and each one may play for more than one team.

    Draw an entity relationship (E-R) diagram to represent this data model in third normal form and label the

    relationships.   [6]

Question 2 Cambridge AS Level & A Level Computing 9691 Paper 3 November 2007

39. State **three** advantages of using a relational database rather than a set of flat files.   [3]

Question 2b Cambridge AS Level & A Level Computing 9691 Paper 3 November 2006

40. Part of a school database consists of a table of student details and a table of teacher details.

    A teacher teaches many students.

    A student is taught by many teachers.

    Explain what is meant by each of the following terms and give an example of each from

    the normalised tables you would produce for this data model.

    i.   Primary key

    ii. Foreign key   [4]

Question 3b Cambridge AS Level & A Level Computing 9691 Paper 3 November 2008

41. A furniture shop sells a large number of different items whose details are stored in the STOCK file.

    Some customers have an account.

    Details of accounts are stored in the ACCOUNTs file.

    The shop has a large number of customers whose details are stored in the CUSTOMER file.

    Discuss the need for controlling access to the database files and how it can be done.   [6]

Question 4d Cambridge AS Level & A Level Computing 9691 Paper 3 June 2009

42. Describe the purpose of the following parts of the database management system:

    i.   the data description language (DDL)   [2]

    ii. the data manipulation language (DML).   [2]

Question 11b Cambridge AS Level & A Level Computing 9691 Paper 3 June 2007

43. i.   State what is meant by a real-time application. [1]
    ii. Give **one** example of a computer application, other than a burglar alarm system, which must be real-time, justifying your choice. [2]

Question 7a Cambridge AS Level & A Level Computing 9691 Paper 3 November 2009

44. A robot is designed to clean a floor.

    It has sensors to learn about its environment and actuators to control its actions.

    State **two** sensors which would be used to give the robot sensible information and say how they would be used.[4]

Question 3a(i) Cambridge AS Level & A Level Computing 9691 Paper 3 June 2008

45. A robot is designed to move over a surface. It must be aware of the immediate environment in order to avoid obstacles.
    a.   The robot is designed to travel around the floor of a factory.

         State **two** input and **two** output devices that would be necessary for the robot to move safely. [4]
    b.   Another robot is designed to travel on the surface of the planet Mars.

         i. Describe how a map of its environment can be created in the computer memory of the robot. [2]

         ii. Explain the need for simulation in the design and testing of this robot. [2]
    c.   Each of the robots can be controlled by a human being.

         Explain why one robot would be controlled in real-time while the other is given instructions as a batch. [2]

Question 8 Cambridge AS Level & A Level Computing 9691 Paper 3 November 2006

46. Simulation is used when a new car is designed.

    State **three** aspects of the design which would be simulated and, for each, give a different reason why simulation is used. [6]

Question 3 Cambridge AS Level & A Level Computing 9691 Paper 3 June 2006

47. a.   A robot is being developed to carry out procedures in a nuclear reactor. Give **three** reasons why simulation would be used in the testing of the design of the robot. [3]
    b.   A robot lawn mower is being developed for sale to the general public. Suggest why simulation is **not** appropriate for the development of this robot. [2]

Question 8 Cambridge AS Level & A Level Computing 9691 Paper 3 June 2007

Question 4b Cambridge AS Level & A Level Computing 9691 Paper 3 November 2009

48. A mail order company employs a number of computer operators who take orders by telephone. There is also a warehouse department from which orders are dispatched. The accounts department need to be able to access customer records to inform their decisions. The computers in all three areas are networked with a central storage facility.

    Discuss the different network components and media available for transmitting data around the network.

    Pay particular attention to their suitability for this example. [8]

Adapted from question 13 Cambridge AS Level & A Level Computing 9691 Paper 3 November 2007

49. The computer systems of all the medical centres in an area are connected to the area hospital. This means that patients can attend any centre and the hospital can access any record in case of emergency.

    Explain why the administrators of the system chose to use an intranet for communication of data rather than the Internet. [4]

Question 2b Cambridge AS Level & A Level Computing 9691 Paper 3 June 2008

50. Customers of a bank have to use the Internet in order to do electronic banking.

    Explain the problem of maintaining confidentiality of data on the Internet and the need for techniques to address the problem. [5]

Adapted from question 2b Cambridge AS Level & A Level Computing 9691 Paper 3 November 2009

4

Computing project

General description of the computing project

The computing project is a major part of the second year of the A level course, accounting for 40% of the total marks for the year and consequently 20% of the A level assessment. It takes on an added importance because it is the only module that gives you the freedom to choose the content yourself.

The volume of work expected should not be underestimated. While the degree of difficulty is largely decided by you in discussion with your teacher and by the problem to be solved, the time required to produce a first-class piece of work is considerable. Most centres will be working to a time-scale where the project work is completed towards the end of the second year of a two-year course. You must realise early that, despite having almost a year to complete the work, there is no scope for time wasting.

You are strongly advised to set interim deadlines in order to structure the time available. A project that is completed in a short period, close to the date for handing in the work, is unlikely to have been completed satisfactorily. You must take into consideration allowing enough time to gain the required degree of involvement of the person whose problem is being solved.

The analysis and design work which will be carried out is not conditional on the level of technical expertise needed later for the implementation.

However, there is a requirement that you should use at least an element of original coding in the solution of the problem that has been set. This is a *Computing* project, not an ICT one, and a proposed project that uses only the tailoring of generic application software to solve the problem has fallen short of the expected requirements. You are expected to play the part of the systems analyst and also the programmer to solve a problem which is owned by someone else, the client.

Project selection

This module is very different from all the others, both because you choose the topic for solution and because there is a single practical task that occupies you over a considerable period of time. The theory modules are examined by a set of questions on a timed examination paper. The practical work in the AS section, which is contained in Module 2, is assessed within a formal examination paper but is also designed to give you the techniques which can be used in the computing project the following year.

The project is very different. It is a single problem which needs to be progressed by you over a relatively long period of time. Because of this, considerable thought must be given to the selection of a suitable problem, that selection being guided by a number of criteria.

Syllabus fit

The syllabus contains a section that documents how the project is going to be marked. It is important to be familiar with this section and choose a problem, the solution to which will require you to complete all the sections mentioned. The purpose of the marking section in the syllabus is to act as a guide to you, indicating what is expected at each stage. It is not intended to be a "straitjacket" and you should realise that many types of project are possible. However, a glance at this appendix in the syllabus shows that there is a specific section, worth five marks, entitled

"Programming". If the project does not contain any original code then these marks cannot be awarded.

Self penalising!

You must select a problem whose solution is within your capabilities. You must not assume that you will know enough about the problem without the assistance of the client for whom you are solving the problem. Many of the marks in the scheme are awarded for you identifying the need for a partnership between the owner of the problem and the analyst (you) and require *evidence* of this. If there is no client, you will be severely handicapped when the marking criteria are applied.

Real end user

The intention of the project is that the problem should be real and consequently the person who has the problem should be a real client. The client is the expert (possibly along with other members of the organisation, the end users) for the problem and knows the background of the problem to be solved. The systems analyst is the expert in computing. The interaction between the client, the end users and you forms a major theme of the project and will largely dictate the order of events and what *evidence* is required in the final coursework report. You should not think of the other people involved just as people who give time for interviews and then will try to use the solution months later. Rather, all the stakeholders should be involved at all stages in the development of the project.

Involvement of the stakeholders

At different stages, you should keep all the stakeholders involved so that they develop ownership of the solution. It is a good idea, for example, if the prototypes of the different parts of the solution are shown to the end user and then altered according to their and the client's feedback. Notice the distinction between the client and the end user. In many cases, this will be the same person. However, a typical project may be to produce a stock-keeping solution for a small store. The client is the owner of the store whereas the end users are the shop assistants. If the problem is to produce a booking system for a hairdresser's salon, the client is probably the owner or the manager, while the end user is the receptionist.

The importance of a "real" problem

You are likely to get more from the work if the problem is a real one and if the end user is unconnected with your institution. However, this is not always possible because of individual circumstances and problems experienced by some centres. In such cases, the use of family members or members of staff within the school is perfectly acceptable, but you must maintain a professional relationship with the person (the "client") in order to make the experience as real as possible. The use of a fellow student as the end user is generally not to be encouraged because the problem is not likely to be real and the fact that you are both students makes it impossible to create the professional working relationship so essential to the project. However, you may want to solve a problem by producing a game. As long as it is done properly, it will require a high level of programming which is to be encouraged for this module and a student or teacher acting as the client can be made to work. The preferable choice would be the teacher because there is already a professional relationship from which to work.

Your interest

As has already been stated, you will be working on the problem for a long time. It is essential that there is plenty of scope for maintaining your interest. The project for the football club is unlikely to be suitable just because it is about football, although it may be if the local football club is considering computerising its manual filing system because the national association states that information in the future must be in electronic form. This is a real problem and the choice of project has changed from a choice based on football to a choice based on the solution of a problem.

Another danger in choosing the project is to choose something that you know something about. This makes the analysis and the information collection problematic. The old adage that a "little knowledge is a dangerous thing" is particularly relevant if you are not aware of the pitfalls. The advantage of a project about which you have no knowledge of the business context is that, in order to find out enough to solve the problem, all the marks will be available. If you already have some knowledge of the business area and problem there is the danger that you do not include it in the documentation because you assume that such knowledge and awareness is general.

Hardware and software

You and your tutor should have some idea what is going to be required by the solution, otherwise there is the danger that partway through the solution you find that the hardware or software required to complete the solution is not available. If you choose a basic data-handling type of project then such problems are unlikely to arise (unless the solution involves specialist hardware such as barcode readers). However, a problem that is a bit more unusual requires that care should be taken to anticipate problems before they arise.

You need to be clear about the software requirements for the development to take place – probably at school or at home. These may not be the same as the hardware and software on which the final solution is to be run in the client's own environment.

What is the role of your teacher?

Computing is a subject unlike most others on the curriculum, in that software which is available for the practical work is constantly changing. Software available now is very different from that available five years ago. Also there are different versions of software types available. Unlike maths, where a division problem is solved in the same way now as it was 50 years ago and everyone does it the same way, computing teachers have great difficulty keeping up with some of the changes in the subject. In particular, your tutor is not expected to be familiar with the facilities provided by all types of database software or spreadsheet programs just because you happen to run it on your machine. Similar problems arise if you decide to use a programming language with which the teacher is not familiar. At the initial stages of the project it is necessary for you and your teacher to have a reasonable idea where the problem solution is going to lead so that, we hope, there are no unpleasant surprises in store later on in the year.

The teacher needs to be honest and realistic about the level of technical support they will be able to offer. Similarly, you need to be aware of the resources which are readily available – in the school or elsewhere – for technical reference.

Problems that may arise

Problems that arise during the solution of the problem are not something to be worried about – but, there will be problems along the way! Parts of the solution may not work as anticipated leading to a possible revisiting of that part of the analysis and design. Hardware may malfunction at particularly awkward times. Such problems should be logged and commented on in the Evaluation section of your report.

If the problem is real, one issue will be the need to use real data for testing of the solution. The organisation supplying the data is almost certainly covered by data protection legislation and at this point compromises may need to be made. An acknowledgement of this, together with a statement that fictional data has been created to allow testing to be done, is acceptable and again needs to be commented on in the final report.

There have been two occasions in the preceding text where the word "evidence" has been used and emphasised. The final report constitutes evidence of the work you have done – probably over a number of months. Often evidence may be handwritten pieces of paper about some design features or remarks made by the end user. A golden rule to follow during the entire development of the project is "don't throw anything away" – that handwritten side of A4 could provide a vital piece of evidence for something you did.

Format of the chapters

This module is very different from the others, both in the way that it is presented in the specification and in the way that centres and you approach it. The syllabus states in some detail the usual learning outcomes as part of the content, but also documents the marking guidelines to be followed for the project. Experience shows that centres and individual students tend to use the marking guidelines to inform their work.

Because of this, the Module 4 discussion that follows is presented according to the marking guidelines rather than the specification itself, although references are made to the learning outcomes throughout.

At the end of each section there is a list of the evidence that the examiner is looking for in the final report. Every item in the evidence list may not be required for every project and there may be specific project types that require additional pieces of evidence specific to that problem solution. However, the evidence list is the first reference point for the expected report content.

4.1 Quality of report

The "quality" of your report is not assessed until the project is finished and the final report submitted. It is worth 3 marks. However, it is an issue that needs to be thought about at the start and kept in mind throughout the production of the report. The assessor is not looking for a short section of the report with a nice heading on it. Rather, the quality is assessed throughout all the work contained in the report.

The examiner will particularly look at documentation sections which are produced specifically for the various stakeholders to use. The assessor is looking for evidence that all the other sections of the project have been completed and that care is taken when producing evidence.

(4.1 a) Organising the report

The report should be *organised*. This means is that it should be easy to read and find important evidence.

The sections in the syllabus have been arranged in a logical order. If you are going to change that order, you need a *very* good reason for doing so. This does not mean that the work has to be carried out in the order shown in the syllabus. For example, if the project is being done properly then the documentation should be created throughout the project. When it comes to presenting the work, use the prescribed order because that makes it more accessible to the reader.

It is important to provide a means of navigating through all the evidence that you are presenting. In most cases, this means including a contents page. Do not make the contents page too long. In most cases, it should include only the section headings in the project (use the ones in the syllabus) and the page numbers in the report where the assessor can find the evidence.

(4.1 b, c) Using word processing features and including evidence

The facilities of a word processor should be used to full effect:

- Ensure there are no errors in spelling, punctuation or grammar.
- Number the pages of the report.

Remember that this is not a single section – the evidence is throughout the report.

Use the facilities of the various pieces of presentation software to produce the report but use them sensibly. In other words, only use them where it makes the report more readable or presentable. The word processed report may well be illustrated with graphics or diagrams that have been produced using graphics software.

Summary

- Organise the report
- Use word processing features where appropriate
- Include the evidence specified in Chapters 4.2 to 4.6

4.2 Definition, investigation and analysis

4.2 a Define the problem [3 marks]

4.2 a Define the problem [3 marks]

The first task is to select a problem to be solved as your project according to the guidance notes in the introductory chapter of this module.

There are two very important points about the problem:

- You should assume that the assessor who has to assess the worth of the project when it is finished knows nothing about the problem and must have it explained to them in detail if they are to understand the following report sections. This is a somewhat artificial suggestion as your teacher will initially mark your report and they will have had an involvement in the life cycle of the project.
- You and the owner of the problem must ensure you have complete agreement about the problem and its boundaries; otherwise you can never be sure that you are solving the intended problem and such differences may only become apparent after a considerable amount of work has already been done.

Background Information – what depth?

You need to explain the organisation with which you are working. The issue is the depth of description that needs to be given. Is it necessary to list the members of the organisation? Probably not. However, it is necessary to identify those members of the organisation that have a specific interest and involvement in the area of the problem and whose views should be sought. In particular, you should clearly identify the client, as this is the person with whom you will be working.

If you are familiar with the area of the problem, you may find it more difficult to gauge how much detail should be given. The teacher's role is essential, to act as a sounding board for you and to ensure that you are providing the right level of information. The teacher may find this difficult if they also have knowledge of the problem area. If this arises then it is sensible for you to discuss your problem with someone else who knows little or nothing about the problem area.

What data are used by the current system?

In order to analyse the situation, you must determine how the present system handles the data. To do this, initial discussions must take place with the users and you to clarify at this early stage:

- methods by which these data are presently stored
- types of data that are used or produced by the system
- how the data are collected and where they come from
- what form the data take and in what form they are stored.

We do not yet want to know, for example, that John Jones (Form 8JHL) hired a school locker (No. 453) on 18/11/10. What we do need to know is that the student name is important, the name must be linked to a locker, that the date the hire began is important in order to calculate the cost, and that the form is important in order to give a point of reference for the student.

The information about how data are collected may be something along the lines of "The school sends a letter home with a tear-off portion that asks for the following information . . .; the lockers are in different areas of the building with those in block 1 starting with the number 1 . . .; different year groups are in different blocks . . . ".

Much of this information may not be known at this stage. The analyst may have to report that the means by which particular locker numbers are assigned to different students is not known, but that it will be necessary to find this information out during the interview with the stakeholders.

Boundaries of the proposed problem

There should be some indication of possible areas that are not performing as well as they should or that are not covered by the present system. If there are no such areas then the project does not have a problem to solve. This discussion must, by definition, be somewhat sketchy because the views are all coming from the systems analyst – the owner of the problem has not yet become fully involved. This is what happens in the next stage of the work.

The syllabus clearly states that you should identify current processes and data structures. It also states that methods currently in use in the area of the problem should be identified and described.

If there are no processes currently in operation, then you are strictly not following the requirements of the syllabus. A student who wants to create a game is not solving a problem and is not working collaboratively with anyone. However, the same student who is approached by a teacher to create a game to teach basic number work to young children is covering all aspects of the syllabus.

Evidence

The report should contain:

- a description of the organisation that has the problem and the place of the problem within its overall operation: This does not have to be in any great detail. As a guide, half a side of A4 should be quite adequate.
- a description of how the chosen problem is dealt with at the moment: This can only be a sketchy description because it is not possible to describe the proposed solution in any detail until the analysis section has been completed.
- a clear description of the data that is used in the area of the problem: The exact data that will form part of the solution is not yet known because the problem has not yet been fully specified; however, it is necessary to be aware of all the data that may be involved.
- a clear statement about the origins of data in the organisation.

Investigation and analysis [8 marks]

This section is really the pivotal section of the whole project. It is in this section that the analyst (i.e. you) and the end user pool their knowledge in order that decisions can be made about the direction that the project should take.

Following the first stage, you will have a number of questions to which you need the answers. The example of school lockers was one from within the experience of most students. The ideal problem is one which you genuinely have to find out about because you know little about it.

Analysis is in essence "finding out" and this is the theme of this section – finding out exactly what is required by the client.

The investigation will be in four parts:

- finding out – in some detail – what the problem is
- learning about the business area within which the problem is situated.
- analysing the present system, including an analysis of the problem itself, though not yet a proposed solution
- defining a requirements specification that will allow you to carry on to the next stage, including a hardware specification and a software specification.

4.2 b, c, d — Finding out about the problem

This is going to involve the client. You need to find out in detail what the client wants from the proposed new system. If this part of the project is not completed carefully, then the project will not be successful because the client and the analyst will have different perceptions of the problem and these may well differ in some very important respects. The normal solution is to arrange an *interview with the client*. This is not a matter of you having a general chat with the client, or even of having detailed discussions where the client has carefully considered all the questions and answers. It must be planned but it will be more than simply reading a prepared list of questions.

The first point to be considered is how the interview is going to be conducted. Will you try to copy down the client's comments as they are being spoken? This is a very poor interviewing technique because it does not allow you to consider what is being said before asking the next question. Two better alternatives are for you to take a third person whose job it is to scribe everything that is said or to use a recorder to tape the interview. Whichever method is used, it is simple politeness to tell the client in advance how you would like to conduct the interview and to seek their agreement (particularly if the interview is to be recorded).

At the same time it is wise to check with the client whether there are any subjects that should not be brought up in the interview. In the real world, there may be sensitive topics to which you are not allowed access. Although it is simple for the client to refuse to answer a question in the interview, it shows an understanding on your part if you are aware of any such issues before the scheduled interview takes place.

You should go into the interview with a series of well-prepared questions. However, they should not be asked as a simple list. If this is all that is done, the interview may be a waste of time and effort; the client could simply have completed a questionnaire. The whole point about an interview is that the questioning can be flexible. You should have "starter" questions on each of the areas in which you are seeking information. You should also have prepared a series of follow-up questions that can be used, dependent upon answers to the initial questioning.

If you find yourself saying something on the lines of "That is interesting, in which case what would you do about . . ." then you are demonstrating flexibility. You are showing that you are listening to the responses and taking an interest in the client and the organisation. In short, you really are playing the role of a systems analyst. In order to do this properly, the questions must be carefully planned.

The typical strategy for questioning could be:

- decide on something that needs to be asked about (If you already know the answer what is the point of asking it?)
- decide on a question to ask which should give you the information
- think of a follow-up question that can be asked for each possible answer that the end user may give.

For example, you may need to know what types of information are important. If the end user states that information needs to be kept on customers, the follow-up question may be to ask about whether this information needs to be protected. If the answer to that is yes, then a further follow-up may be to ask who on the staff is allowed to access the data and who is allowed to alter the data.

The important thing is to have these questions ready and only use the ones that follow on from what the client says in answer to the original question.

In this way, the interview transcript should read like a conversation rather than just the answers to a questionnaire. It will demonstrate that you were playing a full part in the process.

Learning about the business

(4.2 b, c)

You should not forget that there will be different people involved in this organisation. Mrs. Arif may be responsible for the allocation of lockers, so she is the client. However, Mr. Ali is in charge of Year 8 and therefore deals with any problems that may arise with Year 8 students; form teachers actually distribute the keys and collect in the money; students are the actual users of the lockers; and parents may be contacted if there is a problem.

There will be important information to be gleaned from all these stakeholders, which can be found out by using different methods of information gathering. For example, a sample of parents (how are they to be chosen?) could be sent a questionnaire and you may be invited to go to the next Year 8 form teachers' meeting to contribute to a discussion about the present system.

Any existing documentation needs to be collected and analysed. Does the present letter collect all the information which is thought necessary?

Notice that, in the example, a lot of different methods of information collection are used. The important thing to realise is that they are not used to demonstrate to the assessor that you know what they are. They are used because they are a sensible method for information collection for this particular issue and stakeholder.

The interview is mandatory because the project requirement is to solve a problem for a real client and the accepted way to collect information from a single person is to use an interview. Other types of information collection should be justified by reference to the problem.

Analysing the present system

It would be easy to fall into the trap of giving an example of everything you can think of which might be relevant – i.e. to produce a dataflow diagram, a system flowchart and structure diagrams. If you do this without thought then it can be counter-productive.

You are not trying to show the assessor that you know how to draw a DFD, you are showing that you can determine whether a DFD is sensible evidence for this problem. Do not lose sight of what is being assessed – the ability to solve a problem not the ability to draw a DFD or any other form of chart. Some form of charting may well be appropriate but be selective.

You should also document any inefficiencies and problems apparent from the information you collected and write down the information that is required from the system.

Remember, actual paperwork or other documentation you have used to carry out the investigation is the best possible evidence of what you actually did.

Defining the requirements specification

You have now identified the problem and should be able to list the requirements that the client has agreed. This set of requirements should be signed off by the client. It is important to note that this process, like so many others in the work, will probably not be a linear process because the client may not agree exactly when you first show them the requirements list. This is good evidence that the work done so far is "real". In the real world, collaboration does not mean that you state something and the client agrees immediately. Evidence of disagreement which involves you in re-working the evidence is to be applauded and credit is given for it. This can be documented in the Evaluation section on completion of the project.

You must consider the hardware and the software that will be needed to implement the solution. It is at this stage that your teacher must discuss with you the requirements that they consider are going to be necessary. This ensures that the requirements can be implemented and there are no unpleasant surprises later on in the development work. This should make sure that you do not suddenly discover that the chosen software cannot do something that was expected of it.

You must also give attention to the parts of the solution where original code is going to be written in order to satisfy that part of the syllabus requirement.

Hardware and software choices must be justified in relation to the problem solution and should (like all other evidence) be aimed at the correct audience, in this case the client who has to agree with the choices. The justification needs to be approached carefully.

It is not good enough to state that a 19" flat-screen monitor will be used because the question that will be asked is "Why?" The choice needs to be justified. In this case, there may be a lot of detail on the screen so a larger screen size will make it easier for Mr. Ali to read. The use of a flat-screen monitor could be to save space because Mr. Ali only has a small desk. These are simple points but they give a justification for the choice made. All choices should be justified with this level of detail otherwise they simply become your preference and not the solution to a problem! You should appreciate that the best possible outcome for the client is that the proposed solution can be installed and run on their *existing* hardware and software platform. However, this still needs to be justified in the Analysis report.

Notice that everything up to now has been collecting information and about what we propose to do. There has not been any evidence that we have started to *design* how to solve the problem and implement a solution. This comes next . . .

Evidence

The report section should contain:

- detail relating to the planning of the client interview
- the original plan of the question list, showing the issues that were planned to be covered and sensible follow-up questions that had been considered
- transcript of the interview (signed off by the client as accurate)
- other information relevant to the problem and how it was collected (questionnaire, meetings, etc.)
- analysis of the client interview and other information and identification of important facts
- a data flow diagram or some other chart showing how the present system operates (if necessary and appropriate to illustrate the present operation)
- identification – arising from the information gathering – of the areas of the present solution that *will* and *will not* be included in the project
- the list of requirements of the solution (signed off by the client)
- hardware and software requirements of the system with discussion about the likely tools for implementation for each requirement (agreed with the client).

Summary

- Define the nature of the problem to be solved
- Use appropriate methods to investigate the problem and gather information
- Record information or data and gather samples of documents currently used
- Identify the current processes, current data structures and what data is currently stored
- Analyse the data and processes using appropriate techniques to illustrate the analysis
- Specify inefficiencies and problems apparent from the information collection
- Derive the client's requirements and the information requirements of the system
- Specify the required hardware and give reasons for the choices
- Specify the required software and give reasons for the choices
- Develop and document a clear requirements specification

4.3 Design

This section is divided into three parts in the marking guidance:

  i.   Nature of the solution [8 marks]
  ii. Intended benefits [2 marks]
  iii. Limits of the scope of the solution [2 marks]

There are 12 marks available overall for the Design. Most of the discussion below relates to part (i) but you must also address the other two parts in your report.

4.3 a Agreeing a list of objectives

Following the collection of information about the problem to be solved, you should now decide the scope of the project. In other words, you should decide what needs to be done by the time the project is finished. You should draw up a list of required outcomes. This list should not contain subjective points. That is, it should contain points that can be considered at the end of the work as having been achieved or not.

For example, the list might start with the following objectives:

- Mrs. Arif must be able to access all student records.
- Mr. Ali must have complete access to Year 8 records but not to other years.
- It must be possible to pass on, i.e. "migrate", records to the next year/form groupings at the end of each year.
- A form teacher must be able to output a series of letters to the parents of students who are behind with their payments.

The objectives above are all easily quantifiable. When the project is completed it is simple to check to see if form teachers can produce the required letters.

Objectives such as "the solution must be easy to use" or "the solution must be presented in pleasant colours" are very difficult to judge. Indeed, two people can quite reasonably have very different opinions as to whether or not a subjective objective has been met.

The list of objectives must be agreed with the client. This might mean that the original list of objectives may need to be altered when the client sees it. The thing to be remembered is that neither you nor the client should dictate the objectives; they should be agreed. The final list should be signed off by both parties. It will provide the basis both for the final evaluation of how successful the project has been and also for the testing plan that is to be designed and implemented.

Whatever the problem which is being solved, it will involve some form of data entry, some processing and appropriate outputs. We tend to think in terms of data storage and manipulation problems but this applies to all types of project.

4.3 b, c Designing the input and output

The next stage is for you to design the output documents and the input formats with appropriate screen designs. The user does not need to know anything about the processing or the data structures that are to be used because they are not in the realm of the user. However, they do need to know what the input and output formats will look like and agree to their design. These, together with the list of objectives, make up the *design specification* and should all be agreed with the client before development of the system starts.

The process of agreeing the design specification might take some time. If you have one interview with the client who immediately agrees to all your suggestions without needing further discussion or amendment, then the relationship is probably not a real one. Put another way, there is probably no attempt being made at a real project! Remember that the intention is to mirror the real world, in which the design process would need fine tuning.

Later in the project you may find that the original design specification is no longer satisfactory. You should not think that the project is a "disaster" but see this as an opportunity to involve the client again in modifying the design specification. You should document all such occurrences and how they were resolved.

4.3 d Designing the data

The next stage is to determine what data will be processed by the system and stored within it. The simplest way of describing this is to draw it. Students often find this the most difficult part of the project, but it needn't be.

Often difficulties arise because students think that dataflow diagrams or system flowcharts are highly structured. You may think that you do not know the "language" of boxes and how they should relate to one another. The best methodology, for both DFDs and system flowcharts, is to follow the principles laid down in Chapter 1.6. You should use the flowcharting symbols in Module 1. The important thing is to convey to the reader of the project report that there is a clear idea of how the different parts of their system are related and the various data flows.

The locker system example has inputs being made to the system which are different dependent on the user. This means that inputs have to be shown, as does some mechanism for checking the authority of the person to make the inputs (Figure 4.3.1). Also files have to be altered (a DFD is perfect to show this). The files that have to exist seem to be a file of students, a file of lockers with their location, and a file of payment data. All these files will be linked in some way. The outputs include lists of locker data with students grouped by year or form and a complete alphabetical student list.

Although this is not the sort of diagram that you would find in a textbook, what is missing? The ability to draw pretty boxes is not being tested here, simply your understanding of the logic of the intended solution and

of how the various processes and data work together. Individual parts of the logic may need to be considered in more detail: How is the authorisation gained? How does the user select the type of operation? But the basic details are there. Note that the student file is shown, but the payments and lockers files are not. They should be included in a complete diagram.

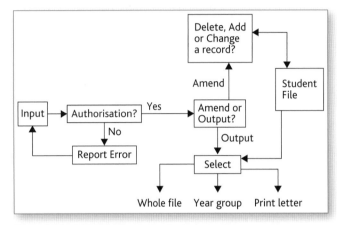

Figure 4.3.1   Initial sketch showing the locker system.

Data storage: files

The data that needs to be stored should be divided up into different groups (files) dependent on the use that will be made of it and the necessary links to other files. An attempt should be made to arrange the data into files so that there is as little duplication of the data as possible. This will inevitably mean that the files will need to be linked so that data from one file can be used in an application area designed for a different file. It is at this point that an *entity–relationship diagram* showing the relationships between the different files or tables should be created (see Chapter 3.6).

If the data are to be organised into files, then we must decide:

- the file organisation, i.e. serial, sequential or direct access
- the methods of file access
- each file's structure, e.g. user-defined "record" data types.

The data fields for each file should be listed. It should be clear what field or fields will be used as the key and also any foreign keys that provide links with the other files in the system. The purpose of storing each of the fields should be explained and the data type that is to be used for each field decided. It is then necessary to calculate the size of the files by giving a size to each of the fields and scaling up to give an indication of size for the whole file.

Data storage: database tables

A popular alternative development route is to implement the E–R model as a set of database tables within a relational database software package.

However the "point and click" features of the database software should only be used to create the tables and set up any relationships. A Microsoft Access database file (`<name>.mdbx`) can be read from programs created in, for example, the Visual Basic .Net programming environment. Any high-level programming language can connect to the database file. This approach provides a perfect vehicle for making sure that the project has a large amount of program coding.

Data validation

Each of the items of data in the file will need to be input. Consequently, there will need to be *validation* performed on much of the data input. These proposed validation checks should be documented in detail. All of this information could be summarised in a table with a row for each field.

These guidelines seem to have veered towards what would be appropriate for a "database type" problem. While most problem solutions include data storage and manipulation in them somewhere it must be remembered that the most important thing is the inclusion of original coding somewhere in the solution.

(4.3 e) Code design

Most problems and their solutions are going to be too large to be implemented with a single program. It is normal to modularise the proposed solution. The different modules may require very different handling. Some will involve the use of applications software while others require the writing of original program code. Modularisation diagrams were described in Chapter 2.1.

It is expected that the Computing project should include an element of coding using a high-level language. Such coding needs to be planned and this is the section where that planning is assessed. The algorithms of the solution should demonstrate how different elements function to provide the desired solution. The intended coding should have preparatory work that allows the coding to be constructed simply by reference to a given algorithm.

The form that algorithms can take can be various, but should always include information or instructions:
- about a stage of the solution
- an implied order that the information or instructions should take.

They can be presented in the form of *pseudocode* (see Chapter 2.1), flowcharts or a written description. The form of presentation is of secondary importance to the logic shown and the perceived usefulness by a third party. Care should be taken that whatever the form of presentation used there is no ambiguity.

(4.3 f) Creating a test plan

In this section you are encouraged to decide the type and nature of the necessary testing. Testing should be related explicitly to the objectives of the solution. The intention of the testing is to provide evidence to the end user that the solution works.

Each test in the test plan should not only specify what data are going to be used and the expected outcome, but also the objective which is being tested. This can normally be included in the "reason for the test" but another method is to have a separate column in the test plan which is headed "objective". If the objectives are numbered appropriately, this linking process is simple. All the objectives should be included in the test plan, in enough detail to persuade the end user that the system works.

Consider an objective of the form "A mark between 1 and 100 should be allowed to be input". It is necessary to ensure that a mark can be entered (normal data), that marks that are too small or too large are not accepted (invalid data, often called 'abnormal' in other books) and that a mark of 1 or 100 is or is not accepted, dependent on where the line is drawn (borderline/boundary data, often called 'extreme' data in other books).

The normal format for a test plan is a tabular presentation because it is the simplest to produce and to understand, but any other form of presentation could be used.

If the test plan is presented as a table, it should have suitable headings. The tests should be numbered in order that they can be cross-referenced to any test evidence which is presented in the report. The table will have blank columns that cannot be filled in until the solution exists. The column for expected results can be filled in but the columns for the actual results and comments about the differences will have to wait until after the solution has been produced.

Assessment is based on completeness and clear presentation.

Activity

When you have finished your test plan, it is sensible to swap with another student and decide whether the test plans are suitable for testing the solution. Would each client be satisfied with the evidence produced in the plan?

Evidence

The report should contain:

- a list of objectives against which the final solution can be evaluated (signed by the client)
- an explanation of the outputs – screen-based or hard copy – and any initial screen designs for the output of data
- an explanation of the way that the data are to be collected and an initial design of data capture forms, input screens and validation
- details of the file structures that are to be used and the links between them, including appropriate diagrams to explain the data design
- explanation of the way the data are manipulated through the system:
  - DFDs showing a diagrammatic representation of the data flows
  - a description of the way the problem has been modularised and how the modules work together
  - a complete set of algorithms in appropriate form which describe the method of solution and the original coding which is intended
  - testing of the algorithms to provide evidence that they produce the intended results ⟶

Evidence continued…

- a test plan covering:
  - sufficient functional testing to persuade the client that the solution will work
  - adequate testing of all the objectives that have been agreed
  - normal, invalid and borderline tests, particularly of validation routines.

The most important sentence about this section in the syllabus is that the specification should be "sufficient for someone to pick up, develop and test an end result". Anyone taking up the project at this stage, with no involvement in the analysis or planning work, should be able to start from the design which has been prepared and produce the required system.

Activity

The syllabus clearly states that the design should be sufficient for someone else to produce the solution with no further analysis or design. Other members of the group can be used to critically view each other's efforts to see if they could consider attempting a solution from the information in the design specification.

Intended benefits   [2 marks]

The introduction of a new system should include changes from the old way of doing things. If there are to be no changes, then what is the point of the system being changed?

It is to be hoped that the time and energy expended on producing a new system will mean that the solution is an improvement on what was there before. It is these expected improvements that need to be documented. The mark scheme mentions that any intended benefits should be relative to the old system but that general points that take the benefit past the scope of the old system are acceptable.

The response on the next page is typical of those expected for this section. It not only gives a benefit of the new system, but also says why it is an improvement on what was done before.

The new system allows the user to search a large number of records for the presence of a particular value far faster than the old system because the user does not have to search through all the individual paper records.

Limits of the scope of the solution   [2 marks]

The effectiveness of any solution will be limited by a number of factors and issues. The hardware that is available to produce the solution may limit the number of options available. If there is no A3 printer available, then it is not possible to produce an A3 version of a large spreadsheet to be used at a board meeting. Software dictates the types of solution possible and the facilities provided with the use of generic software that is available dictate the way that the final product can be presented.

If the solution requires a barcode reader but the school does not have one, you may decide to prototype the solution by using a keyboard to type the barcode into the system to prove that it works. This is a hardware limitation but it does not detract from the solution to the problem – the limitation has been recognised and sensible action has been taken to cope with the shortcoming.

The problem of data protection legislation has already been mentioned and it will, in many cases, limit the solution because real data cannot be used for testing.

Particularly important are the files of data that are to be used as part of the solution. The real-world aspect is that the files will be of a measurable or predictable size. It is necessary to know this predicted size because it will affect many other decisions. An obvious one is the decision about how the file is to be backed up and onto what medium.

Another issue about the size of the data files is that there is a limit to the size of the files that it is sensible to expect a student to produce. It is not a sensible use of time to input *all* the real data into the system, so the idea of creating a file which is a fraction of the size of the real file while retaining its characteristics is sensible and acceptable. However, it is necessary to document the likely file size when it is in actual use.

Summary

- Agree a set of objectives with the client
- Design and document report layouts, screen displays and other forms of output
- Design and document data capture forms or screen layouts
- Design and document the data structures
- Design and document the processing necessary for the solution of the problem
- Design and document a test plan that includes test data and expected outcomes
- Document specific improvements that will result from the adoption of the new system
- Document the expected size of files
- Document any limitations that have been placed on the solution

4.4 Software development, programming, testing and installation

4.4 a, b c, d

Development [4 marks]

The time has arrived to actually use the computer!

The planning of the intended system has been done and the design has been fully documented. The decision has been made whether to use a software package with an element of original coding to manipulate data or to write a solution implemented entirely with program code.

The design section has been completed and the software development should follow the design that was produced. This is particularly important when referring to the coding – the code produced must match the produced algorithms. You should be aware that some problems will inevitably arise only when the actual production of the software is considered.

There is a right way and a wrong way to deal with occasions when it is necessary to depart from the original design. The wrong way is to simply carry on and do something different to the design. It may work, but it is departing from what was agreed with the client and this path leads to a solution which ends up not doing what was agreed with the client. The correct thing to do is to return to the design, change the design to match what is going to be necessary and then get agreement for the change from the client.

Students often think that implementing changes like this demonstrates a failing on their part. Quite the opposite is true. This is what happens in real life. The design is seen to be inadequate in some way, so it is necessary to return to it and adapt it to the new circumstances or needs. A project where it all works perfectly first time is probably very simple. A report on the project (which is what the assessor sees) that shows this continual process of adapting to changing needs shows a real situation and will earn you credit.

Evidence

There must be sufficient hard copy evidence to show that a solution to the original problem has been produced and *implemented*. A table in the report can *describe* the attributes present in a database table, their data type and any validation rules. The evidence that this has been implemented comes from a screenshot of the table design.

The report should include:

- detailed and fully annotated program listing for any original code
- data structures with descriptions and evidence of implementation
- input and output screens printed and annotated to show their effectiveness
- printouts of files or database tables before and after the input of data to show that the data has been populated.

4.4 a, b c, d

Programming [5 marks]

The syllabus makes clear that original code must be produced for at least part of the solution to the problem and it is in this section that credit is given for this coding. This does not mean that the entire solution has to be coded, but it could be. For the parts that have been coded, you need to demonstrate to the assessor that you understand the facilities available in the language that you have chosen to use. You also need to demonstrate that you have used the facilities sensibly.

The code needs to be properly presented. You must demonstrate a sensible use of relevant techniques, such as meaningful variable names, that were covered in Chapter 2.5. The code produced should match the algorithms produced at the design stage of the project and annotation should be used to illustrate this matching up.

The amount of work that needs to be coded is obviously governed by the solution to the problem. However, the syllabus states that for high marks you are expected to make good use of the facilities of a procedural programming language.

Program code annotation

When the program code has been written it is necessary to ensure that the code has been annotated. If you decide to annotate the code by hand, do not be scared of "spoiling" your beautiful printout. The more written explanation on it the better. If you are going to annotate by hand, it is a good idea to do so in pencil because it distinguishes it from the other work and also allows it to be altered easily.

However, the syllabus makes it clear that annotation of the code must use the comment facility in the language that you have used ("a self documenting program listing") if it is to be awarded full credit. All high-level languages have the ability to comment on the program code.

How much annotation is necessary? The definition of "fully annotated" is that, if all the code were removed, a programmer should be able to re-create your code from the annotation alone. In practice, this would be very time-consuming. A more realistic guideline is that the annotation should explain the purpose of each part or line of code to the reader (in this case, the assessor). After all, the algorithms should be sufficient to produce the code if they have been presented in sufficient detail.

Testing [5 marks]

It is essential that the solution is tested in order to make sure that it does all the things expected of it. If the testing is planned after the solution is developed there are two problems. The first is that the testing will tend to be devised in order to show what the solution can do, not whether it can do what was *intended* in the design specification. This leads to the second potential problem, that the original specification may not be tested at all. For these reasons, the testing needs to be planned before the development of the solution and this planning should have already been done in Chapter 4.3.

4.4 e, f

Alpha testing

Testing will be carried out by the developer (i.e. you). Testing done by the person who produced the solution is known as alpha testing. *Alpha testing* is useful because the developer of the solution knows all the different facilities of the software so that all parts of the finished product are tested. However, the developer sometimes misses some things precisely because they know the solution so well. They tend to make assumptions that the final user would not make.

The elements that were detailed in the test plan before the development of the software solution should be executed using the test data specified in the plan. The results should be documented and remedial action planned if the test does not produce the expected result. Remember that it is impossible to fully test a software solution to ensure that it always works because for most problems there will be an infinite number of possible input–process–output combinations. All that can be reasonably expected is that enough test runs have been carried out to show that the different parts of the system work as anticipated and that errors in the data are captured and don't produce any unexpected surprises. If full marks are expected from this section, you should include enough testing to be able to test all the different areas of the solution.

In the real world, software also undergoes *volume testing*. This is where the software is tested with the amount of data that will be used when it is operational. In most cases, this type of testing is not possible when testing the project because there simply is not time to create large enough data files.

4.4 g Beta testing

It is important that the intended users also test the software. This is known as *beta testing*. To just state that the end users have used the system and are happy with it is insufficient. The beta testing must be part of the test plan and hard copy evidence of this testing should be provided.

The mark scheme does state that the assessor "must be left in no doubt the system actually works to the satisfaction of the client". This must be the prime consideration in any testing. It is known as functional testing and basically means that the testing must be comprehensive enough to persuade the client that all their requirements have been met. Also ensure that any error capture routines are thoroughly tested with data which would expect to be recognised as in error.

Evidence

The report should include:
- the test plan with:
  - the objective being tested
  - data used in each test run (normal, invalid and borderline)
  - the expected output in each test run
  - the actual output in each test run
  - comments about each test run including any action which is necessary
- the results of beta testing carried out by the end users and other stakeholders.

4.4 g Installation [4 marks]

In reality, the problem solution will not in most cases be installed in the organisation. However, the assumption is that you must prepare for the installation.

If there is no final meeting with the client this will present problems with collecting the evidence needed for the final section.

Plan the installation

The purchase and installation of any hardware and the installation of software onto the client's computer system must be considered. The installation of the working files must take place. Although none of these stages are actually carried out, you must stress that they have been considered and planned. The location of the hardware and the installation of peripheral software, such as a virus scanner, are included in the planning.

For example, it is unrealistic to expect you to type in data for all 3000 customers in the customer file. However, you are expected to show that you understand the problem by proposing a method for doing this. For example, you may say:

> A word processor operator can be expected to input the details of 50 customers per hour or 400 customers per day. For 3000 customers, this will mean approximately 8 days' work, so employing two temporary word-processor operators for one week should cover the creation of this file and the smaller supplier file.

Training

The end users are going to require training for the new solution. If there are several end-users, a training timetable could be drawn up.

You may prepare training that takes the form of:
- printed materials
- on-screen tutorials with practical exercises that the users can work through themselves, at their own pace and in their own time
- you sitting down with the user and explaining what to do by demonstrating the solution.

Strategy for the implementation

Finally, a method of implementation must be decided and agreed with the client. There are four methods relevant to the introduction of any new computer system (Chapter 1.6):

- direct implementation
- parallel implementation
- phased implementation
- pilot implementation.

The important thing is that the decision about how to implement the new solution should be made by the client but information about the four options should be given to the client by you, along with a recommendation as to which would be the preferred strategy for implementation.

Evidence

The report should include:

- the plan for the installation of the necessary hardware and software
- the plan for creating the data files
- evidence that the different forms of implementation have been explained to the client, that a recommendation has been made and that the client has decided which to use
- reference to evidence that the client has actually used the system

Summary

- Implement the proposed process model using a high-level programming language (and a software package if relevant)
- Develop the data structures of the design
- Develop inputs and outputs appropriate to the design
- Illustrate how the software solution evolves
- Test the software solution
- Produce detailed output from the testing, cross-referenced to the test plan
- Test the software solution with the client
- Provide documented evidence that the solution works
- Devise a strategy for installation and implementation

4.5 Documentation

When deciding what level of explanation is required, think in terms of:

- this is how I created the solution (systems maintenance documentation)
- this is how you use what I have created (user guide).

In the discussion that follows, some of the advised content is not appropriate for some projects. These are decisions that need to be made by you.

4.5 a Systems maintenance documentation [4 marks]

Systems maintenance documentation is designed for use by a developer who understands computer systems. They can be expected to be familiar with and use any underlying software and to be able to follow the code of the high-level language.

Think of the documentation being in three parts:

- hardware and software specifications
- tailoring of the software package
- original programming used in the new system.

A small number of projects will have made no use of generic applications software – all the implementation is done with original program code. In this case there will be no explanation of the way that software was tailored. If software was tailored, this section should include:

- details of the data files including how the data are held as records in files or database tables
- details of the relationships between the data and the information about the data set up in the data dictionary
- the data flows around the system (probably shown in a dataflow diagram)

It is important to realise that the DFD that you produced in the analysis section was of the *original* solution. It is not appropriate here as the requirement is to document data flows for the *new* system.

The section on original programming should include details of the algorithms produced (pseudocode or flowcharts). These need to be properly annotated to explain the thinking behind their production. A full listing of the code, properly annotated so that a programmer can understand it, is also needed. Note that any code produced by an "automatic documenter" facility in the software should *not* be included. Code which has been generated using a "Wizard" facility should not be included as it will gain no credit.

Adaptive maintenance should be acknowledged. Another developer will normally use the documentation either to correct an error which has surfaced or to change the way it works because there is a new or amended requirement after the formal testing stages. Error correction is covered by the detail above. Adaptive maintenance requires the developer to understand things well enough to be able to make the proposed changes. A simple example could be that sales tax changes from 17.5% to 20%, so the solution needs to be changed to reflect this. The documentation should show how to do it. You cannot be expected to provide details about how to do all the possible changes that might occur. However, you should show at least one which can be anticipated. This demonstrates that you understand that it is part of the requirement of the maintenance documentation.

(4.5 b) User guide   [6 marks]

A user guide is simply that. It is a guide for the person who is intending to use the solution and play some part in its operation. Unlike a developer, the user does not want to understand *how* the solution works but they do need to know how to carry out some task.

There are two quite distinct parts to the guide for the user:

- a paper guide
- help available on-screen.

The paper guide is useful because it can be used away from the computer. On-screen help is useful because it can be context-sensitive. The best user guide combines the two types, and that what is required to gain the maximum mark in this section.

Tailored software

You should be wary about including details of software that has been tailored. It is the tailoring of the software that provides the solution to the problem and that the user will use. Consequently, it is the tailoring of the software that should be documented.

As a simple illustration, consider the case of a project that allows the user to search a data file for all customers who live in a certain town and mail merge their details with a standard letter. If the solution is based on the use of a standard query from within the software package itself, then the software has not been "tailored". Inclusion of the necessary techniques in the user guide would mean copying sections from the software guide, which would not be appropriate. However, if the solution has involved the correct degree of tailoring (e.g. the query is launched from a button click on a form) then the user guide must explain the form that has to be loaded and the type of data that is required. Examples of valid data would also be provided and the user would be presented with example outputs so they would know what to expect. The user would not expect to see a long explanation about the way that the software was used to create the query.

Contents of a user guide

There are a number of things that are important in the guide, above and beyond the obvious "How to use it". It could include:

- an initial set-up guide: this may only ever be used once, but it is essential nevertheless; for example, it may include notes on setting up of a file of data for first use
- a troubleshooting guide
- a set of frequently asked questions (FAQs).

You should ensure that the user guide helps the end user to carry out all the tasks that were listed in the objectives. You are expected to illustrate the guide with screenshots help explain the various tasks.

You should explain how to get output from the system. If there is a choice of hard copy output, how is the choice made and what criteria are used to decide which output device to use? You may even include simple instructions such as "ensure that the printer is switched on".

There are, of course, other things which would be needed in most projects as standard content:

- backup procedure
- archiving procedure

- use of the hardware
- error messages and actions necessary following an error message.

The user should be able to find their way around the user guide with ease. It needs an index or contents page. You should not lose sight of the fact that the final user will probably be largely computer illiterate. This means that there are likely to be a number of terms used, in the project and in the guide, that need to be explained. A *glossary* of the terminology used (like a short dictionary) is valuable, though do bear in mind that the appropriate use of technical terms, correct spelling and grammar, form part of the assessment in this section.

The guide should be aimed at the user. It must not assume that the user has any knowledge of the working of this or any other computer system. For example, when stating that a backup routine should be followed, it is insufficient to simply say that a backup should be made to keep the files safe. It is necessary to say which files should be copied; what is the medium to use; how the files are copied; when the copies are made; where they should be stored. The important thing to remember about the user guide is that it is used by a user who has no one to ask, so it must be comprehensive.

Activity

When the user guide is partly finished, show it to someone who does not know anything about the solution that you have produced. Ask them to look at a section (the backup section is a good one to use). If they need to ask you anything while they are reading it, then the guide is incomplete. If, however, they are able to understand what to do, then the guide is suitable for use by a typical user.

On-screen help

There should be on-screen help to supplement any paper-based guide. The sophistication of this help will depend largely on your abilities. It may range from simple on-screen messages to a full user guide, book-marked to allow relevant access from the particular screen that the user is using. Evidence of the on-screen guide must be produced in hard copy form in enough detail to demonstrate its use to the assessor of the project report. There is software available specifically designed for the production of help files.

The solution may be constructed from a number of different software packages. You should ensure that the help includes an explanation of the different types of entry for different types of data. This will normally take the form of a menu screen offering the user a number of forms that can be filled in with the data.

The assessor can only award credit for what they can see, so it is important to ensure that all aspects of the help are evidenced in the final report.

Evidence

The report should include:
- a contents page, an index and possibly a glossary
- details of input requirements including examples of valid and invalid data with explanations
- examples of the input screens so that the user knows the layout of the screens
- information on how to navigate betweens screens
- details of output methods
- explanation of all error messages that may appear
- backup routines and data archiving strategies (if applicable)
- methods that have been used to protect the security of the data (e.g. passwords on files)
- on-screen help facilities
- "getting started" and "troubleshooting" sections
- the security of both the software and the data in use.

Summary

- Develop systems maintenance documentation
- Develop a detailed user guide

4.6 Evaluation

4.6 a Success in meeting the original objectives [3 marks]

This section of the report is often poorly attempted by candidates!

You should compare the hopes that were originally identified for the solution (see Chapters 4.2 and 4.3) with what was achieved on completion of the project. Each of the requirements that were originally agreed with the client should be compared with the final outcome and an assessment made of how well the solution works.

For each objective, you need to discuss the degree of success that you believe has been achieved (with reference to the evidence in the rest of the report), any shortcomings that you have been able to identify and the reasons why such shortcomings occurred.

It is important to provide evidence from the testing of the finished work to support the assertions made. The evidence should either support the assertion that the objective was met or it should be used to generate an explanation of why the objective was not met.

It is also important to evaluate the quality of the solution when it is used. To this end, evidence of the solution being used with real data should be provided, if this is possible. Any problems outlined earlier about restrictions because of data protection issues or similar are still accepted. The distinction between the two types of data should be seen as follows:

- Test data are specially chosen to have a certain characteristic which can be used to test a specific area of the software solution.
- Real data are data that will be used in the actual operation of the system.

Evidence

The report should contain:

- a clear match between the agreed objectives and evidence that the objectives have been met
- a discussion of the success or failure in meeting the objectives
- the results that were obtained using "real" data rather than manufactured test data

4.6 b The user's response to the system [3 marks]

The end user needs to use the finished system. Ideally, the end user is presented with the user guide and a computer with the solution loaded, and is left to get on with it. This is somewhat unreasonable, and you should be on hand to answer any questions and provide support. However, the principle that the end user should use the solution (and not just sit and watch you make it work) is an important one. It is often helpful to present the end user with a worksheet to follow so that they are led through the system gently and there are no areas of the software that they fail to use.

There should be evidence that the end user has used the system, probably in the form of printouts from completed tasks and a letter from the client or end user stating how well they think the solution meets the specification. It is helpful to produce a questionnaire about the solution that would form a framework for the client's feedback.

You should comment on the feedback letter or questionnaire. There may be issues that need further investigation and work.

To obtain full marks in this section, the client or end user must indicate both that the solution is user friendly and that it fully meets the agreed specification.

The syllabus also states that to qualify for full marks for this evaluation section there must be no known faults in the solution.

Evidence

The report should contain:

- a letter from the client or end user stating that they have used the software solution and listing the things that they managed to do and those that they could not or features that need further work
- a completed questionnaire that helps the client or end user structure their responses about the solution
- evidence to support the assertions made in the letter or questionnaire (e.g. a printout showing an amendment to a record in the file)
- an indication of the degree of success that you have achieved in the opinion of the client or end user
- a description of how any inadequacies highlighted by the client or end user could be dealt with.

Summary

- Evaluate the final system against the criteria described in the agreed set of objectives
- Evaluate the client's and user's responses to testing the system

Revision guidelines

Introduction

Sitting for any examination is a stressful experience. Exams don't tend to come singly. You will find yourself not only having to sit one or more of the Computing examination papers, but also exams for some or all of the other subjects you are studying.

You should not start preparing only two or three weeks before the examination. Your teacher will no doubt have stressed to you the importance of learning the work as the course progresses.

For content which has a practical bias (e.g. learning a programming language for Module 2), this is a continual progression of new techniques and features and it tends to be cumulative. For example, you cannot understand how to use procedures and functions until you have studied the design of a modular problem or the use of identifiers and data types.

For some of the more theoretical topics in Module 1 and Module 3, this cumulative effect may be less of an issue, so your learning and revision can be less dependent on other sections of the syllabus.

What resources did you put together as you were taught the course?

There are several things you can read which will help to prepare you for the examinations.

Your own notes

You should have been encouraged by your teacher to produce *your own notes* as each section of new content was introduced to you and to learn the work immediately.

A week before the exam, one of the worst possible feelings would be to realise that you did not understand something you had been taught six months ago and so you are now are faced with learning something – which you did not understand first time around – in less than a week!

Your teacher's notes

Your teacher's notes should fully cover the topic at the right level for *this* syllabus. The teacher will have made clear to you any additions you need to make.

Your task is to ensure the notes are organised. For example, Section 2 of the syllabus has six main headings so you should file your notes in a folder with six dividers. Read them through *before* filing them and ask yourself the following questions:

* Do you understand their content?
* Are there additions you need to make?

Worksheets

Worksheets might not be the first thing to use when the time comes to revise, but they will remind you of the work covered.

What resources are best for revision?

The textbook

This book is the recommended textbook for the Cambridge 9691 Computing A Level. You have, no doubt, used it throughout the course:

* for general background reading
* as the starting point to produce your own notes
* working through the Activity exercises found in every chapter
* attempting some of the suggested Extension activities, especially for topics which have captured your interest.

Revision guide

Ask your teacher if there is a revision guide textbook available which has been endorsed by Cambridge International Examinations.

Revision cards

For factual knowledge, homemade revision cards are probably the most widespread resource used by students. You can dip into them in any odd five minutes you have and they are easy to carry around. Cards are usually available in a variety of colours, so you can use different coloured cards for different topics.

> ## Interrupt
>
> An interrupt is a signal to the processor from a device
> – to indicate that some event has occurred
> – the device is seeking the attention of the processor
>
> Reasons could include :
> – a printer signalling it is out of paper
> – disk drive signalling it has completed the reading of data
>
> All interrupts will have program code called the **interrupt service routine (ISR)** which is called to service the interrupt
>
> See card **Interrupt Handling** for the detailed steps ...

Mind maps

My experience of using mind maps with students is that the reaction is extreme – they either love them or hate them! However, I find students increasingly warm to their use – especially for revision. An example is shown below.

Hand-drawn maps are fine but if you have access to any mind-mapping software then there will be features of the software which really do facilitate revision:

- expanding nodes (for detail of the topic)
- collapsing nodes (for clarity about the "big picture")
- including graphics

Free mind-mapping software is available on the Internet.

The Internet

At the revision stage, this is fraught with potential problems:

- A Google search for a topic such as "lexical analysis" produces 522,000 hits (and you will not have time at this late stage to start trawling through them).
- The web resource you find may not be at the right level for A Level. Many of the articles are likely to be intended for a higher education course or are research papers that are way beyond what you are expected to know for A Level. This is especially true for computing.
- Can you determine what detail is relevant and what is not?
- Is the source reliable?

An Internet search might well be useful when you are first putting your notes together, but definitely *not* at the revision stage.

Past examination papers

The importance of looking at past examination questions cannot be stressed enough.

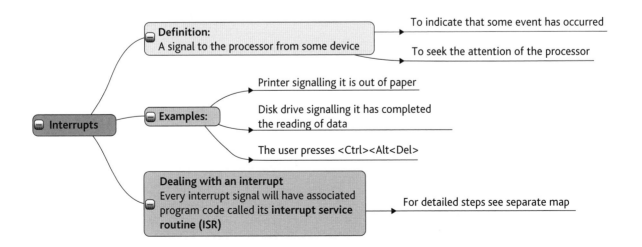

When a paper is set, one of the key questions asked in the quality assurance process is "would a candidate expect to be familiar with the content of each question?" The answer to this question must be "yes" for the paper to pass the quality assurance process. So the examiner and the exam board are very much on your side. The implication of this is that the style and content of questions is likely to be similar to previous papers. So if you have studied a reasonable number of past examination questions, then you are giving yourself the best possible chance of success.

You might be thinking that, as this is a new syllabus, there are only a few past examination papers available. This is true but much of the syllabus content has remained unchanged, so a task for you or your teacher will be to look through the papers from the previous syllabus and carefully select questions which are still "current". That process has definitely taken place in selecting all the questions which appear in this book in the "Exam questions" section at the end of each module.

You are likely to organise your revision into topic areas. At the end of your revision of a topic, attempt all the available questions from past papers. This is the best possible way for you to assess:

- Are there gaps in my knowledge?
- Are there certain concepts where I am not writing enough detail?
- Are there particular questions where I am finding it difficult to express myself?
- Are there topics where I am unable to suggest an application which is relevant to support the theory?
- Am I confusing technical terms?
- Am I using the correct technical terms?

How do you attempt the questions?

Do you simply read the question and then, talking to yourself, convince yourself you could produce a quality answer? Or do you actually *write out* the answer? This will take slightly longer but is what you will actually be doing in the examination. A strategy of writing out the answer is the best possible preparation.

Revision need not be solitary!

Almost certainly, you will have fellow students who are sitting for the examination at the same time as you. If you are using revision cards, why not:

- share out the task of producing them with a fellow student
- test each other using the content of the cards
- meet up regularly and test each other on a topic.

The format of questions

There is a lot of variety in the range of questions you will be asked. There will, however, be indicators in both the wording and layout of the question as to what answer is expected.

- Does the question ask for a specific number of answers?

  Example: State **three** automatic methods for data input.

- What is the key word in the question stem? The introductory text to the question will contain a key word – state, discuss, describe or explain – and this word is a good indicator to the type of answer required.
  - *State, define* and *give* all require only a short, concise answer (one or two words).
  - *Describe* requires more detail. Look at the number of marks for the question. If three marks are available then you must give at least three key points.
  - *Explain* requires some reasoning.

    Examples:
    - State two different output methods.
    - Describe an application where each could be used.
    - Explain why the given algorithm will only output the first matching name found.

- How much space is provided for the answer? All three papers for the 9691 examinations include the questions in the answer booklet. The number of blank lines provided for the answer is a good indicator of the length of answer expected.
- How many marks are allocated for each question? See the example question that follows.
- What is the answer space layout? See the example question that follows.

Example exam question

This example question is assessing your knowledge of interrupts (see Chapter 3.1) and illustrates all the above points about exam technique.

a. A processor is capable of receiving and dealing with interrupts and each interrupt has a priority.

> **Comment**
>
> The text above is the stem for this question – this text therefore applies to both parts (i) and (ii) which follow and it only "sets the scene" for the questions that follow.

i. Describe what is meant by an interrupt.

....

.... [2 marks]

> **Comment**
>
> There are two marks available, so the answer requires at least two key points. The key word is "describe" so we expect to answer the question with full sentences, not just a couple of words.

ii. Describe **two** sources of an interrupt and a possible reason for the interrupt.

1 ....

....

2 ....

.... [4 marks]

> **Comment**
>
> Reading the question carefully makes clear there are two requirements – a "source" and a "reason" for the interrupt. These requirements have to be fulfilled for each of two interrupt sources. The space provided and the numbering 1 and 2 for the answer makes clear the expected organisation of your answer.

Should I revise everything in the syllabus?

You will need to revise everything in the syllabus. There is no choice of question in any of the three examination papers. The rubric of the front sheet of the question booklet will state: **Answer all questions**.

A second reason to cover all of the syllabus content is that some questions may draw on more than one particular section of the syllabus. This is especially true for Section 2. The syllabus has six key topic areas but they are closely related to each other, so we could expect to see questions which use knowledge and skills from more than one of these six areas.

Section 4.3 in the syllabus document makes the following very important statement about Paper 3: "This paper will be set according to the content of Section 3 of the syllabus, but will also assume knowledge learned in Section 1."

This is because some topics will be covered in Section 1 and again in more detail in Section 3. For example, particular network topologies are expected for questions based on Section 1.5.4. Although they are not mentioned again in Section 3.8.2, we have to assume from the above syllabus statement that we would be expected to have knowledge about topologies in Paper 3.

1 Answers to Test yourself questions

Each bullet point represents 1 mark.

1.1 Components of a computer system and modes of use

1. • Hardware comprises the physical electronic components which make up a computer system
   • and software are the programs that make the machine produce useful results.

> **Comment**
>
> Notice that the answer provides a link between the two terms but clearly makes two points. You would not have scored a mark for saying that software are the parts of the system that are not physical because it does not explain *how* they are different. That answer would simply state that software is not the same as hardware, which does not answer the question.

2. Any two from:
   • to store data when the power to the computer system is switched off
   • to store data which are too large to be stored in the processor itself, until they are needed
   • to allow for the transfer of data from one machine to another.

> **Comment**
>
> Notice that there are more than two acceptable answers to the question. If you can think of three answers, you can give the extra one – you will not gain any extra marks but neither will you *lose* marks for it. Do not give more than one extra answer because it might look as if you are not sure and the examiner will choose your first two answers, right or wrong.

3. • System software controls how the computer system works
   • and application software allows the user to make the computer carry out a useful task.

> **Comment**
>
> Notice that the answer provides a link between the two terms but clearly makes two distinct points.

1.2 System software

1. Any three from:
   • to control the hardware
   • to provide a platform for application software to run on
   • to provide an HCI
   • to manage the resources of the computer system.

> **Comment**
>
> Notice that there are many possible responses to the question. You should have three or four specific answers that you will use when this sort of question comes up.

2. a. • A *multi-tasking* operating system is one that gives the user the impression that they can carry out more than one task at the same time.
   • A *multi-access* operating system is one that enables more than one user to access the system at the same time.

> **Comment**
>
> Notice that there are a large number of points that could have been made about both these types of operating system but most of them would not answer the question. Because the question says "distinguish", we have chosen facts that compare the types of system.

   b. • A network system is a system that links a number of computers together.
   • Any one advantage from:
     • Hardware, software and access to files can be shared among the users of the computers on the network.

- Communication between the users of the computers is possible.
- A user's files can be accessed from any machine on the network.

Comment

Notice that the answer gives an advantage by comparing networked computers and stand-alone computers. A more general advantage would not get the marks. Also notice that there is a large number of possible answers for the advantage. This question is generic. What would change if the question text had added "in the computer room in a school"?

3. a.
- In batch processing, data is collected and then processed as a single job.
- In real-time processing, output is produced fast enough to affect the next input.

b.
- The payroll process is run once per week and . . .
- . . . requires no human intervention, so batch processing can be used.
- Enquiries from employees about their pay need to be handled on a one-off basis . . .
- . . . with the result of the enquiry being made available immediately.

Comment

Notice that this question asks about the use of different operating systems at different times to perform different tasks which are part of the same application.

4.
- A form-based interface would be appropriate and it would contain any three of:
  - catalogue number entry field
  - spaces for input of other identifying information (e.g. colour and quantity)
  - space for the description of goods (filled in by the computer)
  - spaces for computer to produce availability and price.

Comment

Notice that this question is more likely to appear in a Module 2 examination because it is more practical. Just as important are the things that would not be on the screen. The question makes it quite clear

that ordering is not taking place, so an answer that suggests spaces for name and address or method of payment will score no marks. You may even be penalised because they show that you have not understood the application in the question.

5. a. A *command line interface* is a:
- series of commands typed at a screen prompt . . .
- which give specific instructions to the computer.

b. Advantages:
- The full range of features is available to the technician.
- An experienced user can elicit a faster response than from a menu-based interface.

Any one disadvantage from:
- The technician needs to learn the commands that are available.
- The technician needs to understand the way the system is designed so that it can be navigated efficiently.

Comment

Notice that the language used in this answer is not necessarily the sort of language that you will use in an examination. Don't worry about this. Answers such as "so that the technician can do tasks quickly" are perfectly acceptable.

6. a. Printer driver software:
- enables successful communication between the device and the OS
- contains the rules for communication.

b. Any three programs and uses from:
- A data transfer program . . .
- . . . to control the transfer of data between hardware devices.
- A file deletion program . . .
- . . . to delete a file which is no longer required to be stored.
- A file retrieval program . . .
- . . . to retrieve a file from storage into the memory of the computer.
- An automatic backup program . . .
- . . . to automatically make copies of files in case of damage to the original.

1.3 Data: Its representation, structure and management

1.

128	64	32	16	8	4	2	1
0	1	1	1	0	0	0	1

113 denary is equivalent to 01110001 in binary.

2.
- Each character is given a code . . .
- . . . as a binary number.
- Each character code occupies one byte.
- Most computers use a standard set of character codes, such as ASCII.

3. a.
- The book file needs to backed up two or three times a year . . .
- . . . when the stock take or book purchasing has made the contents of the file change.
- The member file needs backing up daily (or at least weekly) because of constant changes . . .

- . . . and there also needs to be a transaction log for the member file.
- Backup copies would be stored away from the building with the computer system in it, to ensure that a copy of files survived in case of fire.
- Multiple copies of the book file would be made.
- Member file copies and transaction logs may be kept for a number of backup periods.

b.
- When books are discovered to be missing, or if a book is replaced by a more up-to-date edition, the old records should be kept . . .
- . . . but they are no longer live so are deleted from the file . . .
- . . . after a copy (archive) has been made.
- When members leave the library their data should be archived . . .
- . . . also when they have not taken a book out for a long period of time their record can be considered to be dormant.

4. a.
- Integers are whole numbers . . .
- . . . on which arithmetic can be done.

b. Boolean data can take only two possible values, i.e. true or false.

5. One mark for any three of the following parameters with an extra mark for the explanation:
- The size of the array (how many data items it will hold) . . .
- . . . so that this amount of space can be reserved in memory.

- The type of data to be stored in the array . . .
- . . . so that inappropriate data can be identified, e.g. using validation checks.
- The name of the array . . .
- . . . so that it can be identified when it needs to be used.
- The upper and lower bounds of the array
- . . . so that the program knows the range of valid subscripts for the array.

6. a. i.   The array may be full, consequently no new value can be entered.
    ii. The array may be empty, so there is no value to be removed.
   b. i.   If the array is full, the stack pointer will be pointing outside the array.
    ii. If the array is empty, the stack pointer will be pointing at the first location in the array.

> **Comment**
>
> Notice that when discussing stacks and queues, it is important to have a picture in your mind of what it looks like. The simplest picture is to imagine them being implemented with an array. This is not the only way to store them and you may have been shown other methods, but the array is adequate for this course.

7. a. One mark for any three sensible fields with an extra mark for the explanation:
- ISBN
- . . . to identify the book.
- Shelf number
- . . . to allow a book to be easily located.
- Category (e.g. fiction or reference or children's)
- . . . to decide where in the library the book will be stored.

> **Comment**
>
> Notice that any sensible fields are acceptable (but you must be able to justify your choices). For example, publisher would be a sensible field with the reason that it would allow more copies to be ordered.

   b. • The key would be the book number (ISBN) . . .
- . . . because it is unique to that title and hence can be used as an identifier.

> **Comment**
>
> Notice that you are expected to provide the answer ISBN, although an explanation would be accepted if it was clear what was meant. Try to be aware of the standard key fields – account numbers, ISBN, UPC (barcode), school number, product code.

8. a. • A serial file stores data in the order in which it was received.
- A sequential file holds the data according to some defined order.
   b. • A hashing algorithm is a calculation . . .
- . . . carried out on data . . .
- . . . to determine the location of the data in memory.
- A clash occurs when the calculation performed by the hashing algorithm produces the same record key (and thus the same disk address) as for an existing record.

> **Comment**
>
> Notice that this is a question where it is very easy to give too much detail. Restrict yourself to what the question is asking for. In part (b), don't go into detail about what to do after a collision has occurred – this is not asked for and so would earn no marks.

1.4 Hardware

1. • The arithmetic logic unit carries out arithmetic.
- The arithmetic logic unit enables the processor to make logical decisions.
- The arithmetic logic unit carries out communication with peripheral devices.

> **Comment**
>
> Notice that the expected answers are three single-line responses. However, if the question had said "describe . . ." or "explain . . .", then the question would have been worth 6, or even 9, marks and some extra detail would have been necessary to gain full marks.

2. a. Two differences from:
   - RAM is volatile (loses its contents when the power is switched off) while ROM is non-volatile.
   - The contents of RAM can be altered whereas the data stored in ROM cannot be altered.
   - ROM normally has a smaller capacity than RAM.

Comment

Notice that the way that the answers have been phrased. The question asked for a comparison of ROM and RAM so both need to be mentioned when you are giving your answer. It is true to say that RAM is volatile but it does not answer the question until you say that ROM is not.

   b.
   - RAM would contain user files and software that are in current use . . .
   - . . . because the files will change and the user will want to upgrade the software from time to time. Losing these files when the machine is switched off is not a problem because they will be saved on secondary storage.
   - ROM is used to store the bootstrap program . . .
   - . . . because there must be a program present when the computer is initially switched on that can load up the rest of the operating system from secondary storage. This program must not be altered because without it the computer cannot start to work.

Comment

Notice that the reasons given relate to the answers given in part (a). The part (b) answer is not "user files because there is more space in RAM", although that could be considered correct if phrased a little more carefully.

3.
   - Hard disk . . .
   - . . . to store software and user files (e.g. a word processor and essays).
   - Memory stick . . .
   - . . . to enable work to be transported between school and home so that the student can continue working at home.
   - CD-ROM . . .
   - . . . to allow the installation of new applications software on the PC.

   - CD-RW . . .
   - . . . to back up files so that important work is not lost if the hard disk crashes.

Comment

Notice that the question does not specify how many devices should be mentioned. However, each device has to be named and justified (2 marks), so four devices seems sensible.

You should answer with devices that are appropriate to the given application. In this case, the question refers to a "home computer system". Although magnetic tape is the first type of secondary storage that was mentioned in the textbook, it is not sensible in this example.

Also notice that the justification for each of the devices was linked to the application: for a memory stick, the answer did not just say that it could be used to transport files, but it gave a good reason for wanting to do so in this scenario.

4. We discuss the transfer of data from primary memory to secondary storage:
   - A buffer is an area of fast access storage . . .
   - . . . which can be filled by the processor and then emptied at slower speed by the secondary storage device . . .
   - . . . allowing the processor to continue with other tasks.
   - When the secondary device has used the contents of the buffer . . .
   - . . . it needs to tell the processor that it requires more data . . .
   - . . . this is done by sending a signal to the processor, called an interrupt.

Comment

Notice that the answer describes transfer of data *from* the processor *to* the peripheral. Transfer in the other direction is equally valid and would have a similar answer. However, if the two answers are mixed together then it produces a confused, and often wrong, answer. The first statement is important as it sets the parameters by which the question should be answered. You don't have to state it in your answer but it makes it clear what is being described.

1.5 Data transmission and networking

1. • In a WAN, the computers on the network are remote from each other, e.g. nationwide or global, while in a LAN the computers are geographically close to each other, e.g. in the same building.
   • The method of communication between nodes is likely to be different, with a LAN typically being hard-wired and a WAN being connected by phone lines or satellite communications.

Comment

Notice that you can use the terms LAN and WAN without reference to what they stand for, as it has been stated in the question. In general, be careful when using acronyms – what might be obvious to you may not be familiar to the examiner, so an explanation on first mention is generally a good idea.

The two marks are not given for saying that the WAN is remote while the LAN is confined to a small area. This is really the same thing said the other way around. Be very careful about saying the same thing twice and thinking you have both marks where you have really only said one thing. Notice also that there is no mark for saying that a WAN will have more machines than a LAN. This may be true in many cases, but cannot be assumed.

2. a. • A network card in each of the computers.
   • Cable to carry the signals between different devices.
   • A network server to control access to peripheral devices and to files on the shared hard drive.
   b. • The distances between the computers are further than on a LAN.
   • The cable used to connect up a LAN can only transfer signals over a limited distance.
   • Another communication medium is needed, e.g. telephone line (using a modem).

Comment

Notice that the normal way of stating the point about the communication medium is to say that the method of communication used in a WAN is likely to be owned or controlled by another organisation (the telephone company).

3. a. • Simplex is the transmission of data in only one direction.
   • An example is the transmission of a television picture from the transmitter to the receiving aerial: no signal is sent back.
   b. • Half-duplex is a means of transmitting data in both directions but only in one direction at a time.
   • An example of half-duplex transmission is a walkie-talkie where the handset needs to be set to either send or receive.
   c. • Duplex transmission of data is the ability to send messages over the same link, in both directions, at the same time.
   • An example is a telephone conversation.

Comment

Notice that this is a straightforward question requiring a standard answer. As with so many of these questions, if you try to make up your own examples during the examination you could be making a big mistake!

4. • A colour picture requires more data because each pixel must be defined.
   • A page of text has less data because each character is defined by a single byte of data.
   • The bit rate is the number of bits sent or received per second.

Comment

Notice that this answer is not quite right because it is possible to imagine a page of text written in 2-point font which would use a large amount of data, while a colour picture of alternating stripes of red and blue would not need a lot of data to describe it. Also this answer does not take any account of compression algorithms that many students may know something about. However, in principle this answer is true. As there are only three marks available, any attempt to complicate the answer could be counter productive.

5. • Streaming of a video or a video conference:
  • The large volume of data . . .
  • . . . is time sensitive . . .
  • . . . because it must be used as it is received. If the data is not received quickly enough the video may freeze or the pictures and sound in the conference may not be synchronised.

> **Comment**
> Notice that, again, a standard answer is required. It is not enough just to say "video" as the example because time is not important if the video will be viewed later. The important point is that the data is "time sensitive".

6. a. • The third byte, 10101011, is in error.
  • Bytes should pass a parity check.
  • The other bytes have an even number of ones while this one has an odd number of ones.

> **Comment**
> Notice that you should not call the bytes odd or even.

b. If two bits in the same byte are in error, they will cancel out each other.

c. • All columns should have an even number of ones in order to be of even parity.
  • The first column has an odd number of ones . . .
  • . . . therefore the error is in the first column and the third row.
  • The correct data byte in the third row is 00101011.

> **Comment**
> Notice that you should write the block out completely or at least write the parity byte under the data block so that you can read the values off carefully. With so many 0s and 1s it is very easy to make an error in the pressure of the examination.

d. Checksum:
  • All the bytes of data are added . . .
  • . . . the carry bits of the byte are ignored . . .
  • . . . to supply a checksum.
  • The calculation is repeated at the receiving end and the values are compared.

Echoing back:
  • Data is transmitted and received.
  • Received data is re-transmitted back to the sender.
  • If the original sender receives an exact copy of the original data that was sent then the data has been received correctly.
  • If not, the sender can identify errors and only re-send those blocks.

> **Comment**
> Notice that you have to describe a *checksum*. Be careful not to mix up this term with "check digit".

7. • Packet switching sends a message in equally sized packets in any order so it has to be re-assembled at the destination; circuit switching sends the pieces of the message in order.
  • Circuit switching requires a route to be established before transmission; packet switching sends the individual packets onto the network to be routed by the nodes.

> **Comment**
> Notice that this is a difficult question on which to score two marks. The immediate reaction is to say "Circuit switching needs a route to be established before transmission. Packet switching does not need a route to be established." This is the same point stated in two ways and hence is only worth one mark. The second mark is much more difficult to score.

8. • Baud rate . . .
  • . . . necessary because if the computer transmits at a different speed to that which the printer can receive the message will become jumbled.
  • Parity rules . . .
  • . . . because if the computer transmits using odd parity and the printer checks using even parity correct bytes will never be accepted.

> **Comment**
> Notice that there are many possible answers to this type of question. You may know more than the ones stated in the text of this chapter but if you stay with the ones in the textbook then there is no chance of misunderstanding. Some students, on sight of the word protocol, desperately want to write down TCP/IP or HTTP. Be very careful. It would be difficult to think of a question, at this level, which could possibly require those as answers.

9. a.
- Different rules have to be established to allow the communication to take place.
- These rules are split up into types, for instance the physical connection between devices and the agreement of error trapping routines are handled separately.

b. The rules in one layer can be altered without having to alter those in other layers.

10. a.
- Hardware can be shared.
  - There is no need for a printer for each machine which saves the school money
  - There is a limit to the amount of printing that is required in a lesson.
- Software can be shared.
  - Only one copy of each piece of software is required and the cost to license the network will (probably) not be as much as buying several single copies.
- Students can access their files from any machine on the network; they do not have to use a particular machine or be in a particular computer room.
- Communication can be carried out between machines in the two rooms so that the teacher in one room can send a message to the teacher in the other room.
- Program and system files stored on the server only need to be updated once, so all machines have access to the same resources and the technician can monitor the use of the network by the various users.

Comment

This kind of question is often set. It could have simply been asked in generic form but this adds an extra dimension because the answers should be related to the school context when it is appropriate to do so.

b.
- Files are less secure because of reliance on a single server . . .
- . . . regular backup copies of files should be taken.
- Privacy of files is more difficult to control because of common access to hardware . . .
- . . . passwords are needed to control access to files.

Comment

Notice that this question could have other parts added to it where each part would assess a different section of the Section 1 syllabus.

1.6   Systems development life cycle

1. a.   One mark for each of three from:
- problem identification or definition
- feasibility study
- information collection
- analysis of information collected
- design
- development and testing
- implementation or installation
- evaluation
- documentation
- maintenance or system review.

Comment

Notice that the answers could be one-word answers. No explanation is necessary for answers to questions that start with the keyword "state".

b. Two marks per stage, which must match those in part (a):
- problem definition:
  - the analyst and end user must agree on the problem
  - each will have their own idea as to what the problem is
  - danger of wrong problem being solved if no agreement made
  - the client and the analyst have different areas of expertise which are both relevant to the problem solution
- feasibility study:
  - preliminary investigation in order to determine whether a solution is desirable or possible
  - looks into areas such as technical aspects, economic aspects, resources (both human and software), social consequences of the solution
  - cost–benefit analysis

- information collection:
  - marks for descriptions of interviews, questionnaires, document collection, group meetings and observation of present system
- analysis of information collected:
  - to establish requirements
  - to understand present system
  - to establish data handling requirements and methods
- design:
  - interface
  - software
  - data structures and program modules
  - test plan
- testing:
  - write the program modules
  - test plan carried out
- implementation (or installation):
  - methods and problems of installation
- evaluation:
  - criteria used for evaluation (the requirements specification)
  - degrees of success
  - evaluation from different perspectives of those involved
- documentation:
  - for the user
  - for future maintenance
  - importance of ensuring that documentation is produced throughout the process, not as an add-on
- maintenance:
  - corrective
  - adaptive
  - perfective.

> **Comment**
>
> Notice that a large number of possible responses is available for part (b), for only 6 marks. This is an example of a question which the examiner can aim at different levels of ability. If the question asked for one comment about each of six stages in the life cycle, most candidates would be able to do that. Asking for two things about each of three stages is a

bit more difficult. Asking for three things about each of two stages and it becomes rather difficult to get full marks. In this style of question, it is essential to take your cue from the number of marks available as a guide to the level of detail expected.

Other questions on the systems life cycle could be combined with other syllabus content. For example: "Explain why a feasibility study would be a sensible stage in the construction of a computerised solution of a problem" or "Given XYZ application, explain why the social and economic factors in the feasibility study would be particularly important if a project is suggested which would automate one of the production lines". These can largely be divided into two types of question: the first is based on bookwork, i.e. the recall of knowledge about the topic, and generic answers are expected. The second is very much based around a particular application and answers should be related to that application.

1.7 Choosing appropriate applications software

1. - CAD is used to design an item.
   - The software can be used to carry out tests on the finished design.
   - Completed designs are sent electronically to CAM software . . .
   - . . . that controls robot machinery to produce the item.

> **Comment**
>
> Notice that standard answers are all that is expected from questions about software packages. The facts that are discussed in the textbook are more than adequate for your examination answer.

2. - CAD can be used to design the widget.
   - CAM can be used to produce a prototype or help set up the production line.
   - Spreadsheets can be used to keep track of the firm's accounts.
   - Stock control software can be used to control the stock being stored in the warehouse.
   - Order processing software can be used to keep track of new orders when they arrive.

- Payroll software can be used to pay the workforce.
- Presentation software can be used by the sales team to impress the baking company.

> **Comment**
>
> Notice that this is the only type of question that can be asked about off-the-shelf software. Any other question will be a variant on this, with a different application. The applications will always be fairly simple because this is an examination in computing knowledge, not in your ability to understand a manufacturing process. The important thing is not to choose particular pieces of software but to give a reasonable explanation of why a type of software would be used for a given task.

3.
- The office manager would be keen to go ahead with the purchase as soon as possible because the decision making would have been done and the need has already been established.
- When making the decision to change, current packages available would have been evaluated so there is confidence in a possible replacement.
- The office is likely to be a relatively small operation with few users, hence the relative costs of buying custom software compared to off-the-shelf software would be very high, as would the costs of the staff training.

> **Comment**
>
> Notice that this is a very straightforward section of the syllabus but a difficult question. A question which starts "discuss" is expecting a certain amount of analysis of the situation, not just recall of knowledge. You are also expected to link your answer to the scenario given. The number of marks given for the question indicates the degree of depth required in the answer. There were plenty of other points that could have been made in answer to this question but enough has already been stated to get the four marks. Four marks also means allowing about four minutes to answer the question. When you consider reading and thinking time, you'll certainly use your four minutes.

4.
- This application may need more specialised routines than are available in the readily available software.
- Many of the routines in the readily available software will not be relevant.

> **Comment**
>
> Notice that this is a far simpler question than Question 3, despite the fact that it is about the type of software which is generally more difficult because it tends to be outside your experience. The answer simply needs two statements of fact, the standard answers in the text, with no need to describe or explain, though there is some requirement to relate to the scenario.

1.8 Handling of data in information systems

1. a.
   - Keying in data
   - Optical character recognition (OCR)

   b.
   - Keying in . . .
     - . . . can be used to enter the amount of money for which the cheque was written; this number is then printed in MICR characters.
     - All four data values are now in machine-readable form.
   - Optical character recognition (OCR)
     - OCR – characters are printed in a special font which can be read by a special reader.
     - The data is therefore in machine readable form.

> **Comment**
>
> Notice that although the answer is given as bullet points and the marks would be awarded for such an answer, the response expected would be a prose explanation (a paragraph). Note that although MICR is not stated in section 1.8a of the syllabus, the examiner expects you to have a working knowledge of it and other input types. The syllabus actually says "including". In other words, any input device may be alluded to in the question although, in practice, the devices used in the exam will be ones in widespread use in an application familiar to you.

2.
- Digital camera . . .
  - . . . connected to the computer which uses
  - . . . image editing software to crop and present the image to the printer.
- Camcorder . . .
  - . . . where the image is sent to a video capture card
  - . . . which produces a still image on a screen.

3. a.
- Two operators would . . .
  - . . . independently key in the data.
  - The two copies of the data are then compared . . .
  - . . . by the verification software
  - . . . and any errors are reported.

> **Comment**
>
> Notice that the verification technique of printing out the data so that the customer can check it is inappropriate for a mail order company receiving paper forms.

b.
- The article number can have a length check . . .
  - . . . if there are not exactly five characters then the article number is invalid.
  - The name of the customer can be checked with a character check . . .
  - . . . any characters other than letters, a hyphen or an apostrophe is invalid.
  - The date can be subject to a range check (actually a number of range checks) . . .
  - . . . e.g. the first two digits must be less than 32.

> **Comment**
>
> Notice that there are many possible alternatives. Choose them carefully so that there are three different checks and all *three* pieces of data are used. Notice that there are two marks for each check, meaning that the examiner wants to know what the type of check is and also the rule that has to be followed by the data to be considered valid.

4.
- Graphs (of the temperature, pressure. . .) showing the general state of the reaction vessel . . .
  - . . . to show the operator the trends in the vessel, for example shows clearly whether the temperature is increasing.
  - Report (of temperature). . .
  - . . . while the graph can show a trend, the report gives precise figures.
  - Sound . . .
  - . . . an alarm would sound if the temperature went past a safe limit.

- Hard copy printout. . .
  - . . . to allow investigators to study problems that may cause a shutdown or unacceptably poor product or performance.

> **Comment**
>
> Notice that while knowledge of a chemical reaction is not part of this syllabus, it is reasonable to expect students to realise that heat, or some other sensible parameter, would play an important part in the reaction.

5. a.
- A knowledge-based system is one that has all human knowledge on a specialised topic in the knowledge base . . .
  - together with a number of rules for applied to that knowledge . . . .
  - and an inference engine used to search the knowledge base
  - Communication with the user is provided by a human computer interface where the user can set a goal and ask questions.
  - Answers will typically be accompanied by a measure (often a percentage) of the probability of the response being correct.

> **Comment**
>
> Notice that this is a bookwork (knowledge recall) question.

b.
- Data is given to the system by:
  - a mechanic keying in at an interface and answering questions about the car: age; model; engine size; time since last service; any specific causes for the fault observed
  - sensors applied to the car such as a carbon dioxide sensor placed in the exhaust pipe while the engine is running
  - the on-board computer system which has logged a record of problems since the last service.
  - Inference engine uses rules in the rule base to match the symptoms to known causes.
  - The solutions are be read from the knowledge base and output . . .

- ... with the probabilities of each of the possible faults causing the problems and the remedial action to be taken
- The final decision on what action should be taken is taken by the mechanic.

> **Comment**
>
> Notice that this is an example of the only other type of question that would be asked about knowledge-based systems. It is simply asking about its use in the context of an application. Do not worry about having to have knowledge of these applications, the answers all follow the same pattern:
> - Identify whether data is provided by the user, sensors or other computer systems.
> - Say something about the inference engine using the rules to interrogate the knowledge base.
> - State that the interface shows outputs that are advisory, accompanied by a measure of how likely they are to be correct and the reasoning (i.e. the facts and rules) which were used to arrive at the conclusion.

1.9 Designing the user interface

1. a.
   - Ability of workers with computer systems:
     - have they received training?
     - are they used to computer use?
   - The environment in which the system would be used:
     - lighting conditions on the shop floor may be different to those in the office
     - colours will have to be different on the screen in order to maintain contrast
   - What output will be expected from the computer?
     - The office will probably use text.
     - The shop floor will probably need diagrammatic responses.
   - The hardware that is going to be used to communicate with the HCI
   - ... will determine style of interface, e.g. touch screen or keyboard for input.

> **Comment**
>
> Notice that although the list above includes hardware, the answer must be limited to software because of the question. These are standard answers taken from the text. Each answer needs to be expanded because of the keyword "Describe" in the question.

b.
   - Office:
     - Keyboard/mouse for input because ...
     - ... input is likely to be character-based to carry out typical office tasks.
     - Monitor and laser printer for output because ...
     - ... output needs to be checked and then high-quality printout for documents to be sent outside firm.
     - Hard drive for storage because ...
     - ... of need to store and retrieve documents.
   - Factory:
     - Touch screen for input because ...
     - ... dirty environment could damage other forms of input device.
     - Plotter for output in order to ...
     - ... produce design drawings for use in manufacturing process.
     - Hard drive for storage in order to ...
     - ... store a number of high-quality drawings.
   - Communication:
     - LAN for communication between machines or to some central resource ...
     - ... requiring cabling and network cards.

> **Comment**
>
> Notice the standard style of the hardware question. You should give answers for each of input, output, storage and communication where appropriate. In reality this is too big a question to be asked in an examination. The normal question will have 3, 4, 6 or 8 marks dependent upon whether the question says "state" or "describe" and whether or not communications play a part in the application.

c.
   - The interface will have specific areas to receive the answers to questions ...
     - ... these should match the positions of the answers on the paper form...
     - ... making it difficult to put the details in the wrong place ...
     - ... or to miss any out.
   - Validation routines will be set up where appropriate for some data entries ...
     - ... to check the data entry and reject anything not sensible.
   - Some items will not allow a blank entry.

d. • Menu interface on the screen so that . . .
  • . . . a touch-sensitive screen can be used for input.
  • Hard copy printout of the plans for products . . .
  • . . . produced by a plotter . . .
  • . . . so that they can be taken from the terminal and used at the point of manufacture.
  • Sound . . .
  • . . . so that an alarm can be sounded if there is a problem with the production line.

1.10 Logic gates

1. a. i. One mark for the inputs being correct. One mark for column Z being correct.

A	B	Z
0	0	0
0	1	0
1	0	0
1	1	1

ii. One mark for the inputs being correct. One mark for column Z being correct.

A	B	Z
0	0	0
0	1	1
1	0	1
1	1	1

b. i. One mark for the inputs being correct. One mark for column Z being correct.

A	B	Z
0	0	1
0	1	1
1	0	1
1	1	0

ii. You can replace it with a single NAND gate.

2. One mark for the correct inputs. One mark for each of columns P, Q and Z.

A	B	C	P	Q	Z
0	0	0	1	0	1
0	1	0	1	1	1
1	0	0	1	0	1
1	1	0	0	1	1
0	0	1	1	1	1
0	1	1	1	1	1
1	0	1	1	1	1
1	1	1	0	1	1

3. One mark for the correct inputs. One mark for column L.

S1	S2	L
0	0	0
0	1	1
1	0	1
1	1	1

2 Answers to Test yourself questions

Each bullet point represents 1 mark.

2.1 Designing solutions to problems

1. Any three from:
   - It should be intuitive to know what to do next.
   - On-screen instructions should ensure this is the case.
   - Navigation between screens should be clear.
   - On-screen forms should have the same design as paper-based input forms.
   - Each screen has a similar layout.
   - Few fonts are used.
   - It should take account of the skills of the user.

2. First, list what will be required:
   - a title
   - a box to display the numbers
   - buttons to enter the digits 0 to 7
   - a button for each operation
   - a Cancel button
   - an On/Off button
   - an Execute button.

   The next step is to draw a labelled diagram:

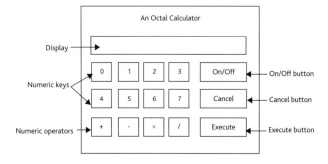

An Octal Calculator

Display

Numeric keys — 0 1 2 3 | On/Off — On/Off button

4 5 6 7 | Cancel — Cancel button

Numeric operators — + - × / | Execute — Execute button

> **Comment**
>
> Marks are given for the contents of the screen and for the layout. Diagrams should be labelled clearly. Remember that you will have to draw these diagrams freehand.

3. Any four from:
   - More than one person can be engaged on solving parts of the same problem.
   - The problem should be solved more quickly.
   - Different people have different skills, so each programmer can be assigned to do what they do best.
   - Modules can be used on many problems.
   - Fewer errors because modules are relatively self-contained
   - Easier to find errors and correct them in smaller modules.
   - This means that the final software should be more reliable when it is being used.

4. Any seven points from:
   - It shows how to calculate wages.
   - It inputs hours worked.
   - It calculates the gross wage:
   - . . . If hours less than or equal to 35 then wage = hours * 15
   - . . . Else wage = hours*35 + (hours-35)*22.5
   - It calculates deductions: tax and other deductions.
   - It calculates take-home pay.
   - It outputs a wage slip.

> **Comment**
>
> Notice that there is one mark for each stage and 8 ways of scoring the 7 available marks.

5.

```
              Start
                │
              INPUT n
                │
        Yes ┌───────────┐
    ┌───────┤  n <= 0?  │
    │       └───────────┘
    │             │ No
    │       Count ← 0
    │       Factorial ← 1
    │             │
    │       ┌─────────────────────────┐
    │       │ Count ← Count + 1        │
    │       │ Factorial ← Factorial * Count │
    │       └─────────────────────────┘
    │             │
    │   No   ┌───────────┐
    └────────┤ Count = n? │
            └───────────┘
                  │ Yes
            OUTPUT
            Factorial
                  │
                End
```

6. One possible solution is:

```
REPEAT
    INPUT n
UNTIL n > 0

Count ← 0
Factorial ← 1

REPEAT
    Count ← Count + 1
    Factorial = Factorial * Count
UNTIL Count = n

OUTPUT Factorial
```

2.2 The structure of procedural programs

1. a. • A statement is an instruction in a program or algorithm.
   • It may be simple like an assignment statement:

   ```
   Total = Number1 + Number2
   ```

   • or more complex like a WHILE... statement:

   ```
   WHILE Number < 0
       INPUT Number
   ENDWHILE
   ```

b. • A procedure is a group of instructions/block of program statements that do a specific task.
   • It has an identifier name.
   • the procedure is called from within the same or another program.
   • It can receive values from the calling program ...
   • ... and may return 0 or more values to the calling program.

c. • A parameter is a variable defined in the header/interface of a procedure or function ...
   • ... that is assigned a value when the procedure/function is called.

d. • Selection is a code construct using an IF or SELECT CASE structure.
   • Selection is when alternative pieces of code can be chosen ...
   • ... according to some condition.

e. • A loop is used when a statement block is to be repeated a number of times.
   • FOR-ENDFOR, REPEAT-UNTIL and WHILE-ENDWHILE are the structures for creating a loop.
   • A loop makes the block of code iterative.

2.

```
lstResult.Items.Clear()              ⎫
Number = InputBox                    ⎬ Sequence
("Enter a number (0 to              ⎪
    end).", "Input")                 ⎭
```

```
⎧ While Number <> 0
⎪     If Number < 0 Then
⎪         lstResult.Items.
⎪         Add("The number is
⎪             negative.")
⎪     Else                          ⎫
⎪         lstResult.Items.          ⎪
Iteration ⎨         Add("The number is      ⎬ Selection
⎪             positive.")           ⎪
⎪     End If                        ⎭
⎪     Number = InputBox
⎪     ("Enter a number (0
⎪         to end).", "Input")
⎩ End While
```

3. The best way to deal with this type of input is using a
   `SELECT CASE` statement:

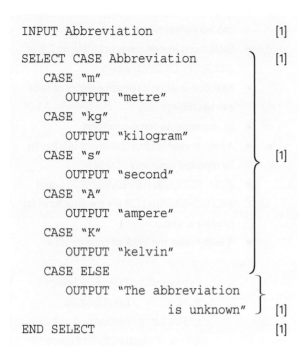

```
INPUT Abbreviation                          [1]

SELECT CASE Abbreviation                    [1]
    CASE "m"
        OUTPUT "metre"
    CASE "kg"
        OUTPUT "kilogram"
    CASE "s"                                [1]
        OUTPUT "second"
    CASE "A"
        OUTPUT "ampere"
    CASE "K"
        OUTPUT "kelvin"
    CASE ELSE
        OUTPUT "The abbreviation
                is unknown"                 [1]
END SELECT                                  [1]
```

> **Comment**
>
> Notice that one mark is given for the input,
> one each for the start and end of the `SELECT`
> statement, one for the specific options of the
> `SELECT` statement and one for the default option.

4. a.
```
INPUT FirstNumber                           [1]
INPUT LastNumber
Number ← FirstNumber
WHILE Number <= LastNumber
    OUTPUT Number
    Number ← Number + 1   [1]      [1]
ENDWHILE
```

> **Comment**
>
> Notice that one mark is given for the input, one for
> the `WHILE` loop and one for the processing inside
> the loop.

b.

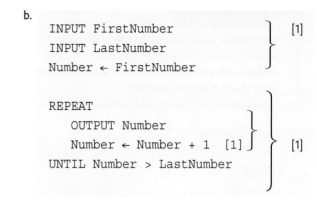

```
INPUT FirstNumber                           [1]
INPUT LastNumber
Number ← FirstNumber

REPEAT
    OUTPUT Number
    Number ← Number + 1   [1]      [1]
UNTIL Number > LastNumber
```

> **Comment**
>
> Notice that one mark is given for the input, one
> for the `REPEAT` loop and one for the processing
> inside the loop.

5.
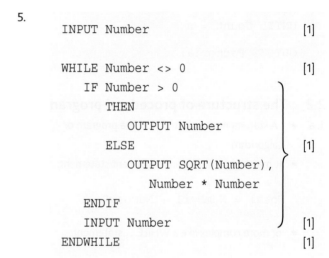
```
INPUT Number                                [1]

WHILE Number <> 0                           [1]
    IF Number > 0
        THEN
            OUTPUT Number
        ELSE                                [1]
            OUTPUT SQRT(Number),
                   Number * Number
    ENDIF
    INPUT Number                            [1]
ENDWHILE                                     [1]
```

> **Comment**
>
> Notice that one mark is given for the input, one
> each for the start and end of `WHILE` loop, one
> for the `IF` statement and one for the input inside
> the loop.

6. Consider the following program and subroutine.
   a. i.   The numbers are 3 and 7
      ii.   The numbers are 4 and 8
   b. The subroutine displays the two numbers input in
      ascending order.

7. • The function does not have a stopping condition . . .
   • therefore it will go on until there is no more memory
     available.

The corrected version is:

```
FUNCTION Sum(BYVAL n : INTEGER)
    IF n = 1 THEN
        RETURN 1
    ELSE
        RETURN n + Sum(n - 1)
    ENDIF
ENDFUNCTION
```

Comment

Notice that one mark is given for each of the bullets and one for the corrected code.

8.
```
Mystery(m = 69, n = 12)
    r ← 69 - INT(69 / 12) * 12 = 9

    IF r = 0
    ELSE
        RETURN mystery(12, 9) = 3    1
    ENDIF
ENDFUNCTION

    Mystery(m = 12, n = 9)
        r ← 12 - INT(12 / 9) * 9 = 3

        IF r = 0
        ELSE
            RETURN mystery(9, 3) = 3   2
        ENDIF
    ENDFUNCTION

        Mystery(m = 9, n = 3)
            r ← 9 - INT(9 / 3) * 3 = 0

            IF r = 0
            THEN
                RETURN n = 3
            ENDIF
    3   ENDFUNCTION
```

(boxes labelled 4, 3 on the left margin indicating return flow)

2.3 Data types and data structures

1. It is a good idea to present the information as a table:

Variable	Data Type	Explanation
ThrowScoreTotal	Array of Integer 1:6	Array to store the total number of 1s, 2s, etc.
i	Integer	Loop counter
NumThrown	Integer	Die value (1 to 6)
AverageScore	Real	Average throw score
TotalScore	Integer	Total throw score

2.
```
FOR i ← 1 TO 6
    ThrowScoreTotal[i] ← 0
NEXT i

TotalScore ← 0

FOR i ← 1 to 1000
    NumThrown ← INT(RND() * 6) + 1
    ThrowScoreTotal[NumThrown] ←
        ThrowScoreTotal[NumThrown] + 1
NEXT i
FOR i ← 1 TO 6
    OUTPUT "Number of ", i,"s is ",
            ThrowScoreTotal[i]
    TotalScore = TotalScore +
            ThrowScoreTotal[i] * i
NEXT i

AverageScore ← TotalScore / 1000
OUTPUT "Total is ", TotalScore
OUTPUT "Average is ", AverageScore
```

Marks are for:
- initialising array to zeros
- initialising total to zero
- generating 1000 random numbers from 1 to 6
- adding 1 to the appropriate running total
- finding the total of all throws
- finding the average
- outputting results.

Comment

There are many alternative solutions but all must have the above components.

3. a.

Field Name	Data Type	Length (bytes)
ModuleCode	Integer	2 (allow 4)
ModuleName	String	25 (allow 15–35)
Credits	Integer	2 (allow 1 or 4)
Room	String	5

> **Comment**
>
> The best way to do this is to draw a table to show the field names and their data types.

b.

```
TYPE ModuleRecord
    ModuleCode   : INTEGER
    ModuleName   : STRING
    Credits      : INTEGER
    Room         : STRING
ENDTYPE
```

> **Comment**
>
> The record structure needs an identifier name such as `ModuleRecord`.

c.
- Bytes per record = 2 + 25 + 2 + 5 = 34
- 500 records = 34 × 500 = 17,000 bytes
- Add 10% for overheads = 17,000 + 1700 = 18,700 bytes
- Size in kilobytes = 18 700 / 1024
- About 19 KB

> **Comment**
>
> The calculation needs to match your data in part (a).

d.

```
OPEN the file for reading (i.e. as
an input file)
IF file is empty
    THEN
        OUTPUT error message "No
                            records"
    ELSE
        Found = FALSE
        WHILE NOT Found AND NOT EOF
            FILEREAD next record
            IF record code ← 3542
                THEN
                    OUTPUT details of
                            this record
                    Found ← TRUE
                ELSE
                    Move to the next
                            record
            ENDIF
        ENDWHILE

        IF Found = FALSE
            THEN
                OUTPUT "This record
                        was not found"
        ENDIF
ENDIF
```

Marks are for:
- checking for empty file
- initialising Found (or similar variable)
- indication of moving to the next record
- setting up a loop . . .
- . . . with a suitable terminator
- checking to see if record is found
- suitable output message "not found".

> **Comment**
>
> Notice that this is not the most efficient algorithm but it would get full marks. Could you improve it? What should happen when we read a code from the file that is greater than 3542?

2.4 Common facilities of procedural languages

1.
```
INPUT SumOfMoney
CentsInDollar = 100
Dollars = SumOfMoney DIV
CentsInDollar
Pence = SumOfMoney MOD CentsInDollar
OUTPUT SumOfMoney, "Cents is $",
                    Dollars, " and ",
    Cents, "cents"
```

Marks are for:
- meaningful name for the constant
- meaningful name for the variables
- correct use of DIV operator
- correct use of MOD operator
- formatted output.

2.
```
REPEAT
    INPUT Mark
UNTIL Mark >= 0 AND Mark <= 100
```

Marks are for:
- correct loop used
- INPUT is inside the loop
- the two Boolean expressions

3. a. a < 5 AND a > 0 OR a = 10
8 < 5 AND 8 > 0 OR 8 = 10
FALSE AND TRUE OR FALSE
FALSE OR FALSE
FALSE

b. a < 5 AND (a > 0 OR a = 10)
8 < 5 AND (8 > 0 OR 8 = 10)
FALSE AND (TRUE OR FALSE)
FALSE AND TRUE
FALSE

4. a. p + q * r
4 + 6 * 10
4 + 60
64

b. (p + q) * r
(4 + 6) * 10
10 * 10
100

c. (q − p) ^ (p + q) / r
(6 − 4) ^ (4 + 6) / 10
2 ^ 10 / 10
1024 / 10
102.4

5. a.
- LOCATE(MyString, Str2) returns the start position of Str2 in MyString; it returns -1 if Str2 is not in MyString. The first character is in position 0.
- RIGHT(MyString, n) returns the last n characters of MyString.
- LENGTH(MyString) returns the number of characters in MyString.

b. This is one possible algorithm:

```
Count ← 0
REPEAT
    PositionOfSpace ← LOCATE
             (MyString, '<Space>')
    Count ← Count + 1
    IF PositionOfSpace <> -1
        THEN
            LengthOfString ← LENGTH
                        (MyString)
            MyString ← RIGHT(MyString, _
            LengthOfString -
                    PositionOfSpace - 1)
    ENDIF
UNTIL PositionOfSpace = -1
OUTPUT Count
```

> **Comment**
>
> Notice that there are many possible solutions. The examiner will accept any algorithm that uses the functions LOCATE(Str1, Str2), RIGHT(Str, n) and LENGTH(Str), provided it works.

2.5 Writing maintainable programs

1. a. A variable is a data item used in a program. Its value is likely to change throughout the execution of the program. All variables are given an identifier name and a data type.

b. A constant is a data item used within a program whose value does not change. Constants are given an identifier name and a value e.g. `RateOfVAT = 0.2`.

c. A reserved word is any word which forms part of the programming language. Examples are `Const`, `Sub`, `If`, `Select Case` (In Visual Basic) or any of the built-in functions, e.g. `INT()` and `RND()`.

2. The examiner will expect you to include references to:
- the use of meaningful names for variables, constants and sub-programs
- the use of constants (rather than using explicit values)
- the use of prefixes on identifier names to indicate their data type
- the initialisation of variables
- the modularisation of programs
- the annotation of code
- the indentation of control structures.

Comment

This is a new type of question. It will be marked on both the content and the accuracy of grammar and the use of technical terms. A bulleted list such as the one above will not be enough. You will be expected to use prose because it is a discussion question. You must explain the advantages of these techniques. It would also help to include some simple examples.

The marks will be banded into three categories. Not every question of this type will have eight marks but for this question, the bands would be:
- high-level response (6–8 marks)
- medium-level response (3–5 marks)
- low-level response (0–2 marks).

2.6 Testing and running a solution

1. a. i. An error in the grammar (language rules) of the program.
   ii. An instruction to perform inappropriate arithmetic.

Comment

An example is not sufficient for part (i) but can be used for part (ii).

b. i. White box testing means:
- Testing logical paths through the code.
- All logical paths scores 1 . . .
- . . . There is a test structure followed scores a second mark
- . . . Mention of a dry run scores a third mark.

ii. Alpha testing:
- Testing is carried out by members of the software house.
- Version may not be finished.
- Testers have knowledge of programming/ software.

2.

Line	X	A	Output	Condition
1	1			
3		1		
4			1, 1	
5	2			
6				2 = 3? FALSE
3		4		
4			2, 4	
5	3			
6				3 = 3? TRUE

3. Any two errors and examples from:
- Syntax error/error in the language or rules of the program . . .
- . . . e.g. PLINT instead of PRINT.
- Logic error/error in the original algorithm or in the transfer of algorithm to the code . . .
- . . . e.g. jump to the wrong instruction.
- Arithmetic error/request to carry out inappropriate or impossible arithmetic . . .
- . . . e.g. divide by zero.

4. Any three from:
- Comments/annotations/within the code/explaining the code/computer will ignore
- Sensible variable and module names
- Indentation/groups of program instructions/identified by some logical connection/start at different point on page from other instructions
- Modularity/code split into smaller groups/allow for local variables or library routines.

3 Answers to Test yourself questions

The answers are sentences or paragraphs that have been separated into bullet points to demonstrate what would score a mark. Each bullet point represents 1 mark. To get full marks you do not need to include all the bullet points listed. You only need to make as many points as there are marks. Make sure your points work together in a written answer though.

3.1 The functions of operating systems

1. • At some point in the cycle/at the end of an instruction . . .
   • . . . the processor checks to see if there are any outstanding interrupts.
   • If there are, the priority of the present task is compared with the highest priority interrupt.
   • If there is a higher priority interrupt, the current job is suspended . . .
   • . . . the contents of the special registers are stored so that the job can be restarted later.
   • Interrupts are then serviced until all have been dealt with.
   • Control is returned to the original job.
   • The processor can be set up to interrupt the current job immediately the current cycle is completed in which case . . .
   • . . . the job is stored at the end of the cycle and the interrupt is dealt with irrespective of its importance.

> **Comment**
> Notice that the handling of interrupts is rather more complex than described here and the manipulation of the special registers has to be explained in more detail, but the above answer covers all the points that were discussed in this section.

Further work may be interesting to you. Areas for discussion might include:
   • Think about how an interrupt queue differs from an ordinary queue and why
   • What will happen if the interrupt queue is full? Under what conditions can this happen?

   • What happens if two interrupts have the same priority?
   • How can the system ensure that even the lowest priority jobs/interrupts are dealt with eventually?

2. • I/O interrupt
   • . . . e.g. printer running out of data to print and wanting the buffer refilling.
   • Timer interrupt
   • . . . where the processor is being forced to switch to some other task.
   • Program interrupt
   • . . . where the processor is stopped from carrying out an illegal operation that has been specified in the program code.
   • Hardware interrupt
   • . . . e.g. power failure.
   • A hardware interrupt is handled first, then a program interrupt, a timer interrupt and finally an I/O interrupt, in order of importance.

> **Comment**
> The most serious interrupt is power failure (or the user pressing the <reset> button) because no other tasks can be carried out if there is no power, so safe powering down of the system must be paramount. Contrast that with the printer wanting more data before it can print. Does it really matter if the printer has to wait a few more seconds?

3. • I/O-bound jobs require relatively little processing but do need peripheral devices.
   • Processor-bound jobs require a large amount of processor time and very little use of peripheral devices.
   • I/O-bound jobs are given the higher priority . . .
   • . . . in order to keep peripherals working as much as possible.
   • I/O-bound jobs would be blocked and never get use of the processor if other jobs had priority over them.

> **Comment**
> Notice that there are far more points to take into account about interrupts. You may find it interesting to investigate vectored interrupts.

4. • Shortest job first:
  • . . . Jobs are queued in order of total processing time.
  • Round robin:
  • . . . Each job is given an equal amount of time before moving on.
  • Shortest remaining time:
  • . . . Jobs are queued in order of remaining processing time.

> **Comment**
>
> Notice that it is an interesting exercise to discuss other scheduling strategies. Consider a student who has to complete three pieces of homework. How does the student decide in what order to do them? There are no right answers here, just ideas. The point is that the OS strategy will be "common sense".

5. • Each job is given a set amount of processor time.
  • At the end of the time available for a job, it is interrupted.
  • The operating system inspects the queue of jobs still to be processed.
  • If it is not empty, the OS allocates the next amount of processor time to the job first in the queue.
  • The previous job goes to the end of the queue.

6. a. • They are both strategies of dividing up the available memory space into more manageable blocks.
  • Paging involves memory being divided into equally sized areas.
  • Segmenting involves areas of different size dependent upon the programs which are waiting to be scheduled.

> **Comment**
>
> Notice that the first mark point does not really answer the question because it does not provide a difference, however it does give a context to the rest of the answer so is worth credit.

  b. • The software code is divided up into parts that have some level of equivalence.
  • The most commonly used routines are kept together
  • . . . and are loaded into memory.
  • Other routines are only loaded when the user calls upon them.
  • Thus they give the impression of being permanently available.

> **Comment**
>
> Notice that it is not simply a standard bookwork question – it also relates specifically to an occurrence seen by computer users every day. A question with a little more detail about the software being used might expect a more detailed answer about the possible contents of each of the pages, but it would also have more marks available.

7. • The disk surface must be divided up into blocks.
  • Files are stored in these blocks.
  • Each file normally uses more than one block.
  • The table of files has an entry pointing to the first area on the disk surface used by that file and
  • . . . a pointer to the next block used.
  • Each subsequent block has a pointer to the next used block, in a linked list with
  • . . . a null value to signify the end of the file.
  • The list of unused blocks must be similarly managed.

3.2 The functions and purposes of translators

1. • Computers can only use binary numbers/understand machine code.
  • Machine code is too confusing for reliable programming by humans.
  • Software is needed to bridge the gap so that both needs are satisfied.
  • Programmers prefer to write programs in a high-level language which mores closely matches with the task or problem.

> **Comment**
>
> Notice that this is an "explain" question. The answer has been approached from two viewpoints and the final mark has been given for the conclusion drawn.

2. a. • Use of mnemonics for operation codes
  • Use of labels for variables
  • Use of labels for addresses
  • Human beings can understand meaningful statements better than binary instructions.
  b. One assembly language instruction is translated directly into one machine code instruction.

> **Comment**
>
> Notice that the last mark point in (a) is not obvious. Despite being an "explain" question, part (b) was only worth one mark.

3. a.
```
IN
STO X
IN
STO Y
IN
STO Z
GET Y
ADD X
DIV Z
OUT
```

The marks are awarded for:
- use of mnemonics and labels
- correct use of mnemonics . . .
- . . . in the correct positions
- sensible labels.

b.
- The value 4 is stored in location 1000 (called X).
- The value 6 is stored in location 1001 (called Y).
- The value 2 is stored in location 1100 (called Z).
- 6 is fetched into the accumulator.
- 4 is added to the accumulator.
- The value in the accumulator is divided by 2.
- The answer 5 is output.
- The code finds the mean of two numbers.

c. i.
- Making code as short/fast to execute as possible
- removing unnecessary lines of code.

ii.
```
IN
STO Z
IN
STO X
IN
ADD X
DIV Z
OUT
```

Note that the first input must be the 2, followed by the two numbers. Marks are awarded for:
- fewer than 10 commands
- working code
- a note of the change in order of input, if necessary.

Comment

Notice that this is a difficult question. The way to attempt a question like this is to start by trying to understand what the algorithm does and you can only do this if you create the assembly language version first.

4. a.
- Multiply . . .
- . . . to allow multiples to be produced
- Increment . . .
- . . . to produce a counter to determine how many times the multiply operation is used
- Comparison . . .
- . . . to compare the counter with the set value X
- Iteration . . .
- . . . to repeat a sequence of statements if a condition is not true.

b.
- Input 10 and X
- Input 1 into a counter variable
- Multiply 10 by the counter/or add 10 to the previous result, if this is done then the previous result must also be stored
- Output the result
- Compare counter with X
- If False then
- . . . increment counter
- repeat from "Multiply 10 . . ."
- End.

Comment

Notice that this is a difficult question. There are many ways of solving the problem and there is no "best solution". The creation of the finished product might be a challenge! Note also the need for far more operations; eight (our current maximum with a three-bit opcode) is simply not enough. The more operations that are required, the smaller the number of memory locations that can be accessed. There must be a compromise between the two, but eight bits for the instruction is obviously unrealistic for a real processor.

5. The computer must be able to hold simultaneously in memory:
- the compiler software/without which the process cannot be carried out

- the source code/the code that needs to be compiled
- the object code/because the compilation process produces the program in machine code form
- working space/processing area for the various lookup tables and table of keywords.

> **Comment**
>
> Notice that this question is trying to make you think about the implications of the creation of a machine code version of a high-level-language program. The size of the memory is not as significant as it used to be because the memory in a microcomputer is now large enough for this not to be a significant issue. In the past, the compilation of programs could cause problems on a microcomputer leading to the alternative translation technique of interpretation.

6. a.
- Interpretation involves the translation and execution of one instruction before translation of the next.
- The compilation of a program involves creating the machine code version of the entire program before the production of the final object code.

 b.
- Interpretation provides the programmer with better error diagnostics. The source code is always present and provides a reference whenever the error occurs.
- When a program is compiled no further translation is necessary no matter how many times the program is run. Consequently, there is nothing to slow down the execution of the program.
- Compilation means the final object code can be widely distributed without the user needing the compiler software or the original source code.

7.
- Lexical analysis
- . . . puts each statement into the form best suited for the syntax analyser
- . . . removes white space and comment text.
- Syntax analysis
- . . . checks language statements against the rules of the language.
- Code generation
- . . . produces the machine code (object code).

> **Comment**
>
> Notice that the number of marks for the question is an indicator of the depth of answer expected. There are six marks, three of which must be for stating the three stages. This means that there is only one mark for describing the purpose of each stage. Do not launch into a long essay, you don't have time in the constraints of the examination – the examiner is simply looking for an outline description of what happens at each stage.
>
> Be careful about writing down all you know about each stage. There is a danger that the first thing you write down may be wrong. There is only one mark available for the description of each stage and, if the answer is very long, the mark is lost immediately. Also, don't think that the marks can be carried across from another part. You may not know anything about code generation, but you do know a lot about lexical analysis – sorry, the marks cannot be transferred over in a question like this.

8.
- Source program is used as the input.
- Tokens are created from the individual characters . . .
- . . . and from the special reserved words in the program.
- A token is a string of binary digits.
- Variable names are stored in a lookup table known as the symbol table.
- Redundant characters (e.g. spaces) are removed.
- Comments are removed.
- Error diagnostics are produced.

> **Comment**
>
> Compare this question with the previous one. This question is asking for the *details*, so it is important to say as much as possible.

3.3 Computer architectures and the fetch–execute cycle

1. a.
- The program counter stores the address . . .
- . . . of the next instruction to be fetched in the sequence of the program.

 b.
- The program counter is incremented . . .
- . . . as part of the fetch–execute cycle.
- The program counter is altered to the value held in the address part of the instruction . . .
- . . . when the instruction alters the normal sequence of instructions in the program.

c. • The Program Counter stores the address of the next instruction to be fetched.
   • Before the program can be executed, the PC must be initialised with the address of the first instruction used by the program.

> **Comment**
>
> Part (a) is often poorly understood. Make sure that you understand its function.
> Part (b) illustrates a characteristic of examination questions. Most questions have more mark points available than there are marks for the question although this is not true for some of these sample questions.

2. • A way of looking at the relationships between the various pieces of hardware in a computer processor.
   • A single memory used to store each program instruction and the data for use with those instructions.
   • A single processor used to process a sequence of instructions.

> **Comment**
>
> Notice that it is not enough to say "that it is the ability to store the instructions and data in the same memory". The mark allocation shows that more is required. Always look at the mark allocation and ask the question – is there enough in the answer to be able score the full number of marks?

3. The steps are:
   • Contents of PC loaded into MAR
   • PC is incremented
   • Contents of address stored in MAR loaded into MDR
   • Contents of MDR copied into CIR
   • Instruction in CIR is decoded.
   OR
   • MAR ← [PC]
   • PC ← [PC] + 1
   • MDR ← [[MAR]]
   • CIR ← [MDR]
   • Decode
   • PC stores the address of the next instruction to be executed.
   • MAR holds the address in memory that is currently being used.
   • MDR holds the data (or instruction) that is being stored in the address accessed by the MAR.

• CIR holds the instruction which is currently being decoded.

> **Comment**
>
> Notice that some questions may ask for the whole cycle but it is more likely to be split up. This is a difficult question but it specifically asks for two parts of the cycle. A candidate who describes the execution of particular types of instruction has demonstrated that they cannot differentiate between the parts of the cycle and would probably gain no credit.
> Remember that the "register transfer notation" is a concise way to describe the stages of fetch–decode–execute cycle.

4. • Data bus
   • . . . is used to transmit data from component to component.
   • Address bus
   • . . . carries address of data destination
   • . . . must synchronise contents with the contents of the data bus.
   • Control bus
   • . . . carries control signals from control unit to parts of the processor.

> **Comment**
>
> Notice that there is very little variation that can be asked beyond the bare knowledge in the syllabus.

5. a. • Registers sufficiently long to handle floating-point numbers as single data values
   • Increases performance by reducing the number of operations that need to be carried out
   • Used in graphics applications as the calculations are time sensitive and the screen requires a rapid refresh.
   b. • More than one processor
   • Able to work on a task by splitting the task into sub-tasks
   • Used to produce weather forecasts.
   c. • Data locations can be processed simultaneously
   • . . . when the calculation is the same for each location.
   • Used to simulate the effect of a single action on a number of points on a car chassis.

3.4 Data representation, data structures and data manipulation

1. a. i.   113 = 01110001.

128	64	32	16	8	4	2	1
0	1	1	1	0	0	0	1

   ii. 1 = 0001

        1 = 0001

        3 = 0011

        Therefore 113 = 000100010011 BCD.

  b. 113 = 0111 0001 in binary = 71 H.

2. i.   Sign and magnitude uses the first bit for the sign and the rest for the magnitude: −27 denary is 10011011 binary.

+/−	64	32	16	8	4	2	1
1	0	0	1	1	0	1	1

   ii. −27 = −128 + 101 = −128 + (64 +32 +4 +1)

−128	64	32	16	8	4	2	1
1	1	1	0	0	1	0	1

    In two's complement, −27 denary is 11100101.

3.   34 = 00100010

    83 = 01010011

```
  0 0 1 0 0 0 1 0
  0 1 0 1 0 0 1 1 +
  0 1 1 1 0 1 0 1
            1
```

01110101 = 117

4. • Available bits divided into fraction part (mantissa) and

    • . . . exponent part (power of 2).

    • Both are stored using two's complement representation.

    • The mantissa is stored as a normalised fraction and

    • . . . the exponent as an integer.

−1	$\frac{1}{2}$	$\frac{1}{4}$	$\frac{1}{8}$	$\frac{1}{16}$	$\frac{1}{32}$	$\frac{1}{64}$	$\frac{1}{128}$	−128	64	32	16	8	4	2	1

5. a. • Digits are moved in the mantissa so that the first two digits are different and

    • . . . there is only one digit before the binary point.

    • A positive number starts 01 and

    • . . . a negative number starts 10.

  b. The accuracy of the representation is maximised.

6. a. i. 01000 100 or ½ * 2⁻⁴ = 1/32
   ii 10001 011 or −1 * 2³ = −8

b. • The larger the number of bits used for the mantissa, the greater the *accuracy*.
   • The larger the number of bits used for the exponent, the greater the *range*.
   • There is always a finite number of bits available.
   • Therefore the more bits used for one part of the representation, the fewer bits can be used for the other.

7. • A dynamic data structure can change in size during the execution of a program and
   • . . . a static data structure maintains a fixed size.
   • A list/tree is a dynamic data structure.
   • An array is a static data structure.

8. a.

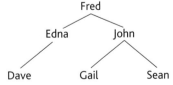

Marks are awarded for:
   • Root node labelled
   • Edna and John correctly positioned in relation to Fred
   • Edna's subtree
   • John's subtree
b. • A data item in a tree serves two purposes: storing the data itself and acting as a reference for the subtree below it.
   • If John is deleted there is the risk that any subtree data below John is lost.
   • Solution 1: Store John's subtree in temporary storage and then rewrite it to the tree after John is deleted. (One member of the subtree takes the place of John in the tree and the other becomes a descendant of this node.)
   • Solution 2: John is marked as deleted but the node remains to provide the right and left pointer links.

9. • Serial search is carried out on data list
   • . . . by comparing each value in sequence with the requested value
   • . . . until item found or no more values.
   • Useful if data items are not in order or the number of items is small.
   • Binary search carried out on data list
   • . . . that has items in order
   • . . . by comparing the middle item in the list with the required value
   • . . . and hence repeatedly splitting the list into two equal halves
   • . . . until middle value is the required value or list is empty.
   • Useful and fast method of searching if the data list is large and the items are sorted.

10. • A value is compared with the values already in the list
    • . . . and is inserted in the correct location.
    • Each value is considered in turn
    • . . . until all the values have been inserted.

> **Comment**
>
> Notice that you could give an example. A typical question could show a number of data items, numerical or alphabetic, and could ask you to explain a sort technique by showing how the data items are moved using a particular sorting method.
>
> The syllabus specifically states that detailed algorithms are not expected and only descriptions of the processes are required. However, any candidate who answers a descriptive question using the appropriate algorithm will be credited.
>
> A good idea would be to practise regularly the techniques of sorting using simple, short, unsorted lists. Show each stage of the sort by writing out the list of items again and again, as was shown in the text. This could be an excellent programming exercise to sort a list of data values stored in an array for each of the algorithms in the syllabus.

11. • Select first value from each list.
    • While neither list is empty . . .
    • . . . compare the values in the lists.
    • . . . copy the smaller value to the new list
    • . . . read the next value in the list that had a value copied.
    • End while loop.
    • When one list is empty . . .
    • . . . copy the remainder of the other list to the new list.

> **Comment**
>
> Notice that the solution takes no notice of what happens if the two original lists contain duplicate values. Neither does the solution consider the case when one of the original lists is empty. Both of these points are worth consideration and would gain credit if mentioned in an exam answer.
>
> The algorithm above is not presented in any formal style but is still acceptable. A prose solution would be acceptable but is not to be encouraged. You should write pseudocode descriptions for algorithms.

3.5 Programming paradigms

1. • Procedural languages expect the programmer to write instructions in sequence
   • . . . telling the computer exactly how to solve a problem.
   • Declarative languages tell the computer the problem which is then solved by

• . . . using a bank of facts and rules and the inference engine.
• Procedural languages can be thought of as being second or third generation languages.
• Declarative languages are fourth generation languages.

> **Comment**
>
> Notice that it would be correct to say that reusing routines from a procedural language program is desirable. As such a comment does not relate to declarative languages, it is not an appropriate answer to the given question.
>
> Always be careful with questions that relate two issues. The relationship implied by the question means that answers must discuss differences and similarities.

2. By value means:
   • A constant or value of a variable is passed to a procedure
   • . . . using the calling stack.
   • The procedure makes a copy of the variable before using it.
   • The original is unaltered.
   By reference means:
   • The address of the value is passed to the procedure
   • . . . using the calling stack.
   • The procedure may change the value because it does not make a separate copy of it.
   • Any changes made inside the procedure or function are passed back to the calling program.

> **Comment**
>
> Notice that the mark for stating that the parameter is passed using the calling stack is only be credited once. It appears twice because it applies to both methods.

3. i • Each class contains data and methods for accessing or using that data.
   • Data can only be accessed by using the methods available to that class.
   ii. • If one class is a subset of another class/a derived class comes from a super-class
   • . . . it can use the methods of that class.
   iii.• An object is an actual instance of an object

- ... referred to with a variable name
- ... with properties and methods defined by the class.

> **Comment**
>
> Notice that the second mark in each case is more difficult to score. If the question was going to be aimed a little lower then it could have given an example of a set of classes and ask for examples for the second mark.

4. a. i. Inheritance means a class can use the data and methods of its parent class/super-class, e.g. a `Teacher` object can use `EmployeeID` defined in the class `Employee`.
   ii. Data encapsulation means the data in a class can only be accessed by using the methods given in that class, e.g. the `HourlyRate` of an `Admin` employee can only be accessed using a method `getHourlyRate` from that class.
   iii. A class defines the methods and properties for a group of similar objects. All people who teach in the school belong to the class `Teacher`; the class is the blueprint from which actual object instances are created.
   iv. An object is an instance of a class, e.g. Mr Amit is a teacher in the school and therefore is an object belonging to the class `Teacher`.

b.

Cleaner
AreaCleaned ...
getAreaCleaned()

c. - `Cleaner` will be placed at the same level as `Teacher` and `Admin`.
   - `HeadOfDept` and `MemberOfDept` will be on the same level
   - ... and have `Teacher` as a super-class from which data and methods can be inherited.

> **Comment**
>
> Notice that the symbol ... has appeared in the diagrams in part (b). This is known as an ellipsis and is used to show that there are more properties or methods than those shown.

5. - Direct addressing means that the value in the operand of a machine code instruction ...
   - ... is the address of the data.
   - Indirect addressing means that the value in the operand of a machine code instruction ...
   - ... is the address of the address of the data.
   - In a standard 32-bit word, 24 bits may be used for the address of the data.
   - This allows 2^{24} locations in memory to be addressed.
   - If this value points to a location which holds nothing but an address then 2^{32} locations in memory can be addressed.

6.
```
<amount_of_money> ::= £<integer> |
           £<integer>.<digit><digit>|
                   £.<digit><digit>
```

> **Comment**
>
> For BNF (Backus Normal Form) questions, it is typical to give a mark for each of the parts of the main statement and then to give a mark for the correct use of notation.

3.6 Databases

1. - All the data are stored on the same structure and can therefore be accessed through it.
   - The data are not duplicated across different files, consequently
   - ... there is less danger of inconsistent data/less risk of data duplication/redundancy.
   - Data manipulation/input can be achieved more quickly as there is only one copy of each piece of data.
   - Data integrity, such as data validation rules, are part of the data design process and so do not have to be implemented with application program code.

2. A table is in second normal form if the following conditions are true:
   - It is already in first normal form i.e. it does not contain a group of repeating attributes.
   - All the non-key attributes are dependent on all of the primary key.

3. a.

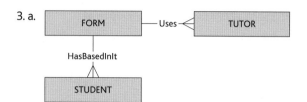

  b. One FORM contains many STUDENTs.

  c. Primary key FormName (in the FORM table) links to foreign key FormName (in the STUDENT table).

4. a.
  - HasBasedInIt (between DEPARTMENT and DEPARTMENT-TUTOR)
  - WorksIn (between TUTOR and DEPARTMENT-TUTOR)

  b. DEPARTMENT-TUTOR contains the list of which tutors are based in which departments.

5.
  - A foreign key is an attribute in one table that
  - ... links to a primary key in another table.
  - It forms, with the primary key, the relationship.

3.7 Simulation and real-time processing

1.
  - The alarm system is working in a closed loop. Once activated, the system is self-contained.
  - Sensors are used as input to the system:
  - ... pressure pads/movement sensors/infra red/sound sensors.
  - The sensors relay data to the processor which then makes a decision based on activation, more than one indicator, indicator of false alarm , etc.
  - Output in many possible forms including:

  - ... direct communication of system to the police/ triggering of an alarm bell.
  - Sensible for system to be a polling system rather than an interrupt system
  - ... a polling system will recognise when the processor cannot communicate with the sensors.

2. Input:
  - Touch sensors . . .
  - ... on some form of "bumper" system so that it can tell if it comes into contact with something.
  - Radar sensor/infra red sensor . . .
  - ... so that it can see things at a distance.

  Ouput:
  - Actuator
  - ... to control the motors that move the wheels.
  - Alarm or warning device (light or sound)
  - ... so that a warning can be given to human workers who come into its vicinity.

3. (For this question, each bullet point is actually worth 2 marks.)
  - Prototype aircraft would be too expensive at an early stage to allow testing of the real thing.
  - There would be too much potential danger to the people involved in testing the real thing.
  - It would take too long to build a prototype and then to alter it when the results of the testing are known.
  - Conditions can be varied easily in order to test the plane design in conditions which may be rare in reality or which cannot be set up as a real test.
  - Individual parts of the design can be isolated away from other factors of the aircraft design.
  - Many different variations for all or various components can be tried to find the best solution.

3.8 Networking

1. (For this question, each bullet point is actually worth 2 marks.)
   - Devices can be added without affecting the existing infrastructure.
   - A breakdown in one communication channel does not affect the remainder of the network.
   - Different communication links may use different data transfer speeds/protocols.

2. a.
   - Changing of the original plain text data
   - . . . using an encryption algorithm and key
   - . . . into cipher text.
   - The cipher text can only be decrypted if the recipient has the algorithm and key.

   b.
   - Each user must be in procession of a digital certificate
   - . . . which contains a public and private key.

   c.
   - User B (the recipient) is in possession of User A's public key from an earlier communication.

   - User A encrypts the plain text using User A's private key.
   - The cipher text is received by User B.
   - User B decrypts the cipher text using User A's public key.

3. a.
   - An intranet is a closed/private network (rather than an open/public network).
   - It is more secure because access is controlled by the bank
   - . . . through user accounts and passwords
   - . . . and levels of access.
   - The intranet contains only relevant, company-specific information.
   - Bank data are likely to be very sensitive.

   b.
   - Problem of hackers gaining unauthorised access to sensitive data.

   Measures to combat:
   - encryption of all data communications
   - use of digital signatures to provide authenticity of source
   - passwords to control users' access to data
   - firewalls to block authorised access to the bank's network
   - portable storage devices not permitted in the workplace
   - workers subject to a strict Code of Conduct.

Answers to Exam questions: Module 1

1.   i.   The physical components/the parts that can be touched   [1]

     ii.   Programs or instructions that can make computer do something   [1]

> **Comment**
>
> This is the first question on the paper and also the first bullet in the syllabus so it is expected to be something simple. These are just simple definitions and the candidates should know them. More marks are lost by trying to elaborate because candidates cannot believe that a question could be so easy. Candidates often say that the hardware is "peripheral" to the computer; this may be true but the computer itself is also hardware.

     iii.   A piece of hardware which prepares data for being sent to the computer   [1]

     iv.   A piece of hardware which reports the results of processing to the user   [1]

     v.   A piece of hardware which keeps data and software while the computer is turned off so that it can be used when the computer is turned on again   [1]

> **Comment**
>
> These last three are the other three possibilities from this bullet point.

2.   i.   To allow the user to give the computer data/change data into computer understandable form

     ii.   To allow the computer to give information/to change information from computer into human understandable form

     iii.   To keep data while the computer is not using it   [3]

> **Comment**
>
> Notice the third answer. There are other things that could be said: "To store data while the computer is switched off/to store data so that the computer can use it when it is switched on". It is even possible to substitute "software" or "operating system" for the word "data". What is not acceptable is to say "To store data" – the memory of the computer does that as well.

3.   i.   Programs that can be used in many different situations/to do something useful/task which would need to be done if no computer available/accept a generic example

     ii.   Programs which run/control the computer/hardware/provide interface between user and hardware   [2]

> **Comment**
>
> A typical starter question. The key word is "state", which simply asks for a simple statement of fact. Notice that the answers are simple definitions of the terms. These need to be learned as part of the exam preparation. Do not be put off by slightly different wording in the question, for example "operating system software", "system software" or "operating system".

4.
- provides environment for application software to be executed
- provides translator software in the form of compiler/interpreter/assembler
- controls the computer system hardware
- allows communication between items of hardware via interrupts
- provides an interface
- provides utility programs to carry out housework
- provides library routines for frequently desired tasks
- makes the computer act in the desired fashion/mention of batch/multi-user . . .
- provides security measures
- memory management

[4]
(1 mark per bullet)

> **Comment**
>
> This is the simplest form of question on this bullet point, requiring only simple statements. More normally the question would require a description and would be allocated 2 marks per purpose.

5.
- User interface . . .
- . . . to allow communication/type of interface
- File handling . . .
- . . . to allow use of secondary storage
- Disk management . . .
- . . . to carry out defragmenting/formatting/storage
- Virus protection . . .
- . . . to protect files on secondary storage
- Security . . .
- . . . and backup procedures
- Privacy to allow each user to protect their files . . .
- . . . logons/passwords
- Access rights . . .
- . . . to allow different users to use different software/hardware
- Access to peripheral devices . . .
- . . . via drivers/allowing hard copy
- Memory management . . .
- . . . to control the way that primary memory is used . . .
- . . . manages application software/installation to system/access to memory . . .
- . . . resource allocation/processor/printer time

[6]
(2 marks per pair of bullets)

6. • The times that the workers come and go need to be collected as a batch
   • Processing cannot be started until all the data is collected
   • Large factory means that there is a large amount of data
   • Data is all very similar . . .
   • . . . needing similar processing
   • Processing required is simple
   • No human intervention is necessary during processing
   • Results are not time sensitive
   • Pay must be calculated for all workers

[4]
(1 mark per bullet)

7. • Playing a computer racing game . . .
   • . . . because the latest input must be processed before the next output

[2]

8. a. i. Consists of:
      • windows
      • icons
      • menus
      • pointer

[2]
(1 mark per bullet)

    ii.   Consists of:
- boxes for input
- . . . in a strict order
- drop-down lists/tick boxes/radio buttons
- help information on screen   **[2]**

(1 mark per bullet)

  b. i.
- School/children/inexperienced users/home computer (almost any application)
- Ease of use   **[2]**

(1 mark per bullet)

    ii.
- Any example where *on-screen* input is necessary
- Allows for instructions/ensures no data is missed/ease of set up of validation routines   **[2]**

(1 mark per bullet)

  c.
- Touch screen
- . . . restrict vandalism/can be weatherproof/acts as both input and output
- . . . menu based
- . . . restricts choices/simple, intuitive to use   **[4]**

(1 mark per bullet)

> **Comment**
>
> A typical set of questions about interfaces. The unusual thing about this question is that it all comes from the same syllabus bullet point. In part (i), descriptions of the words from the scheme are perfectly acceptable. Notice that these are two very easy marks; it is the first question on the paper and would be expected to be straight forward. The type of interface in (a) (ii) has been changed in order to provide an opportunity to consider natural language interfaces which are very badly understood by students, most of whom equate them with spoken language interfaces.

9. i.
- Deletes everything on surface of disk
- Divides surface of disk into smaller areas . . .
- . . . to allow for storage/recovery of data items   **[2]**

(1 mark per bullet)

  ii.
- Scans the files on a computer system/received files . . .
- . . . to detect viruses . . .
- and remove viruses that have been detected   **[2]**

(1 mark per bullet)

> **Comment**
>
> There are many different examples of utility programs. The advice is to stick to the obvious ones. The ones in the syllabus are enough for most questions.

10. i.
- Divides up the surface of the disk . . .
  - . . . to create areas of disk that can be used for different purposes
  - . . . to store all video files in the same area

ii.
- Controls messages to and from the disk and OS
- Makes messages understandable between the disk and the OS
- Installs the disk so that the student can save and load files to and from the disk

iii.
- Changes size of files while maintaining data integrity
- . . . to decompress compressed video to allow faster download from the Internet

iv.
- To ensure files imported to system are virus free
- To check the video files before saving them to system

[8]
(2 marks per part)

> ### Comment
> Notice how the uses are related to the uses that the student in the question requires. In a question like this, always try to answer according to the scenario which is created in the stem.

11.
- (A member of the) character set that a computer recognises
- character on a standard keyboard
- standard to many machines
- stored in binary as . . .
- 7, 8 or 9 bits per character

[2]
(1 mark per bullet)

> ### Comment
> Notice the fact that there is no mark for quoting what the acronym stands for. Many candidates simply state "American Standard Code for Information Interchange" and think that they have answered the question. This answer would score 0.

12. 0101 0011

[2]
(1 mark per nibble)

> ### Comment
> A very long stem for a very simple question. This was originally part of a longer question. There is very little that can be done with this type of question. Other examples can be produced simply by substituting a different number. Questions would normally be restricted to 10 bits.

13

```
INPUT STUDENT
FOR COUNT = 0 TO 19
IF ARRAY(COUNT) = STUDENT THEN REPORT "FOUND", COUNT
END
ENDIF
NEXT
REPORT "ERROR, NOT IN SET"
END
```

- Input of student name
- Loop around selection . . .
- . . . with correct count/condition
- Correct IF . . . THEN . . .
- . . . with correct condition
- Correct output, including COUNT
- Error report

- Identify student
- Compare required student with . . .
- . . . each name in turn
- Keep count of number of names looked at
- If name matches, then report . . .
- . . .count minus one
- If end of array reached then report error

[5]

(1 mark per bullet, from either of the two lists)

14.
- Advantage: Processed/searched more easily/quickly/estimate of file size is easier
- Example: When a customer wants to know the availability of an item, the record can be found quickly/makes selection of storage easier
- Disadvantage: The size of fields must be determined before use so space is often wasted/not sufficient
- Example: The "description" field may not be large enough for a particular item   [4]

(1 mark per bullet)

> **Comment**
>
> Strictly speaking this goes a little bit further than the bullet in the syllabus, which does not ask for advantages and disadvantages. However, if a student knows about fixed length records they should be able to answer this.

15. i.
- Alphabetic/numeric . . .
- . . . records are stored in a logical order
- . . . in this case, in order of employee number   [2]

(1 mark per bullet)

ii.
- All the records have to be updated each time the payroll is run
- Necessary to compare each record with its entry in a file containing hours worked by each worker during the week . . .
- . . . which is in a matching order
- No apparent need for direct access to records   [2]

(1 mark per bullet)

16. a. • Each worker has an employee number which can be stored in a logical order
       • Transaction File (TF) is sorted in the same logical order
       • Records from the two files are easily matched . . .
       • . . . so that workers do not get paid twice
       • . . . so that no worker is missed   [2]
                                                                                                                    (1 mark per bullet)

    b. i. • Large number of records in file . . .
          • . . . make access to an individual record time consuming
          • . . . for the satisfaction of worker/worker demands immediate response   [2]
                                                                                                                    (1 mark per bullet)

       ii. • Indexed sequential. . .
          • . . . because it allow both sequential and direct access to data
          • . . . because it allows fast access to data while maintaining sequential nature
          • Random . . .
          • . . . because it gives direct access to data/faster access to data
          • . . . because immediate access is allowed while payroll may be produced serially   [2]
                                                                      (1 mark for the type and 1 for a relevant justification)

    c. • Serial
       • . . . because there is no logical order to input of data
       • . . . records/fields/items input with no logical structure to file   [2]
                                                                      (1 mark for the type and 1 for a relevant justification)

    d. i. • The production of the payroll
          • . . . because all processing similar/large amount/can be done at off-peak time/no human intervention
            is needed   [2]
       ii. • Individual enquiry made by a worker
          • Time critical because it must be done while worker waits   [2]

17. i. • Algorithm uses all 6 digits.
       • Algorithm has at least 10,000 outcomes/Modular division by 10,000   [2]
    ii. Any two which hash to same address   [1]
    iii. • Values that collide are stored serially . . .
        • . . . after end of file/in a bucket
        • Marker applied to correct address to signify further values

- Original address contains pointer . . .
- . . . which is head of linked list of items . . .
- . . . which hash to same value.
- Locations are searched serially
- . . . until free location found
- . . . value inserted at free location [2]

(1 mark per bullet for any one method)

Comment

This covers everything that is required about direct access to data. There are no "right" answers to part (i), just answers that are sensible. Part (ii) needs the student to give two keys that will clash for their hashing algorithm, so the algorithm shouldn't be too complicated!

18.
- Colour: character/text/string/alphanumeric
- Engine size: integer/real
- Air Con: Boolean
- Price: currency/real/integer [4]

Comment

Notice that there are many alternatives for each answer.

19. i.
- Backing up is making a copy of the entire data file . . .
- . . . in case the working file is corrupted
- Archiving is taking a copy of little used data
- . . . for long-term storage in case reference needs to be made to it in the future
- These redundant files can then be deleted/in order to create space on medium [4]

(1 mark per bullet)

ii.
- Daily (or at least weekly)
- . . . copy of files/to portable medium
- More than one copy made . . .
- . . . at least one copy kept off site
- Transaction log kept between backups [4]

(1 mark per bullet)

Comment

A typical question about backing up data and archiving data. The first part is about comparing the two processes and is a generic question. The second should relate to the scenario. Particularly important here is the concept of an office environment and consequently a regular backup procedure is necessary, as opposed to the records of students in a school which may be backed up once a term because there are so few changes to the data. Candidates should be aware of the concept of an incremental backup procedure.

20. i. • Coordinate the work of the rest of the processor
   • Manage the execution of instructions (not "perform")
   • Choreograph the instruction cycle by using a clock
   ii. • Store OS
   • Store application software in use
   • Store data files in use
   iii. • Carry out processing/calculations
   • Carry out I/O from processor
   • Make logical decisions

[6]
(1 mark per bullet)

> **Comment**
>
> It is difficult to imagine variations to this question, however there are variations in the way that it can be marked. This is perhaps the easiest way, where errors can be compensated for in other parts. The more difficult one is when there are two marks per part, while the most difficult variation is to ask for three marks per part. The question remains the same, the answers remain the same, but the difficulty and hence the grade at which the question is pitched changes.
>
> Notice the importance of the correct way to state the responses here. Too many candidates carelessly suggest that the control unit controls the whole computer, like some hardware version of an operating system, while many candidates state that "the ALU carries out the logic operations and does the arithmetic". This is too close to the wording of the question and is, consequently, not acceptable.

21. • ROM cannot be altered, RAM can
   • ROM is not volatile, RAM is
   • ROM is normally smaller capacity than RAM

[2]
(1 mark per bullet)

> **Comment**
>
> Notice the difference between saying that memory is volatile and saying that the contents can be changed. These are two different things and would gain both marks. Do not say what they are used for – it does not answer the question because their use is dependent upon their features.
>
> Examiners normally give a mark for a single statement such as "RAM is volatile". The question asks for a difference so you should give both parts of the answer for a mark, but the assumption is that if you state this then you know that ROM is not volatile. You must state two differences for the two marks: use bulleted or numbered points to make sure you don't miss one.

22. i. • Data in use/software in use/part of operating system
    • Processor can only use what is stored in RAM/not needed for long [2]
    ii. • Bootstrap/boot loader/loader/startup program
    • It must be available when the computer is switched on/must not be altered [2]

> **Comment**
>
> Notice the need for a second mark point for each part. There are two questions to answer each time: what is stored and why it is appropriate.

23. i. • To store the Files/Software/Operating System which is being used
    • Need to store large volumes of data/semi-permanently/access to data needs to be direct/contents will need to be altered easily
    ii. • Backup/Archive
    • Need to be portable in order to be kept safely away from system/to be rewritable as the backup will be taken often
    iii. • Import software/keep original copies of software
    • Cannot be changed (hence lost)/kept in case of need to reinstall [6]

> **Comment**
>
> The examples of storage may alter (solid-state pen drives is now common) but the basic principles remain the same. Consider the characteristics and decide how those characteristics would be advantageous, for the application given.
>
> Many students will say here that the DVD-RW will be used to take work home and bring it to the office. This is the answer to the question about a student using various devices on their home computer, it is not appropriate here. Notice the specification of CD-ROM in part (iii). Many students will ignore this and state that it is used for taking backups. Similarly "DVD" is often used as shorthand for discs with films stored on them so a popular answer here will be "to watch films", again, not fitting the requirements of the application.

24. • Processor fills buffer with data
    • Processor continues with other jobs
    • Buffer is emptied to storage device
    • When buffer is empty . . .
    • . . . signal is sent to processor (interrupt) . . .
    • . . . requesting further data to be sent to buffer
    • . . . dependent on priority
    • Processor interrupts present job to refill buffer
    • Mention of double buffering [6]
    (1 mark per bullet)

> ## Comment
>
> This is a standard answer. Problems arise when candidates are unsure of what produces the interrupt and where it is sent. The memory is often given more power than it deserves, candidates suggesting that the memory controls the process. Candidates should also be aware that sometimes the memory is called main memory or primary memory and that the storage device can be any peripheral.

25.
- Black and white laser
  - . . . used in office to produce letters
  - . . . produces high quality/speedy so does not develop large queue on a LAN
- Colour laser
  - . . . used to produce reports for a meeting
  - . . . high-quality outputs/can produce large quantity quickly
- Dot matrix
  - . . . used to print receipts at checkout/tickets on railway
  - . . . produces more than one copy at a time, one for customer + one for shop
- Inkjet
  - . . . used to do homework at home to hand in at school
  - . . . relatively cheap and slowness does not matter
- Plotter
  - . . . used to produce architect's plans
  - . . . produces very accurate drawings to scale
- Braille printer
  - . . . used to produce documents for blind people
  - . . . outputs 3D data

[9]

(1 mark per bullet for each type of printer)

> ## Comment
>
> Notice the example uses. There are many others but candidates would be advised to think about a characteristic of the printer they have chosen and then to think of a use which would need that characteristic. Better still, there are certain standard answers about which there can be no argument. They are highlighted in bold in the mark scheme and students are advised to stick to these.

26. ATM:
- Restricted characters
- Fewer keys . . .
- . . . simplifies input required
- Meaning of key alters according to place in sequence
- Use of output device to explain meaning of keys
- Braille characters on keys

- ... to allow blind people to use ATM
- Keys are touch sensitive
- Protected from elements/vandalism
- Made of more resilient material because of position/volume of use/users [6]

(1 mark per bullet for each type of printer)

Note: All these mark points are from the point of view of the ATM. Equivalent points are acceptable from the point of view of a QWERTY keyboard.

Comment

The list of peripheral devices is enormous. Candidates may be asked to provide their own examples for given situations. Questions that ask about particular types of peripheral will be restricted to the main types.

The question could have been asked in the form of "State the features of . . . " or "Explain why it is necessary to have . . . " but this question is more difficult because it asks for comparisons to be made so there is an element of having to produce two sets of work at a time. The content of the question is at a lower level but the way it has been asked has elevated it to a middle grade question. This is the sort of question where it is essential to answer as a set of bullet points so that you can keep track of the number of points you have made.

27.
- Storage that allows reading of professionally produced material (CD ROM drive, DVD)
- ... necessary to input game instructions to her hard drive
- Joystick/gamespad
- ... to play the game
- Memory stick (floppy disk, CDRW)
- ... to save her half-finished work and transport it to a different machine
- (Colour) printer/Inkjet/Bubble jet
- ... to produce hard copy of her work to hand in.
- Network Card/Modem and phone line/Broadband, ADSL, ISDN
- ... to allow access to Internet to facilitate use of e-mail
- Webcam/Microphone and speakers
- ... to allow conversation and vision [8]

(1 mark for the device and the explanation, per peripheral)

Comment

This question is within the experience of most students. This should make it a simple question to answer but unfortunately too many do not take advantage of the information given in the question about what the student uses the computer for. There is a lot of scope there for a lot of peripheral devices. (Note that there are 8 marks for the question, which means four peripherals and reasons why they are necessary. Any more than that can't score because all the marks have been given.) Any peripheral which can be justified is awarded marks, but too many students give unsuitable peripherals for the application (barcode reader?).

28. a.
- The user is far slower than the processor in making decisions
- The peripherals are slower than the processor
- This means that the processor has to wait

[2]
(1 mark per bullet)

> **Comment**
>
> Standard question. There is little else that can be asked about the speed mismatch!

b. Any suitable for batch processing, e.g. utility bills/bank statements . . .

[1]

> **Comment**
>
> Notice the ones listed are standard. "Payroll" could be added to them but don't use any others as answers. These examples are accepted, others may not be. For example, the transactions at a cash machine (ATM) may be batched (statement requests) but may also be real-time (checking of funds). If the candidate states ATM then it will not gain credit, as the answer is not precise enough – the safe option is to choose one of the standard ones!

c.
- Data is prepared offline/input at speed of peripheral
- User is not provided direct access to processor/user is offline
- Processor services more than 1 peripheral
- Carried out at off-peak times so that processor time not so important

[2]
(1 mark per bullet)

> **Comment**
>
> Once again, a standard answer. It is difficult to think up a different question for this! Parts (b) and (c) could have been placed in a number of bullets in the syllabus, notably 1.2.c, but have been placed here because the question is basically about speed mismatch and only secondarily about batch processing.

29.
- LAN is geographically small area/WAN over a larger area
- LAN may be hard wired/WAN requires other medium for communication
- LAN much easier to keep secure/WAN is prone to hacking

[2]
(1 mark per bullet)

> **Comment**
>
> There are not many ways to ask a question about this. Strictly the answers to this question should have a comment from the point of view of the LAN *and* from the point of view of the WAN, but the examiner will accept the single statement as meaning the other type will be opposite.

30. Hardware:
    - (Wireless) network cards
    - Hub/switch if describing a star network
    - Cable/Radio transmitters
    - (File/Network/Printer) server   [2]

(1 mark per bullet)

Software:
    - Network operating system
    - Communications software
    - Network versions of the software   [1]

> **Comment**
>
> This is the standard question for hardware and software for creating a network from a number of stand-alone machines. If the question is about adding a LAN to the Internet the above answers are not relevant because the LAN has already been created. Candidates should be considering Gateway/Router/Modem and web browser software.

31. a. i.   The transfer of data in only one direction
        ii. The transfer of data in both directions but only one direction at a time
        iii. The transfer of data one bit at a time down a single (wire)
        iv. The transfer of data down a number of wires/bits being sent simultaneously/normally one byte at a time   [4]

> **Comment**
>
> These are intended to be very basic marks which a grade E candidate should be able to get. They are basic definitions which should be known. The ones that cause difficulty are serial and parallel because candidates are prone to confusing them with serial data storage.

   b. - Parallel
       - . . . because the processor requires the data to be downloaded as quickly as possible
       - Half duplex
       - . . . because there needs to be communication in both directions though only one at a time because data cannot be read to and written from at the same time   [4]

> **Comment**
>
> This question is more difficult because it requires some thought to apply the basic knowledge to a situation.

32. - Different applications require different bit rates
    - To ensure that data is read at the same rate as it is sent
    - To avoid bits becoming jumbled up when they are transmitted . . .
    - . . . which can lead to one bit being interpreted as two bits   [2]

(1 mark per bullet)

33.
- Data sent as binary bytes which are added up before transmission
- ... with no carry out of byte
- Added again after transmission/the two values are compared [3]

34. a. i. 10111100/the second one [1]

   ii.
- This has an odd number of ones.
- The others all have an even number of ones.
- Even parity is being used [2]

                   (1 mark per bullet)

   iii. There may be two (or an even number of) errors in one byte [1]

   iv.
- Data is sent in blocks of bytes
- Each byte has a parity bit
- Each column of bits (from each byte) has a parity bit as an individual parity byte which is sent along with the data block
- An error in the parity bit s of the data byte and the parity byte give coordinates of a bit in the block
- This is the location of the error [4]

                   (1 mark per bullet)

  b.
- When the data is received it is stored
- A copy of the data is then sent back to the transmitting station
- The returned data is compared to the data that was originally sent
- If there is a difference then an error has occurred
- The data is retransmitted [4]

                   (1 mark per bullet)

35. i.
- Message is split into equal-sized packets
- Each packet is labelled
- Each packet travels independently
- At each node label checked and packet redirected
- Must be ordered at destination and reassembled [3]

                   (1 mark per bullet)

ii. Advantages:
- Allows optimum use of network
- Less chance of message being intercepted
- If a route is congested or blocked an alternative route is used

Disadvantages:
- Travels at speed of slowest packet
- Must be reordered at destination   [2]

(1 mark for the advantage and 1 for the disadvantage)

Comment

The advantages and disadvantages are no longer explicitly required by the syllabus. As packet switching and circuit switching are alternative methods, the advantages and disadvantages are comparisons and consequently make up an important part of the differences between them.

36. • A set of rules
- . . . to (control) communication   [2]

(1 mark per bullet)

37. A set of rules/instructions
. . . to govern data communication   [2]

(1 mark per bullet)

Comment

Again, not much more can be asked for this bullet. The syllabus specifically states that particular protocols are not expected, although elements of a protocol are. For example the other part of this bullet would be the need for a handshake signal to set up the communication. All this does is to introduce the protocol to the two devices and ensure that they are ready for communication.

38. • Commissioner is the expert in the field of the problem while the analyst is the expert in what is possible with a computer
- Need to ensure that both understand the scale of the solution planned . . .
- otherwise a different problem may be solved   [2]

(1 mark per bullet)

Comment

The basic point is that you have two different people who, because they see the problem from different perspectives, have two different expectations on the problem. This is poorly understood by students meaning that what should be a question that is aimed at grade E candidates is in reality aimed at a much higher level.

39. • Is the solution technically possible?
- . . . Is there access to hardware that is appropriate for the proposed solution?
- Is the solution economic to produce?

- ... Can a member of staff be made redundant, thus saving money?
- Is the solution economic to run?
- ... Will the purchase of e.g. a new printer save money on ink?
- What will be the social implications of change?
- ... Will a valued colleague is going to be put out of work?
- ... Is the skill level in the available workforce high enough?
- ... Training the staff to be able to use the new system is an additional cost
- ... Will the staff be capable of using the new system?
- What will be the effect on the customer?
- ... Will the introduction increase the profits?
- ... Will they complain about the new system?
- Time constraints
- ... The new system and all the training must be completed during a quiet period [4]

(1 mark per top-level bullet)

> **Comment**
>
> This question is very basic. However, the question is more instructive (and will attract more marks) when it is put in a context. If the question is part of a scenario then it is important to relate the standard answers to the scenario and additional credit is given every time it is done. Notice that not every one of the standard answers is easy to relate to a specific scenario.

40.
- Interview client/manager/key personnel
- ... allows questions to alter according to the answers given
- Questionnaires
- ... allows a large number of people to give their views in a short period of time/maintains anonymity
- Meetings
- ... partially combines the good points of interviews and questionnaires/allows discussion between people in meeting
- Collect present documentation
- ... shows what form the input and output is expected to take
- Observe present system in action
- ... can see first-hand/unbiased view of what actually happens [6]

(1 mark per bullet would be awarded: 1 mark for method and 1 for adavantage)

> **Comment**
>
> Standard question. Marks tend to be lost here through carelessness and also misconceptions, most common of which concerns the advantage of interviewing. Typical answer is "Can get information directly from the manager" or similar. This is wrong because the same information can be obtained by using a questionnaire, in fact the questionnaire is better because it would give the manager time to think carefully about their responses. The only reason is that it allows the person who is asking the questions to change a question when they hear an unexpected answer.

41. • Interview:
    • . . . interviewee can think about responses
    • . . . interviewer can alter questions dependent on the response to previous ones
    • Questionnaire:
    • . . . large number of people's views can be included in short time
    • Existing documentation:
    • . . . see all the necessary inputs and outputs required for the system
    • . . . obtain ideas for the formatting.
    • Observation:
    • . . . obtain an unbiased view of what goes on in present solution   [4]

                                      (1 mark per method and 1 for suitable advantage)

Comment

Notice how it seems to be the advantages that are asked for each time rather than the disadvantages. It is normal to ask for positive effects in questions because students find negative points very much more difficult to make. If the disadvantages are required, the question will normally ask for the advantages and the disadvantages.

42. • Information collection
    • . . . Use of interview/questionnaire/document collection/observation/meetings
    • Analysis of information collected
    • . . . Produces clear view of present system
    • Diagrams to show how present system works
    • . . . Example diagrams DFD/flowcharts
    • Requirements specification
    • . . . "Wish list" of requirements from user
    • . . . Subjective list of requirements
    • . . . Hardware and software requirements of the user should be included
    • Consideration of alternative solutions
    • . . . Investigate different types of software solution
    • Matching of alternative solutions to needs of requirements specification
    • Justify one solution against others   [6]

                                (1 mark per area, up to 3 areas, and 1 for the description of the area)

Comment

The restriction on the number of areas alluded to and the requirement to discuss expansions in each area was not stated in the question but arises because the question stated "describe", so simply stating an area which needs addressing is not enough for more than a single mark.

43. • Site map
    • . . . a diagram showing the way the different screens fit together
    • . . . shows the links between screens

- Gantt chart /progress chart
- . . . shows the different parts that need to be developed
- . . . shows which parts of the development are independent and which are reliant on each other
- Spider diagram
- . . . to show interaction between the different elements of the solution
- . . . and those parts which are independent of each other
- Flow diagram
- . . . to show the order of producing the parts of the solution
- . . . or to show the flow through the proposed site

[4]
(1 mark per group)

44. i. Ensures that all users' requirements have been met
     ii. Acts as a contract/makes sure analyst is paid.

[2]
(1 mark per bullet)

> **Comment**
>
> The answer should be clearly from the points of view of both the people involved in the contract: the client and the analyst. That is where the two marks come from.

45.
- Documentation for owner of system/website
- . . . will be paper based
- . . . will contain instructions for changing/maintaining system
- Documentation for user/viewer/visitor to website
- . . . will be on-screen
- . . . will give detailed help on searches/use of facilities/communication with site owner

[4]
(2 marks per documentation type)

46.
- Creation of files necessary to run software/machine
- System testing
- Training of personnel
- Decision on changeover strategy/direct changeover

[3]
(1 mark per bullet)

47.
- Corrective maintenance
- . . . to correct faults that are found after commissioning
- . . . to debug errors in the code
- Adaptive maintenance
- . . . to institute necessary changes
- . . . because of changes in the way the organisation works/tax changes/law changes
- Perfective maintenance
- . . . to improve the performance of the system
- . . . despite the fact that it does all it needs to

[4]
(2 marks per type)

48. i.   One off software/specially written to fit a specific application
    ii. Software is appropriate to many areas/can be tailored to requirements.   [2]

49. i.
    - Custom-written software is especially written/according to the requirements of the customer
    - Off-the-shelf is readily available/needs tailoring to the needs of the customer   [2]

    (1 mark per bullet)

    ii.
    - No delay as it is ready immediately
    - No shortage of experienced users/ready trained/no learning curve
    - Software should be error free
    - Help available through Internet/colleagues/courses
    - Compatible with other users/software   [2]

    (1 mark per bullet)

50.
- Barcodes of items are read as they arrive/leave
- If arriving the number in stock is incremented
- If leaving the number in stock is decremented
- Software checks number in stock against reorder number after every transaction
- When number in stock falls below reorder level then order created
- Linked to supplier table for automatic ordering
- Note that the order made is stored as Boolean 1 until it is delivered   [5]

(1 mark per bullet)

51. i.   Word processor/database/communication software/email
    ii. Spreadsheet/accounting
    iii. Database/spreadsheet   [3]

(1 mark per par)

> ### Comment
> A simple question with no hidden problems. Note the number of acceptable alternative answers. Notice, also, the lack of proprietary brand names: "a word processor" is fine for part (i) but "MS Word" is not.
>
> This sort of question can be asked in two ways: this way round, where the candidate is expected to supply the software for a task, or the candidate may have to supply the task for the software (e.g. "State a use for a word processor in this office").

52. a. • Data is numerical
        • Allows for predictions to be made and formulae to applied to the data/ease of calculation
        • Tabular/graphical representation of data/for ease of understanding   [3]

(1 mark per bullet)

    b. • Animation to maintain interest
        • Use of video to show sites
        • Sound to explain decisions
        • Ability to present to a large audience all at once.   [2]

(1 mark per bullet)

> ### Comment
> Notice that the expectation is at quite a low level because this is not IT but Computing. The level of understanding of the facilities of different software is not expected to be anything more than fairly superficial.

53. Custom-written:
    • Machine is unique/product of machine unique/performs single task
    • Generic software will not exist
    • . . . has extra facilities not required
    • . . . will not allow software to run at maximum efficiency   [3]

(1 mark for the type and 1 per bullet)

54.
- File of records of car sales . . .
- . . . searched for date = required date
- Standard form of letter exists . . .
- . . . with fields identified
- . . . which are completed with reference to data on data fields.
- Takes data from customer file
- Finished letters are then printed ready for sending [5]

(1 mark per bullet; if not related to scenario, max 2 marks)

55. a. Hardware:
- OMR reader
- Disk drive for storage
- Screen, keyboard, etc. to provide user interface

Method:
- Data read off OMR sheets by light reflection
- Position of marks corresponds to replies
- Data stored on hard drive until . . .
- . . . batch of data ready for input [4]

(1 mark per bullet; max 2 marks for hardware)

b.
- No prose answers
- Answers in form of tick boxes/underlining/ . . .
- . . . with limited choice of responses to each question
- Probably restricted to one sheet

- Need to keep sheet unfolded/clean
- Text on form is invisible to the reader

[3]
(1 mark per bullet)

> **Comment**
>
> The same sort of question can be asked about any of the automatic methods of data capture. Common are OCR and barcode readers.

56.
- Picture taken with digital camera/customer brings in hard copy picture
- Downloaded to computer through USB port/graphical picture scanned in
- Picture stored as JPEG (or other suitable format)
- Picture edited to a standard size using tools in software, such as cropping and contrast
- Picture pasted into software used to produce rest of card (word processor)
- Card printed out using colour printer

[5]
(1 mark per bullet)

> **Comment**
>
> This type of question is a good discriminator. The marks are aimed across the ability range with some accessible to all candidates but only the most able candidates gaining 5 marks for the question.

57. a.
- Ensuring that data input matches data collected
- Done by double entry/on-screen techniques

[2]
(1 mark per bullet)

b.
- Any sensible application needing data to be accurate, e.g. inputting details of bank cheques
- . . . because whole application based on accuracy/bank needs to be trusted

[2]
(1 mark per bullet)

> **Comment**
>
> The big problem with this type of question is the confusion between validation and verification. The concepts are simple and most candidates understand them but they mix them up too easily.

58. i.
- Check data input to ensure it matches source data
- Typed in twice . . .
- . . . by different people/at different times
- . . . inputs checked against each other for errors
- Manual check by comparing . . .
- . . . screen output of input with original document.

[3]
(1 mark for first bullet and any other two)

ii.
- Check data input is sensible/follows set rules/is reasonable
- Data type
- . . . should be numeric
- Data format
- . . . should be in currency form (xxx.xx)

- Length check
- ... input should be < x characters
- Presence check
- ... something has been input
- Range check
- ... value between 0 and some upper limit   [3]

(1 mark for first bullet and any other two)

59.
- Sound
  - ... set alarm for immediate response
- On-screen
  - ... to provide visual representation of where/what problem is
- Hard copy text
  - ... to provide evidence for later study
- Graphical
  - ... to indicate (quickly) whether still within parameters
  - ... to provide visual comparison across sets of data
- Tabular
  - ... to provide exact figures which can be compared with adjacent readings
- Analogue/digital meters
  - ... to provide readings from equipment
- Lights
  - ... to indicate state of the process/alert operator   [6]

(2 marks per pair of bullets)

> **Comment**
>
> Note that some types of output format are not relevant, e.g. video and animations would be difficult to justify on a production line.

60. i.
- Hard copy output
- Larger scale printout
- Graphical output
- High level of accuracy   [2]

(1 mark per bullet)

ii.
- Sound/Beeper
  - ... emergency or urgent information/to draw attention to new radar data
- Hard copy
  - ... tabular/numeric/to study the data in detail/to search for anomaly in geology
- On-screen/graphical to show
  - ... snapshot of situation/result of one radar sweep/comparison of data   [4]

(2 marks per pair of bullets)

> **Comment**
>
> The bullet points tend to run into each other but this time there is little doubt that the question is about fitting the different forms of output to specific users.

61. a.
- Knowledge base
  - . . . all the information about the particular study/about different formations and what they mean
- Rule base
  - . . . a set of definitions/algorithms to apply to the knowledge base
  - . . . rules about interpreting the collected data
- Inference engine
  - . . . does the searching of the knowledge base using rules from the rule base
- Human–computer Interface
  - . . . to allow data/enquiries to be input and results to be output [6]

(2 marks per pair of bullets)

> **Comment**
>
> Standard set of answers. This used to be a difficult question but is now one for which you should really have little difficulty picking up the marks.

b. Set up:
- The knowledge of a number of experts is collected . . .
- . . . and collated/edited
- Knowledge is stored in system
- Algorithms are developed/to use rules collected from experts
- HCI developed (to suit users)

Use:
- System matches patterns/data from survey with patterns/data in knowledge base
- Uses rules (in rule base) to interpret (meanings of) patterns/data found
- Produces probabilities of successful drilling [5]

(1 mark per bullet, max 3 for either section)

> **Comment**
>
> Notice that this question covers work from syllabus bullet points 1.8.f and 1.8.g.

62.
- Data collected on site/by drilling /observation/explosions
- Data collected remotely/by satellite/by electronic means
- Collected data input to system via HCI/automatically
- Data input is compared to library of data to find matches . . .
- by inference engine . . .
- Using rules found in rule base
- Decisions made about geological structure reported through HCI [4]

(1 mark per bullet)

> **Comment**
>
> Another example of the use of knowledge-based systems, a topic which students find very difficult.

63. Interface must be good because:
    - Single operator
    - Large quantity of information
    - Importance of some of the information
    - Features: colour, layout, video reverse/flashing/bold, graphics, sound [5]

    (1 mark per bullet or feature)

64. - Who will be using the interface
    - What experience/knowledge do they have
    - What is the system requirement/time sensitive or not
    - What is the information that needs to be shown
    - How much information is needed
    - What is the best way to show the information required
    - Colours that should/should not be used
    - What other forms of output are sensible/possible in the environment of the control room
    - What technology is available
    - Layout/language to be used [6]

    (1 mark per bullet)

Comment

Notice that this question could equally well have been asked about the syllabus bullets 1.9.a and 1.9.b. The content contains a lot of overlap.

65. a.

A	B	Output
0	0	1
0	1	1
1	0	1
1	1	0

[2]

(1 mark for the 1s and 1 mark for the 0 in the output column)

b.

A	B	Output
0	0	1
0	1	0
1	0	0
1	1	0

[2]

(1 mark for the 1 and 1 mark for the 0s in the output column)

c. - NOT AND, or NAND, is not the same as NOT the inputs and then add the results.
   - The order of the NOT and the AND gates is important. [2]

   (1 mark per bullet)

Comment

Logic gates is a new topic and consequently there are no past paper questions available. The question here is typical of what may be asked in the papers. You can expect to be asked one of the standard gates and then to work out a combination of gates. Finally, you may be asked to comment on the results.

Answers to Exam questions: Module 2

University of Cambridge Local Examinations Syndicate bears no responsibility for the example answers to questions taken from its past question papers which are contained in this publication.

1. Advantages:

    - There are fewer bugs because each set of programming commands is shorter
    - Algorithm is more easily understood
    - Many programmers can be employed, one on each of the modules
    - Programmers can use their expertise on particular techniques
    - Testing can be more thorough on each of the modules
    - Library programs can be inserted/allowing reuse of modules
    - All of which saves time and means the finished program can be completed more quickly

    Disadvantages:

    - can lead to problems with variable names
    - documentation of modules must be thorough
    - can lead to problems when modules are linked because links must be thoroughly tested   [5]

    (1 mark per bullet, maximum 4 advantages)

    > **Comment**
    >
    > These are standard answers but it is a large-reaching question, so it is not easy. You should notice that the question requires both *advantages* and *disadvantages*. The sensible form of response is to bullet the answers.

2. The following diagram is an example. A flowchart is just as acceptable.

    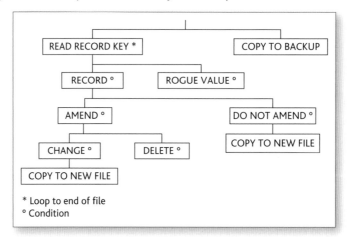

    Marks are awarded for:

    - distinct layers or modules
    - most important problem at top
    - use of repeat
    - correct condition to end loop
    - backup as separate module
    - condition to amend or not
    - condition to alter or delete
    - result copied to new file   [5]

    (1 mark per bullet, maximum 3 if no diagram attempted)

3.

```
WHILE CONTROL SYSTEM ON DO
    WHILE M NOT TRIGGERED DO
        IF FAN ON THEN
            FAN OFF
        ENDIF
    ENDWHILE
    IF T > D THEN
        IF FAN OFF THEN
            FAN ON
        ENDIF
    ELSE
        IF FAN ON THEN
            FAN OFF
        ENDIF
    ENDIF
ENDWHILE
END
```

Marks are awarded for:
- loop for system switched on
- loop to wait for M to be triggered
- switch off fan in loop
- condition on temperature
- two correct outcomes: fan on and fan off
- condition to reverse current state of fan
- correct positioning of loops
- correct structure (e.g. end statements)

[6]
(1 mark per bullet)

4.

```
WHILE DOOR NOT SHUT
    SHUT DOOR
END WHILE
IF HOT WASH THEN
    T = 80
ELSE
    T = 40
END IF
HEATER ON
REPEAT
    INPUT WATERTEMP
UNTIL WATERTEMP = T
HEATER OFF
TURN M ON
FOR TIME = 1 TO 20 STEP 5
    IF WATERTEMP < T THEN
        SUSPEND TIMER
        REPEAT
            TURN HEATER ON
        UNTIL WATERTEMP = T
        HEATER OFF
        RESTART TIMER
    ENDIF
NEXT TIME
TURN OFF M
SOUND BUZZER
```

Marks are awarded for:

- condition (door is shut) with action/loop to shut door
- condition hot or cool to set parameter
- for loop with correct count . . .
- . . . and correct step
- sound buzzer
- turn on heater H
- loop until temperature met
- turn M on
- check for temperature in loop and correct action

[7]

(1 mark per top five bullets and up to two other bullets)

> ### Comment
>
> Notice that the mark scheme contains two classes of mark, ones that are required and ones that are optional. The solution can be presented as a flowchart.

5. • A small program/subprogram
   • . . . designed to do a defined task
   • Called by a name/identifier   [2]
                                                         (1 mark per bullet)

6. • User selection from menu is compared with possibilities
   • Each possibility gives the name of a procedure
   • . . . which is run if possibility chosen
   • Procedure is code which carries out user's desires   [3]
                                                         (1 mark per bullet)

7. i. • 8,2
       • 4
                                                         (1 mark per bullet)

   ii. • 6,0
       • 6
                                                         (1 mark per bullet)

> **Comment**
>
> Notice the font of the pseudocode. You can expect algorithms printed on the exam paper to use Courier font. This question tests two things: the understanding of the IF statement and the ability to dry-run an algorithm.
>
> Notice that the question is specific about writing down the outputs from the algorithm. If you include extra material (e.g. A = 8 instead of just stating 8), the answer is strictly wrong. One mark would be deducted in each case for this error.

8. An example algorithm is:

```
IF MARK < 0 or MARK > 100 THEN
   REPORT ERROR
   GO TO READ MARK
END IF
```

Marks are awarded for:
   • condition MARK < 0
   • condition MARK >100
   • error report
   • loop back to read next MARK
   • algorithm is to be inserted into given algorithm after READ MARK   [5]
                                                         (1 mark per bullet)

9. a. 7, 0, 4   [3]

    (1 mark per bullet in correct order. If > 3 answers, mark first 3 and deduct 1 for error)

    b. • 4, 6, 3, 7, 1
        • . . . F is not a whole number
        • 0
        • . . . can algorithm cope with no input
        • 4, −6, 3, 7, 1
        • . . . can algorithm cope with negative numbers
        • 4, 6, 6, 6, 6
        • . . . can algorithm cope with equal values for B and C   [3]

    (1 mark per pair of bullets)

10. • Colour: character/text/string/alphanumeric
    • Engine size: integer/real
    • Air Con: Boolean
    • Price: currency/real/integer   [4]

    (1 mark per bullet)

11. a. • Text/character/string
        • Text/character/string/alphanumeric/integer (if an example makes it clear that an integer is appropriate)
        • Date/integer
        • Boolean/yes or no   [4]

    (1 mark per bullet)

b.
- 10–30
- 5–20
- 2,4,6,8
- 1 (total = 18–59 bytes per record)
- plus 10%
- multiply by 1000
- divide 1024 (1000)
- Answer = 19–64 KB

[4]
(1 mark per bullet)

12.
- – Comments/annotations (in code) . . .
  – . . . which machine ignores/explains rest of code
- – declare variable names
  – explain the scope of each variable
- – meaningful names . . .
  – . . . which explain meaning of variable/function/procedure
- – indentation
  – . . . to show which lines of code have something in common
- – modularisation
  – . . . small blocks of code are easier to understand

[4]
(2 marks per bullet i.e. 1 mark per dash)

13.
- Comments or annotations/within the code/explaining the code/computer will ignore
- Sensible variable and module names/so that the reader does not have to resort to a table to understand what they stand for
- Indentation/groups of program instructions/identified by some logical connection/start at different point on page from other instructions
- Modularity/code split into smaller groups/allow for local variables or library routines

[6]
(up to 2 marks per bullet)

14. • Syntax error/error in the language or rules of the program/e.g. A + B = C
    • Logic error/error in the original algorithm or in the transfer of algorithm to the code/e.g. call to the wrong procedure
    • Arithmetic error/request to carry out inappropriate or impossible arithmetic/e.g. divide by zero   [6]

    (up to 3 marks per bullet)

15. i. • Testing of all logical routes through program code . . .
       • . . . to ensure that code follows the algorithm
       • Desk checking/dry running   [2]

       (1 mark per bullet)

    ii. • – Translator diagnostics . . .
          – . . . produced by translator program/when code transgresses rules
       • – Debugging tools . . .
          – . . . programmer investigates conditions where error occurs
       • – Use of test data . . .
          – . . . to identify which inputs produce errors/Tracing of variable values
       • – Break points/variable dump . . .
          – . . . to find values of all variables/at specific point in code
       • – Black box testing . . .
          – . . . to test functionality of code/expected results compared with actual results
       • – Cross referencer . . .
          – . . . to report different modules/procedures/functions using the same variable names   [4]

       (up to 2 marks per bullet i.e. 1 mark per dash)

16.

A	B	C	D	E	F	I	X	Output
			1					
				6			4	
	6	6						
						1		
3								
		3						
			2					
				9				
						2		
7								
	7							
			3					
				16				
						3		
0								
		0						
			4					
				16				
					4			
								7,0,4

> **Comment**
>
> This is not a past paper question but it shows how easy it is to practice ideas like a dry run. New questions can be given simply by altering the data to be used.

17.

NUMBER	COUNTER	MARK	OUTPUT
4			
	1	40	1,FAIL
	2	90	2,MERIT
	3	60	3,PASS
	4	50	4,PASS

[8]

(1 mark per correct input and 1 for correct output; −2 if more lines are added)

18. •   – Translator diagnostics . . .
       – . . . when the source code is translated, the translator spots syntax errors
    •   – Desk checking/white box testing . . .
       – . . . following the logic of the code (manually)
    •   – Debugging tools . . .
       – . . . range of tools to study characteristics when the code fails
    •   – Bottom-up programming . . .
       – . . . code is in small modules making it easy to check
    •   – Black box testing . . .
       – . . . choosing test data to study the results produced/set results against expectations
    •   – Trace tables/step mode . . .
       – . . . trace the values of variables through a program run
    •   – Variable dump . . .
       – . . . see values of all variables at a particular place in the code
    •   – Break points . . .
       – . . . to stop execution at significant points
    •   – Cross referencer . . .
       – . . . identifies errors caused by duplication of variable names across procedures   [6]

(2 marks per bullet i.e. 1 mark per dash)

Answers to Exam questions: Module 3

University of Cambridge Local Examinations Syndicate bears no responsibility for the example answers to questions taken from its past question papers which are contained in this publication.

1.
   - Interrupt is given a priority
   - . . . placed in a queue with other interrupts to be done
   - . . . according to priority
   - When it becomes the highest priority interrupt, it is dealt with
   - Contents of registers are placed on a stack/saved
   - Interrupt (and others) dealt with
   - . . . values read from stack into special registers
   - Check for interrupts at end of each cycle before fetching next instruction
   - Vectored interrupts

   [6]
   (1 mark per bullet)

   > **Comment**
   >
   > Don't forget: the queue of interrupts with individual priorities; use of the stack to hold values from registers (important because they need to be used in reverse order to being placed on stack); and check for interrupts at end of cycle.

2. a.
   - When more than one program is resident, the operating system uses scheduling to decide on processing to be done
   - Allocation of processing in a multi-access/multi programming environment
   - . . . to be "fair" to all programs/users
   - . . . to use the peripherals efficiently
   - . . . to prevent system failure
   - . . . to maximise use of processor

   [2]
   (1 mark per bullet)

   b.
   - First Come First Served
   - . . . first job to enter ready queue is first to enter running queue/favours long jobs
   - Shortest Job First
   - . . . sort jobs into time expected to run, shortest first/new jobs placed in queue in correct order
   - Round Robin
   - . . . gives time slice to each job in turn/after slice job returns to back of queue
   - Shortest Remaining Time
   - . . . jobs sorted according to run time left to do/long jobs may never be done

   [6]
   (2 marks per pair of bullets)

3. i.
   - Memory is divided into fixed sized units
   - IAS is organised into physical pages
   - Programs/data are divided into page sized pieces
   - OS keeps an index of which programs/data are in which pages
   - Pages requiring processing need to be in memory
   - Address may be in form of page and distance from start of page

   [3]
   (1 mark per bullet)

ii. • Programs/data are divided up into logical amounts
   • . . . each of which is of a different size
   • Memory tends to become fractured
   • . . . leading to compaction of memory being necessary
   • Address complicated by need to calculate from start of segment [3]
   (1 mark per bullet)

iii. • Used when there is not enough space in memory
   • Part of backing store is used as though it were memory
   • Contents must be copied to memory to be used
   • Previous contents must be saved first
   • Too much use of virtual memory leads to disk thrashing [3]
   (1 mark per bullet)

> **Comment**
>
> A standard question which covers the whole of this syllabus learning outcome.

4. i. • The temporary storage of (input or output) data
   • . . . on some form of backing storage [2]
   (1 mark per bullet)

   ii. • Jobs are stored on backing store
   • . . . with a reference to the job and its location stored on a spool/print queue
   • The jobs in the spool queue can be prioritised and
   • . . . the job reference can enter the queue at a position according to its priority [3]
   (1 mark per bullet)

5. • – HCI
      – . . . type/to allow communication
   • – Utility programs
      – . . . routines that the OS makes available to the user/example
   • – Hardware control/Input and Output
      – . . . software routines to control the hardware/device drivers
   • – Multi-tasking capability
      – . . . allows different windows/user can carry on more than one task at a time
   • – Spooling
      – . . . to queue jobs for input/printing, etc.
   • – Security
      – . . . to ensure that different users can keep files confidential
   • – FAT
      – . . . contains details of where files are stored on the backing store
   • – . . . is also stored on the same backing store
      – Boot file
   • – . . . commands that allow users to make the computer start up as they want
      – . . . automatically executed by the computer after it has booted the operating system [4]
   (2 marks per bullet i.e. 1 mark per dash)

6.
   - An interpreter translates one line of code and runs it before translating the next line
   - The original code is always present
   - The interpreter needs to be present whenever code is run
   - The compiler translates the entire code
   - . . . before allowing it to be run
   - It creates object code

[4]
(1 mark per bullet)

7. Lexical analysis:
   - Instructions are tokenised
   - Some of characters must be combined to create token for keyword
   - If keyword does not exist in internal dictionary of keywords
   - . . . error is reported

Syntax analysis:
   - Each keyword has a syntactic structure
   - Tokens are checked to ensure that they match the syntax for that keyword
   - e.g. Do left and right brackets match?/Does punctuation for Print keyword match rules?

[5]
(1 mark per bullet)

8. The purpose of code generation is:
   - . . . the production of a machine code program/intermediate code that
   - . . . produces the results intended by the source code
   - Optimisation reduces the size of the object code by
   - . . . removing any duplicate or redundant instructions (which improves the speed of execution)

[3]
(1 mark per bullet)

9. i.
    - Linkers join (compiled) modules of code
    - . . . to produce an executable file
    - . . . and match up address references between modules.

    ii.
    - Loaders take a set of code from storage and copies it into memory
    - . . . resolving problems with addresses
    - Mention linking loader

    [4]
    (1 mark per bullet)

10. i.
    - A dictionary of reserved words is maintained
    - . . . if the reserved word used is not in this dictionary then an error has been made
    - Checks use of variable name against those in the variable table
    - A message may be given that suggests one close to spelling provided

    ii.
    - Variable names must follow the rules of the language
    - The rules are applied to the variable names used and reports any errors
    - The contents of variables are checked to ensure they are of specified type
    - An error is created by the attempted use of anything else

    [4]
    (1 mark per bullet)

11.
    - Instructions and data stored together in same memory
    - Single processor
    - Serial processing of instructions

    [2]
    (1 mark per bullet)

12.
    - Value in PC
    - . . . is copied into MAR
    - Value in PC is incremented
    - Instruction in the address referred to in MAR
    - . . . is copied into MDR
    - Instruction in MDR is copied into CIR

- Contents of CIR are split into operation code and address
- Instruction/operation code is decoded as unconditional jump
- Value in address part of instruction is copied into PC   [7]
                                                    (1 mark per bullet)

> **Comment**
> A standard question which expects a similarly standard answer. Problems
> to be wary of are mixing up the MAR and the MDR and the stage at
> which the instruction is copied from memory into the MDR. If this is not
> phrased properly, it often states that the contents of the MAR are copied
> into the MDR, which effectively says that the address of the instruction is
> now in two registers.

13. i. • Stores the instruction that is currently being processed
      • . . . while the operation code is decoded
      • Splits the binary code into operation code and address   [2]
                                                    (1 mark per bullet)

    ii. • Stores the address (in memory)
      • . . . of data to be accessed (from memory)
      • Data to be accessed is either instruction or raw data   [2]
                                                    (1 mark per bullet)

    iii. • Stores the address of the next instruction to be accessed
      • . . . is incremented (after contents are copied to MAR)
      • . . . is altered to allow for jump instructions   [2]
                                                    (1 mark per bullet)

    iv. • Contains a value that is added to the address (in the CIR)
      • . . . in order to make the address of the data
      • Incremented after use so that a set of data can be read one after the other without altering
        the raw address   [2]
                                                    (1 mark per bullet)

> **Comment**
> These are two ways of asking the same question about this bullet point –
> either to ask for the fetch–execute cycle or to ask what the individual registers
> do. Effectively they are the same question as they rely on the same body of
> knowledge about the uses of registers in the processor.

14. i. • 201/202 (sensible value)
      • Once sent to MAR the value in the PC is incremented   [2]
                                                    (1 mark per bullet)

    ii. • It is the result of a jump instruction which . . .
      • . . . requires that the next instruction is not to be handled in sequence/specifically, that held in 180   [2]
                                                    (1 mark per bullet)

15. i. • Weather forecasting
    • ... requires a large number of calculations
    • ... the results are time sensitive [3]
    (1 mark per bullet)

    ii. • Special operating system (to control) several processors simultaneously
    • ... array processor/co-processor
    • ... specially written/non-serial (application) software [3]
    (1 mark per bullet)

16. a. i. 01011101 [2]
       ii. 5D [2]
    b. • Hexadecimal is groups of four bits
       • Taken from the least significant bit (LSB) give hexadecimal values [2]
       (1 mark per bullet)

17. i. 11011010
    ii. 10100110 [2]
    (1 mark per point)

18. Result = (1)00101111 = +47
    • A positive and negative have been added together and the result is positive
    • ... because the larger value was positive
    • There was carry in and out of the MSB therefore ignore carry out (result is correct) [3]
    (1 mark per bullet)

19. a.
    - ½ × 2^0 (1 mark for each part)
    - ½ or .5 (2 marks) [2]

    b
    - A normalised value must have the first two bits of the mantissa different
    - Therefore one must be a 1
    - . . . which must represent either −1 or + ½ , but not zero [2]

    (1 mark per bullet)

20. i.
    - The fractional part of the representation
    - Place value of MSB is −1 . . .
    - Remainder of bits are ½, ¼ . . .
    - Holds the magnitude of the data [2]

    (1 mark per bullet)

    ii.
    - A twos complement integer which
    - . . . holds the power of 2
    - . . . by which the mantissa must be multiplied
    - . . . to give the original value [2]

    (1 mark per bullet)

    iii. 0.0101011 * 10 ^ 0101 = 1010.11 = 8+2+ ½ + ¼

    Alternative:

    10 = 1010 and .75 = .11

    10.75 = 00101011 × 10^101

    Point moves 5 places [3]

    iv. 01010110 0100

    (1 for mantissa, 1 for exponent) [2]

21.
- Range is decreased
- . . . because power of two which the mantissa is multiplying by is decreased
- Accuracy is increased . . .
- . . . because more digits are represented after the binary point [4]

(1 mark per bullet)

> **Comment**
>
> This is a standard answer to a standard question.

22. a. The following points would be looked for in the diagram drawn by the candidate:

Start: 4

4	AMOR	2		2	DIPO	3		3	GHIA	1		1	SIHA	0

- Start point/head of list table
- Data in alphabetic order
- Pointers used properly
- Null pointer to terminate
- Evidence of free space [4]

(1 mark per bullet)

> **Comment**
>
> Notice that the use of an array to represent the list with pointers from each element of the array to the next element in the list is perfectly acceptable. However, you should be aware that the use of an array restricts the size of the list to the size of the array. The main reason for using a list is that it is of variable size.

b.
- Find correct list in head of lists table
- Follow pointer to data
- If data = THEO then report found, End
- If data > THEO then report error, THEO not present, End
- If pointer = null then report error, THEO not present, End
- Repeat from the second line. [4]

(1 mark per bullet; 1 mark for the correct use of "End" twice)

> **Comment**
>
> The form of the algorithm is secondary to the logic exhibited. It is not written as an algorithm above – there are no indentations, for example. You should try to write the stages in an acceptable way if you use pseudocode.

23. a.
- Array may become full because of a lot of print jobs being sent together
- Linked list does not needlessly take up space in memory
- Print jobs may be inserted into queue in any position if they have a high priority [2]

(1 mark per bullet)

b. Find the head of the print queue

    i.   •   Insert data into free space
          •   Head of list points to new node
          •   New node points to old first value
          •   Mention inserting high-priority jobs into queue

    ii.   •   Follow pointers to null pointer
          •   Read address of print job
          •   Move null pointer to previous node
          •   Return node to free space

[5]
(1 mark per bullet)

24. i   •   Would take too long to search
       •   . . . because there is no indication of where to start
       •   . . . because data is not in order

[2]
(1 mark per bullet)

  ii. Alternative 1

       •   Binary search which
       •   . . . requires array to be sorted into alphabetical order
       •   Continual halving and take appropriate half
       •   . . . mean length of search is 500 searches for serial search
       •   . . . max length of search for binary search is 12 searches
       •   Non existence in array makes the length of serial increase to 1000
       •   . . . while the binary search remains at 12

     Alternative 2

       •   Indexed sequential search
       •   . . . array must be sorted into alphabetical order
       •   . . . initial letters stored in index
       •   . . . serial search from initial index given
       •   . . . length of search is dependent on the number of students with that initial, will be < 1000

Alternative 3
- Hashing algorithm
- . . . using Mod 1000
- . . . to give index in the array
- . . . must use linked list to deal with clashes
- . . . Immediate finding of name, no searching necessary   [3]

(1 mark per bullet; one is reserved for comparison with serial method)

> **Comment**
>
> The expected alternative is the binary search because that is the one listed in the syllabus. Others options are accepted if they answer the question.

25. 15,3,8,10,1
    - Compare 3 with those before   3,15
    - Compare 8 with those before   3,8,15,
    - Compare 10 with those before   3,8,10,15,
    - Compare 1 with those before   1,3,8,10,15

    Marks are awarded for:
    - Compare each number in turn
    - . . . starting with second in list
    - . . . with those before it
    - . . . to find its final place in list
    - . . . ending with final answer   [4]

(1 mark per bullet)

> **Comment**
>
> You need to be careful what you say. If you say "15 is compared with 3 and they are swapped", the word "swapped" demonstrates that you do not understand an insertion sort and no mark is given. Note that this is a very simple sort algorithm and it should be seen as such. It simply inserts the values in the correct place in turn through the list of values.

26. - While root node exists
    - Compare new value with root value
    - If > root value then follow right subtree
    - Else follow left subtree
    - Endwhile
    - Insert new value as root of new subtree (allow symmetric algorithm)   [4]

(1 mark per bullet)

27.

1st List	2nd List	Compare	New List
2,4,7,9	1,3,8,10,15	2,1	1
		2,3	1,2
		4,3	1,2,3
		4,8	1,2,3,4
		7,8	1,2,3,4,7
		9,8	1,2,3,4,7,8
		9,10	1,2,3,4,7,8,9
		Copy remaining	1,2,3,4,7,8,9,10,15

Marks are awarded for clearly showing:

- First from each list compared
- Smallest put into new list
- . . . and replaced by next from its original list
- Repeat until one list empty
- Copy remains of other list to new list

[4]

(1 mark per bullet)

28. i.
- Data and the permitted operations on that data are defined together
- . . . mention of class/encapsulation
- Objects in classes can pass messages from one to another/data can be manipulated within the object
- Classes can share some characteristics/mention of inheritance/derivation

[2]

(1 mark per bullet)

ii.
- Programs are expressed as a number of rules/relationships and a set of facts
- Program specifies what must be done, not how to do it/ mention of backtracking/goals [2]

(1 mark per bullet)

> **Comment**
>
> There are only two other paradigms that could be chosen: low-level and procedural.
>
> Low-level languages are close to the machine code representation needed by the computer. The instructions are one to one with machine code and they are very close to the architecture of the machine, consequently programs written in low-level languages are very easily translated, normally done by an assembler. The language statements comprise labels and mnemonics with names for variables. This explanation is the clearest as it is simple, however, it does suggest that machine code is always another step from a low-level language and while an assembly language program is low-level, so is a machine code version.
>
> Procedural languages state the necessary steps to be taken, in sequence, to solve a problem.

29. i.
- Split original problem into smaller parts
- Continue splitting into smaller and smaller parts until
- . . . each part can be considered to be a single process/matches one step in the algorithm [2]

(1 mark per bullet)

ii.
- A procedure/small section of code that returns a specific value
- A value is returned whenever the function name appears [2]

(1 mark per bullet)

> **Comment**
>
> This is a standard function type of question. It repeats some of the work from Module 2 (Chapter 2.1 about stepwise refinement and Chapter 2.2 about the definition of functions).

30. i. A variable whose value only applies in a particular procedure
ii. A variable whose value applies throughout a program
iii. A value which is applied to a variable within a procedure
iv. The value to be applied is stored in a memory location which is passed to the procedure. Any change is carried out of the procedure because the change will be stored in the memory location [4]

(1 mark per bullet)

> **Comment**
>
> This is a set of definitions which should be known.

31.
- Return address is placed on stack
- . . . along with values of parameters
- Parameters are read off stack by procedure

- Any returning values are placed on stack by procedure
- Return to address at top of stack at end of procedure [4]
(1 mark per bullet)

> ### Comment
> Notice that the order of the steps is important otherwise the parameters and the return addresses will become confused. This should be learned at the same time as the arrow diagrams for showing sequence in the calling of procedures, as shown in the text Module 3.5d on page 237.

32. i.
- Data can only be accessed using specific methods
- . . . provided by the class
- Objects cannot be corrupted by the user [2]
(1 mark per bullet)

ii.
- One class can include the data and methods of another
- . . . plus some of its own
- Allows for simple reuse of code/extension of original data and methods without affecting the code [2]
(1 mark per bullet)

33. i.
- A particular fact that fits the rule
- e.g. if salt (X) then salmon is an instance of X/X is instantiated to salmon [2]
(1 mark per bullet)

ii.
- The intention to find all instances that satisfy a rule/fact
- e.g. if goal is salt (X) then the result is to find shrimp, herring, salmon [2]
(1 mark per bullet)

iii.
- If the result of one rule does not apply in a second rule, then go back to find another result of the first rule
- For example, find a salt water eater of roach:
- eats (guppy, roach) is found
- fresh (guppy) shows guppy is a fresh water fish
- eats (salmon, roach)
- salt (salmon) shows salmon is a salt water fish
- salmon satisfies the rule [4]
(1 mark per bullet)

> ### Comment
> Students tend to solve these questions by common sense. If you look at the question and the answers then a very rudimentary understanding of the three concepts is enough to provide adequate detail to answer the three questions. Nowhere will you be asked to write program code in the exam.

34. i.
- The address in the instruction is
- . . . the address of the address of the data
- . . . used to access areas of memory that are not accessible due to the fact that there is not room in the instruction for the address to be directly addressed [3]
(1 mark per bullet; suitable diagram is worth two marks)

ii. • The address in the instruction is added to

    • ... a value held in a special register called the index register

    • ... allows a set of contiguous data (an array) to be accessed without altering the instruction   **[3]**

(1 mark per bullet; suitable diagram is worth two marks)

35.

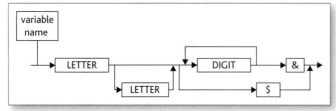

Marks are awarded for:

- Single letter possible
- Two letters possible
- Single digit possible
- Loop for multiple digits ...
- $ loop correctly positioned to miss digits and &
- & after digits loop

> ### Comment
> This sort of diagram should be straightforward as you only have to draw the statements in the question in sequence, but invariably candidates find this more difficult than the BNF work.

36. i. Lower case letters are not defined.   **[1]**

    ii. <TERMINATOR> : : = . | ?

       <SPACE> : : = ^

       <GROUP> : : = <WORD> <SPACE>

       <SET> : : = <GROUP> <WORD> | <GROUP> <SET>

       <SENTENCE> : : = <SET> <TERMINATOR>

       Marks are awarded for defining:

- Terminator
- Space
- Group
- Set
- Sentence
- and for correct use of notation   **[5]**

(1 mark per bullet)

> ### Comment
> There are a number of different ways in which the question can be answered. Most errors are caused by a failure to divide the words from each other. Those who do provide a space between words tend to forget that there is one fewer space in a sentence than there are words. This is a very difficult question and was designed to be so, however, there are still marks that can be picked up even for a part answer.

37. i. • Most items of data only need to be stored once
     • . . . because tables/files are linked allowing the contents of all tables to be used via access to one   [2]
     (1 mark per bullet)

   ii. • Access to areas of data can be easily controlled
      • . . . because users each have their own view of data
      • . . . DBMS can control views using access rights
      OR:
      • Regular backups of the data can be made
      • . . . automatically by the DBMS to alternative hardware   [2]
      (1 mark per bullet)

   iii. • As most information is only stored once there is less chance of contradictions being caused
        by the data being stored as different values
      • Data is protected from misguided or malicious processing/alteration
      • . . . leading user to trust in the correctness of the data   [2]
      (1 mark per bullet)

38.

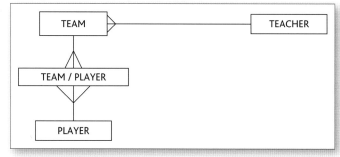

Marks are awarded for:
• The three original entities
• Link entity with acceptable name
• Relationship Team to Teacher
• Relationship Team to Player as many to many
• Relationship Team to Link as one to many
• Relationship Link to Player as many to one
• At least one relationship descriptor   [6]
(1 mark per bullet)

> **Comment**
> This is a typical E–R diagram question. These are questions set in a relatively short exam and consequently they cannot be too complex. Questions normally contain at least one many-to-many relationship, which means there is a need to create a link table.

39. • Reduces duplication of data/no duplication of data
   • Improves data integrity because only a single copy of data to be updated
   • Allows for different users to have different views of the data easily
   • More simple to control access to data
   • Simpler/faster/easier to access specific data through searches/queries   [3]
   (1 mark per bullet)

40. i. • Field or attribute in each record which uniquely/identifies the record.

   • e.g. StudentID/TeacherID

   ii. • a field or attribute in one table which is the primary key in another table

   • e.g. Student ID in the link table   [4]
   (1 mark per bullet)

41. • Confidential data of a sensitive type

   • Customers need to have the privacy of their accounts/details guaranteed

   • Must comply with legislation protecting data

   • Customers do not want data to be accessed or have data maliciously altered/used

   • Important to store to maintain data integrity

   • Passwords needed to access system . . .

   • . . . and different tables . . .

   • . . . giving different access rights/RO or RW . . .

   • . . . and providing different views of the data dependent on person's requirements

   • Physical protection by, e.g. locking system terminals away/iris recognition/fingerprints

   • Protecting system with firewall, etc.   [6]
   (1 mark per bullet)

42. i. Allows the user to:

   • define the data tables

   • specify data types and structures

   • specify constraints on the data   [2]

   ii. Allows the user to:

   • Insert/Update/Delete data

   • Modify/Retrieve data   [2]
   (1 mark per bullet)

> ### Comment
>
> Such a question could also ask about the data dictionary, for which marks would be allocated for:
> - A file containing information about the structure of the data held in the database
> - Typically not accessible to users/used by the database manager . . .
> - when it becomes necessary to alter the way in which data is being stored.

43. i.   An application where the output is produced quickly enough to affect the next input   [1]

ii.   Any sensible example, e.g. Check the state of a customer's account at an ATM machine before offering a service on the card proffered.   [2]

(1 mark per bullet)

> ### Comment
>
> Any suitable example is perfectly acceptable but be careful to make sure that there is no ambiguity. Are all computer games real-time? In this example answer, notice that to say "An ATM machine" or even "Using an ATM machine" is not good enough because some uses of an ATM machine are batched.

44.
- Radar or Sound
- . . . to build up a picture of surroundings
- . . . to warn when something is in front of robot
- Pressure sensor
- . . . on front of robot to tell processor that a solid object has been touched
- Light sensor/infra-red sensor
- . . . to detect light intensity which will warn robot of change of surroundings
- . . . to warn when something is in front of robot
- Sound sensor
- . . . may hear human or other machine approaching   [4]

(2 marks per pair of bullets)

> ### Comment
>
> Be careful of using the correct names to identify sensors. "Heat" sensor is an example of a response for which the examiner knows what the candidate is trying to say but cannot award credit because it is not possible to sense "heat" whereas a temperature sensor is allowed because it senses a temperature. Temperature is a measurable value, but heat is not – it needs to be set to a specific temperature first.

45. a.
- Input: Any two from touch/radar/proximity/infra-red sensors
- Output: Any two from alarm/speakers/lights/motors to activate wheels/steering/actuators   [4]

(1 mark per bullet)

b. i. • Optical sensors/radar
   • ... used to detect obstacles
   • Positions determined by
   • ... angular bearing from reference point
   • ... distance from radar   [2]
                                                     (1 mark per bullet)

   ii. • Design must be created using simulation because of large cost of real thing
    • Testing also simulated because not possible to test in real environment   [2]
                                                     (1 mark per bullet)

c. • Factory robot is physically available to people to control it/commands acted upon immediately/
   need to have immediate action because of proximity to humans
   • Mars robot cannot be controlled in real-time because of the time taken for instructions to reach
   it/instructions need to be sent as a batch and then acted upon and results sent back to the operator
   on earth   [2]
                                                     (1 mark per bullet)

> ## Comment
>
> Notice in (a) that "heat" sensor is not acceptable. These are four easy
> marks and it is a shame to see students missing the mark here. It is not
> a trick question; stick to the standard examples that we are sure will be
> accepted. In part (b) the clue is "Mars". You should immediately be asking
> the question "Why Mars?" and the answer is a simple one: "It is a long
> way away and commands will take a long time to get there". We can
> go on to think that no human has ever been there so, unlike a factory
> floor, nobody knows what it looks like or what obstructions there may
> be. Additionally there is the problem of testing in conditions which are
> not understood and have to be recreated, consequently the need for
> simulation. Finally, there is the delay in communications which give the
> need for batch-processing of instructions and the ability to control a local
> robot using real-time.
>
> This is not an easy question and was not designed as such; it was
> intended to be challenging to all candidates. However, all candidates
> should have been able to score some marks, even if only in part (a).

46. • To test out new parts without building them
    • ... saves time in development
    • To test safety features in crashes
    • ... saves money/saves risk of injury to humans
    • To give immediate readout of costings
    • ... as modifications are made the costs are shown immediately/no need for further work
    • To measure how the car interacts with the environment
    • ... may not be possible to find that particular environment
    • To predict the performance of car
    • ... saves cost/time/allows for comparisons to be made in different conditions
    • Test different materials in different conditions

- . . . to ensure cost/safety/time to test in reality
- Long-term testing of the design to destruction of important parts
- . . . can be done in short time/less cost [6]

(1 mark per bullet)

> **Comment**
>
> Plenty of scope here for answers. The one thing that you must be very careful of is to ensure that your answers relate to the example application given and that they are not just generic values.

47. a. • Production of a test prototype would be very expensive
- Time taken to produce and test a prototype may be too long/immediate need
- Need to test in circumstances unable to be reproduced
- May be too dangerous to test in reality
- Situations can be reproduced which may never arise in ordinary testing [3]

(1 mark per bullet)

b. • No positive reasons of time/danger
- Impossible to simulate a physical action like cutting grass
- Lawn mower can be produced easily
- Large quantity will be sold so prototype costs easily covered [2]

(1 mark per bullet)

> **Comment**
>
> It is important to understand that there are situations where it is simply not worth producing a simulation to do tests on because the product or situation is mundane and does not provide any of the advantages of using simulation to test the design.

48. • Three LANS necessary for security reasons
- Three LANS connected by bridges/routers to allow intelligent directing of data
- UTP/Twisted Pair/Fibre optic/Coaxial/Wireless (mention of any 2)
- . . . Sensible are either UTP or Twisted pair for the operators and the accounts department
- . . . because of low level of traffic/confidential nature of data
- . . . the wired network is more secure
- . . . Wireless is sensible in warehouse
- . . . so that operatives can move about and still be connected to the network
- Switches may be used to create a star network for the telephone operators so that the volume of data sent across the network is kept to a minimum
- Modem/gateway used to connect the accounts department to Internet to allow communication with banks/suppliers. [8]

(1 mark per bullet)

49.
- Restricted access/keeps patient records secure
- Sensitive nature of data/less chance of hacking
- Limited volume of data/makes searches simpler, quicker/all data is relevant
- Only relevant people have access/so communications can be considered secure
- Any comments on the intranet can be considered relevant, accurate, informed.

[4]
(1 mark per bullet)

> **Comment**
>
> Students tend to understand the ideas of data being sensitive and the intranet allowing greater security for the data, but fail to understand the importance of the positive points, such as comments on the intranet being more easily accessible, more relevant and more trustworthy.

50.
- Hackers attack communications/customer data
- Data being distributed leading to unsolicited communications
- Encrypting data on database files
- Digital signatures to guarantee reliability of source
- Passwords to enter user's area/database
- Use of firewall to block unwanted access
- Workers subject to DP legislation
- Portable storage devices not allowed
- Use of authorisation and authentication techniques

[5]
(1 mark per bullet)

Glossary

A

Acceptance testing   Testing done when the software is delivered to the client on their computer system. The performance of the software is monitored against the requirements specification

Accumulator   Single general-purpose register in the CPU. *See also* Special-purpose register

Actuator   Device that receives signals from a computer system and responds with some form of movement. *See also* Sensor

Adaptive maintenance   Maintenance to a computer system occasioned by changes to conditions, e.g. new tax legislation. *See also* Corrective maintenance, Perfective maintenance

Address bus   Unidirectional bus used to address main memory and input/output devices. *See also* Bus, Control bus, Data bus

Algorithm   Sequence of steps designed to perform some task

Alpha testing   The software is tested at the development company by a number of testers. At this stage it may well still have faults. *See also* Beta testing

ALU   *See* Arithmetic and logic unit

Analogue data   Data values that may take any continuous value between some range, e.g. speech input to the computer system from a microphone using a sound wave produces analogue data. *See also* Digital data

AND gate   Output is TRUE only when both inputs are TRUE

Animation   Still pictures which are presented in a rapid sequence to create the appearance of movement

Annotation   Text, usually in the form of comment statements, added to a source program

Anti-virus software   Utility software designed to detect and deal with virus malware

Application software   Does a task that would be carried out even if there were no computer. For instance, business letters are sent without technology, so a word processor is an applications program. *See also* Software

Archive   Copy of data that is no longer in use on the computer system, kept on offline storage. *See also* Backup

Argument   Value passed to a function or procedure when it is called. *See also* By reference, By value, Parameter

Arithmetic and logic unit (ALU)   Part of the processor that performs arithmetic calculations and makes logical decisions

Array   Data structure that refers to a set of data items with a common identifier name and individual items with an index (subscript)

Array processor   Processor that is designed to allow a single machine instruction to operate on a number of memory locations (i.e. an array) simultaneously

ASCII   American Standard Code for Information Interchange – widely used 7-bit coding system used for character data

Assembler   Software that translates assembly language source code into an object file once the source code has no errors. *See also* Assembly language, Machine code

Assembly language   Second-generation low-level programming language with instructions made up of an op(eration) code and an operand; every assembly language instruction translates into one machine code instruction. *See also* Assembler, Low-level programming, Machine code

Assignment statement   Code that gives a value to a variable or constant, e.g. `MyAge ← 4`, in pseudocode, assigns the value 4 to the variable `MyAge`

Asymmetric encryption   Both the sender and receiver have their own pair of keys called the public key and private key; also called "public key encryption"

Attribute   Data item recorded in database design, e.g. the `CustomerName` attribute in the `Customer` table. *See also* Entity, Table

Authentication   Checking that a user is who they say they are; digital signatures attached to an email are designed to check that the sender is who they appear to be. *See also* Authorisation

Authorisation   Granting permission to a user, e.g. for access to a data file or a directory. *See also* Authentication

B

Backtracking   The process of working back through a solution to establish steps used to arrive at the final solution; used in expert systems to explain how a goal was satisfied. *See also* Declarative programming language, Goal

Backup   Copy of data stored for security reasons and used in the event of the loss or corruption of the live data. *See also* Archive

Backus–Naur Form (BNF)   Formal language that uses "replacement rules" to describe how elements of a language are built up from simpler elements. *See also* Syntax diagram, Terminal symbol

Bandwidth   Measure of the amount of data that can be transferred in a given time

Barcode   Series of bars that represent a numerical code, such as a Universal Product Code; used extensively in retailing

Batch processing   Applications that run without human intervention, processing a set of data and producing output

Bespoke software   *See* Custom-written software

Beta testing   The software under development is released to a number of privileged customers for their feedback, before it is commercially released. *See also* Alpha testing

Binary   Number system that has two digits, 0 and 1

Binary chop   *See* Binary search

Binary coded decimal (BCD)   Representation of a number that uses a group of four binary digits to represent each digit in a denary number, e.g. 78 in denary is 0111 1000 0011 in BCD.

Binary search   Searching technique that repeatedly divides a list in half until the required value is found; the list values must be in order; also called "Binary chop". *See also* Serial search

Binary tree   Data structure in which values are called nodes and links exist between each node and its descendants; links between nodes are called branches; the original value in the tree is called the root node

Bitmap graphic   Image made up of a number of small "picture elements" called pixels. *See also* Vector graphic

Black box testing   Testing that considers only the inputs to the program and the outputs produced; the detailed code is not considered. *See also* White box testing

Blocked status   In multiprogramming, a process that is not yet able to use the processor. *See also* Ready status, Running status

Bluetooth   Short range communications technology typically used in hi-fi (HD) equipment, mobile devices and car radios

Blu-ray   Secondary optical storage technology using a laser; much higher storage capacity than DVD, suitable for high-definition media

Boolean   Data type that allows two values, TRUE or FALSE

Boot up   The process of accessing and executing the boot file stored in the ROM of the computer system

Borderline (Boundary) data   Data values that are on the boundary of a range of permitted values. For example, if a menu selection has valid options 1, 2, 3, 4 and 5, the borderline values are 1 and 5. *See also* Invalid data, Normal data

Break point   Debugging technique in which a marker is inserted in the source code. When executed, the program terminates at the marked statement and the developer can study the variables at this point in the execution

Bridge   Hardware device that allows communication between two LAN segments. *See also* Local area network

Buffer   Temporary storage area used to counteract the difference in speeds between the processor and an I/O device

Built-in function   Function that is part of the programming language, e.g. all the string-handling functions. *See also* User-defined function

Bus   Set of wires in parallel that connect various architecture components and provides communication between them. *See also* Address bus, Control bus, Data bus

Bus topology   Local area network where all devices are connected directly to a communication cable. *See also* Bridge, Segment, Star topology, Topology

By reference   Variable is used as the argument to a procedure or function; if its value changes within the subroutine, the changed value is available in the main program. *See also* By value, Argument, Function, Parameter, Procedure

By value Copy of a variable's value is used as the argument to a procedure or function; if its value changes within the subroutine, the change is local and the original variable's value is not changed in the main program. *See also* By reference, Argument, Function, Parameter, Procedure

Byte Number of bits to store one character. Generally considered as eight bits.

`Byte` **(data type)** Data type used for variables or constants with a value in the range 0 to +255. *See also* Integer

C

CD-R Secondary storage media with data read and written with a laser; data contents cannot be changed; used for archiving backups

CD-ROM Secondary storage media with data read and written with a laser; data contents cannot be changed; used for software distribution

CD-RW Secondary storage media with data read and written with a laser; data contents can be changed; used for backup and data transfer

`Char` Data type used for values of a single character, usually enclosed in single quotes, e.g. `MyJobCode = 'P'`

Character Single character from a character set. Includes; upper and lower case letters, digits, punctuation and 'control' characters (e.g. <Carriage Return>) Note: the pseudocode examples in the book use single quotes to denote a single character. *See also* function (CHAR), ASCII

Character set Complete set of characters that the computer uses

Check digit Validation technique that involves calculating an additional digit from the ones that proceed it. *See also* Validation check

Checksum Technique used in data transmission to validate data by sending a block of data calculated from the contents of preceding blocks. *See also* Validation check

Chip and PIN Plastic card with an embedded chip used for debit and credit cards

Cipher text The message text after encryption. *See also* Encryption, Plain text

Circuit switching System in which sending and receiving devices set up a route (circuit) before data

transfer starts and maintains it until transmission is complete. *See also* Packet switching

Class In object-oriented programming, the blueprint design of an object that describes the properties and methods of the object. *See also* Method, Object, Property

Class diagram In object-oriented programming, a diagram that shows how actual instances of one or more objects are related to an instance of another class

Client–server model Application that uses a central service from a server, that is provided to a number of client computers; many applications are based on this model, e.g. email server, web server, FTP server. *See also* Server

Coaxial cable Cable made up of a single central wire that is insulated from an outer conductor made up of many strands. *See also* Twisted pair

Code generation The final stage in the compilation process. *See also* Lexical analysis, Syntax analysis

Code optimisation Final stage in the compilation process that aims to produce an object file that uses the optimum amount of main memory and processing speed. *See also* Lexical analysis, Syntax analysis

Command line interface (CLI) Interface through which the user communicates with the computer by keying in text commands

Compiler Software for the translation of a high-level language source program into an object file, i.e. machine code. *See also* Interpreter, Translator

Composite key Primary key made up of more than one attribute

Computer aided design (CAD) Software that enables design, e.g. of a new building

Computer aided manufacture (CAM) Software that enables the automated production of items, e.g. in a milling machine

Computer architecture In this syllabus, the term is used for "machine-level" architecture (widely used in computing to also include systems design)

Concatenation Joining together two or more strings, e.g. `FullName = Initials & " " & Surname,` where & is the concatenation operator

Constant Identifier for some data value that is fixed. *See also* Variable

Control bus Wires that are dedicated to provide a particular control signal between the processor, main memory and I/O devices. *See also* Address bus, Bus, Data bus

Control unit   Processor component that manages the execution of instructions during the fetch–execute cycle. *See also* Control bus

Co-processor   Component added to the CPU to speed up the manipulation of floating point numbers

Corrective maintenance   Maintenance to a computer system occasioned by errors that surface after the system is live, i.e. after the formal testing stages. *See also* Adaptive maintenance, Perfective maintenance

Current instruction register (CIR)   Stores the current instruction that has been fetched and is about to be decoded and executed. *See also* Special-purpose register

Custom-written software   Software written for a specific client, also called "bespoke software"

D

Data bus   Bidirectional bus used to communicate a data value to and from main memory and the processor. *See also* Address bus, Bus, Control bus

Data capture   The input stage of a data processing application

Data definition language (DDL)   In database software, SQL statements that allow the creation of a database. *See also* Data manipulation language (DML)

Data dictionary   File that is part of the DBMS that stores a description of the data held in a database. *See also* Database, Database management system

Data item   Single data value

Data manipulation language (DML)   In database software, SQL statements that allow querying of a database and insertion, amendment and deletion of data. *See also* Data definition language (DDL)

Database   Collection of related data where all records have the same structure. *See also* Database management system (DBMS), Relational database

Database management system (DBMS)   Software that provides a layer between software that manages the databases and the application programs that access the data. *See also* Database, Relational database

Dataflow diagram (DFD)   Charting technique used to describe data flowing through a system: inputs, processes and outputs. *See also* System flowchart

Data logging   Collection and storage of data values (from sensing devices) for processing by a computer system. *See also* Sensor

Debugging tool   Software utility for checking and testing code; it is designed to find errors in the code and report them to the developer; also called a diagnostic program or a debugger. *See also* Integrated development environment (IDE)

Declaration statement   Code that declares an identifier and its data type to be used in the code that follows; a programming language that requires variables to be declared before they are used is said to be "strongly typed"

Declarative programming language   Programming paradigm that sets up a knowledge base of facts and rules and then extracts information with the setting of a goal. *See also* Fact, Knowledge base, Prolog, Rule

Decryption   The process of translating cipher text back to the original plain text. *See also* Cipher text, Encryption, Plain text

Denary   Number system that has ten digits: 0, 1, 2, 3, 4, 5, 6, 7, 8 and 9

Dependency   In relational databases, a non-key attribute that is not fully dependent on the primary key

Design specification   Formal document that shows how the features of the requirements specification (inputs, processing and outputs) will be implemented

Desktop publishing (DTP) software   Software that allows for the presentation of text and graphics in a printed publication, such as a newsletter or a product catalogue

Digital data   Data that takes the form of discrete values (i.e. not continuous). *See also* Analogue data

Direct addressing   The operand part of the low-level instruction is the actual address to be used. *See also* Indexed addressing, Indirect addressing, Relative addressing, Symbolic addressing

Direct changeover   The new system is introduced at the same time as the old system is withdrawn. *See also* Parallel running, Phased implementation, Pilot running, Systems development life cycle

Directory   A virtual area of file storage referred to by name. Folder creation and management is done by the file manager module of the operating system. Also called "Folder"

Disk formatter   Utility program that formats the surface of a disk to prepare it for use

DIV function   "Modular arithmetic" function that operates on two numbers X and Y and returns the

whole number of times that Y divides into X,
e.g. `11 DIV 4` returns 2

Domain name server (DNS) Server on the Internet that matches fully qualified domain names to their corresponding IP address. *See also* Server

Dry run Process in which a programmer checks by hand the execution of a program by recording the changing values of all variables in a trace table. *See also* Trace table

Duplex Data transmission in both directions at the same time, also called "full duplex". *See also* Half-duplex, Simplex

DVD-R Secondary storage media with data read and written with a laser; data contents cannot be changed; used for archiving and backups

DVD-RAM Rewriteable DVD that uses a different technology from a DVD-RW

DVD-ROM Secondary storage media with data read and written with a laser; data contents cannot be changed; used for software distribution

DVD-RW Secondary storage media with data read and written with a laser; data contents can be changed; used for backup and data transfer

Dynamic data structure Data storage that is created only when it is needed, e.g. the pointer available in some high-level languages. *See also* Static data structure

Dynamic RAM (DRAM) Random access memory which has to be continually refreshed – about every 2 milliseconds – by reading and rewriting the contents. Data is stored as charge. Most popular type of memory for PCs and laptops. *See also* RAM, Static RAM

E

Electronic point-of-sale (EPOS) system The checkout facility in a shop that records all aspects of the transaction

Embedded system Computer system dedicated to one task and embedded in a machine, e.g. a washing machine

Encapsulation In object-oriented programming, combining an object's properties and its methods to form a class. Access to data must be through methods of the class

Encryption Process whereby a message when transmitted can only be understood by the sender and receiver. *See also* Asymmetric encryption, Decryption, Symmetric encryption

Entity In database design, something about which we store data, e.g. a customer. *See also* Table

Entity-Relationship (E-R) diagram Used in database design to show the entities and the relationships between them

Expert system Software application that captures the knowledge of some area of human expertise (e.g. medicine) and allows the setting of queries (goals) by a non-expert user. *See* Knowledge base, Fact, Rule

Expert system shell Software that enables an expert system application to be created. *See* Fact, Knowledge base, Rule

Exponent The "to the power of" part of a floating point representation of a real number. *See also* Floating point representation, Mantissa

Extranet Private network that uses Internet protocols and where access from the outside is carefully controlled

F

Fact Item of data encoded in an expert system or declarative programming database. *See* Knowledge base

Feasibility study Report on whether or not a computerised solution is feasible

Feedback loop Use in real-time processing to describe the way in which the latest outputs are feed back to act as input to the next processing cycle

Fetch–execute cycle The sequence of execution of a program based on the von Neumann stored program concept. *See also* von Neumann architecture

Fibre-optic cable Cabling made up of several fibre-optic glass strands that each transmit a modulated light beam

Field Component of a record, e.g. `CustomerName` is a field in a `Customer` record. *See also* Key field, Record

File Collection of data items that are stored under a file name

File allocation table (FAT) Table for a secondary storage device that stores data about the file allocation units used by the stored files

File allocation unit The basic unit of storage allocation to files by the operating system. One file allocation unit will consist of a number of contiguous sectors on the disk. Also called "Cluster". *See also* File allocation table (FAT)

File compression software Utility software that produces a version of the input file with a reduced size

File handling General term to describe the use of files in a high-level programming language

File size The number of bytes that make up a file

Firewall Application designed to control unauthorised access to a computer or computer network; a "personal firewall" describes the software used when a single PC user is accessing the Internet

First-generation programming language Machine code programming. *See also* Second-generation programming language, Third-generation programming language

Fixed-length record Collection of fields relating to the same object where the size is standardised; a field such as surname may stored with a fixed size, e.g. 30 characters. *See also* Record, Variable-length record

Flat file File of data records, as used by all applications before the arrival of relational database software. *See also* Field, Record

Floating point representation Representation used for real numbers, based on the idea that any number can be expressed as: number = mantissa $\times 2^{exponent}$; floating point stores the mantissa and the exponent. *See also* Exponent, Mantissa

Flowchart Flowcharting techniques are used in many areas of computing; a *program* flowchart is used to describe the sequential steps in an algorithm

Folder A virtual area of storage referred to by name. Folder creation and management is done by the file manager module of the operating system. Also called "Directory"

Foreign key Attribute in a table that links back to the same attribute in another table; the primary key–foreign key link forms a relationship between the tables. *See also* Primary key, Relationship

Form-based interface Interface through which the user communicates with the computer by entering data into controls (possibly arranged similar to a paper-based form), e.g. text boxes, radio buttons, check boxes and drop-down lists

Function Block of program code (referred to by an identifier name and with none or more parameters) that returns a value to some variable in the main program. *See also* Argument, Built-in function, Parameter, Subroutine, User-defined functions

function (`ASCII`) Built-in function that computes the ASCII number value for the given character parameter, e.g. `MyCode ← ASCII('A')` assigns 65 to `MyCode`. *See also* function (`CHAR`)

function (`CHAR`) Built-in function which computes the character from the given ASCII code parameter, e.g. `MyCharacter = CHAR(65)` assigns 'A' to `MyCharacter`. *See also* function (`ASCII`)

Function (as procedure) header The first line of a function definition that contains the identifier name and parameters; also called the "function interface"

Function Interface *See* Function header

G

Gateway Hardware device that acts as a node on a network to handle communication with other networks. *See also* Firewall

General-purpose applications software Software which is the 'starting point' from which a variety of applications can be developed. Examples are a word processor and a spreadsheet. Also called "Generic software"

General-purpose register One or more registers in the CPU that temporarily store data; the simplest processor has one general-purpose register, the accumulator. *See also* Accumulator

Generic applications software Software that can be the starting point for a variety of different tasks, also called "generic software"

Generic software *See* Generic applications software

Global variable Variable that exists within the entire program. *See also* Local variable, Scope

Goal The query set when interrogating a knowledge base in a declarative programming language, e.g. `Car (X, >2000)` displays all values of X with an engine size greater than 2000 cc

Graphical user interface (GUI) Interface through which the user communicates with the computer by using windows, icons, menus and a pointing device, e.g. a mouse

Graphics tablet Input device used to capture an image hand-drawn on the tablet with a stylus

H

Half-duplex Data transmission is possible in both directions, but at any time in one direction only. *See also* Duplex, Simplex

Handshake signal   Signal sent between the sending and receiving devices to establish whether or not they are ready to begin data transfer. *See also* Protocol

Hard copy   Printed output. *See also* Soft copy

Hard disk   Secondary storage device consisting of disk platters that rotate at high speed

Hardware   The physical – mostly electrical and electronic – components that make up a computer system, e.g. a device controller or motherboard

Hardware driver   Software that allows for successful communication between a device (e.g. printer) and the operating system

Hexadecimal   Number system that uses base 16; possible digits are 0, 1, 2, 3, 4, . . ., 8, 9, A, B, C, D, E and F

High-level scheduler   The program module in the operating system that decides which process is loaded next into main memory. *See also* Low-level scheduler

High-level scheduling   the management of new programs loaded into primary memory by the operating system in a multiprogramming environment

Hub   Hardware device used to connect computers in a network; it may be a computer (e.g. in a star network) but could be only a wiring connector (e.g. to form a bus network)

Human–computer interface (HCI)   *See* Command line interface, Form-based interface, Graphical user interface, Menu-based interface, Natural language interface, User interface

I

I/O-bound job   Process that spends most of its time doing input and output and very little time processing, e.g. a program that prints a catalogue of 4000 products reads data records from the disk and outputs them to the printer. *See also* Processor-bound job

Identifier   Name or label used by a programmer to represent an object (e.g. a variable, a constant, a user-defined function and a procedure) or address within a program

IF statement   Program structure used for selection that has several variants:

```
IF <condition> THEN <statement(s)> ENDIF
IF <condition> THEN <statement(s)> ELSE
<statement(s)> ENDIF.
```
See also Select Case, Selection

Immediate access store   *See* Main memory

Indentation   Programming style designed to help the "readability" of the source code, e.g. by indenting all the statements inside a loop or a selection structure

Index number   Subscript that identifies an array entry. *See also* Array

Index register   Special-purpose register that contains a number that is used with an indexed addressing instruction. *See also* Indexed addressing

Indexed addressing   The address to use for a low-level instruction is formed by the operand plus the number in the Index Register. *See also* Direct addressing, Indirect addressing, Relative addressing, Symbolic addressing

Indexed sequential   Method of file organisation and access that provides both sequential access and direct access to individual records using an index

Indexing   In database software, creating a secondary key on an attribute to provide fast access when searching on that attribute; the indexing data must be updated when the table data changes. *See also* Primary key, Secondary key

Indirect addressing   The operand part of the low-level instruction is a "forwarding address" to the actual address to be used. *See also* Direct addressing, Indexed addressing, Relative addressing, Symbolic addressing

Inference engine   Heart of an expert system that applies rules to facts to answer queries by a non-expert user. *See* Expert system, Fact, Knowledge base, Rule

Infix notation   Common representation for an expression in maths that positions the operator between the two operands, e.g. $12 + 67$. *See also* Postfix notation

Infra-red communication   Communication using a particular range of frequencies of electromagnetic radiation over a short distance and in a straight line; applications include a television remote controller and a remote computer keyboard

Inheritance   In object-oriented programming, a subclass ("child" class) takes on all the properties and methods of a super-class ("parent" class). *See also* Class

Initialising   In program code, assigning an initial value to an identifier, e.g. all values in an integer array could be assigned the value zero

Inkjet printer   Printer has a number of ink cartridges – usually cyan, magenta, yellow and black – and ink is forced onto the paper forming the image as a series of coloured dots

Input device   Hardware that allows data to be captured and then transmitted to the processor

Insertion sort   Algorithm used to sort a data set. *See also* Quick sort

Instance   Used in object-oriented programming to describe an actual object which the program code has created. Typically `MyCustomer` (the variable) is an instance of the class `Customer`. *See also* Object-oriented programming, Class, Object

Integer   Whole number; a data type in most programming languages that stores values in two bytes (i.e. from –2768 to +2767). *See also* Byte

Integrated development environment (IDE)   Software tool that assists with the development and testing of programs; contains an editor, a translator and debugging features "integrated" into a single software application

Internet   Infrastructure of computers, networks and routers that uses various communications methods to link devices globally

Internet protocol (IP) address   32-bit number arranged as four bytes, e.g. 192.168.67.3, that identifies a particular device on the Internet. *See also* Internet, Router

Interpreter   Software that identifies a programmer's source code and executes it. *See also* Compiler, Translator

Interrupt   Signal from a device to the processor to seek its attention

Interrupt Service Routine (ISR)   Program code which is executed to service as interrupt. E.g. the 'printer out of paper' interrupt signal will trigger the running of the appropriate ISR code

Intranet   Information system using Internet protocols that provides a service similar to the Internet but where content is available only within the company or organisation. *See also* Extranet

Invalid data   Data that is outside the range of normal and borderline data; also called "erroneous data"

Iteration   One of the fundamentals constructs of a procedural high-level language in which a block of code is repeated a number of times; also called "repetition"

J

Jackson diagram   Charting technique that describes the modular design of a problem

K

Key field   Field that determines the sequence order of a set of data values. *See also* Field

Knowledge base (1)   Set of facts and rules used in declarative programming and by an expert system. *See* Expert system, Fact, Rule, Prolog

Knowledge base (2)   A knowledge base is also described as a depositary of faults/fixes which is created by a software home for an item of software

L

Label   Used in assembly language programming to mark a particular instruction. *See also* Symbolic addressing

Leaf node   Node of a tree with no sub-trees. *See* Binary tree

LEFT function   String-handling function. *See also* `LENGTH, LOCATE, MID, RIGHT`

LENGTH function   String-handling function. *See also* `LEFT, LOCATE, MID, RIGHT`

Lexical analysis   The first stage carried out by compiler software. *See also* Code generation, Code optimisation, Syntax analysis

Linked list   Data structure in which each node consists of the data value and a link pointer; the pointers produce ordering of the data

Linker   Software that links program modules to produce object code. *See also* Loader

Loader   Software that copies a program from secondary storage into main memory ready for execution. *See also* Linker

Local area network (LAN)   Computers and other devices that are connected and communicate over a small geographical area, e.g. the same building. *See also* Wide area network

Local variable   Variable that exists only within the block of program code (typically a procedure or function) in which it was declared. *See also* Global variable, Scope

LOCATE function   String-handling function. *See also* `LEFT, LENGTH, MID, RIGHT`

Logic error   Error such that the programmer's logic is incorrect, e.g. a loop does 21 iterations, when it should be 20

Logic gate   Basic component used to construct a logic circuit. *See also* AND, NAND, NOR, NOT, and OR gates

Logic programming   See Declarative programming language

Loop   *See* Iteration

Loop counter   Variable that is used to count the number of iterations performed by a loop

Lower bound   Lowest value used as an array index

Low-level programming   Programming in machine code or assembly language. *See also* Assembly language, Machine code

Low-level scheduler   Program module in the operating system that decides which of the processes in the "ready state" uses the processor next. *See also* High-level scheduler, Multiprogramming

Low-level scheduling   the allocation of processor time by the operating system in a multiprogramming environment

M

MAC address   Stands for Media Access Control and is a unique address assigned to the network interface card by the manufacturer. It is a 6-byte number

Machine code   Code written in binary that uses the processor's basic machine operations, i.e. the instruction set. *See also* Assembly language, Low-level programming

Magnetic tape   Secondary storage media usually used for backup

Main memory   The primary memory in the central processing unit, also called primary memory, random access memory (RAM), immediate access store

Maintenance   Changes that may need to take place to a system after it has become operational. *See also* Adaptive maintenance, Corrective maintenance, Perfective maintenance

Mantissa   The "fraction" part of a floating point representation. *See also* Exponent, Floating point representation

Memory address register (MAR)   Special-purpose register that stores the address to be used for the current instruction. *See also* Fetch–execute cycle, Memory data register

Memory data register (MDR)   Special-purpose register that stores the data value that has just been read from main memory or is about to be written to memory; also called memory buffer register (MBR). *See also* Fetch–execute cycle, Memory address register

Memory management   Program module in the operating system that manages the main memory and the processes that use it. *See also* Paging, Segmentation

Memory refresh   *See* Dynamic RAM. *See also* RAM, static RAM

Menu-based interface   Interface through which the user communicates with the computer using a set of menus; menu items often contain sub-menus

Method   In object-oriented programming, the things an object can do, e.g. assigning a property a value and using it. *See also* Class, Object, Property

Microwave transmission   Communication technology that uses radio waves with a very short wavelength, ideal for use in radio and television broadcasting

`MID` **function**   String-handling function. *See also* `LEFT, LENGTH, LOCATE, RIGHT`

`MOD` **function**   Modular arithmetic function that operates on two numbers X and Y and returns the remainder when Y is divided by X, e.g. `11 MOD 4` returns 3

Modem   Hardware device that converts signals from analogue to digital and vice versa; typically used to convert signals sent over the public service telephone network. *See* Analogue data, Digital data

Modular approach   The design methodology of taking a problem and breaking it down in smaller related tasks. *See also* Module

Module   Self-contained part of a large computer program that provides features that are accessed by or integrated with other sections of program code; also called "program module"

Multiprogramming   Several processes concurrently loaded into main memory that give the *illusion* that more than one program is executing at the same time

Multi-tasking operating system   Operating system (e.g. Microsoft Windows) that supports several processes concurrently loaded into main memory

Multi-user operating system   Operating system for a single central computer that provides a service to a number of "dumb" terminals

N

NAND gate   Single logic gate that is equivalent to an AND gate followed by a NOT gate. *See also* Logic gate

Natural language interface   Interface through which the user communicates with the computer using natural language keywords or phrases

Navigation   The movement from one screen/feature to another within a software program

Nested structure   Program structure (such as a loop or an IF statement) that is contained inside another such structure

Network interface card   Hardware that provides the connection from the network cable to the computer (motherboard), also called "network interface card (NIC)"

Network operating system   Operating system that supports a network of computers that share resources including hardware devices and software

Node   Data item in a binary tree. *See also* Binary tree

NOR gate   Logic gate that is equivalent to an OR gate followed by a NOT gate. *See also* Logic gate

Normal data   Set of (test) data values that the final software is expected to use

Normalisation   Formal process of checking a relational database design to ensure it does not have duplicated or redundant data

Normalised   Floating point representation of a real number that gives the maximum possible accuracy; don't confuse with normalisation in database design

NOT gate   Logic gate with a single input that it inverts. *See also* Logic gate

O

Object   Instance of a class. *See also* Class

Object code/program   Executable (.exe) file that is output from a compiler. *See also* Compiler, Source code

Object-oriented programming (OOP)   Programming paradigm that uses a bottom-up approach by first defining the objects used by the problem. *See also* Class, Object

Obsolescence   End of the lifetime of the system. *See also* Systems development life cycle

Off-the-shelf software   Software that can be bought in a shop or on a website and can be used without customisation

On-screen help   Instructions for using a system that are built into it and are displayed on the screen

Op(eration) code   In low-level programming, a basic machine operation, e.g. Store, Load direct, Add, Jump. *See also* Assembly language, Operand

Operand   In low-level programming, an address or number on which the opcode operates. *See also* Assembly language, Operation code

Operating system (OS) software   Software that makes computer hardware useable and provides an interface between the hardware and the user

Operator   Symbol used to describe how two data values are to be manipulated, e.g. high-level language have arithmetic, relational and Boolean operators

Optical character recognition (OCR)   Automatic data entry method in which characters are read from a paper document and converted to text, e.g. a utility bill; don't confuse with optical *mark* recognition

Optical mark recognition (OMR)   Automatic data entry method in which the position of marks are read from an input document, e.g. multiple choice examination answer sheets

OR gate   Logic gate in which the output is TRUE if either or both inputs are TRUE. *See also* Logic gate

Output device   Hardware that conveys the results of some processing to the user

P

Packet switching   System in which data are divided into packets that are sent between sending and receiving devices using a variety of routes. *See also* Circuit switching

Page   In paged memory management, a fixed-size unit of main memory. *See also* Paging, Page frame

Page frame   In paged memory management, a fixed size unit of main memory into which a program's pages are loaded. *See also* Page, Paging

Paging   Strategy for managing the main memory when multiprogramming. *See* Page, Page frame

Paradigm   Something that serves as a pattern or model; a programming paradigm is a way of considering a problem. *See also* Declarative programming language, Object-oriented programming, Procedural programming language

Parallel data transmission   Bits are sent concurrently along a set of parallel wires

Parallel processor   The simultaneous use of more than one processor to perform a task. *See also* Array processor, Co-processor

Parallel running   Implementation in which the new system runs alongside the old system for a limited period of time. *See also* Direct changeover, Phased implementation, Pilot running, Systems development life cycle

Parameter   Value to be passed to a function or procedure; it appears in the function/procedure header; built-in functions require zero or more parameters. *See also* Argument, By reference, By value

Parity block   A parity check carried out on a sequence of bytes. The parity block is an additional byte where the bits are computed from the proceding data bytes. The bytes are arranged in a grid and each parity byte bit is calculated from the bits in the column above. *See also* Parity check

Parity check   Technique used in data transmission to validate data by sending an additional bit determined by the contents of the preceding bits to make the total number of 1s odd or even.

Parsing   Breaking a statement (in a high-level programming language or BNF) down into its component parts; the breakdown shown as a sequence of steps is called a parse tree. *See also* Backus–Naur Form

Perfective maintenance   Maintenance to a computer system that improves the performance of the system. *See also* Adaptive maintenance, Corrective maintenance

Peripheral device   Hardware device outside the central processing unit

Phased implementation   Implementation in which the component parts of the new system is gradually introduced. *See also* Direct changeover, Parallel running, Pilot running, Systems development life cycle

Pilot running   Implementation in which the new system is introduced to a subset of the business, e.g. in one shop. *See also* Direct changeover, Parallel running, Phased changeover, Systems development life cycle

Pipelining   Processor that allows the concurrent decoding of two or more program instructions to speed up program execution

Plain text   Original message text before encryption. *See also* Cipher text, Encryption

Postfix notation   Writing an expression with the operator following the two operands, e.g. x y + (to describe the addition of x and y) ; also called "reverse Polish notation"

Prefix notation   Writing an expression with the operator preceding the two operands, e.g. + x y (to describe the addition of x and y)

Presentation software   Software that creates and displays a number of information slides usually in sequence

Primary key   In database software, an attribute (or combination of attributes) chosen to ensure that all records in a table are unique. *See also* Foreign key, Secondary key

Primary memory   *See* Main memory

Priority queue   Queue data structure in which the items are linked in priority order; the first item to leave the queue is the one with the highest priority. *See also* Linked list

Private key   In asymmetric encryption, the private key is only ever known by the owner. *See also* Encryption, Public key

Procedural programming language   High-level language that allows the programmer to express an algorithm as a hierarchy of tasks. *See also* Declarative programming language

Procedure   Block of program code referred to with an identifier name; it can be "called" many times throughout the program; it may or may not have parameters. *See also* Argument, Function, Parameter, Subroutine, Function header

Processor-bound job   Process that spends the majority of its time using the processor (and doing very little input or output). *See also* I/O-bound job

Program counter (PC)   Register that stores the address of the next instruction to be fetched; also called "sequence control register". *See also* Special-purpose register

Program instruction   In low-level programming, one line of a program. *See also* Low-level programming

Program library   A collection of previously written programs which are available for the development of new applications. For example, code to sort an array of string data might be needed in many applications and so is made available from a program library

Program specification   Documentation of the algorithms needed for program modules, following from the design specification. *See also* Systems development life cycle, Design specification

Prolog   Declarative programming language. *See also* Declarative programming language, Logic programming

Property   In object-oriented programming, a data item that is part of a class description, e.g. `CustomerAddress` is one of the properties in the `Customer` class definition. *See also* Class

Protocol   Set of rules for data communication. *See also* Handshake signal

Proxy server   Server that acts as a gateway between a network and the Internet. *See also* Gateway

Pseudo real-time operating system   Operating system that supports a real-time application but on a timescale much slower than a process control application, e.g. a ticketing system

Pseudocode   Methodology for describing an algorithm by writing steps – using keywords and identifiers – that are general enough to implement the description in a high-level language

Public key   In asymmetric encryption, the key given to a recipient before any secure communication can take place. *See also* Encryption, Private key

Q

Query   Structured question used to retrieve information from a database or knowledge base. *See also* Goal

Queue   Data structure in which the first item to join is the first item to leave. *See also* Priority queue

Quick sort   Algorithm used to sort a data set. *See also* Insertion sort

R

Random access memory (RAM)   *See* Main memory

Random (file) access   Each record is allocated a record key and the record is stored at an address calculated from this record key using a hashing function

Read-only memory (ROM)   Memory whose contents cannot be changed or erased. *See also* Random access memory

Ready status   In multiprogramming, a process that is capable of using the processor immediately. *See also* Blocked status, Running status

Real number   Number that may have a fractional part; also a data type in some programming languages

Real-time operating system   Operating system that processes data fast enough to influence some real-world application in a continuous input–processing–output cycle. *See also* Pseudo real-time operating system

Record   Collection of items (fields) relating to the same object and treated as a single unit for processing. *See also* Fixed-length record, Variable-length record

`Record` **data type**   User-defined data type that describes several fields that make up a record

Recursion   Algorithm that is defined in terms of itself, i.e. the algorithm definition calls itself. *See also* Unwinding

Relational database   Database where data are organised in one or more tables with relationships between them. *See also* Database, Database management system

Relationship   Link between two database tables made using a primary key and foreign key. *See also* Foreign key, Primary key

Relative addressing   The operand part of the low-level instruction is the address to be used, shown as a number "relative" to the address storing the instruction. *See also* Direct addressing, Indexed addressing, Indirect addressing, Symbolic addressing

Repetition   *See* Iteration

Report   Hard or soft copy output – usually providing summary information

Requirements specification   Formal document produced by the systems analyst following the analysis stage. *See also* Program specification

Reserved word   Word that is part of the syntax of the programming language (and therefore cannot be used as an identifier)

Reverse Polish notation   *See* Postfix notation; *See also* Infix notation

`RIGHT` **function**   String-handling function. *See also* `LEFT`, `LENGTH`, `LOCATE`, `MID`

Round robin   *See* Time sharing

Router   Hardware device used on a packet switching network to direct packets from the sending device to the receiving device. *See also* Domain name server, Internet protocol (IP) address

Rule   Data about some area of human expertise used by an inference engine to answer queries by a non-expert user. *See* Knowledge base, Expert system

Running status   In multiprogramming, the process that is currently using the processor. *See also* Blocked status, Ready status

Run-time error   Error that only becomes apparent when the program is executed, e.g. caused by an attempted division by zero

S

Sampling   Selection of a subset of data values used to perform some calculation

Scanner   Hardware device that scans a paper document with a laser and produces a bitmap image as output

Scheduling   *See* High-level scheduling, Low-level scheduling

Scope   Range of program code statements for which a variable is recognised. *See also* Local variable, Global variable

Screen resolution   Size of a monitor display screen, measured in number of pixels

Secondary key   Index created for an attribute in a database table that allows the data to be accessed fast in an order other than the primary key field order. *See also* Indexing, Primary key

Secondary storage   Hardware device that allows data to be permanently stored

Second-generation programming language Assembly language. *See also* First-generation programming language, Third-generation programming language

Sector A fixed size portion of a track on a magnetic disk. Modern hard disks use sectors of size 4096 bytes. Also called "Block"

Segment (networking) When a bus network has two or more communication lines, each cable is called a segment. *See also* Bridge, Bus, Local area network

Segment (memory management) Portion of a program which has been organised into smaller parts

Segmentation Strategy for managing the main memory when multiprogramming

Select Case Program structure used for selection when the problem has a large number of alternatives. *See also* IF statement, Selection

Selection One of the fundamental programming constructs for procedural languages; any program statement in which a decision is made. *See also* IF statement, Select Case

Semantic check Check on the meaning of an expression or program statement. *See also* Syntax

Sensor Electrical component that converts one form of energy into another, e.g. a thermistor converts temperature into electrical energy measured as a voltage. *See also* Actuator

Sequence One of the fundamental constructs of procedural programming; statements are executed in sequence until told otherwise, e.g. when there is a loop. *See also* Iteration, Selection

Sequential file Data items stored in some key field order. *See also* Serial file, Key field

Serial file Data items stored in no particular order. *See also* Sequential file

Serial search Searching a collection of data values – e.g. a file or array – starting with the first item and then looking at items in sequence. *See also* Binary search

Serial transmission Data transmission where individual bits are sent in sequence along a single wire

Server Computer that provides a service to "client" computers. The most basic server would be a file server. *See also* Client–server model

Sign and magnitude Representation of an integer where the most significant bit indicates the sign (0 for positive and 1 for negative) and the remaining bits represent the size (or magnitude) of the integer. *See also* Integer, Two's complement

Simplex Data transmission in one direction only. *See also* Duplex, Half-duplex

Simulation Software model of a problem that predicts the behaviour of a real-life system

Single-user operating system Operating system that supports a single user, e.g. a personal computer

Soft copy Output that is viewed by the user on screen. *See also* Hard copy

Software Sequence of instructions designed to make a computer system perform some task

Source code/program Program code (in assembly language or a high-level language) as written by the programmer. A source program is made up of source code. *See also* Object code/program, Translator

Special-purpose applications software Software designed for one specific task. *See also* Software

Special-purpose register Register inside the CPU that has a dedicated role, e.g. the program counter (PC). *See also* Fetch–execute cycle, General-purpose register

Spooling Temporary storage of program output, that is queued and only sent to the output device when it becomes available

Spreadsheet Software that provides a grid for the presentation of data and does calculations. *See also* General-purpose applications software

Stack Data structure in which the last item to join is the first item to leave

Star topology LAN or WAN where a computer or other network is connected to a central computer system. *See also* Bus topology, Topology

Static data structure Data structure for which a fixed amount of memory is pre-allocated, e.g. an array. *See also* Dynamic data structure

Static RAM Random access memory which holds its contents as long as there is a power supply. Data is stored using a switchable current. Typical application is for cache memory (as SRAM has faster access times than DRAM). *See also* RAM, dynamic RAM

Storage device Hardware on which data are stored

Streaming Buffering technique that allows media content to be displayed without excessive delay whilst the file is being downloaded. *See also* Buffer

String Data type used for values that contain text characters; data is usually enclosed in double quotes, e.g. `MyOccupation = "Consultant"` High-level programming languages will use a string data type

Structured Query Language (SQL)   Industry-standard data description language and data manipulation language used by database and database management software. *See also* Data definition language, Data manipulation language

Subroutine   Self-contained block of program code that is implemented as a procedure or function. *See also* Function, Procedure

Subscript   Index number that identifies an array entry. *See also* Array

Switch   Hardware device used on an Ethernet bus network that queues data packets and avoids collisions; all devices are wired as a star network to the central switch although the network behaves as a bus. *See also* Bus topology

Symbolic addressing   Mode of addressing used in assembly language programming where the programmer uses labels for specific addresses in the program. *See also* Label

Symmetric encryption   Encryption method in which the recipient must have the algorithm and key that created the cipher text. *See also* Asymmetric encryption, Cipher text, Plain text

Syntax   Set of rules for combining the elements (i.e. identifiers, keywords, punctuation) that make up a programming language; correct syntax means a statement is accepted by the translator

Syntax analysis   Second stage carried out by compiler software. *See also* Code generation, Code optimisation, Lexical analysis

Syntax diagram   Diagram that describes the permitted syntax of one of the rules of a high-level programming language. *See also* Backus–Naur form

Systems analyst   Job title of the computing professional who does the fact finding and designs a new computer system. *See also* Systems development life cycle

Systems development life cycle   All the stages in the analysis, design, development, testing, implementation and maintenance of a computer system. *See also* Systems analyst

System flowchart   Diagram that focuses on the programs and files used by a system. *See also* Dataflow diagram (DFD)

System software   Operating system, programming language translators, utility programs and library programs. *See also* Library program, Operating system software, Translator, Utility software

T

Table   In relational database software, a table is the implementation of an entity in the problem. *See also* Attribute

Terminal symbol   Symbol that cannot be further broken down using the rules of the language, e.g.
`<digit> ::- 0|1|2||4|6|7|8|9`; the digits 0, 1, ..., 9 are all terminal symbols. *See also* Backus–Naur form

Third-generation programming language   Procedural high-level languages such as Pascal, Visual Basic, Java, etc. *See also* First-generation programming language, Second-generation programming language

Time sharing   Strategy for implementing a multi-user operating system; programs are allocated a slice of time in sequence

Time slice   In a multiprogramming environment, one strategy the low level scheduler can use is to allocate each program in the ready state a fixed amount of processor time called a time slice

Token   Used at the lexical analysis stage of compilation. Each language keyword is replaced by a single character or 'shorthand' character sequence, called a token. The source file is said to be 'tokenised' after this process. *See also* compiler, lexical analysis

Top-down design   Methodology for the design of a problem by successively breaking stages of the problem into more detailed steps; the sub-tasks may be implemented as program modules

Topology   The logical arrangement of all devices connected to a network. *See also* Bus topology, Star topology

Touch screen   Monitor screen that acts as both an input and output device. Finger contact with a particular position on the screen is mapped by software to an action

Trace table   Table with a column for each of the variables in the program code; the programmer traces changes in the value assigned to each variable at each stage of the program

Transaction log   Record of the transactions applied to a file since the last backup

Transcription error   Data input error caused by the user incorrectly copying a value from a paper document to the computer system

Translator   Software that translates a programmer's source code into a form that can be executed. *See also* Assembler, Compiler, Interpreter

Truth table   Table of all possible combinations of inputs and outputs for a logic circuit. *See also* Logic gate

Turnaround document   Document (e.g. a utility bill) that is output from a computer system and is later used for input

Twisted pair   Cable used for data transmission formed from a pair of insulated copper wires. *See also* Coaxial cable

Two's complement   Representation used for integers and fractions that allow both positive and negative values to be represented. *See also* Sign and magnitude

U

Unicode   16-bit character coding system. *See also* ASCII

Universal resource locator (URL)   The standard format for referring to a resource on the Internet; also called Uniform Resource Indicator (URI); made up of:

- the protocol, e.g. http
- the server, e.g. www
- the domain name, e.g. cie.org.uk
- the file path – folder and file

Unwinding   Flow of control on the completion of a recursive function call to the previous call. *See also* Recursion

Upper bound   Highest value used as an array index

User interface   Software interface that allows the user to communicate with the computer system, also called human–computer interface (HCI). *See also* Command line interface, Form-based interface, Graphical user interface, Menu-based interface, Natural language interface

User-defined function   Function that is written by a programmer. *See also* Built-in function

Utility software   System software that performs a specific task, e.g. file backup, file compression or virus-checking

V

Validation check   Checking the correctness (or validity) of a data value: presence, format, length, "from a list", unique, range and check digit

Variable   Data value with an identifier that may change during the execution of a program. *See also* Constant, Identifier

Variable-length record   Collection of fields relating to the same object where the size varies between records; a field such as surname is stored with only as many characters as required. *See also* Fixed-length record

Vector graphic   Image made up of numerous vectored shapes that can be re-sized without a reduction in resolution. *See also* Bitmap graphic

Verification check   Checking the validity of a data value by keying in the value twice to check that both attempts match

Video capture card   Analogue-to-digital converter device that receives input analogue video signals (e.g. from a camcorder) and converts them to digital data

Virtual memory   Storage space on a disk drive that behaves like an area of main memory. *See also* Paging

Voice recognition   Software that converts the human voice to digital text

von Neumann architecture   Model of computer architecture based on the stored program concept. *See also* Fetch–execute cycle

W

White box testing   Testing designed to analyse the structure of a program; test data are devised that test all possible routes through the code

White space   Blank lines and other spacing of program source code that make it more "readable"

Wide area network (WAN)   Computers, other devices and networks that are connected and communicate over a wide geographical area (national or global), such as the Internet. *See also* Local area network

Wi-fi   Trademark for wireless communication

Wireless network   Network which uses radio wires for all communications, i.e. "without wires". *See also* Wi-fi

Word processor   Software for the creation, editing and storage of text documents. *See also* General-purpose applications software

Index

project work *see* computing project
Prolog, 235–36, 246–49
properties of objects, 235, 243–45
protocols, data transmission, 50–51
proxy servers, 288
pseudo real-time operating system, 5
pseudocode, 118–19
    functions, 158
public keys, encryption, 288–89

queries
    declarative programming, 235
    flat file, 263
    relational database, 271–72
questionnaires, 56
queues, 20–21
    implementation of, 221–22
    interrupts, 185
    job scheduling, 185–87
    print spooling, 189–90
quick sort, 225–28
QWERTY keyboards, 35–36

random access memory (RAM), 31
    dynamic and static, 95
random (file) access, 23
    methods of, 24–25
range check, data validation, 81
rate of data transmission, 47
read-only memory (ROM), 31
reading from a file, 150
ready status of job, 187
real numbers, 142, 214–15
real-time applications, 274
real-time operating system, 5
real-time processing, 7
records, 22, 146
    data type for, VB.NET, 147–48
    designing format of, 146–47
    flat file, 262–63
    relational database, 263–64
recursion, 134–37
    binary trees, 228–29, 256–58
    definitions, BNF, 252, 254
    quick sort algorithms, 227–28
    rules, Prolog, 247–49

"refreshable" memory, logic gates, 95–96
registers, CPU, 206–8
relational databases, 263–64
    advantages over flat files, 267
    and DBMS software, 269–72
    designing, 264–67
    keys: primary, secondary & foreign,
        267–68
    user access restrictions, 26–29
relational operators, 155–56
    using on alphanumeric strings,
        158–59
relationships between entities, 267–68
relative addressing, 250–51
remainder, MOD function, 155
repetition *see* iteration
reports, 82
    database, 263, 267
    design of, 113–15
requirements specification, 58, 61
reserved words, 163
resolution, screen, 39
return addresses, storage of, 241
reverse Polish notation, 255
revision cards, 325
revision guidelines, 324–28
RIGHT function, 158
robots, 276–77
ROM (read-only memory), 31
round robin scheduling, 5, 187
routers, 45, 284–85, 286
rule base, 84
rules, 84
run-time errors, 172
running status of job, 187

sampling, 76
scanners, 38, 79
scheduling, 183, 185–86
    and job status, 187
    objectives of, 186–87
    strategies, 187
scope of variables, 163–65, 239–41
screen layout, interface design, 109–13
screen resolution, 39
screens, 39–40

searching algorithms
    binary, 223–25
    linked lists, 218
    serial/sequential/linear, 223
second-generation programming
        languages, 233
secondary keys, 268
secondary storage media, 32–34
sectors, 192
security of data, 287–90
segmentation, 188–89
segments
    memory management, 188–89
    network, 283, 284, 285
Select Case construct, 124
selection constructs, 124–26
    nested, 128–29
semantic checks, 200
sensors, 41, 76–77, 274–75
sequence of instructions, 124
sequence control register (SCR), 206
sequential access, 23
    methods of, 23–24
sequential files, 23
    inserting data into, 151–52
sequential search, 223
serial access of data, 22–23
serial files, 23
    inserting data into, 151
serial search, 223, 224
serial transmission of data, 46
servers, 6, 45, 283
    domain name, 287
    proxy, 288
    web server, 286, 287
sign bit, negative numbers, 213
simplex transmission of data, 46
simulation
    reasons for using, 277–79
    in testing design feasibility, 279
single-user operating system, 5
soft copy, 82
software, 2
software lifespan, 64
software requirements, 58
solid state technology, 33, 34